Wound Care

A Collaborative Practice Manual
for Physical Therapists and Nurses

Edited by

Carrie Sussman, PT
Sussman Physical Therapy Inc.
Torrance, California

Barbara M. Bates-Jensen, MN, RN, CETN
Assistant Professor of Clinical Nursing
Department of Nursing
University of Southern California
Los Angeles, California

AN ASPEN PUBLICATION®
Aspen Publishers, Inc.
Gaithersburg, Maryland
1998

The authors have made every effort to ensure the accuracy of the information herein. However, appropriate information sources should be consulted, especially for new or unfamiliar procedures. It is the responsibility of every practitioner to evaluate the appropriateness of a particular opinion in the context of actual clinical situations and with due considerations to new developments. Authors, editors, and the publisher cannot be held responsible for any typographical or other errors found in this book.

Library of Congress Cataloging-in-Publication Data

Wound care : a collaborative practice manual for physical therapists
and nurses / edited by Carrie Sussman, Barbara M. Bates-Jensen.
p. cm.
Includes bibliographical references and index.
ISBN 0-8342-0748-6
1. Wounds and injures—Treatment. 2. Physical therapy.
3. Nursing. I. Sussman, Carrie. II. Bates-Jensen, Barbara M.
[DNLM: 1. Wounds and Injuries—rehabilitation. 2. Wounds and Injuries—nursing.
3. Wounds and Injuries—diagnosis. 4. Physical therapy—methods.
WO 700 W9384 1998]
RD93.W683   1998
617.1—dc21
DNLM/DLC
for Library of Congress
97-40496
CIP

Aspen Publishers, Inc., grants permission for photocopying for limited personal or internal use. This consent does not extend to other kinds of copying, such as copying for general distribution, for advertising or promotional purposes, for creating new collective works, or for resale. For information, address Aspen Publishers, Inc., Permissions Department, 200 Orchard Ridge Drive, Suite 200, Gaithersburg, Maryland 20878.

Orders: (800) 638-8437
Customer Service: (800) 234-1660

About Aspen Publishers • For more than 35 years, Aspen has been a leading professional publisher in a variety of disciplines. Aspen's vast information resources are available in both print and electronic formats. We are committed to providing the highest quality information available in the most appropriate format for our customers. Visit Aspen's Internet site for more information resources, directories, articles, and a searchable version of Aspen's full catalog, including the most recent publications: **http://www.aspenpub.com**
Aspen Publishers, Inc. • The hallmark of quality in publishing
Member of the worldwide Wolters Kluwer group.

Editorial Services: Ruth Bloom
Library of Congress Catalog Card Number: 97-40496
ISBN: 0-8342-0748-6

Printed in the United States of America

2 3 4 5

Table of Contents

Color Plates

Contributors

Barbara M. Bates-Jensen, MN, RN, CETN
Assistant Professor of Clinical Nursing
Department of Nursing
University of Southern California
Los Angeles, California

Nancy Byl, PhD, PT
Director
Program in Physical Therapy
University of California at San Francisco
Oakland, California

Carlos E. Donayre, MD
Assistant Professor of Surgery
University of California, Los Angeles
School of Medicine
Harbor/UCLA Medical Center
Department of Vascular and General Surgery
Torrance, California

Mary Dyson, BSc, PhD, CBiol, MIBiol
Division of Anatomy and Cell Biology
UMDS Medical School
Guys Hospital
London England

Nancy Elftman, CO, C.Ped.
Certified Orthotist, Certified Pedorthist
Cosmos Extremity
Hands on Foot
LaVerne, California
Rancho Los Amigos Medical Center (Retired)
Downey, California

Evonne Fowler, MN, RN, CETN
Wound/Ostomy/Skin Care Specialist
Bellflower Kaiser Hospital
Bellflower, California

Diane Krasner, PhD, RN, CETN
Consultant
Nursing Care of Patients
Wound Care, Ostomies, Incontinence
Baltimore, Maryland

Harriett Baugh Loehne, PT
Staff Physical Therapist
The North Carolina Baptist Hospitals, Inc.
Winston-Salem, North Carolina

Laurie M. Rappl, PT
Clinical Support Manager
Span-America Medical Systems, Inc.
Greenville, South Carolina

Anne Siegel, RN, RVT, CVN
Vascular Surgery Nurse Coordinator
University Hospital
Los Angeles, California

Carrie Sussman, PT
Sussman Physical Therapy, Inc.
Torrance, California

Geoffrey Sussman, PhC, MPS, MSHPA, AFAIPM, MSMA, JP
Director, Wound Dressing Education and Research
Department of Pharmacy Practice
Victorian College of Pharmacy
Monash University
Parkville, Victoria, Australia

Melisa Tiffany, BSN, RN, CETN
Graduate Student
ET Nursing
University of Southern California
Los Angeles, California

James Wethe, MD
South Bay Plastic Surgery
Torrance, California

Laurel A. Wiersema-Bryant, MSN, RN, CS
Clinical Nurse Specialist
Barnes-Jewish Hospital
at Washington University Medical Center
St. Louis, Missouri

Foreword

I was delighted to be given the opportunity to write a foreword to this unique manual about wound care. As a strong supporter of collaboration and community and deeply embedded in wound management, I commend the authors for giving us this excellent wound care resource manual. An environment that supports a collaborative spirit allows clinicians from both disciplines to provide their unique perspective to best meet the needs for each individual patient with a wound problem. Chronic wounds are a major problem for the person who has one, for the significant others involved with them, and the health care providers who care for them.

Wound management is carried out in all care settings: acute and long-term care facilities, in the home, and in outpatient clinics. In most settings, the care is often provided by health care professionals not formally educated in wound healing. However, when wound healing has not been achieved, the wound is difficult to treat, or time consuming and costly, often the patient will be seen by a wound care specialist. Usually first called is the nurse wound care specialist or physical therapist wound care specialist. The specialist may assess the situation, and recommend a management plan using advanced care products and techniques or alternative methods of management or provide the care. Having a wound care resource manual on hand would be a direct aid to practice.

Wound Care: A Collaborative Practice Manual for Physical Therapists and Nurses is a much needed resource for the health care providers who work daily to manage these troublesome wounds. It is a user-friendly resource volume, formatted for quick reference as a guide in any clinical setting. The procedures and guidelines included in the chapters provide the clinician with a tool box for daily practice in wound management.

This resource manual is a collaborative effort, written by Carrie Sussman, PT, a physical therapist, and Barbara M. Bates-Jensen, MN, CETN, a nurse wound care specialist. Both are recognized throughout the country for their clinical knowledge, practical expertise, and unwavering dedication to wound care. Both have national reputations as superb teachers who emphasize critical thinking/deductive reasoning in decision making. Their purpose for writing the book is to provide basic and advanced information on wound healing and wound care therapies, to promote collaborative wound management between nurses and physical therapists by providing a better understanding of the similarities and differences between disciplines, and to promote an understanding of wound management by challenging the thinking process.

The chapters are written by wound care specialists from many disciplines, who are on the forefront of wound healing practice and research. They have joined together to share their accumulated knowledge base, wisdom, and diverse experiences and expertise in wound management.

Wound management is multifaceted: the causes and consequences of non-healing wounds are complex and multidimensional and resolutions require an aggressive interdisciplinary approach to management. The best approach for handling chronic wounds is management by a multidisciplinary team working in a collaborating, supporting manner and using a science-based practice. This wound care manual provides a beginning for a living resource for excellence in wound management.

Evonne Fowler, RN, MN, CETN
Wound/Ostomy/Skin Care Specialist
Bellflower Kaiser Hospital
Bellflower, California

Preface

THE MULTIDISCIPLINARY TEAM

Writing this book has been a collaborative effort between the two editors and the 13 contributors. Early on in the writing it was recognized that, just as in the real world, the skills and expertise of a multidisciplinary team were needed to provide the scope of information needed for wound management. The writing team represents the disciplines usually found on the wound management team. Our authors include two surgeons, two researchers (one is a physical therapist), five nurses, one certified pedorthist, one pharmacist, and three physical therapists. What's more, a number of the chapters are coauthored by representatives of different disciplines. Two authors are from outside the United States. Wound management is a global problem and a multidisciplinary challenge, and collaboration across all borders must be encouraged. Yes, at times collaborating was challenging, but it has been very rewarding. Yet it seemed very logical that we should prepare this work as a collaborative effort and thus set the stage for collaborative practice.

ORGANIZATION OF THE BOOK

The book is organized into four parts. Part I reviews the diagnostic process used by both nurses and physical therapists when evaluating the patient with a wound. Why start with diagnosis? Nurses and physical therapists have extensive education with unique bodies of knowledge and, as professionals, have a level of autonomy and self-regulation. The use of a process to arrive at a diagnosis for the patient with a wound provides clarity in communication and collaborative practice. Clear communication assists with accountability and greater professional autonomy. Historically, nurses and physi-

cal therapists have used the medical diagnosis of the patient to describe the focus of their practice. There is better nursing and physical therapy–related terminology to describe the impairments, risk factors, and functional deficits for which nurses and physical therapists intervene. As it turns out, terminologies used by nurses and physical therapists are very similar—all the better to foster communication and collaboration between the two groups.

The rest of Part I reviews implementation of the diagnostic process and includes chapters on review of wound healing biology, chronic wound healing, assessment of the wound and surrounding skin, specific examinations and tests for wounds, and the complication factors of vascular disease. These chapters form the assessment foundation for the patient with a wound.

Part II describes management of the wound by specific wound characteristics. Recently, the American Physical Therapy Association convened a panel of five integumentary subject matter expert physical therapists to develop proactive patterns for management of integumentary impairments and disabilities. It was the consensus of the panel that wounds and burns are managed similarly, and that the factors that affect management of the wound are the depth of the injury (partial versus full thickness and extending into deep tissues) and the wound-associated characteristics of necrosis, edema, and infection. Everything else revolves around management of the wound environment or the factors influencing healing. Chapters include Management of Necrotic Tissue, Management of Exudate and Infection, Management of Edema, and Management of the Wound Environment. Three wound characteristics, necrotic tissue, exudate and infection, and edema, are the wound characteristics that most often drive interventions and cause concerns for clinicians. Each chapter begins with a definition of the characteristic, the significance of the findings, assessment for the characteristic, and basic interventions appropriate for the wound characteristic. Each chapter ends with outcome measures, self-care teaching guidelines, and referral criteria for the specific wound characteristic. Where appropriate, procedures and protocols for interventions are included.

Part III focuses on management of the wound by etiology. This section includes chapters on management of acute surgical wounds, management and prevention of pressure ulcers, management of pressure with therapeutic positioning, and management and diagnosis of vascular and neuropathic ulcers. The chapters focus on pathophysiology, prevention, classification, and intervention.

Part IV, Management of Wounds with Physical Therapy Technologies, applies the diagnostic process to selection of wound treatment interventions with physical therapy technologies including electrical stimulation, pulsed shortwave diathermy, pulsed radiofrequency stimulation, ultrasound, pulsatile lavage with suction, and whirlpool. Each physical therapy technology chapter begins with a definition of the intervention, the science and theory of the intervention as it relates to wound healing, and application of the diagnostic process to appropriate selection of candidates for treatment. Each chapter includes protocols and expected outcome results for the therapy described, as well as case studies.

Carrie Sussman
Barbara M. Bates-Jensen

Acknowledgments

We would like to express our appreciation to the many individuals who have made this book possible including:

— The individuals who have contributed their clinical and academic knowledge,
— Mary Anne Langdon, Ruth Bloom, Laura Smith, Jan Kortkamp and the rest of the staff at Aspen Publishers for their help and support in production,
— The reviewers and consultants whose suggestions were invaluable during development: Michelle Cameron, PT, OCS, Linda Frankenberger, MS, PT, Deborth Hagler, PT, Robert Kellogg, PhD, PT, Marko Markov, PhD, Gretchen Swanson, MPH, PT, Eleanor Price, PhD, Nancy A. Stotts, EdD, RN,

— Kris Johnson and Erin McEntyre who took care of many of the details associated with preparation of the manuscript,
— The authors, publishers, companies, and colleagues who have allowed us to publish their art work, photographs, and tables to illustrate the information.

Our husbands and children—Robert Sussman and Ronald, Holly, and Thomas Jensen, who have sweated the big and small stuff with us during the years of development and preparation of the manuscript and without whom completion of this project would not have been possible.

Carrie Sussman
Barbara M. Bates-Jensen

Introduction: The Need for Collaborative Practice

Carrie Sussman and Barbara M. Bates-Jensen

COLLABORATION

Physical therapy and nursing are the two health care disciplines most often involved in providing care for the patient with a wound. We believe one key to providing optimal wound care management to individuals with chronic wounds is collaborative practice between the health care disciplines of nursing and physical therapy. It has been our experience that in clinical practice, true collaboration is not the standard, and in many instances there exists some level of conflict between nursing and physical therapy. Conflicts may arise from misconceptions about the "other" discipline's ability, education level, or experience with wounds, from interpersonal differences, or from "turf battles" wherein one discipline is fighting with the other for greater control over the wound care segment of health care. Much of the conflict may be related to simple misunderstanding about the true nature of collaborative practice. True interdisciplinary collaboration does not require that one discipline "give up control" of wound care, nor does it require that clinicians always agree upon management options for patients. An environment that supports a collaborative spirit allows clinicians from both disciplines to provide their unique perspectives to best meet the needs for each individual patient with a wound problem.

Collaboration is challenging. The challenges to collaboration include the wide variety of clinical settings in which patients with wounds are managed, the variety of education and experience of clinicians, and the struggles of each discipline to clarify and better define professional roles. Yet when collaboration is implemented successfully, the rewards to clinicians, payers, health care agencies, and patients are numerous. Clinicians benefit from the free exchange of ideas from differing perspectives and the excitement of working

as a team to solve patient problems. Payers and health care settings benefit from fewer duplicated services and better patient outcomes at lower costs. Patients benefit from improved wound healing management, including better wound healing outcomes as a result of health care service integration. To practice in a collaborative spirit, each discipline must understand the process of wound healing, chronic wound difficulties, and the skills and services offered by each discipline. Each practitioner has areas of knowledge that by definition are not shared by others. Yet both physical therapy and nursing practice have many similarities.

The main purpose of this book is to provide basic information on wound healing and wound care therapies to nurses and physical therapists in a user-friendly resource volume for clinicians who deal with wounds on a daily basis and who do not have access to a "wound care expert." A secondary purpose of this manual is to promote collaborative wound management between nurses and physical therapists by providing a better understanding of the similarities and differences between disciplines. This book is for nurses and physical therapists in acute care, long-term care, outpatient care, and home health care settings. The book is formatted for use as a quick reference guide in any clinical setting. The book is designed to appeal to several groups of nurses. Enterostomal therapy (ET) nurses are often consulted on wound care and have additional education in wound care. ET nurses may find the book a direct aid to their practice and a valuable educational tool for use with other clinicians involved in wound care. Home health care nurses and nurses in long-term care settings in conjunction with physical therapists provide direct wound care in the home and long-term care setting with minimal support or education in new technologies for wound care diagnosis or management. Rehabilitation nurses work with spinal cord–injured patients; these patients are a high-risk group for pressure ulcer wounds, and treatment of pressure ulcers is one of the main points in the book. Physical therapists will find the text valuable as a reference for therapy and also as an educational tool for use with other health care professionals. Physical therapists are being asked to do more in the wound care arena, and many feel the need for additional education in this dynamic area.

EDUCATION OF NURSES AND PHYSICAL THERAPISTS

Nurses are licensed health care professionals who diagnose and treat human responses to health and illness.[1] The nursing profession is committed to the care and nurturing of both healthy and ill people, individually or in groups and communities. There are four essential features of contemporary nursing practice as defined by the American Nurses' Association Social Policy Statement: ". . . Attention to the full range of human experiences and responses to health and illness without restriction to a problem-focused orientation, integration of objective data with knowledge gained from an understanding of the patient or group's subjective experience, application of scientific knowledge to the processes of diagnosis and treatment, and provision of a caring relationship that facilitates health and healing."[2(p6)] The difference between professional and technical nurses is the depth and breadth of clinical nursing practice based on the knowledge foundation of the nurse, the nurse's role, and the type of patient service.[3] Nurses study biologic, physical, and social sciences in addition to nursing theory and the science of nursing practice. Nurses acquire knowledge in anatomy, physiology, pathophysiology, pharmacology, microbiology, chemistry, and statistics, as well as nursing science. Nursing education includes the traditional focus on illness and acute care clinical practice and the more pressing current focus on health promotion and community nursing.

Nurses practice at a variety of educational levels. The vocational or practical nurse education programs are located in technical or vocational schools. The vocational nurse education program is typically 1 year in length and leads to a certificate of completion and eligibility to take the state licensure examination to be designated as a licensed vocational nurse (LVN) or a licensed practical nurse (LPN). LPNs and LVNs are prepared to work with registered nurses (RNs) and to be supervised by RNs. The purpose of the vocational nurse programs is to prepare assistant licensed nurse workers.[4] These programs generally do not articulate well with collegiate nursing programs, although LPNs/LVNs may receive advanced placement in collegiate programs.

The first formal nursing education in the United States was in diploma programs. Diploma programs are typically hospital based and were the predominant model for nursing education in this country. Diploma programs are usually 2 to 3 years in length, and many include summer sessions. Graduates of diploma programs are eligible to take the RN licensure examination. The purpose of the diploma programs is to prepare clinically competent bedside nurses.[4] Some diploma programs have now aligned with other academic institutions, and many now offer an associate degree in nursing, ADN or AA.[5] Associate degree programs are community or junior college based, and the nursing portion is 2 years in length. The purpose of the associate degree nursing programs is to prepare competent technical bedside nurses for secondary care settings.[4] Many nurses enter associate degree programs with future intentions of continuing their education in nursing at the baccalaureate level.[5] Some 4-year university programs also offer combination degree programs to allow flexibility.

Baccalaureate programs in nursing are 4 years in length, with the nursing curriculum concentrated at the upper division. Graduates of baccalaureate programs are prepared as nurse generalists to practice nursing in beginning leadership positions in a variety of settings. In 1965, the American Nurses' Association designated the baccalaureate degree as the entry level for professional nursing practice. The majority of programs admit both prelicensure students and RNs who are graduates of diploma or associate degree programs. The general education requirements are the same for all students, and those with prior nursing education or experience are allowed to progress through the nursing curriculum by designs that capitalize on prior learning.

Master's degree education in nursing is typically 2 years in length and builds on the baccalaureate nursing major. Program content usually includes a group of core graduate-level courses, research course work, and specialty nursing courses. Master's-prepared nurses function at an advanced practice level and include nurse anesthetists, nurse midwives, nurse practitioners, and clinical nurse specialists. The degree most often awarded on completion of a master's program is the MSN (master of science in nursing) or the MN (master of nursing) degree. The purpose of master's education in nursing is to prepare advanced practice nurses in a specialty area such as psychiatric mental health nursing or nursing management.[5] In addition, advanced practice nurses serve as mentors, consultants, and educators of nurses in basic practice. They conduct research to expand the knowledge base of nursing practice, provide leadership for practice changes, and contribute to the advancement of the profession, health care, and society in general.[2]

Doctoral programs in nursing range from 3 to 5 years of full-time study. Doctoral programs include advanced content in concept development, theoretical analysis, research, advanced nursing, and supporting cognates. Doctoral programs prepare leaders for programs in education, administration, clinical practice, and research.

In addition to formal education programs, many nurses are specialty certified. The need for specialization in nursing developed as technologic advances in health care occurred over the last 10 years. Specialty programs are varied in scope, length of time, and requirements. Most specialty programs prepare RNs to take a certification examination as a part of credentialing in the specialty area. Certification requirements vary, depending on the specialty area, and may include completion of an education or training program, as well as clinical experience requirements. National certification examinations are offered through professional organizations in a variety of specialties, including wound care and ET nursing. In most states, RNs are required to maintain currency in their practice by completing specified amounts of continuing education.

Physical therapists (PTs) are licensed health care professionals who evaluate and treat people with health problems resulting from disease or injury. The American Physical Therapy Association (APTA) is the national organization representing the physical therapy profession, which accredits education programs for PTs and PT assistants (PTAs). Professional education required for PTs includes a minimum 4 years of college or university level training resulting in a baccalaureate degree in physical therapy from an accredited professional education program. The information explosion in the health-related sciences has led to current requirements that most therapists enter the profession as master's level–prepared clinicians, and now some are entering with a professional doctoral degree. Following graduation, PTs must pass a national licensing examination to qualify for state licensure. Like nurses, PTs may be specialty certified in a variety of areas of practice. Although there is no current specialty certification for wound care, instruction in wound management skills is a requirement for accreditation of physical therapist and physical therapist assistant programs. The requirements for continuing education for relicensure by PTs varies by state. The fact is that most PTs seek continuing education so as to be at the cutting edge of practice, even though it may not be a mandated requirement. Specialty certification in wound management is a targeted goal of the Wound Management Special Interest Group within the Section on Clinical Electrophysiology of the APTA. The special interest group was formed to bring together PTs and PTAs from many practice settings who have special interest in wound management.

PTAs are trained and licensed paraprofessionals with 2 years of educational training in an approved PTA program or who have worked as a physical therapy aide for a specific period of time and then passed a qualifying examination. The PTA provides services under the supervision of a PT.

The PTA can perform various tests and measures for which the assistant is trained, such as wound measurements, tissue attribute recording, and provision of treatment services with physical agents and electrotherapeutic modalities. In some states, the PTA may also perform sharp debridement. Both PTs and PTAs are qualified to apply topical agents and dressings to wounds.

Many individuals are surprised that the PT is included in the wound management team. Reports of wound management, including burn and wound interventions, by PTs appeared in the physical therapy literature for more than three decades. By education and training, PTs learn anatomy, physiology, and pathophysiology related to body systems responsible for repair and regeneration of soft tissue. For example, human cadaver dissection is part of the basic anatomy education of the PT and provides a foundation for the skills needed in sharp debridement of nonviable tissue. Courses in cardiopulmonary and vascular system physiology are required. These two systems are critical to wound healing. Neuropathy plays an important part in development of chronic wounds. PTs take courses in neurology and learn neurologic testing and effects of insensitivity on the integumentary system. The PT is expected to examine the integument as part of an overall evaluation. Postsurgical wounds are routinely seen and evaluated by the PT as part of the rehabilitation service. For example, dehiscence of a wound on an amputated limb requires wound management before prosthetic training is initiated. PTs also are skilled in the use of physical agents (heat, light, sound, and water), electrotherapeutic modalities, and therapeutic exercise, all of which are used in wound healing strategies. The PT can manage the wound as well as the prosthetic training and an exercise program to achieve the desired outcomes. PTs are interested in evidence-based health care choices, and many research studies by PTs on wound healing that demonstrate treatment efficacy are cited in this book.

Physical therapy is the care and services provided by or under the direct supervision of a PT.[6] Services provided by others using technologies generically referred to as physical therapy should not be confused with the services of a PT. Outcomes research studies show that expected outcomes may not be equivalent.[7] PTs are important players in the provision of primary care, defined as "integrated accessible health care services by clinicians who are accountable for addressing a large majority of personal health care need, developing a sustained partnership with patients and practicing in the context of family and community."[8(p712)] In 30 states, direct access to physical therapy services from a licensed PT is part of the practice acts. PTs play major roles in secondary and tertiary care as well. For example, patients with wounds are often seen initially by another health care practitioner and then referred to the PT. PTs provide tertiary care in highly specialized, complex, and technologically advanced settings. In such situations, a patient may have a traumatic wound, surgical wound, or burn plus complicating medical problems, and the PT is called upon to manage the wound as well as the other aspects of patient rehabilitation.

REFERENCES

1. American Nurses' Association. *Nursing A Social Policy Statement.* Kansas City, MO; 1980.

2. American Nurses' Association. *Nursing's Social Policy Statement.* Washington, DC; 1995.

3. American Nurses' Association. *Facts about Nursing.* Kansas City, MO; 1987.

4. Hart SE. Pathways of nursing education. In: Creasia JL, Parker B, eds. *Conceptual Foundations of Professional Nursing Practice.* 2nd ed. St. Louis, MO: Mosby; 1996:26–45.

5. Kozier B, Erb G, Blais K. *Professional Nursing Practice: Concepts and Perspectives.* 3rd ed. Menlo Park, CA: Addison-Wesley; 1997: 2–27.

6. American Physical Therapy Association. A guide to physical therapist practice, I: a description of patient management. *Phys Ther.* 1995;75:707–764.

7. American Physical Therapy Association. *Outcomes Effectiveness of Physical Therapy: An Annotated Bibliography.* Alexandria, VA; 1994.

8. Donaldson M, Yordy K, Vanselow N. *Defining Primary Care: An Interim Report.* Washington, DC: National Academy Press; 1994.

PART I

Introduction to Wound Diagnosis

Carrie Sussman

Development of diagnoses to direct and guide treatment by nurses and physical therapists has been growing over the last 15 to 20 years. Both disciplines recognize that use of a diagnostic process applies the skills and knowledge of the professional nurse and physical therapist to the appropriate treatment of client situations they can and should treat legally and independently. The role of diagnostician is unfamiliar to many, and practice experience in the area of diagnosis varies from nonexistent to full-practice integration for many years. Because the incorporation of diagnosis into the health care professions is still in its infancy, there is much variance in understanding of the process. Therefore, there are a number of questions that need to be clarified as the process begins:

- What does a diagnosis really mean?
- What kinds of information need to be collected to yield a diagnosis?
- How are diagnoses differentiated from each other?
- How is a diagnosis tailored to the patient's functional problem or human response to health or illness?
- How does diagnosis relate to prognosis and outcomes?
- How does the nursing or physical therapy diagnosis direct interventions?

Advanced clinicians who are more familiar with classification systems and diagnostic methods will have other types of questions:

- Can and should the medical diagnosis be part of the physical therapy diagnostic statement?
- What kind of functional diagnostic statement should be written for a person at risk for wounds?
- What is the difference between diagnosis and classification?

Part I begins with an introduction to the diagnostic process. It seeks to answer these questions, including specifics about wound diagnosis. Guidelines for writing functional diagnoses that are meaningful and related to the prognosis and treatment interventions are included for both disciplines. One of the things that became clear to the authors as Chapter 1 was crafted is that the diagnostic process and the terms of the diagnosis of the nurse and physical therapist are very similar. Both incorporate functional impairment and disability into the diagnostic process. For example, the nurse determines the client's response to health or illness as positive functioning, altered functioning, or at risk for altered functioning.[1] Nurses use a diagnosis that incorporates risk that could work equally well for the physical therapist. Nursing diagnosis specifically identifies collaborative problems and then the health care practitioner needed for joint management. The most appropriate joint manager for wounds may be the dietitian, the physician, or the physical therapist. Nurses already have taxomony for *impaired tissue integrity* and *impaired skin integrity.* Physical therapists use disablement terminology, including the terms *impairment, disability,* and *handicap* in their management model.[2]

Functional diagnosis requires understanding of functional impairment. Functional impairment differs from the pathogenesis or etiology of the problem and describes a functional change as physiologic, anatomic, structural, or functional at the tissue, organ, or body system level.[3] Functional impairments are the system or organ impairments that prevent normal function.[4] In impaired wound healing there is a functional impairment of wound healing that occurs at a system, organ, or tissue level in the body. Chapter 2 is devoted to understanding the system functions related to wound healing biology and chronic wound healing. Assessment, examinations, tests, and measurements are an integral part of establishing a diagnosis. Chapters 3, 4, 5, and 6 describe techniques to perform the procedures and how to interpret the findings.

At the conclusion of Part I, clinicians will be able to perform the tests and measures necessary to determine functional wound diagnosis, develop a prognosis, and state the expected outcome. They will be able to document the diagnostic process and the findings with a functional outcomes report. The clinician will then be ready to go to Parts II, III, and IV to learn the management skills for different wound-related problems and interventions.

REFERENCES

1. Carpenito LJ. *Nursing Diagnosis: Application to Clinical Practice.* 6th ed. Philadelphia: J.B. Lippincott; 1994.

2. American Physical Therapy Association. A guide to physical therapy practice, I: a description of patient management. *Phys Ther.* 1995;75:707–764.

3. World Health Organization. *International Classification of Impairments, Disabilities, and Handicaps.* Geneva, Switzerland; 1980.

4. Jette AM. Physical disablement concepts for physical therapy research and practice. *Phys Ther.* 1994;74:380–386.

CHAPTER 1

The Diagnostic Process

Carrie Sussman, Barbara M. Bates-Jensen, and Melisa Tiffany

This chapter describes the diagnostic process for management of patients with chronic wounds. Nurses and physical therapists use essentially the same decision-making process in diagnosing patient problems, although the terms used to describe the process may differ slightly. Nurses use the nursing process and nursing diagnosis as the framework for planning and evaluating patient care. The nursing process includes the following steps: assessment, diagnosis, goals, interventions, and evaluation. Physical therapy uses a process that includes the steps of assessment, examination, diagnosis, prognosis, and outcomes. To simplify and guide the reader, the diagnostic process has been broken into four steps, each with two or three parts. Step I, assessment, includes review of the reason for referral, history, systems review/physical assessment, and wound assessment. Step II, diagnosis, includes examination strategy, evaluation, and diagnosis. Step III, goals, includes prognosis, goals, and outcomes. Step IV, intervention, is described in subsequent chapters. Examinations and specific measurements plus special test procedures are found in Chapters 6 and 8, as well as in others.

STEP I: ASSESSMENT PROCESS

The assessment process is the first step in wound care management. Assessment is done for all patients before determining the need for special testing examinations and interventions. For nurses, this process begins when the patient is admitted to the agency. For physical therapists, this process begins with the reason for referral, which is part of the patient history. The assessment process involves gathering data from the patient history and physical examination. The patient history determines which relevant systems reviews are needed in the physical examination. For physical therapists, the history and systems review determine the candidacy or noncandidacy for services; for nurses, the history and systems review determine the direction for the treatment plan. Many physical therapists retain the belief that all referrals automatically show candidacy for wound care. The reality is that not all patients are appropriately referred for physical therapy. To some physical therapists this will sound like heresy, but proper utilization management is mandatory in today's health care environment.

Utilization management is part of the process of prospective management and is designed to ensure that only medically necessary, reasonable, and appropriate services are provided. Utilization management attempts to influence the treatment pathway to ensure optimal clinical outcomes.[1] For nurses, the assessment process provides the framework for planning comprehensive wound care incorporating utilization management, and may include making a referral for physical therapy.

Utilization management for the patient with the wound and for comorbidities and coimpairment are separate but related. Collaborative interdisciplinary management of comorbidities and coimpairments will reduce iatrogenic effects from inappropriate selection of interventions or handling of the wound, and will lessen extrinsic and intrinsic complications. Chapter 2 explains and discusses comorbidities and coimpairments as well as the iatrogenic extrinsic and intrinsic factors that affect wound healing. The interdisciplinary nature inherent in caring for the patient with a wound requires clinicians to carefully determine candidacy for services before initiating referral or treatment. The assessment process assists in clinical decision making by avoiding undirected care and inappropriate treatment.

Assessment with attention to utilization management allows selection of a path for referral for another intervention or to other health care disciplines and practitioners. For example, the physical therapist may determine that the patient is not a candidate for whirlpool therapy as ordered by the physician, and sends the findings with an alternative recommendation to the referring physician. An additional example is provided when the history and physical examination of the wound suggest to the nurse that vascular examination and testing procedures are needed.

The use of standardized forms is the best method of collecting assessment data quickly and efficiently, thus ensuring that important information is not lost. Use of a form that the clinician completes and a form that the patient completes ensures data maintenance from the interview. A self-administered patient history form helps the clinician to focus the interview and can save time. Samples of an assessment form for a self-administered history and an interview form for physical therapists and nurses are presented in Appendixes 1–A and 1–B. The forms include reason for admission/referral, past medical history, physical examination findings, and a place to list suggested examinations to follow based on the intake information. Forms may be completed by both the clinician and the patient or significant other. Some information will be found in the patient's medical record, but many times the patient or significant other can provide additional insights and information not otherwise available. Partnering or engaging the patient in his or her own care from the beginning is essential to achieving mutually satisfactory outcomes.

Review of Admission/Referral

It is essential for a physical therapist to know the reason why a patient is referred. This referral is the first step in documenting patient history. The initial referral for wound care management is usually to the nurse; if the nurse determines a need for physical therapy services, the physical therapist is brought into the team. It is critical for nurses to know expectations and projected outcomes from a physical therapy referral in order to refer appropriately. In some health care settings, a wound care team decides the services necessary for wound management and makes the appropriate referrals. The patient referred to the physical therapist for wound healing is usually an individual who has not shown signs of normal wound repair. Most often other treatment interventions are in use or have been tried with limited or no success. Physical therapy services usually involve an additional fee.

The referral to physical therapy is regarded as an attempt to maximize and enhance wound repair. However, expectations of referral may be for reasons beyond improved wound healing. For example, the patient may be referred for help in cleaning and debriding a necrotic wound, for enhancement of the inflammatory process and to reinitiate wound repair, or for recurrent infection. The patient may not have the physi-

cal capacity necessary for healing because of multiple comorbidities that impair wound healing, such as chronic pulmonary disease or end-stage cancer. For the patient who presents with factors that impair wound healing, the reason for referral is to achieve a clean, stable wound that can be managed easily by the nurse or caregiver at home. Pain management may be the underlying reason for referral, with physical agents and electrotherapeutic modalities prescribed to help control pain. Thus, for both the nurse and the physical therapist, wound closure may not be the highest priority. Both nurses and physical therapists must understand the reason for the referral and the expected outcomes. There must be a match between selected intervention and expected outcomes to meet the referral objectives. For example, the patient with a foot ulcer secondary to pressure and insensitivity is fearful of amputation and loss of ability to walk. The patient's main concern is limb salvage, and expectations are high. In contrast, the family of a debilitated nursing home patient may only desire comfort for their family member with no expectations of wound closure. Family and caregiver perceptions of various interventions may differ from the clinician's view. What is perceived by one to be heroic and painful measures may in truth be normal procedures. The nurse must address these issues before a referral to physical therapy is made.

Patient History

Patient history information is commonly collected by an interview process with the patient, family, significant others, and caregivers; by consultation with other health care practitioners; and by reviewing the medical record. Ideally, in the continuum of care, the information about the patient history will be transmitted with the patient. Unfortunately, this is not always the case. The clinician may have to piece together the history from the many sources listed above. If a limited amount of medical and social information is available, the clinician may have to choose diagnostic options based on available data. It is easier to plan appropriate care with a complete history.

Clinical Wisdom: *Patient History Needed To Determine Care Direction*

- Reason for admission or referral
- Expectations and perceptions about wound healing
- Psychosocial-cultural-economic history
- Present medical comorbidities
- Current wound status

Remember that one of the primary goals during the patient interview is to begin to develop a therapeutic relationship with the patient and family. The history taking allows the clinician to assess and diagnose patient problems and place the problem within the context of the individual patient's life. The skills used by clinicians during the patient history are those of listening, observing, and asking questions. Several types of questions are useful to the clinician conducting the patient history. Closed-ended questions require a brief response, usually yes or no, and are useful when specific information is required, such as age, marital status, or presence of a specific health risk such as smoking. Open-ended questions aim to elicit more information in patient responses. An example of an open-ended question is "Can you tell me about your wound?" Questions can be directive, to lead the patient to focus on a specific area, and are most useful during the systems review portion of the history. An example of a directive question is "Have you experienced any problems with venous disease in the past, such as lower leg edema or swelling, previous ulcers, or skin color changes on the lower leg?" The last type of question is the permission-giving question. Permission-giving questions are especially useful when dealing with difficult topics. An example of a permission-giving question is "Many patients I see have questions or concerns about sexual activity with a wound. What are your questions?" The clinician also uses active listening and observation skills during the interview. For example, when questioning a patient about alcohol or tobacco use the clinician also observes for signs of alcohol or tobacco use such as an odor of alcohol or smoking.

Chief Complaint and Health History

Begin the patient history by finding out the patient's chief complaint or major reason for seeking care and the duration of the problem. Find out why the patient is seeking help at this time. It may be simple convenience or it may be that the wound problem was worsening and the patient felt that treatment was needed at this time. Investigate other agendas the patient may have other than the obvious problem by asking a question such as "How did you hope I could help you today?" Explore the meaning of the wound with the patient. Questions such as "What do you think caused your wound?" and "Why do you think it started when it did?" and "What do you think your wound does to you and how long do you think the wound will last?" help reveal the patient's level of understanding of the health problem. Based on answers obtained, care can be planned that is sensitive to the patient's needs and level of understanding. The clinician seeks a complete understanding of the patient's symptoms (symptoms are the subjective feelings of the patient) during the interview. Seven criteria can be used to describe symptoms: location, character, severity, timing, setting in which the symp-

tom occurs, antecedents and consequences of the symptom, and other associated symptoms.

Clinical Wisdom: *Questions To Ask To Elicit Extent of Wound Symptoms*

Location:	Where do you feel the wound? Do you feel it anywhere else? Show me where it hurts.
Character:	What does it feel like?
Severity:	On a scale of 0 to 10, with 10 being the worst pain you could imagine, how would you rate the discomfort you have now? How does the wound interfere with your usual activities? How bad is it?
Timing:	When did you first notice the wound? How often have you had wounds?
Setting:	Does the wound occur in a certain place or under certain circumstances? Is it associated with any specific activity?
Antecedents and consequences:	What makes it better? What makes it worse?
Other associated symptoms:	Have you noticed any other changes?

During the patient interview, answers to these questions should provide a thorough understanding of the patient's wound symptoms. Review the patient's present health and present illness status. This provides information relevant to the patient's reasons for seeking care. Describe the patient's usual health and then focus on the present problem, investigating the chief complaint thoroughly as described above. For interpretation and analysis of the patient's problem, it is helpful to document the chief complaint data in chronologic order.

Next, review the patient's past health history. The purpose of the past health history is to identify major past health problems that may have some effect on the patient's current problem. Information about management of and response to past problems provides an indication of the patient's potential response to current treatment of the problem. Much of this information may be available in the patient's medical record. If not available, the following information should be obtained: past general health, childhood illnesses, accidents or injuries with any associated disabilities, hospitalizations, surgeries, major acute or chronic illnesses, immunizations, medications and transfusions, and allergies. Current health information includes allergies, habits, medications, and sleep and exercise patterns, all of which provide information on the patient's health habits. Investigate environmental, food, drug, animal, or other allergies. Specific allergies may have a bearing on interventions chosen for the patient's wound care regimen. Allergic reactions usually affect the gastrointestinal tract, the respiratory tract, and the skin. Allergic reactions involve the release of histamine from the mast cells. The clinician should be aware of signs and symptoms of an allergic reaction, which is a type of inflammatory response. The allergic inflammatory response can be erroneously interpreted as cellulitis or infection. It can also cause a contact dermatitis or pruritus and scratching with resultant excoriation of the skin. The excoriation lesions can become infected and may be the pathogenesis of the wound. Some products used for wound care can contribute to an allergic reaction. One is latex that is found in dressings, gloves, and plastic tubing. Tape is another notorious culprit often associated with skin allergies. The clinician should be aware of warning signs and take necessary measures to control the offending allergen. Sulfonamide is a common drug allergen, and Silvadene is a common topical therapy for wound care that contains sulfonamide, so the clinician would need to choose another topical agent to accomplish the goals for that patient.

Evaluate current and past habits relevant to the health of the patient including alcohol, tobacco, substance, drug, and caffeine use. Alcohol, tobacco, and substance use in particular present significant problems with tissue perfusion and nutrition for wound healing. Complete a full medication profile, including both prescription and over-the-counter medications, names, dosages, frequency, intended effect, and compliance with the regimen. Many medications interfere with wound healing or may interact with wound therapy.

Evaluate the patient's usual routine for patterns of physical and sedentary activities. Ask the patient to describe a usual day's activities. Exercise patterns influence healing in several wound types, such as venous disease ulcers. Finally, describe the patient's sleep pattern and whether the patient perceives the sleep to be adequate and satisfactory. Ask the patient where he or she usually sleeps. Patients with severe arterial insufficiency may sleep sitting up in recliner chairs because of the pain associated with the disease. Likewise, patients with chronic obstructive pulmonary disease may sleep sitting up because of difficulty breathing in the supine position.

The family health history provides information about the general health of the patient's relatives and family. Family health information is helpful in identification of genetic, familial, or environmental illnesses. Specific areas to target are diabetes mellitus, heart disease, and stroke. Each of these diseases can impair wound healing in an existing wound and are risk factors for further wounding. If the patient has a family history of these diseases, he or she may have early signs of the disease as yet undiagnosed and is at higher risk of eventual disease development.

Sociologic History

Diagnosis and management of the patient's wound problem is best accomplished within the context of the whole person. It is important to gather information about the patient's sociologic, psychologic, and nutritional status. Many patients are unaccustomed to questions about nonphysical matters, and it may be necessary to explain the purpose of gathering this information to the patient. For example, the clinician can simply state, "To be effective in caring for your wound, it is important for me to know something about you as a person." Sociologic data fall into seven areas: relationships with family and significant others, environment, occupational history, economic status and resources, educational level, daily life, and patterns of health care.

Relationships with family and significant others includes gathering information on the patient's position and role in the family, the persons living with the patient, the persons to whom the patient relates, and any recent family changes or crisis. The role of the patient within the family may dictate treatment decisions. For example, the grandmother with venous disease ulcers may also be the prime caregiver of young grandchildren, thus it is unrealistic to expect compliance with a therapeutic regimen that includes frequent periods of elevating lower extremities. The family support system may be a critical component when determining wound care management programs and answers to questions such as "Who will change the wound dressing and perform procedures?" "Who prepares meals?" and "Who will transport the patient to the clinic?" may influence treatment options. Personal relationship information gathering can extend to discussion of how the wound affects the patient's sexuality. Sexually active patients are going to need treatment considerations that will not interfere with their sexual functions. For example, a paraplegic patient with a sacral ulcer is going to need pressure relief and a dressing that will not impede sexual activity, cause trauma to the wound, or leak.

The environment plays a significant role in health and illness of individuals. Ask questions about the home, community, and work environments. Home care patients present challenging environments for wound repair. For example, the elderly woman living alone with four cats in a two-room trailer with minimal bathroom facilities will require different management strategies than the middle-aged man living with a spouse and family in a three-bedroom house in the suburbs. The community environment may provide additional resources for the patient, such as senior citizens' centers, health fairs, or the neighborhood grocery store that delivers to the home. The work environment along with the occupational history provides information on the ability of the patient to eliminate certain risk factors for impaired healing. For example, the grocery clerk with a venous disease ulcer will need help with work adjustment of a job when standing for long periods of time is required. Occupational history can pinpoint health-risk jobs such as those that require prolonged standing.

Economic status and resources are important to determine adequacy for therapy compliance. It is not necessary to know the patient's exact income; instead, ask whether the patient feels the income is adequate and elicit the source of the income. It is important to identify patients with inadequate resources and make appropriate referrals for financial assistance. Be sure to include an assessment of the patient's health insurance resources. If the expectation is prolonged wound healing, a discussion of financial reserves may be desirable. The economic history needs to include not only the patient's payer source for insurance coverage, but also the resources the patient has available to obtain necessary dressing supplies. Some patients have insurance coverage that pays for all dressing supplies, other patients have insurance coverage that pays for only certain types of supplies (gauze, but not tape), and yet other patients have no coverage for supplies at all. The economic history is also needed to determine whether the patient has adequate resources available to pay for a caregiver, if one is needed to come in to help with caregiving or changing dressings.

The educational level of the patient and judgment of age-appropriateness of intellect is helpful in planning future education on self-care of the wound. Ask the patient to describe a typical day and to identify any differences on the weekend. The daily profile allows the clinician to perceive the whole patient. Questions about the social and recreational activities of the patient as well as typical daily routines provide valuable insights into the patient's lifestyle and possible health risks. Evaluation of previous health care access and use assists with clinical judgment of past health promotion and prevention activities and whether the patient's care has had continuity.

Psychologic History

The psychologic history includes an assessment of the patient's cognitive abilities (including learning style, memory, comprehension), responses to illness (coping patterns, reaction to illness), response to care (compliance), and cultural implications for care. Usually at this point the clinician has some idea of the patient's comprehension, memory, and overall cognitive status. If mental function is still unclear, the clinician may want to administer a mental status examination such as the mini–mental status exam. Previous coping patterns and reactions to illness provide insight to possible

reactions to the current situation. Has the patient had difficulties with wound healing in the past? Is there a history of chronic wounds? How has the patient responded to previous chronic wounds? All are important questions to ask the patient. Response to previous care and compliance with other therapy regimens may indicate potential adherence difficulties with the current treatment plan.

Cultural History

People come from different walks of life, and often have belief systems significantly different from those of the clinician. It is therefore very important to take nothing for granted and to assess the patient's and caregiver's values and beliefs about health and wellness. For example, Hinduism espouses the belief that if something was wrong in a past life, then karma is bad and the patient deserves the wound. Asian cultures may believe that the body should go back to where it came from whole, and the wound causes the body to be not whole. Hispanics often believe that if patients are unable to make their own decisions regarding their care, then the eldest son should direct the care, even if a middle daughter has been performing direct hands-on care for 6 months. Patients from Sweden often believe that if a problem is ignored it doesn't exist, and thus they may delay seeking appropriate care. These examples are not provided so that the clinician can jump to conclusions about a patient or family belief system, but rather as a reminder that we all have different values and beliefs about health care, healing, and wellness. As clinicians, we need to be particularly sensitive in our assessment of the patient's culture and values.

Nutritional History

Nutrition plays a major role in wound healing. During the patient interview, determine the patient's usual daily food intake, risk for malnutrition, and specific nutritional deficiencies. Evaluate the patient's weight in comparison to the usual weight of the patient. Ask the patient to recall all foods eaten in the past 24 hours and determine whether this is a normal pattern for the patient. Evaluate intake of fruits, vegetables, meats, dairy products, and breads and cereals. Look for high-risk food behaviors such as high intake of red meat; low amounts of fiber, fruits, and vegetables; or high intake of calories.

Medication History

An accurate and complete medication history is an important element of a complete patient history. Medications can have a significant impact on wound progress. Determine all prescription and over-the-counter medications in use by the patient. Clarify the dose, frequency, and reason for the medication. Is the patient compliant with the medication regimen? Why or why not? What over-the-counter medications does the patient take and for what reasons? Is there evidence of polypharmacy, overmedication, drug-drug interactions, or drug-condition interactions? The physical therapist will need to work with the nurse to better understand the medication regimen and the effects of drugs in use on potential wound healing. This is a wonderful opportunity for collaboration.

Systems Review and Physical Assessment

The systems review portion of the patient history and the physical assessment of each system provide information on comorbidities that may impair wound healing. The individual's capacity to heal may be limited by specific disease effects on tissue integrity and perfusion, patient mobility, compliance, nutrition, and risk for wound infection. Throughout the patient history, systems review, and physical assessment the clinician considers host factors that affect wound healing. The physical assessment of relevant systems offers the clinician insight into factors that determine patient candidacy, selection of appropriate tests, and ultimately wound prognosis. Generally, physical therapists review the medical record and query the patient during the systems review. Nurses usually gather the pertinent history from the patient and perform a physical assessment of each system. The pertinent factors for each body system are presented below, along with guidelines for history taking, followed by a brief discussion of physical assessment parameters to look for in each system.

Respiratory System

The respiratory system is critical for delivery of oxygen and nutrients to the tissues to promote wound healing and control infection. Pulmonary disease may be progressive in conditions such as cystic fibrosis, chronic obstructive pulmonary disease (COPD), and lung cancer. Nonprogressive disease states to consider are pneumonia, postcardiac or postthoracic surgery, and traumatic injury. Specific respiratory diseases affect wound healing. Considerations related to major pulmonary pathology are presented.

Chronic Obstructive Pulmonary Disease. Patients with COPD have problems of pulmonary secretion retention, which fills alveolar sacks and reduces the surface area for transference of oxygen through the alveolar membrane into the blood stream. Assessment includes evaluation of pulse oximetry, pulmonary function tests, and mode and amount of oxygen delivery. Transcutaneous oxygen transport measurements are also helpful (see Chapter 6). If noninvasive vascular test results are not available, they should be considered as part of the examination strategy for patients with COPD. It is critical for clinicians to know the status of avail-

able oxygen for wound healing and infection control. Oxygen delivery is even more compromised for COPD patients on bed rest. Oxygen delivery is severely reduced when the body is in the horizontal position. In the supine position the diaphragm has reduced excursion space that decreases the thoracic expansion and tidal volume of air into the lungs. Elevating the head of the bed and placing the patient in semi–Fowler's position may improve air flow into the lungs. However, skin over the sacrococcygeal area will be at risk for pressure ulcer formation because of shearing and friction forces present in the typical semi–Fowler's position. Decreased mobility is often an additional complication of COPD because of poor endurance, deconditioning, and difficulty of breathing during activity. Decreased mobility is an indicator for positioning and risk reduction examinations.

Pneumonia. The patient with pneumonia should be assessed for etiologic factors and pulmonary status. The patient most at risk for pneumonia is the elderly, frail, institutionalized patient with multiple health deficits. Check chest radiograph reports to determine onset date and location of the infiltrate. Patients with swallowing disorders and those with nasogastric tube feedings are at high risk for aspiration pneumonia, and radiographic studies may demonstrate aspiration into the lungs. The patient may have a history of recurrent pneumonia. Patients with pneumonia have elevated temperatures, chest congestion, and decreased lung sounds, and appear acutely ill. The stress of the illness and the related signs and symptoms lead to impaired wound healing. Wounds will generally plateau, fail to continue healing, or deteriorate until the pneumonia is resolved. Wound repair may not be an option for this patient until the underlying disease is under control. Maintaining current wound status and preparing the wound for healing may be goals for this time frame. Prevention of wound trauma and further skin breakdown would be expected outcomes from therapeutic positioning.

Asthma. Asthma is a collection of respiratory symptoms caused by infections, hypersensitivity to irritants (pollutants, allergens) psychologic stress, cold air, exercise, or drug use. Asthma may be symptom-controlled with medications including steroids such as prednisone. Inquire about the time of onset of the asthma and the start of steriod therapy. Some individuals have a long history of steroid use and this will affect ability to heal. Steroids repress the inflammatory response, and without inflammation wound healing will not progress. The effects of steroids can be mitigated by use of oral or topical vitamin A. The physician should be contacted with recommendations for vitamin A administration as soon as possible.

Respiratory System Physical Assessment. As previously discussed, the patient history determines the physical assessment needed. A respiratory physical examination includes a thorough assessment using observation, palpation, percussion, and auscultation. The findings will help determine etiology and plan of care. The clinician needs to pay particular attention to overall clinical status. Is the patient having labored respirations at rest, talking, or ambulating short distances? This indicates potential for decreased oxygenation to the wound bed. Clinicians should evaluate laboratory values such as arterial blood gases (ABGs). The clinician palpates for crepitus, uses percussion for areas of dullness, and auscultates for adventitious breath sounds such as crackles or rales, rhonchi, or wheezes. Document abnormal findings and monitor for adequate breath sounds.

Cardiovascular System

Patients with cardiac disease have poor pump function. There may be dysfunction of the coronary arteries, the valves, or the cardiac electrical conduction system. In general, any dysfunction of the cardiac system poses significant difficulties related to wound healing. The heart is responsible for pumping oxygenated blood through the circulatory system to all body tissues. Thus, if the heart is not functional, all body tissues suffer. Specific pathology with concerns for wound patients include coronary artery disease and congestive heart failure.

Clinical Wisdom: *Pacemaker Caution for Physical Therapists*

Some patients have pacemaker implants to support or replace the dysfunction of the cardiac system. This is important information for physical therapists when selecting a treatment intervention with electrotherapeutic agents.

Coronary Artery Disease. In coronary artery disease, blood vessels may become clogged, producing signs and symptoms of angina pectoris or myocardial infarction. In either case, the effect is to shunt blood flow away from the periphery of the body. This impedes circulation to the tissues. Impaired blood flow reduces oxygen and nutrients. A questioning guideline is to determine whether the patient is a candidate for cardiac bypass surgery or valvular surgery. If surgery is indicated, it should precede aggressive intervention by the clinician. The wound should be managed conservatively during the presurgical phase.

Congestive Heart Failure. Congestive heart failure (CHF) is the heart's inability to pump enough blood for body functioning. In CHF the right or left side of the heart can fail. Either case generally involves the other side, and symptoms

of both right- and left-sided failure relate to fluid overload. Diuretic therapy is commonly prescribed to assist in fluid balance, decrease the burden on the heart, and thus improve heart pumping action. Is diuretic therapy successful? Information on severity of heart failure and effectiveness of therapeutic management guides the clinician's examination strategy. For example, in evaluation of the patient with CHF and concomitant lower leg ulcers and lower extremity edema, it is essential to differentiate the edema associated with CHF from edema associated with venous disease. Treatment for the edema in the patient with both CHF and venous disease may differ from treatment for the patient with edema related to venous disease only.

Cardiovascular System Physical Assessment. Cardiac system physical assessment includes palpation of pulses and auscultation of the heart. Physical assessment includes evaluation for dependent edema (in lower extremities if ambulatory or in a chair, and in sacral area if patient is supine), pitting edema of the lower extremities, weight gain from fluid retention, muscle weakness, and fatigue. The effects of edema on wound healing include slowed or impaired wound healing response. Interventions must incorporate management of blood flow within the body's capacity to handle fluid movement. For instance, a patient with CHF and a necrotic heel ulcer is referred to physical therapy for whirlpool therapy. The clinician should know that placing a leg in a dependent position in a warm whirlpool will aggravate an already overloaded vascular and interstitial fluid system, and alternative therapy should be recommended. The patient with CHF and a wound will need significant help to progress, and the outcome may be limited to a clean stable wound.

Gastrointestinal System

The anatomy of the gastrointestinal (GI) tract includes the esophagus, stomach, small intestine, and large intestine. The GI system is responsible for digestion and absorption of nutrients and fluids. Specific disorders of concern for patients with wounds include GI bleeding or problems with digestion and absorption of nutrients. Gastrointestinal bleeding weakens the patient and decreases blood supply. Any disease causing GI malfunctioning leads to poor absorption of nutrients and fluids for the patient. Patients with gastrostomy tubes receive enteral nutrition directly into the stomach, bypassing the mouth. Tube feedings may be accompanied by loose stools, which can irritate skin and seep into wounds in the pelvic area, resulting in wound contamination. A dietary consultation may be helpful in the optimal management of patients with GI tube feedings or malnutrition related to GI pathology.

Clinical Wisdom: *Diarrhea with GI Tube Feedings*

Diarrhea associated with tube feedings requires investigation. Sometimes slowing the rate of the feeding infusion, diluting the formula, or using a formula containing fiber may help decrease or eliminate the diarrhea. Wound therapy choices for patients with diarrhea from tube feedings include attention to dressings that protect the wound area from fecal contamination.

Gastrointestinal System Physical Assessment. Physical assessment of the GI system uses skills of palpation, percussion, and auscultation. Palpate the abdomen with attention to areas causing pain or tenderness and any masses or lumps palpated. Percuss the abdominal fields and, finally, auscultate for bowel sounds and arterial bruits. Check the medical record for the pattern of stool evacuation and interpret the stool data for diarrhea or constipation patterns.

Nutrition and Hydration. Nutritional screening is an important component of assessment because of the relationship among malnutrition, pressure ulcer development, and impaired wound healing. Nutritional data may be found in the medical record as a single assessment or as pieces of information that need to be brought together by the clinician. A sample nutritional assessment guide and diagram can be found in Chapter 2. If no standardized nutrition assessment form exists within the agency or setting, the following should be evaluated by the clinician: current weight, prior weight, weight change, and percentage change in weight, height, and body mass index. Body weight is a commonly used indicator of nutrition. An involuntary increase or decrease in weight of 5% is predictive of a drop in serum albumin.[2] Serum albumin is a measure of protein available for healing; a normal level is greater than 3.5 mg/dL. Other laboratory tests to evaluate include prealbumin levels and total lymphocyte count.

Malnutrition may be a consequence of several factors, including chronic disease, cognitive impairment, or social isolation. Each requires a separate assessment. Some individuals are unable or unwilling to take nutrition by mouth and refuse other means of obtaining nutrition such as tube feedings. Some individuals have difficulty obtaining healthful food or preparing meals, or are socially isolated for meals with resultant poor intake. Likewise, the cognitively impaired individual may be unable to prepare meals or simply forget to eat available food. It is essential that patients and family caregivers receive education on nutritional needs and the effects of malnutrition on wound healing. The patient and caregiver response to nutrition information has an impact on wound prognosis and wound recurrence as well as the aggressiveness of treatment interventions.

Hydration status can be determined by interpreting intake and output sheets. Intake and output sheets are often kept in the patient's room and may be completed by nurses or nursing assistants, depending on the health care setting. Signs of dehydration include thirst, tongue dryness in non–mouth breathers, and decreased skin turgor.

Clinical Wisdom: *Skin Turgor Assessment*

Assess skin turgor by evaluating for tenting of the skin. Gently pinch the skin and release; observe tissues for the speed of return to normal contours. It is best to check for tenting of the skin on the patient's forehead or sternal (chest) areas.

Dehydration affects wound healing by reducing the blood volume available to transport oxygen and nutrients to healing tissues. The state of hydration affects weight and albumin levels. Jugular vein distention may indicate overhydration. The thirst reflex is diminished in older adults, placing them at higher risk of dehydration. Nutrition and hydration intake history that indicates inadequate dietary or fluid intake should trigger assessment of the physical and psychosocial barriers to good nutrition. Ask questions such as: Is the gut functioning properly? Can the patient swallow? Is the patient depressed? Is the patient at an end-stage of life? Until these matters are addressed the patient may not respond positively to aggressive wound healing interventions, and palliative or preventive therapy may be most appropriate.

Case Study: *Malnutrition and Wound Management in End-Stage Illness*

A malnourished patient with a pressure ulcer on the coccyx is in the end-stage of life. The patient and family refuse tube feedings and understand the consequences of the minimally nourished and dehydrated condition. In this case, palliative and prevention treatment is indicated. The wound can be kept clean and dressed to control drainage and odor. Yet the patient is also a candidate for a pressure-relief mattress replacement or specialty bed for prevention of additional skin breakdown. A turning schedule and training of the caregivers is also part of the prevention intervention strategy.

Case Study: *Cognitively Impaired Patient with Leg Ulcers*

A patient who was cognitively impaired with a history of venous disease and recurrent ulceration of her legs can demonstrate how the change in nutritional status affected her recurrent ulcers. Emma was an elderly nursing home patient with a diagnosis of Alzheimer's disease and was confined for her safety to a secure medical unit. She was labeled "Mrs. Houdini" because she could undo any restraint, including climbing the bedrails. Emma walked all day long with negative consequences on her venous disease. Compression stockings were out of the question. She would not tolerate putting them on or wearing them. Emma was hyperactive and a very poor eater.

The director of nurses decided to investigate her nutritional status. She reviewed Emma's weight status and found progressive loss of weight over the previous 3 to 4 months. Consultation with the physician led to further evaluation and revealed a low albumin level of 2.5 mg/dL. Evaluation by the speech pathologist demonstrated delayed swallowing response and resulted in a recommendation for a videofluoroscopic examination.

The nutritional assessment with the resultant recommendation for gastrostomy tube placement was shared with the family. Emma tolerated the procedure well. A benefit of the gastrostomy tube placement for Emma was that it could be covered by her clothing and was out of sight and therefore out of mind for this individual, so she left it alone.

In a couple of weeks the added nutrition to her diet made her much less irritable and hyperactive. Emma could be placed in a gerichair with a restraint tray and her legs were elevated part of the day. She walked with assistance a couple of times a day. She was transferred from the secure unit to the long-term care custodial area of the facility and had more social interaction. She gained weight and had no further episodes of venous dermatitis or ulceration during the next year.

Genitourinary System

The genitourinary system is divided into the upper tract (kidneys and ureters) and the lower tract (bladder, sphincters, and urethra). Patients with kidney failure may require treatment involving some form of dialysis and a special diet that may impair wound healing. The patient with kidney failure often has multiple system failure. Evaluation for other diseases such as diabetes and hypertension is warranted, as they often coincide with kidney dysfunction.

Urinary Incontinence. Bladder dysfunction, outlet problems, or sphincter dysfunction can cause urinary incontinence. Urinary incontinence has implications for skin damage, including maceration from moisture on the skin, softening and separating the epidermal layers, and irritation related to increased friction and shearing. Wound contamination is also an issue for patients with sacrococcygeal wounds and concomitant incontinence. There are several types of urinary incontinence. The most prevalent type of incontinence in institutionalized older adults is urge incontinence. Urge incontinence involves involuntary bladder contractions with loss of large amounts of urine with or without a strong urge to void. Stress incontinence occurs predominantly in women and involves loss of a small volume of urine associated with increased intra-abdominal pressures such as laughing, coughing, or sneezing. Overflow incontinence is associated with outlet obstruction such as an enlarged prostate in men and manifests with constant dribbling and feelings of incomplete bladder emptying after voiding. Functional incontinence is urine loss due to cognitive impairment, physical functioning, environmental barriers (no access to toileting facilities), or psychologic unwillingness (depression). The type of incontinence influences the treatment. Some incontinence may be reversible, such as incontinence caused by a medication side effect or infection. In reversible incontinence, when the causative factor is removed the incontinence resolves. Persistent incontinence can often be managed or cured by behavioral interventions, medications, and sometimes surgery. It is important to remember that incontinence is not a normal response to aging; it is a symptom of an underlying pathologic condition and as such should be investigated.

Urinary Tract Infection. Bladder or urinary tract infection is an additional stressor to the body and may slow wound repair. Management of urinary tract infections usually involves systemic antibiotic therapy. Treatment of a urinary tract infection will influence the amount of time predicted for the wound to respond to therapy. For example, if a urinary tract infection is present, the clinician may add a week to progress through the initial phase of wound healing.

Genitourinary System Physical Assessment. Physical examination of the urinary system occurs in tandem with assessment of the gastrointestinal system. During the abdominal examination, the clinician is attuned to location of the bladder and the presence of any abnormalities. Specific assessment of the perineal area involves primarily observation, and the focus is on the external skin. Look for indications of urinary incontinence–related skin damage. Specific assessments for determining type of urinary incontinence are usually indicated, and laboratory values should also be evaluated. Standard urine analysis and culture and sensitivity reports may indicate the pathogen involved in a urinary tract infection and direct the appropriate treatment.

Peripheral Vascular System

The peripheral vascular system includes the venous, arterial, and lymphatic circulatory systems. Chapter 14 describes the pathogenesis and differential diagnosis of peripheral vascular disease (PVD). The clinician should pay particular attention to all medical chart notations or comments by and questions asked of the patient or family about vascular disorders, including history of hypertension, deep vein thrombosis, claudication, cold feet, and chronic swelling of the lower extremities. Patients with PVD are at high risk for development of chronic wounds and resultant impaired wound healing. The diagnosis of PVD guides the clinician's examination strategy for observational and noninvasive vascular testing. The important observations and testing procedures for patients with PVD are outlined in Chapter 6, Noninvasive Vascular Testing Procedures.

Peripheral Vascular System Physical Assessment. Physical examination involves assessment of temperature, color, capillary refill, and edema of both lower extremities. Compare one side with the other with attention to detection of deficits that are bilateral or unilateral in nature. Note nail growth. Are the nails hypertrophic or discolored? Note skin color of both extremities. Is there evidence of hemosiderin staining or dependent rubor present (see Chapter 3)? Is the extremity shiny, flaky, moist, dry, odorous, or deformed? Evaluate range of motion and strength in the lower extremities. Check lower extremity pulses and reflexes. The presence of lower extremity symptoms may be clinical indicators of peripheral vascular disease and necessitate a more focused assessment.

Neurologic and Musculoskeletal System

An imbalance or insufficient movement of body segments, limbs, or the whole body due to impairment or disability of the neurologic or musculoskeletal system are known factors for predicting certain wound development such as pressure ulcers and neuropathic ulcers. Neurologic disorders and dysfunction of the musculoskeletal system include a broad range of medical diagnoses such as spinal cord injury, cerebrovascular accidents, Parkinson's disease, arthritis, and multiple sclerosis. See Chapters 12, 13, and 15 for more information about the impact of movement disability on pathogenesis of pressure ulcers, pressure ulcer prevention, therapeutic positioning, and problems of the neuropathic foot. The neurologic or musculoskeletal deficit guides examination strategies for the clinician. For example, the nurse caring for a patient with limited body movements and neurologic deficits performs a pressure ulcer risk assessment to evaluate

risk factors for pressure ulcer development, which may trigger referrals for therapeutic positioning evaluation by a physical therapist and a nutritional consultation. In another example, patients who have had a cerebrovascular accident or stroke may have decreased activity and mobility, increasing their risk for pressure ulcer development or reducing the healing capacity of current wounds.

Cerebrovascular Accident. Cerebrovascular accidents (CVAs) or strokes are caused by disruption in blood flow to the brain. CVAs usually affect one hemisphere of the brain, causing deficits on the contralateral side of the body. Stroke can result in impaired ability to walk, impaired ability to use an upper limb, and inability to communicate, think, or see adequately. The patient's limited ability to move body parts places the patient at risk of developing pressure ulcers, skin tears, or friction and shearing injury.

Arthritis. Arthritic disorders affect the joints of the body. The two main types are rheumatoid arthritis and osteoarthritis. Osteoarthritis affects older adults and is associated with painful joints, particularly knees, ankles, and hips (weight-bearing joints). Evaluation of the wound patient with arthritis may be more difficult because of pain on positioning for adequate view of the wound. Treatment of arthritis commonly includes nonsteroidal anti-inflammatory drugs and steroids, both of which can impair or slow wound healing. Rheumatoid arthritis affects the joints of the hands and fingers, making self-care of wounds difficult or impossible.

Neurologic and Musculoskeletal System Physical Assessment. The clinician assesses cranial nerves I to XII and reflexes to determine the level of involvement of the stroke. The clinician needs to assess gait, balance, tremors, ataxia, one-sided weakness, and cognition. Joints involved in arthritis should be evaluated for pain and range of motion. Assessment of the patient with a stroke includes examination of the affected side of the body for strength and range of motion, flaccidity or spasticity, and hemineglect syndrome. Hemineglect can cause a patient to bump into objects on the neglected side of the body or fail to attend to one side of the body, resulting in injury. Assessment should also include evaluation of the patient's gait, mobility, and balance. Assessment of the neurologic and musculoskeletal systems includes completion of a functional assessment. It is important to evaluate the patient's ability to perform activities of daily living and instrumental activities of daily living.

Hematologic System

Disease processes such as anemia, fluid and electrolyte imbalance, or other blood dyscrasias associated with medication side effects or disease pathology affect wound healing capacity. Evaluation of laboratory values to rule out anemia, electrolyte imbalance, or infections is the key to hematologic system assessment. The patient may require iron supplements or blood transfusions to correct the deficit.

Hematologic System Physical Assessment. Assess for skin color. Is it pale? Does the patient have multiple bruises? Does the skin seem "thin"? Look at the mucous membranes. Are they pale? Does the patient report bleeding gums or frequent nosebleeds? Does the patient complain of fatigue? Evaluate laboratory data for evidence of anemia such as low hemoglobin, hematocrit, or iron.

Endocrine System

The endocrine system includes numerous glands that secrete body-regulating hormones. One of those glands is the pancreas, which controls insulin levels in the body. Diabetes mellitus is the disease of most concern in the endocrine system. Diabetes impairs wound healing and poses significant risk for wound development. Glucose levels alter wound healing and immune system functioning to control infection. Check for a diagnosis of diabetes mellitus. Is it type I insulin dependent or type II non–insulin dependent? The type of diabetes signals whether the patient will use insulin or diet and exercise to control glucose. Type I diabetics require insulin for glucose management. Type II diabetics manage glucose control initially with diet and exercise, then if unsuccessful, with oral hypoglycemic agents or insulin.

Endocrine System Physical Assessment. This is the time to review the record for glucose levels. Normal glucose levels are 80 mg/dL. Levels of 180 to 250 mg/dL or greater are indicators that glucose levels are out of control. Levels of greater than 200 mg/dL are known to have an impact on wound healing.[3] Review of laboratory values is prudent to determine level of diabetic control. Look specifically for a fasting blood glucose level <140 mg/dL and a glycosylated hemoglobin (HbA$_{1c}$) of less than 7%. The HbA$_{1c}$ helps determine the level of glucose control the patient has had over the last 2 to 3 months. The diabetic patient will need both medical and nursing management to bring glucose levels within normal limits. Many diabetics monitor their blood sugar at home with a blood sugar monitor such as One-Touch or Accu-Check, or they perform self-monitoring with simple fingerstick glucose testing. The clinician will want to know about the method of management and success of the control measures. This will help predict the success of wound therapy interventions.

Additional information can be used to guide therapy. Answers to key questions, Is the patient elderly?" and "Is diabetes of recent onset?" provide a history of the diabetes. Complications from diabetes generally occur the longer the patient has the disease. Patients with relatively new onset of diabetes may not exhibit neuropathic or vascular complications related to diabetes. Patients with diabetes over longer periods of time and those with type I diabetes are more at risk for complications associated with the disease, such as neuropathy, retinopathy, and vascular changes. The diabetic with a wound should trigger examination of sensation in the feet and vision testing. Patients with diabetic neuropathy may present with ulcers on the soles of the feet, and care should be taken to examine the plantar surfaces for callus formation, cracking, and bony deformities. Additional information on management of the patient with vascular and neuropathic disabilities related to diabetes is discussed in Chapters 14 and 15.

Although this review of systems with physical assessment guidelines is not inclusive, it provides a framework of those areas of most concern to the clinician managing patients with wounds. A complete history and physical examination provides the context for the wound itself. After completing the history and physical examination the clinician can turn attention to planning interventions. If the information is very limited, the clinician will have to make a clinical decision about the appropriateness of the referral from the reason for referral, expected outcomes, and personal observations of the patient. Clinicians can complete the general history, systems review, and physical assessment in about 30 to 40 minutes for a single wound. An experienced clinician can perform the basic physical assessment in 10 to 15 minutes. Typically all information is not gathered at the same time. Portions of the history and physical assessment may be gathered over a period of several days after several clinic visits or home visits. By the end of a 1-hour evaluation the clinician should be able to complete the history and physical assessment, evaluate the wound, determine candidacy of the patient for service (if clinician is physical therapist), and develop a strategy for specific examinations or referrals. (See the Case Study in the following section for an example of patient history influencing wound care management.) An experienced nurse should be able to evaluate the history for risk factors for impaired healing, perform the necessary physical assessment and wound evaluation, and develop a strategy for intervention in about 40 minutes.

Wound Assessment

Wound assessment involves evaluation of a composite of wound characteristics, including location, shape, size, depth, edges, undermining and tunneling, necrotic tissue characteristics, exudate characteristics, surrounding skin color, peripheral tissue edema and induration, and the presence of granulation tissue and epithelialization (see Chapter 3 on wound assessment, Chapter 4 on wound measurement, and Chapter 5 on tools).

Wound History

The next questions are directed toward acquiring information about the history of the wound. How long has the wound been present? Is there a history of previous wounds? What interventions have been used and have they been successful? What disciplines have been involved in the management of the wound? For instance, if the patient has been seen by many disciplines and has had multiple interventions without successful progress toward healing, the patient's candidacy for more aggressive intervention is questionable. What factors have impaired the wound response so far? Previous therapy and response to therapy must be carefully examined to avoid repeating unsuccessful intervention. Some patients may not heal. However, evaluation of past interventions with attention to appropriateness of topical wound care, prevention strategies, risk factor and comorbidity management, and use of adjunct therapy such as a whirlpool or electrical stimulation may reveal inconsistencies in treatment approach.

Patient Candidacy for Physical Therapy Services

During the assessment process, the clinician focuses on how the medical history and systems review will affect the candidacy of the patient. Physical therapists may determine the candidacy of the patient for services; with nursing, the option of determining candidacy for nursing services does not exist. The nurse usually has no choice in determining whether or not to provide nursing services to the patient. However, the nurse does have the option of assisting in determination of appropriate therapy for the patient involving other disciplines. The medical history and systems review findings may suggest to the clinician that the patient's problem requires consultation; is outside the scope of the clinician's knowledge, experience, or expertise; or the intervention originally suggested is inappropriate. In physical therapy, the patient is then identified as a noncandidate for the referred physical therapy service. It then becomes the responsibility of the clinician to refer to another practitioner who is more skilled, more knowledgeable, or better able to manage the identified problem or recommend an alternative treatment and management strategy. Below are examples of some criteria that would trigger a referral:

- Vascular testing should be considered if assessment findings include hair loss, skin pallor or cyanosis, and cold temperature of the feet.
- Callus and hemorrhagic spots on the callus are indicators of deeper tissue damage and a need for further assessment.

Case Study: *Example of Patient History Influencing Wound Care Management*

An 83-year-old Spanish-speaking illiterate gentleman was referred by the vascular department to the leg ulcer clinic of the county hospital for healing the ulcer on his leg. The patient presented with a large, full-thickness ulcer on his left leg due to underlying venous disease. He lived alone, had no family to help, was on county welfare, and had no regular transportation to the clinic except for a monthly clinic visit. He was embarrassed about having the ulcer on his leg and did not want to involve neighbors in his care. During the interview it was observed that he was ambulatory, alert, and able to learn.

The clinician performed the evaluation following the diagnostic process and decided that the patient was not a candidate for the leg ulcer clinic because he lacked transportation to the clinic. There were no caregivers available other than the patient himself. Therefore, the patient would have to be taught self-care. Financial resources were very limited. He was eligible to receive wound care supplies and he could come in to the clinic monthly for supplies and to have the ulcer evaluated. He was alert and motivated and demonstrated the ability to learn self-care if he was given simple instruction in Spanish. The teaching plan involved demonstration and return demonstration, and the patient returned home to self-manage the wound with monthly follow-up appointments at the clinic.

The medical history guided the wound examination. It was examined for drainage, size, status of surrounding skin, and healing status of the wound. Since he had had a prior vascular examination determining the presence of venous disease, further vascular testing was ruled out. A treatment intervention that he could safely perform and that was appropriate for his wound problem and underlying pathology needed to be selected. Since his underlying disease was venous insufficiency, compression of the venous system was needed. Since the wound was draining he needed a dressing to control exudate and keep the wound and surrounding skin clean.

The clinician elected to clean the wound with normal saline and apply a hydrocolloid dressing under an Unna's boot treatment to be changed every 4 days. The patient demonstrated that he understood wound care instructions and dressing techniques. He required support in case he developed problems. Instructions about potential problems he might encounter and the phone number of the Spanish-speaking nurse assigned to his case were given to him with instructions to call with any questions or to report problems with the ulcer. With this approach to wound care, ulcer healing progressed.

- Toenail abnormalities; if not an area of expertise of the examiner, should be referred.
- Assessment of an abscess in a tunnel or sinus tract requires immediate referral for surgical management.
- Undermining or tunneling that is a black hole without a bottom should be immediately referred for surgical management.
- Signs of granulation tissue infection (superficial bridging, friable tissue, bleeding on contact, pain in the wound, or regression of healing) need medical intervention.

STEP II: DIAGNOSIS

Examination Strategy

Utilization management requires close attention to the management of factors that prolong healing. The risk factors for impaired healing are identified at this point in the examination based on data collected during the history and systems review. Because the information about the patient determines the examination strategy, all patients will *not* receive the same examination.

Examination: Part I

There are two parts to the examination. Part I includes testing for factors related to the physiologic or anatomic status of the comorbidities that impair healing, such as vascular impairment or sensory impairment. For example, the patient is a candidate for noninvasive vascular testing if there is an ulcer on the ankle with the following characteristics: slow healing, cold foot, symptoms of claudication, pallor of the limb, and no report of an ankle-brachial index in the medical record. Sensory testing should have a high priority in the testing scheme if the patient has a history of long-term type I insulin-dependent diabetes, history of ulceration of the foot, or a history of prior amputation of a segment of the foot on the same or opposite limb. These tests have significant weight in the prediction of healing and development of the prognosis. For example, a low ankle-brachial index score indicates severe occlusive disease and is a predictor of failure to heal without reperfusion. Loss of protective sensation in the feet is an indicator of high risk for ulceration of the feet from pressure or trauma and leads to the intervention strategy. The patient with a low ankle-brachial index would not be considered a candidate for physical therapy services or aggressive wound healing interventions because of the severity of the vascular system impairment. The nurse would manage the patient's wound and refer the patient to the vascular surgeon. The patient with the insensitive foot due to neuropathy would be a candidate for physical therapy because this would constitute a medical necessity requiring the skills of a physical therapist. The physical therapist prognoses an expected functional outcome of risk reduction following interventions of pressure elimination and stimulation leading to healing. In both cases, the ulcerations are related to underlying medical pathology. In the former case the ulcer would not be expected to respond unless the underlying pathology was addressed. In the second case, the ulcer management was appropriate along with risk reduction management. The interpretation of the data from the history and physical examinations sets the stage for the functional diagnosis and allows triage of cases that should be referred or managed conservatively.

Examination: Part II

Part II of the examination strategy is to look at four key features of the wound assessment. The four key features are evaluation of the surrounding skin, assessment of the wound tissue, observation of wound drainage, and size measurements. All four characteristics have several aspects to include in the assessment. Surrounding skin examination includes evaluation of color, texture, temperature, edema, and pain in the tissues around the wound site. Assessment of wound tissue includes color, tissue status, and visible structures. Observation of wound drainage includes odor, color, and quantity. Size measurements taken include open surface area, depth, and undermining. Methods of performing wound assessment are described in Chapters 3, 4, and 5. For example a wound with an open surface area, depth, and undermining present should have all three characteristics measured. A partial-thickness wound will require only measurement of the open surface area.

Sequencing the examination will depend on visual observation and palpation of the impaired tissues. The examiner chooses those tests and measures specific to the wound situation. For example, temperature testing may be the best way to distinguish the presence of inflammatory processes in a pressure ulcer in persons with darkly pigmented skin. A wound tracing may be best method to measure the irregular shape of a venous ulcer. If signs of redness, heat, edema, pain, and loss of function are observed, the wound is in an inflammatory phase. The wound history provides information about wound etiology, duration of the wound status, and recent wound change in status. If the wound status has not changed significantly in 28 days it is in a chronic phase of repair and needs help to restart the biologic cascade.

After completing the examination part of the diagnostic process, the clinician interprets the physiologic and anatomic systems information and wound assessment data. The clinician brings all the data together like the pieces of a puzzle to develop functional diagnosis.[4]

Evaluation and Diagnosis

The evaluation aspect of the diagnostic process includes evaluation and analysis of findings collected during the examination and leads to clinical judgments based on the data collected. Diagnosis includes the process and is also the conclusion reached after the evaluation data has been organized.[5] Physical therapists are expected to use the diagnostic process to establish a diagnosis for the specific conditions requiring attention. If the findings of the diagnostic process are such that the management of the patient is outside the physical therapist's knowledge, experience, or expertise, the patient should be referred to the appropriate practitioner.[5] The nurse may reach a diagnostic conclusion that a referral to another practitioner is needed, but as mentioned previously, the nurse usually cannot bow out while waiting for a referral and is required to provide a plan of care for the patient in the interim. The purpose of data analysis is to draw conclusions about a patient's specific problems or needs so that effective interventions can be implemented. Problem identification is a process of diagnostic reasoning in which judgments, decisions, and conclusions are made about the meaning of the data collected, in order to determine whether or not intervention is needed.[6] Diagnosis involves forming a clinical judgment identifying a disease/condition or human response through scientific evaluation of signs and symptoms, history, and diagnostic studies. In many respects a diagnosis is analogous to a research hypothesis. For example, a research hypothesis directs the research study and a diagnosis directs the patient's care plan. Both a research hypothesis and a diagnosis are chosen based on available data and information, and both research hypotheses and diagnoses may be proven correct or incorrect as the study or care plan progresses.

Physical therapy diagnosis is defined as ". . . a label encompassing a cluster of signs, symptoms, syndromes, or categories."[5(p715)] The purpose of a diagnosis is to guide the clinician in determining the most appropriate intervention strategy for the individual. In the event that the diagnostic process does not provide adequate information, intervention may be based on alleviation of symptoms and remediation of deficits.

Nursing diagnosis can be defined as both a noun and a verb. As a verb, nursing diagnosis is the process of identifying specific patient problems or needs in the second step of the nursing process. As a noun, nursing diagnosis refers to labels or terminology that identify specific patient problems or needs or the means of describing health problems amenable to treatment by nurses. Health problems may be physical, sociologic, or psychologic. Nursing diagnosis is typically stated in three parts: the problem, the etiology, and the signs and symptoms. Problem statements are drawn from the North American Nursing Diagnosis Association (NANDA) approved list of nursing diagnoses. Both nurses and physical therapists make diagnoses based on the symptoms or the sequelae of the injurious process such as impaired wound healing. Physical therapists evaluate the functional implications of impairments and disabilities leading to a functional diagnosis. Impairment is loss or abnormality of psychological, physiological, or anatomical structure or function.[7] Impairment describes the loss of function of a body system or organ due to illness or injury.[8] An example is loss of function of the skin and underlying soft tissue due to wounding or due to underlying pathology. Additional impairment characteristics include the effect of pathology/disease without attributing cause or the loss of a body part such as by amputation. Underlying pathology creates the susceptibility to loss of function, eg, "undue susceptibility to pressure ulcers" and "undue insensitivity to pain."[8]

The definition of a disability is any restriction or lack (resulting from an impairment) of ability to perform an activity in the manner or within the range considered normal for a human being. Disability may result from impairment or be caused by the person's response to the impairment. Disability may be permanent, reversible, or irreversible. Disability reflects a deviation in performance or behavior within a task or activity.[8] Examples are the disabled person who has musculoskeletal disablement leading to difficulty walking or difficulty moving or integumentary disablement related to the inability of the body to progress from the inflammatory phase of healing to the proliferative phase.

Functional Diagnosis

Functional diagnosis is defined as an assessment of the related impairments and associated disabilities that affect wound status and its ability to heal. Examples of functional diagnosis are the following:

- Impaired sensation (unable to detect pressure or light touch)
- Impaired circulation (Ankle-Brachial Index below 0.8) of lower extremities
- Impaired lower extremity strength and joint range of motion (including manual muscle test and range of motion) resulting in persistent pressure to buttocks
- Impaired healing associated with chronic inflammation phase.

Physical therapists use functional diagnosis to describe the consequence of disease and as a justification of medical necessity requiring the skills of the physical therapist. With respect to wounds, the wound healing phase can be used as a functional diagnosis to describe the status of wound healing (see wound healing phases described in Chapter 2).

Each phase of healing can be impaired. Impaired wound healing can be described as prolonged, chronic or failure to occur, meaning absent. For example, a wound with prolonged or chronic inflammation has impaired functioning of the body system(s) needed to progress to the next phase of repair. The particular phase of wound healing that is dysfunctional helps predict the interventions needed to restart the repair process.[9]

The impairments in wound healing can be labeled with a diagnosis. The *wound healing phase diagnosis* is a diagnosis of impaired status regarding the biologic phase of wound healing. ***There are 12 possible wound healing phase diagnoses:***

1. Chronic inflammation
2. Inflammation
3. Absence of inflammation
4. Chronic proliferation
5. Proliferation
6. Absence of proliferation
7. Chronic epithelialization
8. Epithelialization
9. Absence of epithelialization
10. Chronic remodeling
11. Remodeling
12. Absence of remodeling

The wound healing phase diagnosis describes the biologic phase of repair observed by examination of the wound. Wounds become chronic and lacking in the function necessary to progress to the next phase of repair. This can occur in any of the phases of healing. For example, when wound edges curl in and become fibrotic the wound demonstrates absence of epithelialization due to impairment in the epithelialization process. Wounds can become "stuck" in the proliferation phase when infection is present and impairs the proliferative process, thus demonstrating chronic proliferation. Wounds can become chronically inflamed when tissue trauma is prolonged. The wound healing phase diagnosis describes the current status of the wound and can be used to predict how the wound healing should progress. This is logical because wound healing is an orderly series of events. A wound in one phase should progress to and through each successive phase. (See Chapter 2 for information about biologic cascade of healing.)

A question frequently asked is how to state the wound healing phase diagnosis of a wound in transition from one phase to another. The transition is usually gradual and because phases overlap it is appropriate to describe the change by using a ratio of the *dominant phase* to the *recessive phase*. *Dominant* refers to the most active phase observed. *Recessive* refers to the less active phase. A ratio is simply a relationship between two variables, in this case the relationship between two phases of healing. The way it can be used to describe a wound with the dominate phase active inflammation and the recessive phase active proliferation is to write the description as in the following sample: The wound healing phase diagnosis is INFLAMMATION/proliferation. The use of capital letters for the dominant phase emphasizes its dominance. Small letters show the relationship of the recessive phase. If the two phases are equal they can both be capitalized (eg, INFLAMMATION/PROLIFERATION). The prognosis is that the wound healing phase would progress from inflammation to proliferation. A last example is the newly reepithelialized wound. This can be written: EPITHELIALIZATION/absence of remodeling. It will gradually progress through the remodeling phase to develop a mature scar.

STEP III: PROGNOSIS AND GOALS

Once the diagnosis is established, the clinician predicts or prognoses the expected outcome goals and selects an intervention. Prediction is a useful tool for goal setting. Prediction of the maximal improvement expected from an intervention and how long it will take is the *prognosis*. Prognosis may include prediction of *improvement* at different intervals during treatment.[5] For example, the biologic model using phases to monitor acute wound healing described in Chapter 2, is organized and predictable. The phases of repair are benchmarks that can be used to determine the effectiveness of treatment interventions.

Many clinicians are intimidated by the idea of predicting outcomes. The clinician must be familiar with treatment effects of interventions they prescribe and administer. If the clinician cannot predict the effects of an intervention, who can? Why would a patient want to expose himself or herself to the intervention with unpredictable results? Why should a payer reimburse for services with unexpected benefit and indefinite cost? The successful clinician is able to predict the patient outcomes. In the current health care environment, familiarity with prognosis and outcomes is important for both nurses and physical therapists.

Wound Prognosis Options

For wounds, the prognosis options are limited. One system for evaluating secondary intention wound healing defines healing as minimally, acceptably, or ideally healed. An ideally healed wound results in return of the fully restored dermis and epidermis with intact barrier function. The prognosis is ideally healed closed wound. An acceptably healed wound has a resurfaced epithelium capable of sustained functional integrity during activities of daily living. The prognosis is acceptably healed closed wound. A minimally healed wound is characterized by reepithelialization but does not establish a sustained functional result and may recur. The prognosis is minimally healed wound. In all of these definitions of healing, complete closure of the wound is expected.[10]

For some individuals and some wounds, closure is not an option. The best prognosis that can be made is for a change in the wound healing phase from an impaired or early phase of repair to a more advanced phase of repair. For example, a wound that is chronically inflamed is impaired from progressing to more advanced phases of healing. A predicted outcome can be that the chronic inflammation will progress to acute inflammation. An acutely inflamed wound prognosis is to progress to a proliferation phase. Some wounds progress to the proliferation phase, and it is not expected nor is it preferred for the wound to close by secondary intention; the prognosis is a clean and stable wound or prepared for surgical closure. A change in phase is a functional outcome prediction. This method monitors a real change in the organ function of the skin and soft tissues, which is a measure of reduced functional impairment.

A prognosis that the wound is not expected to improve based on the results of the diagnostic process may determine referral for other management. Nursing may be expected to care for the wound, but this patient may not be a candidate for physical therapy intervention. Prognosis is not an option for physical therapists; it is a requirement. Medicare has mandated that a functional outcome prediction be established by the physical therapist at the start of care. This is part of utilization management of medical services.

Goals

Nurses' Goals

In determining goals for the patient, the nurse must set priorities, establish the goals, and identify the desired outcomes. Goals are determined in the planning stage of the nursing process. Goals are important because they assist in determining outcomes of care and effectiveness of intervention. To set goals, the nurse must first determine the priority of needs. Priorities are fluid and dynamic. The priorities for a patient can change day to day and even hour to hour in the course of a day. Certain essential survival needs overshadow lesser needs. For example, a patient presents with an ulcer on the lower extremity and severe pain from the lesion. The priority will be management of acute pain, and wound management becomes a secondary priority. Basic survival needs and safety needs must be met before dealing with higher-level needs such as self-esteem or social interaction.

Once the needs are prioritized, the nurse can establish patient goals. A goal is a broad guideline indicating the overall direction of movement as a result of intervention. Goals can be short term or long term. Short-term goals are usually actions that must be met before the patient is discharged or moved to another level of care. Long-term goals may require continued attention by the patient and the caregiver long after discharge. Short-term goals should move the patient toward the long-term goal. Short term-goals are small steps to the long-term goal.

Physical Therapists' Goals

Physical therapists also have a historical requirement to document short- and long-term goals. Physical therapists' goals are expected to be measurable, objective, and functional. Unlike nursing goals that are broad guidelines indicating the overall direction of progress, goals used by physical therapists must be very specific. Traditionally, a short-term goal has been one that is expected to be achieved in 30 days or less and usually corresponds to the end of the billing period or length of stay. Long-term goals are those predicted to be attainable by the time of discharge. With the shift to short lengths of stay in different care settings, the time frames have also changed to correspond to the setting. Today there is a terminology shift away from using the term *goal* and replacing it with *expected outcome*. A goal is a desired or expected result of an intervention. An outcome is the result or status after the intervention. Completing the diagnostic process with recommendations is one outcome of the services of the physical therapist. The physical therapist is able to target specific measurable outcomes for specific interventions. To make them functional outcomes, they must meet the criteria described below. Target outcomes are short-term specific expectations of change in impairment status. *Prognosis* is the expected outcome after a course of care and is the long-term goal. Examples of wound healing prognosis are the following:

1. Ideally healed closure
2. Acceptably healed closure
3. Minimally healed closure
4. Clean and stable open wound
5. Ready for surgical closure
6. Not expected to improve

Outcomes

Outcomes are now well-established quality management tools, yet there is considerable confusion about the term *outcome* and how to report it. *An outcome* is the result of what is done. The intervention or activity that is done to achieve the result is the *process* to get an outcome. How are outcomes measured? Performance indicators are objective measurements that are used to benchmark change as a result of an intervention. Providers, payers, regulators, and clinicians are all working toward establishing reliable performance indicators that are useful for reporting clinical outcomes. Exhibit 1–1 lists examples of some wound-related performance indicators, wound outcomes, and functional outcomes for each. Methods and procedures for testing and relevance of the performance indicators are presented throughout the text.

Assessing patient outcomes provides the nurse and physical therapist with a means for assessing how the intervention altered the problem. There are several types of outcomes, two types of which will be described: behavioral and functional. Payer groups have an interest in both the behavioral and functional outcomes.[11] The purpose of this section is to help the clinician begin to formulate documentation for reporting outcomes.

Reporting Outcomes

The reporting of outcomes is frequently confused with process. There has been much discussion about outcomes, but what is being reported is mainly process. This section will discuss some commonly misused terms and the appropriate way to report the outcome. Terms that will be discussed include:

- Prevention
- Reduced
- Maintained
- Controlled
- Maximized
- Minimized
- Improved
- Provided
- Promoted

Prevention is often the target of a intervention. Prevention is the process to reduce or buffer risk. Risk factors usually exist prior to or at the onset of a problem (eg, immobility, deformities, smoking). Buffers are those attempts to reduce or intervene so as to alter the progression of an impairment, disability, or handicap (eg, take pressure off a diabetic ulcer).[7] There are many reliable performance indicators that measure risk and intervention-related changes used by both nurses and physical therapists. As part of the initial assessment, apply instruments with performance indicators to test the current status and then retest status after applying the chosen intervention to measure achievement of the predicted outcome. Instead of saying the prognosis is "prevention of pressure ulcers" or "minimized risk of pressure ulcers," it would be more appropriate to say "risk of pressure ulcers will be reduced from high to moderate based on the Braden scale."

For example, the Braden scale (see Chapter 12) is used to measure risk for development of pressure ulcers. Mobility is one portion of the Braden scale. If a patient on admission has a low mobility score on the Braden scale, indicating complete immobility, the patient is judged at high risk for development of a pressure ulcer. The patient receives an intervention for mobility training, and the mobility score improves. Now the patient is slightly limited in mobility and makes frequent changes in body position. There has been a functional change in the mobility of the patient. The functional outcome is improved mobility status, which leads to the consequence of reduced risk of pressure ulceration.

Another topic of confusion is about reduced risk of infection. This is also not an outcome. Infection free or reduced by assessment of the exudate, odor, or culture results are measurable outcomes. However, in order for any of these outcomes to be functional outcomes, they must change the way the body system functions. Infection free may be an outcome of wound cleansing, and it becomes a functional outcome if the wound healing progresses to the next phase of repair. The written functional outcome should be stated as "the wound is infection free and the wound healing has progressed from the inflammatory phase to the proliferative phase."

A troublesome word in health care is *maintained.* Maintained is a process that implies no change. *Controlled* should not be mistaken for *maintained.* If the edema is fluctuating, for instance, from treatment to treatment and then stabilizes as a result of intervention, the outcome is edema controlled. A functional outcome for edema controlled would be stated as "the edema in the tissues surrounding the wound is controlled and the wound is epithelializing." The functional outcome of control of the edema is that the wound progresses to the next phase of healing.

Maximized and *minimized* is similarly confused with outcomes. For example, "maximized participation in activities of daily living" is not about the functional outcome of an intervention with an orthotic device. A functional outcome reports the result of the intervention, such as "the patient performs ADL wearing/using orthotic equipment, has returned to work and/or resumed leisure activities." An example of misuse of *minimized* as an outcome is "minimized stresses precipitating or perpetuating injury." Correct use is: Functional outcome—patient/caregiver identified stress-reduction methods to minimize risk or injury.

Improved is defined as to make better or enhance in value. Improved is a subjective measure, not a measurable outcome. An outcome reports the objective result of improvement. For example, increased vital capacity measured in liters (performance indicator) is a measurable change in the pulmonary system with a result of increased oxygenation of tissues for wound healing. The functional outcome is "wound progresses to next phase of healing."

Provided is a sometimes confused with an outcome. This is an action by the clinician, not the outcome of the intervention. An example of improper use is "provided electrical stimulation to enhance circulation." This describes the rationale for the intervention, not the outcome. A predicted functional outcome addresses the changes expected in the wound from the intervention, such as change of wound phase from inflammation to proliferation. *Promoted* is another inappropriately used word. "Promoted angiogenesis" is a process. Angiogenesis is an expected outcome from treatment and represents an attribute of wound healing. The performance indicators of angiogenesis are change in wound attributes, phase, or size. The outcome is wound progression through proliferation phase.

Behavioral Outcomes

Behavioral outcomes are written by listing behaviors. Outcomes must be specific, realistic, time oriented, objective, patient centered, and measurable. Write outcomes by listing behaviors or items that can be observed or monitored to determine whether an acceptable or positive outcome is achieved within the desired time frame. The outcome then serves as the evaluation tool. Use measurable action verbs to describe behavioral outcomes. For example, the verb *understand* is not measurable; we cannot measure a person's understanding. But the verb *identify* is measurable; the patient can be tested to determine whether or not he or she can identify. Other action verbs include *list, record, name, state, describe, explain, demonstrate, use, schedule, differentiate, compare, relate, design, prepare, formulate, select, choose, increase, decrease, stand, walk,* and *participate.* Contrast these action verbs with the verbs *understand, feel, learn, know,* and *accept,* all of which are not measurable. Examples of expected behavioral outcomes for a wound patient are the following: The patient will describe the signs of wound infection and identify correct action within 24 hours, the patient will demonstrate wound dressing application within 2 days. Documenting that the target outcome was met would include a statement: Patient is able to describe the signs of infection and lists the steps for corrective action. Patient is able to demonstrate correct wound dressing application. These are behavioral outcomes. What implication do they have for the patient's function? To become functional outcomes these behavioral outcomes need to include the implications for the patient.

Functional Outcomes

What is a functional outcome? A functional outcomes helps to communicate the change in function to the patient, caregiver, or payer. Physical therapists usually deal with patients who have loss of functional abilities and use functional tests that measure physical attributes to predict the function the patient is expected to achieve after a course of treatment. What is *function?* Function in this context refers to those activities or actions that are meaningful to the patient or caregiver. Meaningful function is determined while completing the reason for referral portion of the assessment. To be a functional outcome, the results must meet three tests[12]:

1. Is the result meaningful?
2. Is the result practical?
3. Will the result be sustained outside the treatment setting?

Meaningful is defined as of value to the patient, caregiver, or both. Function is achieved by the patient through the services of the physical therapist or nurse so that the patient can perform activities effectively at home or work (eg, wound exudate is controlled or eliminated so the patient can return to work). *Practical* means that the outcome is applicable to the patient's life situation. *Sustainable over time* refers to functional abilities achieved through the intervention maintained by the patient or caregiver outside the clinical setting (eg, patient-demonstrated ability to apply dressing and stocking during two follow-up visits).[13]

Standardized tests and measurement tools are quite useful to monitor and track change over time. The Pressure Sore Status Tool (PSST) and the Sussman Wound Healing Tool (SWHT) are described in Chapter 5 and can be used to document outcomes of change in wound attributes by change in test scores. Although these tools report outcomes as they affect wound attributes, to be functional outcomes the dots need to be connected between the items on the test and the meaningful, the practical, and the sustainable implications. In the example described above, if the PSST is used to monitor exudate amounts, there would be a change in score on that test item from 4 (moderate exudate) to 2 (scant exudate) indicating reduced drainage. This outcome is measurable, objective, and meets all the criteria listed for a valid outcome, but this information alone is not a functional outcome. To interpret this score as a functional outcome, a statement is needed that connects the findings with meaning to the patient, practical effect, and sustainable result. A resulting statement of functional outcomes is: Wound exudate PSST score has reduced from 4 (moderate) to 2 (scant) exudate, patient demonstrates ability to monitor for signs of infection and action to take, patient is now able to return to work and will be seen for intermittent follow-up.

Functional outcomes should be documented throughout the course of care, not just at discharge. Statements that can be used to demonstrate intermittent functional change include change in patient lifestyle, change in patient safety, adaptation to the impairment or disability. These statements should be patient-centered and measurable. For instance, a functional outcome statement would be: *Initial statement:* Patient is unable to sit in wheelchair without trauma to integument. *Initial target outcome:* sitting for two hours in adaptive seating system in 2 weeks. *Interim outcome after 1 week:* patient sits for 1 hour in adaptive seating system. *Discharge statement:* sits in adaptive seating system for 2 hours without disruption of integumentary integrity. Change in wound tissue attributes and size can also be used as functional outcome: Necrosis free, reduced risk of infection, and size reduced 50%, wound is clean and stable, decreased frequency of visits required.

Exhibit 1–1 Examples of Performance Indicators, Wound Outcomes, and Functional Wound Outcomes

Performance Indicators	*Wound Outcomes*	*Functional Outcome*
1. Change of wound and surrounding skin attributes 2. Reduced severity of wound: depth, size 3. Change in wound exudate characteristics, or undermining 4. Closure	Progression through the phases of wound healing (inflammation, proliferation, epithelialization)	1. Clean stable wound ready for surgical closure 2. Dressing changes needed biweekly instead of daily 3. Exudate managed; patient returns to work 4. Return to work/leisure activities
1. Temperature comparison 2. Transcutaneous partial pressure of oxygen level 3. Laser doppler	Oxygenation or perfusion of tissue	1. Progress to next wound healing phase 2. Pain level no longer interferes with ADL
1. Girth measurements 2. Volume meter measurements 3. Palpation grading system	Edema reduction or controlled	1. Patient able to don compression hose 2. Leg ulcers are smaller, require less frequent dressing changes
1. Wound exudate characteristics 2. Wound and surrounding skin attributes 3. Culture	Infection controlled	1. Wound exudate odor controlled, able to return to community 2. Pain alleviated, patient resumes walking
1. Necrosis free 2. Proliferation phase tissue attributes 3. Change in depth or size	Clean stable wound	1. Frequency of visits reduced 2. Physical therapy intervention no longer required 3. Patient can now manage wound dressing changes
1. Braden Scale score 2. Functional activities performance 3. Comprehension testing	Reduced risk of pressure ulceration	1. Patient performing self-care activities while up in wheelchair 2. Patient demonstrates use of hand mirror to monitor skin
1. Wound closure 2. Functional activities performed related to use of scar tissue	Acceptably healed scar	1. Patient identifies risk factors for reulceration 2. Patient uses protective equipment correctly under scar tissue to perform functional activities in wheelchair

Summary: How To Write Outcome Statement. When reporting outcome, use the following guidelines:

- An outcome expresses the *result* of an intervention, not the intervention or the process to reach an outcome (eg, wound resurfacing/closure).
- A behavioral outcome may be learned information (eg, demonstrates application of wound dressing). This outcome would follow an intervention of instruction.
- Coordination, communication, and documentation are behavioral outcomes used to ensure proper utilization management.

Functional outcomes are written to describe function results of treatment. A functional outcome includes three parts:

1. A functional outcome statement describes a meaningful functional change to a body system (eg, progression through the phases of healing).
2. A functional outcome statement describes a practical result of the change in the body system (eg, wound is minimally exudative).
3. A functional outcome statement describes the sustainable result or change in the impairment status or disability resulting from the intervention (eg, pressure elimination allows the patient to sit up in wheelchair 2 hours twice a day).

THE FUNCTIONAL OUTCOME REPORT

This chapter has described three of the four steps needed to complete the diagnostic process. The functional outcome report (FOR) developed by Swanson, described below, is a written report describing the diagnostic process.[4] Swanson's FOR helps the therapist project clinical reasoning that is clear, logical, and understandable to the reader. As previously explained, payers want to know about functional outcomes, not wound measurements and tissue color. The FOR process helps communicate treatment strategies to justify the intervention and lead to a predictable functional outcome.[13] Exhibit 1–2 is a completed example of the report. There are additional examples of the FOR in Chapter 14 and the case studies in Part IV.

The FOR document has six parts. **Part I** begins with the *reason for referral*. Here the clinician establishes patient needs. The report will read in one of the following manners:

- Patient/family seek services for . . .
- The patient/family reports . . .
- The following medical problems are associated with this request for service . . .

It is not unusual that following a course of therapy there will be residual impairments and disabilities in conjunction with a meaningful functional outcome that is important to the patient (eg, a clean, edema-free wound). This may be the most important goal and the reason for the referral because it is meaningful to the patient.

Part II is an analysis of *functional limitations.* Function implies many different activities or actions. With respect to wounds, this includes identification and analysis of the functional limits of the local tissues to perform the activities necessary to initiate repair. Function also implies that the body systems have the ability to perform the repair. For instance, the current status of the tissue assessment identifies tissue activity (eg, inflammation phase) and the circulatory system response to injury (eg, erythema, edema, pain, and heat). An impaired circulatory system function will impair the healing process. The clinician writes the report with the following leads:

- The specific functional items that are causing the patient's need for service are (eg, impaired healing response)
- Patient's functional loss of healing is due to (eg, impairment of the circulatory system)
- The loss of function causes the following (eg, inability to progress through the phases of repair without intervention)
- Patient has improvement potential (eg, patient has improvement potential but remains at risk for ischemic ulceration)

In **Part III,** *clinical assessment or diagnosis* is the clinical impression based on the results of the tests and measures selected by the clinician. The clinician chooses tests and measures that have performance indicators for wounds. This is defined differently from the medical diagnosis because it focuses on the functional consequence of the disease rather than the etiology. See the section on functional diagnosis described earlier.

Part IV is the justification of *need for skilled service or the therapy problem*. Utilization management requires that there be an identification of the specific elements that will be changed as a result of the intervention and once changed will improve the patient's functional status. An example of a wound problem that can be expected to change as a result of an intervention is a change in the phase of wound healing as a result of an intervention (eg, whirlpool). Change can also be expected in the wound symptoms (eg, erythema free, pain free), which will demonstrate improved functional status of the tissues.

In **Part V,** *prediction of a functional outcome* is expected because clinicians have a responsibility to know the effect of the selected treatment interventions. Patients and referral

Exhibit 1–2 Sample FOR

Patient ID: J.J. **AGE:** 59

Patient History:

Reason for Referral:

Patient/family seeks services for: Return to social activities and concern about a pressure ulcer on a heel.
Caregiver's report: Less time is now spent out of bed and patient has episodes of confusion. Patient is usually alert and oriented and has adequate communication skills to make needs, wants, and discomforts known.

Medical History:

Medical Impairments, Taken from Medical History:

- Limited respiratory capacity due to chronic obstructive pulmonary disease.
- Requires continuous oxygen from a concentrator.

Systems Review:

The Following Systems Are Impaired:

Cardiopulmonary System:

- Pulse oximetry: 98%–good oxygen saturation achieved with supplemental oxygen.

Musculoskeletal System:

- Contracted to 90° at hips and knees and has limited bed mobility.

Vascular System:

- Impaired circulation of the lower extremities: coldness, pallor, absence of hair, and poor pulses.

Integumentary System:

- Skin intact but impaired by eschar over a pressure ulcer on the right heel.

Evaluation:

1. Specific functional losses causing the patient's need for service are: loss of wound healing capacity.
2. Patient's functional loss is due to
   - Respiratory impairment and circulatory impairment.
   - Mechanical impairments of the lower extremities (contractures of hips and knees).
   - Motor impairment (unable to reposition in bed and unable to transfer to wheelchair).

Functional Diagnosis:

The loss of function causes the following:
- Undue susceptibility for pressure wound on lower feet.
- Inability to heal without integumentary intervention.

Prognosis:

Patient has improvement potential; will heal following intervention but will continue to be at risk for pressure ulceration.

---

sources have a right to this information when they expose themselves to an episode of care. Prediction is not new. Previously, prediction was known as short- and long-term goals. A short-term goal usually refers to a 2- to 4-week period of care and a long-term goal is what will be achieved at discharge. The functional outcomes goal section of the report has three components related to the predicted functional outcome: the activity that will occur, the performance expected, and the due date. For example, with respect to wounds the "activity" may be erythema free, the "performance" change

to proliferation phase, and the "due date" 2 to 4 weeks. This segment of the report promotes continuity of care when different or multiple clinicians are involved in the patient's care.

In **Part VI**, the final step in the FOR is to present the *treatment plan with rationale.* Subsequent chapters will provide the rationale for many different interventions based on established theory and science. This is the place where the clinician reveals the clinical judgment used to select a treatment plan. For example, the clinician writes that the wound is in a chronic inflammatory phase related to a large amount of necrotic tissue, has failed to respond to prior treatment interventions, and requires debridement to initiate the healing process. This becomes the rationale for selecting the treatment strategy (eg, pulsatile lavage with suction) to clean up the necrotic debris.

Applying FOR to Form HCFA-700

To become familiar with the diagnostic process and the FOR method, review the sample case in Exhibit 1–2. Physical therapists are accustomed to using the Form HCFA-700 (11-91) for documentation (see Appendix 1-C). The HCFA-700 and the FOR method of reporting were designed to work together. A template added to the HCFA-700 (Appendix 1-D) guides the physical therapist through documentation of the diagnostic process and FOR methodology. Appendix 1-E is a sample case report on the HCFA-700 using FOR methodology.

Clinical Wisdom

Some facilities have the HCFA-700 form on computer. If a template can be added to the form with the items as listed formatted to fit the computer field, it would help the physical therapist complete the documentation in an orderly and consistent manner. For those using a hard copy of HCFA-700, a template can still be useful to ensure that all items are recorded following the format.

Reevaluation

Once the target outcomes and goals have been determined, the reevaluation process is really quite simple. The clinician uses performance indicators to measure the patient's progress toward the outcome within the desired time frame. For example, if the target outcome is *patient's wound will demonstrate 25% reduction in size within 2 weeks,* then the clinician simply monitors wound size over the 2-week period of time and then determines whether the wound has reduced surface area size by 25% at the end of week 2. If the wound has decreased in size more than 25%, the outcome has been exceeded. If the wound has just decreased in size by 25%, the outcome has been acceptably met. If the wound has failed to decrease in size by 25%, the outcome has not been met

and the goals must be adjusted and interventions reviewed. Reevaluation is an ongoing dynamic process that will recur on a regular basis following reexamination of the effects of treatment. At that time, goals and outcomes may be adjusted, new goals developed, and interventions modified. The PSST and SWHT tools described in Chapter 5 are validated methods for monitoring wound healing outcomes that are used throughout the evaluation and reevaluation process. The tools provide a quick checkup at regular intervals to determine efficacy of treatment or to alert the clinician to deviations from the expected course.

Since utilization management attempts to influence the clinical path from the beginning so as to reduce deviation from an expected course and to produce optimal outcomes, the adjustment of goals and expected outcomes should be minimal. The clinician must make accurate predictions at baseline. Multiple approximations to reach the target outcome will not be tolerated by patients or third-party payers. For example, the *APTA Guide to PT Practice*[14] lists wound management guidelines regarding range of visits and length of episode of care by physical therapists for patients with wounds. This range represents the lower and upper limits of services that it is anticipated that 80% of the patients/clients with such wounds will need to achieve the predicted goals and outcomes (prognosis) listed. Multiple factors may modify the duration of the episode of care, frequency, and number of visits. Wounds extending into fascia, muscle, or bone (integumentary pattern E), for instance, will require 4 to 16 weeks (12-112 visits) for an episode of care (all types of etiologies included). The prognosis for wounds of this severity is that over the course of 4 to 16 weeks of care by the PT that one of the following will occur:

- Wound will be clean and stable.
- Wound will be prepared for closure.
- Wound will be closed.
- Immature scar will be evident.[14(p1605)]

CONCLUSION

The diagnostic process described in this chapter is intended as a framework for clinicians working with patients with wounds. The information may or may not be new, but there are times when review of material may be helpful. This chapter is meant to assist those clinicians new to the diagnostic process or unfamiliar with its use. Use of clinical judgment with diagnostic reasoning is one of the essential practice tools that nurses and physical therapists use with the patients they serve.

REFERENCES

1. Clifton. DW. Utilization management: whose job is it? *Rehab Manage.* June/July 1996;38:44.

2. Bergstrom N, Bennett MA, Carlson C, et al. Treatment of pressure ulcers. *Clinical Practice Guideline,* No. 15. Rockville, MD: US Department of Health and Human Services, AHCPR Publication No. 95-0652, December 1994.

3. Hisch IB, White PF. Medical management of surgical patients with diabetes. In: Levin ME, O'Neal LW, Bowker JH, eds, *The Diabetic Foot.* Chicago: CV Mosby; 1993.

4. Swanson G. *The Guide to Physical Therapist Practice,* vol 1. Presentation at California chapter, APTA, San Diego, CA, October 1995.

5. American Physical Therapy Association. A guide to physical therapy practice, I: a description of patient management. *Phys Ther.* 1995;75:707–764.

6. Doenges MD, Moorhouse MF, Burley JT. *Application of Nursing Process and Nursing Diagnosis.* 2nd ed. Philadelphia: F.A. Davis; 1995.

7. Jette AM. Physical disablement concepts for physical therapy research and practice. *Phys Ther.* 1994;74:380–386.

8. Swanson G. *The IDH Guidebook for Physical Therapy.* Long Beach, CA: Swanson and Company; 1995.

9. Sussman C. Case presentation: patient with a pressure ulcer on the coccyx. Paper presented at APTA Scientific Meeting and Exposition, Minneapolis, MN, June 1996.

10. Lazarus GS, Cooper DM, Knighton DR, et al. Definitions and guidelines for assessment of wounds and evaluation of healing. *Arch Dermatol.* 1994;130:489–493.

11. Swanson G. What is an outcome? And what does it mean to you? *Ultra/sounds.* (California Private Practice Special Interest Group—California APTA). 1995; 94-51:7.

12. Swanson G. Functional outcome report: The next generation in physical therapy reporting in documenting physical therapy outcomes. In: Stuart D, Ablen S, eds, *Documenting Physical Therapy Outcomes.* Chicago: CV Mosby; 1993:101–134.

13. Staley M, Richard R, et al. Functional outcomes for the patient with burn injuries. *J Burn Care Rehab.* 1996;17(4):362–367.

14. Guide to physical therapist practice. *Phys Ther.* 1997;77:1593–1605.

Appendix 1–A: Patient History Form

Medical Record #_____ Name_____

Street Address_____

City, State, Zip_____

Telephone Number (_____)_____

Sex: M/F_____Height: _____Weight: _____

Religious Preference: _____

What is your primary reason for seeking wound care today? _____

_____

How long has your wound existed? _____

_____

_____

Who referred you here? _____

Who has been treating you before today? _____

Can you describe what you have been using on your wound? _____

_____

Who has been helping you with your wound care? _____

How have you been paying for your supplies? _____

Have you ever had surgery? _____Type: _____

Do you have any allergies? Medications (Sulfa, Penicillin) _____Other? _____

Do you smoke? _____Packs per day: _____# of years: _____

How often do you use recreational or illicit drugs? _____

How often do you drink alcohol? _____

Do you have any pain? _____

On a scale of 0–10 (0 = No Pain, 10 = Severe Pain), what is your pain level now? 0 - 1 - 2 - 3 - 4 - 5 - 6 - 7 - 8 - 9 - 10

What over-the-counter medications are you taking (Tylenol, aspirin, antacids, vitamins, etc.): _____

_____

What prescription medications are you taking? Please include drug, dose, and frequency: _____

_____

Have you ever been told you had or do you currently have any of the following:

	Past	Present		Past	Present
Stroke:			Hypertension:		
Gangrene:			Cancer:		
Problems with circulation:			Chemotherapy:		
Arterial:			Radiation therapy:		
Venous:			Alternative treatments:		
Diabetes:			Swollen glands:		
Parkinson's:			Muscle spasms:		
Alzheimer's:			Polio or post-polio syndrome:		
Congestive heart failure:			Quadriplegia/paraplegia:		
Problems sleeping:			Myelomeningocele:		
Emphysema:			Decreased sensation:		
Bronchitis:			Arthritis:		
Chronic obstructive pulmonary disease:			Decreased activity:		
Problems controlling urine:			HIV or AIDS:		
Problems controlling bowels:			Hepatitis B:		
Atherosclerosis/arteriosclerosis			Decreased appetite:		
Malnutrition:			Problems with mobility:		
Dehydration:			Changes in weight greater than 10 pounds:		
Thyroid disorder:			Pacemaker:		

Appendix 1–B: Focused Assessment for Wounds

Medical Record # _____ Name _____

Attending Physician: _____

Referral Source: _____MD _____Nurse _____Other

Site: __Office ___Acute Hospital ___Subacute Center ___Nursing Home ___Assisted Living ___Home __Other

   Facility Name / Address / Pts. bed #: _____

Physical Exam: _____year old M F acquired non-healing wound(s) on   /   / .

Prior wound management includes:

_____

Past Medical History is positive for the following:

Allergies: _____	Alcoholism _____
CVA _____	NIDDM _____
Gangrene _____	Complications of DM _____
PVD _____	Weakness _____
Arterial insufficiency_____	Paraplegia/quadriplegia _____
CAD _____	Immobility/contractures _____
IDDM _____	Parkinson's _____

Vitals: T/P/R _____ BP: L/R_____(sit/stand/lying)

Braden Scale:

Sensory/MS	1. totally limited	2. very limited	3. slightly limited	4. no impairment
Moisture	1. constantly moist	2. very moist	3. occasionally moist	4. dry
Activity	1. bedfast	2. chairfast	3. walks w/assist	4. walks frequently
Mobility	1. 100% immobile	2. very limited	3. slightly limited	4. full mobility
Nutrition	1. very poor	2. < 1/2 daily portion	3. most of portion	4. eats everything
Friction/Shear	1. frequent sliding	2. feeble corrections	3. independent correction	

Braden Scale Total: _____

Mental Status: <u>Alert & Oriented X 3 : Other</u> _____

Skin: (moist, dry, flaky, scaly, condition of nails): _____ Turgor: <u>good / med / poor</u>

  <u>Rubor, cyanosis, atrophy, dermatitis, hair loss, rash, erythema.</u>

EENT (Eyes sunken, swollen lymph nodes) _____ Mucous Membranes Moist: _____

Neuro (Cranial nerves, sensation): _____

Endocrine (Blood sugar/other): _____

Respiratory: <u>Lungs Clear: Other:</u> _____

Cardiac: <u>Regular Rate & Rhythm: Other:</u> _____

Abdomen: <u>G-Tube: Soft/Supple/Without Masses or Tenderness:</u> _____ Other: _____

Perineal: <u>Skin intact</u> _____Other: _____

Lower Extremities: Ankle Brachial Index: _____

  Pulses Palpable: Dorsalis Pedis _____ Posterior Tibial _____ Popliteal _____

  Pulse Quality: Bounding _____ Strong _____ Weak _____ Barely Palpable _____

  Doppler: L + _____: R + _____

  Edema_____ Circumference: (L) _____:(R) _____

Functional Assessment: ADLs: Independent _____ Minimal Assist _____ Mod Assist _____ Total Assist _____

Labs/Nutrition: Hct: _____%: TP _____: Alb _____: Prealbumin _____: Other _____

            WBC_____ : % O_2 Sat_____: Lytes _____

Suggested Tests/Examinations: _____

Source: Adapted with permission of Dean P. Kane, MD, FACS, PA.

Appendix 1–C: Form HCFA-700

Department Of Health And Human Services Health Care Financing Administration	Medicare Part ☐ A ☐ B	FORM APPROVED

PLAN OF TREATMENT FOR OUTPATIENT REHABILITATION *(COMPLETE FOR INITIAL CLAIMS ONLY)*

1. PATIENT'S LAST NAME	FIRST NAME	M.I.	2. PROVIDER NO.	3. HICN
4. PROVIDER NAME	5. MEDICAL RECORD NO. *(Optional)*		6. ONSET DATE	7. SOC. DATE
8. TYPE:	9. PRIMARY DIAGNOSIS *(Pertinent Medical D.X.)*		10. TREATMENT DIAGNOSIS	11. VISITS FROM SOC.

12. PLAN OF TREATMENT FUNCTIONAL GOALS OUTCOME *(Long Term)*	PLAN
13. SIGNATURE *(professional established POC including prof. designation)*	14. FREQ/DURATION *(e.g., 3/Wk × 4 Wk.)*

I CERTIFY THE NEED FOR THESE SERVICES FURNISHED UNDER THIS PLAN OF TREATMENT 15. PHYSICIAN SIGNATURE	17. CERTIFICATION FROM THROUGH ☐ N/A
	18. ON FILE *(Print/type physician's name)* ☐

20. INITIAL ASSESSMENT *(History, medical complications, level of function at start of care. Reason for referral)*	19. PRIOR HOSPITALIZATION FROM TO ☐ N/A

21. FUNCTIONAL LEVEL *(End of billing period)*   PROGRESS REPORT   ☐ CONTINUE SERVICES *OR*   ☐ DC SERVICES

	22. SERVICE DATES FROM THROUGH

FORM HCFA-700 (11-91)

Source: Reprinted from Form HCFA-700 (11-91), Department of Health and Human Services, Health Care Financing Administration.

Appendix 1–D: HCFA-700 Form with FOR Template
To Guide Documentation in Italics

Department Of Health And Human Services
Health Care Financing Administration   MEDICARE PART ☒ A   ☐ B   OMB NO. 09380227

PLAN OF TREATMENT FOR OUTPATIENT REHABILITATION *(COMPLETE FOR INITIAL CLAIMS ONLY)*

1. PATIENT'S LAST NAME FIRST NAME M.I.	2. PROVIDER NO.	3. HICN
4. PROVIDER NAME	5. MEDICAL RECORD NO. *(Optional)*	6. ONSET DATE	7. SOC. DATE
8. TYPE	9. PRIMARY DIAGNOSIS *(Pertinent Medical Dx)*	10. TREATMENT DIAGNOSIS *(Functional Dx)*	11. VISITS FROM SOC.

12. PLAN OF TREATMENT FUNCTIONAL GOALS
   GOALS (Short-Term) *(Target Outcomes)*

   Outcomes (Long-Term) *(Prognosis)*

PLAN (Need for skilled services)

13. SIGNATURE (professional established POC including prof. designation)

14. FREQ/DURATION (eg, 3/wk × 4 wk) *(Due Date)*

I CERTIFY THE NEED FOR THESE SERVICES FURNISHED UNDER THIS PLAN OF TREATMENT AND WHILE UNDER MY CARE   ☒ N/A

15. PHYSICIAN SIGNATURE | 16. DATE

17. CERTIFICATION   ☐ N/A
FROM   THROUH

18. ON FILE (Print/type physician's name)
   ☐

20. INITIAL ASSESSMENT (History, medical complications, level of function at start of care. Reason for referral)

19. PRIOR HOSPITALIZATION   ☐ N/A
FROM   TO

Reason for Referral:

Hx:

Systems Review:

Results of Test and Measures:

Wound Healing Tissue Assessment:

Wound Size:

21. FUNCTIONAL LEVEL *(End of billing period)*   PROGRESS REPORT *(Verify functional outcomes):*
   ☐ CONTINUE SERVICES or   ☐ DC SERVICES

Change in Wound Functional Status:

Change in Mobility Functional Status:

22. Service Dates: FROM   THROUGH

Source: Reprinted from Form HCFA-700 (11-91), Department of Health and Human Services, Health Care Financing Administration.

Appendix 1–E: Sample Case Report Using HCFA-700

Department Of Health And Human Services
Health Care Financing Administration   MEDICARE PART ☒ A   ☐ B   OMB NO. 09380227

PLAN OF TREATMENT FOR OUTPATIENT REHABILITATION (COMPLETE FOR INITIAL CLAIMS ONLY)

1. PATIENT'S LAST NAME Luck	FIRST NAME M.I. George	2. PROVIDER NO.	3. HICN
4. PROVIDER NAME	5. MEDICAL RECORD NO. *(Optional)*	6. ONSET DATE 10/09/97	7. SOC. DATE 11/27/96
8. TYPE	9. PRIMARY DIAGNOSIS *(Pertinent Medical Dx)* CHF, COPD, multiple decubitus, weakness, debility	10. TREATMENT DIAGNOSIS *(Functional Dx)* 2 wounds with impaired wound healing secondary to eschar and chronic inflammation phase. Impaired mobility, transfers, gait (707; 710.7)	11. VISITS FROM SOC. 15

12. PLAN OF TREATMENT FUNCTIONAL GOALS
GOALS (Short-Term) *(Target Outcomes)*
Tissue Attribute changes expected:
   Necrosis free and wound healing progression to Proliferation
     phase Wound #1 & 2   21 days
   Reduce risk of pressure ulcers (Reduce Braden score to 19/22)   15 days
   Transfers and Gait with FWW to bathroom SBA   15 days
Outcomes (Long-term goals-prognosis of Functional Outcomes)
Target Performance Status:
Patient has improvement potential: Wounds will heal following intervention. Functional independent bed mobility, transfers and gait with assist device will be restored to enable patient to return to prior living situation in 6 weeks.

PLAN *(Need for skilled PT services)*
1. Wound not improving with routine dressing changes, pressure relief & enzymatic debriding
2. Wounds #1 & 2 require a) sharp debride b) HVPC to stimulate cells of repair and circulation for healing
3. Ther ex., balance, gait training to reduce risk of pressure ulcers and enhance circulation for healing current ulcers

---

13. SIGNATURE (professional established POC including prof. designation)

14. FREQ/DURATION (Due Date)
6x/wk daily × 6 wks (36 days)

I CERTIFY THE NEED FOR THESE SERVICES FURNISHED UNDER THIS PLAN OF TREATMENT AND WHILE UNDER MY CARE   ☒ N/A

15. PHYSICIAN SIGNATURE | 16. DATE

17. CERTIFICATION   ☒ N/A
FROM   THROUH

18. ON FILE (Print/type physician's name)
☐

---

20. INITIAL ASSESSMENT (History, medical complications, level of function at start of care. Reason for referral)

19. PRIOR HOSPITALIZATION   ☐ N/A
FROM   10/08/96   TO   11/26/96

Reason for Referral: Loss of mobility, (e.g., unable to reposition in bed, or ambulate); necrotic pressure ulcers R upper back and coccyx. Wants regain prior level of indep. Gait with cane. Heal pressure ulcers for return to retirement home.
Hx: Mild dementia, indep in gait w/cane; fell in shower and was unable to move; sustained pressure ulcers R upper back and coccyx, CHF, COPD.

Systems Review: 1) Cardiopulmonary system disabilities affect oxygen transport to tissues for repair. 2) Musculoskeletal impairments due to weakness (MMS BLE 3-/5 limit bed mobility, inability to transfer or ambulate without assist of 2 w/4ww × few feet. Diminished balance. 3) Neuromuscular impairment due to reduced cerebral oxygen causes mild functional loss of mentation, impaired mobility and awareness of need to reposition. Risk of Pressure ulcers is moderate (Braden Risk score 17/23). *Results of test and measures:* Wound Severity Dx (stage) delayed until both wounds are debrided. *Wound healing tissue assessment:* 1) R upper Back: presence of tissue attributes "good for healing"; adherence of wound edges; and "not good for healing": necrosis and depth of 0.2cm; 2) coccyx: presence of attributes "not for healing": erythema, necrosis, absence of attributes "good for healing." *Wound Size:* R Up Back: 17.7cm^2 Coccyx: 4.3cm^2 .depth >0.2

21. FUNCTIONAL LEVEL PROGRESS REPORT *(End of billing period) (Verify functional outcomes):* ☐ CONTINUE   ☐ DC Services
1) *Change in Wound Status:* a) R upper back: progressed to profileration phase of healing. Wound is erythema free, necrosis free and has factors "good for healing": Contraction sustained × 2 weeks, edges are adhered. Wound is reduced in size from 17.5cm^2 to 12.3cm^2 (decreased 25%), b) Coccyx: increased size and extent from 34.4cm^2 to 37.41cm^2 after debriding. Severity Dx: Stage IV Pressure ulcer. Tissue attributes present: "not good for healing" include: Undermining at 9:00 position, necrosis and erythema; good for heaing attributes include: granulation-significant reduction in depth from 2.0 cm to 1.5 cm, appearance of contraction and sustained wound contraction for 2 weeks (reduced size). Wound is at end of acute inflammation phase and progressing to proliferation phase. 2) *Change in Mobility Status:* a) Braden risk socre 19/23; b) Performs transfers and gait with min-assist using FWW for 15 feet; c) *Change in Balance* improved from fair to fair+ with functional change. Reduced risk of falling and pressure ulcers

22. Service Dates: FROM 11/10/99   **THROUGH** 11/30/99

Source: Reprinted from Department of Health and Human Services, Health Care Financing Administration Medicare.

CHAPTER 2

Wound Healing Biology and Chronic Wound Healing

Carrie Sussman

This chapter reviews five basic wound healing models, the biology of acute wound healing, fetal wound healing, and factors that affect chronic wound healing. The clinician must first understand the normal acute healing biology so as to recognize the current status of the wound and to diagnose abnormal wound healing leading to chronicity.

WOUND HEALING MODELS

There are five basic wound healing models for acute wounds, and similarities exist in all: (1) superficial wound healing, (2) primary intention wound healing, (3) delayed primary intention wound healing, (4) partial-thickness wound healing, and (5) secondary intention healing.

Superficial Wound Healing

An alteration in the superficial skin such as by pressure, including shearing and friction (stage I pressure ulcers), first-degree burns, and contusion, produces an inflammatory repair process. There is reason to believe that this begins, within hours, the response to trauma seen in wound healing of open wounds that are described below.[1] Superficial skin involvement may be an indicator of deeper soft tissue trauma and needs to be investigated for changes in skin color, temperature (warmth, followed by coolness, indicating tissue devitalization), tension, and sensation indicating tissue congestion. If deep tissue death occurs a few days after first observation, the tissues may rupture and become a deep cavity. This is a well-known phenomenon of pressure ulceration. The soft tissues usually heal by themselves over time, but intervention at this stage may hasten return to functional activities such as work and homemaking. For instance, ath-

letes are seen and treated immediately for superficial soft tissue injuries with reduced loss of playing time and pain. In patients with functional impairments, pain and tissue tension from congestion in the tissues often limit functional activities and result in diminished mobility, placing the individual at risk for further wounding. Part IV, Management of Wounds with Physical Therapy Technologies, points out benefits from intervention for superficial wounds (eg, reabsorption of hematoma for faster healing, including stage I pressure ulcers and grade I neuropathic ulcers). *Color Plates 65 to 71* illustrate how early intervention reduces hematoma. Case studies are described in Chapter 19, Ultrasound.

Primary and Delayed Primary Healing

Primary healing is drawing the wound edges together to achieve closure (eg, surgical wounds). There are three considerations in closing wounds by primary intention: there is no major loss of subcutaneous tissue, the edges are smooth and clean cut, and the wound is not contaminated with microorganisms or foreign bodies. Primary intention healing normally occurs quickly but less visibly than partial-thickness or secondary intention healing. The result is minimal residual scarring with closure in 3 to 7 days. Delayed primary intention healing is chosen for wounds that are contaminated with microorganisms or debris, where there is a large tissue loss, and closure by primary intention would result in intolerable tissue tension or put the patient at risk of infection.[2] In delayed primary intention, the wound is left open, although stitches are placed in the subcutaneous and fascial layers. The wound is usually closed in 5 to 7 days, after the risk of infection is significantly decreased or part of the tissue loss has been replaced.

Partial-Thickness Wound Healing

Wounds that have partial-thickness loss of the dermis heal by repair, which is the resurfacing of the wound by new epidermal cells. Immediately after injury, the body starts the process of closing the wound to protect the body from invasion by infection or debris, beginning with the inflammation phase. Epidermal cells at the edges as well as from the dermal appendages—sebaceous glands, sweat glands, and hair follicles—provide a supply of intact epithelial cells to assist in resurfacing of the wound by migration.[3,4] If the dermal appendages are present, islands of epidermis may appear on the wound surface and speed the resurfacing process. The resulting resurfacing is often indistinguishable from the surrounding skin. Examples of partial-thickness wounds are abrasions, skin tears, stage II pressure ulcers, and second-degree burns.

Secondary Intention Healing

Secondary intention healing is the chosen method of healing when the wound extends through the full thickness of the skin and may extend into underlying tissues. For instance, when a large amount of tissue is removed and a gap occurs, the wound has irregular edges that cannot be approximated, or there are nonviable wound margins, it is left to close by secondary intention. Wounds with a high microorganism count, debris, or skin necrosis are also left to close by secondary intention. Healing by secondary intention, or by contraction, as it is frequently called, occurs when the contractile forces produced by the myofibroblasts draw the wound together. Wounds healed by secondary intention go through a regeneration process that is nominally divided into four overlapping phases of repair: inflammation, proliferation, epithelialization, and remodeling. Wounds that regenerate by secondary intention and contraction have little epithelialization. Regeneration of tissue by secondary intention involves scar tissue formation. In this process, the anatomic structure of the scar tissue does not replicate the tissue replaced (eg, muscles, tendons, and nerves). In addition, the surface tissue will not be equal in elasticity or tensile strength to the original. After wound closure, the remodeling phase continues for 6 months to 2 years.[3]

Sometimes there is a defect that is too small to close by primary intention and healing by secondary intention is preferred. Some wounds are incompletely covered by split-thickness skin grafts and are best healed by secondary intention. If a wound is in an area where contraction will produce disfiguring or nonfunctional deformities, the process of healing by secondary intention may be allowed to develop a good, healthy wound bed. Then it may be interrupted and a split-thickness skin graft placed on the granulating wound bed.

Secondary intention is the mechanism for healing associated with chronic wounds.[2]

ACUTE WOUND HEALING BIOLOGY

The process of healing by different phases has been described by Hunt et al.[5] as a cascade of overlapping events that occur in a reasonably predictable fashion. Even though the events overlap, the series of events can be divided into phases. The literature describes the phases of repair as either three or four phases depending on whether epithelialization is included as part of proliferation or as a separate phase. In the proliferation phase, the fibroblasts are the cells of regeneration that build the collagen matrix referred to as granulation tissue and contract the wound opening. In the epithelialization phase, the function of the epidermal cells is to close the wound by resurfacing.[5]

A diagram by Hunt and Van Winkle[6] (Figure 2–1) shows inflammation, the central activity of wound healing, located in the center of the diagram. On either sides are the concurrent events that occur as a consequence of injury, proliferation and epithelialization. The lower portion of the diagram represents the coming together of the phases leading to the remodeling phase of wound healing. The interpretation of the diagram is that four phases—inflammation, proliferation, epithelialization, and remodeling—occur in an orderly overlapping fashion. The wound healing model used in this text is based on four phases. The biologic repair process is the same for all wounds, open and closed, regardless of etiology. However, the sequence of repair is completed more quickly in primary healing, and when there is superficial and partial-thickness skin involvement. Slower healing occurs when there is full-thickness skin loss extending into and through subcutaneous tissue.

Phase I: Inflammation

The classic observable signs and symptoms of inflammation, where recognized, are change in color from surrounding skin (red, blue, purple), temperature (heat), turgor (swelling), and sensation (pain), plus a loss of function (*Color Plates 1, 19, and 21*). The inflammation response is sometimes referred to as a "flare" because of the suddenness of the response, the color, and the associated temperature changes that are reminiscent of the flaring up of a fire. Inflammation is the body's immune system reaction and is essential for healing. The biology of inflammation is well regulated in the normal acute healing wound. The process lasts 3 to 7 days. Acute inflammation begins at the moment of injury, setting into motion a biologic cascade that functions, according to Knighton,[7] like a three-compartment system (see

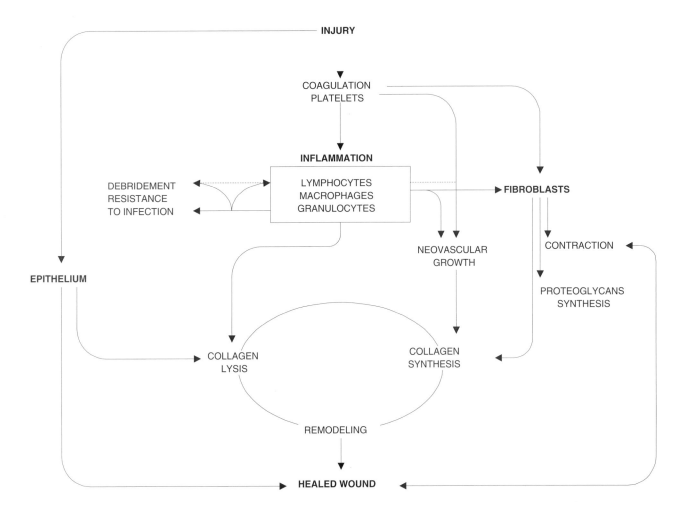

Figure 2–1 Wound repair diagram. Reprinted with permission from TK Hunt and W Van Winkle, *Fundamentals of Wound Management in Surgery, Wound Healing: Normal Repair,* p. 1e, © 1976, South Plainfield, NJ: Chirurgecom, Inc.

Table 2–1). Knighton's three-compartment system is used and adapted in this chapter to explain the actions of the key components and the sequence of events occurring during three phases of healing: inflammation, proliferation, and epithelialization. In all phases, the battle zone is the center of the action.[7–10] Signal sources attract responder cells and regulate the repair process.

Battle Zone

The battle zone is defined as the area of tissue trauma where the vascular response to wounding begins. It is the location of the central activity, which includes perfusion, pain, temperature, infection, and nutrition. First there is clotting and vasoconstriction, or hemostasis, to reduce blood loss at the site of injury. Hemostasis is a major function of the platelets. Platelets, which are normally present in the intravascular space, are activated by collagen or microfibrils from the subendothelial layers exposed when injury occurs. In addition, activated platelets release biologically active substances, or signal sources known as platelet-derived growth factor and epidermal growth factor, both of which facilitate cell migration of granulocytes and macrophages to the area of injury. They have a life span of approximately 8 to 12 days.

Perfusion and Nutrition. Vasodilatation is accompanied by perfusion and increased capillary pressure and permeability, which permits the plasma protein molecules to migrate into the surrounding tissues. Fibrin plugs seal off the lymphatic flow to prevent spreading of infection. Increased

Table 2–1 Three-Compartment System—Inflammation Phase

Battle Zone	Signal Source	Responder Cells
Trauma	Wound space	Fibroblasts
Perfusion	Hypoxia	Endothelial cells
Pain	Hyperlactic environment	Epithelial cells
Temperature	Current of Injury	
Infection	Neutrophils	
Nutrition	Mast cells	
	Macrophages	

Source: Adapted with permission from tables of the Three Compartment Concept for Inflammation Phase of Wound Healing, presented at San Diego, California, May 2, 1995, as part of a lecture, *The Role of Oxygen in Wound Healing,* © David Knighton, M.D.

perfusion or blood flow brings needed nutrients to meet the increased metabolic demands of the tissues. High metabolic activities and the increased blood flow raises tissue temperatures. This cascade of events is the biologic basis for the familiar signs and symptoms of inflammation: a reddening of the surrounding tissues or, in individuals with darkly pigmented skin, a purple or violaceous discoloration, pain, heat, and edema. The rise in tissue temperature provides an environment favorable for cell mitosis and enhanced cellular activities.[8,9]

Pain. Bleeding into the tissues releases histamine and prostaglandins, which stimulate dilation of injured vessels in adjacent tissues and pain afferents of the sympathetic nervous system. This phenomenon is called reflex hyperemia.

Infection. An oxygen tension gradient develops across the wound that is used for regulatory purposes. Oxygen is essential to prevent infection and to meet metabolic demands of the tissues, as well as hydroxylation of proline necessary for useful collagen production in the remodeled wound. Oxygen supplementation by nasal cannula is one way to enhance oxygen available for these tissue functions; oxygen has been demonstrated to function as an "antibiotic" and prevent wound infections.[10–12]

Signal Source

The second compartment in the system are the signal source(s). Signal sources include indicators from environmental conditions or from some cells to other cells of repair signalling them to migrate to the wound to begin repair or regeneration. During inflammation, the signal sources are

> **Research Wisdom:** *Supplemental Oxygen*
>
> Oxygen can be supplemented through a nasal cannula at 40%, or 5 L/min. If chronic obstructive pulmonary disease (COPD) is present it can be safely supplemented at 2 L/min. This is a simple and useful method of enhancing the available oxygen.[10,11]

the wound space, hypoxia and hyperlactic environment, current of injury, neutrophils, mast cells, and macrophages.

Wound Space Hypoxia and Hyperlactic Environment. The process of hemostasis is to curtail blood flow directly to the site of injury which reduces oxygen delivery to the wound space, producing an environmental change to a state of hypoxia. Hypoxia in the wound space is a key signal that controls wound healing. Too much oxygen in the wound space will *impede* wound healing. Hypoxia is a signal that recruits endothelial responder cells and serves as a stimulant for angiogenesis or the process of new blood vessel growth by the endothelial cells that occurs during the proliferation phase. Local hypoxia also causes a shift to anaerobic glycolysis with increased lactate production that also is involved in activation of both angiogenesis and collagen synthesis. The wound space thus becomes hyperlactic and acidotic.[5,13]

Current of Injury. Another component of healing is endogenous biologic electrical currents. Becker,[14] in the 1960s, demonstrated the existence of a direct-current electrical system that controls tissue healing. He called this the "current of injury." The human body has an average charge on the skin surface of −23 mV.[15] Multiple experiments demonstrate that a negative charge exists on the surface of the skin with respect to the deeper skin layers. This results in weak electrical potentials across the skin, creating a "skin battery" effect. The battery is driven by a sodium ion pump initiated by the sodium ions passing through the cells of the epithelium via specific channels in the outer membrane. Once in the cell they diffuse to other cells of the epithelium and then they can be actively transported from these cells via electrogenic "pumps," located in all of the plasma membranes of the epithelium except the outer membrane. The result is a transport of NA[+] from the water bathing the epithelium to the internal body fluids and generation of a potential in the order of 50 mV across the epithelium.[16] If there is a break in the integrity of the skin, there will be a net flow of ionic current through the low-resistance pathway of the injured cells and fluid exudate that line the wound; if the wound space becomes dry, the voltage gradient will be eliminated.[12] Use of moist wound healing methods is clinical application of this theory.[17] The ionic current flowing between the normal and injured tissue is a stimulus for the repair process. During the repair process there is a distinct pattern of current flow and polarity switching, and when healing is complete the current ceases. The bioelectric repair process is polarity regulated, and cells of repair are attracted by the positive or negative pole. This is called galvanotaxis. The macrophages and neutrophils are attracted to the positive pole.[18,19] Mast cells seem to be inhibited by the positive pole.[20] Weiss et al.[20] found reduced mast cell representation in wounds after positive polarity stimulation and suggested that as a mechanism for reduced fibrotic scarring. When the wound is inflamed or infected, neutrophils are attracted to the negative pole.[21] The negative pole attracts fibroblasts,[22] which stimulates protein and DNA synthesis and increases CA[2+] uptake, fibroblast proliferation, and collagen synthesis.[23–25] Negative polarity facilitates migration of epidermal cells.[26] Negative polarity is also associated with suppression of bacterial growth.[27–30] In chronic wound healing, it is proposed that the current of injury fails to occur. One rationale for the use of electrical stimulation for wound healing initially is based on the theory that electrical stimulation mimics the current of injury and will restart or accelerate the repair process. Clearly, there are significant research data to support the concept that electrical current plays an important role in the cell physiology of wound healing. The use of electrical stimulation for wound healing is explained in Chapter 16, Electrical Stimulation.

Neutrophils. Neutrophils (polymorphonuclear neutrophilic leukocytes) migrate into the wound space usually within the first 24 hours after wounding and remain from 6 hours to several days. Neutrophils are granulocytic leuko-

---

> **Research Wisdom:** *Attraction of Neutrophils and Macrophages*
>
> Electrical stimulation has the ability to attract neutrophils and macrophages to the wound site and stimulate fibroblasts. See Chapter 16, Electrical Stimulation, for more information.

cytes that function as phagocytic cells that proliferate in the hypoxic acidotic environment and produce superoxide to fight bacteria and enhance effectiveness of antibiotics. Length of stay of the neutrophils is minimal if the bacterial count is low or declines. High bacterial counts prolong neutrophil activation and inflammation.[31] The neutrophil is considered to be a primary cell responsible for cleansing the wound of microorganisms, and lack of adequate numbers of neutrophils will retard healing in infected wounds. When bacterial counts in the wound exceeds 10[5], infection becomes apparent in the wound site. The wound begins to pour forth pus, which is the accumulation of dead neutrophils that have phagocytized debris in the wound. The neutrophil has a short life span because it is unable to regenerate spent lysosomal and other enzymes used in the destruction of foreign substances. In addition to pus formation, the neutrophil produces numerous toxic byproducts that, if there is excessive neutrophil activity due to high bacterial counts, will negatively affect the wound tissue and even healthy tissue.[3]

Mast Cells. Mast cells are specialized secretory cells that, in the resting state, contain granules that are largely a heparin-protein complex in which the protein carboxyl groups serve as histamine-binding sites. There are a number of biologically active substances in mast cell granules, including neutrophil chemotactic factor.[32] Histamine is initially released from the mast cells after injury and plays an important role in vascular dilation and permeability, inducing temporary mild edema. In low doses histamine may stimulate collagen formation and healing.[32,33] Once the body has produced enough platelet and prothrombin reaction, the mast cell will produce heparin. Heparin stimulates the migration of endothelial cells. Other substances in the mast cells, eosinophil and neutrophil chemotactic factors, attract the leukocytic cells that in turn act as chemical signals for the recruitment of macrophages, leading to a modulation of the inflammatory phase. Macrophages promote later phases in the repair process through recruitment of fibroblasts.[32,34] The effect of the heparin is to accelerate the activity of the leukocytes (neutrophils and eosinophils) in the phagocytosis of the hematoma that occurs in the wound following damage to the blood vessels at the time of wounding.[35]

Macrophages. Both neutrophils and macrophages function in a low-oxygen, high-acidotic environment. Macrophages perform several important functions during the inflammatory phase. Macrophages phagocytose debris and
control infection by ingestion of microorganisms and excre-
tion of ascorbic acid, hydrogen peroxide, and lactic acid. The
body interprets the buildup of these excreted byproducts as
a signal to send more macrophages, and the result of the
increased macrophage population is a prolonged, more intense inflammatory response. Macrophages are the essential
cells for the transition between the inflammation phase and
the proliferative phase of repair. The secretion of angiogenesis growth factor (AGF) by the macrophage is well established. AGF is a signal source that stimulates the budding of
the endothelial cells from the damaged blood vessels and
subsequent angiogenesis. Reestablishment of the blood supply is essential to deliver nutrients to the newly forming tissue. Together, secretions of the macrophages and the dead
platelets combine to produce a fibroblast-stimulating factor,
which signals a chemotactic message to the fibroblasts during the late phases of inflammation. The life span of the
macrophage is thought to be months to years and is a component of wound fluid for a long period of time, transcend-
ing all phases of healing.

Responder Cells

Fibroblasts. Responder cells include the fibroblasts that
respond to the chemotactic signals from the macrophages.
The fibroblasts are the cells that build the collagen matrix
produced during the proliferative phase. Fibroblast cells begin to differentiate, and some transform into myofibroblasts
during the later part of the inflammatory phase.
Myofibroblasts are able to contract and extend. They draw
the edges of the wound together like the drawstring on a purse,
and influence the rate and amount of wound contraction.
Drawing together too tightly causes deformity of the repaired
scar and an impairment of function.

Endothelial Cells. Endothelial cells respond to the AGF
secretions of the macrophages and from the signal of the
hypoxic environment that induces angiogenesis. Angiogenesis is development of the new blood vessels or vasculariza-

tion of the tissue that will grow on the collagen matrix and
gives the bright red appearance of granulation tissue seen in
the proliferative phase.

Epithelial Cells. Epithelial cells respond to the signal of
trauma from a break in the skin from the wound edges and,
if a partial-thickness skin trauma, from the dermal appendages. Epithelial cells begin the resurfacing process immediately after injury. The process is described later in the section on the epithelialization phase. A specialized function of
the epithelial cells is debridement of necrotic tissue by release of lytic enzymes, which lyse the attachment of the necrotic tissue that may be present in the wound bed. The migration of the epithelial cells is also oxygen dependent. When
there are low levels of oxygen, epithelial migration cannot
debride the wound. Wound resurfacing is hampered if there
is a full-thickness wound that has lost the dermal appendages and as a consequence epithelial cells can only migrate
from the wound edges. For example, full-thickness pressure
wounds develop a buildup of the epithelial cells at the wound
edges, forming an epidermal ridge that curls under the edges
and slows closure. It is as if the epithelial cells get tired of
waiting for granulation tissue to fill in the wound defect, so
they prematurely proliferate and migrate over the edge.

Phase II: Proliferation Phase

The proliferation phase consists of two overlapping phenomena. Fibroplasia, or the laying down of the collagen
matrix known as granulation tissue, is one phenomenon and
wound contraction is the other. The granulation is first seen
as pale pink buds, which, as it fills with new blood vessels,
becomes bright, beefy, red tissue. The thick capillary bed,
which fills the matrix, supplies the nutrients and oxygen
necessary for the wound to heal. This tissue is structurally
and functionally different from the tissues it replaces and
will not differentiate into the nerves, muscles, tendons, and
other tissue that it replaces.[3] Wound contraction is seen as
the change in wound shape and reduction in the open area of
the wound. The three-compartment system (Table 2–2) is
used to describe the next sequence of events that occur during the proliferation phase in the battle zone, by the signal
sources and from the responder cells.

Battle Zone

The battle zone remains the center of activity for wound
healing during the proliferation phase. The vascular response
started in the inflammation phase now is responsible for sustaining the perfusion to the new tissue formation, bringing
necessary nutrition and oxygen. Oxygen and nutrition demand remains very high to support the cells of repair, fibro-

Table 2–2 Three-Compartment System—Proliferation

Battle Zone	Signal Sources	Responder Cells
Perfusion	Current of injury	Fibroblasts
Infection	Neutrophils	Myofibroblasts
Oxygen	Macrophages	Endothelial cells
Nutrition	Moist environment	Epidermal cells
Trauma		
Temperature		

Source: Adapted with permission from tables of the Three Compartment Concept for Inflammation Phase of Wound Healing, presented at San Diego, California, May 2, 1995, as part of a lecture, *The Role of Oxygen in Wound Healing,* © David Knighton, M.D.

blasts, myofibroblasts, endothelial cells, and epidermal cells, which are reproducing at a rapid rate to create the collagen matrix. Nutrients, including zinc, iron, copper and vitamin C, and oxygen, are essential for fibroblast synthesis of the collagen matrix. The macrophages and neutrophils work to control infection as long as the wound remains open. The combination of activities raises tissue temperatures. The wound needs warmth at this time to promote cellular division and management of infection.

Signal Source

The current of injury remains a signal source to attract cells of repair as long as the wound surface remains open. Macrophages continue to produce growth factors that are chemotactic signal sources to fibroblasts. A moist wound environment contains ions that attract the cells required for current flow and migration.

Responder Cells

Fibroblasts. The activities of the responder cells, fibroblasts, myofibroblasts, endothelial cells, and epidermal cells during this phase are very high. Fibroblasts extrude collagen matrix as polypeptide chains that aggregate into a triple helix, called procollagen. The procollagen undergoes a process of cleavage and become tropocollagen molecules. The tropocollagen molecules spontaneously associate with other tropocollagen molecules to form a collagen fibril, producing an array of disorganized filaments. The organization and bonding of the filaments is called intermolecular cross-linkage. Cross-linkage is the welding together of the collagen matrix for wound durability and tensile strength. The better the degree of organization and cross-linkage of the collagen matrix, the better the tensile strength or strength of the remodeled scar tissue. The process is called fibroplasia.

Elastin is another connective tissue that is synthesized by the fibroblast. It derives its name from its elastic properties.

It is found in skin, lungs, blood vessels, and the bladder and functions to maintain tissue shape. A third fibrous connective tissue component is the structural glycoproteins. Laminin and fibronectin are two of these fiber-forming molecules. Together these connective tissues provide structural and metabolic support to other tissues.

Collagen matrix, which is elastin together with the new vascular network produced by the endothelial cells, looks like red granules piled on top of each other (see *Color Plates 2, 4, and 8* for examples) and give the tissue the name "granulation tissue." Pink "granulation buds" may be the first sign of repair seen in the wound bed, as seen in *Color Plate 7.* Notice how the granulation starts at one side of the wound and then "marches" across the wound bed as shown in *Color Plates 8 and 9.* At this time, the granulation tissue is very fragile and unable to withstand any trauma. Trauma may reinitiate the inflammatory process and cause the laying down of excessive collagen, resulting in poor elasticity and a less desirable scar.

Clinical Wisdom: *Granulation Tissue Complications*

1. Change *from* beefy, red granulation tissue to a dusky pink is an evaluation point. Wound fluid may also change at the same time in either color or quantity, or both. This is often a sign of infection.
2. Trauma to the new granulation tissue will cause bleeding, which will lead to scarring. Protection of the new granulation tissue is very important.

Myofibroblasts and Wound Contraction. During the inflammation phase, it was described how the fibroblasts differentiate into a specialized cell called the myofibroblast. These cells contain the contractile properties of smooth muscle cells. The myofibroblast connects itself to the wound skin margins and pulls the epidermal layer inward. The myofibroblast ring forms what has been described as a "picture frame" beneath the skin of the contracting wound. The contracting forces start out equal in all wounds, but the shape of the "picture frame" predicts the resultant speed of contraction. Linear wounds contract rapidly, square or rectangular wounds contract at a moderate pace, and circular wounds contract slowly. One characteristic of pressure ulcers is that they take on a circular shape, and this is an indicator that they will contract slowly.[36]

Wound contraction is a process that pulls the wound edges together for the purpose of closing the wound. In effect, this will reduce the open area and, if successful, will result in a smaller wound with less need for repair by scar formation. Wound contraction can be very beneficial in the closure of wounds in areas such as the buttocks or trochanter but can be very harmful in areas such as the hand or around the neck and face, where it can cause disfigurement and excessive scarring. Rapid, uncontrolled wound contraction in these areas must be avoided.

Surgical wounds that are closed by primary intention have minimal contraction response. Skin grafting is used to reduce avoided contraction in undesirable locations. The thickness of the skin graft influences the degree of contraction suppression. Pressure garments are another method of controlling wound contraction.

Research Wisdom: *Best Time To Apply Skin Grafts*

Split-thickness skin grafts suppress contraction by 31% and full-thickness skin grafts diminish contraction by 55%. The best time for application of skin grafts is during the inflammatory phase before contraction begins.[36]

Phase III: Epithelialization

The epithelialization phase commences immediately after trauma as a priority for the body to protect itself from invasion by outside organisms and occurs concurrently with the other phases. Once again the three-compartment system model (Table 2–3) is used to describe the activities that occur in the three aspects of the reepithelialization process.

Battle Zone

Trauma, as described, triggers perfusion to the "battle zone" area. During this phase, as during all of the wound healing processes, perfusion is a key component for delivery of the oxygen, nutrients, and warmth necessary for cell mitosis.

Signal Source

The signals for epithelialization begin during the inflammation phase from the macrophages, neutrophils, and current of injury to stimulate the response of the epithelial cells to migrate from the wound edges and dermal appendages.

Responder Cells

Epithelial cells make up the layers of the dermis and epidermis as well as lining various body organs and dermal appendages (eg, sebaceous glands, sweat glands, and hair follicles). Epithelial cells respond to signals from the macrophages, neutrophils, and current of injury. Responding epithelial cells advance in a sheet to resurface the open space. The leading edges of the advancing epidermal cells become phagocytic and clean the debris, including clotted material, from their path. A moist wound environment will speed the migration toward one another from the edges of the wound and from the dermal appendages. Full-thickness skin loss injuries suffer loss of the dermal appendages as an important source of new epithelial cells. The advancing front of epidermal cells cannot cover a cavity, so they dive down and curl under at the edges.

In surgical wounds that are sutured, epidermal migration begins within the first 24 hours and is usually complete, in healthy adults, within 48 to 72 hours postoperatively. In other wounds, trauma to skin results in tissue degeneration with broad, indistinct areas, where any edge is difficult to see.

Table 2–3 Three-Compartment System—Epithelialization

Battle Zone	Signal Source	Responder Cells
Perfusion	Current of injury	Epidermal
Temperature	Moist wound environment	Stem cells
Nutrition	Macrophages	
Trauma	Neutrophils	

Source: Adapted with permission from tables of the Three Compartment Concept for Inflammation Phase of Wound Healing, presented at San Diego, California, May 2, 1995, as part of a lecture, *The Role of Oxygen in Wound Healing,* © David Knighton, M.D.

This forms a shallow lesion with more distinct, thin, separate edges. As tissue trauma progresses, the reaction intensifies with a thickening and rolling inward of the epidermis. The edge is well defined and sharply outlines the ulcer with little or no evidence of new tissue growth. Repeated trauma and attempts at repair to the wound edges result in fibrosis and scarring. The edges of the wound become indurated and firm,[37] which results in possible impairment of the migratory ability of the epithelial cells.[38] If the epithelialization process becomes arrested, the result is a chronic wound.

Elasticity of the replaced epidermal layers will affect the function of the skin as it overrides bony prominences and moving muscles or tendons. Once the wound has been resurfaced by epithelial cells, the cells begin the process of differentiating and maturing into type I collagen. The tensile strength of the remodeled skin will not exceed 70% to 80% of the original. The quality of the scar tissue is an indication of the final outcome. Because closure had been achieved by epithelialization, it does not mean that the wound is fully healed. The new skin at this time has a tensile strength of only roughly 15% of normal. The new skin must be treated carefully to avoid trauma, which can cause edema and infection and lead to reinflammation. Chronic inflammation will cause a thickening of the skin and less-elastic remodeled tissue.[36]

Phase IV: Remodeling Phase

Collagen Lysis

Collagenase is an enzyme produced during the inflammation phase and throughout the proliferation phase as a regulator of fibroplasia. Collagenase has the capability of cleaving or breaking the cross-linkage of the tropocollagen molecules. This is called collagen lysis. In the healthy wound, collagenase is a regulator of the balance between synthesis and lysis of collagen. It is this ability to break down collagen that makes collagenase useful as a debriding agent. Breaking of the cross-linkage has the effect of making the tropocollagen molecule soluble so that it can be excreted from the body. The balance between collagen synthesis and collagen lysis is fine tuned with a goal that one process should not exceed the other. However, as the wound matures during remodeling, collagen lysis increases. The organization of the collagen fibers as they are laid down by the fibroblasts is part of this regulatory process. Better organization produces a better functional outcome of more elastic, smoother, and stronger fibers for the repaired scar tissues.

Collagen synthesis is oxygen dependent, but collagen lysis is not. Too much oxygen is believed to cause hypertrophy of the granulation tissues, called hypergranulation. Hypergranulation creates a humping of the tissue that inhib-

its the epidermal cell movements against gravity to cover and resurface the wound (see *Color Plate 23*). This is usually the result of an imbalance of collagen synthesis to collagen lysis. Some individuals have a genetic inhibition of lysis, meaning that the balance between collagen synthesis and collagen lysis is not balanced, and hypertrophic scars and keloid scars form. One way to control hypertrophic granulation and hypertrophic scarring is by application of pressure garments to the scar tissue area to reduce profusion and oxygen inflow. In the ischemic area, synthesis is suppressed and lysis continues. This is an accepted method for flattening scar bulk. Continuation of this process is required until the remodeling is complete.

Clinical Wisdom:
Controlling Hypergranulation Tissue

If proliferation of granulation tissue overlaps the wound edges due to hypertrophic granulation, cauterizing the undesired tissue with a silver nitrate stick should be tried to suppress the overgrowth. Repeated applications may be necessary. This will knock down the granulation tissue and allow the epithelial cells to migrate over the granulation tissue base.

Scar Formation

Scar formation progresses during the remodeling phase, when the fibronectin laid down in the granulation phase is eliminated and large bundles of type I collagen accumulate. Mature scar is formed from type I collagen. The external scar undergoes contraction, and the small vessels that gave the new scar its red appearance gradually retract. As long as the scar exhibits a rosier appearance than normal, remodeling is under way.[36] The purpose of this process is an attempt by the scar to blend in both cosmetically and functionally. An example is the surgical scar on the incision line that initially is bright red and then over time blanches and conforms to the body contours. The entire process of remodeling of wounds is described as taking from 3 weeks postinjury to 2 years.[36]

At this time, the clinician has limited ability to control the amount and location of scarring, but this may change in the near future. Much research is being done on pharmacologic interventions that may be used to manipulate the scar formation. Two theories are being tested on the forces that direct the alignment of the collagen fibers. These two theories are induction theory and tension theory. Briefly stated, according to induction theory scar tissue attempts to mimic the characteristics of the tissue it is healing. Tension theory refers to internal and external stresses that affect the wound during the remodeling phase. Several studies of the tension theory suggest that adding tension during the healing process increases the tensile strength of all soft tissue structures, as well as bone, and that immobilization and stress deprivation have been shown to produce loss of tensile strength and collagen fiber organization. Dynamic splinting, serial casting, repetitive motion devices, and exercise are ways of applying long-duration stress on healing scar tissues to remodel to new positions. Physical therapists are often involved in selecting and providing these interventions. They are, however, beyond the scope of this book and are not included in the interventions for wound healing.

FETAL WOUND HEALING

Researchers are looking to see what can be learned from fetal wound healing. It has been known for some time that there is a lack of scar formation in fetuses that have fetal surgery in utero.[39–41] One feature of fetal wounds is that they are continually bathed in amniotic fluid, which has a rich content of hyaluronic acid (HA) and fibronectin as well as growth factors crucial to fetal development. HA is a key structural and functional component of the extracellular matrix and fosters an environment that promotes cell proliferation and tissue regeneration and repair.[42] HA is laid down in the matrix of both fetal and adult wounds, but the sustained deposition of HA is unique to fetal wounds. An example of the effects of HA and amniotic fluid on healing of surgical wounds was reported by Byl et al. in two studies.[43,44] Amniotic fluid, HA, and normal saline were applied to controlled incisional wounds. The surgeons were blinded to the fluids applied. Both the amniotic fluid– and HA-treated incisions healed faster than the saline-treated wounds. In fact, the wounds treated with the amniotic fluid and HA appeared to close within minutes of the application. The healing was quicker and the quality of the scar was better in the HA and amniotic fluid groups than in the saline-treated incisions. The tensile strengths of the amniotic fluid– and HA-treated wounds were slightly weaker than those of the saline-treated group at the end of 1 week, but after 2 weeks all groups had equal tensile strength.

There remain many questions to be answered about fetal wound healing. There are many differences between fetal development and adult repair and regeneration. For example, the transplacental circulation provides a partial pressure of oxygen of 20 mm Hg, which is markedly lower than that in adults, signifying that the fetus lives in a hypoxic environment.[45] This is in marked contrast to the adult environment, where oxygen is a critical factor in prevention of infection and in the repair process. Other factors are the differences in the fetal and adult immune systems, the histology of fetal skin during development, the function of adult versus fetal

fibroblasts in collagen synthesis, and the absence of myofibroblasts.[46,47]

CHRONIC WOUND HEALING

A chronic wound is defined as one that deviates from the expected sequence of repair in terms of time, appearance, and response to aggressive and appropriate treatment.[48] When the response to wounding does not conform to the described cycle of wound recovery after a period of 2 to 4 weeks, the wound may become stuck and unable to progress through the phases of healing without intervention. The chronic wound often does not have the cardinal signs of heat, swelling, redness, and pain observed in acute wounds. Chronic wounds may be surrounded with a halo of redness or a purple/violaceous color around the wound caused by overactive macrophages and mast cells, which release histamine. A brown staining of the skin by hemosiderin from the lysing of red blood cells often surrounds chronic wounds or scars (eg, pressure ulcers or venous ulcers).

The typical way to diagnose chronic wounds is to use the pathophysiology leading to the ulcer and apply that as the medical diagnosis. For example, there are ischemic arterial ulcers, diabetic ulcers (both vascular and neuropathic), pressure ulcers, vasculitis ulcers, venous ulcers, and rheumatoid ulcers (Exhibit 2–1). The disease processes are contributing factors to the ulceration. For example, diabetes and peripheral vascular disease are comorbidities. The impairment of functions such as impairment of sensation due to long-term diabetes or the impaired circulation due to the vascular disease process are the coimpairments. Intrinsic factors are usually comorbidities. Extrinsic factors and iatrogenic factors are impairments to healing. This book uses both management strategies for the wound pathophysiology and comorbidities and for the wound coimpairments to guide the nurse and physical therapist to interventions.

There are a number of factors, including intrinsic, extrinsic, and iatrogenic factors (Table 2–4), that influence whether the wound will go on to heal or will become chronic. Intrinsic factors are those that are related to medical status or physiologic properties within the patient that may effect the healing. Examples of intrinsic factors include age, chronic disease, circulatory disease, malnutrition, neuropathy, and immunosuppression. Extrinsic factors are those that come from sources in the environment that affect the body or the wound such as medication, irradiation, psychophysiologic stress, wound bioburden from necrotic tissue or infection, or other therapies that are impairments of healing. Iatrogenic factors are those factors related to the specific way that the wound is managed. These include local ischemia, inappropriate wound care, trauma, pressure, inattention to contributing pathology, and patient noncompliance.[49] These are also im-

Exhibit 2–1 Examples of Chronic Wounds

- Ischemic arterial ulcers
- Diabetic vascular and neuropathic ulcers
- Venous insufficiency
- Vasculitis ulcers
- Rheumatoid arthritis
- Pressure ulcers

pairments of healing. These items are not an all-inclusive listing of factors that impair wound healing and contribute to chronic wounds, but are presented to raise awareness of the nurse and the physical therapist to some common factors that have been implicated in the problem.

The nurse and the physical therapist have responsibility in management of the patient with a chronic wound to evaluate the comorbidities and impairment factors that may contribute to chronic wound healing. Much of this information is available in the medical history, from the systems review, or the physical examination as described in Chapter 1. The following information describes factors listed in the three groups. Early identification of wound healing factors that contribute to chronicity will help the clinician to triage cases, reduce variability in cost and care, and improve the prognosis and outcomes for planned interventions.

Intrinsic Factors in Chronic Wound Healing

Aging

Skin changes occur with aging. The epidermis becomes thinner with increased risk of injury from shearing and friction, resulting in ulceration and skin tears. The skin also loses its impenetrability to substances in the environment. Irritants and certain drugs are more readily absorbed. The reproduc-

tive function of epidermal cells diminishes with age and replacement is slowed. Elastin fibers are lost, and the skin becomes less elastic. The dermis atrophies, which slows wound contraction and increases risk of wound dehiscence. There is diminished vascularity of the dermis.[49] Aging and chronic disease states often go together, and both delay repair processes due to delayed cellular response to the stimulus of injury, delayed collagen deposition, and decreased tensile strength in the remodeled tissue. The regeneration process may be diminished as a result of impaired circulatory function. Aging alone is not a major factor in chronic wound healing. Research now demonstrates that in elderly persons without chronic disease states, healing is only slightly retarded compared with that of a young population.[50]

Chronic Disease

Chronic diseases of all kinds, renal, pulmonary, and other systemic diseases, affect the cardiopulmonary system and the oxygen transport pathway that delivers oxygen from the lungs to the tissues and removes carbon dioxide. The cardiopulmonary system is affected by conditions that are hematologic, neuromuscular, musculoskeletal, endocrine, and immunologic.[51] For example, depending on the location or level of a neuromuscular lesion, breathing functions will be affected. This may contribute to reduced respiratory muscle function, which will affect lung volumes, flow rates, inspiratory and expiratory lung functions, and the delivery of oxygen to and removal of carbon dioxide from the tissues that are required for healing. Impaired cardiopulmonary function will affect mobility and must be considered as a risk for skin ulceration. In this case, the nurse and physical therapist must be aware of how to optimize the positioning and mobility of the patient to compensate for the effects of chronic disease on the body. More discussion about chronic diseases and their effects on wound healing follow under specific categories.

Table 2–4 Factors in Chronic Wound Healing

Intrinsic—Related to Medical Status	Extrinsic—Related to Environment	Iatrogenic—Local Wound Management
Age	Medication	Local ischemia
Circulatory disease	Irradiation	Inappropriate wound care
Neuropathy	Psychophysiologic stress	Trauma
Malnutrition	Wound bioburden: necrosis or infection	Pressure
Immunosuppression		Inattention to contributing pathology
		Patient noncompliance

Circulatory Disease

Circulatory disease is a comorbidity of chronic wounds that results in vascular changes that are coimpairments of wound healing because of decreased delivery of blood supply bringing oxygen and nutrients. All phases of wound healing require adequate oxygen. Oxygen is carried in the blood and dissolved in the plasma by the red blood cells bound to the hemoglobin. In anemia, there is reduced hemoglobin and reduced oxygen-carrying capacity of the blood. However, research data suggest that anemia does not impair wound healing when there is adequate *perfusion* and *blood volume*.[52] Hypovolemia, the lack of adequate intravascular volume, has been shown to impair healing because of insufficient volume to transport the oxygen and nutrients to the tissues and remove waste products.[52] Prolonged hypovolemia impairs collagen production and diminishes leukocyte activities.[50] External signs of mild hypovolemia are not evident. Diagnosis of hypovolemia is made by measurement of trans-cutaneous partial pressure of oxygen in the blood. Hypovolemia should be considered in situations that are common to the chronic wound population, such as use of diuretics, renal dialysis, or blood loss. Fluid administration can be used to correct for hypovolemia, but care must be taken to maximize intravascular volume without causing fluid overload.[50]

Theories and research abound in looking at reasons why there is a failure to respond to the signals of injury. In Chapter 14, Diagnosis and Management of Vascular Ulcers, the theory about white blood cell inhibition is explained. Another theory of the etiology of venous ulcer chronicity attributes the problem to a dysfunctional fibrinolytic system.[53] According to this theory, lipodermatosclerosis is part of the pathogenesis of venous ulcers that impairs the progression of the inflammation phase, progressing to the proliferation phase.

Malnutrition

Malnutrition of protein and insufficient calories is a comorbidity related to chronic wound healing. Multiple studies cite malnutrition as a risk factor for wound healing.[54–56] A nutritional assessment should be considered for all patients with chronic wounds and is required for those individuals who are unable to take food by mouth or who experience weight loss. The Agency for Health Care Policy and Research (AHCPR) published an algorithm for nutritional assessment and support as a guide for clinicians to manage nutritional needs of persons with pressure ulcers.[57] Serum albumin levels below 3.5 mg/dL is a clinical indicator of a diagnosis of significant malnutrition if accompanied by total lymphocyte count less than 1,800 mm³ or body weight has decreased more than 15%.[57] Inadequate absorption may be a part of the problem. Dietary restriction such as renal diets will effect the protein available for wound repair. Vitamin C and zinc

supplementation have been encouraged for wound healing. Hydration should also be considered as part of the nutritional assessment. Malnutrition, which has long been recognized as a problem for pressure ulcer patients, is now being considered as a problem for the patient with venous ulcer disease.[50] Figure 2–2 is an algorithm from the AHCPR guideline for treatment of pressure ulcers[57] to guide management of nutritional needs. Exhibit 2–2 is an assessment form from the same source.

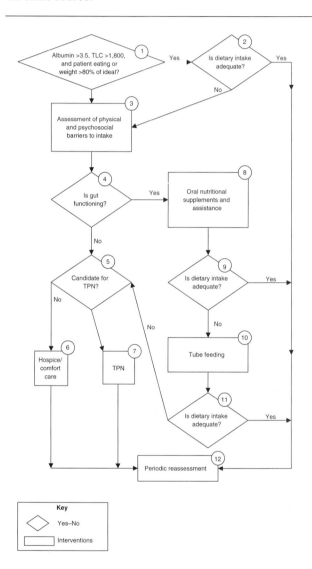

Note: TLC = total lymphocyte count; TPN = total parenteral nutrition.

Figure 2–2 Nutritional assessment and support. *Source:* Reprinted from N. Bergstrom, M.A. Bennett, C.E. Carlson, et al., *Treatment of Pressure Ulcers,* Clinical Practice Guideline No. 15, December, 1994, U.S. Department of Health and Human Services, Public Health Service, Agency for Health Care Policy and Research, AHCPR Publication No. 95-0652.

Exhibit 2–2 Sample Nutritional Assessment Guide for Patients with Pressure Ulcers

---

Patient Name: _____ **Date:** _____ **Time:** _____

To be filled out for all patients at risk on initial evaluation and every 12 weeks thereafter, as indicated. Trends will document the efficacy of nutritional support therapy.

Protein Compartments

Somatic:

Current Weight (kg)	_____	
Previous Weight (kg)	_____	(_____ date)
Percent Change in Weight	_____	
Height (cm)	_____	
Height/Weight	_____	
Current Body Mass Index (BMI)	_____	[wt/(ht)^2]
Previous BMI	_____	(_____ date)
Percent Change in BMI	_____	

Visceral:

Serum Albumin _____
   (Normal ≥ 3.5 mg/dL)
Total Lymphocyte Count (TLC) _____ (optional)
   (White Blood Cell count × percent Lymphocytes/100)

   Guide to TLC:
   - Immune competence   ≥ 1,800 mm^3
   - Immunity partly impaired   < 1,800 but ≥ 900 mm^3
   - Anergy   > 900 mm^3

State of Hydration

24-Hour Intake _____ mL   24-Hour Output _____ mL

Note: Thirst, tongue dryness in non–mouth breathers, and tenting of cervical skin may indicate dehydration. Jugular vein distention may indicate overhydration.

Estimated Nutritional Requirement

Estimated Nonprotein Calories (NPC) _____/kg   Estimated Protein _____ (g/kg)

Actual NPC _____ /kg   Actual Protein _____ (g/kg)

Recommendations/Plan

1.
2.
3.
4.

Source: Reprinted from N. Bergstrom, M.A. Bennett, C.E. Carlson, et al., *Treatment of Pressure Ulcers,* Clinical Practice Guideline No. 15, December, 1994, U.S. Department of Health and Human Services, Public Health Service, Agency for Health Care Policy and Research, AHCPR Publication No. 95-0652.

Neuropathy

Neuropathy is a common complication of chronic diabetes and alcoholism. Three types of neuropathy are found in individuals with neuropathy: sensory, motor, and autonomic. Neuropathy affects autonomic nervous system function of the sweat and sebaceous glands, resulting in impairments of these sweat and sebaceous glands. When sweat and sebaceous gland function in the feet is impaired, the skin becomes dry and cracked, providing a portal of entry for infection. The skin acidity is also changed, resulting in impairment of the skin's ability to control surface bacteria normally controlled by the skin acidity. Patients with diabetes also have an impairment of the body's immune system, which is simply unable to generate an inflammatory phase of repair and subsequently unable to overcome infection. Combining all of these functional impairments results in a chronic infected wound in a patient with a comorbidity of diabetes. Chapter 15 describes the examinations to test for and the consequences of the trineuropathy, including photos of the consequences.

Extrinsic Factors in Chronic Wound Healing

Medication and Immune Suppression

In body systems suffering immune suppression, such as is common in those who have diabetes, human immunodeficiency virus infection, and acquired immune deficiency syndrome, the body lacks the ability to produce an inflammation phase, which is the body's immune response to injury. As described above, the inflammatory response sets off the cascade of repair. Absence or impairment of inflammation at the onset of trauma will impair the healing cascade. Medications are often prescribed to control inflammatory responses in the body including anticoagulants, immunosuppressive agents, antiprostaglandins, and antineoplastics. Steroids are immunosuppression medications that may be applied topically or systemically. Steroids are prescribed for diverse disorders ranging from asthma to polymyalgia rheumatica. Steroids inhibit macrophage levels and delay wound repair.[58] Application of topical vitamin A and systemic vitamin A supplementation have proven efficient in counteracting the effects of steroid medication. Vitamin A should be part of the medical management of the wound patient on steroids.[59]

Irradiation

The purpose of radiation therapy is to kill cells. The damage may not be visible on the surface. Injuries to the cells of repair, fibroblasts and endothelial cells, and to the vasculature of the area make tissues that have been irradiated at risk

---

> **Research Wisdom:** *Topical Vitamin A to Restart Inflammation*
>
> Application of topical Vitamin A will effectively counteract the effects of steroid and restart the inflammation process in chronic wounds and set them back on track.

---

for breakdown and poor healing. The extent, dosage, frequency, and location of irradiation in relation to the wound site will determine the effect on wound healing. The effects of irradiation on tissue are not easily reversed.[49]

Psychophysiologic Stress

Understanding the role of psychophysiologic stress is another area of chronic wound research. Psychophysiologic stress has been shown to lengthen the time for wounds to heal. Paraplegics who were college students were found to have more skin breakdown during final examination periods than at other times of the school year.[60] Caregivers of chronically ill patients who experienced wounds were found to take longer to heal than persons not living in such stressful situations. The chronically ill patient with multiple comorbidities has psychophysiologic stress from multiple disease processes.

Bioburden and Infection

Excessive bioburden from necrotic tissue and infection have been associated with development of a chronic wound. For example, epidermal cells normally march forward as a sheet and lyse the necrotic debris from the wound edges, but they are impaired in this process of phagocytosis if obstructed by a large quantity of devitalized material. Devitalized tissue and foreign matter debris contribute to the proliferation of bacteria in the wound, which in turn will overwhelm the body with infection, possibly leading to sepsis. In such situations, the body will not be able to cleanse the wound without intervention. It is imperative to clean the wound down to healthy bleeding tissue to restart the inflammatory phase and the biologic cascade of healing. Bleeding creates a new acute battle zone and signal source for the responder cells. However, the response may fail to occur or be inadequate to initiate a new inflammation response if there is inadequate circulation.

Iatrogenic Factors in Chronic Wound Healing

Ischemia

Ischemia is the result of constricting blood supply to tissues. Ischemia occurs in different ways, such as from pressure over a bony prominence or an inadequate vascular function, and may result in mixed venous and arterial disease. If the patient is then inappropriately placed on compression treatment, ischemic trauma may ensue.[50]

Inappropriate Wound Care Management

Inappropriate wound management, including a misuse of topical agents (eg, antiseptics) or poor technique in application of dressings and tapes that results in tears and blisters on surrounding skin or wound bed, have all been implicated as factors in development of a chronic wound.[49,50] Wound desiccation, from lack of a dressing or inappropriate dressing choice, is not uncommon. Drying out of the wound interferes with the "current of injury" function as well as the mitotic and migratory function of cells.[10]

Trauma

Trauma to wound tissue occurs frequently and impedes wound repair. Trauma can be attributed to many different causes, including the following:

- High-pressure irrigation such as in the whirlpool or with WaterPik™ or removal of wet to dry dressings used for cleaning granulating wounds can cause trauma.
- Improper pressure to new granulation tissue traumatizes the fragile tissue and initiates a new inflammatory response, which retards healing and causes abnormal scarring.
- Improper handling during removal of dressings, compression wraps, or stockings, frequently results in trauma to venous ulcers whose surrounding skin is often extremely fragile.

Clinical Wisdom:
Avoiding Adverse Treatment Effects

Careful evaluation of each treatment and technique based on wound assessment can avoid adverse treatment effects and change the course of the wound.

CONCLUSION

The beginning of this chapter explains five methods by which wounds heal: superficial, partial thickness, primary intention, delayed primary intention, and secondary intention. Biologically they all heal similarly. The biologic sequence of healing was described for four phases of acute wound healing: inflammation, proliferation, epithelialization, and remodeling. The chapter has focused on the four phases subdivided into three compartments to differentiate the activities occurring in the wound space, called the battle zone; these are the signal sources—chemical and bioelectric—produced by the body and by the responder cells. The intent has been to describe key aspects of each phase and then connect the relationships to the clinical management. Much more has been written about the biologic process of wound healing than is presented here, and further reading is suggested.

The goal of wound management is to provide interventions that progress wounds through the biologic sequence of repair or regeneration in an orderly and timely manner. In order for the nurse and physical therapist to have successful wound healing outcomes, it is critical to understand and be able to recognize this key sequence of events. The ability to recognize the benchmarks of wound phase change are critical to monitoring the effects of treatment interventions and recognizing when the intervention is successful or not successful. Early identification that the wound has become "stuck" and unable to progress should trigger an appropriate response to avoid chronicity. Chronicity can happen during any phase of recovery. A wound can also have an absence of a phase of repair. This occurs when the body simply fails to initiate the phase (eg, when there is inadaquate circulation). These concepts are expanded in Chapter 3, Assessment of Surrounding Skin and Wound Tissue.

In the section on chronic wounds, three major factors (intrinsic, extrinsic, and iatrogenic) were described. Careful assessment of the patient with respect to these three factors in connection with the wound are required to identify potential interference with the process of healing. The following chapters are arranged so as to guide the nurse and physical therapist through assessment and diagnosis, management strategies to manage the factors that are coimpairments to healing, and selection of interventions that will provide optimal wound healing outcomes.

REFERENCES

1. Hunt TK, Hussain M. Can wound healing be a paradigm for tissue repair? *Med Sci Sports Exerc.* 1994;26:755–758.
2. Cohen K. *Principles of Wound Healing* (video). Richmond, VA, Wound Healing Center, Medical College of Virginia, Virginia Commonwealth University; 1990.
3. Cooper D. The physiology of wound healing: an overview. In: Krassner D, ed. *Chronic Wound Care.* King of Prussia, PA: Health Management Publication; 1990:1–11.
4. Winter GD. Epidermal regeneration studied in the domestic pig. In: Hunt TK, Dunphy JE, eds. *Fundamentals of Wound Management.* New York: Appleton-Century-Crofts; 1979:71–111.
5. Hunt TK, Heppenstall RB, Pines E, Rovee D, eds. *Soft and Hard Tissue Repair: Biological and Clinical Aspects.* New York: Praegar Publishing; 1984.

6. Hunt TK, Van Winkle W. *Fundamentals of Wound Management in Surgery, Wound Healing: Normal Repair.* South Plainfield, NJ: Chirurgecom Inc.; 1976:1e.

7. Knighton D. The role of oxygen in wound healing. Presented at the Symposium for Advanced Wound Care, San Diego, CA, 1995.

8. Lock PM. The effect of temperature on mitotic activity at the edge of experimental wounds. In Sandell B, ed. *Symposium on Wound Healing: Plastic, Surgical and Dermatologic Aspects.* Sweden: Molndal; 1979:103–107.

9. Myers JA. Wound healing and the use of modern surgical dressing. *Pharm J.* 1982;229:103–104.

10. Knighton DR, et al. Oxygen as an antibiotic: the effect of inspired oxygen on infection. *Arch Surg.* 1984;119:199–204.

11. Hohn DC, et al. Effect of O_2 tension on microbicidal function of leukocytes in wounds and in vitro. *Surg Forum.* 1976;27:18–20.

12. Goodson WH, et al. Wound oxygen tension of large vs small wounds in man. *Surg Forum.* 1979;30:92–95.

13. Knighton DR, Silver IA, Hunt TK. Regulation of wound-angiogenesis: effect of oxygen gradients and inspired oxygen concentration. *Surgery.* 1981;90:262.

14. Becker RO. The significance of bioelectric potentials. *Med Times.* 1967;95:657–659.

15. Foulds IS, Barker AT. Human skin battery potentials and their possible role in wound healing. *Br J Dermatol.* 1983;109:515–522.

16. Vanable J Jr. Natural and applied voltages in vertebrate regeneration and healing. In: *Integumentary Potentials and Wound Healing.* New York: Alan R. Liss; 1989: chap 5.

17. Jaffe LP, Vanable JW. Electric field and wound healing. *Clin Dermatol.* 1984;3:233–234.

18. Orinda N, Feldman JD. Directional protrusive pseudopodial activity and motility in macrophages induced by extracellular electric fields. *Cell Motil.* 1982;2:243–255.

19. Fukushima K, et al. Studies of galvanotaxis of leukocytes. *Med J Osaka Univ.* 1953;4:195–208.

20. Weiss DS, et al. Pulsed electrical stimulation decreases scar thickness at split-thickness graft donor sites. *J Invest Dermatol.* 1989;92:539.

21. Kloth LC. Electrical stimulation in tissue repair. In: McColloch JM, Kloth LC, Feeder JA, eds., *Wound Healing Alternatives in Management.* 2nd ed. Philadelphia: F.A. Davis; 1995:292.

22. Erickson CA, Nuccitelli R. Embryonic fibroblast motility and orientation can be influenced by physiological electric fields. *Cell Biol.* 1981;98:296–307.

23. Bourguignon GJ, Bourguignon LYW. Electric stimulation of protein and DNA synthesis in human fibroblasts. *FASEB J.* 1987;1:398.

24. Bourguignon GJ, Jy W, Bourguignon LYW. Electric stimulation of human fibroblasts causes an increase in Ca^{2+} influx and the exposure of additional insulin receptors. *J Cell Physiol.* 1989; 140:379–385.

25. Bourguignon LYW, Jy W, Majercik MH, et al. Lymphocyte activation and capping of hormone receptors. *J Cell Biochem.* 1988;37:131–150.

26. Cooper MS, Schliwa M. Electrical and ionic controls of tissue cell locomotion in DC electric fields. *J Neurosci Res.* 1985;13:223–244.

27. Rowley BA, McKenna J, Chase G. The influence of electrical current on an infecting microorganism in wounds. *Ann N Y Acad Sci.* 1974;238:543–551.

28. Barranco S, Spadaro J, et al. In vitro effect of weak direct current on staphylococcus aureus. *Clin Orthop.* 1974;100:250–255.

29. Kincaid C, Lavoie K. Inhibition of bacterial growth in vitro following stimulation with high voltage, monophasic, pulsed current. *Phys Ther.* 1989;69:29–33.

30. Zuminksky S, et al. Effect of narrow, pulsed high voltages on bacterial viability. *Phys Ther.* 1994;74:660–667.

31. Knighton DR, Hunt TK. The defenses of the wound. In: Howard RJ, Simmons RI, eds. *Surgical Infectious Diseases.* 2nd ed. Norwalk, CT: Appleton & Lange; 1988:188–193.

32. Dyson M, Luke D. Induction of mast cell degranulation in skin by ultrasound. *IEEE Trans Ultrasonics, Ferroelectronics, Frequency Control.* 1986;33:194–201.

33. Dabrowski R, Masinski C, Olczak A. The role of histamine in wound healing: the effect of high doses of histamine on collagen and glycosaminoglycan in wounds. *Agents Actions.* 1997;7:219–224.

34. Dexter TM, Stoddart RW, Quazzaz STA. What are mast cells for? *Nature.* 1981;291:110–111.

35. Ross J. Utilization of pulsed high peak power electromagnetic energy (diapulse therapy) to accelerate healing processes. Presented at the Digest International Symposium, Antennas and Propagation Society, Stanford, CA; Stanford University, June 20–22, 1977: 146–149.

36. Hardy M. The biology of scar formation. *Phys Ther.* 1989;69:22/ 1014–1023/32.

37. Shea JD. Pressure sores: classification and management. *Clin Orthop.* 1975;112:89–100.

38. Seiler WD, Stahelin HB. Implications for research. *Wounds.* 1994;6:101–106.

39. Adzick NS, Harrison MR, Glick PI, et al. Comparison of fetal, newborn and adult wound healing by histologic, enzyme-histochemical and hydroxyproline determination. *J Pediatr Surg.* 1985;20:315.

40. Harrison MR, Langer JC, Adzick, NS, et al. Correction of congenital diaphragmatic hernia in utero, V: initial clinical experience. *J Pediatr Surg.* 1990;25:47.

41. Harrison MR, Adzick NS, Longaker MT, et al. Successful repair in utero of a fetal diaphragmatic hernia after removal of herniated viscera from the left thorax. *N Engl J Med.* 1990;322:1582.

42. Harris MC, Mennuti MT, Kline JA, et al. Amniotic fluid fibronectin concentrations with advancing gestational age. *Obstet Gynecol.* 1988;72:593.

43. Byl N, McKenzie A, Stern R, et al. Amniotic fluid modulates wound healing. *Eur J Rehab Med.* 1993;2:184–190.

44. Byl N, McKenzie A, et al. Pulsed micro amperage stimulation: a controlled study of healing of surgically induced wounds in Yucatan pigs. *Phys Ther.* 1994;74:201–218.

45. Hock RJ. The physiology of high altitude. *Aci Amer.* 1987;22:52.

46. Chang B, Longaker MT, Tuchler RE, et al. Do human fetal wounds contract? Presented at the 35th Annual Meeting of the Plastic Surgery Research Council, Washington, DC, April 1990.

47. Longaker MT, Adzick, NS, et al. Studies in fetal wound healing, VII: fetal wound healing may be modulated by elevated hyaluronic acid stimulating activity in amniotic fluid. *J Pediatr Surg.* 1990;25:430.

48. Mulder GD, Jeter KF, Fairchild PA, eds. *Clinician's Pocket Guide to Chronic Wound Repair.* Spartanburg, SC: Wound Healing Publications; 1991.

49. Mulder G, Brazinsky BA, Seeley J. Factors complicating wound repair. In: McCulloch JM, Kloth LC, Feeder JA, eds. *Wound Heal-*

ing Alternatives in Management. 2nd ed. Philadelphia: F.A. Davis; 1995;47–59.

50. Stotts NA, Wipke-Tevis D. Co-factors in impaired wound healing. *Ostomy/Wound Manage.* March 1996;42:44–56.

51. Dean E. Oxygen transport deficits in systemic disease and implications for physical therapy. *Phys Ther.* 1997;77:187–202.

52. Hunt TK, Rabkin J, von Smitten K. Effects of edema and anemia on wound healing and infection. *Curr Stud Hematol Blood Transf.* 1986;53:101–111.

53. McCulloch JM. Treatment of wounds caused by vascular insufficiency. In: McCulloch JM, Kloth LC, Feeder JA, eds. *Wound Healing Alternatives in Management.* 2nd ed. Philadelphia: F.A. Davis; 1995: 216–217.

54. Allman RM, Laprade CA, Noel LB, et al. Pressure sores among hospitalized patients. *Ann Intern Med.* 1987;105:337–342.

55. Bergstrom N, Braden B. A prospective study of pressure sore risk among institutionalized elderly. *J Am Geriatr Soc.* 1992;40: 747–758.

56. Breslow RA, Hallfrisch J, Goldberg AP. Malnutrition in tubefed nursing home patients with pressure sores. *J Parenter Enteral Nutr.* 1991;15:663–668.

57. Bergstrom N, Bennett MA, Carlson C, et al. Treatment of pressure ulcers. *Clinical Practice Guideline,* no. 15. Rockville, MD: US Dept of Health and Human Services, AHCPR Publication No. 95-0652, December 1994.

58. Leiebowitch SJ, Ross R. The role of the macrophage in wound repair. *Am J Pathol.* 1975;78:71–91.

59. Hunt TK. Vitamin A and wound healing. *J Am Acad Dermatol.* 1986;15:817.

60. Crenshaw R, Vistnes L. A decade of pressure sore research. *J Rehab Res Dev.* 1989;26:63–74.

CHAPTER 3

Assessment of the Skin and Wound

Carrie Sussman

This chapter continues the methodology of the diagnostic process described in Chapter 1 with step II, the assessment and functional diagnosis of the wound. Assessment is a process of assigning numbers or grades to events systematically. Tests are the instruments or means by which events are assessed or measured. Examination is the process of determining the values of the tests. To evaluate something properly or accurately, skills of evaluation are necessary. That is, a background is required in selecting appropriate tests, understanding the significance of the tests and measurements, and knowing how to interpret them. Both the examination and the evaluation require specific skills and understanding of the condition, how the information will be used to recognize its importance and value, and how to collect it appropriately and in an organized manner.[1] Examination and performance of tests are within the scope of practice of both physical therapist assistants and licensed practical/vocational nurses; however, evaluation of the data is a skill that is the purview of licensed physical therapists and registered nurses who have some knowledge of wound management. Simple monitoring of tissue attributes can be performed by unskilled persons after instruction and then reported back to the professional. The purpose of this chapter is to instruct the clinician in the why, who, when, where, what, and how to assess wound attributes leading to a functional diagnosis. Accepted terminology and the significance of each tissue attribute to be assessed are described and illustrated with color plates located in this book. Chapter 4 describes techniques for measurement of size and extent of wounding. Chapter 5, Tools To Measure Wound Healing, teaches how to use two methods to assign numbers or grades to the attributes described in this chapter.

Assessment of the wound and surrounding tissues through examination of various attributes provides data leading to two diagnoses—wound severity and biologic phase of wound healing. Additional examinations that are related to the wound etiology or coimpairments are described in chapters related to specific problems such as the chapters on noninvasive vascular testing, management of exudate and infection, management of edema, and therapeutic positioning.

During the initial assessment, the clinician may find that data collected trigger concerns that require another opinion or a different level of care. For example, the initial assessment may indicate that the patient is not a candidate for sharp debridement because of concerns about circulatory or medical status. The nurse or physical therapist communicates these findings to the referring physician. The term for this is *prospective management,* and physical therapists and nurses are clinicians who have the ability to do prospective management of wound cases. Utilization management begins at baseline and is really prospective management because it is management of services to be delivered to the patient ahead of the actual delivery. Utilization management continues with every follow-up reassessment. At the end of this chapter, referral criteria are discussed. Why list referral criteria in a chapter on assessment? Utilization management mandates that at the earliest possible time the patient be diagnosed, appropriate medically necessary services identified, and proper referral made. Prospective, appropriate utilization management of health care services is critical under prospective payment and capitated delivery systems.

THE ASSESSMENT PROCESS

Purpose and Frequency

Wound assessment data are collected for three purposes: (1) to examine the severity of the lesion, (2) to determine the phase of wound healing, and (3) to establish a baseline for the wound and to report observed changes in the wound over time. Assessment data enable clinicians to communicate clearly about a patient's wound, provide for continuity in the plan of care, and allow evaluation of treatment modalities. Baseline assessment, monitoring, and reassessment are the keys to establishing the plan of care and evaluating achievement of target outcomes and progress toward goals. Valid, significant tests and measurements should be selected for the assessment process. Use the tests selected initially and for each retest throughout the course of care to evaluate progress toward target outcomes and to revise the treatment plan as required.

Attributes are assessed at the initial or baseline examination and at regular intervals, usually weekly or at most biweekly, to measure progress or deterioration of the ulcer. Reassessment is done to measure change in either the status of the ulcer or change in risk factors.[2] One study of stage III and stage IV pressure ulcers found that the percentage reduction in the ulcer area after 2 weeks of treatment was predictive of time to heal.[2] Expect improved status in 2 to 4 weeks.[3] If the reassessment indicates that the wound has deteriorated or has failed to improve with appropriate treatment after 2 to 4 weeks, the physician should be notified.

Monitoring is a means of checking the wound frequently for signs and symptoms that may trigger a full reassessment such as increased wound exudate or bruising of the adjacent or periwound skin. Monitoring includes gross evaluation for signs and symptoms of wound complications such as erythema (change in color) of periwound skin and pus secondary to infection and progress toward wound healing, such as granulation tissue growth (red color) and reepithelialization (new skin). Less skill is required for monitoring than for assessment and may be performed by unskilled caregivers such as the patient's family or a nurse attendant. Monitoring takes place at dressing changes or other treatment application times.

Different care settings will have different requirements and will designate specific individuals to perform the assessment function. For example, in the home setting the nurse or physical therapist may function as professional wound "case manager" who assesses the findings but they may instruct a nonprofessional caregiver in wound attributes to be monitored. The caregiver would gather the data at dressing changes and predetermined intervals and report changes to the professional wound case manager who would evaluate the results of the treatment plan. The professional wound case manager may see the patient's wound only intermittently for a complete reassessment. In a skilled nursing facility (SNF), there are usually requirements by federal licensing agencies that prescribe intervals for reassessment. If the patient is in an acute or subacute setting where there are very short lengths of stay, there may be only a single assessment.

Clinical Wisdom: *Monitoring Wound Progress*

Teach family and other caregivers to *monitor* the wound at each dressing change, looking for the following: signs of wound infection such as large amounts of purulent exudate (pus), periwound erythema (reddish, purplish), warmth, increased tenderness or pain at the site or elevated temperature, and signs of healing characteristics (bright red color and new skin).

Attributes to Assess

Evaluation of the severity of the wound by observation of the depth of tissue destruction, tissue response to injury, and signs of wound healing phase are presented. These components are used to provide a wound severity diagnosis and wound healing phase diagnosis. Assessment of the wound is separate from the assessment of the etiology of the wound, although the examinations chosen for the assessment may relate to or provide clues to the etiology. Wound etiologies are presented in Part III. For example, wounds with an etiology of venous insufficiency will have characteristics of the adjacent and periwound skin that are different from those of a pressure ulcer. A patient with a diagnosis of diabetic ulcer and insensitivity will have distinctive adjacent skin and tissue characteristics. Therefore, soft tissues adjacent to the area of wounding should be assessed for attributes of sensation, circulation, texture, and color. Findings of the adjacent soft tissues will be useful in determining medical necessity, establishing a treatment plan, and predicting outcomes of care for the wound. *Adjacent* refers to tissues extending away from the periwound. Therefore, it is a good clinical practice to include examination of the adjacent skin characteristics as well as periwound skin characteristics.

Assessment encompasses a composite of characteristics. A single characteristic cannot provide the data necessary to determine the treatment plan nor will it allow for monitoring progress or degradation of the wound. The indexes for wound assessment include all of the following: location, size of the wound, stage or depth of tissue involvement, presence of undermining or tunneling, presence or absence of tissue attributes not good for healing (such as necrotic tissue in the wound and erythema of the periwound tissue), and attributes good for wound healing such as condition of the wound edges, granulation tissue, and epithelialization. For many clinicians, the wound exudate characteristics are also essential indexes.

There are two schools of thought regarding tissue assessment. One looks only at the wound tissue. The second examines both the wound tissue and periwound skin and soft tissue structures. Because the periwound skin is intimately involved in the circulatory response to wounding as well as the risk for infection, it is prudent to evaluate both areas. The examination of the wound and periwound skin provides the data related to the wound healing phase diagnosis described later in this chapter.

Wound severity attributes to assess include determination of the tissue layers involved in the wound. Wounds that penetrate through more tissue layers are more severe than those that are less deep. This is the wound severity diagnosis. Depth of tissue involvement indicates the wound severity and has an impact on further wound assessment strategies and determination of an appropriate treatment plan. For example, a partial-thickness wound would not be assessed for tunneling or undermining. It also has impact on prediction of risk for nonhealing and on reimbursement. For example, third-party payers know that a stage IV pressure ulcer requires more care and a longer length of stay than a stage II pressure ulcer and that the risk of complications is greater. The most commonly used method of diagnosing wound severity is with classification systems.

Wound Classification Systems

At the present time, a variety of wound classification systems is used to describe wound severity for different wound etiology. Although the classification systems were designed and researched with one specific wound type, they are often (sometimes inappropriately) used for any wound type. Although there are many wound classification systems, such as methods of classifying surgical wounds and severity scoring of lower leg ulcers, four wound classification systems are presented in this chapter. The National Pressure Ulcer Advisory Panel (NPUAP) pressure ulcer staging criteria developed for use with pressure ulcers, the Wagner staging system for grading severity of dysvascular ulcers, partial-thickness/full-thickness skin loss criteria, and Marion Laboratories red/yellow/black color system are described and discussed.[4,5] The NPUAP pressure ulcer staging system and the Wagner staging system are classifications based on tissue layers and depth of tissue destruction. The partial-thickness and full-thickness skin loss classifications are tissue layer descriptions of skin loss that are also commonly used. The final method discussed groups wounds based on color of the tissue. Marion Laboratories, in Europe, developed a system that classifies the wound based on the color of the wound surface—red, yellow, or black. No wound classification system when used in isolation is an appropriate method of measuring wound healing (see Table 3–5).

NPUAP Pressure Ulcer Staging System

Classification by stages is used to describe the anatomic depth of soft tissue damage observed after the pathology has declared itself.[4] The pressure ulcer staging system is prob-

ably one of the most widely known wound classification systems. The staging system is most often applied to pressure ulcers, but it is used (sometimes inappropriately) to classify other types of wounds as well. It is best used for wounds with a pressure or tissue perfusion etiologic factor such as arterial/ischemic wounds or diabetic neuropathic ulcers. The NPUAP and the Agency for Health Care Policy and Research (AHCPR) used the initial pressure ulcer staging system proposed by Shea[6] as a basis for recommending a universal four-stage system for describing pressure ulcers by anatomic depth and soft tissue layers involved. The pressure ulcer staging system does not describe the whole wound and is limited to a description of the anatomic tissue loss and is a diagnosis of severity of tissue insult before healing starts. The AHCPR adopted the NPUAP staging system for use in two sets of clinical practice guidelines.[3,7] It is widely accepted and commonly used to communicate wound severity, to organize treatment protocols, and as criteria for selection and reimbursement of treatment products for pressure ulcers. Table 3–1 presents the staging criteria for pressure ulcers.

Table 3–1 Pressure Ulcer Staging Criteria

Stage	Definition
I*	Nonblanchable erythema of intact skin, the heralding lesion of skin ulceration. In individuals with darker skin, discoloration of the skin, warmth, edema, induration, or hardness may also be indicators.*
II	Partial-thickness skin loss involving epidermis and/or dermis. The ulcer is superficial and presents clinically as an abrasion, a blister, or a shallow crater.
III	Full-thickness skin loss involving damage or necrosis of subcutaneous tissue that may extend down to, but not through, underlying fascia. The ulcer presents clinically as a deep crater with or without undermining of adjacent tissue.
IV	Full-thickness skin loss with extensive destruction, tissue necrosis or damage to muscle, bone, or supporting structures (eg, tendon, joint capsule).

*In 1997 the NPUAP proposed a new definition of stage I pressure ulcers to reflect better the ethnic diversity of persons with pressure ulcers. The new definition under review is as follows: "an observable pressure related alteration of intact skin whose indicators as compared to an adjacent or opposite area on the body may include changes in skin color (red, blue, purple tones), skin temperature (warmth or coolness), skin stiffness (hardness, edema) and/or sensation (pain)."[8(p18)] *Source:* Reprinted with permission from Pressure Ulcer Staging Criteria from Pressure Ulcers: Prevalence, Cost, and Risk Assessment, *Consensus Development Conference Statement,* © 1989, National Pressure Ulcer Advisory Panel.

The pressure ulcer staging system is not an ideal system. It has many problems. Staging systems measure only one characteristic of the wound and should not be viewed as a complete assessment independent of other indicators. Staging classification systems do not assess for criteria in the healing process and hinder tracking of progress because of the inability of the staging system to demonstrate change over time. The definition of a stage I pressure ulcer does not account for the severity of soft tissue trauma beneath the unbroken skin such as is seen with purple stage I ulcers. Stage I lesions vary in presentation and pose validity concerns. Some stage I lesions may be the indicator of deep tissue damage just beginning to manifest on the skin, and others may indicate only superficial insult where damage is somewhat reversible and not indicative of underlying tissue death. There are problems with the reliability of assessment of stage I ulcers in dark-skinned patients. In fact, in 1997 the NPUAP proposed a new definition of Stage I pressure ulcers to reflect better the ethnic diversity of persons with pressure ulcers (see footnote to Table 3–1). Identification and meaningful interpretation of skin color changes in darkly pigmented skin requires special assessment strategies. These strategies are described in the section on assessment of the periwound and wound tissues.

Stage II pressure ulcers are lesions that are not necessarily caused by pressure and are more likely due to shearing, friction, or incontinence. The latter should be distinguished and treated in a different manner than pressure ulcers. Theoretically, pressure ulcer trauma starts at the bony tissue interface and works outward, eventually manifesting damage at the skin. However, stage II lesions are usually caused by friction or shearing of the tissues, causing superficial and partial-thickness damage to the epidermis and dermis. Stage II lesions start at the epidermis or skin and may progress to deeper layers.

Staging of pressure ulcers covered by eschar and necrotic tissue cannot be accomplished until removal of necrotic tissue allows determination of the extent of depth of tissue involvement. Pressure ulcers with necrotic tissue filling the wound bed are full-thickness wounds or stage III or stage IV wounds. The clinician cannot determine the level of tissue insult until the necrotic debris is removed. Another difficulty with staging occurs with patients with supportive devices because of the difficulty in accurately assessing the wound without removal of the supportive device. Finally, accurate,

meaningful communication is difficult, as clinicians may not have the experience necessary to recognize the various tissue layers that identify the stage or grade. In addition, clinicians may be defining stages differently. Staging requires practice and a certain amount of skill that develops with time spent examining wounds

Unfortunately, the staging system has been misinterpreted and applied in clinical practice as a way to monitor healing. It was not designed to do this. Biologically wounds do not heal in the manner suggested by reversing the staging system. For example, a stage IV pressure ulcer cannot "heal" and become a stage II pressure ulcer. Staging pressure ulcers is used to document the maximum anatomic depth of tissue involved after all necrotic tissue is removed. Staging of pressure ulcers is a diagnostic tool useful to determine the extent of tissue damage only. Staging is a diagnostic tool to aid examination of the *wounding* severity and not *wound healing*. Elimination of reverse staging has left a void in the system to report and document wound healing quickly and efficiently. The situation has been complicated because of a reporting system developed by the Health Care Financing Administration (HCFA) that requires that providers must continue to reverse stage in order to stay in compliance with HCFA regulations. Specifically, the Minimum Data Set (MDS) developed by HCFA relies on the reverse staging of wounds, both pressure ulcers and venous ulcers, to demonstrate progress of a wound toward healing. This has created a dilemma for the conscientious practitioner. One pragmatic suggestion is to stage for the wound severity at baseline and then on subsequent reassessment report with decreasing stages as the wound shows attributes of healing (eg, initial stage IV wound has bad-for-healing attributes of eschar, slough, and exposure of tendon, muscle, or bone indicators progressing to a stage III wound with presence of some good-for-healing attributes: absence of necrosis and presence of granulation tissue to a stage II reepithelialization beginning and stage I healed).[9] While this is a misuse of the staging system, it does have some merit, and until there is broad acceptance of a research-based tool to monitor healing and a change in the government reporting system, this may be the only route open to the thoughtful clinician. The MDS documenting system can be supported by using the Pressure Sore Status Tool, or the Sussman Wound Healing Tool, which are research-based tools for monitoring wound healing attributes. The tools are presented in Chapter 5.

Wagner Ulcer Grade Classification

The Wagner Ulcer Grade Classification system is used to establish the presence of depth and infection in a wound. The Wagner grading system was developed for the diagnosis and treatment of the dysvascular foot.[5] It is commonly used as an assessment instrument in the evaluation of diabetic foot ulcers. It is useful for both neuropathic and arterial/ischemic ulcer classification. There are six grades progressing from 0 to 5 in order of severity. Table 3–2 presents the Wagner grading criteria and Figure 3–1 shows how the natural history of breakdown in the diabetic, neuropathic foot corresponds to the Wagner 0 to 5 classification. The 0 classification evaluates for predisposing factors leading to breakdown and, along with grades 1 to 3, is used for risk management as described in Chapter 15.

Table 3–2 Wagner Ulcer Grade Classification

Grade	Characteristics
0	Preulcerative lesions; healed ulcers; presence of bony deformity
1	Superficial ulcer without subcutaneous tissue involvement
2	Penetration through the subcutaneous tissue; may expose bone, tendon, ligament, or joint capsule
3	Osteitis, abscess or osteomyelitis
4	Gangrene of digit
5	Gangrene of the foot requiring disarticulation

Source: Reprinted with permission from F.E.W. Wagner, The dysvascular foot: a system for diagnosis and treatment. *Foot and Ankle*, 2:64–122, © 1981, Williams & Wilkins.

Classification by Thickness of Skin Loss

Classification by thickness of skin loss, partial- or full-thickness skin loss, is another classification system and is commonly used for wounds whose etiology is other than pressure wounds such as skin tears, donor sites, vascular ulcers (venous ulcers in particular), surgical wounds, and burns. Wound thickness refers to partial-thickness or full-thickness loss of the skin with or without penetration into subcutaneous tissues and deeper structures. Partial-thickness wounds extend through the first layer of the skin or epidermis, and into, but not through, the second layer of the skin or dermis. Full-thickness wounds extend through the epidermis, the dermis, and beyond. Full-thickness wounds may be further categorized according to depth of involvement by using the term *subcutaneous tissue wounds*. Subcutaneous tissue wounds extend into or through subcutaneous tissues and may extend into muscles, tendons, and possibly down to the bone. Depth of injury classification identifies the specific anatomic level of tissues involved but does not report their condition or color.

Anatomic depth is predictive of healing.[1,10] Partial-thickness wounds heal by epithelialization and heal faster than full-thickness and subcutaneous wounds. Full-thickness and subcutaneous wounds heal by secondary intention, which is a combination of fibroplasia or granulation tissue formation and contraction. Table 3–3 provides the definitions of partial- and full-thickness skin loss.

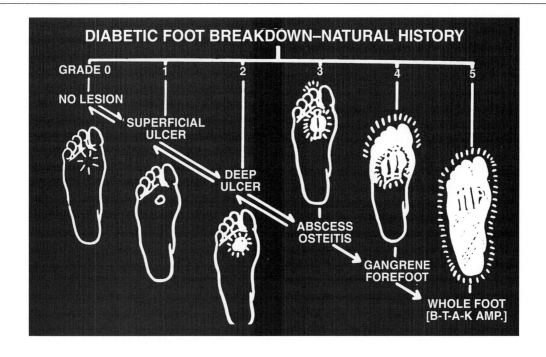

Figure 3–1 Diabetic neuropathic progression of foot breakdown. Courtesy of William Wagner, MD.

Table 3–3 Partial-Thickness and Full-Thickness Skin Loss

Thickness of Skin Loss	Definition	Clinical Examples
Partial-thickness skin loss	Extends through the epidermis, into but not through the dermis	Skin tears, abrasions, tape damage, blisters, perineal dermatitis from incontinence; heal by epidermal resurfacing or epithelialization
Full-thickness skin loss	Extends through the epidermis and the dermis, extending into subcutaneous fat and deeper structures	Donor sites, venous ulcers, surgical wounds; heal by granulation tissue formation and contraction
Subcutaneous tissue wounds	Additional classification level for full-thickness wounds, extending into or beyond the subcutaneous tissue	Surgical wounds, arterial/ischemic wounds; heal by granulation tissue formation and contraction

Marion Laboratories Red, Yellow, Black Wound Classification

Classification by color is a popular system because of the simplicity of the concept and the ease of use of the system. A three-color concept, red, yellow, or black, is used for assessing the wound surface color.[11] The three-color system was originally conceived as a tool to direct treatment, with each color corresponding to specific therapy needs. The red wound is clean, healing, and granulating. Yellow signals possible infection, need for cleaning or debridement, or the presence of necrotic tissue. Finally, the black wound is necrotic and needs cleaning and debridement. Red is considered most desired, yellow less desirable, and black least desirable. If all three types are present, select the least desirable as the basis for treatment. Table 3–4 shows the red, yellow, and black classification system with clinical manifestations.

The four wound classification systems discussed in this section and the type of wound most appropriate for use with each system are presented in Table 3–5.

Wound Severity Diagnosis

Nurses use nursing diagnoses to classify skin and tissue impairments and assist with developing care plans for wound care patients. Nursing diagnoses are expressed as specific diagnostic statements, which include the diagnostic category and the related to stem statement. *Impaired tissue integrity* is the broad diagnosis and would be correctly applied to stage III and stage IV pressure ulcers, for example. *Impaired skin integrity* is a subcategory and correctly applies to partial-thickness or full-thickness loss of skin. *Impaired skin integrity* should not be used for surgical incisions or deep tissue wounds. The diagnosis *risk for infection related to surgical incision* is more appropriate because of the disruption of the skin during surgery, making it more vulnerable to infection.

Table 3–4 Red, Yellow, and Black Wound Classification System

Color	Indication
Red	Clean; healing; granulation
Yellow	Possible infection; needs cleaning; necrotic
Black	Needs cleaning; necrotic

Source: Data from J.Z. Cuzzell, The New RYB Color Code, *American Journal of Nursing,* Vol. 88, pp. 1342–1346, © 1988, American Nurses Association and N.A. Stotts, Seeing Red & Yellow & Black, The Three Color Concept of Wound Care, *Nursing,* Vol. 2, pp. 59–61, © 1990, Springhouse Corporation.

The related to stem statements aid in communicating with other health care professionals and in planning care by targeting the defining characteristics for the diagnostic statement. For example, the diagnosis statement *impaired skin integrity* would be followed by a related to stem statement such as *impaired skin integrity related to friction and moisture from urinary incontinence.* For nurses, the related to stem statement usually reflects etiologic factors in wound development and directs the plan of care and specific interventions.[12]

Physical therapists will also use a wound severity diagnosis that relates to depth of penetration of wounding. The wound diagnosis statement will have a stem statement *impaired integumentary integrity secondary to———.* The ending part of the statement will include the depth of skin involvement. End statements read *superficial skin involvement or partial-thickness skin involvement and scar formation, full-thickness skin involvement and scar formation,* or *involvement extending into fascia, muscle, or bone.* A total statement would read *impaired integumentary integrity secondary to partial-thickness skin involvement and scar formation.*[13] The statement refers to the functional impairment

Table 3–5 Wound Classification Systems and Wound Types

Wound Classification Systems	Pressure Ulcers	Venous Ulcers	Arterial, Ischemic Ulcers	Diabetic Ulcers (Neuropathic)	Other Wounds
NPUAP pressure ulcer stages	X		X (Those with pressure component)	X (Those with pressure component)	Stage II classification will be appropriate for skin tears and tape damage.
Wagner grades		X	X	X	
Depth of skin loss (partial-thickness to full-thickness skin loss)	X If the wound is full thickness, it requires examination of level of deep tissue involvement.	X If the wound is full thickness, it requires examination of level of deep tissue involvement.	X If the wound is full thickness, it requires examination of level of deep tissue involvement.	X If the wound is full thickness, it requires examination of level of deep tissue involvement.	Useful for skin tears, burns, and other skin wounds. If the wound is full thickness, it requires examination of level of deep tissue involvement.
Marion Laboratories red, yellow, and black system	X	X	X	X	Surgical wound is healing by secondary intention.

of the integument and different tissues, which has implications for functional impairment and disability. Physical therapists use the severity diagnosis to select examinations, plan treatment, and predict functional outcomes.

Diagnosis statements for both nurses and physical therapists are similar. Both use impairment diagnoses that affect function of the involved tissues.

ASSESSMENT OF WOUND STATUS

Data Collection and Documentation Forms

Information collection is easier, better organized, and more consistent when a form is used as a collection instrument. Forms may be paper-and-pencil instruments or templates on the computer screen. There are many forms being used, with the most common being the skin care flow sheet used by nurses. Methods of recording assessment data should allow for tracking of each assessment item over time in objective and measurable terms that show changes in the wound sta-

tus. Two tools, the Pressure Sore Status Tool (PSST) and the Sussman Wound Healing Tool (SWHT), can be used to record the findings and to measure each attribute objectively. Both are described, with forms and instruction provided, in Chapter 5. Useful forms for assessment of tissue will usually include the following items:

- Periwound skin attributes
- Wound tissue attributes
- Wound exudate characteristics

Regardless of which instrument is used to collect findings, all attributes on the form should be considered. If the attribute is not applicable the notation N/A should fill the blank. If an attribute is absent, record a 0. If present, a grade or check is required. Leaving a blank space on the form implies the attribute was not considered or assessed.

If the patient's medical diagnosis suggests possible related impairments associated with the wound and periwound skin (eg, neuropathy or vascular disease), multiple forms may be required to report all the necessary elements that relate to the patient's condition. Chapter 6, Noninvasive Vascular Testing, and Chapter 15, Management of the Neuropathic Foot, have sample forms specific to recording data related to those problems.

Documentation requirements for wound assessment should be part of the facility policies and procedures. Documentation should be accurate and should clearly reflect the patient's condition, the examinations performed, the findings, the care rendered, and proper notification of the physician of significant findings. Documentation of similar findings by practitioners in the same department or facility should be consistent and reflect the facility policies.[14] Remember that some day, maybe 5 years from the time of initial assessment, the medical records may be subpoenaed into court. "Documentation can be either your shield against a potential malpractice lawsuit or the sword that strikes you down."[14(p40)]

Case Study: *Dangers of Differing Clinical Procedure and Facility Policy*

A physical therapist (PT) debrided a toenail on a patient with a medical history of neuropathy associated with diabetes. The toe went on to become infected, leading to below-the-knee amputation of the leg. The PT's action was called into question in a malpractice lawsuit. The debridement procedure followed by the PT was acceptable and documented, but it was the facility policy to have a patient with diabetic neuropathy evaluated in the vascular laboratory for transcutaneous oxygen levels before debridement. The PT did not document anything about evaluating the patient for circulatory status prior to performing the procedure. The case is pending.

Observation and Palpation Techniques

Observation and palpation are classic components of physical diagnosis used to determine alteration in soft tissue characteristics, including the skin, subcutaneous fascia, and muscles leading to a soft tissue or structural diagnosis.[15] Proper lighting and positioning of the patient and tissue to be assessed will improve observation.

Begin the examination of tissues by evaluating for symmetry with the opposite side of the body and adjacent structures by both observation and palpation. Look for consistency of symmetry of tissues in color, texture, contour, hardness/softness, temperature that represent changes in the attributes of the skin, subcutaneous tissue, fascia, and muscle compared with an area of normal skin and soft tissue.

Palpation requires the use of the hands as important sensitive diagnostic instruments. The hands should be clean and the fingernails of appropriate length. It is important for the clinician to development a palpatory sense in the hands. For example, different parts of the hands are valuable for different tests. The back of the hand is more sensitive to temperature, the palms of the hands are best used to detect changes in tissue contours (induration, edema), and the fingerpads are more sensitive to texture (fibrotic tissues) and fine discrimination. The thumbs are useful to apply pressure to check for hardness or softness at different tissue depths. Techniques of palpation include the use of slow, light movements. Avoid pressing too hard and trying to cover the area of examination too quickly. This will provide confusing messages to the sensory receptors of the examiner's hands.

Palpation skills require practice to refine the practitioner's palpatory sense. The first requirement is for the examiner to reduce other sensory inputs in the environment (noise, traffic, conversation) so as to concentrate and focus on the palpation examination. The next requirement is a common language to communicate the findings, in easily understood terms. Paired descriptors such as superficial-deep, moist-dry, warm-cold, painful-nonpainful, rough-smooth, hard-soft, thick-thin are useful. The state of tissue changes can be reported as acute, subacute, chronic, or absent. They can also be graded on a scale of 0 to 3+ as a way of diagnosing the severity of the problem. A familiar example of this type of grading system is pitting edema; another is pulse strength. The use of this type of grading system is also helpful in reporting response to treatment intervention.

Clinical Wisdom:
Four Requirements for Palpatory Examination

1. Concentration
2. Language to communicate findings
3. Light pressure
4. Slow movement

Assessment of Adjacent Tissues

The tissues adjacent to and surrounding a closed or open wound provide many clues that identify the health of the skin, the phase of wound healing, and the patient's overall health status. For clarity, the term *adjacent* is used to separate the tissues that may not show signs of wounding but that are predictive of healing from the tissues immediately surrounding the wounded tissue, referred to as periwound skin. Skin or trophic changes are important predictors of the body's ability to respond to wounding. The attributes of the adjacent tissues that should be assessed are described in the following sections including:

- Anatomy of the skin
- Skin texture (eg, dryness, thickness, turgor)
- Scar tissue
- Callus
- Maceration
- Edema
- Color
- Sensation (pain, thermal, touch, protective)
- Temperature
- Hair distribution
- Toenails
- Blisters

Anatomy of the Skin

The skin is composed of two primary layers: the epidermis, which is about 0.04 mm thick, and the dermis, which is about 0.5 mm thick (Figure 3–2). Each of the primary layers is stratified into several layers. The dermis is the true skin. It is tough, flexible, and elastic. The thickness of the skin varies from extremely thin over the eyelids to one third of an inch thick over the palms of the hands and soles of the feet.

The epidermis is avascular, whereas the dermis is well vascularized and contains the lymphatics, epithelial cells, connective tissue, muscle, fat, and nerve tissue. The vascular supply of the dermis is responsible for nourishing the epidermis and regulating body temperature. The well-vascularized dermis will withstand pressure for longer periods of time than will subcutaneous tissue or muscle. The collagen in the dermis gives the skin its toughness. Hair follicles and sebaceous and sweat glands, located in the dermis, contribute epithelial cells for rapid reepithelialization of partial-thickness wounds. The sebaceous glands are responsible for secretions that lubricate the skin and keep it soft and flexible. They are most numerous in the face, and sparse in the palms of the hands and soles of the feet. The sweat gland secretions control skin pH to prevent dermal

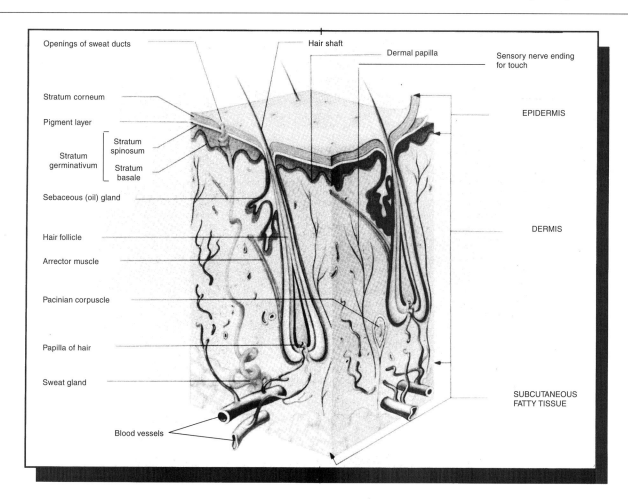

Figure 3–2 Anatomy of the skin. Courtesy of Knoll Pharmaceuticals, Mount Olive, New Jersey.

infections. They are numerous in the soles of the feet and palms of the hands. The three together are referred to as dermal appendages. The sweat glands, dermal blood vessels, and small muscles in the skin (responsible for goose pimples) control temperature on the surface of the body. The nerve endings in the skin include receptors for pain, touch, heat, and cold. Loss of the nerve endings in the skin increases risk for skin breakdown by decreasing the tolerance of the tissues to external forces. Nails are also considered as appendages of the skin. The deep or reticular layer of the dermis consists of fibroelastic connective tissue that is yellow and composed mainly of collagen. Fibroblasts are present in this tissue layer. The deep layer of the dermis merges with the subcutaneous fat and fascia and may be confused with yellow slough, but it should be evaluated for texture and vitality. A healthy reticular layer will be adhered and firm, not soft, mushy, or stringy like slough. Often granulation buds are seen protruding through the mesh of the reticular layer. *Color Plate 17* shows the reticular layer of the dermis with the red granulation buds poking through the mesh layer in a partial-thickness wound.

Skin color varies greatly in humans, but the structure and the skin are very similar. Melanin produced from melanocytes account for the variation in pigmentation from very light to extremely dark. Numbers of melanocytes in dark and light skin are similar, but the size and activity of the melanocytes are greater in black skin than in light skin. The melanin pigmentation is concentrated in the stratum corneum layer in a dark horny layer that can be wiped off when washing clean, black skin. Of course, this does not mean that all the color is removed, just the superficial layer. The thickness of the stratum corneum in both dark and light skin is the same, but the cells in dark skin are more compact with more cell layers. For this reason, dark skin is more resistant to external irritants. Healthy dark skin is usually smooth and dry. Dry dark skin may have an ashen appearance.[16]

Clinical Wisdom: *Care of Darkly Pigmented Skin*

Care of darkly pigmented skin requires keeping the skin lubricated. Petrolatum, lanolin-based lotions, and sparing use of soaps are recommended.[16]

Skin Texture

Smooth, flexible skin has a feeling of fullness and resistance to tissue deformation that is called turgor. Turgor is a sign of skin health. Aging skin often shows signs of dryness due to atrophy and thinning of both the epithelial and fatty layers of tissue in the dermis. The feel of the skin reflects a

loss of turgor. The areas most affected by loss of subcutaneous fat are the upper and lower extremities. This thinning of subcutaneous fat results in more prominent bony protuberances on the hips, knees, ankles, and bony areas of the feet with a higher risk of pressure ulcer formation. Elderly skin also experiences a loss of elasticity due to shrinkage of both collagen and elastin. There is a weakening of the juncture between the epidermis and dermis, making the skin layers "slide" across each other and placing the person at risk for skin tears. Sebaceous glands and their secretions are diminished, resulting in skin that is dry, often itchy, and easily torn.[17] Impaired circulation also contributes to changes in the skin; it is usually associated with aging but may be due to a disease process such as neuropathy associated with diabetes. Neuropathy impairs the secretion of sweat and sebaceous glands. Death of sweat and sebaceous glands contributes to slow resurfacing of partial-thickness dermal ulcers. Loss of sweat changes the pH of the skin, making it more susceptible to infection and bacterial penetration.

To assess skin texture the clinician uses observation and palpation. Observe the skin, looking for evidence of dryness such as flaking or scaling. To check skin turgor, gently pick up the tissues with thumb and forefinger and observe how the tissues respond. For example, in older patients loss of elasticity may be exhibited by the tissues' slow return to normal after pinching. In older patients it is best to check for general skin turgor on the forehead or sternal area. Palpate by gently rubbing your fingers across the patient's skin and feel for sliding of the epidermis away from the dermis.

Clinical Wisdom: *Skin Texture Assessment*

Observe skin for moisture content; look for evidence of dryness such as flaking, scaling, and excoriations (linear scratches). Palpate the skin to assess turgor; gently grasp the tissues between thumb and forefinger and observe for any delay in the tissues' return to normal position. Finally, rub your fingers across the patient's skin and feel the sliding of the epidermis from the dermis due to weakened epidermal-dermal juncture.

Scar Tissue

Inspection of the adjacent skin should include checking for scar tissue. Check scar for smoothness, flexibility, thickness, and toughness. Scar tissue that is mature has greater density and toughness and is less resilient than surrounding skin. New scar tissue is thinner and more flexible than mature scar and is less resilient to stress. Wounding in an area of scarring will have less tensile strength when healed than a new wound and will be more likely to break down (see *Color Plate 37*).

New scar tissue will be bright pink. As the scar tissue matures it will become nearly the same color as the periwound skin except in persons with darkly pigmented skin. Hypopigmentation frequently follows injuries to dark skin. Loss of skin color may create more anxiety for the individual than the wound itself. If the wounding disruption is less than full-thickness loss of the epidermis, repigmentation will usually occur over time. However, new skin covering deeper lesions and new lesions will appear pink.[18] The area of scar may even turn white. Hypopigmented areas are more susceptible to sunburn than are normally pigmented areas. For some individuals, burns and physical trauma may be followed by localized areas of hyperpigmentation. Like hypopigmention, hyperpigmentation leads to anxiety for many individuals.

Observe for abnormal scarring characteristics. Hypertrophic scarring results from excessive collagen deposition, causing a very thick scar mass that remains within the area of the original wound. These scars are ugly and disfiguring and may be bothered by itching or pain that may interfere with functional mobility. The scars are differentiated from keloid scars, which are also thickened scars, but keloid scars extend beyond the boundaries of the original wound.[19] Although keloids are known in persons of all races, scarring is of special concern to persons of the Negro race and some Asians as opposed to other dark-skinned individuals because of frequency of keloid formation in this population, thus suggesting a genetic factor. Frequency of occurrence is equal among men and women. Keloids are like benign tumor growths. Keloids continue to grow long after the wound is closed and may reach large size. Any attempt to cut or use dermabrasion to buff away the keloid will only result in even more scarring.[18] The mechanism of collagen deposition is totally out of control. Areas with keloids may be itchy and may be tender or painful.[16] New therapies are being used to control this phenomenon, but if a patient reports having had this problem or reports a familial tendency to form keloids, special attention should be made to address this problem at the time of initial assessment. Hyperkerototic scarring is hypertrophy of the horny layer of the epidermis. It is commonly seen in diabetic patients and may be located in adjacent and periwound tissue (see *Color Plate 24*).

Callus

The most commonly encountered calluses occur on the plantar surface of the foot. They are usually found along the medial side of the great toe, over the metatarsal heads, and around the heel margin. Callus formation is a protective function of the skin to shearing forces of a prominent bone against an unyielding shoe surface. Neuropathy often leads to muscle imbalance and subsequent uneven weight distribution along the metatarsal heads resulting in callus formation in those areas. The location of the callus is a clue to the underlying bony pathologic condition.[20] Untreated, the callus buildup will continue creating additional shear forces between the bony prominence and soft tissues, resulting in breakdown of the interposing soft tissues. Hemorrhaging seen on a callus indicates probable ulceration beneath. Callus is an indicator of need for further assessment of the foot. Chapter 15 contains more information about callus management, and pictures of callus.

Clinical Wisdom:
Observation and Palpation of Callus

The callus will appear as a thickened area on the sole of the foot and it will usually be lighter in color (often yellow) when compared with the adjacent areas. When palpated, the callus area will feel firm or hard to the touch. There may also be some scaling or flaking, roughness, or cracking of the callus. Cracked callus is a portal for infection. Further examination is recommended.

Maceration

Maceration is defined as "the softening of a tissue by soaking until the connective tissue fibers are so dissolved that the tissue components can be teased apart."[17(p198)] Macerated skin is drained of its pigment and has a white appearance and a very soft, sometimes soggy, texture (see *Color Plate 15*). The skin is often described as being wrinkled like a prune. A familiar example is dishpan hands. Softened tissue is easily traumatized by pressure and is a contributing factor in the development of pressure ulcers.[17] The source of moisture that soaks and macerates the skin may be perspiration, soaking in a tub, wound exudate, or incontinence, as well as from wound dressing products. Macerated skin will be thinner than adjacent skin. Palpate very gently so as to avoid trauma. Protect from pressure and shear.

Edema

Presence of edema may be associated with the inflammatory phase, the result of dependency of a limb or an indication of circulatory impairment or congestive heart failure. Edema is defined as fluid excess in the tissues due to overload of interstitial or intracellular fluid, causing congestion. A consequence of trauma is increased extracellular fluids in the tissues that both blocks the lymphatic system and causes increased capillary permeability. The function of edema following injury is to block the spread of infection. The result is a swelling that is hard, and the application of pressure to the swollen area does not distort the tissues. The term "brawny edema" refers to this type of swelling and is associated with the inflammatory phase. Traumatic edema is usually accompanied by pain. Swelling resulting from lymphedema or from systemic causes is usually painless.[21]

There are two types of edema—nonpitting and pitting. Nonpitting edema is identified by skin that is stretched and shiny, with hardness of underlying tissues. Pitting edema is identified by firmly pressing a finger down into the tissues and waiting 5 seconds. When pressure is released, if tissues fail to resume the previous position and an indentation remains, there is pitting edema. Pitting edema is observed when there is tissue congestion associated with congestive heart failure, venous insufficiency, and lymphedema, or dependency of a limb. It is measured on a severity scale of 0 to 3+, where 0 = not present, 1+ = minimal, 2+ = moderate, and 3+ = severe.

Evaluate for body symmetry when examining for edema and also refer to the patient's medical history. Bilateral edema of the lower extremities can be a sign of a systemic problem such as congestive heart failure, cirrhosis, malnutrition, or obesity or may be caused by dependency or use of certain drugs. Drug-induced edema is often pitting edema and may be caused by hormonal drugs, including corticosteroids, estrogens, progesterones, and testosterone. Other drugs to consider include nonsteroidal antinflammatory and antihypertensive drugs. Symptoms usually resolve if the drug is withdrawn.[21] Systemic edema may extend from the lower extremities up into the abdomen. Unilateral edema of the lower extremity of sudden onset may be due to acute deep vein thrombophlebitis and requires immediate referral to the physician. Other causes of unilateral edema are chronic venous insufficiency, lymphedema, cellulitis, abscess, osteomyelitis, Charcot's joint, popliteal aneurysm, dependency, and revascularizaion. Deep vein thrombophlebitis, chronic venous insufficiency, and lymphedema are the three most common causes.[21] If in doubt about the etiology of the edema, consult with the physician before planning further testing or an intervention. If edema is left in the tissue the large-protein molecules will clog the lymphatic channels and cause fibrosis. Chapter 9, Management of Edema, describes the management of edema with compression.

Measurement of Edema. Tissue volume increases when edema is present. Edema can be evaluated by palpation for change in contour of the tissues and by photographs. Two methods used for measurement of the extent of edema formation are girth and volume. Girth measurement of the limb is the most common method used in clinical practice because it is simple to perform. Although limbs are most easily measured, the torso can also be assessed for edema by taking girth measurements. Volumetric measurement is made by using water displacement. This is a quick and accurate measurement using a volumometer filled with water. Volumometers are made of a heavy Lucite and come in different sizes for immersion of a foot and ankle, leg above the knee, and the hand (see Figure 3–3). They are strong and durable. Both methods work best when edema in a limb is being measured.

A simple form, such as Exhibit 3–1, either handwritten or preprinted, listing the measurements of both limbs side by side is a useful guide for consistency and completeness of the measurements and to make comparison between baseline and retest measurements quick and easy. Change in edema measurements is one way to assess the treatment outcomes.

The procedure for girth measurements is as follows:

1. Mark and record the bony landmarks on the limb to guide the measurements, including the metatarsal heads, both malleoli, 3 cm above the lateral malleolus, 12 cm above the lateral malleolus, 18 cm above the lateral malleolus, and the lower edge of the patella.
2. Use a flexible tape measure to measure the circumference around these landmarks.
3. Measure both limbs.
4. Record measurements (for both limbs) side by side. Repeat at next assessment. Compare.

Figure 3–3 Volumetric Edema Measurement. *Source:* Reprinted with permission from G.M. Pennington, D.L. Danley, and M.H. Sumko, Pulsed, Non-Thermal, High-Frequency Electromagnetic Energy (DIAPULSE) in the Treatment of Grade I and Grade II Ankle Sprains, *Military Medicine: The Official Journal of AMSOS,* Vol. 158, No. 2, p. 102, © 1993, Association of Miliary Surgeons of the United States.

Exhibit 3–1 Lower Extremity Girth Measurements Form

Date						
	Right	Left	Right	Left	Right	Left
Metatarsal heads						
Both malleoli						
3 cm ↑ lateral malleolus						
12 cm ↑ lateral malleolus						
18 cm ↑ lateral malleolus						
Lower edge of patella						

The procedure for volume displacement measurements is as follows:

1. Fill volumometer with tepid water (about 95° F).
2. Immerse the affected extremity into water.
3. Catch overflow in a graduated cylinder to measure volume displaced.
4. Repeat with both limbs.
5. Record volume displacements to both limbs side by side on a form.

Target Outcomes for Edema Interventions. The edema will be absent, reduced, or controlled. Baseline girth or volume measurements were larger for the affected limb or area at baseline and are now equal to or closer to the measurements of the unaffected limbs.

If both limbs are affected, it will not be possible to do an opposite limb comparison. Measurements will be compared to the same limb or area. Palpation and observation as well as decreased measurements are used for evaluating change in edema. Change in severity of the pitting edema would be another measurement to report change in edema. Controlled edema means that following an initial reduction the edema has not returned to the prior level but remains in the tissues.

Edema Increased. Edema is increased when retested girth or volume measurements are *increased* in the affected limb compared with the unaffected limb or area when compared with baseline. Again, if both limbs are affected, it will not be possible to do an opposite limb comparison. Palpation and observation as well as increased girth measurements will need to be used for evaluating change in edema. The skin will be taut and the tissues hard and uncompressible. Increased edema could be an indication of change from absence of the inflammation phase to the acute inflammation phase. The increased edema would be accounted for by increased perfusion to the tissue. This edematous reaction may be more appropriately palpated than measured by instruments. The edema should be transitory and reduce as the inflammation phase passes.

Color

Assessment of adjacent skin color is a clue to skin circulation and disruptions in circulation associated with trauma or infection. Skin color tones reflect the condition of underlying blood vessels. In lightly pigmented skin, pressure closes capillaries and induces a blanching of the skin color that returns to normal color tones when pressure is released. If the color does not return to the color of the adjacent skin within 20 minutes after removal of pressure, this is called unblanchable erythema. Unblanchable erythema in lightly pigmented skin is redness that does not disappear when pressure is removed. Histology of unblanchable erythema shows erythrostasis in the capillaries and venules, followed by hemorrhage[22] (see *Color Plates 1, 17, and 25* for unblanchable erythema). The same indexes cannot be used in darkly pigmented skin.

Color Assessment for Darkly Pigmented Skin. Identification of stage I pressure ulcers has historically relied heavily on color changes in the skin. Erythema may be seen in some situations in lighter-toned persons of color, but in darkly pigmented skin the redness may not be seen.[18] Darkly pigmented skin is defined as skin tones that "remain unchanged (does not blanch) when pressure is applied over a bony prominence, irrespective of the patient's race or ethnicity."[23(p35)] Darkly pigmented skin is usually found in African Americans, Africans, Caribbeans, Hispanics, Asians, Pacific Islanders, Middle Easterners, Native Americans, and Eskimos. When assessment is made of darkly pigmented skin in patients with high risk for pressure ulcers, careful attention should be paid to color changes at sites located over bony prominences. Look for color changes that differ from the patient's usual skin color (as described by the patient or those who are familiar with the patient's usual skin color or as observed in an area of healthy tissue).[23] Consider conditions that can cause changes in skin color, such as vasoconstriction (pallor) caused by lying on a cold surface or hyperemia (redness or deepening of skin tones) from lying on a bony prominence. Allow the area to be assessed to be exposed to ambient room temperature for 5 to 10 minutes before examining. When darkly pigmented skin is inflamed, the site of inflammation becomes darker and appears bluish or purplish (eggplant-like color; see *Color Plates 19 and 21*). This is comparable to the erythema or redness seen in persons with lighter skin tones.[23] Change in color, as mentioned, is an indicator of hemorrhage of the microvasculature in the skin and may also be an indicator of deep tissue trauma that will later rupture and form a crater. When there is an extremely high melanin content, the color of the skin may be so dark that it is hard to assess changes in color at all.[17]

Another complicating factor in identifying erythema in darkly pigmented skin is differentiating inflammation from the darkening of the skin caused by hemosiderin staining. Hemosiderin staining usually occurs close to the wound edges, whereas injury-related color changes usually extend out a considerable distance and are accompanied by the other signs of inflammation. *Color Plate 10* shows hemosiderin staining at the margins of a wound in a dark-skinned person. Hemosiderin staining is a symptom of wound chronicity or repeated injury. The mechanism of hemosiderin staining is described later.

Color changes are apparent around acute (inflamed) and chronic open wounds (pigmentation). If color is not a reliable indicator, use other clinical indicators such as sensation (pain), temperature (heat, coolness), tissue tension (edema or induration and hardness) to confirm the diagnosis of inflammation in darkly pigmented skin.

Assessment of tissue circulatory status by use of color is also difficult in darkly pigmented skin. Consider the effects of gravity on vasomotor changes in the tissues of the extremities in elevated and dependent positions. Color changes will appear more subtle than those in light skin. Assess from a neutral position, then with the area elevated about 15° and dependent for about 5 minutes and compare.[24] Assessment

of capillary refill time for persons with darkly pigmented skin should be tried at the tips of the second or third fingers.[11] Also consider the examining the nail beds. If they are not pigmented, apply pressure to the second or third finger; if the skin under the nail blanches, it will give a color comparision for assessing pallor or cyanosis. The speed of color return following the slow release of pressure is an indicator of the quality of vasomotor function. The slower the return of color the more diminished the vasomotor function. Compare the speed of return with that in your own nail bed or that of another person with normal vascularity.[24]

Assessment should be made with good lighting. Avoid fluorescent light, which casts a blue color to the skin. Use natural or halogen lighting to assess skin tones. Flash photographs are recommended because the flash makes the demarcation between normal skin tones and those that are traumatized easier to see and the picture provides a visual record of the patient's skin status.[23] Notice the demarcation between the normal skin tones and the traumatized area in *Color Plate 19*. The patient or family member who is familiar with the patient's natural skin tones should be the primary person to provide information relative to skin color changes.

Ecchymosis (Hemorrhage). Trauma to the skin and subcutaneous tissue causes rupture of the blood vessels and subcutaneous bleeding or hemorrhage called ecchymosis. Ecchymosis is seen as a purple discoloration in white skin and a deepening to a purple color in darkly pigmented skin. The skin over the hemorrhagic area may be taut, shiny, and edematous (see *Color Plate 34*). Hemorrhage and clotting occur as a consequence of an acute injury such as trauma from pressure, a bump, or shearing and includes trauma to new granulation tissue as well as venous leakage from venous insufficiency (see *Color Plate 65*). Clotting cuts off oxygen to the tissues with subsequent hypoxia and ischemia. If the blood is not reabsorbed into the tissues in a timely fashion, tissue necrosis will occur. It is not known exactly how long clotted blood can remain in the tissues before necrosis occurs, but electrical stimulation, pulsed radio frequency stimulation, and ultrasound facilitate reabsorption of hemorrhagic materials if started soon after injury (eg, 48 to 72 hours). Efficacy studies reported in the literature and photographs that show the effects of these interventions are described in Chapters 16, 18, and 19.

Rupture of the vessels around a wound and also seepage from venous hypertension cause deposition of blood in the subcutaneous tissues. The blood stains the tissues by deposition of hemosiderin from lysed red blood cells and turns the skin a rust brown color. Hemosiderin staining is seen as a ring around pressure ulcers (see *Color Plate 2*) or as the brown discoloration of the skin of the lower leg in patients with venous disease (see *Color Plates 49 and 50*). The discoloration may be permanent or it may gradually disappear.

Sensation

Sensory testing procedures and expected outcomes are described in this section. They include pain, protective sensation, and thermal sensation.

Pain. Severe pain or tenderness either within or around the wound may indicate the presence of infection, deep tissue destruction, or vascular insufficiency. Use of a pin to test for pain sensation is considered outdated and is not recommended. Absence of pain or insensitivity to touch and temperature may indicate neuropathy. Sometimes pain-level reports are more a report of anxiety than pain. Observation of movements by the patient in the area of reported pain and reaction to gentle palpation are useful in distinguishing between the two.

Ideally the best and most reliable way to determine the intensity of pain is by report of the patient. Of course, this is not always possible. Several methods can be used to test and retest for pain. Retesting is very important if one of the expected outcomes from treatment is pain reduced, eliminated, or controlled. Use the same testing measures before and after the use of an intervention. Commonly used tests for pain include pain questionnaires that are either verbal or pictorial, visual analog scale, pain diary, or palpation and observation for those who cannot communicate except by response to noxious stimuli.

Testing with a Pain Questionnaire: If the patient can communicate verbally, ask the patient to describe the pain. Guiding questions would include the following:

- Where is the pain?
- When do you have the pain? How long does it last?
- What type of pain do you have? Is it burning, throbbing, cramping, or prickling?
- Does the pain affect your sleep?
- Does it affect your mood?
- Do you take medication for the pain? What do you take?
- What are the effects of the medication?
- What positions or activities affect the pain?

For those who cannot communicate verbally, but who can understand and respond, cue with questions such as, Show me where it hurts? Does it feel like it is burning?

In noncommunicating patients, observe during guided movement and palpation for facial grimacing, tenseness, and/or withdrawal response to noxious stimuli.

Testing with a Visual Analog Scale: A visual analog scale (Exhibit 3–2) is a line marked with 10 perpendicular lines and numbered 0 to 10, where 0 = no pain and 10 = the worst pain imaginable. Ask the patient to give a number on the line or point to a number to indicate pain severity. Record. This is a common procedure for assessing pain severity. It can be repeated to determine change in pain severity as a measure of treatment effect. Reliability may be questionable. Patients with either very high or very low pain thresholds may more accurately report pain level by another method.

Keeping a Pain Diary: The patient or caregiver can record the information on a pain diary form such as Exhibit 3–3. This will be a valuable tool to measure change in pain over time and will provide feedback to the patient that pain is altered. If test results indicate that pain is present and a problem, management of the pain with an intervention would be indicated with a target outcome of pain free, pain reduced, or pain controlled. A change in pain status will be a functional outcome if there is a change in the patient's functional activities as a result of the change in pain status, such as the patient is able to tolerate active assistive range of motion to the wounded area and is able to sit up in a wheelchair.

Outcome measures to report after an intervention for pain management include the following:

- Pain free—the patient is pain free by observation or report of the patient or caregiver.
- Tension free—tissue tension reduction is tested by palpation or by checking for increased mobility of the area.
- Pain medication free—the patient may no longer require pain medication, or the amount or frequency may be reduced.
- Sleeping—the patient's pain is controlled and he or she has more hours of undisturbed sleep.
- Unreactive (to noxious stimuli)—the patient no longer responds to movement or palpation that produced pain.

Exhibit 3–2 Visual Analog Scale for Pain Measurement

0	1	2	3	4	5	6	7	8	9	10

Exhibit 3–3 Pain Diary Form

Date	Time	Location	Activity	Pain intensity	Medication	Other symptoms

---

Clinical Wisdom: *Premedication for Pain*

Response to the pain testing will guide the clinician about the need to premedicate the patient before performing a procedure. Sometimes relaxation and anti-anxiety medication will be more appropriate than pain medication.

Protective Sensation. If neuropathy is suspected by medical history or observation, testing for sensation is indicated. A safe, accurate method for testing sensation has been developed using Semmes-Weinstein monofilaments. The monofilaments come in different force levels. Levels 4.17, 5.07, and 6.10 are used to check for protective sensation. Force levels increase as the numbers increase. The object of the test is to see if the patient can detect pressure when the monofilament is placed against the skin and force applied that is sufficient to buckle the monofilament. Testing is usually performed on the sole of the foot. The procedure for measurement of sensation with Semmes-Weinstein monofilaments is as follows:

1. Start by applying to the sole of the foot.
2. Place the monofilament against skin.
3. Apply pressure until the filament buckles.
4. Ask the patient to identify where the monofilament was applied.

The patient should be able to detect the monofilament at the time it buckles.

The inability to detect the 5.07-level monofilament indicates a limited ability to use protective sensations. If the patient can distinguish this level of sensation at several points on the feet, the protective sensation is considered to be adequate to avoid risk of trauma.[25] A photograph of Semmes-Weinstein filaments and the appropriate interventions for patients with loss of protective sensation are given in Chapter 15.

Thermal Sensation. The test for thermal sensation is performed by using test tubes or small narrow bottles filled with warm and cold water. Be sure to test in a normal area before applying to possible insensate areas to avoid burns. Research reports that the lateral aspect of the foot is the area most sensitive to thermal sensation.[26] If the patient is unable to sense warmth, there will be a high risk of burns if heat is applied to the skin. If the patient is unable to sense cold, there is a risk of injury from exposure to cold; the feet should be protected from frostbite if the patient is going to be exposed to very cold temperatures.

Adjacent Skin Temperature

Baseline skin temperature is one objective measurement of circulation. The baseline can be used to monitor circulatory response to treatment or to evaluate inflammation. Temperature can be tested by palpation or by a skin surface thermometer. If greater accuracy is required, there are several commercial instruments available. A thermistor is the least costly of the three commercial devices described here for measurement of skin surface temperature. A probe is placed against the skin and a reading taken. Another device is a radiometer, which determines temperature by measurement of surface reflection of infared radiation. Another way of taking temperature is with liquid crystal thermography, which produces multicolor picture maps of the wound and adjacent tissues. These devices have good reliability but are usually used for research. The thermistor and the infrared scanner, however, could be used in the clinic easily with minimal training. Use of the infrared scanner is described in Chapter 15.

Use of an inexpensive (about $2) skin fever thermometer strip that changes color with temperature change is a simple and useful way to assess the temperature of periwound skin. This is best done in areas that have adequate circulation, such as on the trunk. It is more sensitive to changes in temperature than the back of the hand, although not sensitive enough to record temperatures below 95°F, which are found in the distal parts of extremities. Skin fever thermometers usually have six thermochromic liquid crystal indicator lights in shades of brown, tan, green, and blue, which respond to temperature shifts. To read the temperature use the *highest* temperature window indicated by a color. Skin temperature is shown in 1°F intervals. The normal skin temperature in areas of good circulation is usually about 95°F. An increase in temperature of the surrounding skin measured on the fever thermometer, compared with adjacent area temperature, is an indication of an area of circulatory perfusion. This is the heat described as a classic sign of inflammation. Absence of an increase in periwound skin temperature from adjacent skin may be an indicator of an impaired or absent inflammatory response. Skin temperature below 95°F will not record on this thermometer. Other more sensitive tests for temperature or blood flow should be considered.

Skin temperature is a useful measure for assessing many kinds of wounds, including stage I pressure ulcers. An increase in skin temperature may indicate pressure ulcer formation or the presence of infection. It is a very useful tool for assessing inflammation in darkly pigmented individuals, in whom the margins of erythema are hard to see. Skin temperature can be taken at locations on the margins of discoloration and at the center. The clock method, taking the temperature at the 12-, 3-, 6-, and 9-o'clock positions around the wounded tissue, is useful for recording this measurement. The procedure for measuring skin temperature is as follows:

1. Make sure that the area of skin to be tested has been pressure free and exposed to ambient air temperature for at least 5 to 10 minutes before testing its temperature (a sheet can cover the patient for privacy).
2. Place a single layer of plastic against the skin as a hygienic barrier (this does not interfere with temperature accuracy).
3. Lay temperature strip flat on the plastic barrier.
4. Hold the strip in place at both ends lightly so as not to compress capillaries, and wait for color of strip to change color. Allow at least 1 full minute for the color change to occur. In very inflamed tissues, it may occur immediately, but may change further as it is held for the full minute.
5. Read the temperature while the strip is still against the skin.
6. Measure at the wound edge at the 12- and the 6-o'clock positions and near the expected outer margin of the periwound erythema/discoloration. Repeat at the 3- and the 9-o'clock positions.
7. Record temperature at each point.

Interventions affect tissue perfusion and thus skin temperature. Skin temperature would be expected to increase if there is enhanced perfusion following superficial heating with whirlpool. Temperature changes in deeper tissues may occur following pulsed short wave diathermy. However, the fever strip may not be sufficiently sensitive to measure any of these changes. If that is the case, the thermistor or infrared scanner thermometer is recommended. To measure the effects of an intervention, take a baseline measurement before treatment and repeat the measurement after treatment. Skin temperature should rise after treatment. If there is an absence of inflammation and the target outcome is to initiate the acute inflammation phase, repeated measurement of tissue temperatures would help verify the outcome.

Coolness also can be used as an assessment of circulation. Sometimes there is an initial increase in skin temperature followed by coolness after trauma. Like warmth, coolness without trauma may be an indicator of circulatory status. Some areas of the body naturally have less warmth, including the feet, toes, and fingers. The areas of the trunk or over well-perfused muscle tissues have greater warmth. If there is coolness in the digits or the feet, it is important to evaluate other signs and symptoms such as hair growth, skin color, pulses, and skin texture for circulation. If those signs are also suggestive of circulatory impairment, they should trigger further circulatory examination as described in Chapter 6. Coolness may also be an indicator of impaired tissue viability or tissue death following ischemia. A quantitative measure of tissue temperature as part of the assessment of wounds is not yet a standard of clinical practice. However, articles are appearing regularly in journals describing temperature measurement as an assessment procedure for inflammatory processes and tissue viability. All of the procedures described are simple, noninvasive, and quick but most importantly have clinical significance.

Hair Distribution

Normal body hair is distributed over all four extremities, extending down to the digits. Over time body hair diminishes and is eventually lost. A diminished presence of hair is seen in aging skin or where there is impaired circulation. As circulation in a leg decreases, hair is lost distally. Hair distribution may be used as an indicator of the level of vascular impairment and an indication for vascular testing. Hair follicles are important to wound healing because they contribute epidermal cells for resurfacing partial-thickness wounds. Absence of hair should be considered a factor in the prognosis of wound healing if there is a partial-thickness wound in an area where hair is usually found, such as the lower leg.

Clinical Wisdom: *Assessment of Hair Distribution as an Indicator of Peripheral Circulation*

1. An easy checkpoint for adequate tissue perfusion to the lower extremities is examination of the great toe for hair growth. Hair growth on the great toes implies adequate circulation to support the hair follicles. When working with female patients, prior to examination remember to ask whether they shave the hair on the great toe.
2. Move up the leg proximally from the ankle and assess the most distal point where hair distribution stops. Then palpate for skin temperature and pulses, and observe skin color in the area denuded of hair for circulatory changes.

Toenails

Part of a comprehensive examination of the feet includes not only the skin but also the toenails. Look at the color, thickness, shape, and any irregularities. Toenail pathology commonly seen includes hypertrophic, thick nails. Some toenails may look like a ram's horn. Ingrown toenails and fungal and pseudomonas infection, which give the toenail a green color, may be observed. Findings of toenail abnormalities, as described, are referral criteria unless the clinician has knowledge and training in foot and nail care.[27]

Blisters

Trauma to the epidermis gives rise to a blister. The blister may be filled with clear fluid or, if the trauma is deeper than the epidermis and ruptures blood vessels, the blister fluid may be bloody or brown (see *Color Plate 68*). The blister roof is nature's best dressing, but it can hide deep tissue damage. Removal of the blister roof is controversial. If the blister fluid is clear, tissue damage may not extend into the dermis or deeper, and the wound will heal under the blister roof; the epidermis will eventually just fall off. It should not be disturbed and in fact may require protection. However, if the fluid is bloody, brown, or cloudy, as shown in *Color Plate 68,* deep tissue damage may be present, and unroofing the blister may be the only way to determine the extent of trauma, as shown in *Color Plate 69.*

Assessment of the tissue under the blister without breaking the blister is helpful in evaluating when the blister needs to be unroofed. Gently press down with a fingertip on the tissue beneath the blister roof and compress it; release, and feel for the resiliency of the subcutaneous tissues. If there is good resilience, that is, it bounces back when the pressure is removed, the deep tissues may be mildly congested, but if the tissue feels soft, spongy, or boggy there is high probability of tissue congestion and probable necrosis. Practice and careful concentration are needed to perform this palpation examination. One tip is to try pressing down on the skin on the opposite side of the body in the same location (eg, on the heel) and compare the resiliency when compressed.

ASSESSMENT OF THE PERIWOUND AND WOUND TISSUES

Assessment of the periwound and wound tissues is described in the following sections according to clinical signs and symptoms that would be expected in each wound healing phase. There is a close relationship between assessment of the wound and periwound tissues and diagnosis of wound healing phase. Careful assessment of the wound and periwound tissue establishes the present, predominant wound healing phase. The *predominant* wound healing phase is the primary functional diagnosis for the wound at that time. There will also be a secondary functional diagnosis signifying transition to the next phase(s) or absence of subsequent phases(s). In this section, tissue assessment is presented by describing three aspects of healing, acute, chronic, or absent, for each phase of wound healing (inflammation, proliferation, and epithelialization). Each aspect of each phase is a potential wound healing phase diagnosis. Table 3–6 lists the wound healing phase and the related wound healing phase diagnosis. Also an expected prognosis applies to each diagnosis and is also listed.

Table 3–6 Wound Healing Phase Diagnosis and Prognosis

Wound Healing Phase	Acute Wound Healing Phase Diagnosis	Chronic Wound Healing Phase Diagnosis	Absence of Wound Healing Phase Diagnosis
Inflammation	Acute inflammation	Chronic inflammation	Absence of inflammation
Proliferation	Acute proliferation	Chronic proliferation	Absence of proliferation
Epithelialization	Acute epithelialization	Chronic epithelialization	Absence of epithelialization
Prognosis	Progression through phases of healing	Reinitiate acute phase, then progress through phases of healing. Reinitiate acute phase of healing and progress to a clean, stable wound.	Initiate healing phase, if able, and progress through phases. If able to initiate healing phase, progress to a clean, stable wound. If unable to initiate healing phase, refer.

Acute Phase

As normal acute wounds heal, there is an orderly progression through the wound healing phases (inflammation, proliferation, epithelialization, and remodeling). Chapter 2 describes the normal biologic phases of wound repair.

Chronic Phase

Failure of the orderly progression of healing results in a chronic wound. The chronic wound may fail to initiate or stall in any phase of wound healing. When a wound stalls, plateaus, or simply gets stuck in one wound healing phase, the wound becomes chronic with respect to that phase. For example, a pressure ulcer often will become stuck in the inflammatory phase of wound healing, thus the term *chronic inflammation*. Another example is the wound that fills with granulation tissue but does not stop proliferating and goes on to form hypergranulation tissue *(Color Plate 23)*. This is termed *chronic proliferation*. A final example is the wound with impaired scarring, such as with hypertrophic scars or keloid formation. A wound in this condition does not stop laying down collagen. This is termed *chronic epithelialization*.

Absent Phase

The wound that fails to pass through a wound healing phase is lacking attributes of that phase and is referred to as absence of inflammation, absence of proliferation, or absence of epithelialization. Wounds that fail to progress through a wound healing phase differ from those that get stuck or exhibit characteristics of chronicity in one phase. Those wounds that are absent an inflammatory response, for example, will not demonstrate signs of inflammation, whereas wounds with chronic inflammation will show signs of a continued inflammatory response. Absence of the wound healing phase is a way of indicating that the wound has not initiated the phase for whatever reasons. Absence of the wound healing phase signifies either the inability to heal or the need of help from an intervention to initiate the acute phase leading to progression through phases, for example, reperfusion through surgical intervention or enhanced blood flow from a physical agent.

WOUND HEALING PHASE DIAGNOSIS AND PROGNOSIS

When the periwound and wound tissue assessment is completed the clinician will be able to review attributes present or absent, interpret the wound healing phase status observed, and create a care plan based on a diagnosis of wound healing phase. The wound healing phase diagnosis is used for the prognosis and to target treatment outcomes. Prognosis for a wound with a diagnosis of the acute healing phase (inflammation, proliferation, or epithelialization) is progression through the phases of healing. A chronic wound healing phase diagnosis indicates a prognosis that the wound will progress through the phases of healing following reinitiation of the acute phase of healing that is impaired. Alternatively, the prognosis may be a clean, stable wound that may not heal or may need another intervention to achieve closure. If there is inability to initiate the absent phase and progress through the phases, the prognosis for the wound is nonhealing. Such a finding may suggest referral to another practitioner. More than one predominant wound healing phase can be apparent at the same time. For example, a wound with the chronic inflammation phase is also in absence of the proliferation phase and in absence of the epithelialization phase. Chronic inflammation would be the primary wound healing phase diagnosis and absence of the proliferation phase and the epithelialization phase would be the secondary functional diagnosis, signifying that the wound is not progressing through the phases of healing. The wound healing phase diagnosis is useful to demonstrate medical necessity for intervention by the nurse or physical therapist.

Inflammation Phase

Assessment of the periwound and wound tissues during the inflammation phase includes attributes associated with the vascular response to wounding described in Chapter 2. The appearance of periwound and wound tissue will change as the wound progresses through the phases of healing. *Color Plates 1 and 2* show a wound that went from the chronic inflammation phase to the acute inflammation phase and subsequent progression to the proliferation phase. Four categories of wound characteristics are considered: periwound and adjacent tissue appearance (color, edema/induration, temperature), wound tissue appearance (color and texture), wound edges, and exudate characteristics (odor, type, and quantity). The major attributes of adjacent and periwound tissue that are observed and palpated in the inflammatory phase include color, temperature, firmness/texture, sensation, and ecchymosis (hemorrhage)—bruising. In this section, the attributes of the wound and the periwound tissues are described during acute inflammation, chronic inflammation, and absence of inflammation.

Acute Inflammation

Signs of acute inflammation often extend well beyond the immediate wound and periwound tissues and extend into adjacent tissues as well; they indicate a healthy response and are a prerequisite to normal healing. Compare the characteristics seen during acute inflammation as a reference point for the evaluation of impaired responses.

Adjacent Tissues.

Skin Color. Erythema is defined as redness of the skin and is one of the classic characteristics of the inflammatory phase. Skin color attributes found in light and darkly pigmented skin are described in the section on assessment of adjacent tissue, discussed earlier. Reddened skin with streaks leading away from the area may indicate the presence of cellulitis. If assessed, check the patient's history for fever, chills, history of recurrent cellulitis, or medications being used to treat the condition. If no treatment has been initiated, these findings should be reported immediately to the physician.

Edema and Induration. The edema of acute inflammation phase is a localized brawny edema that feels firm and distorts the swollen tissues causing the skin to become taut, shiny, and raised from the contours of the surrounding tissues. This edema results from trauma (eg, pressure ulcers, burns, and surgical debridement) and is related to release of histamines. Histamines cause vasodilatation and increase vascular permeability resulting in the movement of fluid in the interstitial spaces. It is usually accompanied by pain. Induration is abnormal hardening of the tissue at the wound margin by consolidation of edema in the tissues. A test for induration is to pinch the tissues gently; if induration is present the tissues cannot be pinched. Induration follows reflex hyperemia or chronic venous congestion.[17]

Skin Temperature. Skin temperature should be palpated manually by using the back of the hand or a liquid crystal skin fever thermometer if the temperature is at least 95°F. More precise measurement can be made with an infrared scanner. See earlier description of measuring skin temperature. During acute inflammation expect the temperature of periwound to be greater than adjacent tissues, and then gradually decline as inflammation progresses.

Pain. Spontaneous or induced pain in the adjacent tissues should be assessed by either palpation or by report or both. Pain may indicate infection or subcutaneous tissue damage that is not visible, such as in pressure ulcers or vascular disease. Report of a sudden onset of pain accompanied by edema in a leg is a common indicator of a deep vein thrombosis. Unilateral edema accompanied by pain in the calf or to palpation over a vein are indicators of thrombophlebitis. Immediate referral for vascular assessment should follow these findings. More pain testing measures are described under assessment of sensation, in an earlier section. Absence of pain in an obviously infected or inflamed wound should be investigated as an indication of neuropathy and need for further assessment of sensation.

Differential Diagnosis of Inflammation and Infection

A differential diagnosis between inflammation and infection should be performed by the nurse or physical therapist during the tissue assessment. Inflammation with periwound characteristic symptoms of color change (red or purple), edema, pain, heat, and loss of function may progress to infection and necrosis. If the inflammatory process alone is present, there will be exquisite tenderness over the involved area. If, however, there is cellulitis or other infection, there will be streaks of redness extending away from the wound and pain may become intense (see *Color Plate 47*). Wound exudate may be thick, yellow, tan, brown, or green color with malodor. Amount may be moderate to large. Monitor for signs of systemic infection that can lead to sepsis including fever of 101°F (39.4°C) or higher, chills, manifestation of shock including restlessness, lethargy, confusion, and decreased systolic blood pressure.[11] Management and diagnosis of infection is discussed in Chapter 8.

Wound Tissue Assessment. A partial-thickness skin loss creates a shallow crater that looks red or pink or shows the yellow reticular layer, a thin, yellow, meshlike covering, that is the deep layer of the dermis (see *Color Plate 17*). If it is bright and shiny, it is healthy and viable and should be left intact. *Color Plate 13* shows the anatomy of the tissues beneath the skin. If the wound penetrates through the dermis into the subcutaneous tissue, the wound will look as if it contains yellow fat, such as chicken fat, or white connective tissue called fascia. The fascia is a connnective tissue that covers and wraps around all muscles, tendons, blood vessels, and nerves. Wounds that extend through the subcutaneous tissue into the muscle may have a pink or dark red appearance with a shiny layer of fascia on top.

Undermining/Tunneling. Excavation of the subcutaneous tissues during debridement creates a "cave" or undermining of the wound edges. Undermining can lead to separation of fascial planes (see *Color Plate 37*). Muscles lie together in bundles held together by fascia. Separation of the muscle bundles occurs when the fascia is cut. Separation of the fascial layers opens tunnels along the fascial planes between the muscles under the skin (see *Color Plate 37*). Tunnels may join together and form sinus tracts (see *Color Plate 36*). The tunnels are areas where infection can travel, leading to abscess. A wound in the acute inflammation phase with undermining/tunneling will not have signs of infection or necrosis in those species. Differential diagnoses of inflammation and infection has been discussed previously. Muscle tissue is striated and jumps or twitches when palpated. Muscles are connected to bones by tendons. Tendons are covered with white fascia and look like ropes. The sheath of fascia covering the tendon is called peritenon. New granulation tissue will grow over intact peritenon.

Penetration of a wound into the joint may expose several anatomic structures, including ligaments that are white and striated, joint capsule that is white and shiny, and cartilage that is white, hard, and smooth and is on the end of bones. Bone is white, hard, and covered with a clear or white membrane called periosteum. The level of tissue exposed is used to stage or grade the wound severity as described previously. Loss of peritenon or periosteum will compromise a skin graft.

Wound Edges. During acute inflammation the wound edges are often indistinct or diffuse and change shape as wound contraction and epithelialization begins. Wound edges may be attached to the wound base or may be separated from it, forming walls with the base of the wound at a depth from the skin surface. Wound edges should be palpated for firmness and texture. Observe the margins for curling. See *Color Plates 31 and 32* to observe wound edges.

Wound Drainage. Wound drainage during the acute inflammation phase is an indication of the status of the clotting mechanisms and of infection. Wound drainage that contains dead cells and debris is called exudate. Clear fluid drainage is called transudate. See Chapter 8 for more descriptions of exudate characteristics. During assessment record the presence or absence, color, odor, and quantity and quality of the wound drainage.

Sanguineous. Initially there will be bleeding into the wound space that is controlled by clotting. Wounds that have bloody exudate are called sanguineous and may have impaired clotting. This may be due to anticoagulant pharmacologic products that contain substances such as heparin or to disease processes such as hemophilia. The amount of exudate will vary. Medical history, including a pharmacy history, and systems review should clarify the causes of the sanguineous drainage. Copious or persistent sanguineous drainage should be reported to the physician.

Research Wisdom:
Management of Heavy Sanguineous Drainage

If there is heavy sanguineous drainage, a dressing that promotes hemostasis and is very absorptive, such as an alginate, should be considered.

Serous. Serous transudate is clear fluid that exudes from the wound. It is usually yellow and odorless and is seen in varying amounts during the inflammation phase (see *Color Plates 41 and 43*).

Chronic Inflammation

Inflammation that persists for weeks and months is referred to as chronic inflammation. Chronic inflammation occurs when the macrophages and neutrophils fail to phagocytose necrotic matter, ingest foreign debris, and fight infection.[28] Therefore, necrotic matter or foreign debris is the type of material that would be expected to be found in the wound bed. Chronic inflammation is also related to the release of histamine from the mast cells and reflex hyperemia associated with vasodilatation of the surrounding vasculature. Repeated trauma to the wound will also develop into chronic inflammation.

Periwound Skin. Chronic inflammation is seen as a halo of erythema in lightly pigmented skin or a dark halo in darkly pigmented skin located in the periwound area. The latter may be easily mistaken because of its similar appearance with hemosiderin staining. There is minimal temperature change or cooling compared with adjacent uninjured tissues. There may be some minimal firmness from edema in the periwound tissues. There is usually minimal pain response or there may be intense pain associated with arterial vascular disease or infection. Arterial ulcers over the malleolus and pressure ulcers are frequently seen with a halo of erythema but lack the blood flow to progress the wound (see *Color Plate 47*).

Wound Tissue. Wounds in the chronic inflammation phase usually have necrotic tissue covering all or part of the wound surface. Necrotic tissue varies in color and may be black, yellow, tan, brown, or gray. Soft necrotic tissue, such as fibrin or slough, may be present in the wound bed. Fibrin forms on the wound surface and is associated with venous disease. Slough is necrotic fat and fascia adhering to the layer beneath it. See *Color Plates 25 to 30* for different appearances of necrotic tissues. Pale pink wounds may have chronic infection (see *Color Plate 24*). Chapter 7 describes the significance of the different qualities of necrotic tissue. Wounds that are chronically inflamed often have a portion of the wound surface that is in the proliferation phase with granulation tissue present, but the proliferation fails to progress. Not all pink tissue is granulation, however, as muscle tissue that is beneath newly removed necrotic tissue is pink or dark red (see *Color Plate 13*). During assessment record the presence of necrotic tissue and the color. Wounds in the chronic inflammation phase of healing often have a combination of several attributes present. For example, a wound can have black and yellow necrotic tissue as well as pink granulation tissue or healthy muscle tissue (See *Color Plate 7*).

Clinical Wisdom: *Distinguishing Granulation Tissue from Muscle*

To distinguish granulation tissue from healthy muscle, palpate the tissue with a gloved finger. Granulation tissue is soft and spongy and will not jump if pinched, but it may bleed. Muscle tissue is firm and resilient to pressure and will jump or twitch if pinched or probed.

Wound Drainage.

Color and Odor. Wound drainage that is foul smelling and/or viscous yellow/gray or green exudate is often referred to as pus. The pus is a result of the demise of neutrophils after they have phagocytosed debris and excessive bacterial loads. When there is a high bacterial count (greater than 10^5), signs of active infection will be seen. Prolonged, chronic inflammation is the result when there is a bacteria-filled wound.[28]

Not all malodorous or yellow/gray exudate signifies infection. The odor and fluid may come from solubilization of necrotic tissue by enzymatic debriding agents or autolysis. Enzymatic and autolytic debridement are described in Chapter 7. Cleanse exudate from the wound to determine whether odor is transient or internal. If enzymatic or autolytic methods of debridement are used, the odor and debris should be removed by the cleansing. If odor remains or if exudate can be expressed from the wound or adjacent tissues that has color or odor, consider infection. Check for other symptoms of infection such as heat, fever, and lethargy. Exudate color can suggest the type of infection. Normally, wound exudate is serous—a clear or light-yellow fluid. Green is usually associated with an anaerobic infection (see *Color Plates 40 to 45* and Chapter 8). Record color, texture, and odor on the assessment form.

Volume. Exudate volume is considered an indicator of wound outcome.[2] The amount of wound exudate volume should be estimated as scant/minimal, small, moderate, or large/copious. It is hard to record exudate quantity from a dressing or by expressing it from a wound, so these estimates are considered appropriate ways to record estimated quantity. Absence of exudate or dryness of the wound bed may indicate desiccation and the need for adding moisture. During assessment record the presence or absence, color, odor, and quantity of exudate. The PSST has a Likert scale to rate each one of these aspects (Chapter 5).

Gelatinous Edema. Following a secondary trauma to the wound bed such as sharp debridement or enzymatic debridement, wound edema forms as a result of the leakage of plasma proteins from damaged or irritated capillaries, allowing moisture to accumulate and form an opaque gelatinous mass in the base of the wound. The edematous mass contains many substances, all of which are contributory to sustaining a chronic inflammatory response. This mass is visible on examination.[29] Record if present (see *Color Plate 42*).

Absence of Inflammation

Absence of the inflammation phase or inability of the body to present an immune response to wounding may be due to many causes, including an immune-suppression state (eg, human immunodeficiency virus infection/acquired immune deficiency syndrome, cancer, diabetes, drug or radiation therapy, overuse of antiseptics, or severe ischemia). Absence of an inflammatory response prevents the wound from progressing through the biologic phases of repair. It is different from chronic inflammation, with distinct signs and symptoms. In order for the wound to heal, interventions need to be considered to restart the inflammatory response. However, because of the coimpairments related to the problem this may not be realistic. For example, a patient with an ischemic foot and an eschar over a wound on the heel has an absence of inflammation. This is nature's best protection from entry of infection. Protection of the eschar and the limb from trauma to prevent opening of the body to infection and new wounding would be the preferred treatment strategy[3] (see *Color Plate 46*).

Periwound Skin. Absence of an inflammation phase is recognized by absence of a vascular response to wounding, including absence of color changes in the periwound skin and absence of tension or hardness; however, there may be a boggy feeling, and minimal temperature difference or coolness compared with adjacent tissue. Minimal pulses are palpable. Such findings would trigger further investigation of vascular status of the patient (see *Color Plate 46*).

Wound Bed Tissue. Wound bed tissue may be covered with hard, dry eschar to seal off debris and infection from the wound (see *Color Plate 46*).

Wound Drainage. Wound drainage may be scant or the tissues may be dry. Dryness may be due to sealing off of tissues or due to improper treatment.

Summary of Three Inflammation Phase Diagnosis and Prognosis

A diagnosis is the summary of data collected during the assessment process. Wound healing phase diagnosis is a diagnosis of the functional status of healing.[30] Table 3–7 summarizes the findings for each aspect of the inflammation phase. The presence of edema, induration, erythema, elevated temperature, pain, or diffuse or indistinct wound edges is an indicator that the wound healing phase diagnosis is *acute inflammation*. The *chronic inflammation* wound healing phase diagnosis will be recognized by an inadequate circulatory response to the area of trauma. There will be a mild or limited erythema, minimal or absent edema and induration, and no elevation in tissue temperature. Often the assessment findings include a wound with a large bioburden of necrotic tissue. There may be a copious and malodorous exudate signifying an infection that the body cannot adequately suppress. *Absence of inflammation* wound healing phase diagnosis is recognized by an absence of circulatory response to trauma. Sealing off the wound from the rest of the body by a hard, dry eschar gangrene is often nature's way of protecting the body from invasion. Absence of the inflammation phase may also be due to scabbing over the wound surface or letting the deep wound tissues dry out.

Because the phases of healing overlap, the wound healing phase diagnosis if the wound is transitioning from one phase to the next is defined by the *primary* phase appearance. *Inflammation* is the wound healing phase diagnosis if the attributes of inflammation are at least 50% to 75% of what would be expected in an acute inflammatory response (see *Color Plate 1*). If the wound attributes are chronic inflammation for at least 50% to 75% of the symptoms associated with chronic inflammation, the diagnosis is *chronic inflammation* (see *Color Plate 7*). When the wound attributes of acute inflammation are less than 50% of what are expected and there is significant proliferation of granulation tissue in the wound bed, the primary wound phase diagnosis changes to proliferation phase (see *Color Plate 8*).

Proliferation Phase

Like the inflammation phase, the proliferation phase is broken into three aspects: acute proliferation (the active biologic process of proliferation, including granulation tissue formation and contraction), chronic proliferation (the wound is stuck in the proliferation phase and not progressing to the next phase of epithelialization and remodeling), and absence of proliferation (the wound bed is clean but the wound is not proliferating or is not contracting). Each of the three aspect characteristics of proliferation are described.

Acute Proliferation Phase

Periwound Skin. Periwound skin during proliferation regains color and contour symmetry with that of adjacent skin (edema resolved); if it is a recovering chronic wound, however, expect to see hemosiderin staining (pigmentation) around the wound margins (see *Color Plate 2*). Ecchymosis should be resolved. Skin turgor is normal and is not stretched

Table 3–7 Wound Healing Phase Diagnosis: Tissue Characteristics for Inflammation Phase

Periwound Skin and Wound Tissue Characteristics	Acute Inflammation	Chronic Inflammation	Absence of Inflammation
Periwound skin color	• Unblanchable erythema in light-skinned patients • Discoloration or deepening of normal ethnic color in dark-skinned patients • Ecchymosis (purplish bruising) • Hemosiderin (rust brown) staining	• Halo of erythema or darkening • Hemosiderin (rust brown) staining • Ecchymosis (purplish bruising)	• Pale or ashen skin color • Absence of erythema or darkening • Hemosiderin (rust brown) staining • Ecchymosis (purplish bruising)
Edema and induration	• Firmness • Taut, shiny skin • Localized swelling • Consolidation (hardness) between adjacent tissues	• Gelatinous edema may be seen on wound tissue • Minimal firmness • Absent • May feel boggy	

continues

Table 3–7 continued

Periwound Skin and Wound Tissue Characteristics	Acute Inflammation	Chronic Inflammation	Absence of Inflammation
Tissue temperature	• Elevated initially, decreases as inflammation progresses	• Minimal change or coolness	• Minimal change or coolness
Pain	• Present; wound is tender and painful unless neuropathy is present	• Minimal pain unless arterial etiology or infection, then may have intense pain	• Minimal or no pain unless arterial etiology, then may have intense pain
Wound tissue	• Blister with clear or bloody fluid • Shallow or deep crater with red to pink color • Red muscle • White shiny fascia • Yellow reticular layer of dermis with granulation buds	• Necrotic, varies in color from yellow to brown to black • Necrotic tissue covering full or partial surface area • Soft or hard necrotic tissue • Yellow fibrin or slough • Portion of wound may have granulation tissue • May also appear as clean, pale pink	• Covered with hard, dry eschar • Necrotic, varies in color from yellow to brown to black • Scab
Undermining/tunneling	• May be present in deep wounds • Has potential for infection and abscess	• May be present in deep wounds • May extend potential for infection and abscess	• May be present in deep wounds • Has potential for infection and abscess
Wound edges	• Diffuse, indistinct, may still be demarcating from healthy tissues	• Distinct, edges may be rolled or thickened • Is not continuous with wound bed if deep wound cavity	• Has distinct well-defined wound edges • May be attached to necrotic tissue
Wound drainage	• Serous or serosanguineous	• Infection • Viscous • Malodor • Pus (yellow, tan, gray, or green) • Moderate to large amount	• Scant or dry
Color Plates	1, 14, 15, 17, 19, 36, 37, 39, 68	20, 25, 27, 42, 47	26, 29, 46

COLOR PLATES

PROGRESSION THROUGH THREE PHASES OF WOUND HEALING
Plates 1–6

The patient is a 97-year-old nursing home resident with Stage IV pressure ulcers in the bilateral rib cage and sacral area.

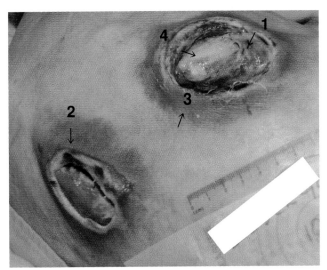

1. Chronic wound converted to acute inflammation phase.
   (1) Yellow, stringy slough;
   (2) Edema;
   (3) Skin color changes (red), erythema;
   (4) Rib bone noted in superior ulcer.
   Wound healing phase diagnosis: acute inflammation phase.
   Wound severity diagnosis: Impaired integumentary integrity secondary to skin involvement extending into fascia, muscle, bone.
   Source: Reprinted with permission, copyright © C. Sussman.

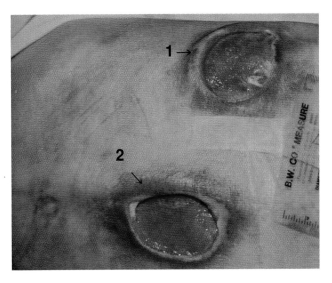

2. Same wound as in Plate 1.
   (1) Rolled epidermal ridge around granulation base;
   (2) Brown hemosiderin staining.
   Wound healing phase: proliferation phase.
   Source: Reprinted with permission, copyright © C. Sussman.

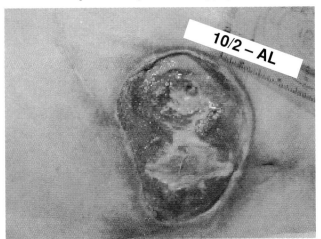

3. Same patient as in Plate 1. Chronic wound: converted to acute proliferation phase. This is a sacral wound with stringy, yellow slough evident. Predominant wound healing phase diagnosis: Proliferation phase. Wound severity diagnosis: same as in Plate 1.
   Source: Reprinted with permission, copyright © C. Sussman.

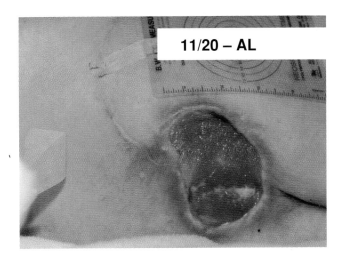

4. Same wound as Plate 3 progressing through the proliferation phase of healing. Wound contracting and proliferating. Note change in size, shape, and depth compared to Plate 3.
   Source: Reprinted with permission, copyright © C. Sussman.

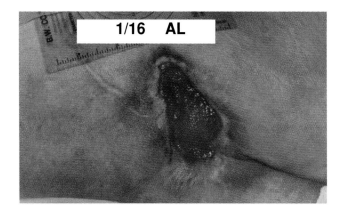

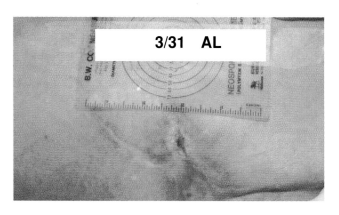

5. Note sustained wound contraction evident between Plates 4 and 5. Wound is in both epithelialization and proliferation phases.
Source: Reprinted with permission, copyright © C. Sussman.

6. The wound is completely resurfaced. It is in the remodeling phase.
Source: Reprinted with permission, copyright © C. Sussman.

PROGRESSION THROUGH PROLIFERATION PHASE
Plates 7–9

Plates 7 to 9 show a sacral pressure ulcer progressing from chronic inflammation phase through the proliferation phase of wound healing. In Plates 8 and 9 the wound edges demonstrate epithelial migration with new epidermis clearly visible as bright pink in this dark-skinned patient in Plates 7 to 9.

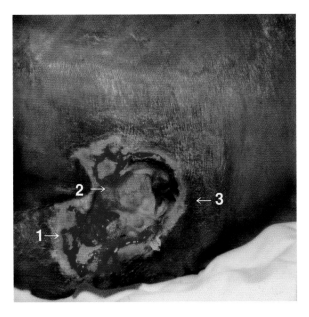

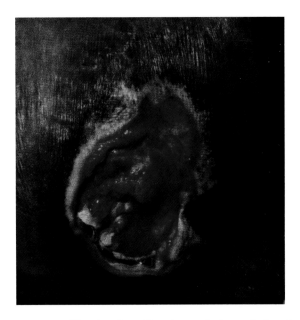

7. Chronic inflammation phase. Note the following wound characteristics:
   (1) Sanguineous drainage;
   (2) Muscle exposure;
   (3) Hemosiderin staining surrounding the wound.
   Source: Reprinted with permission, copyright © B.M. Bates-Jensen.

8. Acute proliferation phase. Note the attached wound edges from the 12-o'clock to 6-o'clock positions and how granulation tissue fills up one side of the ulcer.
   Source: Reprinted with permission, copyright © B.M. Bates-Jensen.

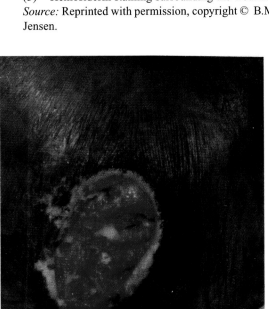

9. All of the wound edges are now attached to wound base. Note the presence of fibrin (yellow) within the granulation tissue. Ready for epithelialization phase.
   Source: Reprinted with permission, copyright © B.M. Bates-Jensen.

ABNORMAL PROLIFERATION PHASE
Plates 10 and 11

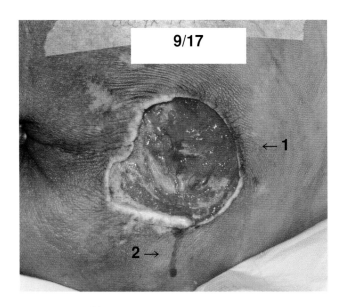

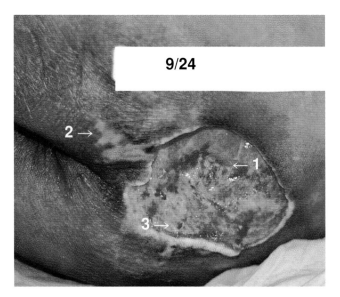

10. Acute proliferation phase.
    (1) Hemosiderin staining;
    (2) Sanguineous drainage.
    Source: Reprinted with permission, copyright © B.M. Bates-Jensen.

11. Chronic proliferation phase with attributes of infection.
    (1) Hemorrhagic area of trauma;
    (2) Hypopigmentation;
    (3) Dull pink granulation tissue.
    Source: Reprinted with permission, copyright © B.M. Bates-Jensen.

WOUND IN REMODELING PHASE
Plate 12

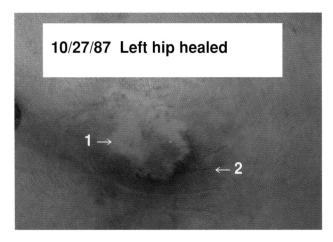

12. An example of a wound in the remodeling phase of wound healing.
    (1) New epithelium (scar);
    (2) Hyperpigmentation (Hemosiderin-staining).
    Source: Reprinted with permission, copyright © B.M. Bates-Jensen.

ANATOMY OF SOFT TISSUE
Plate 13

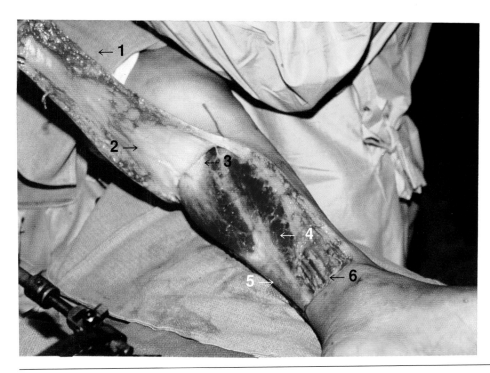

13. Full-thickness skin resected from calf.
    (1) Vascularized dermis;
    (2) Yellow healthy fat tissue;
    (3) White fibrous fascia;
    (4) Dark red muscle tissue;
    (5) Tendon covered with peritenon;
    (6) Blood vessel.
    Source: Reprinted with permission, copyright © J. Wethe.

WOUNDING OF THE SKIN
Plates 14–18

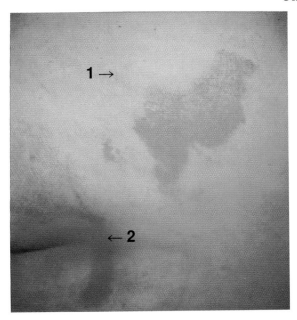

14. Superficial wounding of skin.
    (1) This wound would be classified as a stage I pressure ulcer;
    (2) This wound is perineal dermatitis. Note location over rectum.
    Source: Reprinted with permission, copyright © B.M. Bates-Jensen.

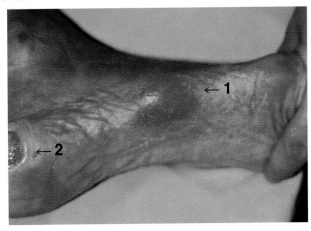

15. (1) Intact skin with subcutaneous microvascular bleeding suggesting deeper trauma located over a bony surface, and would be classified as a stage I pressure ulcer;
    (2) Maceration of periwound skin.
    Source: Reprinted with permission, copyright © B.M. Bates-Jensen.

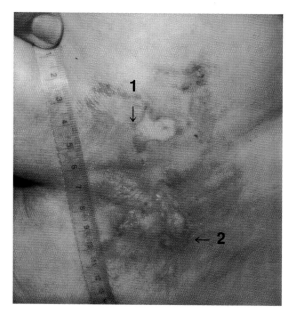

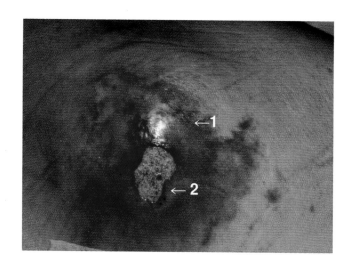

16. Perineal dermatitis with classic differentiating characteristics of diffuse erythema across buttocks and perineal area and partial-thickness skin loss. This wound is in the acute inflammation phase and was not staged.
(1) Multiple, partial-thickness lesions with irregular borders;
(2) Lesions occur across area singly and in groups and may or may not be over a bony prominence.
Source: Reprinted with permission, copyright © B.M. Bates-Jensen.

17. Acute inflammation phase, partial thickness stage II pressure ulcer located over bony prominence.
(1) Erythema and edema;
(2) Reticular layer of dermis.
Source: Reprinted with permission, copyright © B.M. Bates-Jensen.

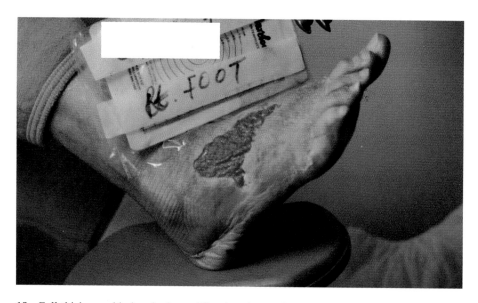

18. Full-thickness skin loss in the proliferation phase. The wound was not due to pressure and was not staged.
Source: Reprinted with permission, copyright © C. Sussman.

ASSESSMENT OF DARKLY PIGMENTED SKIN
Plates 19–22

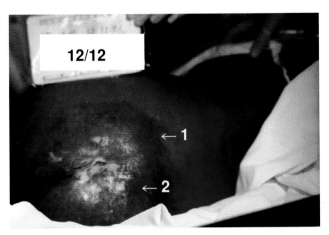

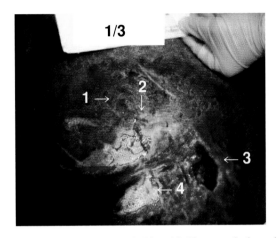

19. Pressure ulceration with multiple, small, stage II open areas. Wound is in acute inflammation phase. Note onset date 12/12.
    (1) There is a clear line of dermarcation between healthy tissues and inflammation;
    (2) Evidence of discoloration, edema, and induration suggest underlying tissue death. Assess tissue temperature and pain.
    Source: Reprinted with permission, copyright © C. Sussman.

20. Same pressure ulceration as in Plate 19. Three weeks later the skin now shows evidence of the severe tissue destruction that occurred at the time of trauma. Note delayed manifestation of injury at the skin level. The date was 1/3.
    (1) Continued demarcation of inflammation;
    (2) Irregular diffuse wound edges;
    (3) Eschar, black and adherent;
    (4) Partial-thickness skin loss. There is enlargement of stage II ulcers compared with those in Plate 19.
    The correct staging for this sacrococcygeal pressure ulcer is at minimum a stage III. Once eschar is removed, true depth of tissue loss can be determined. Documentation should reflect a combined area of wounding, including all three visible ulcers and the area of inflammation. This is the overall size estimate for the pressure ulcer. Inflammation now chronic.
    Source: Reprinted with permission, copyright © C. Sussman.

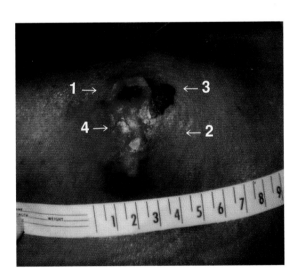

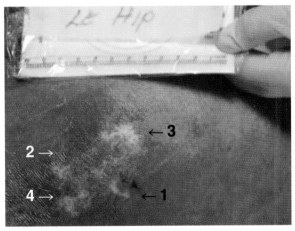

21. Assessment of inflammation attributes in darkly pigmented skin.
    (1) Erythema gives skin a reddish brown glow;
    (2) Hemorrhage of microvasculature gives skin purplish gray hue;
    (3) Eschar—note tissue texture change to hard black;
    (4) Use skin color of adjacent skin for reference of normal skin tones.
    Source: Reprinted with permission, copyright © B.M. Bates-Jensen.

22. Assessment of epithelialization and remodeling attributes in darkly pigmented skin.
    (1) New epithelial tissue that is light red;
    (2) New scar tissue that lacks melanin and is bright pink;
    (3) Old scar tissue that lacks melanin and is silvery white;
    (4) Residual hemosiderin staining.
    Source: Reprinted with permission, copyright © C. Sussman.

ABNORMAL WOUND ATTRIBUTES
Plates 23 and 24

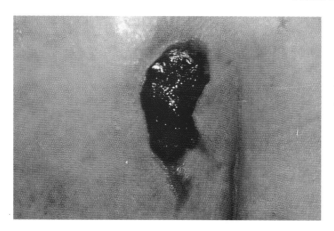

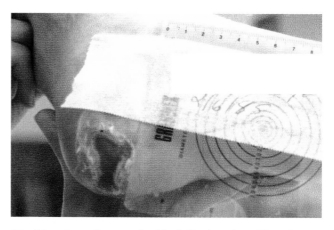

23. Wound is in chronic proliferation phase. Hypergranulation tissue; absence of epithelialization phase.
Source: Reprinted with permission, copyright © B.M. Bates-Jensen.

24. There is an absence of epithelialization phase. Hyperkeratosis on heel ulcer of a 100-year-old woman.
Source: Reprinted with permission, copyright © C. Sussman.

NECROTIC TISSUE TYPES
Plates 25–30

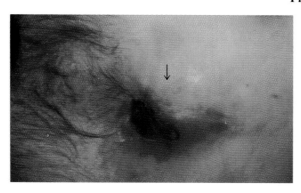

25. Hard, leathery eschar in the chronic inflammation phase. Notice how the eschar looks similar to a scab.
Source: Reprinted with permission, copyright © B.M. Bates-Jensen.

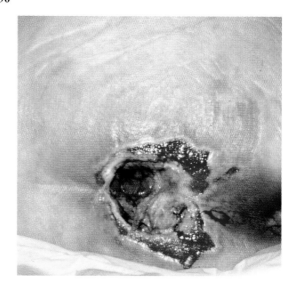

26. Soft, soggy, black eschar in the absence of inflammation phase.
Source: Reprinted with permission, copyright © B.M. Bates-Jensen.

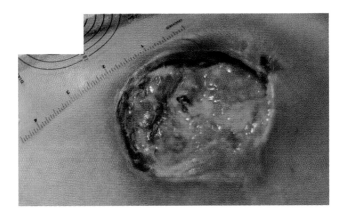

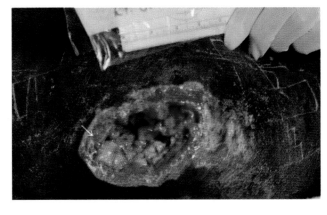

27. Chronic wound converted to acute inflammation phase with yellow, mucinous slough.
Source: Reprinted with permission, copyright © C.Sussman.

28. Necrotic fatty tissue.
Source: Reprinted with permission, copyright © C.Sussman.

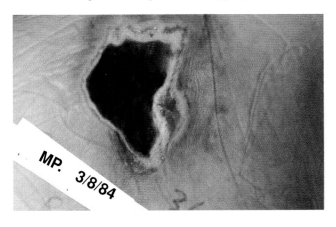

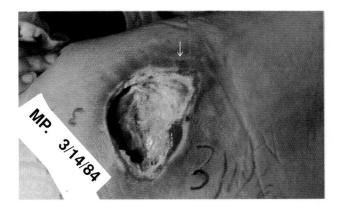

29. Eschar before debridement. Absence of inflammation phase.
Source: Reprinted with permission, copyright © C.Sussman.

30. Eschar after debridement. Necrotic fat and fascia often called slough. Restart of inflammation phase.
Source: Reprinted with permission, copyright © C.Sussman.

WOUND EDGES
Plates 31–34

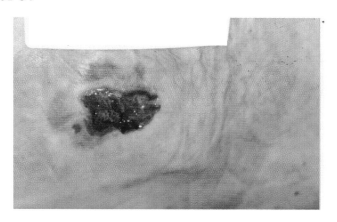

31. Absence of proliferation phase. Wound with no epithelialization present. The wound is clean, but nonprofilerating.
Source: Reprinted with permission, copyright © B.M. Bates-Jensen.

32. Same wound as in Plate 31. Wound is in acute proliferation phase with evidence of new epithelial migration.
Source: Reprinted with permission, copyright © B.M. Bates-Jensen.

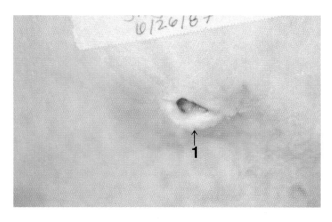

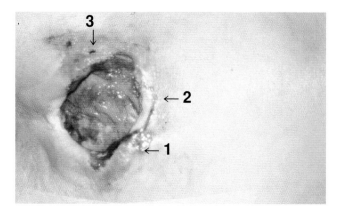

33. There is an absence of epithelialization phase.
(1) Wound lacking epithelialization due to chronic fibrosis and scarring at wound edge. Chronic proliferation phase.
Source: Reprinted with permission, copyright © B.M. Bates-Jensen.

34. An example of knowledge gained from careful examination of the wound edge. Wound is in chronic proliferation phase.
(1) New pressure-induced damage (hemorrhage);
(2) Maceration from wound fluid;
(3) Friction injury with signs of inflammation.
Source: Reprinted with permission, copyright © B.M. Bates-Jensen.

SURGICAL DISSECTION FOR TUNNELING
Plates 35 and 36

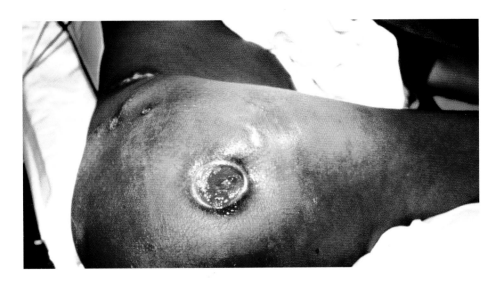

35. Unobservable tunneling.
Source: Reprinted with permission, copyright © J. Wethe.

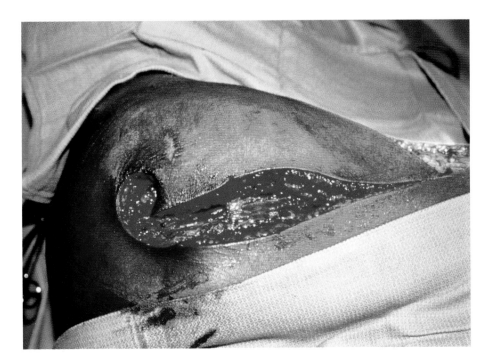

36. Same wound as Plate 35 with surgical dissection demonstrating the extent of the tunneling process.
Source: Reprinted with permission, copyright © J. Wethe.

UNDERMINING AND TUNNELING
Plates 37–39

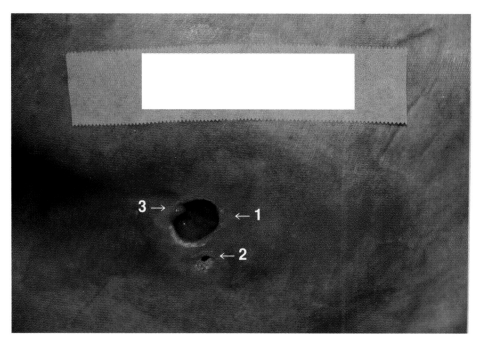

37. Wound with tunneling before insertion of a cotton-tipped applicator.
    (1) Ulcer reoccurrence at site of old scar tissue;
    (2) Skin bridge between two open ulcers;
    (3) Surrounding skin has unblanchable erythema. Wound edges rolled under demonstrate chronic inflammation phase.
    Source: Reprinted with permission, copyright © B.M. Bates-Jensen.

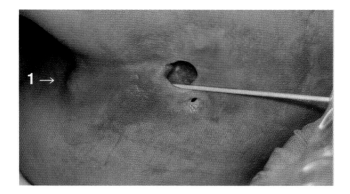

38. Same wound as in Plate 37. The wound overall size is much larger than the surface open area. Tunneling is present.
    (1) Note bulge from end of cotton-tipped applicator.
    Source: Reprinted with permission, copyright © B.M. Bates-Jensen.

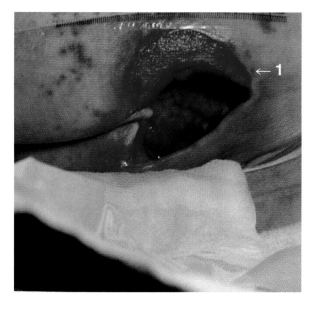

39. Undermined wound.
    (1) Note shelf.
    Source: Reprinted with permission, copyright © C. Sussman.

READING THE DRESSING: WOUND EXUDATE ASSESSMENT
Plates 40–45

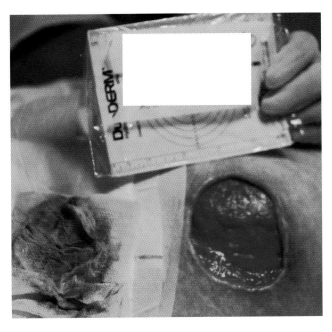

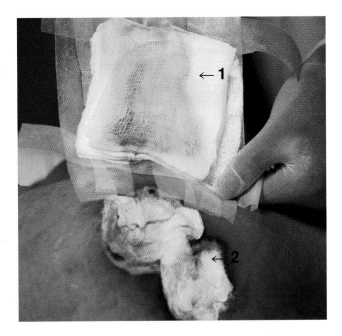

40. Clean wound in chronic proliferation phase. The quantity of exudate is determined by the amount of dressing saturated by the drainage.
(1)   Moderate to large amount of sanguineous exudate;
(2)   Moderate to large amount of purulent exudate;
(3)   Evaluate for infection.
Source: Reprinted with permission, copyright © C. Sussman.

41. Wound with packing still present.
(1)   Moderate amount of serous exudate on dressing;
(2)   Green color of exudate suggests possible infection.
Source: Reprinted with permission, copyright © C. Sussman.

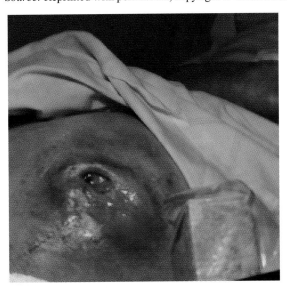

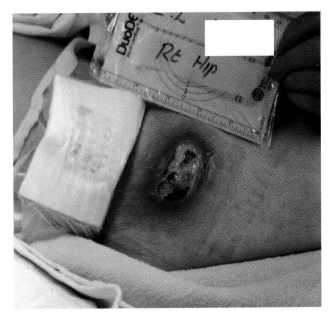

42. Wound with composite dressing. Dressing shows moderate amount of serosanguineous exudate. The wound bed shows gelatinous mass that may be gelatinous edema. Evaluate for trauma. Bright pink skin is scar tissue.
Source: Reprinted with permission, copyright © C. Sussman.

43. Wound with composite dressing shows scant amount of serous exudate. Wound is in chronic inflammation phase. There is an absence of proliferation phase.
Source: Reprinted with permission, copyright © C. Sussman.

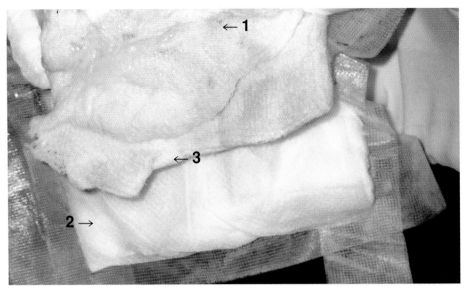

44. (1) Large amount of serous drainage;
(2) Note how drainage flows into secondary dressing;
(3) Note green tinge to edges of dressing, suggesting anaerobic infection (eg, pseudomonas). Monitor for a degenerative change in exudate type from present serous to purulent (eg, greener, thicker, and more opaque).

Source: Reprinted with permission, copyright © C. Sussman.

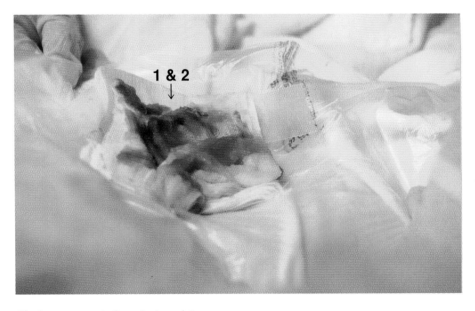

45. Large amount of purulent exudate.
(1) Thick, opaque cloudy appearance;
(2) Note green color. Assess for odor.

Source: Reprinted with permission, copyright © C. Sussman.

ARTERIAL ISCHEMIC WOUNDS
Plates 46–48

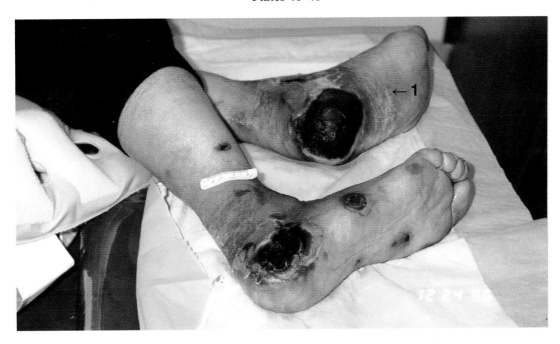

46. Severe arterial ischemic disease with multiple ischemic ulcers below the ankle bilaterally. Wounds are in absence of inflammation phase with hard, dry, black eschar covering.
(1)   Note trophic changes on foot, evidence of scaling.
Source: Reprinted with permission, copyright © E. Fowler.

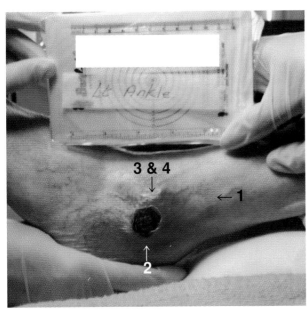

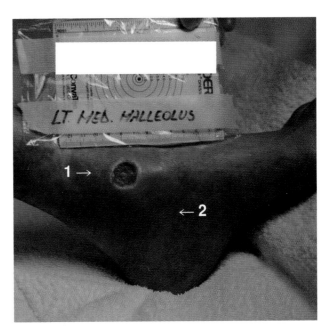

47. Classic ischemic ulcer. Note:
  (1)   Chronic inflammation with cellulitis;
  (2)   Punched-out ulcer edges;
  (3)   Covering of dry, black eschar;
  (4)   Location over lateral malleolus.
Source: Reprinted with permission, copyright © C. Sussman.

48. Ischemic ulcer in chronic proliferation and absence of epithelialization phase. Note:
  (1)   Punched-out ulcer appearance with rolled wound edges;
  (2)   Dependent rubor.
Source: Reprinted with permission, copyright © C. Sussman.

VENOUS DISEASE
Plates 49–54

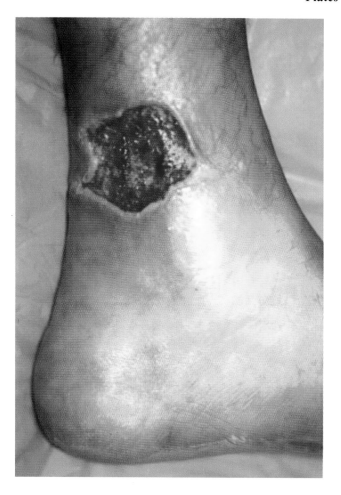

49. Ischemic ulcer in a 55-year-old male smoker with a 4-month history of having "blistered" his ankle with the subsequent formation of a painful ulcer. He was diagnosed as having a venous stasis ulcer and was treated with wet-to-dry dressing changes three times per day. Despite good compliance his ulcer failed to improve. The physical exam revealed absent femoral, popliteal, and pedal pulses with an ABI of 0.35. The ulcer edge was irregular, but the base was clean and had adequate granulation tissue. Even though the ulcer was located proximal to the medial malleolus, the typical location of chronic venous stasis ulcers, this patient did not exhibit any of the physical signs of chronic venous insufficiency such as brawny edema, hyperpigmentation, or stasis dermatitis. See Chapter 14, Diagnosis and Management of Vascular Ulcers, for photos of angiogram on same patient (Figure 14–4).
Source: Reprinted with permission, copyright © C. Donayre.

50. Structure of the venous wall. Cross-section of a venous branch of lower extremity reveals a relative standard wall structure. The intima is covered by uninterrupted endothelium which is connected to a thin connective tissue layer. The media is structured much more loosely than corresponding arteries, and is composed of distinct layers of collagenous and elastic fibers between which narrow strips of smooth muscle are found.
Source: Reprinted with permission, copyright © C. Donayre.

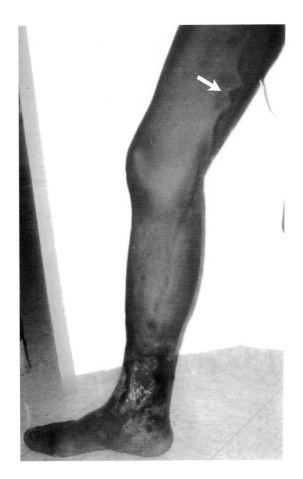

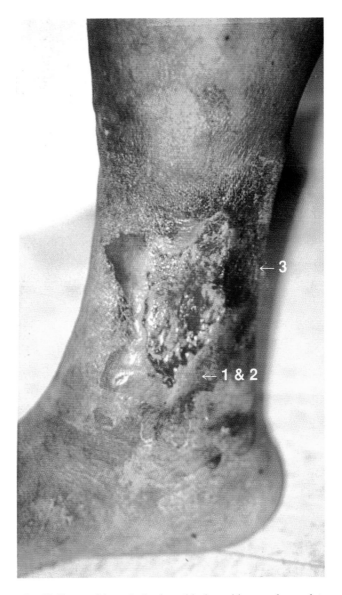

51. Venous stasis ulceration. This 49-year-old male with a 3-year history of recurrent venous ulceration was being treated with Unna boot changes once a week. Physical exam revealed patent femoral, popliteal, and pedal pulses. An enlarged, dilated, and tortuous greater saphenous vein was easily visualized with the patient in a standing position (white arrow). A duplex scan confirmed isolated greater saphenous vein incompetence, with a normal deep and perforator vein system.
Source: Reprinted with permission, copyright © C. Donayre.

52. Shallow and irregularly shaped lesion with a good granulating base and the associated physical signs of chronic venous insufficiency such as hyperpigmentation, chronic scarring, and skin contraction in the ankle region are readily identified. Note the classic characteristics of venous disease:
(1)   Irregular edges;
(2)   Shallow ulcer;
(3)   Evidence of hyperpigmentation (hemosiderin staining) surrounding ulcer;
(4)   Location above the medial malleolus.
Source: Reprinted with permission, copyright © C. Donayre.

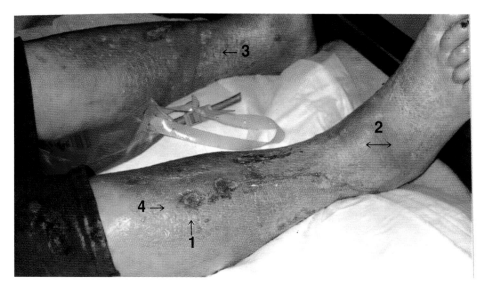

53. Stasis dermatitis. There is an absence of epithilialization phase. Evidence of:
   (1)   Brawny edema;
   (2)   Trophic skin changes;
   (3)   Hemosiderin staining (hyperpigmentation);
   (4)   Multiple shallow ulcers.
   Source: Reprinted with permission, copyright © B.M. Bates-Jensen.

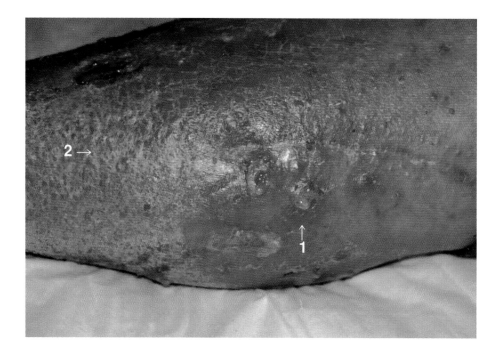

54. Close-up view of same leg as in Plate 53 and shows evidence of:
   (1)   Edema leakage through wounds;
   (2)   Scaling and crusting (trophic changes) due to lipodermatosclerosis.
   Source: Reprinted with permission, copyright © B.M. Bates-Jensen.

WOUND HEALING WITH ELECTRICAL STIMULATION—CHAPTER 16
Plates 55 and 56

Patient with vascular ulcer treated with ED and HV PC (see Chapter 16 for details).

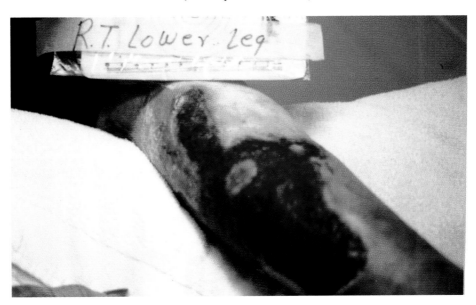

55. Note beefy red granulation tissue and island of epidermal tissue in full thickness wound. The wound is in acute proliferation phase on 12/28.
Source: Reprinted with permission, copyright © C. Sussman.

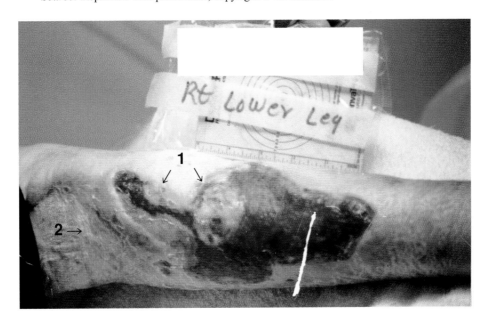

56. Same wound as in Plate 55. Note epidermal migration from wound edges, island and wound shape changes.
(1) It had progressed to the acute epithelialization phase by 2/17;
(2) Note hyperkeratotic skin changes due to old burn wounds and poor circulation.
Source: Reprinted with permission, copyright © C. Sussman.

WOUND HEALING WITH PULSATILE LAVAGE WITH SUCTION—CHAPTER 17
Plates 57–59

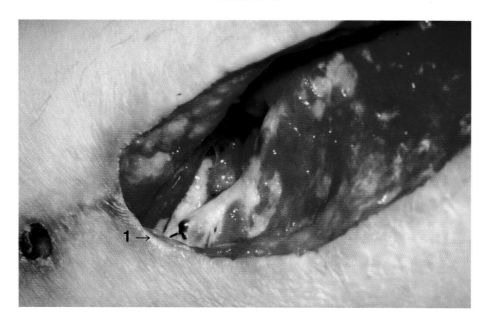

57. (1) Exposed artery in infected bypass graft donor site in lower leg.
Source: Reprinted with permission, copyright © H. Loehne.

Case Study

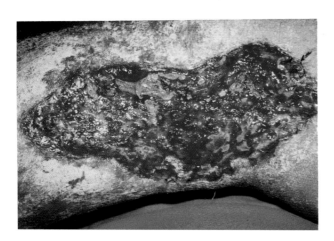

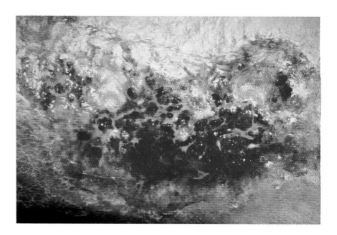

58. Pyoderma gangrenosum ulcer on medial lower leg of 8 years' duration.
Source: Reprinted with permission, copyright © H. Loehne.

59. Pyoderma gangrenosum ulcer (same ulcer as Plate 58) on medial lower leg after 2 weeks of treatment with Pulsavac® System.
Source: Reprinted with permission, copyright © H. Loehne.

WOUND HEALING WITH PULSED SHORT WAVE DIATHERMY
CASE STUDY 1—CHAPTER 18
Plates 60–62

Patient with pressure ulcers treated with PSWD (see Chapter 18 for details).

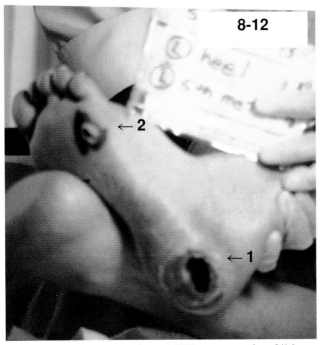

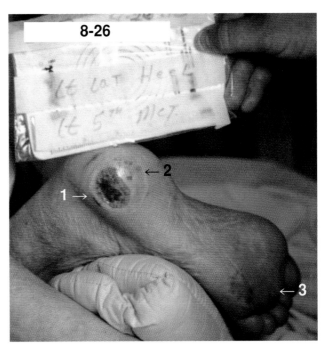

60. Patient with pressure ulcers. PSWD was started on 8/16.
   (1) Black eschar on heel wound surrounded by partial-thickness skin loss. There is an absence of inflammation phase;
   (2) Black eschar over the 5th metatarsal head. There is an absence of inflammation phase.
   Source: Reprinted with permission, copyright © C. Sussman.

61. Same ulcer as seen on heel in Plate 62 10 days after start of PSWD.
   (1) Eschar removed to soft necrosis;
   (2) Reepithelialization of partial-thickness skin loss;
   (3) Eschar removed 5th matatarsal. Wound healed.
   Source: Reprinted with permission, copyright © C. Sussman.

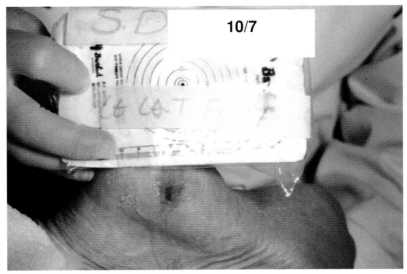

62. Same heel ulcer as in Plates 62 and 63 (10/7). The ulcer healed and is shown in the remodeling phase.
   Source: Reprinted with permission, copyright © C. Sussman.

WOUND HEALING WITH PULSED RADIO FREQUENCY STIMULATION
CASE STUDY 2—CHAPTER 18
Plates 63 and 64

Patient with incisional wound treated with PRFS (see Chapter 18 for details).

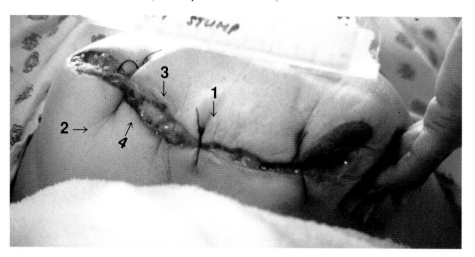

63. Patient with an incision from an above-the-knee amputation left open for delayed primary intention healing. Wound is in acute inflammation phase. Start of treatment with PRFS 8/3.
    (1) Sutures placed;
    (2) Edema;
    (3) Erythema and tissue tension;
    (4) Yellow mucinous slough in incision line.
    Source: Reprinted with permission, copyright © C. Sussman.

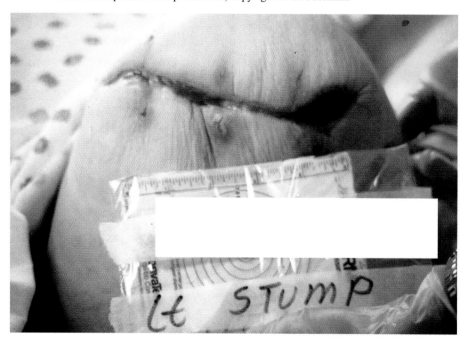

64. Same incision wound as in Plate 63 on 8/17 (14 days later). Note outcomes: edema free, necrosis free, wound contraction and granulation. The wound is in acute proliferation phase and epithelialization phase.
    Source: Reprinted with permission, copyright © C. Sussman.

**WOUND HEALING WITH ULTRASOUND
CASE STUDY 1—CHAPTER 19
Plates 65–67**

Patient with a venous ulcer 24 hours after onset. (See Chapter 19 for details.)

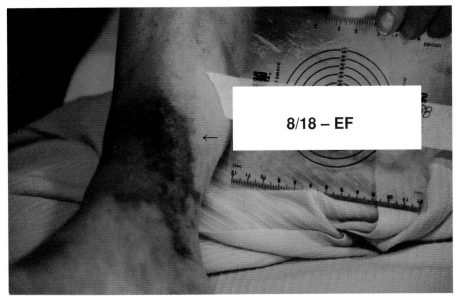

65. Wound is in acute inflammation phase and shows subcutaneous hemorrhage (ecchymosis) associated with venous disease.
Source: Reprinted with permission, copyright © C. Sussman.

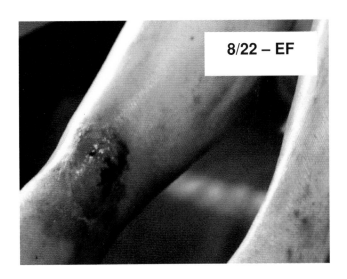

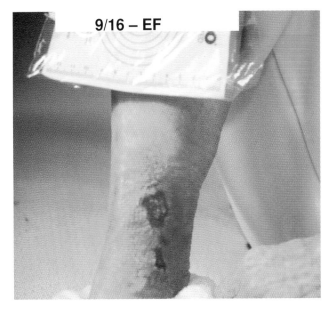

66. Same wound as Plate 65, 4 days after 2 treatments with ultrasound. Shows absorption of ecchymosis seen earlier. There is partial-thickness skin loss. The wound is in acute inflammation phase.
Source: Reprinted with permission, copyright © C. Sussman.

67. Same ulcer as in Plates 65 and 66, 4 weeks after start of ultrasound. Note wound contraction compared with that in Plate 66. There are soft irregular wound edges and new epithelization. The wound is in epithelialization phase.
Source: Reprinted with permission, copyright © C. Sussman.

WOUND HEALING WITH ULTRASOUND
CASE STUDY 2—CHAPTER 19
Plates 68–71

Patient with blood blister on heel secondary to pressure, treated with ultrasound (US).

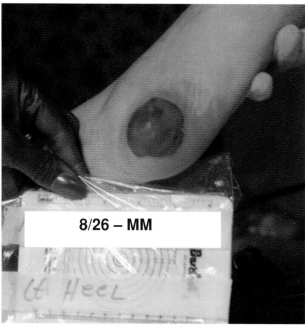

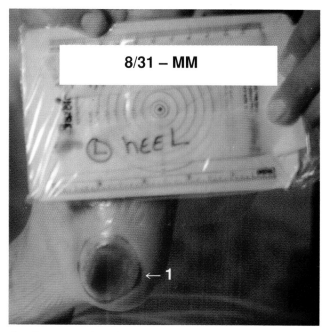

68. Acute inflammation phase. Blister with bloody fluid at day of identification.
Source: Reprinted with permission, copyright © C. Sussman.

69. Same wound as Plate 68 without blister roof. The periwound skin was treated with daily US for 4 days prior.
(1) Note area of apparent necrosis, hematoma. There is an absence of inflammation phase.
Source: Reprinted with permission, copyright © C. Sussman.

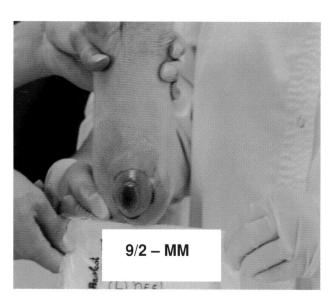

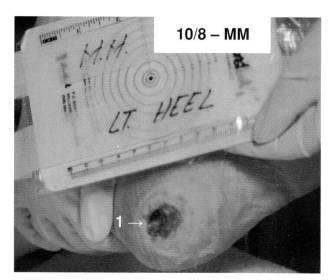

70. Same wound as Plates 68 and 69 after 2 additional periwound US treatments. Note absorption of hematoma by reduced size of necrotic area and mild erythema surrounding the area of necrosis. The wound is in acute inflammation phase.
Source: Reprinted with permission, copyright © C. Sussman.

71. Same wound as Plates 68, 69, and 70.
(1) Note focal area of necrosis. Time of change in treatment to ES and sharp debridement. The wound shows the start of proliferation phase.
Source: Reprinted with permission, copyright © C. Sussman.

or taut because the edema and induration are resolved (absent). Firmness is absent or minimal.

Periwound Skin Temperature. Periwound skin temperature when palpated or measured on a skin thermometer is the same as skin in adjacent areas or may be slightly elevated due to enhanced perfusion of the tissues and higher metabolic activities associated with healing.

Pain. Minimal or no pain is experienced during this phase. It is an inappropriate indicator if there is neuropathy.

Undermining/Tunneling. The acute proliferation phase progresses after the wound has been debrided of necrotic tissue. Debridement of necrotic tissue creates a disruption of the tissue integrity of the skin and the underlying structures. The proliferation phase is concluding when the wound tissue integrity is reestablished. Undermining is defined as a closed passageway under the surface of the skin that is open only at the skin surface.[2] As previously described, wound undermining occurs following debridement of the skin and subcutaneous tissue and is erosion of the tissue, forming a cave under the wound edge (see *Color Plate 39*). Both undermining and tunneling are loss of tissue integrity. The loss of tissue integrity allows separation of the fascial planes between the bundles of muscles. Tunneling is like a subway progressing from the initial undermined excavation and occurs when there is debridement into the fascial and muscle layers. Tunneling may be unobservable from the surface and yet have a great extent, as shown in *Color Plates 35 and 36* of the same wound. Undermining and tunneling close as the tissues reestablish continuity during the laying down of the collagen matrix and granulation tissue during the proliferation phase. The extent of undermining is a measure of the total soft tissue involved in the wound. Reduction of the extent of undermining/tunneling is a measure of the progression of proliferation and reduced overall wound size. Note findings of undermining and tunneling as part of the tissue assessment. If the tunneling extends beyond about 15 cm, this is cause to notify the physician. Chapter 4 describes how to measure undermining/tunneling and then calculate the extent of the overall wound.

Wound Tissue. Wounds that have a bowl-like shaped cavity will fill with granulation tissue during the acute proliferative phase to create a surface across which epidermal cells may migrate. Tissue that develops during this phase has been given the term *granulation tissue* because the tissue has the appearance of granules piled upon one another. Biologically, this tissue is the collagen matrix. Granulation buds are clearly seen in *Color Plates 4 and 8*. Note how the cavity is filling in those photos to create a level surface with the adjacent skin. Acute proliferation starts when the wound bed tissue begins to show red or pink granulation buds and overlaps the late inflammatory phase. The collagen matrix is laid down and is infiltrated by and supports the growing capillary bed, giving it the red color. Reduced depth in a full-thickness wound is a measure of proliferation activity. The collagen matrix does not replace the structures or functions of the tissues that occupied the cavity prior to injury. This is scar tissue. The prevailing opinion is that this deep red color indicates a healthy healing wound. A contrary opinion is explained later under Chronic Proliferation Phase.

Another feature that has been reported to appear during the acute proliferation phase of healing in a number of patients is the development of a yellow, fibrinous membrane on the surface of the granulation tissue. Removal of this membrane has been attempted, but it will recur in a few days. Wounds that develop this yellow membrane appear to be less susceptible to infection. These wounds continue to heal in a normal fashion. Recognizing this membrane during examination will prevent unnecessary disruption of the wound bed.[31]

Wound Edges. The wound edges are soft to firm and are flexible to touch. Edges will roll if the wound is full thickness, but when the wound tissue fills the cavity even with the edge of the wound, the edges will flatten and epithelialization and contraction will continue together (see *Color Plates 3 to 5 and 8 to 9*). At this point, the wound acquires a distinctive wound shape or "picture frame." The cells that control the movement of the picture frame, the myofibroblasts, are located beneath the wound edge. The cells are contractile and will move forward, drawing the wound together. During this process the wound edges are drawn together like the drawing together of purse strings, shrinking the size of the open area measurably. The shape that the wound now assumes predicts the resulting speed of contraction. Linear wounds contract rapidly. Square or rectangular wounds contract at a moderate pace. Circular wounds contract slowly.

Clinical Wisdom:
Assessment of Abscess by Palpation

Palpation to assess for an abscess is done by pressing down over the undermined area. If there is a lump accompanied by pain or fluid expressed by the compression, an abscess should be suspected and referral made to the physician.

Wound contraction is a major activity of the acute proliferation phase of healing. Contraction reduces the areas needing to close by epithelialization. Contraction in areas such as the gluteals and abdomen will be fine, but examples of locations where contracture is troublesome include the head, neck, and hand. Drawing together too tightly in those areas will cause a defect or contracture that will impair function and cosmesis. Wounds that would have a poor outcome if allowed to close by contraction would have a prognosis of need for surgical intervention at the start of the proliferation phase.[32]

Wound Drainage. During the acute proliferation phase the wound drainage is serosanguineous and of moderate to minimal quantity and odor.

Chronic Proliferation Phase

Periwound Skin Color and Edema. Color of the skin at the wound edge may blanch or begin to draw together very tightly (see *Color Plate 34*). Gelatinous edema may be present, signifying an episode of trauma.

Periwound Skin Temperature and Pain. Compared to the temperature of the adjacent skin, periwound skin during the chronic proliferation phase may be cool or mildly elevated, and there may be some signs of intense pain. This could indicate that the wound has been traumatized and is having another episode of acute inflammation, or there may be presence of infection.

Undermining and Tunneling. Chronic proliferation develops when the tissue integrity is not reestablished. The tunneling can extend a long distance and presents an opportunity for infection to travel up the fascial plane. Tissues in the tunnel may be necrotic. Tunneling can become a sinus tract, which is defined as a cavity or channel underlying a wound that involves an area larger than the visible surface of the wound. An abscess may form in the tunnel or sinus tract.[2] When undermining/tunneling persists in a proliferating wound and the assessment findings include a black hole that has no reachable bottom, the wound needs urgent medical management.

Wound Tissue. A wound in chronic proliferation may exhibit attributes of infection, poor vascular supply, desiccation, or hypergranulation. Poor vascular supply will appear as a pale pink, minimally granulating wound. A contrary opinion of some clinicians is that certain wounds that develop a livid red surface color may be infected and slow to heal (see *Color Plate 40*). Infection in granulating wounds is disruptive to healing. The features of infection that may be observed in granulating wounds are superficial bridging, friable tissue, bleeding on contact, pain in the wound, and a delay in healing. There are two stages in the proliferation

phase when the granulation tissue may show these characteristics of infection, about 10 days postoperatively and at the end stage of healing, when the wound has progressed satisfactorily and then becomes indolent.[31] *Color Plates 10 and 11* show the same wound. In *Color Plate 10* the wound was progressing through the proliferation phase. Seven days later the wound has attributes of infection, the proliferation has ceased, and the wound is now in the chronic proliferation phase. Trauma can also retard proliferation. Pale pink, blanched to dull dusky red granulation tissue indicates poor vascular supply. Desiccated granulation tissue is dark, dull garnet red. Hemorrhaging or bleeding of the granulation tissue vessels causes an acute inflammation to the area and promotes scarring. Hemorrhaging on the granulation tissue looks like a purple bruise on the surface. In *Color Plate 11* note the small hemorrhagic area at the center of the wound, indicating rupture of blood vessels.

In Chapter 2 the processes that result in disruption of granulation tissue regulation that allow hypergranulation to occur are explained. Normally, the process of granulation decreases as the wound space decreases and the wound integrity is recovered. The granulation tissue fills the wound space to the surface; the epithelialization process then covers the wound. But when the "flowering" of the granulation tissue overflows the wound bed, the epithelial cells cannot climb the hill of granulation tissue against gravity and the result is that the epithelialization process is halted. See *Color Plate 23* for hypergranulation. If hypergranulation persists, the wound moves into a chronic proliferation phase. The Clinical Wisdom below describes some methods that are commonly used to control hypergranulation. There have been some suggestions about the use of dressings to control hypergranulation, but these methods are unproven and remain anecdotal.

Wound Edges. The chronic proliferation phase develops when the wound edges roll in and become hard and fibrotic, which inhibits further wound contraction. See *Color Plate 33* for an example of rolled fibrotic edges. Wounds of different pathogeneses develop this problem, including pressure ulcers and venous ulcers. This finding may trigger a referral to a surgeon to excise the rolled edge to restart the healing process.

Wound Drainage. Chronic proliferation exudate may be a yellow, gelatinous, viscous material on the wound granulation base that indicates the wound has been traumatized. This should not be confused with wound dressings such as amorphous hydrogels or treatments such as antimicrobial ointments. An infected wound in chronic proliferation may have a malodorous, viscous, reddish brown, green, or gray exudate. *Color Plate 40* shows an apparently clean wound, but the wound dressing shows signs of moderate to large amounts of sanguineous and purulent reddish brown exudate. This wound is in the chronic proliferation phase and needs treatment to recover.

Absence of Proliferation Phase

Periwound Skin: Color, Edema, Pain, and Temperature. The presence of hemosiderin staining or a halo of erythema will surround the wound, signifying a wound that is also in the chronic inflammation phase. The skin may show signs of ecchymosis. Edema and pain will be minimal or absent. Temperature change is minimal increase or coolness.

Wound Tissue. A wound in an absence of proliferation phase is either not producing granulation tissue or not contracting (see *Color Plate 31*). The wound tissue may look dry, dull red, and desiccated or may contain pale pink granulation tissue. There is lack of change in wound depth. Not much is written describing an absence of proliferation. The wound that is in the chronic inflammation phase or absence of inflammation phase also has absence of a proliferation phase. The wound is not progressing through the proliferative phase. Wounds in this situation often have a surface appearance of necrotic tissue and/or hemorrhage/ecchymosis. Any signs of ecchymosis would signify a restart of an inflammatory process within the wound. The chronic inflammation phase and absence of the proliferation phase can both be used as functional diagnoses for the same wound. The prognosis would be for the wound to progress to the acute proliferation phase. The medical history and systems review should guide the clinician to investigate the impairments to the proliferation process.

Wound Edges. Wound edges may be rolled or jagged and the shape is irregular. The wound does not change shape, signifying lack of wound contraction. Deep wounds may have absence of continuity of wound bed and edges. The wound is not reducing in size.

Wound Drainage. Wounds have absence of exudate or scant serous exudate. The wound in *Color Plate 43* is in the chronic inflammation phase and has absence of a proliferation phase. Note the scant amount of serous exudate on the wound dressing. Treatment interventions should be reviewed to see why the wound lacks moisture.

Summary of Three Proliferation Phase Diagnosis and Prognosis

Table 3–8 summarizes the findings for each aspect of the proliferation phase. The presence of the following attributes signifies that the wound healing phase diagnosis is *acute proliferation phase*: beefy red granulation tissue in the wound bed (reduced depth); wound contraction (reduced surface open area, regular wound edges and shape); serous or serosanguineous exudate of moderate to minimal amount; and normalized peripheral skin temperature, turgor, and color. The prognosis is that reassessment will show reduction in depth and closing of the undermined/tunneled space with measurable reduction in overall size estimate as the integrity of the tissue is reestablished.

Failure to progress as expected through the proliferation phase signifies a wound healing phase diagnosis of *chronic proliferation* or *absence of proliferation*. The evaluation of a halt to proliferation should be given careful consideration. For example, infection during proliferation retards healing and causes a chronic proliferation phase. If superficial bridging, friable tissue, bleeding on contact, pain in the wound, and a delay in healing are observed, the evaluation would be positive for infection. Wounds with early signs of infection are treated with a regimen of oral antibiotics for 2 to 4 weeks and those that have late healing signs of infection are treated with topical antibiotics.[31] The prognosis is that the wound will resume progression through the phases of healing following intervention with antibiotics. Failure to initiate an inflammatory phase will cause absence of a proliferation phase. Iatrogenic wound care may also cause the wound to have absence of a proliferation phase. The prognosis is that the inflammation phase will be initiated (if body systems can support it) and will progress to the proliferation phase. Another possibility of prognosis is that the proliferation phase will be initiated following change in treatment.

Once again, the phases of healing overlap; the wound healing phase diagnosis if the wound is transitioning from one phase to the next is defined by the *primary* phase appearance. A wound healing phase diagnosis of *acute proliferation phase* means that most (50% or greater) of the wound surface appearance attributes, granulation tissue and contraction, are observed. If less than 50% of the proliferation attributes are identified, the wound is primarily in an inflammatory phase and has not yet reached the proliferative phase

Table 3–8 Wound Healing Phase Diagnosis: Tissue Characteristics for Proliferation Phase

Periwound Skin and Wound Tissue Characteristics	Acute Proliferation	Chronic Proliferation	Absence of Proliferation
Periwound skin color	• Continuity with adjacent skin • Hemosiderin staining if recovering chronic wound	• Continuity with adjacent skin • Paler than adjacent skin • Hemosiderin staining • Ecchymosis (purple bruising)	• Hemosiderin staining if chronic wound • Halo of erythema if in chronic inflammatory phase • Ecchymosis (purple bruising)
Edema and induration	• Absent	• Gelatinous edema may be present signifying trauma	• Minimal edema present
Tissue temperature	• Temperature may be minimally elevated if wound is well perfused	• Minimal change or coolness	• Minimal change or coolness
Pain	• Pain free or minimal • Inappropriate indicator in presence of neuropathy	• Painful, may be indicator of local inflammation; if intense, consider infection	• Minimal or absent • Intense if infection present
Wound tissue	• Shiny bright red to pink granulation • Sustained reduction in wound depth • Sustained wound contraction • Reduced size • Covering of yellow fibrinous membrane on granulation tissue	• Livid red • Hypergranulation • Desiccation (dark red color) • Poor vascularization (pale pink) • Ecchymosis (purple bruising) on granulation	• Necrotic tissue—stuck in chronic inflammation phase • Ecchymosis (purple bruising) on granulation inflammation restarting • Dull red—desiccated granulation • Pale pink granulation • Lacking change in wound depth • Unsustained contraction—no reduction in size of surface area
Undermining/tunneling	• May be present in deep wounds • Closes as proliferation progresses	• May be present in deep wounds • Fails to close or may extend • Has potential for infection and abscess	• May be present in deep wounds • Fails to close or may extend • Has potential for infection and abscess
Wound edges	• Soft to firm • Flexible to touch • Rolled if full thickness • Change in wound shape from irregular to regular • Reduction in size of surface area • Drawing together • Adherence of wound edges by end of phase	• Tight drawing together to reduce size—contracture • Absence of continuity of wound bed and edges • Rolled • Fibrotic • Ecchymosis (purple bruising) on wound edge	• Unchanged size • Rolled or jagged irregular edges • Fibrotic • No change of shape—not drawing together • Absence of continuity of wound bed and edges

continues

Table 3–8 continued

Periwound Skin and Wound Tissue Characteristics	Acute Proliferation	Chronic Proliferation	Absence of Proliferation
Wound drainage	• Serosanguineous or serous in moderate to minimal amount for wound size	• Yellow gelatinous following trauma • Infection: viscous malodorous, red/brown, green, purulent • Large amount	• Serous drainage scant to minimal amounts • Desiccated and dry
Color Plates	3 to 5, 8 to 10, 18	11, 34 to 36, 39, 40	30, 31, 43

for diagnostic purposes. The diagnosis would be written *inflammation phase/proliferation phase*.

A wound with infection of the granulation tissue has impaired healing and would carry a wound healing phase diagnosis of *chronic proliferation*. A clean wound that is not producing granulation tissue or contracting is in a wound healing phase of *absence of proliferation*.

Clinical Wisdom: *Describing a Wound in the Proliferation Phase*

Example of a narrative note describing a wound in the acute proliferation phase:

Evaluation: A wound on the right hip has beefy red granulation tissue. The wound edges are firm and soft. Wound is contracting into a rectangular shape.

Wound healing phase diagnosis: The wound healing phase diagnosis is *proliferation* phase.

Epithelialization Phase

Acute Epithelialization Phase

Periwound Skin. Since acute epithelialization begins at the time of wounding concurrently with the inflammation phase and overlaps the other phases, expect the signs of acute inflammation to also be observed in the periwound skin. As the acute inflammation process subsides, the periwound skin should return to the usual color for ethnicity, temperature of adjacent tissues, and should be firm but not hard, edematous, or fibrotic. Maceration of the periwound skin and new

epidermis may occur from leakage of wound exudate or use of products that moisten the skin and saturate the cells. Maceration is especially damaging to new epithelium. Macerated skin looks pale and wrinkled and feels soft and thin to touch, making it very susceptible to trauma such as from pressure.

Clinical Wisdom:
Protection of Skin from Maceration

Skin barriers are products that can be used over the periwound skin and new scar tissue to protect them from maceration.

Wound Edges and Wound Bed Tissue. Epithelial cells start migrating toward the center from the wound edges to cover the defect with new skin within hours of wounding. Epithelialization occurs from several directions. The edges are a source of keratinocytes that cover the wound surface with epithelium. The wound edges must be adhered to the wound base for epithelial cell migration to cover the wound. The leading edge of the migrating cells is one cell thick. Gradually the epithelium spreads across the wound bed, as shown in *Color Plates 5 and 6* of the same wound. The migrating tissue is connected to the adjacent skin and will pull it along to cover the opening.[33] The new skin will be bright pink regardless of normal pigmentation and may never regain the melanin factors that color skin (see *Color Plates 8 and 22*). New skin is formed as a very thin sheet, and it takes several weeks for the new skin to thicken. If the wound is less than full thickness, islands of pink epithelium may appear in the wound bed from migrating cells donated by the dermal appendages, the hair follicles, and the sweat glands. Cells from these islands and edges spread out and cover the open area. *Color Plate 55* shows a wound with an island of epithelium. *Color Plate 56* of the same wound shows the migration of the epithelium across the wound from the edges and from the island. Notice in *Color Plate 56* how the edges of the new epithelium are jagged. Full-thickness wounds lose these island contributors and they never regenerate.[32] Full-thickness wounds begin to epithelialize when the edges are attached and even with the wound so that there are no sides or walls, and the epithelial cells can migrate from the edge across the wound surface. Edges are soft to firm and are flexible to touch, as shown in *Color Plate 18*. This wound went on to heal by epithelialization from the wound edges. The wound environment is critical to a successful epithelialization phase. The wound must be kept warm, moist, and free of trauma at all times.

Wounds may bypass this phase of repair if it is preferable to place a skin graft or muscle flap to close the wound. Large wounds and wounds in areas where contraction will be harmful or where it will simply take too long to cover the wound may benefit from surgical repair. The wound shown in *Color Plate 56* was closed at that time by a split-thickness skin graft to speed the repair process.

Clinical Wisdom: *Maintaining a Moist Wound Bed for Epithelialization*

Amorphous hydrogel dressings are useful wound moisturizers and, along with moisture-permeable films and sheet hydrogels, provide the warm, moist homeostatic environment critical for epithelialization.

Wound Drainage. A scant or small amount of serous or serosanguineous wound exudate is expected. The wound must be kept moist during this phase of healing because desiccation will destroy the epithelial cells.

Chronic Epithelialization Phase

Periwound Skin. The characteristics of the skin may be the same as chronic or absence of inflammation phase. The periwound skin may show signs of ischemia such as a pale or ashen color in the elevated position, which deepens to dark purple with dependency (rubor). Pain may be a constant, throbbing pain or intermittent claudication during walking, if it is associated with arterial occlusive disease. The appearance of the adjacent skin is usually dry, shiny, taut, and/or hairless. These are indicators of loss of hair fol-licles, sweat, and/or sebaceous glands. The wound shown in *Color Plate 57* is in the chronic epithelialization and chronic inflammation phase. The appearance of adjacent and periwound skin changed as chronicity was altered and acute epithelialization and proliferation phases were initiated (*Color Plate 59*).

Wound Edges. Epithelialization of deep wounds occurs only at the edges and may involve thickening and rolling under of the edges. If the cells cannot continue to migrate across the wound they will build up an epithelial ridge along the edge of the wound, as seen in *Color Plate 40*. Pressure ulcers typically develop a round shape when this occurs. Wounds in chronic epithelialization have cells piled on each until the rolled, thickened edges become fibrotic. The wound edges need to be modified and the wound bed filled before wound epithelialization will be reinitiated. Hyperkeratosis is another abnormality of the epithelialization phase. Hyperkeratosis is overgrowth of the horny layer of the skin. *Color Plate 24* shows a wound with hyperkeratosis and an irregular shape of a heel ulcer of a 100-year-old woman.

Scar Tissue. The majority of wound closure in humans is by granulation tissue formation followed by epithelialization.[32] New epithelium of scar tissue is bright pink, regardless of the pigmentation of normal skin. In darkly pigmented skin, the scar tissue may never be repigmented. The bright pink color may fade over time to a lighter shade of pink as the vascular system is fully reestablished.

Wound Tissue. The wound bed tissue that is hypergranulating may develop a chronic epithelialization phase because the epithelial cells cannot migrate over the hump of granulation tissue against gravity (see *Color Plate 23*). The granulation tissue must be trimmed back to be level with the periwound skin for epithelialization to resume.

Wound Drainage. Wound drainage may be nonexistent and the wound dry. If no or scanty exudate is assessed, additional moisture may be needed to facilitate the migration of the epithelial cells. Epidermal cells migrate best in a warm moist environment. Wound dryness can be due to improper dressing selection, loss of dressing, dehydration of the wound or patient, or other iatrogenic conditions. On the other hand, there may be heavy exudate from a partial-thickness ulcer that should be epithelializing, but the exudate washes out of the epidermal cells faster than they can migrate and attach to the wound surface. Excessive moisture associated with wound products may also cause this to occur. Management of the wound moisture would be required.

Absence of Epithelialization Phase

Absence of the epithelialization phase may be due to intrinsic, extrinsic, or iatrogenic causes that may be identified during the assessment.

Color. The color of the adjacent and periwound skin offers clues to the etiology of absence of the epithelialization phase. Absence of the epithelialization phase may be related to an intrinsic condition such as arterial obstructive disease (AOD). AOD limits blood supply and oxygen to the tissues and impairs the function of the skin to repair itself. Examination of adjacent skin will reveal absence of hair, dependent rubor, and pallor on elevation. The wound will have a punched-out appearance and a very limited ring of epidermal tissue around the wound that will not migrate across the wound, as shown in *Color Plate 48*. If no prior vascular testing is reported, these findings would indicate the need for further assessment of the vascular system. Chapter 6 should be consulted for testing suggestions.

Texture. Periwound skin that is dry and flaky, has an irregular texture, or is macerated provides limited epidermal cells to resurface the wound. The wound will lack epithelialization activity.

Skin Temperature. Skin temperature is a reflection of blood supply. Skin temperature cooler than 92°F to 96°F on the torso and lower in the extremities (75°F to 80°F) is an indicator that blood supply to the skin may be limited; warmer skin may be due to infection.

Edema. Chronic edema caused by tissue congestion such as lymphedema, congestive heart failure, or venous insufficiency stretches the skin and fills interstitial spaces with excess fluid, including large protein molecules. When the capacity of the tissue to hold fluid is exceeded, the fluid leaks through the skin. Because of the disease process, changes occur in the vascularity of the tissues, leading to loss of dermal appendages and dry stasis eczema. The changes are known as lipodermatosclerosis.[34] Skin changes associated with this disease process are shown in *Color Plates 53 and 54*. Patients with lipodermatosclerosis may show absence of epithelialization phase. More information on lipodermatosclerosis is presented in Chapter 14.

Wound Edges. Another example of an intrinsic factor that causes absence of epithelialization is decreased epidermal proliferation due to delayed cellular migration attributed to aging. There is slow or absence of new skin growth from edges or islands. Absence of epithelialization attributes include dry, flaky, hyperkeratotic skin at the wound edges. The dryness may be associated with a dry wound environment.

Wound Tissue. Hypogranulation results from an absence of the proliferation phase and failure to fill the wound bed and provide a surface for the epidermal cells to migrate across to cover the wound.

Summary of Three Epithelialization Phase Diagnosis and Prognosis

The *epithelialization phase* of healing begins with epithelial migration during the inflammation phase of healing. Partial-thickness wound epithelialization may progress from islands in the center of the wound as well as from the wound edges. Full-thickness and deeper wound healing by epithelialization will be arrested if a large amount of wound debris interferes or if the wound edges fall off into a deep wound bed with steep walls or are nonadhered to the wound bed. Throughout the wound healing process the phases overlap, and it is not at all unusual for the epithelialization, inflammation, and proliferation phases to overlap and attributes of each to be identified. Table 3–9 summarizes the findings during the epithelialization phase.

A wound phase diagnosis of *epithelialization phase* is based on findings that the wound is resurfacing. Partial-thickness wounds that are resurfacing from the middle or edges are in the *epithelialization phase*. Wounds that are greater than 50% attached at the edges and do not have steep walls that are epithelializing are also diagnosed as being in the *epithelialization phase*. Wounds in the acute epithelialization phase have an excellent prognosis for healing. Wounds in the chronic epithelialization phase need an intervention that will restart the healing process. The prognosis then would be wound will heal with intervention. For example, the surgeon may need to excise the fibrotic wound edges. An absent or chronic proliferation phase may need initiation before cells can migrate over the surface. Wounds that have absence of the epithelialization phase of healing have high risk for nonhealing unless intrinsic or iatrogenic conditions can be altered, for example, by reperfusion or application of moisture-retentive dressings.

Clinical Wisdom: *Describing a Wound in the Epithelialization Phase*

Example of narrative note describing a wound in the epithelialization phase:

Evaluation: A wound on the left medial ankle is adhered at 75% of the edges and epithelialization is progressing over 50% of the open area.

Wound healing phase diagnosis: The wound is in the the epithelialization phase.

Table 3–9 Wound Healing Phase Diagnosis: Tissue Characteristics for Epithelialization Phase

Periwound Skin and Wound Tissue Characteristics	Acute Epithelialization	Chronic Epithelialization	Absence of Epithelialization
Periwound skin	• Early phase has same characteristics as acute inflammation phase • Returns to normal color for ethnicity as inflammation subsides • Hemosiderin stain if chronic wound	• May be same as chronic or absence of inflammation phase • May be ischemic (pale) or ashen • May be purplish with dependency • Dry, flaky (hyperkeratotic—may be due to desiccation or aging skin) • Maceration: pale, wrinkled, soft, thin • Hemosiderin stain	• Scar tissue • Same as chronic or absence of inflammation phase • Dry with hyperkeratosis or lipodermatosclerosis
Wound tissue	• Even with wound edges • Pink/red granulation • Reduction in wound surface area	• Not connected with wound edge • Hypergranulation	• Absence of resurfacing from edges or dermal appendages • Hypogranulation • Presence of scab or necrotic tissue
Undermining/tunneling	• Steep walls limit migration	• Steep walls limit migration	• Steep walls limit migration
Wound edges	• New skin moves out from wound edge and dermal appendages in irregular pattern • Bright pink color regardless of usual skin pigmentation • Texture is soft to firm and flexible to touch, thin	• Epithelial ridge • Rolled under or thickened • Dry flaky skin • Rounding off of wound shape	• Fibrotic wound edge • Rounding off of wound shape and edges • Macerated • Dry flaky skin
Wound drainage	• Minimal to scant serous or serosanguineous	• Absent, dry; if hypergranulation, minimal/moderate	• Absent, dry
Scar tissue	• Thin layers of scar tissue • Thickens over time • Deep pink color initially; changes to bright pink color regardless of usual skin pigmentation	• Hypertrophic scarring • Keloid scarring • Hyperkeratotic scarring	• Weak, friable epithelial tissue • Breaks or washes out
Color Plates	5, 22, 55, 56, 59	24, 48	33, 37, 48, 54 58

REFERRAL CRITERIA

Utilization management requires that the patient's problems be identified and triaged early to the medical care provider most appropriate to the patient's wound severity or wound healing phase diagnosis. Referral should be made when there are findings that require the attention of another discipline more skilled or more knowledgeable in management of the identified problem. Referral will depend on where the patient is to be seen, the available resources, and other very significant factors. For instance, skin lesions that have not been described in this chapter include scales associated with psoriasis, papules such as warts and tumors, vesicles such as chickenpox, and shingles, which are examples of skin conditions that may be seen on the adjacent skin and should be referred to a dermatologist. Wounds that have a history of nonhealing for long periods of time may be cancerous, and they should be referred to a dermatologist for biopsy evaluation. Deep wounds that can be probed to the bone should be considered positive for osteomyelitis and need evaluation by the orthopaedic surgeon. Wounds that are in the chronic inflammation phase need enhanced perfusion to achieve conversion to an acute inflammation phase. Vascular assessment would be a primary consideration, and the vascular technician may be the most qualified to provide the service. Reperfusion requires the expertise of the vascular surgeon. A wound with deep tunneling should be referred to the plastic surgeon. The physical therapist has skills in exercise, use of physical agents, and electrotherapeutic modalities, all of which enhance perfusion to tissues. Exhibit 3–4 is a list of possible referral sources.

CONCLUSION

Wound classification systems are used to identify the wound severity by the depth of tissue impairment leading to a functional diagnosis of *impaired skin integrity* (if the dermis is not penetrated) or *impaired tissue integrity* (if the wound extends through the dermis and deeper). Wound healing assessment by biologic wound healing phase includes three aspects for each biologic phase: acute, chronic, or absent. Each phase describes the attributes of the acute, chronic, or absent state of the phase by symptoms found in the periwound skin and the wound tissues. The nurse or physical therapist needs to know where in the trajectory of healing the wound is at baseline assessment to plan treatment, make a diagnosis and prognosis of healing, select interventions, predict outcomes, and triage patients.

The assessment is usually completed by the same person, but this is not always the case. The evaluator may be a person more highly skilled and trained in interpretive skills than

Exhibit 3–4 Referral Sources

Physicians	Nursing	Allied Health
Dermatologist	Dermatology Nurse	Physical Therapist
Orthopaedic Surgeon	Enterostomal Nurse	Podiatrist
Plastic Surgeon	Geriatric Nurse Practitioner	Vascular Technician
Vascular Surgeon	Vascular Nurse	

the collector. For example, examination and recording of the different wound characteristics may be collected by a properly trained physical therapist assistant or a licensed practical nurse, and the evaluation of the findings, the wound healing diagnosis, and the prognosis may be completed by the physical therapist, the registered nurse, or the enterostomal nurse. Collection tools to grade, record, and monitor findings are described in Chapter 5. Documentation requirements for wound assessment should be part of the facility policies and procedures. Documentation should be accurate, clearly reflect the patient's condition, and be consistent with documentation by others in the same department or facility. If it is not documented, it did not happen.

REFERENCES

1. van Rijswijk L. Frequency of reassessment of pressure ulcers, NPUAP Proceedings. *Adv Wound Care.* July/August 1995; 8(4 Supp):19–24.

2. van Rijswijk L, Polansky M. Predictors of time to healing deep pressure ulcers. *Ostomy Wound Manage.* 1994;40(8):40–42.

3. Bergstrom N, et al. *Treatment of Pressure Ulcers.* Clinical Practice Guideline No. 15. AHCPR Publication No. 95-0652. Rockville, MD: Agency for Health Care Policy and Research, U.S. Department of Health and Human Services; December 1994.

4. National Pressure Ulcer Advisory Panel (NPUAP). Pressure ulcers: prevalence, cost and risk assessment: consensus development conference statement. *Decubitus.* 1989;2(2):24–28.

5. Wagner FW. The dysvascular foot: a system for diagnosis and treatment. *Foot Ankle.* 1981;3:64–122.

6. Shea JD. Pressure sore: classification and management. *Clin Orthop.* 1975;112:89–100.

7. Bergstrom N, et al. *Pressure Ulcers in Adults: Prediction and Prevention.* Rockville, MD: Agency for Health Care Policy and Research, U.S. Department of Health and Human Services; May 1992.

8. Henderson CT, et al. Draft definition of stage I pressure ulcers: inclusion of persons with darkly pigmented skin. *Adv Wound Care.* 1997;10(5):16–19.

9. Krasner D, Weir D. Recommendations for using reverse staging to complete the M.D.S.-2. *Ostomy Wound Manage.* 1997;43(3):14–17.

10. Ferrell BA, Osterweil D, Christenson P. A randomized clinical trial of low-air-loss beds for treatment of pressure ulcers. *JAMA.* 1993;269:494–497.

11. Cuzzell J.Z. The new RYB color code. *AJN.* 1988;88(10):1342–1346.

12. Carpenito LJ. *Nursing Diagnosis, Application to Clinical Practice.* 6th ed. Philadelphia: JB Lippincott Co; 1995:701–713.

13. Integumentary Panel. Guide to physical therapist practice, II. *Phys Ther.* 1997;77:1163–1650.

14. Abeln S. Reporting risk check-up. *PT Magazine.* October 1997; 5(10):38.

15. Greenman PE. Principles of structured diagnosis. In: *Principles of Manual Medicine.* 2nd ed. Baltimore: Williams & Wilkins; 1996:13–20.

16. Mackelbust J, Siegreen M. Glossary, pressure ulcers. In: *Guidelines for Prevention and Nursing Management.* 2nd ed. Springhouse, PA: Springhouse; 1996:8–9.

17. Mackelbust J, Siegreen M. Glossary, pressure ulcers. In: *Guidelines for Prevention and Nursing Management.* West Dundee, IL: S.N. Publications; 1991:14–15.

18. Throne N. The problem of the black skin. *Nursing Times.* August 1969;999–1001.

19. Weiss EL. Connective tissue in wound healing. In: McCulloch J, Kloth L, Feedar J, eds. *Wound Healing Alternatives in Management.* 2nd ed. Philadelphia: F.A. Davis; 1995:26–28.

20. Harkless LB, Dennis K. Role of the podiatrist. In: Levin ME, O'Neal LW, Bowker JH, eds. *The Diabetic Foot.* 5th ed. St. Louis, MO: Mosby–Year Book; 1993:516–517.

21. Ruschhaupt WF III. Vascular disease of diverse origin. In: Young JR, et al., eds. *Peripheral Vascular Diseases.* St. Louis, MO: Mosby–Year Book; 1991:639–650.

22. Parish CP, Witkowski JA. Decubitus ulcers: how to intervene effectively. *Drug Ther.* May 1983.

23. Bennett MA. Report of the task force on the implications for darkly pigmented intact skin in the prediction and prevention of pressure ulcers. *Adv Wound Care.* 1995;8(6):34–35.

24. Roach LB. Assessment: color changes in dark skin. *Nursing 77.* January 1977:48–51.

25. Cavanagh PR, Ulbricht JS. Biomechanics of the foot in diabetes mellitus. In: Levin ME, O'Neal LW, Bowker JH, eds. *The Diabetic Foot.* 5th ed. St. Louis, MO: Mosby–Year Book; 1993:225.

26. Levin ME. Pathogenesis and management of diabetic foot lesions. In: Levin ME, O'Neal LW, Bowker JH, eds. *The Diabetic Foot.* 5th ed. St. Louis, MO: Mosby–Year Book; 1993:43.

27. Fishman T. *Foot and Nail Care.* Presented at the First Annual Wound Management Workshop, Deerfield Beach, Boca Raton, FL, October 1995.

28. Cooper D. The physiology of wound healing: an overview. In: *Chronic Wound Care.* Wayne, PA: Health Management Publications; 1990:1–11.

29. Feedar J. Clinical management of chronic wounds. In: McCulloch J, Kloth L, Feedar J, eds. *Wound Healing Alternatives in Management.* 2nd ed. Philadelphia: F.A. Davis; 1995:140.

30. Sussman C. *Case Presentation: Patient with a Pressure Ulcer;* APTA Scientific Meeting; Minneapolis, MN; June 1996.

31. Harding KG. Wound care: putting theory into clinical practice. In: Krasner D, ed. *Chronic Wound Care: A Clinical Source Book for Health Care Professionals.* 1st ed. Wayne, PA: Health Management Publications; 1990:24.

32. Knighton D, Fiegel VD, Doucette MM. Wound repair: the growth factor revolution. In: Krasner D, ed. *Chronic Wound Care: A Clinical Source Book for Health Care Professionals.* Wayne, PA: Health Management Publications; 1990:441–445.

33. Hardy MA. The biology of scar formation. *Phys Ther.* 1989;69:1014–1024.

34. Micheletti G. Ulcers of the lower extremities. In: Gogia PP, ed. *Clinical Wound Management.* Thorofare, NJ: Slack; 1995:100–101.

CHAPTER 4

Wound Measurements

Carrie Sussman

BASELINE ASSESSMENT

This chapter describes quantitative measurements to measure size and change in size of wounds and extent. Assessment means to test and measure, to perform an examination. It is important to distinguish between examination and evaluation. The examination provides the data that are evaluated. The data may be collected by the physical therapist assistant or the licensed practical nurse. The evaluation of the significance of change in size measurements requires skilled judgment of the registered nurse or licensed physical therapist.

This chapter provides information and step-by-step procedures for performing many measurements of wounds and the surrounding tissues. It also provides a guide to the most commonly used measurements, benefits, and disadvantages. User-friendly helpful hints and clinical wisdoms are sprinkled throughout.

Measurement done at the start of care establishes a baseline wound size. Measurements are performed at regular intervals. The rationale for measurement is to quantify and measure the progression of wound healing.[1] In the home care or long-term care settings measurement is usually recommended at least weekly. The professional case manager, nurse, or physical therapist may choose to select measurements that can be made easily, after training, by an unskilled individual in the home and reported to the skilled professional at a specified interval such as weekly. Linear measurement of the size of an open surface area is an example of a type of measure that might be delegated. Significance would be interpreted by the professional case manager.

Tests and measurements of wound size and extent are important to providers, payers, and regulators, as well as the patient and the family. Well-documented wound measurements can be used as the best legal defense. They also provide strokes for the clinician, who can review the measurements and feel a sense of accomplishment. They may also be the alarm that all is not well. Because the information gathered is important to the interdisciplinary team, the language used requires uniform and consistent terminology to encourage good communication between all.

ACCEPTED MEASUREMENTS

Table 4–1 is an overview of the three different commonly used methods to monitor healing.[2] The table highlights purpose, requirements, and information derived from each method. Many measurement methods and suggestions are included in this chapter. Not all will be useful in all settings. Different skill and interest will determine the methods and measurements used. A table of common usage patterns for wound test and measurements (Table 4–2) is a guide to current practice patterns. Measuring with planimetry and sophisticated computer-assisted or technologic equipment has been omitted because these devices are usually research tools rather than clinical practice approaches.

MEASUREMENT ASSESSMENT FORMS

Examination must be consistent, complete, and accurate. One way to manage uniformity, consistency, and completeness is with the use of forms. Forms guide the examination in a logical sequence and organize the information gathering. Forms may be paper-and-pencil instruments or templates on the computer screen. They are real timesavers because one simply fills in the appropriate information on the preprinted form. Forms become a part of the documentation

Table 4–1 Monitoring Recovery of Chronic Wounds: Photo, Tracing, Measurements

Purpose	Photo	Tracing	Measurements
Objective	Records change in recovery phase or wound stage	Records change within a recovery phase	Linear: estimates size Perimeter: estimates boundary Digitization: approximates surface area
Treatment planning	Validates overall treatment plan	Demonstrates short-term response to treatment plan	Demonstrates rate of recovery
Frequency	Monthly or change in phase/condition	Weekly	Weekly
Time reference	Retrospective	Interim	Ongoing/interim
Requirements	**Photo**	**Tracing**	**Measurements**
Conditions	Correct light, body position, and device to indicate relative size	Use of standard anatomic landmarks and method to transfer tracing to medical record	Use of standard anatomic landmarks
Equipment	Camera and film	Tracing kit	Measurement tool and recording notebook
Information	**Photo**	**Tracing**	**Measurements**
Type	Displays full color picture	Gives black and white three-dimensional picture on two-dimensional form	Provides numeric information
Comparison	Provides color comparison	Represents topographic effects	Summarizes quantitative changes for use in a graph
Use	Clinical medical review, program management, referral source, reports, survey team, legal	Clinical medical review, program management, referral source, reports, survey team, legal	Clinical medical review, program management, referral source, reports, survey team, legal

record. There are numerous forms in use for documenting wound measurements. Exhibit 4–1 is a sample form for performing the wound measurement examination. The form fits into a 4 × 6-in pocket notebook. A new form is used each week, and the forms are kept together in the notebook during the course of care for easy reference to prior week measurements. A sample completed form is given in Exhibit 4–2. Having the measurements together in one place facilitates monitoring of the size changes on a weekly or biweekly basis. When the case is completed, the measurement sheets

are tiled onto pages of note paper with tape and put into the permanent record. This notebook functions like the nurses' treatment or drug record books. When not in use it can be kept in a specific location at the nurses' station or in the physical therapy department for reference. The form uses the clock method described later for monitoring wound depth and undermining. Other measurements can also be taken, using that method or another. Methods of measurement are described later in this chaper. The sample wound form includes the following items:

Table 4–2 Common Usage Patterns for Recording Wound Measurements

Always	Often	Sometimes	Rarely	New
L × W area	Clock L × W area	Depth—greatest	Polaroid grid photo	Depth four points of clock
Tracing shape	Undermining—longest and "mapping"	Tracing on grid	Stereophotography	Undermining four points of clock
	Instant photo with flash		Planimetry	Undermined estimate
	Point and shoot with flash		Digital photography with computer technology	Area of erythema or discoloration in darkly pigmented skin
				Tracing "wound map"
				Tracing "wound map" with graph report

- Wound anatomic location is noted, which on the form is called the wound ID.
- Size is given, including length by width open area, length by width area of erythema (color change), depth, undermining/tunneling, and overall wound size estimate (explained below).
- Period of the wound assessment is given: initial, interim observation week number (OB), and discharge (DC).
- The form also captures information about the wound healing phase. Initials are inserted next to *wound phase* to identify the current wound phase. The initials stand for the phase as follows: I for inflammation phase, P for proliferation, and E for epithelialization as described in Chapter 3.
- Discharge outcome status also should be checked as healed or not healed.

The sample form works well when used in conjunction with the Sussman wound healing tool (SWHT)[3] described in Chapter 5. Data can be entered into a computer database and program outcomes monitored.

Exhibit 4–1 Wound Measurement Form

```
                              Wound Measurements

                                                    Initial      _____
                                                    Discharge    _____
                                                    OBWK#:       _____
                                                    DC Status:   _____

Date: _____     Patient Name: _____

Wound ID:_____ Med Rec #_____

Wound Phase:_____
(all measurements in cm)

Linear Size (cm²):   12:00–6:00   (A)_____  ×  3:00–9:00   (B)_____  = _____
Erythema Size (cm²): 12:00–6:00   (A)_____  ×  3:00–9:00   (B)_____  = _____
Undermined:          12:00 (A1)____  6:00 (A2)____  3:00 (B1)____  9:00 (B2)____
Depth:               12:00 _____   3:00 _____    6:00 _____    9:00 _____
Overall Undermined Estimate:
                     A + A1 + A2 = (a)_____
                     B + B1 + B2 = (b)_____
                     (a) × (b) = _____ cm²

Examiner_____

(OB = the observation week # since start of care)
```

Exhibit 4–2 Completed Wound Measurement Form

```
                              Wound Measurements

                                                    Initial       X
                                                    Discharge    _____
                                                    OBWK#:        O
                                                    DC Status:   _____

Date: 01/03/99      Patient Name: G. Lucky _____

Wound ID: R Trochanter _____ Med Rec# 0397 _____
Wound Phase: Chronic inflammation _____
(all measurements in cm)

Linear Size:      12:00–6:00   (A) 4.4 cm  ×  3:00–9:00   (B) 3.3 cm = 14.52 cm²
Erythema Size:    12:00–6:00   (A) 6.5 cm  ×  3:00–9:00   (B) 4.5cm = 29.25 cm²
Undermined:       12:00 (A1) O   6:00 (A2) 0.5   3:00 (B1) 1.5   9:00 (B2) O
Depth:            12:00 0.3    3:00 0.3    6:00 O    9:00 O
Overall Undermined Estimate:
                  A + A1 + A2 = (a) 4.9
                  B + B1 + B2 = (b) 4.8
                  (a) × (b) = 23.52 cm²

Examiner: B Sweet, PT

(OB = the observation week # since start of care)
```

LOCATION

Document the wound's anatomic location. Location can be an indication of the wound etiology (Table 4–3). For example, wounds located over bony prominences are usually pressure wounds, wounds on the soles of the feet may be due to pressure and insensitivity (diabetic wounds), and wounds over the medial side of the ankle often are venous ulcers. Location provides important information about the expected wound healing. Wounds in areas of diminished blood flow, such as over the tibia, heal slowly.

The anatomic name that clearly describes the wound location should be written. For example, *trochanter* is a clearer descriptor than *hip* and signifies that the wound lies over the bony prominence (Figure 4–1). A circle over the anatomic site on the body diagram gives quick, easy identification of wound location on the documentation form (see sample of recording form, Exhibit 4–3).

If several wounds are clustered close together in a location, they should be noted by either different letters or by references such as outer, inner, upper, or lower. It is important to keep the same reference location ID for all the wounds by name throughout the course of care. If one of the wounds in the cluster heals, this should be noted in the documentation, and the same reference names for the remaining wounds should be retained for further documentation. If several wounds join together and become one, this should be recorded and a new ID name given to the revised wound site. Exhibit 4–3 shows documentation of wound location for multiple wounds.

WOUND SIZE MEASUREMENT ACCURACY AND RELIABILITY

Accurate, complete, uniform, and consistent wound measurements are required to establish a wound diagnosis, plan treatment, and document results. Ways to maximize accuracy include the following:

- Take the measurement the same way each time, from a noted reference point on the body.
- Use the same terminology and units of measure for each measurement.
- When possible, have the same person do repeat measurements.

Careful measurement records even small changes and shows the improved wound status or deterioration.

Recording the wound measurement is also an important part of accurate, consistent measurements. If it isn't recorded, it didn't happen.

- An assistant is helpful as a recorder of the measurements as they are taken. Use a prepared form and then fill in a measurement number at each space indicated on the form. This form can be preprinted or handwritten so nothing is forgotten. Record as soon as each parameter is measured. Memory is not accurate.
- Record a 0 if a characteristic is assessed and found absent. The 0 says that you observed the characteristic and assessed it. For example, partial-thickness wounds are superficial. By the depth measures spaces, a 0 should be written. A blank space does not show that this characteristic was assessed.

Table 4–3 Common Locations for Chronic Wounds by Etiology

Arterial Ulcers	*Pressure Ulcers*	*Neuropathic Ulcers*	*Venous Ulcers*
Lower leg dorsum	Bony prominences:	Plantar surface of foot	Above the ankle
Foot	Ears	Metatarsal heads	Medial lower leg
Malleolus	Shoulder	Heel	
Toe joints	Scapulae	Lateral border of foot	
Lateral border of foot	Sacrum		
	Coccyx		
	Trochanter		
	Ischial tuberosity		
	Knees—condyles, patella		
	Tibia/fibula		
	Malleolus		
	Heel		
	Metatarsal heads		
	Toes		

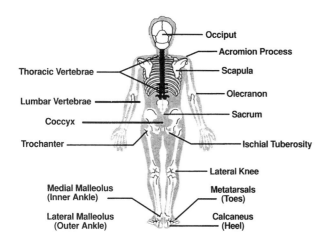

Figure 4–1 Common locations for chronic wounds. Courtesy of Knoll Pharmaceutical Company, Mount Olive, NJ.

Exhibit 4–3 Documenting Wound Location

Documenting Wound Location with Narrative Note:

Example:

1. Single wound location: coccyx
2. Multiple wounds at a location:

Initial note: *Three wounds are located upper, middle, and outer side on the right trochanter.*
    The upper and middle wounds merge. Since they are upper to the outer wound, the same term upper is retained and the merger noted as in this example:
Follow-up note: The upper and middle wounds have merged and will in the future be referred to as the upper wound on the right trochanter.

LINEAR WOUND SIZE MEASUREMENTS

Three types of wound measurements that track the change in the wound size over time are described in this section: open area (OA) measurements (length by width), undermining or tunnels, and depth. The most common wound measurements are the open area length and open area width. The open area length and width of the wound are measured from wound edge to wound edge. The *greatest length and greatest width method* of measurement means that the wound is measured across the diameter of the greatest length and the greatest width. Then the length is multiplied by the width, which gives the estimated square area of the wound or OA. This measurement inflates the size area of the wound. The product results in a single number that can be easily monitored for change in size. These two dimensions are always measured and may be the only measurement recorded. Less frequently measured are undermining/tunnels and depth.

Another way to measure is called the *clock method*. The face of the clock is used to guide the measurement (see Figure 4–2). Select a 12:00 reference position on the wound. Twelve o'clock is usually toward the head of the body but in situations such as severe contractures of the trunk and lower extremities it may be more convenient and easier to reproduce the measurements if another convenient anatomic landmark is selected. For example, measurements in the foot may use the heel or the toes as the 12:00 reference point. In a fetally contracted person, a trochanteric pressure ulcer may be more easily tracked if the 12:00 reference point is toward the knee. Use a clock face and take the measurement from 12:00 to 6:00 and from 3:00 to 9:00.

Both wound measurement methods are acceptable. Choose a method that is comfortable and record which method is used, then use it *consistently*. Exhibit 4–4 lists some advantages and disadvantages of each.

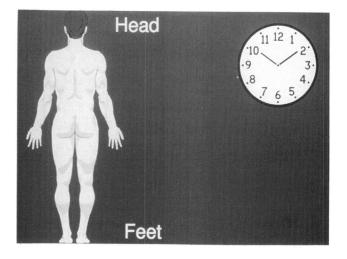

Figure 4–2 Orientation of 12:00 to 6:00 position on the body related to a clock face. Courtesy of Knoll Pharmaceutical Company, Mt. Olive, NJ.

Exhibit 4–4 Comparison of Two Wound Measurement Methods

GREATEST LENGTH BY GREATEST WIDTH METHOD

Advantages

- Simple and easy to learn and use
- Most common method
- Reliable

Disadvantages

- Diameters change as size and shape change, so different diameters are measured each time
- Wound open area will be larger than in clock method

CLOCK METHOD

Advantages

- Simple and easy to learn and use
- Tracks same place on the wound over time
- More conservative measure of area

Disadvantages

- Requires more steps to perform
- More precision required to line up wound points along the clock "face"
- Less commonly used

Supplies Needed for Linear Measurement

Supplies assembled in advance help improve efficiency and reduce examiner and patient fatigue (see Helpful Hints for Measuring).

- Pen or pencil
- Disposable plastic straight edge ruler with linear measure ruled in centimeters
- Disposable gloves
- Normal saline
- Disposable syringe with 18-gauge needle or angiocatheter (for cleaning)

- Gauze paper, form, or pocket-size notebook to record data (see Exhibits 4–1 and 4–2)

How To Measure

Before measuring, the wound should be cleaned and examined closely. Look carefully at the wound edges and see if they are distinct so you are measuring from wound edge to wound edge. Use the following steps:

1. Position patient.
2. Don gloves and remove wound dressing and packing.
3. Place in disposable infectious waste bag.
4. Clean wound with normal saline and syringe with 18-gauge needle or angiocatheter (see Chapter 8 for wound cleansing procedure).
5. Take measurements with disposable wound measurement ruler.
6. Measure the open area greatest length and greatest width from wound edge to wound edge.
7. Record each measurement *as it is taken.*
8. Dispose of wound dressing, measurement instrument, dressing, and gloves in infectious waste container after the procedure is completed.
9. Dispose of the syringe with 18-gauge needle in sharps container.
10. Calculate wound open area.
11. Repeat weekly or more frequently if indicated.

The Clock Method To Measure Open Area

Replace step 6 with the following. Everything else remains the same.

6a. Establish the 12:00 position by choosing an anatomic landmark that will be easy to identify, and make a record for all following measurements. Example ✔ 12:00 toward head.
6b. Mark 12:00 with arrow on the skin. Repeat with marks at 6:00, 3:00, and 9:00.
6c. Measure from wound edge at 12:00 to wound edge at 6:00 position.
6d. Measure from wound edge at 3:00 to wound edge at 9:00 position.

Clinical Wisdom: *Using a Template To Improve Measurement Accuracy*

To improve accuracy and keep the measurements better aligned, cut a circle from paper folded in half twice and mark the four clock points at the four paper folds. Place over wound to use as a guide. Tape paper guide to the periwound skin to keep from shifting.[4] Take all measurements with the template in place for uniformity of tracking the same wound locations for open area, undermining, and depth (see Figure 4–3).

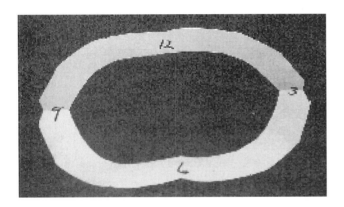

Figure 4–3 Using a template to improve measurement accuracy.

Measurement of Undermining/Tunneling

Measurement of undermining/tunneling shows the extent of wound damage into surrounding deep tissue. Three methods to measure undermining/tunneling are described. Choose one and use it consistently (see *Color Plates 37 and 38*).

Method 1

1. Map undermining around the *entire* wound perimeter by inserting a moist, cotton-tipped applicator into the length of the undermined/tunneled space and continuing around the perimeter. Dip the cotton tip into normal saline before insertion to make it slide in easier and be less likely to cause tissue trauma (see Figure 4–4).
2. At the end point *do not force* further entry but gently push upward until there is a bulge in the skin. Mark the points on the skin with a pen and connect them. Measure two diameters as in the length by width. Calculate by multiplying length by width for *overall undermined estimate* (explained later).

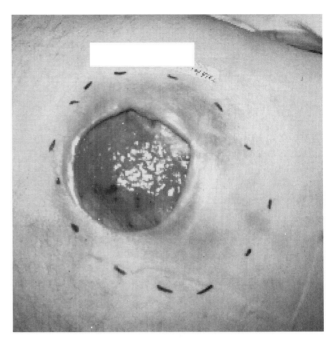

Figure 4–4 Mapping undermining around the entire wound perimeter. *Source:* Copyright © Evonne Fowler, MN, RN, CETN.

Method 2

1. The Sussman method for wound measurement applies the four points of the clock method to measurement of undermining/tunneling.[2] The four cardinal points of the clock, 12, 3, 6, and 9, are used. Twelve o'clock will be toward the head unless otherwise noted (see section on clock method of measurement).
2. Wet the cotton-tipped applicator with normal saline and insert gently into tunnel. The place on the skin where the cotton tip causes a bulge can be marked and the cotton-tipped applicator can be withdrawn.
3. The cotton-tipped applicator is gripped at the point where the skin and the wound edge meet and withdrawn. This is the length of the tunnel.
4. Next place the length of the cotton-tipped applicator up to the withdrawal point against a centimeter ruler or measure from wound edge to mark on skin. Record length.

Method 3

1. Test the perimeter for undermining with a cotton-tipped applicator and then select the longest tunnel to record.
2. Use the clock to identify the location(s) on the wound perimeter where there is tunneling and then track the tunnel over time.

Taylor[4] studied the variability of the measurements of wound undermining among physical therapists trained to use the Sussman wound undermining measurement method. Her findings show that the biggest variation occurred when 12:00 was chosen to coincide with the greatest length of the wound open surface area. This produced an inflation of the area measurements. Her results of reviewing measurements by 39 physical therapists over the 4-week study period demonstrated some interesting findings. For instance, there were three common errors: misreading the measuring device, errors in transferring the numbers, and calculation errors. As would be expected, there was more error in measurement when the wounds were smaller compared with larger wounds. Overall the coefficient of variation for open wound area measurements was 5% or less for intratester replication for 69% of the physical therapists and between 5% and 10% for the balance. The wound overall estimate had intertester variance of 10.5% or less for 100% of the study participants. Validation of the measuring technique was proven as highly reliable and suggests that this measurement can be used to document progress in the healing of undermined wounds.[4]

Two devices are available to aid in wound measurement: the Wound Stick Tunneler and the Wand. Both devices are long, thin rulers. The Tunneler is made of very thin, flat metal (see Figure 4–5). The Wand prototype resembles a fever thermometer and is made of smooth, unbreakable plastic. Both devices have centimeter ruling along the length of the device and can be gently inserted into the undermined space to the point of tissue resistance. ***Never force the instrument into the space.*** To use either device, insert the "1 cm" end into the length of the undermined space. The distance from the inside point of resistance to the edge of the wound is read on the ruler. Read the length from ***under*** the wound edge, ***not*** the visible number. Otherwise extent of undermining will be overstated. These devices can also be used to measure across the open area and from the wound bed to the skin surface for measurement of the depth as described. The depth is read directly from the ruler device. Both devices come in sterile packages and are for single-use application.[4] If the wound undermining/tunneling exceeds the length of the instrument it would signify that a physician should be notified of possible sinus tract formation. Figure 4–6 shows how undermining is measured on a mock latex wound model. Extent can be read to nearest millimeter. See section on accuracy of measurements for more information.

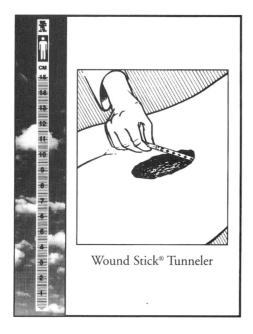

Wound Stick® Tunneler

Figure 4–5 Wound Stick Tunneler. Courtesy of USMS, Miami, Florida.

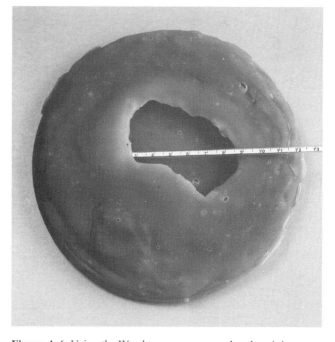

Figure 4–6 Using the Wand to measure wound undermining on a latex wound model. Courtesy of Desmyrna R. Taylor, Loma Linda, California.

Overall Undermined Estimated Size

Undermining/tunneling adds to the extent of tissue involved in the wound. The linear measurement of the extent of the wound undermining/tunneling at the same four points on the clock is added to the open area length and width. This is the overall length and overall width. Next the overall length is multiplied by the overall width to derive an estimate of the *overall undermined estimated size* of the wound area[2] (calculation is shown below). The product is a single number that can be monitored and graphed over time in the manner shown in Figure 4–7. Figure 4–7 shows graphically how the overall undermined estimated size compares with the surface area estimate.[2] If only the open surface area is monitored as change in size, the wound appears significantly smaller than it actually is, and incremental changes in size information are lost.

Other information can be read from the graph. For example, large variations in the extent of the wound noted earlier, between May and July. Whereas notice the linear reduction in wound extent from September to December. As the wound healed, undermined/tunneled spaces closed and tissue integrity was restored, the overall size reduced. Another finding observed from graphing is how the change in undermined estimate also parallels the change in wound phase. Note the abrubt jump in wound overall undermined estimate from 42.25 cm to 122.43 cm. This is frequently coincident with the early proliferative phase. The expansion of the wound extent reflects the effects of wound debridement on loss of subcutaneous tissue integrity (the separation of fascial planes), producing tunneling. Loss of subcutaneous tissue integrity produces increased risk of infection. Subcutaneous tissue integrity is restored as the wound progresses through the proliferative phase to the remodeling phase.

Graphs, like the one illustrated (Figure 4–7), are a very useful visual method to monitor healing over time. The graph can be generated as part of a database program or can be manually drawn on a piece of graph paper.

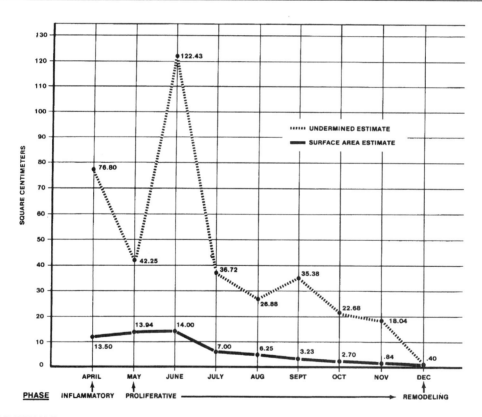

66-YEAR-OLD FEMALE
WOUND TYPE: PRESSURE WOUND
LOCATION: LEFT HIP

Figure 4–7 Wound healing profile: recovery of a pressure wound.

Calculating the Overall Estimate

1. Add the length of the open area from 12:00 to 6:00 to the undermined lengths at both 12:00 and 6:00. This is the overall length of the wound.
2. Add the width of the open area from 3:00 to 9:00 to the undermined lengths at both 3:00 and 9:00. This is the overall width of the wound.
3. Multiply the overall length by the overall width.
4. This equals the overall size estimate of the wound.

Example: Overall Size Estimate

12:00–6:00 length + 12:00 undermining + 6:00 undermining = overall length

3:00–9:00 width + 3:00 undermining + 9:00 undermining = overall width

Overall length × overall width = overall estimated area

☞ **Helpful Hints for Measuring**

1. Wound Measurement Kit

If wound measurements are taken frequently, the job may be easier if you assemble a kit made up of the supplies in the *supplies needed* list for wound measurement that you keep with you in a small plastic carrier.

2. Use An Assistant

An assistant is helpful to:

- Position patient
- Comfort patient
- Act as recorder
- Control wound "sagging" (see below)
- Seek additional supplies or assistance

3. Patient Positioning

It is easier for everyone if both the patient and measurer are comfortable during the procedure. Some patients and some wounds are difficult to position for accurate measuring. Once a convenient and comfortable position to measure is found, record the position that works best. This will save time and effort and improve the uniformity of measures from time to time.
Example: coccyx wound—position: right sidelying; heel wound—position: left sidelying.

4. Order of Measuring

If measurements are always taken in the same order, the tracking of the wound will be more consistent. Suggestion is to take the length first, the width second. If the clock method is used, take 12:00, 6:00, 3:00, and 9:00 in that order for improved consistency.

5. Controlling Sagging Wounds

Full-thickness wounds with undermining may sag because of lack of subcutaneous support and the pull of gravity. Tension on the tissue is hard to maintain. Try to keep sagging to a minimum and maintain uniform tension for accurate length and width measurements.

6. Wound Measurement Pocket Notebook (see Exhibits 4–1 and 4–2)

A 4 × 6-in pocket notebook is useful for recording wound measurements. This can be a spiral notebook or a ring binder. If the information to be gathered is listed in the spiral notebook before doing the measurement, sort of like a handwritten form, it will help consistency, uniformity, and completeness. Another way is to use a preprinted form (see sample) with holes punched to fit a loose leaf notebook. An alphabetic index is also helpful in keeping the records separated by patient name. The small sheets can be taped to a large sheet and placed in the medical record in a cascading fashion. Then numbers do not have to be rewritten. They can also be entered into a computer.

Calculating Percentage Rate of Change in Wound Size

An interesting way to see how a wound is progressing is to look at the percentage rate of change. This is a way to measure and predict successful outcomes. It is a simple statistical calculation that uses the following formula:

1. Baseline (week 0) wound size (OA or overall OA size) measurement is used as the original size.
2. Subtract the next wound size OA or overall OA size measurement (interim) taken from the baseline.
3. Divide by baseline wound measurement and multiply by 100%.

Formula for computing rate of change in wound open area:

$$(\text{Baseline open area (OA)} - \text{Interim open area (OA)}/\text{Baseline open area}) \times 100\%$$

Example:

Wound open area (OA) baseline week 0	$= 30 \text{ cm}^2$
Wound open area (OA) week 1 (interim)	$= 28 \text{ cm}^2$
OA baseline–OA week 1 (interim)	$= 30–28 = 2$
Divide the remainder by the baseline OA	$= 2/30 = 0.066$
To calculate percentage multiply $0.066 \times 100\%$	$= 6.6\%$ = Percentage rate of change

Note: A weekly percentage of change would use the prior week size measurement instead of baseline. Wounds often change drastically in size from one week to another in the early phases of healing and then the rate slows. Referring to the percentage of change measure on a weekly or biweekly basis is a good guide to how the wound is healing.

Measurement of Wound Depth

Wound depth is defined as distance from the visible skin surface to the wound bed.[5] A method to track wound depth is desirable and needed because this measurement is an important indication of the proliferation phase of wound healing. Wound bed surfaces are irregular, and repair is not uniform. It is common practice to try to find the deepest site in the wound bed. This method is difficult to reproduce from measurement to measurement because the wound bed fills in irregularly and what is the deepest spot one time may not be the same spot at the next measurement. Depth measurement accuracy is limited regardless of how this measurement is made; however, the clock method sets repeated measurement sites that can be more closely reproduced at each measurement test than the use of a single "deepest" spot measurement. There is controversy, especially among researchers, about usefulness of the depth measures because of the inaccuracies recorded.[6]

The Clock Method for Measuring Wound Depth

1. Take depth measurements at the 12:00, 3:00, 6:00, and 9:00 positions.[2]
2. Insert a cotton-tipped applicator perpendicular to the wound edge.
3. Grab stick of applicator with fingers at wound skin surface edge.
4. Holding this position on the applicator stick, place applicator stick along a centimeter-ruled edge. Record for each position.
5. These depth measurements may or may *not* be at the deepest area.
6. A separate measurement may be taken and noted at the deepest area.

Partial-thickness wounds have a depth less than 0.2 cm. Wounds with >0.2 cm depth are difficult to measure, and should be recorded as >0.2 cm. Measure the depth of full-thickness wounds of greater than 0.2 cm depth. When a wound is undergoing debridement of nonviable tissue, the wound depth usually increases; but then as the wound bed fills with granulation tissue, the depth decreases. Reduction in wound depth is a measurement of progression through the proliferation phase of healing.

Measurement of wound volume is difficult and is usually reserved for research. Two methods have been reported. One method involves filling the wound with a measured amount of normal saline from a syringe. This works best for wounds that can be positioned horizontally so liquid doesn't spill out. Another method is the use of Jeltrate, an alginate hydrocolloid used by dentists. It has been reported that by pouring the rapidly setting plastic into the wound a mold of the wound can be made. Jeltrate is reported to be well tolerated by the wound tissue.[6] Regardless of which method of measuring wound volume is used, there will be significant inaccuracies. Is it necessary to measure wound volume? At this time, there is questionable value to the taking of volume measurements. Use of this parameter of measurement appears to be of most concern in the research arena and should not be of concern to the clinician.[6]

Measurement of Surrounding Skin Erythema

Erythema of the skin surrounding a wound may be a measure of the inflammation phase of healing or a sign of infection. Chronic wounds often show a halo of erythema but lack the other signs of inflammation. The periwound erythema can be identified as unblanchable redness or a darkening of the skin in darkly pigmented skin. See the Clinical Wisdom box regarding measurement of erythema in darkly pigmented skin. Streaking or significant signs of erythema projecting out a distance from the wound may be an indication of cellulitis, and medical measures are needed. Measurement can be taken using the greatest length and greatest width method, or the clock method can be used. The clock method is described.

The Clock Method To Measure Surrounding Skin Erythema

1. Measure across the wound open area at the 12:00 to the 6:00 position to the outer margin of the periwound erythema.
2. Measure across the wound open area at the 3:00 to the 9:00 position to the outer margin of the periwound erythema.
3. Compute the periwound area of erythema.

Estimated area of erythema:

12:00 to 6:00 length × 3:00 to 9:00 width = _____ cm^2

Example: 9:0 cm × 6.0 cm = 54 cm^2

Wound Tracings

Making a wound tracing is reported to be the most popular and practical method for measuring wound area. It is easy to learn, inexpensive, and readily available.[8] Measuring the wound area from transparency tracings and placing it on graph paper to determine size by counting the centimeters have shown high intra- and intertester reliability (0.99). Compared with linear measurements with a ruler there is less overestimation of the real wound area, although some error can be expected. Using the 1-cm graph paper to count squares has been reported to be quick and efficient.[9] Tracing can be made on acetate measuring sheets such as those that are given out free by many companies for measuring wounds or on

---

Clinical Wisdom: *Measurement of Erythema in Darkly Pigmented Skin*

Skin color changes reported by clinicians and in the literature[7] indicate that, when inflamed, the skin color of darkly pigmented people darkens to an eggplant/purplish color. It may be difficult to differentiate darkening of inflammation from hemosiderin staining. If this is true, proceed with temperature and edema examinations. For a full description of assessment of darkly pigmented skin, see the section on assessment of darkly pigmented skin in Chapter 3. The following are guidelines for measuring the extent of inflammation/trauma in darkly pigmented skin:

- Use natural light or halogen light, not fluorescent light.
- Outline the margins of color change on the surrounding skin with a marking pen.
- Select a reference point for future measures.
- Measure the greatest length and the greatest width or use the clock method.
- Calculate the area of color change (as described for all length-by-width measurements).

---

household plastic wrap with a plastic transparency marking pen (the ink does not bead up). Tracings taped to a sheet of paper can be put in the patient record. However, because taped-on tracings can come loose or ragged in a chart, the tracing and form can be photocopied and the copy placed in the chart. A tracing is a picture of the wound shape. Repeated tracings show change of size and shape over the course of recovery. Accuracy of measurement with tracing is dependent on how carefully the wound edges are followed as the tracing is drawn. Kloth and Feedar[10] documented measurements for patients in a research study. Sussman[11] suggested use of tracings applied to a graph form with a key for tissue assessment called wound assessment form[11] for clinical practice reporting wound healing progression. Following are suggested ways that tracings can be used:

- Tracings show change in the wound perimeter shape over time. Wound shape is a helpful indicator of the rate of healing. As described in Chapter 2, linear wounds contract rapidly, square or rectangular wounds contract at a moderate pace, and circular wounds contract slowly.[9]
- Tracings can be placed on a metric graph form. This shows the wound size as well as shape and provides a three-dimensional pictograph of the wound on a two-dimensional form[11] (see Exhibit 4–5).
- A tracing can become a "wound map" showing features of the wound bed such as necrotic tissue and adjacent tissue characteristics such as erythema (see Exhibit 4–6). Household plastic wrap is better for this because it is clear.

Exhibit 4–5 Wound Assessment Form

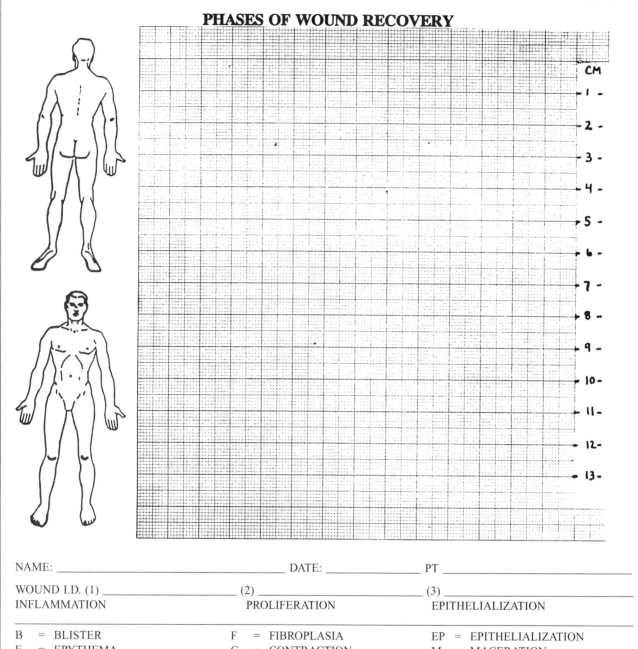

PHASES OF WOUND RECOVERY

NAME: _____ DATE: _____ PT _____

WOUND I.D. (1) _____ (2) _____ (3) _____

INFLAMMATION	PROLIFERATION	EPITHELIALIZATION
B = BLISTER	F = FIBROPLASIA	EP = EPITHELIALIZATION
E = ERYTHEMA	C = CONTRACTION	M = MACERATION
H = HEMORRHAGIC	FT = FULL THICKNESS	R = REMODELED
SB = SCAB	PT = PARTIAL THICKNESS	I = INTACT
N = NECROSIS	U = UNDERMINING	

DRAINAGE:	DRAINAGE:	DRAINAGE:
V = VISCOUS	S = SEROUS	S = SEROUS
PU = PURULENT	SS = SEROSANGUINOUS	DY = DRY

Source: Adapted from Sussman, CA: Physical Therapy Choices for Wound Recovery, *Ostomy/Wound Management,* 1990; 29:20–28, © 1990. Health Management Publications, Inc.

Exhibit 4–6 Wound Assessment Form with Tracing

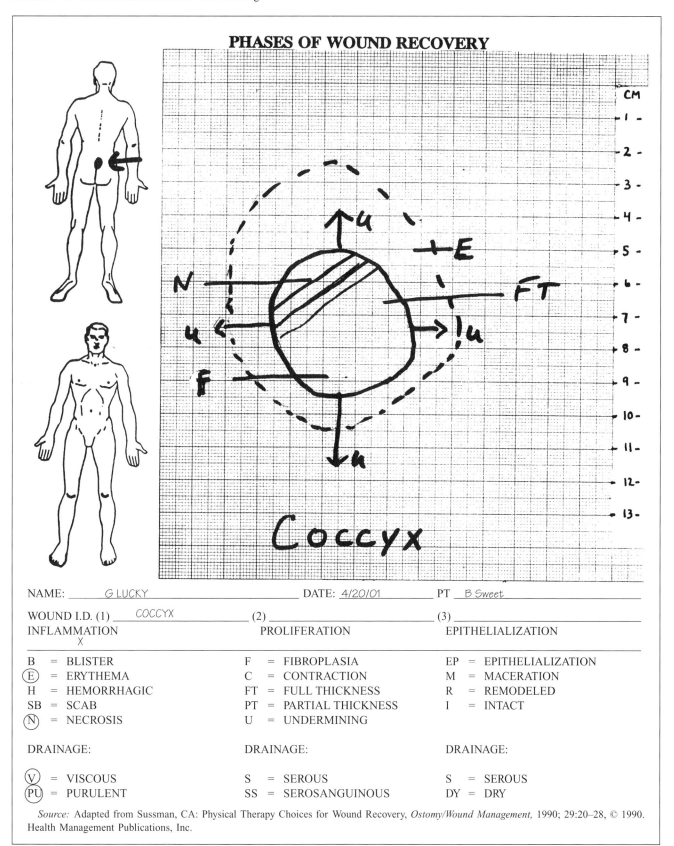

PHASES OF WOUND RECOVERY

Coccyx

NAME: _____ G LUCKY _____ DATE: _4/20/01_ PT _B Sweet_

WOUND I.D. (1) _____ COCCYX _____ (2) _____ (3) _____

INFLAMMATION X   PROLIFERATION   EPITHELIALIZATION

B = BLISTER   F = FIBROPLASIA   EP = EPITHELIALIZATION
Ⓔ = ERYTHEMA   C = CONTRACTION   M = MACERATION
H = HEMORRHAGIC   FT = FULL THICKNESS   R = REMODELED
SB = SCAB   PT = PARTIAL THICKNESS   I = INTACT
Ⓝ = NECROSIS   U = UNDERMINING

DRAINAGE: DRAINAGE: DRAINAGE:

Ⓥ = VISCOUS   S = SEROUS   S = SEROUS
ⓅⓊ = PURULENT   SS = SEROSANGUINOUS   DY = DRY

Source: Adapted from Sussman, CA: Physical Therapy Choices for Wound Recovery, *Ostomy/Wound Management,* 1990; 29:20–28, © 1990. Health Management Publications, Inc.

- The wound map, if placed on the metric graph paper, can have features such as *actual* amount of undermining/tunneling around the wound perimeter drawn in using the actual measurements and a ruler.
- The wound map tracing becomes the tissue attributes assessment documentation by the addition of information about the tissue. A key of tissue attributes with assigned letters for each attribute at the bottom of the graph form makes this an easy way to mark the tissue in the drawing. This is then a paper-and-pencil instrument to track wound healing over time. *Note:* The tissue attributes are the same as those represented in the Sussman wound healing tool described in Chapter 5.
- The wound tracing can be scanned into a computer and a digitized measurement of the wound can be made, the area calculated, and stored in the computer.

Supplies Needed

Assemble all equipment needed:

- Two acetate measuring guides or one each plastic wrap over wound topped by measuring guide
- Two pieces of plastic wrap cut to approximately 6 × 8-in pieces or larger if wound plus periwound erythema is larger
- Fine-point transparent film–type marking pen so ink won't bead up on the plastic (Dark Pentel or Vis a Vis)
- Paper towel, folded in half lengthwise
- Paper or graph form
- Transparent tape

Make a Wound Tracing

1. Place two acetate measuring guides or two pieces of plastic wrap over wound so that the bottom piece is going across wound from 3:00 to 9:00 and the second piece is going from 12:00 to 6:00. This helps when separating the top layer from the bottom layer. Smooth each one to avoid wrinkles. Two layers are used to prevent contamination of the layer with the drawing. The layer that was in contact with the wound will be discarded with infectious waste after tracing is completed.

☞ **Helpful Hints for Tracings**

1. A grid printed on an acetate film that peels off a plastic backing sheet can be used to make wound tracings. The sheet acts as a barrier to infection and is discarded. The tracing is then ready to place in the medical record.
2. The Polaroid Wound Photograph system has a grid available to be used when taking a wound photograph.

2. Draw an arrow on the plastic wrap in the location and direction of the 12:00 position.
3. Trace the wound edges.

Clinical Wisdom: *Tracings on Plastic Sandwich Bags*

A plastic sandwich bag can be placed over the wound and tracing made on top layer. The bottom layer of the bag makes a wound barrier. Slit the bag in half and discard the contaminated layer with infectious waste. The top layer can be put on the graph form or placed in a zippered sandwich bag and kept for comparison measurements. This is very useful for home care.

Optional Additions to Tracings

1. Draw any notable features within or around the wound open area such as outline of the necrotic tissue, exposed bone, etc. Label with a letter from wound assessment form[11] key.
2. Mark areas of erythema/darkened darkly pigmented skin with broken lines around the wound open area.
3. Mark area of necrotic tissue or eschar with diagonal lines.
4. Mark other features with a circle and dots and label.
5. Place the film with drawing so the 12:00 arrow is in the conventional 12:00 position on the graph form. Tape wound tracing onto graph form. Make sure that plastic is taut and free of wrinkles. See instructions for completing the wound assessment form which follows.
6. Copy wound tracing with copier for permanent record. Discard graph with plastic tracing.
7. Mark wound features with lines drawn at right angles to the feature and label.

Wound Assessment Form

The wound assessment form[11] is a paper-and-pencil instrument that consists of a centimeter graph sheet, a linear measurer lined up with the graph coordinates to show size, and an anatomic figure front and back to mark location. The tissue characteristics are listed by phase: inflammation, proliferation, and epithelialization. The key assists the clinician in the evaluation and the development of the wound phase healing diagnosis. The form is shown in Exhibit 4–5 and the completed tracing is shown in Exhibit 4–6.

Supplies Needed

- Wound assessment form
- Wound tracing
- Transparent tape
- Fine-tip marking pen
- Copier (optional)

Use the Wound Assessment Graph Form

1. Prepare wound tracing (see above).
2. Place tracing on assessment form graph with arrow lined up with lines at 12:00 position.
3. Tape tracing in place unless adhesive backed.
4. Draw lines exactly the same length as length measurement taken from the undermining at clock points around wound perimeter starting at wound edges outward.
5. Draw lines from tissue characteristic out to side of graph and label with letter from key.
6. Print wound location at bottom of picture. Mark location on anatomical figures.
7. This "wound map" is also a tissue assessment report.

Note: Tissue characteristics are described in Chapter 3.

Clinical Wisdom:
Using the Wound Tracing for Compliance

The wound tracing is used as an incentive for compliance in diabetic patients. Two wound tracings are made on acetate film or plastic wrap. A date is placed on the tracing next to the wound edge. One copy is placed in the patient records and the other is given to the patient. The next assessment day the patient brings in his or her copy and the copy from the chart is also presented. The wound is redrawn on both pieces of film and dated. The size change is then visually compared. Patients receive positive reinforcement for their compliance by seeing their wounds getting smaller (N. Elftman, personal communication, 1996).

WOUND PHOTOGRAPHY

"A picture is worth a thousand words" best describes the value of wound photography. Serial color photographs record wound tissue characteristics. The lighting will affect the color. Flash photography tends to give a blue tone to the photograph. Incandescent light gives a yellow tone. Photographs are used also to measure the wound size. The accuracy of wound measurement taken from a photograph is compro-

mised by the problem caused by measuring wound area on curved surfaces.[8] Periodic photography is a method often used to validate the overall treatment outcome. Serial photos are great teaching tools for in-services, for referral sources, and for patient encouragement. Photography can be done as simply as shooting an instant camera or by using more complex camera equipment. For example, an instant camera with a grid printed on the film is one method. See Figure 4–8, A to C, for an example of grid photography. Digital camera equipment is now available that interfaces with computer software and performs wound measurements as well as records the color. The cost of such equipment is still high and not readily available to the clinician. Another new option is color print film, which can be shot with a standard 35-mm camera and is processed and returned in three forms: photos, slides and computer disc. One company that offers this service also sells inexpensive (about $20 to $25) software that can read the disc and upload the photos on screen. The computer could store the photographic records. Additional information can be added to each photo for record keeping. Scanning is yet another method for computer inputting of photographs. Complex camera set ups are usually used by researchers. Regardless of which method is used, for good pictures follow these tested suggestions:

- Use a good light source.
- Position patient and wound carefully, ensuring that the patient's private areas are screened from the camera.
- Position a linear measure (ruler) in the photo to show relative size.
- Use a string of known length to measure distance from the camera to the wound for more uniform recording.
- Use an identification sign with patient ID, wound location, and date in the photograph (unless dated by the camera).
- Select a camera with a close-up feature if possible to take the best close-up view of the wound.
- Use an assistant to help maintain the position and perhaps to position the marker.
- Record wound and patient position for repeated photographing sessions, ie, right sidelying.

☞ **Helpful Hint:** *Making an Identification Marker for Photographs*

1. Tape plastic measuring sheet to a 3 × 5-in index card.
2. Put card into a plastic sandwich bag.
3. Put two strips of white tape on plastic sandwich bag.
   — Write patient ID, wound location on first strip (example: W.J., coccyx).
   — Write date on second strip (example: 1/23/99).
4. Throw away the plastic bag.
5. Reuse the card with measuring information.

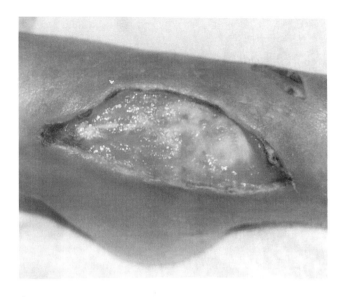

A

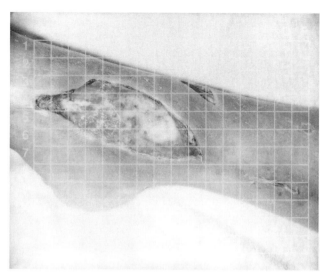

B

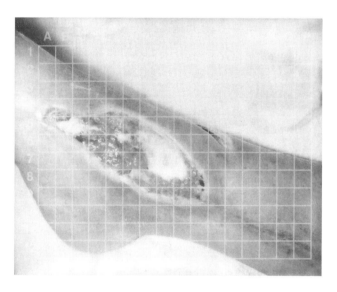

C

Figure 4–8 Grid photography **(A–C).** Shows change in wound size and attributes over time.

REFERRAL CRITERIA

Why include referral criteria with the chapter on measurement? As wound measurements and remeasurements are performed, it may become immediately apparent that a prompt referral is necessary. Following is a list of referral criteria to guide clinical decisions:

- Extent of wound involves bone and/or deep subcutaneous spaces—may indicate osteomyelitis or other infection.
- Impending exposure of a named anatomic structure—wound extent should be evaluated medically.
- Black holes or tunnels that cannot be measured—high-risk situation.
- Wound tunneling may perforate the peritoneal cavity either in the abdomen or rectum.
- Wound size is enlarging more than expected.

REFERRAL SOURCES

There are many health care practitioners who have experience in complex wound management. One or more of these professionals should be contacted for follow-up management if any of the referral criteria listed above are met. Some choices include the following:

Physicians	Nursing	Allied Health
Dermatologist	Dermatology nurse	Physical therapist
Orthopaedic surgeon	Enterostomal	Vascular technician
Plastic surgeon	registered nurse	Podiatrist
Vascular surgeon	Geriatric nurse	
	practitioner	
	Vascular nurse	

SELF-CARE TEACHING GUIDELINES

In today's health care environment, many levels of caregivers may be called upon to measure and monitor the wound size parameters discussed in this chapter and then report to the expert clinician their findings for interpretation. The most successful results occur when step-by-step instructions and return demonstration are given by the designated data collector. Prepare an instruction sheet for measuring and/or for tracing. Include a chart like the one in Exhibit 4–7 for recording the data. First, make an assessment of the person's abilities to follow the directions. If the patient or a lay caregiver is to do the measuring, limit the measurements to length and width. Teach the simple length by width multiplication so that only one number needs to be reported. Making a wound tracing is also within the ability

of many caregivers. Tracing the wound will also help the caregiver to see that the wound is getting smaller as the report number decreases or to see the changes in drawing shape and size. This reinforces both the caregiver's and the patient's compliance. If the wound is not getting smaller, it will be an attention getter and encourage change in treatment planning. A form such as the one illustrated (see Exhibit 4–7) can be faxed to the wound case manager if visits cannot be made on a frequent basis, and the progress of the wound can be followed. If the person to monitor the wound is a paraprofessional, physical therapist assistant, or licensed practical nurse, other wound measurements can be taught and with a high level of expected reliability and confidence.

Sample Instruction Sheet

Wound Measurements

Supplies: plastic measuring sheet, pen, plastic wrap, plastic sandwich bag (one or two), hand-held pocket calculator. Wound measurements are taken once a week or biweekly.

1. Note the date.
2. Measure the longest diameter of the wound in each direction, head to toe (length) and side to side (width). Record the length and width in the appropriate boxes on the form as the measurements are taken.
3. Then multiply the two numbers together for a single total size measurement.

Instructions To Make a Wound Tracing at Home

1. Use either two pieces of plastic wrap or a plastic sandwich bag.
2. Place one layer of plastic against the clean wound. If the plastic becomes foggy, that is, like warm air condensing on eyeglasses, lift a corner of the plastic to

---

Exhibit 4–7 Wound Measurement Record

Name: _____ Medical Record # _____

Date	Length	Width	Total
4/30/04	5 cm	3 cm	15 cm^2
5/15/04	4.5 cm	2.5 cm	11.25 cm^2
5/30/04	4.0 cm	1.75 cm	8.8 cm^2
6/15/04	2.5 cm	1.25 cm	3.13 cm^2

allow the heat and moisture to escape and the fog will go away.

3. When you can see the edges of the wound, use a felt-tip marking pen and draw around the wound edges.
4. Mark the date of the drawing next to the edge of the wound. After the ink is dry (about 10 seconds), lift the top layer of plastic wrap or cut off the top layer of the plastic bag.
5. Save the wound tracing in another clean plastic lunch bag.
6. Discard the dirty plastic sheet.

CONCLUSION

This chapter described a number of different measurement strategies for monitoring wound extent and wound healing by tracking change in four different parameters of size: open surface area, undermining/tunneling, depth, and overall wound estimate. Obviously, to perform all of the above measurements would be overload for most people. All are used commonly. One method will appeal to one facility's practitioners and another to another facility's. This is an opportunity for collaboration. Have a team meeting and decide on the method that meets the needs of the majority of practitioners and conveys the desired information. There is enough similarity between methods that the information communicated through the continuum of care can and will be readily interpreted. The key to successful measurements are consistency and accuracy. Once a method is selected, use it with rigor by all clinicians. Report on a regular, consistent basis.

RESOURCES

- The Wound Stick Tunneler, USMS, Inc., 1172 S. Dixie Highway, Coral Gables, FL 33146
- The Wand and latex wound models: D. Taylor, Loma Linda University, School of Allied Health Professions, Loma Linda, CA
- Plastic/acetate measuring sheets are available from many wound care products companies listed in Appendix A.

REFERENCES

1. van Rijswijk L. Frequency of reassessment of pressure ulcers: National Pressure Ulcer Advisory Panel Proceedings, 1995. *Adv Wound Care.* July/August 1995:19–24.
2. Sussman C, Swanson G. A uniform method to trace and measure chronic wounds. Poster presentation, Symposium for Advanced Wound Care, San Francisco, CA, April 1991.
3. Sussman C, Swanson GH. The utility of Sussman wound healing tool in predicting wound healing outcomes in physical therapy. Presented at the National Pressure Ulcer Advisory Panel Fifth Biennial Conference, Washington DC, February 1997.
4. Taylor DR. Reliability of the Sussman method of measuring wounds that contain undermining. Poster presentation at American Physical Therapy Association Scientific Meeting, San Diego, CA, June 1997.
5. Hess CT. *Nurse's Clinical Guide, Wound Care.* Springhouse, PA: Springhouse; 1995.
6. Gentzkow G. Methods for measuring size in pressure ulcers, National Pressure Ulcer Advisory Panel Proceedings, 1995. *Adv Wound Care.* July/August 1995:43–45.
7. Bennett MA. Report of the task force on implications for darkly pigmented intact skin in the prediction and prevention of pressure ulcers. *Adv Wound Care.* November/December 1995:34–35.
8. Harding K. Methods for assessing change in ulcer status. *Adv Wound Care.* July/August 1995:37–42.
9. Majeske C. Reliability of wound surface area measurement. *Phys Ther.* 1992;72:138–141.
10. Kloth L, Feedar J. Acceleration of wound healing with high voltage, monophasic, pulsed current. *Phys Ther.* 1988;68:503–508.
11. Sussman C. Physical therapy choices for wound recovery. *Ostomy/Wound Manage.* July/August 1990:20–28.

SUGGESTED READING

Hardy MA. Biology of scar formation. *Phys Ther.* 1989;69:1014–1024.

CHAPTER 5

Tools To Measure Wound Healing

Carrie Sussman and Barbara M. Bates-Jensen

INTRODUCTION

Various instruments have been proposed to address the question of monitoring healing, including the Pressure Sore Status Tool (PSST),[1] the Sessing scale,[2] the National Pressure Ulcer Advisory Panel (NPUAP) Pressure Ulcer Scale for Healing (PUSH),[3] the Wound Healing Scale (WHS),[4] and the Sussman Wound Healing Tool (SWHT).[5] None has demonstrated predictive validity for wound healing and none has been validated for measuring healing or worsening of ulcers over time. Table 5–1 shows the factors of wounds and surrounding skin and other factors used in these tools as well as the scoring system used by each. Each of the tools is in development at this time with the idea of deriving a tool that will be valid, reliable, responsive, and practical for the wound care community including providers and payers.

Historically, measurements used to evaluate improvement over time include change in ulcer size, change in surface appearance, tissue type present, and surrounding skin characteristics (see Table 5–2). No single measurement or combination of measurements has been satisfactorily combined into a tool to monitor healing.

Staging systems such as the NPUAP staging system[6] and the Wagner scale,[7] (see Chapter 4) are appropriate for determining initial severity at tissue trauma based on depth of tissue destruction. The information that is reported by assigning a stage of severity is static as opposed to healing, which is dynamic. Staging systems are used in many ways; some are appropriate and others are not. For example, wound stage is used as a criterion for inclusion or exclusion in research studies. The reimbursement system uses the staging system as a criterion for eligibility for products and services.

Product manufacturers also apply the staging system as a criteria for product selection and use as well as marketing. Staging systems have been misapplied as methods of evaluating healing by using a down or reverse staging system to signify healing. The assumption has been made that stage III and stage IV pressure ulcers heal by replacing lost tissue with tissue of the same type and quality as the original. This method of monitoring healing is biologically inaccurate because granulation tissue and scar tissue are not the same structures and lack the function of tissues such as muscle, tendons, subcutaneous fat, and dermis that they replace.[6] There is a need, therefore, for a validated tool that measures healing in a biologically accurate manner.

Criteria for a Wound Healing Tool

Criteria to evaluate the appropriateness and utility of a tool include reliability, validity, responsiveness, sensitivity to change, and clinical practicality.[8]

Validity

For an instrument to be valid the instrument should measure what it is supposed to measure. For instance, a wound healing tool must measure change in attributes highly correlated with wound healing. To be useful, the measurements must be *current*. In order for a tool to have predictive validity, the tool must predict outcomes characteristic of healing. Predictive validity is of great importance. Screening tools that have predictive validity are based on the assumption that after detecting specific variables, an intervention can be applied that would affect the predicted outcome.

Table 5–1 Factors and Scoring Methods Used in Wound Healing Tools

Factors	PSST	Sessing Scale	PUSH	WHS	SWHT
Wound Factors					
Size	x		x		x
Depth/Stage	x	x		x	x
Edges	x			x	x
Necrotic Tissue	x	x	x	x	x
Type	x	x	x		
Amount	x				
Slough	x	x	x		
Exudate	x	x	x		
Type	x	x			
Amount	x	x	x		
Odor	x	x		x	
Infection	x	x		x	
Granulation	x	x	x	x	x
Contraction				x	x
Undermining	x				x
Epithelialization	x	x	x	x	x
Surrounding Skin Factors					
Color	x	x			x
Edema	x				
Induration	x				
Maceration					x
Hemorrhage					x
Other Factors					
Location	x				x
Risk of Skin					
Breakdown		x			
Wound Healing					
Phase					x
Sharp Debridement				x	
Healed				x	
Scoring:	Likert scale: 1=best; 5=worst. Scores for 13 items are added. Score changes as wound improves or worsens.	Scale 0–6 Uses the numerical value most closely associated with description. Score by calculating change in numberic value over successive assessments. Positive score = improvement; negative score = worsening.	3 Weighted subscores for: surface area, exudate, and surface appearance are added to obtain total score. Score changes as wound heals or worsens.	Eight letter modifiers are used with the Pressure Ulcer Staging System (eg, 4N-Stage IV necrotic). Method to measure change in status over time not clear.	Scores presence or absence of each of 19 wound attributes, "good for healing" or "not good for healing" and other factors. Measures change by noting change from "not good" to "good for healing" attributes.

Table 5–2 Historical Measures of Pressure Ulcer Improvement

Measures	Definitions
Change in ulcer size	• Area (length × width) • Depth (for volume) • Perimeter/circumference
Surface appearance	• Red • Yellow • Black
Tissue type	• Necrotic • Granulation • Epithelial • Singly or in combination
Surrounding skin characteristics	• Erythema (color change) • Edema • Undermining or Tunneling

Source: Sussman C, Swanson GH. The utility of Sussman Wound Healing Tool in predicting wound healing outcomes in physical therapy. *Advances in Wound Care*, September 1997.

Reliability

Reliability of a tool is its ability to be used with minimum error. There are several kinds of reliability tests for a tool. Intrarater reliability means that the same rater gets the same score with repeated measurements. Interrater reliability means that two or more individuals get the same results after administering the same instrument.

Responsiveness/Sensitivity to Change

Responsiveness or sensitivity to change is the next test criterion for a tool. An appropriate tool or method must be able to detect changes in the condition of the wound over time with repeated administrations.

Clinical Practicality

Clinical practicality means the tool must be simple, easy to learn and to use with clear instructions, and must be reliable with the same and multiple users. It must be time efficient and cost effective.

Two Tools To Monitor Wound Healing

This chapter describes two tools to monitor wound healing, the Sussman Wound Healing Tool (SWHT) and the Pressure Sore Status Tool (PSST), each developed by one of the authors of this chapter. Both clinicians recognized many years ago that the ability to monitor healing outcomes was essen-

tial. Both tools are in various stages of development and their reliability, validity, responsiveness, sensitivity to change, and clinical practicality for monitoring wound healing are still to be determined. There are similarities in some aspects of the tools: both tools evaluate tissue attributes of the wound and surrounding skin. Methods of evaluation and scoring are different. At this time, neither author knows for certain that all items listed in the tools are useful. The processes of development and application of the two tools will now be presented.

SUSSMAN WOUND HEALING TOOL

Introduction and Development of the Sussman Wound Healing Tool

The SWHT was developed by Sussman and Swanson[5] as a physical therapy (PT) diagnostic tool to monitor and track the effectiveness of PT technologies used for pressure ulcer healing. The ability to predict pressure ulcer healing and treatment outcomes in PT has yet to be done reliably. The monitoring and tracking of healing and treatment outcomes is essential for clinical decision making and triage and provides payers and providers improved utilization management.

The basis for the SWHT is the acute wound healing model (see Chapter 2) that describes the changes in tissue status and size over time as the wound progresses through the biologic phases of wound healing. Some attributes of the wound that are observed during each phase are considered related to failure to heal or "not good for healing" and others are considered indicators of improvement or "good for healing." For example, a tissue attribute such as necrosis is thought to be negative or not good for healing, whereas wound attributes such as granulation tissue, which represents fibroplasia, and adherence of the wound edges are considered good for healing. The concept of the SWHT is to benchmark the wound attributes as it recovers and progresses throughout the healing phases. For example, the "not good" attribute, necrosis, should change over time from *present* to *absent,* thus moving from "not good for healing" to "good for healing." The "good for healing" attribute, fibroplasia—significant reduction in depth, should be granulation observed as the wound heals and changes from *absent* to *present*, in-dicating improved tissue status.

The initial design of the SWHT is a qualitative instrument, meaning that a wound would be described as having certain tissue attributes. Subsequently, the tool will be refined and each SWHT variable will be measured, weighted, and ranked to produce a quantitative tool. In total, 19 attributes are defined. It is composed of 10 wound attributes combined with 9 descriptive attributes of size, extent of tissue damage plus location, and acute wound healing phase, which are not measurable. The 10 wound tissue attributes described were each assigned a score as *present* or *absent* and ranked as *not good* or *good* for healing. Five attributes ranked as *not good* include hemorrhage, maceration, erythema, undermining, and necrosis. Five attributes ranked as *good* include adherence at the wound edge, fibroplasia, appearance of contraction, sustained contraction, and epithelialization. The lists defining and describing each attribute are shown in Exhibit 5–1.

Sussman Wound Healing Tool Attribute Definitions

Part I: Tissue Attributes

The first five attributes described are classified as "not good for healing" and the second five listed are classified as "good for healing." The "not good for healing" attributes are all related to the inflammatory phase of healing. The attributes that are "good for healing" are related to the proliferation and epithelialization phases of healing. As the wound attributes change from "not good" to "good" the wound is progressing through the phases corresponding to those of acute wound healing.

1. Hemorrhage. Hemorrhage is defined as a purple ecchymosis of wound tissue or surrounding skin (see *Color Plates 65 and 68*). The color plates show the deepening of tissue color or distinguishable purple ecchymosis which is an indicator of significant subcutaneous bleeding or hemorrhage. Wounds with hemorrhage have high probability of tissue death and thus enlargement of the wound. This attribute is classified as "not good for healing."

Clinical Wisdom: *Assessment of Hemorrhage Triggers Further Examination*

The presence of hemorrhage would be a trigger for further examination, including temperature testing as described in Chapter 3 to determine tissue vitality. Hemorrhage may trigger vascular consultation. The chapters in Part IV on electrical stimulation, pulsed short wave diathermy/pulsed radio frequency, and ultrasound describe how these interventions promote absorption of hemorrhagic material.

---

2. Maceration. Maceration is defined as a softening of connective tissue fibers by soaking until they are soft and friable.[9] Macerated tissue loses its pigmentation, and even darkly pigmented skin looks blanched. This weakened tissue is highly susceptible to trauma, leading to breakdown of the macerated tissue and enlargement of the wound. Maceration is an attribute classified as "not good for healing."

3. Undermining/Tunneling. Undermining is defined as erosion under the edge of the wound, and tunneling is defined as separation of the fascial planes leading to sinus tracts. Location of undermining for this attribute means undermining at any location around the wound perimeter. *Color Plates 37 to 39* show wounds that are undermined or with tunneling. The extent of the undermining/tunneling is not recorded or included as part of the assessment, only the presence or absence of this attribute. If undermining is present, it is an attribute that is classified as "not good for healing."

4. Erythema. Erythema is defined as reddening or darkening of the skin compared with surrounding skin. Erythema following trauma is due to rupture of small venules and capillaries or may be caused by inflow of blood to start the inflammatory process, or both events. Distinguishing between the two is often difficult. Erythema is usually accompanied by heat, but it may be accompanied by cooling, indicating devitalization of tissue.[10] Distinguishing and assessing erythema in darkly pigmented skin is described in detail in Chapter 3 (see *Color Plate 19*). The ability to see the margins of the change in skin color is enhanced by lighting and may be seen more easily in a photograph than in the living tissues, especially in very dark skin tones. *Color Plates 6, 14, and 15* show erythema in both lightly and darkly pigmented skin. Erythema is an attribute that is classified as "not good for healing."

Clinical Wisdom: *Differentiation between Erythema and Reactive Hyperemia*

Erythema should be assessed after pressure has been relieved from the area for about 20 minutes so as to eliminate effects of reactive hyperemia.

---

5. Necrosis. All types of necrotic tissue, including eschar and slough, are included when assessing for presence or absence of this attribute. Necrosis is defined as dead devitalized tissue. Color may be black, brown, gray, or yellow. Texture may be dry and leathery, soft, moist, or stringy. Odor may be present or absent. To determine if the tissue being assessed is necrotic, see Chapter 7, Management of Necrotic Tissue, and *Color Plates 3, 25 to 30, 46, and 47.* One common error in assessing necrotic tissue is to assess all yellow and white tissue as necrotic. Yellow tissue may be either healthy yellow fat, the reticular membrane of the dermis, or a tendon. White tissue may be connective tissue, fascia, or a ligament. *Color Plate 13* shows healthy yellow and white tissue. Healthy tissue usually has a gleam not seen in devitalized tissue. Note, however, that the topical treatment or exudate is not the source of the "gleam." Healthy tissue is not friable and has resilience when compressed. Dead tissue tears and does not spring back when compressed. Waiting 24 hours helps to see if the tissue changes color to gray or brown, indicating loss of vitality. Reassess. Necrosis is an attribute that is classified as "not good for healing."

6. Adherence at Wound Edge. Adherence at the wound edge means that there is continuity of the wound edge and the base of the wound at any location along the wound perimeter (*Color Plates 8, 9, 56, and 57*). A partial-thickness wound will be adhered at the wound edge by definition. A full-thickness or deeper wound will have closed by either granulation or contraction to the point where some area of the wound edge will be even with the skin surface. Some wound edges curl under because of epithelial migration over the edge of the wound. This can halt wound contraction and lead to fibrosis of the scar tissue. Edges may not adhere when this occurs, and wound healing will not proceed. Adherence of the wound edges is an attribute that is classified as "good for healing."

7. Granulation Tissue (Fibroplasia—Significant Reduction in Depth). Granulation tissue formation or fibroplasia is the action of the fibroblasts laying down collagen matrix during the proliferation phase of healing. The collagen matrix fills the wound, causing a measurable or significant reduction in wound depth. For determining the presence of fibroplasia—significant reduction in depth, a linear measurement of this attribute is required (see Chapter 4). A significant reduction in depth is at least 0.2 cm since the prior assessment. *Color Plates 7 to 9* show a significant reduction in depth. Granulation is an attribute that is classified as "good for healing."

8. Appearance of Contraction. The appearance of contraction is defined as the first measurement of the wound drawing together, resulting in reduction of wound open surface area size. Compare *Color Plate 3* with *Color Plates 4 and 5* to see the onset and progression of contraction. It is identified by a change in wound open area size and may be identified as a change in wound shape (eg, from irregular to symmetric, such as the circular or oval formation and rounding off the edges of the wound seen in pressure ulcers; see *Color Plate 2*). This item is scored at subsequent assessments as the contraction continues or if it has stopped. If the wound enlarges, however, this item would change from present to absent, and a new appearance of contraction would be required to have a score of "present" again. When present, adherence at the wound edge is an attribute that is classified as "good for healing."

9. Sustained Contraction. Sustained contraction means there is a continued drawing together of the wound edges that is measured by a reduction in wound surface open area size. It is usually accompanied by a change in wound shape.

Color Plates 3 to 5 show the same wound as it goes through wound contraction. Sustained contraction is scored 0 at the appearance of the contraction benchmark and then scored 1 at subsequent reassessment following the appearance of contraction. Occasionally something interferes with the wound contraction and the wound does not reduce in size or increases. This attribute would be marked 0, absent, if the wound size does not reduce or enlarges after the appearance of contraction. Sustained contraction is an attribute that is classified as "good for healing."

10. Epithelialization. Epithelialization refers to the appearance of and continuation of resurfacing of the wound with new skin at the wound edges or surface. *Color Plate 5* shows the same case as *Color Plates 3 to 5,* now in the epithelialization phase. Epithelialization may first be noticed during the inflammation or proliferation phase of healing as a lightly pigmented pink tissue, even in individuals with darkly pigmented skin (*Color Plates 7 to 9*). In partial-thickness wounds, the epithelial cells may migrate from islands on the wound surface or from the wound edges, or both. *Color Plates 55 and 56* show an example. Full-thickness and deeper wounds have epithelial migration, usually from the edges only. *Color Plates 5 and 6* show the same full-thickness wound as seen in *Color Plates 3 and 4*, that is, resurfacing from the wound edges. Many people confuse new bright pink scar tissue or skin as erythema. *Color Plate 22* shows new pink scar tissue in a person with darkly pigmented skin. Epithelialization is an attribute that is classified as "good for healing."

Part II: Size Location and Wound Healing Phase Measures

Wound depth and undermining indicate extent of wound. If a wound has a depth less than 0.2 cm it is scored as 0 at all four points and at general depth. Depth and undermining are two indicators of "not good for healing."

11–15. Wound Depth. Five items on part II of the SWHT are related to presence of depth of at least 0.2 cm both in general depth and at the four points of the clock, 12-, 3-, 6-, and 9-o'clock positions. Depth is measured as described in Chapter 4, and if it is at least 0.2 cm it is recorded as present. Extent of depth is not significant for this assessment as long as it is at least 0.2 cm. (See *Color Plates 2, 7, 27, and 30* for full-thickness depth.)

16–19. Tunneling/Undermining. Undermining and tunneling are measured at all four points of the clock, like depth. However, the objective measure used to report this attribute is also present or absent. With further testing and analysis this attribute may prove to be redundant with part I. For the present time, it remains a part of the tool.

Additional Descriptive Attributes

Wound Location. Wound location is noted as the anatomic description most closely related to the wound site. Because lower torso and lower extremity wounds are most frequently seen, the locations have been broken down into the common sites for chronic wounds and they have been clustered together for the upper body. Letters are also used to represent the wound location: *UB* for upper body, *C* for coccyx, *T* for trochanter, *I* for ischial, *H* for heel, and *F* for foot. Wounds in other locations can be added to the list if they are commonly seen in the practice setting by using letters on the form and adding a location descriptor to the key (eg, *K* = knee, *A* = abdomen, *Th* = Thigh). One needs to be sure to include the side of the body where the wound is located, right or left, by putting an *R* or an *L* next to the location letter. Wound location has been shown to be an indicator of healing. However, the specific locations that indicate healing are still to be determined.

Wound Healing Phase. The wound healing phase refers to the four biologic phases of wound healing: inflammatory, proliferative, epithelialization, and remodeling. Letters are used to represent the current wound healing phase: *I* for inflammation, *P* for proliferation, *E* for epithelialization, and *R* for remodeling. As described in Chapter 2 the wound healing phase may be chronic, acute, or absent. A letter is placed before the phase such as the letter *C* before the phase for chronic, no letter before acute, or the letter *L* for lacking or absent can be used as modifiers of the current phase. A change in phase over time is an expected outcome. Chronicity of a phase should change to an active state of the phase followed by progression to the next phase in the trajectory. Absence of a phase indicates need for investigation as to why the phase has not been achieved. This item is listed but unscored.

Testing the SWHT

One of the first questions applied to the SWHT was whether a tool design based on the four phase acute wound healing model could be applied to chronic wounds such as pressure ulcers. The SWHT is in the process of being tested on a dataset of 112 pressure ulcer cases. All of the patients who were included in the dataset were long-term care residents with pressure ulcers. Many experts consider pressure ulcers to be chronic wounds from the time of onset. The analyses are as yet incomplete.

SWHT for Monitoring and Tracking Wound Healing

The utility of the SWHT in the clinical setting for monitoring and tracking healing is easy and practical. Each of the attributes of the SWHT is scored if tissue attributes of the wound or surrounding skin are present or absent. The total number of present (1) "not good" for healing attributes should diminish as the wound heals, and the total number of present (1) "good" for healing attributes should increase in number. Change of score measures the change in healing and reduced severity of the wound. The scores are also useful for measuring the level of healing indicating progress, lack of progress, or regression of healing. The SWHT has proven utility both as a diagnostic tool that differentiates phases by assessment of healing attributes and as a tool for measurement of *change* in tissue status (eg, tissue attribute) and size (eg, change in depth and undermining) over time. Thus, the SWHT is designed to monitor and track healing based on the acute wound healing model, and can be applied to acute or chronic wounds such as pressure ulcers.

SWHT Reliability and Practicality

The SWHT has been clinically tested for reliability and clinical practicality by physical therapists and physical therapists' assistants working in a long-term care facility during its 5 years of development and found to be very reliable for monitoring and tracking healing and nonhealing of pressure ulcers. It relies primarily on visual observation skills. No linear measurements, arithmetic calculations, or estimates of amount of tissue characteristic present are required. To health care professionals who treat wounds, the SWHT information communicates clearly wound progress or risk. Documentation is very simple and outcomes are visual. For example, it takes the clinician about 5 minutes to complete the assessment. In a trial educational session to train new learners to use the SWHT, a group of 10 physical therapists and physical therapists' assistants who received 1 hour of training in the classroom using verbal description and photos to teach the method of assessment and definitions of the attributes, followed by 1 hour of clinical practice on pressure ulcer patients, learned to use it well.

Assessment of Treatment Outcomes

Assessment of treatment outcome was the initial reason for development of the SWHT. Most patients are referred to the physical therapist by the nurse for treatment after conventional treatments failed to heal the wound. To qualify for an intervention by the physical therapist, the patient and the wound often need to meet a criterion of no progress or regression or a halt of healing. Therefore, it is critical for the physical therapist and the nurse to be able to set target outcomes and then assess the response to the treatment intervention. A wound assessed with the SWHT as not progressing after a course of conventional care by the nurse would meet the criterion for referral. Once referred, the SWHT is useful for reporting wound outcomes associated with the intervention prescribed by the physical therapist, such as physical therapy technologies. Response to treatment with these interventions should demonstrate consistent change in tissue status that corresponds to the biologic model for acute wound healing. A change in tissue status benchmarks the healing process and becomes a target functional outcome for reporting purposes, such as the wound will be hemorrhage free, undermining free, necrosis free, and so forth. Reviewers can quickly determine a change in wound tissue status during the course of care because, as already described, the wound attributes should change from those "not good for healing" to those "good for healing."

Using the SWHT

Two Parts of SWHT

Exhibit 5–1 shows the two parts of the SWHT. The SWHT is a paper-and-pencil instrument comprising 19 attributes. Part I is the collection form of 10 tissue attributes. Part II is the list of 11 other attributes, including extent, location, and wound healing phase. All items on the SWHT are scored except location and the wound healing phase. Omission of a score indicates that the assessment was not completed. Scoring begins at baseline, week 0. The method of scoring for the tool is a number 1 for present and a 0 for absent. This reporting format is readily compatible with computer technology and simplifies using the tool to build a database such as the one described later. Completion of the form requires understanding of the definitions for each of the scored items (see Exhibit 5–2 for definitions of attributes). The assessment process is visual except for determining the presence of undermining/tunneling, which cannot be seen at the surface, and measurement of the open surface area of the wound.

Procedure for Using the SWHT (see Exhibit 5–1)

Completion of the SWHT is by observation and physical assessment, as follows:

1. Each wound of each patient needs its own SWHT attributes form.
2. The patient's name and medical record number and date of assessment are written at the top of the form.
3. The examiner has a place to sign the document.
4. As the wound is assessed, the rater marks a 1 or a 0 to signify present or absent on the form next to each of the 19 attributes. The squares in the column must be marked with one of the two scores.
5. The wound location and the current wound healing phase are marked with the appropriate letter. Choose the appropriate letter to represent the anatomic location of the wound and place it in the square at the time of the initial assessment and subsequent reassessments. The location will not change.
6. Letters are also used to represent the current wound healing phase: mark an *I* for inflammation, *P* for proliferation, *E* for epithelialization, and *R* for remodeling. In the appropriate box, the phase is noted initially and at each reassessment. The wound healing phase should change as the wound heals.
7. Undermining and depth require some physical assessment to determine presence or absence.
8. Open area measurements are made and listed on a separate form (see Chapter 4) and then compared with subsequent measurements of these characteristics to determine contraction and sustained contraction, measured as reduction in linear size.
9. Scoring part I. Add the number of "not good for healing" attributes and the number of "good for healing" attributes listed. The score of "not good for healing" should diminish as the wound heals, and the score of "good for healing" attributes should increase.
10. A graphic representation of the change is shown in Exhibit 5–4.

SWHT Forms

Long Form

Two SWHT forms are shown (Exhibits 5–2A and 5–2B). Part I of the long form (Exhibit 5–1) contains the 10 tissue attributes, listed in descending order of severity, next to definitions, followed by a column listing the rating option for the attribute as present or not present. The next column ranks the relationship to healing as "not good" or "good." The last column is where the rating is listed as a score of present or absent. Part II lists measures and extent. The same scoring system of "present" or "absent" for 19 attributes of extent is applied. The attributes are the general depth of greater than 0.2 cm, the depth at the four clock points, and undermining at the four clock points. Date and week of care should be noted on the form. The benefit of the long form is having the definitions on the form. This would be helpful to a nurse or physical therapist learning the system or for medical reviewers and surveyors looking for information about the rating system used for documentation.

Short Form

The short form (Exhibits 5–2A and 5–2B) of the SWHT is the same as the long form except that the short form lacks the definitions printed on the form. The short form lists only the attributes and has columns to record data for multiple

Exhibit 5–1 Long Form SWHT

Sussman Wound Healing Tool (SWHT)
WOUND ASSESSMENT FORM

NAME: _____

DATE: _____

EXAMINER: _____

MEDICAL RECORD NO.: _____

CIRCLE WEEK OF CARE: B   1   2   3   4   5   6   7   8   9   10   11   12

SWHT Variable	Tissue Attribute	Attribute Definition	Rating	Relationship to Healing	Score
1	Hemorrhage	Purple ecchymosis of wound tissue or surrounding skin	Present or absent	Not good	
2	Maceration	Softening of a tissue by soaking until the connective tissue fibers are soft and friable	Present or absent	Not good	
3	Undermining	Includes both undermining and tunneling	Present or absent	Not good	
4	Erythema	Reddening or darkening of the skin compared to surrounding skin; usually accompanied by heat	Present or absent	Not good	
5	Necrosis	All types of necrotic tissue, including eschar and slough	Present or absent	Not good	
6	Adherence at wound edge	Continuity of wound edge and the base of the wound	Present or absent	Good	
7	Granulation (Fibroplasia—significant reduction in depth)	Pink/red granulation tissue filling in the wound bed, reducing wound depth	Present or absent	Good	
8	Appearance of contraction (reduced size)	First measurement of the wound drawing together, resulting in reduction in wound open surface area	Present or absent	Good	
9	Sustained contraction (more reduced size)	Continued drawing together of wound edges, measured by reduced wound open surface area	Present or absent	Good	
10	Epithelialization	Appearance and continuation of resurfacing with new skin or scar at the wound edges or surface	Present or absent	Good	

	Other	Letter
	Location	
	Wound healing phase	
	Total "Not Good"	
	Total "Good"	

MEASURES AND EXTENT (Depth and Undermining: Not Good)

	Depth/Location	SCORE		Undermining/Location	SCORE
11	General depth >0.2 cm		16	Underm @ 12:00	
12	General depth @ 12:00 >0.2 cm		17	Underm @ 3:00	
13	General depth @ 3:00 >0.2 cm		18	Underm @ 6:00	
14	General depth @ 6:00 >0.2 cm		19	Underm @ 9:00	
15	General depth @ 9:00 >0.2 cm				

Key: **Present = 1. Absent = 0.** Location choices: upper body (UB), coccyx (C), trochanter (T), ischial (I), heel (H), foot (F); add right or left (R or L). Wound healing phase: inflammation (I), proliferation (P), epithelialization (E), remodeling (R).

Source: Copyright © 1997, Sussman Physical Therapy Inc.

Exhibit 5–2A SWHT Short Form Part I: Wound Tissue Attributes

Name: _____ Med Rec # _____ Examiner: _____

Week	0	1	2	3	4
1. Hemorrhage					
2. Maceration					
3. Undermining					
4. Erythema					
5. Necrosis					
6. Adherence					
7. Granulation (decreased deth)					
8. Appearance of contraction (Reduced size)					
9. Sustained contraction (More reduced size)					
10. Epithelialization					
Total Not Good					
Total Good					

Key: Present = 1. Not present = 0.

Source: Copyright © 1997, Sussman Physical Therapy Inc.

Exhibit 5–2B SWHT Short Form Part II: Size, Location, Wound Healing Phase Measures, and Extent

Date	0	1	2	3	4
11. General Depth >0.2 cm					
12. Depth @ 12:00 > 0.2 cm					
13. Depth @ 3:00 >0.2 cm					
14. Depth @ 6:00 >0.2 cm					
15. Depth @ 9:00 >0.2 cm					
16. Underm @ 12:00 >0.2 cm					
17. Underm @ 3:00 >0.2 cm					
18. Underm @ 6:00 >0.2 cm					
19. Underm @ 9:00 >0.2 cm					
Location					
Wound healing phase					

Key: Present = 1. Not present = 0. Location choices: upper body (UB), coccyx (C), trochanter (T), ischial (I), heel (H), and foot (F); add right or left (R or L). Wound healing phase: absent (A), chronic (C), inflammation (I), proliferation (P), epithelialization (E), remodeling (R).

Source: Copyright © 1997, Sussman Physical Therapy Inc.

Exhibit 5–3A SWHT Part I: Wound Tissue Attributes

Week	0	1	2	3	4
Date: 2010	1/7	1/14	1/21	1/28	2/4
1. Hemorrhage	1	0	0	0	0
2. Maceration	0	0	0	0	0
3. Undermining	0	0	1	1	1
4. Erythema	1	1	1	0	0
5. Necrosis	1	1	1	0	0
6. Adherence	0	0	0	1	1
7. Granulation (decreased depth)	0	0	1	1	1
8. Appearance of contraction (reduced size)	0	0	1	1	1
9. Sustained contraction (more reduced size)	0	0	0	1	1
10. Epithelialization	0	0	0	1	1
Total "Not Good"	3	2	3	1	1
Total "Good"	0	0	2	5	5

Key: **Present = 1. Absent = 0.**

Source: Copyright © 1997, Sussman Physical Therapy Inc.

Exhibit 5–3B SWHT Part II: Size, Location, Wound Healing Phase Measures, and Extent

Week	0	1	2	3	4
Date:	1/7	1/14	1/21	1/28	2/4
11. General depth >0.2 cm	0	1	1	1	1
12. Depth @ 12:00 >0.2 cm	0	1	1	1	1
13. Depth @ 3:00 >0.2 cm	0	1	1	1	1
14. Depth @ 6:00 >0.2 cm	0	1	1	1	1
15. Depth @ 9:00 >0.2 cm	1	1	1	1	1
16. Underm @ 12:00 >0.2 cm	0	0	1	1	0
17. Underm @ 3:00 >0.2 cm	0	1	1	0	0
18. Underm @ 6:00 >0.2 cm	0	1	1	1	0
19. Underm @ 9:00 >0.2 cm	0	0	1	1	1
Location	RT	RT	RT	RT	RT
Wound healing phase	I	I	I	P	P

Key: Present = 1. Not present = 0. Location choices: upper body (UB), coccyx (C), trochanter (T), ischial (I), heel (H), and foot (F); add right or left (R or L). Wound healing phase: inflammation (I), proliferation (P), epithelialization (E), remodeling (R).

Source: Copyright © 1997, Sussman Physical Therapy Inc.

weeks. Part I can be printed on one side and part II on the other and the paper can be cut to fit in a small pocket-size 4 × 6-inch looseleaf notebook. Printing the forms as a pad punched with a hole pattern to match the notebook makes it easy and convenient to keep forms on hand. A printed set of the definitions and scoring can be printed on the same size paper and then kept in the notebook for reference. The notebook functions most smoothly if an alphabetic index the size of the notebook is used. The wound progress notebook can then be kept like a nursing treatment record book with records alphabetically filed. The current patient wound healing records would then be readily available. The benefit of the notebook is that it will usually fit in a lab coat pocket and can be carried to the bedside or home. In a facility, like the treatment record book, it can be kept at the nurses' station, when not in use, for easy reference. An additional benefit of the short form is that it is easy to see a complete history of the change in tissue status over multiple weeks of assessment. Reading the report over time provides a quick and clear evaluation to monitor wound healing progress. Exhibits 5–3A and 5–3B show a completed case record. At the time of discharge or monthly the completed record of wound attributes is then taped in tiling fashion like telephone order prescription sheets onto a sheet of paper and filed in the medical record.

Clinical Wisdom: *Use of Forms for Wound Measurement along with the SWHT*

Since wound measurement and tissue assessment or reassessment are usually done at the same time it makes sense to record the information in the same record book. A wound measurement recording short form that fits in the same notebook as the SWHT meets this need. This form is used to record the size, depth, and undermining linear measurements. Each week a new measurement form is added behind the SWHT form. By having the two forms together in the notebook the examiner can check at a glance to see whether there is reduction in depth and open area. Chapter 4, Exhibit 4–1, shows a sample wound measurement form designed to fit this model.

Case Example Using the SWHT

Exhibits 5–3A and 5–3B show an example of a case where wound healing was monitored over a 5-week course of care as reported on the short form of the SWHT parts I and II. A summary, Exhibit 5–4, of the case example shows how the SWHT can be used to document a change in wound tissue status from a predominance of "not good for healing" to a predominance of "good attributes." Exhibit 5–4 reflects the following:

- The patient had the presence at baseline, week 0, hemorrhage, necrosis, and erythema, and absence of any attributes "good for healing." The presence of these attributes at baseline is an indication that this wound will need aggressive intervention to improve.
- At week 2 there were multiple attributes that were indicators that this patient will be in the "risk for not healing" group, including undermining and depth at all four clock points, further indicating the medical necessity for aggressive intervention to put the wound on a course of healing.
- Assuming that aggressive intervention was undertaken at week 2, the improvement in the wound tissue status from "not good" to "good" is significant by week 4.

Sussman Wound Healing Tool Database

Although the SWHT is a paper-and-pencil instrument, the SWHT wound database is maintained in a computer. The scoring system of using a 1 or a 0 is computer compatible for data management and data entry. The SWHT forms are printed on the computer as screens, and data are entered either prospectively or retrospectively. Data reports can be printed and the captured data can be analyzed on an individual patient basis or by group. Further testing of the SWHT is planned at different sites.

Summary

Physical therapists and nurses can utilize the SWHT present/absent scoring system to triage the case, guide treatment intervention, and report functional outcomes. The SWHT is a simple, easy-to-follow, and complete documentation system that provides payers and providers improved utilization management.

Exhibit 5–4 Summary of Wound Attribute Change over a Five-Week Course of Care

WEEK 0	WEEK 2	WEEK 4
"NOT GOOD" for healing	*"NOT GOOD" for healing*	*"NOT GOOD" for healing*
Hemorrhage Undermining Erythema Necrosis Depth 9:00	Necrosis Undermining Erythema Depth 12, 3, 6, 9:00 Undermining 12, 3, 6, 9:00	Undermining Depth 12, 3, 6, 9:00 Undermining 9:00
"GOOD" for healing	*"GOOD" for healing*	*"GOOD" for healing*
None	Fibroplasia Appearance of contraction	Fibroplasia Appearance of contraction Sustained contraction Adherence Epithelialization
Wound healing phase	*Wound healing phase*	*Wound healing phase*
Inflammation phase	Inflammation phase	Proliferation phase

Source: Copyright © 1997, Sussman Physical Therapy, Inc.

THE PRESSURE SORE STATUS TOOL

Introduction and Development of the Pressure Sore Status Tool

The Pressure Sore Status Tool (PSST) is a pencil-and-paper instrument comprising 15 items (see Exhibit 5–5). Two items that are not scored are location and shape. The remaining 13 items are scored and appear with descriptors of each item rated on a modified Likert scale (1 being the healthiest attribute of that characteristic and 5 being the worst attribute of the characteristic). The tool has a one-page sheet of instructions for use in addition to the item descriptions (Appendix 5–A). The PSST was developed to measure wound healing in pressure ulcers based on a clinical and research need in this area.

The items on the PSST were developed through the use of experts participating in a modified Delphi panel. The content validity of the tool was established with the use of a nine-member expert judge panel (mean overall content validity index = 0.91, p = 0.05). Reliability was demonstrated on adult patients in an acute care hospital with enterostomal therapy (ET) nurses. The mean interrater reliability coefficient was 0.91.[11] Intrarater reliability estimates yielded a mean of 0.975. Although high reliability estimates had been established with ET nurses, a question remained as to the efficacy of the tool's use with practitioners who did not have extraordinary education or experience in wound assessment and management. The issue of reliability of the PSST when used by "regular" health care practitioners was addressed in a long-term care facility. Fifteen practitioners participated in the study. Their educational background and experience with wounds varied. Two physical therapists, three licensed practical nurses, and 10 registered nurses participated in the study. Pairs independently assessed 16 wounds across a broad spectrum of severity on two occasions (2 hours apart). An expert ET nurse also independently assessed the same wounds as the practitioner pairs. Interrater reliability estimates were calculated between practitioners themselves and between practitioners and the expert rater. Intrarater reliability estimates were calculated in a similar manner except that each rater's recordings were compared with a second assessment

Exhibit 5–5 Pressure Sore Status Tool Form

PRESSURE SORE STATUS TOOL   NAME _____

Complete the rating sheet to assess pressure sore status. Evaluate each item by picking the response that best describes the wound and entering the score in the item score column for the appropriate date.

Location: Anatomic site. Circle, identify right (R) or left (L) and use "X" to mark site on body diagrams:

_____	Sacrum and coccyx	_____	Lateral ankle
_____	Trochanter	_____	Medial ankle
_____	Ischial tuberosity	_____	Heel Other site _____

Shape: Overall wound pattern; assess by observing perimeter and depth. Circle and *date* appropriate description:

_____	Irregular	_____	Linear or elongated
_____	Round/oval	_____	Bowl/boat
_____	Square/rectangle	_____	Butterfly Other shape _____

Item	Assessment	Date	Date	Date
		Score	Score	Score
1. Size	1 = Length × width <4 cm^2 2 = Length × width 4–16 cm^2 3 = Length × width 16.1–36 cm^2 4 = Length × width 36.1–80 cm^2 5 = Length × width >80 cm^2			
2. Depth	1 = Nonblanchable erythema on intact skin 2 = Partial-thickness skin loss involving epidermis and/or dermis 3 = Full-thickness skin loss involving damage or necrosis of subcutaneous tissue; may extend down to but not through underlying fascia; and/or mixed partial and full thickness and/or tissue layers obscured by granulation tissue 4 = Obscured by necrosis 5 = Full-thickness skin loss with extensive destruction, tissue necrosis, or damage to muscle, bone, or supporting structures			
3. Edges	1 = Indistinct, diffuse, none clearly visible 2 = Distinct, outline clearly visible, attached, even with wound base 3 = Well-defined, not attached to wound base 4 = Well-defined, not attached to base, rolled under, thickened 5 = Well-defined, fibrotic, scarred or hyperkeratotic			
4. Undermining	1 = Undermining <2 cm in any area 2 = Undermining 2–4 cm involving <50% wound margins 3 = Undermining 2–4 cm involving >50% wound margins 4 = Undermining >4 cm in any area 5 = Tunneling and/or sinus tract formation			
5. Necrotic Tissue Type	1 = None visible 2 = White/gray nonviable tissue and/or nonadherent yellow slough 3 = Loosely adherent yellow slough 4 = Adherent, soft, black eschar 5 = Firmly adherent, hard, black eschar			
6. Necrotic Tissue Amount	1 = None visible 2 = <25% of wound bed covered 3 = 25% to 50% of wound covered 4 = >50% and <75% of wound covered 5 = 75% to 100% of wound covered			

continues

Exhibit 5–5 continued

Item	Assessment	Date Score	Date Score	Date Score
7. Exudate Type	1 = None or bloody 2 = Serosanguineous: thin, watery, pale red/pink 3 = Serous: thin, watery, clear 4 = Purulent: thin or thick, opaque, tan/yellow 5 = Foul purulent: thick, opaque, yellow/green with odor			
8. Exudate Amount	1 = None 2 = Scant 3 = Small 4 = Moderate 5 = Large			
9. Skin Color Surrounding Wound	1 = Pink or normal for ethnic group 2 = Bright red and/or blanches to touch 3 = White or gray pallor or hypopigmented 4 = Dark red or purple and/or nonblanchable 5 = Black or hyperpigmented			
10. Peripheral Tissue Edema	1 = Minimal swelling around wound 2 = Nonpitting edema extends <4 cm around wound 3 = Nonpitting edema extends ≥4 cm around wound 4 = Pitting edema extends <4 cm around wound 5 = Crepitus and/or pitting edema extends ≥4 cm			
11. Peripheral Tissue Induration	1 = Minimal firmness around wound 2 = Induration <2 cm around wound 3 = Induration 2–4 cm extending <50% around wound 4 = Induration 2–4 cm extending ≥50% around wound 5 = Induration >4 cm in any area			
12. Granulation Tissue	1 = Skin intact or partial-thickness wound 2 = Bright, beefy red; 75% to 100% of wound filled and/or tissue overgrowth 3 = Bright, beefy red; <75% and >25% of wound filled 4 = Pink, and/or dull, dusky red and/or fills ≤25% of wound 5 = No granulation tissue present			
13. Epithelialization	1 = 100% wound covered, surface intact 2 = 75% to <100% wound covered and/or epithelial tissue extends >0.5 cm into wound bed 3 = 50% to <75% wound covered and/or epithelial tissue extends to <0.5 cm into wound bed 4 = 25% to <50% wound covered 5 = <25% wound covered			
TOTAL SCORE				
SIGNATURE				

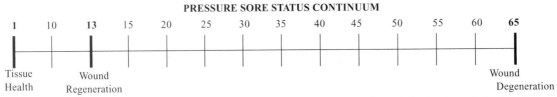

PRESSURE SORE STATUS CONTINUUM

1   10   **13**   15   20   25   30   35   40   45   50   55   60   **65**

Tissue Health   Wound Regeneration   Wound Degeneration

Plot the total score on the Pressure Sore Status Continuum by putting an "X" on the line and the date beneath the line. Plot multiple scores with their dates to see at a glance regeneration or degeneration of the wound.

Source: Copyright © 1990, Barbara M. Bates-Jensen.

(taken within 2 hours of the first) for the same wound. Interrater reliability for the practitioners yielded a mean of 0.78. Reliability estimates for the practitioners versus the ET expert yielded a mean of 0.82. Intrarater reliability for the practitioners averaged 0.89.[12]

Since the PSST involves a Likert-type ordinal scale and the probability of chance agreements between two raters is 0.20 for any item, the data were also subjected to analyses using a polychotomous data stratagem. Resulting κ statistics for each item on the scale yielded coefficients above 0.60. Collectively, the results from the long-term care setting suggested that use of the PSST by general health care practitioners resulted in lower reliability than use by ET nurses, but certainly within an acceptable range.

The Pressure Sore Status Tool Items

The PSST is meant to be used once a pressure sore has developed; it is not a risk assessment tool. It is recommended that the pressure sore be scored initially for a baseline assessment and at regular intervals to evaluate therapy. Once a lesion has been assessed for each item on the PSST, the 13 item scores can be added to obtain a total score for the wound. The total score can then be plotted on the pressure sore continuum at the bottom of the tool to see at a glance regeneration or degeneration of the wound. Total scores range from 13 (skin intact but always at risk) to 65 (profound tissue degeneration). Each of the items is discussed below in terms of how the PSST item measures the characteristic.

Location. Assess the location of the pressure sore by identifying where the lesion occurs on the patient's anatomy and using the body diagram on the tool. Remember, the sacrococcygeal area is the most common area for pressure sores; more severe pressure ulcers often occur over the greater trochanter and there are very few pressure sores on the hips (usually someone has mislabeled the lesion—it most often is the greater trochanter that caused the pressure sore).

Shape. As wounds heal they often begin to assume a more regular, circular/oval shape. The shape also helps determine the overall size of the wound. Butterfly-shaped wounds occur in the sacrococcygeal area and are wounds with mirror images on each side of the coccyx. *Color Plates 3 and 4* show butterfly-shaped ulcers on the coccyx. To determine the shape of the pressure sore, evaluate the perimeter of the wound. Is the wound circular or oval?

Size. Use a transparent measuring guide to measure in centimeters the longest and widest aspect of the wound surface that is visible; multiply the length by the width to determine the surface area of the wound. It can be difficult to determine where to measure size on some wounds, because the edge of the wound may be hard to visualize or the edge may be irregular. This is a skill that simply takes some practice. Always look for the *longest* aspect and the perpendicular *widest* portion of the wound; the measurements then will be more reliable.

Depth. Measure the depth of the wound using a cotton-tipped applicator. Insert the applicator in the deepest portion of the wound; mark the applicator with a pen, and measure the distance from the tip to the mark, using a metric measuring guide. Pick the depth of tissue layers involved with the wound or the thickness of the wound most appropriate using the additional guidelines on the PSST form (Exhibit 5–5).

Edges. The edges of the wound reflect some of the most important characteristics of the wound. The wound edges can be a window to the history and health of the wound. When assessing edges look for how clear and distinct the wound outline appears. If the edges are indistinct and diffuse, there are areas where the normal tissues blend into the wound bed and the edges are not clearly visible. Edges that are even with the skin surface and the wound base are edges that are attached to the base of the wound. This means that the wound is flat, with no appreciable depth. Well-defined edges are clear and distinct and can be outlined on a transparent piece of plastic easily. Edges that are not attached to the base of the wound imply a wound with some depth of tissue involvement (*Color Plate 31*). The wound that is a crater or has a bowl/boat shape is a wound with edges that are not attached to the wound base (*Color Plate 39*). The wound has walls or sides. There is depth to the wound. As the wound ages, the edges become rolled under and thickened to palpation. The edge achieves a unique coloring. The pigment turns a grayish hue in both dark- and light-skinned persons (*Color Plate 33*). Wounds of long duration may continue to thicken, with scar tissue and fibrosis developing in the wound edge, causing the edge to feel hard, rigid, and indurated. Hyperkeratosis is the callus-like tissue that may form around the wound edges (see *Color Plate 24*). Evaluate the wound edges by visual inspection and palpation. *Color Plates 31 to 34* show wounds with different edges.

Clinical Wisdom: *Tips for Assessing Wound Edges*

Definitions for help in assessing wound edges:

Indistinct, diffuse—unable to clearly distinguish wound outline

Attached—even or flush with wound base, *no* sides or walls present, flat

Not attached—sides or walls are present; floor or base of wound is deeper than edge

Rolled under, thickened—soft to firm and flexible to touch

Hyperkeratosis—callus-like tissue formation around wound and at edges

Undermining. Undermining and tunneling are the loss of tissue underneath an intact skin surface. Undermining usually involves a greater percentage of the wound margins with more shallow length than tunneling. Undermining usually involves subcutaneous tissues and follows the fascial planes next to the wound. An undermined area can be likened to a cave, whereas a tunnel is more like a subway. Tunneling usually involves a small percentage of the wound margins; it is narrow and quite long and it seems to have a destination.

Assess for undermining by inserting a cotton-tipped applicator under the wound edge and advancing it as far as it will go without using undue force. Raise the tip of the applicator so that it may be seen or felt on the surface of the skin and mark the surface with a pen. Measure the distance from the mark on the skin to the edge of the wound. Continue this process all around the wound. Then use a transparent metric measuring guide with concentric circles divided into four (25%) pie-shaped quadrants to help determine percentage of the wound involved (see *Color Plates 37 to 39*).

Necrotic Tissue Type. Assess necrotic tissue for the color, consistency, and adherence to the wound bed. Choose the *predominant* characteristic present in the wound. Necrotic tissue type changes as it ages in the wound, as debridement occurs, and as further tissue trauma causes increased cellular death. There are two main types of necrotic tissue: slough and eschar. Slough generally indicates less severity than eschar. Slough usually appears as a yellow to tan mucinous or stringy material that is nonadherent to loosely adherent to the healthy tissues of the wound bed (*Color Plates 3, 27, and 38*). Nonadherent material is defined as appearing scattered throughout the wound; it looks as though the tissue could be removed easily with a gauze sponge. Loosely adherent refers to tissue that is attached to the wound bed; it is thick and stringy and may appear as clumps of debris attached to wound tissue.

Eschar signifies deeper tissue damage. Eschar may be black, gray, or brown in color. Eschar is usually adherent or firmly adherent to the wound tissues and may be soggy and soft or hard and leathery in texture. A soft, soggy eschar is usually strongly attached to the base of the wound but may be lifting from and loose from the edges of the wound (*Color Plate 26*). Hard, crusty eschars are strongly attached to the base and the edges of the wound (*Color Plates 25, 29, and 46*).

Clinical Wisdom: *Eschar Appearance*

Hard eschars are often mistaken for scabs. A scab is a collection of dried blood cells and serum on top of the skin surface, whereas an eschar is a collection of dead tissue within the wound.

Sometimes nonviable tissue appears prior to a wound's appearance. This can be seen on the skin as a white or gray area on the surface of the skin. The area usually demarcates within a few days and the wound appears and interrupts the skin surface.

Necrotic Tissue Amount. The amount of necrotic tissue present in the wound is one of the easier characteristics to assess. Place a transparent measuring guide with concentric circles divided into four (25%) pie-shaped quadrants over the wound. Look at each quadrant and judge how much necrosis is present. Add up the total percentage from judgments of each quadrant; this determines the percentage of the wound involved. Also measure the length and width of the necrosis and determine surface area.

Exudate Type. Evaluating exudate type can be tricky because of the moist wound healing dressings used on most wounds. Some dressings interact with wound drainage to produce a gel or fluid, and others may trap liquid and drainage at the wound site. Before assessing exudate type, gently cleanse the wound with normal saline or water and evaluate fresh exudate. Pick the exudate type that is *predominant* in the wound according to color and consistency. Remember that a wound with necrotic tissue present will almost always have an odor and this may not be true exudate odor.

Exudate Amount. Exudate amount can be difficult to assess accurately for the same reasons it is difficult to determine the type of exudate in the wound. Moist wound healing dressings interact with wound drainage to trap drainage at the wound site. Others may absorb varying amounts of exudate. To judge the amount of exudate in the wound, observe two areas: the wound itself and the dressing used on the wound. Observe the wound for the moisture present. Are the tissues dry and desiccated? Are they swimming in exudate? Is the drainage spread throughout the wound? Use clinical judgment to determine how wet the wound is. Evaluate the dressing used on the wound for how much it interacts with exudate. *Color Plates 40 to 45* show different exudate characteristics.

Skin Color Surrounding Wound. The tissues surrounding the wound are often the first indication of impending further tissue damage. The color of the surrounding skin may indicate further injury from pressure, friction, or shearing. Assess the tissues within 4 cm of the wound edge. Dark-skinned persons show the colors "bright red" and "dark red" as a deepening of normal ethnic skin color or a purple or blacker hue (*Color Plates 19 to 21*). As healing occurs in dark-skinned persons, the new skin is pink and may never darken. In both light- and dark-skinned patients, new epithelium must be differentiated from tissues that are erythemic. To assess for blanchability, press firmly on the skin with a finger; lift the finger and look for blanching (sudden whitening of the tissues) followed by prompt return of color to the area. Nonblanchable erythema signals more severe tissue damage.

Peripheral Tissue Edema. Edema in the surrounding tissues will delay wound healing in the pressure ulcer (*Color Plates 17 to 19*). It is difficult for neoangiogenesis, or the growth of new blood vessels into the wound, to occur in edematous tissues. Assess tissues within 4 cm of the wound edge. Nonpitting edema appears as skin that is shiny and taut, almost glistening. Identify pitting edema by firmly pressing a finger down into the tissues and waiting for 5 seconds; on release of pressure, tissues fail to resume normal position and an indentation appears. Crepitus is accumulation of air or gas in tissues. Measure how far edema extends beyond the wound edges.

Peripheral Tissue Induration. Induration is a sign of impending damage to the tissues. Along with skin color changes, induration is an omen of further pressure-induced tissue trauma. Assess tissues within 4 cm of the wound edge. Induration is an abnormal firmness of tissues with margins. Palpate where the induration starts and where it ends. Assess by gently pinching the tissues. Induration results in an inability to pinch the tissues. Palpate from healthy tissue, moving toward the wound margins. It is usual to feel slight firmness at the wound edge itself. Normal tissues feel soft and spongy; induration feels hard and firm to the touch.

Granulation Tissue. Granulation tissue is a marker of wound health. It signals the proliferative phase of wound healing and usually heralds the eventual closure of the wound. Granulation tissue is the growth of small blood vessels and connective tissue into the wound cavity. It is more observable in full-thickness wounds because of the tissue defect that occurs with full-thickness wounds. In partial-thickness wounds granulation tissue may occur so quickly and in concert with epithelialization that it is unobservable in most cases. Granulation tissue is healthy when it is bright, beefy red, shiny, and granular with a velvety appearance. The tissue looks bumpy and may bleed easily. Granulation tissue can be seen in *Color Plates 8, 9, and 18.*

Clinical Wisdom:
Appearance of Unhealthy Granulation Tissue

Unhealthy granulation tissue due to poor vascular supply appears as pale pink or blanched to dull, dusky red color. Usually the first layer of granulation tissue to be laid down in the wound is pale pink; as the granulation tissue deepens and thickens; the color becomes the bright, beefy red color.

Try to judge what percentage of the wound has been filled with granulation tissue. This is much easier if there is history with the wound. If the same person follows the wound over multiple observations, it is simple to judge the amount of granulation tissue present in the wound. If the initial observation of the wound was done by a different observer or if the data are not available, simply use best judgment to determine the amount of tissue present.

Epithelialization. Epithelialization is the process of epidermal resurfacing and appears as pink or red skin. Visualizing the new epithelium takes practice. *Color Plates 5, 6, 55, and 56* show the process of epidermal resurfacing. In partial-thickness wounds it can occur throughout the wound bed as well as from the wound edges. In full-thickness wounds epidermal resurfacing occurs from the edges only, usually after the wound has almost completely filled with granulation tissue. Use a transparent measuring guide to help determine percentage of the wound involved and to measure the distance the epithelial tissue extends into the wound.

The assessment and ultimately the quantification of clinical judgment forms the foundation for determining treatments and for evaluating effectiveness of therapy.

Clinical Wisdom: *Evaluation of Reepithelialization in Partial-Thickness Wounds*

In partial-thickness wounds, reepithelialization will occur from the wound edges and from throughout the wound bed where portions of hair follicles and accessory glands remain.

Assessment of Treatment Response

The PSST tool allows for temporal tracking of individual characteristics as well as the total score. Each characteristic is assessed as described above and given a value from the Likert scale; thus the scores can be monitored for improvement or deterioration in each characteristic. Additionally, the 13 item scores can be summed and the total score tracked over time to determine the wound status. This quantification of observations allows for monitoring not only individual items and total score but also groups of characteristics. For example, the characteristics of necrotic tissue type and amount and exudate type and amount may be tracked to evaluate debridement or infection management.

Another benefit associated with the assignment of numeric values to items on the tool is the ability to set realistic goals. Clinical experience shows that not all pressure ulcers heal and certainly not always in the same setting. The PSST allows for more realistic goal setting as appropriate to the health care setting and the individual patient and pressure ulcer. For example, the patient with a large necrotic full-thickness ulcer in acute care will probably not be in the facility long enough for the wound to heal completely. However, the tool enables clinicians to set smaller goals, such as "The wound will decrease in type and amount of necrotic tissue."

Clinical Wisdom: *Realistic Goal Setting*

In some instances a pressure ulcer may never heal because of host factors or other contextual circumstances, so an example of a goal might be to maintain the total wound score between 20 and 22.

Use of the PSST or a similar instrument should enhance communication between health care professionals involved in pressure ulcer care. By providing a framework for assessment and documentation with an attempt at quantification, the communication process becomes more meaningful. An objective method of assessing pressure ulcers and monitoring changes over time allows for evaluation of the therapeutic plan of care and may be used to guide and direct therapy. This is particularly true now that health care is moving into a managed care environment. For example, if a specific treatment modality is in use and the patient's wound status as determined with the PSST has not changed in 2 weeks, reevaluation of the plan of care is warranted. Several studies have demonstrated that wounds with a 50% reduction in surface area within 2 weeks healed more expediently than those without a 50% surface area reduction.[13] These data become an expectation with chronic wound healing. Use of the PSST may uncover other outcome criteria that will help identify critical attributes during the course of healing.

The PSST has been fully automated as the Wound and Skin Intelligence System® and now incorporates graphic capabilities and tracking ability for all 13 pressure ulcer assessment items for monitoring progress or deterioration of the pressure ulcers. The system uses relational databases and provides ongoing monitoring capabilities for determining changes in pressure ulcer status over time, produces essential documentation, and automatically reminds users when additional assessments should be completed. The purposes of the Wound and Skin Intelligence System® are clinical assessment; management and documentation, providing feedback based on aggregate data within the system; and monitoring. Data are collected routinely on patients in the system (usually weekly) on standardized forms and then transferred to the computer file by the nurse or designated clerk. Patient files consist of demographic and clinical data, types and costs of treatments and support surfaces, and agency/facility and staff data. All data are entered into the system through a fixed-

format screen. The clinical assessment data fields provide basic treatment guidelines based on the Agency for Health Care Policy and Research pressure ulcer treatment guidelines. Out-of-range values and certain illogical entries are not permitted.

The Wound and Skin Intelligence System® captures related risk factor data and evaluates the overall wound status in relation to risk factor data as well as the assessment data discussed. Development of a large database with the system is currently being explored.

An automated system with the advantages discussed will have significant regulatory implications. Third-party payers and managed care groups are looking for the most cost-effective methods of treating chronic wounds. Use of a quantified tool can assist the clinician in proving the effectiveness of a chosen therapy plan, explain the course of the wound more clearly to payers, and provide rationale for therapy decisions, thus expediting reimbursement in particular cases.

Use of this tool or a similar research-based tool can improve health care practitioner communication and the generalizability of research studies, allow discrimination in studies dealing with treatment modalities, and may help improve understanding of wound healing in pressure ulcers. It can provide increased sensitivity, allowing greater precision and clarity in studies related to the treatment and development of pressure ulcers. An instrument that is sensitive to change in wound status will be helpful in the development of critical pathways for pressure ulcers and is useful as an outcome measure.

REFERENCES

1. Bates-Jensen BM. Indices to include in wound healing assessment. *Adv Wound Care.* 1995;8:25–33.
2. Ferrell BA, Artinian BM, Sessing D. The Sessing scale for assessment of pressure ulcer healing. *J Am Geriatr Soc.* 1995;43:37–40.
3. Thomas D, Rodeheaver G, et al. *Pressure Ulcer Scale for Healing: Derivation and Validation of the Push Tool.* Washington, DC: Fifth National Pressure Ulcer Advisory Panel Consensus Conference; February 1997.
4. Krasner D. *WHS. Wound Healing Scale Version 1.0: A Proposal.* Washington, DC: Fifth National Pressure Ulcer Advisory Panel Consensus Conference; February 1997.
5. Sussman C, Swanson G. The utility of Sussman Wound Healing Tool in predicting wound healing outcomes in physical therapy. *Adv Wound Care.* 1997;10(5):74–77.
6. Maklebust J. Pressure ulcer staging systems: NPUAP proceedings. *Adv Wound Care.* 1995;8(4):1–14.
7. Wagner FW. The dysvascular foot: a system for diagnosis and treatment. *Foot Ankle.* 1981;64:122.
8. Cuddigan J. *Pressure Ulcer Classification: What Do We Have? What Do We Need?* Washington, DC: Fifth National Pressure Ulcer Advisory Panel Consensus Conference; Feburary 1997.
9. Maklebust J, Sieggreen M. *Pressure Ulcer Guideline for Prevention and Nursing Management.* West Dundee, IL: S-N Publications; 1991:198.

10. Bennett A. Report on the task force on the implications for darkly pigmented intact skin in the prediction and prevention of pressure ulcers. *Adv Wound Care.* 1996;8(6):35.

11. Bates-Jensen BM, Vredevoe DL, Brecht ML. Validity and reliability of the Pressure Sore Status Tool. *Decubitus.* 1992;5(6):20–28.

12. Bates-Jensen B, McNees P. Toward an intelligent wound assessment system. *Ostomy Wound Manage.* 1995;41(suppl 7A): 80–88.

13. van Rijswijk L, Polansky M. Predictors of time to healing deep pressure ulcers. *Ostomy Wound Manage.* 1994;40(8):40–50.

Appendix 5–A

Instructions for Pressure Sore Status Tool

GENERAL GUIDELINES

Fill out the attached rating sheet to assess a pressure sore's status after reading the definitions and methods of assessment described below. Evaluate once a week and whenever a change occurs in the wound. Rate according to each item by picking the response that best describes the wound and entering that score in the item score column for the appropriate date. When you have rated the pressure sore on all items, determine the total score by adding together the 13 item scores. The HIGHER the total score, the more severe the pressure sore status. Plot total score on the Pressure Sore Status Continuum to determine progress.

SPECIFIC INSTRUCTIONS

1. **Size:** Use a ruler to measure the longest and widest aspect of the wound surface in centimeters; multiply length by width.
2. **Depth:** Pick the depth and thickness most appropriate to the wound using these additional descriptions:
   1 = Tissues damaged but no break in skin surface
   2 = Superficial, abrasion, blister, or shallow crater. Even with and/or elevated above skin surface (eg, hyperplasia)
   3 = Deep crater with or without undermining of adjacent tissue
   4 = Visualization of tissue layers not possible due to necrosis
   5 = Supporting structures include tendon, joint capsule
3. **Edges:** Use this guide:

Indistinct, diffuse	=	unable to clearly distinguish wound outline
Attached	=	even or flush with wound base, *no* sides or walls present; flat
Not attached	=	sides or walls *are* present; floor or base of wound is deeper than edge
Rolled under, thickened	=	soft to firm and flexible to touch
Hyperkeratosis	=	callus-like tissue formation around wound and at edges
Fibrotic, scarred	=	hard, rigid to touch

4. **Undermining:** Assess by inserting a cotton-tipped applicator under the wound edge. Advance it as far as it will go without using undue force. Raise the tip of the applicator so that it may be seen or felt on the surface of the skin and mark the surface with a pen. Measure the distance from the mark on the skin to the edge of the wound. Continue the process around the wound. Then use a transparent metric measuring guide with concentric circles divided into four (25%) pie-shaped quadrants to help determine percentage of wound involved.
5. **Necrotic Tissue Type:** Pick the type of necrotic tissue that is *predominant* in the wound according to color, consistency, and adherence using this guide:

White/gray, nonviable tissue	=	may appear prior to wound opening; skin surface is white or gray
Nonadherent, yellow slough	=	thin, mucinous substance; scattered throughout wound bed; easily separated from wound tissue
Loosely adherent, yellow slough	=	thick, stringy clumps of debris; attached to wound tissue
Adherent, soft, black eschar	=	soggy tissue; strongly attached to tissue in center or base of wound
Firmly adherent, hard/black eschar	=	firm, crusty tissue; strongly attached to wound base *and* edges (like a hard scab)

6. **Necrotic Tissue Amount:** Use a transparent metric measuring guide with concentric circles divided into four (25%) pie-shaped quadrants to help determine percentage of wound involved.

continues

7. **Exudate Type:** Some dressings interact with wound drainage to produce a gel or trap liquid. Before assessing exudate type, gently cleanse wound with normal saline or water. Pick the exudate type that is *predominant* in the wound according to color and consistency, using this guide:

   Bloody   =   thin, bright red
   Serosanguineous   =   thin, watery, pale red to pink
   Serous   =   thin, watery, clear
   Purulent   =   thin or thick, opaque tan to yellow
   Foul purulent   =   thick, opaque yellow to green with offensive odor

8. **Exudate Amount:** Use a transparent metric measuring guide with concentric circles divided into four (25%) pie-shaped quadrants to determine percentage of dressing involved with exudate. Use this guide:

   None   =   wound tissues dry
   Scant   =   wound tissues moist; no measurable exudate
   Small   =   wound tissues wet; moisture evenly distributed in wound; drainage involves ≤25% dressing
   Moderate   =   wound tissues saturated; drainage may or may not be evenly distributed in wound; drainage involves >25% to ≤75% dressing
   Large   =   wound tissues bathed in fluid; drainage freely expressed; may or may not be evenly distributed in wound; drainage involves >75% of dressing

9. **Skin Color Surrounding Wound:** Assess tissues within 4 cm of wound edge. Dark-skinned persons show the colors "bright red" and "dark red" as a deepening of normal ethnic skin color or a purple hue. As healing occurs in dark-skinned persons, the new skin is pink and may never darken.

10. **Peripheral Tissue Edema:** Asses tissues within 4 cm of wound edge. Nonpitting edema appears as skin that is shiny and taut. Identify pitting edema by firmly pressing a finger down into the tissues and waiting for 5 seconds; on release of pressure, tissues fail to resume previous position and an indentation appears. Crepitus is accumulation of air or gas in tissues. Use a transparent metric measuring guide to determine how far edema extends beyond wound.

11. **Peripheral Tissue Induration:** Assess tissues within 4 cm of wound edge. Induration is abnormal firmness of tissues with margins. Assess by gently pinching the tissues. Induration results in an inability to pinch the tissues. Use a transparent metric measuring guide with concentric circles divided into four (25%) pie-shaped quadrants to determine percentage of wound and area involved.

12. **Granulation Tissue:** Granulation tissue is the growth of small blood vessels and connective tissue to fill in full-thickness wounds. Tissue is healthy when bright, beefy red, shiny, and granular with a velvety appearance. Poor vascular supply appears as pale pink or blanched to dull, dusky red color.

13. **Epithelialization:** Epithelialization is the process of epidermal resurfacing and appears as pink or red skin. In partial-thickness wounds it can occur throughout the wound bed as well as from the wound edges. In full-thickness wounds it occurs from the edges only. Use a transparent metric measuring guide with concentric circles divided into four (25%) pie-shaped quadrants to help determine percentage of wound involved and to measure the distance the epithelial tissue extends into the wound.

CHAPTER 6

Noninvasive Vascular Testing

Anne Siegel

INTRODUCTION

In the past decade, many advances have been made in the diagnosis and treatment of vascular disease. The key to preventing debilitating circulatory problems is prevention and early diagnosis. Noninvasive vascular evaluations are used to detect the presence or absence of arterial occlusive or venous disease. They are used to evaluate the healing potential of ulcers/wounds, as an aid in determining wound care management plans, and as a guide in determining which patients need referral to a vascular surgeon for further evaluation.

The first step in a vascular evaluation is to obtain a complete medical history from the patient. This information is imperative in the overall assessment and treatment of the patient's condition. The patient's history provides a guide in determining the etiology of the wound being evaluating. A careful, thorough history is the key in vascular assessment. The history should include the areas discussed below.

CHIEF COMPLAINT

The chief complaint is the combination of symptoms that prompted the patient to seek medical attention.[1] Focus on the symptoms that concern the patient and then ask the patient to describe those symptoms in more detail. Spending time listening to the patient is as important as the physical examination.

A detailed pain history is essential in determining the urgency and type of treatment the patient will receive. Investigate the pain. Where is the location of the pain? When did the pain start? What factors aggravate or relieve the pain: elevation? dependency? walking? resting? standing? sitting?

What time of the day is the pain experienced? Describe the pain: aching? burning? constant? intermittent?

For example, venous ulcers are not very painful and the patient may find relief from elevation of the leg. Arterial ulcers are very painful because of the lack of circulation. Keep in mind that there are always exceptions.

The patient may have a combination of arterial and venous disease. The patient can have diabetic neuropathy and have an arterial ulcer without any pain. Pain on the plantar aspect of the foot usually signals a diabetic neuropathic foot. Arterial rest pain is found on the dorsum of the foot and is usually described as a burning ache type of pain (like a toothache). Sometimes the patient will find some relief with dependency of the leg. Rest pain indicates that the patient has significant arterial insufficiency and will need intervention from a vascular surgeon to heal the wounds. Claudication is exercise-induced pain in the major muscle groups that is relieved with rest (usually described as a cramplike pain in the calf, thigh, or buttock). If the patient has a history of claudication, this should guide the clinician's thinking that the ulcer being evaluated may have an arterial etiology.

PAST MEDICAL HISTORY

Exhibit 6–1 lists areas of medical history questioning used to identify risk factors for vascular disease, both arterial and venous. It goes beyond the general medical history discussed in Chapter 1 and focuses on specific vascular-related factors.

PHYSICAL EXAMINATION

After obtaining a complete history from the patient, the next step is the physical exam. A careful physical exam used

Exhibit 6–1 Past Medical History

Risk Factors for Peripheral Vascular Disease[1]

Cardiac history

- Heart disease (cardiac catheterization? results?)
- Heart attack (date of last event)
- Chest pain (note location of the pain, how is pain relieved? onset?)
- Stroke (date of event, note location of weakness or speech deficit)

Hypertension (severity, medications, age at onset, highest blood pressure reading)

Hyperlipidemia (last cholesterol level, medication, number of years)

Smoking history (number of packs per day × years smoked = number of pack-years) (For example: a patient smoking two packs per day for 20 years has a 40-pack-year smoking history.) (quit? year quit)

Diabetes (number of years, medications)

Concomitant illnesses (renal disease, collagen vascular disease, arthritis, pulmonary disease, malignancy [type of malignancy] back [spine] problems, etc)

Family history of arterial disease

Risk Factors for Venous Disease

Trauma (type, date)
Deep vein thrombosis (date, anticoagulants)
Prolonged inactivity
Pregnancies
Family history of venous disease
Obesity
Clotting disorders

Past Surgical History

Vascular surgery (date of procedure, indication)
Angiogram/venogram (dates, indication, intervention?)
General surgery (date of procedure, indication)

---

in conjunction with a thorough history can usually determine the etiology of the wound and determine the wound care plan or establish the need for further vascular testing. The first step to the physical exam is *inspection* of the extremity. Note the presence and location of any ulcers, wounds, or gangrene. Describe the wound: color, wound bed, drainage (color of drainage), size, and odor. Note the presence or absence of swelling (compare both legs, and document the location of any swelling). Ask the patient how long the ulcer has been present. Look at the skin color. Are there any pigment changes? Feel the texture of the patient's skin: dry? moist? Feel the temperature of the skin, comparing both legs. Using the back of the hand to assess temperature, note the level at which the limb is cool or warm. Note the presence or absence of hair (legs, toes). Note the appearance of the toenails (thickened?). Check for the presence and distribution of varicose veins.

Clinical Wisdom: *Severe Arterial Insufficiency*

If arterial disease is severe, elevating the leg while the patient is supine will cause the patient's leg to become pale, which is known as *elevation pallor.* The pale color is due to lack of blood flow in the patient's leg. If the patient then hangs the leg over the side of the examining table, the color of the foot will change to a deep red or purple color, known as *dependent rubor.* This is also due to the lack of blood flow and vasodilatation of the arterioles. Be careful not to confuse dependent rubor with cellulitis. If the patient has cellulitis, the leg will not become pale with elevation.[1]

Differentiation between Arterial and Venous Disease

Patients with arterial insufficiency have classic characteristics that will enable the examiner to distinguish easily between arterial and venous ulcers. Always remember that patients can have a combination of arterial and venous diseases, and the whole clinical picture may not fit into one specific category. Use the following lists of characteristics as a guide.

Characteristics of Arterial Disease

- Pain (walking and/or at rest)
- Foot cool or cold
- Weak or absent pulses
- Absence of leg hair
- Skin shiny, dry, pale
- Thickened toenails
- Ulcer location: usually below ankle (pressure areas, toes)
- Ulcer: necrotic, minimal drainage
- Ankle-brachial index (ABI) less than 0.5 (*note:* if diabetic, can be greater than 1.0)
- Elevation pallor/dependent rubor
- History of diabetes, hypertension, smoking, claudication
- History of foot trauma (tight shoes, toenails cut too short, object falling on foot)

Clinical Wisdom: *Trophic Changes*

Trophic changes are skin changes that occur over time in patients with chronic arterial insufficiency. Trophic changes include absence of leg hair; shiny, dry, pale skin; and thickened toenails. These symptoms are due to the chronic lack of nutrition from a good blood supply to the extremity. Some of these changes occur naturally in elderly patients.

Characteristics of Venous Disease[2]

- Foot warm
- Edema
- Brawny skin pigment changes
- Varicose veins
- Ulcer location usually above ankle (medial malleolus)
- Venous ulcers generally not painful
- Ulcer: granulating, drainage
- ABI greater than 1.0
- History of trauma, deep vein thrombosis, varicose veins, malignancy

PULSE EXAM

The next step in the physical examination is the *pulse exam.*[3] The pulse exam includes locating and grading bilateral femoral, popliteal, dorsalis pedis, and posterior tibial artery pulses. The following system should be used to grade pulses:

0	=	No pulse
1+	=	Barely felt
2+	=	Diminished
3+	=	Normal pulse ("easily felt)
4+	=	Bounding, aneurysmal ("pulse hits you in the face")

Pulse Table

	Femoral	Popliteal	Dorsalis Pedis	Posterior Tibial
RLE				
LLE				

The pulse exam algorithm (Figure 6–1) is the clinician's guide to triage patients for appropriate pathways for examination, referral and patient teaching.

The lower extremity pulse exam can accurately assess for the presence, absence, and location of arterial disease. The patient should be supine with head and legs adequately supported. The *common femoral artery* (CFA) is easily palpated with the second, third, and fourth fingers in the groin below and medial to the inguinal ligament. If the patient is obese, the CFA pulse may be difficult to palpate. If the pulse is diminished or absent, the patient may have aortic/iliac disease. Figure 6–2 indicates the location of arteries to palpate and to use for main probe sites when taking Doppler readings (described later).

The *popliteal artery* is the most difficult to palpate. The artery is located midline behind the knee in the popliteal fossa. Have the patient slightly flex at the knee. Have the clinician place both hands behind the patient's knee in a cupped fashion and allow the pulse to bounce back into the clinician's hands. *Note:* If the popliteal pulse is easy to palpate, this could indicate a popliteal aneurysm, and further investigation is needed from a vascular lab.

The *dorsalis pedis pulse* is examined by sitting or standing facing the patient. Using the second and third fingers, palpate the dorsum of the foot. Place the thumb on the plantar surface of the foot to anchor the hand. Do not press hard because the pressure can occlude the artery. Use a light touch. The *posterior tibial artery* is palpated at the level of the ankle (medial and posterior). While facing the patient, use the sec-

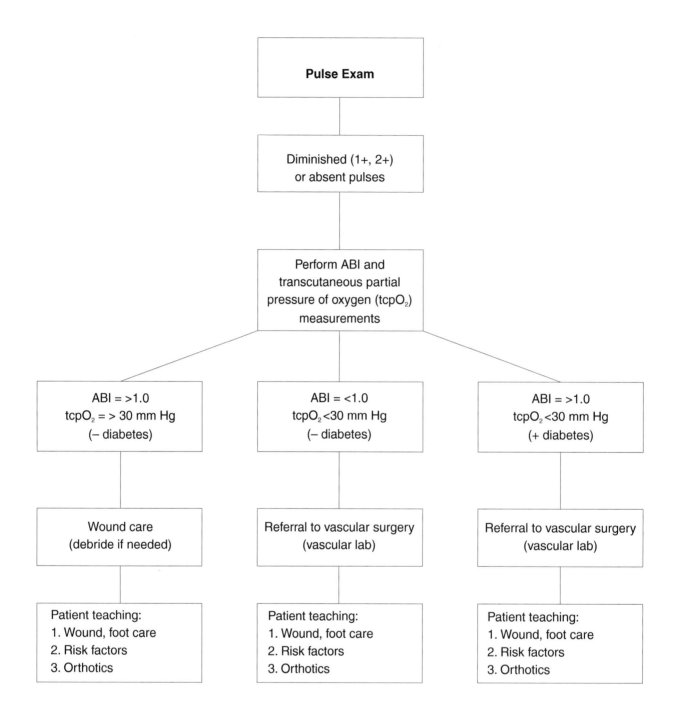

Figure 6–1 Pulse exam.

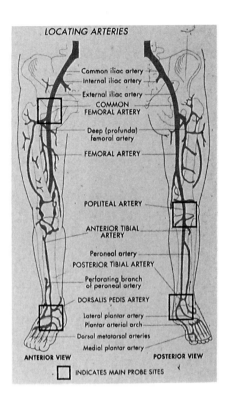

LOCATING ARTERIES

Common iliac artery
Internal iliac artery
External iliac artery
COMMON
FEMORAL ARTERY
Deep (profunda)
femoral artery
FEMORAL ARTERY
POPLITEAL ARTERY
ANTERIOR TIBIAL
ARTERY
Peroneal artery
POSTERIOR TIBIAL ARTERY
Perforating branch
of peroneal artery
DORSALIS PEDIS ARTERY
Lateral plantar artery
Plantar arterial arch
Dorsal metatarsal arteries
Medial plantar artery
ANTERIOR VIEW   POSTERIOR VIEW
☐ INDICATES MAIN PROBE SITES

Figure 6–2 Locating arteries. Courtesy of Huntleigh Diagnostics Ltd., Cardiff, United Kingdom.

ond and third fingers to palpate the pulse. Place the thumb on the lateral malleolus to anchor the hand. The other hand can be used to support the patient's heel.

NONINVASIVE VASCULAR TESTING

After completing the history and physical exam, the clinician may already know the etiology of the patient's ulcer or wound. If more information is needed, the patient will require noninvasive testing. If the patient has a venous ulcer and has 3+ normal pulses, it is possible to safely treat the ulcer with wound care, compression, and debridement. If the patient has decreased pulses and has an arterial or venous ulcer, an ABI will need to be performed and, if available, a tcpO$_2$ measurement should be obtained.

The ABI measures the systolic blood pressure in the ankles and provides objective information as to the presence and severity of arterial occlusive disease.[4] It is sometimes called the ankle pressure index (API). The equipment needed to obtain an ABI is a Doppler probe (ultrasound stethoscope), blood pressure (BP) cuff, and ultrasound gel (Exhibit 6–2). The Doppler works on the principle that ultrasound waves that strike a moving object (blood) at one frequency are reflected back at a different frequency. Figure 6–3 illustrates the procedure for performing ABI.

Significance of ABI Values

ABI values are predictors of healing (Table 6–1). Wounds will heal if the ABI is 0.8 or greater; an ABI of 0.5 to 0.8 means high risk for a nonhealing limb, which needs perfusion. If ABI is below 0.8 wounds should not be debrided because of high risk for necrosis and infection or treated with compression.

Exhibit 6–2 Ankle-Brachial Index Procedure

Ankle-Brachial Index Procedure

1. Lay patient flat.
2. Apply BP cuff around the patient's arm (above elbow).
3. Apply ultrasound gel.
4. Hold Doppler probe at a 45° angle and place over brachial pulse.
5. Identify the arterial signal and inflate the cuff until the signal disappears.
6. Slowly deflate the cuff until the arterial sound returns. The first sound that is heard is the systolic brachial pressure.
7. Obtain brachial pressures in both upper extremities.
8. To obtain ankle pressures, place the cuff above the ankle and place Doppler probe over the dorsalis pedis or the posterior tibial artery.
9. Repeat steps 3 to 6.

Calculating the ABI

$$ABI = \frac{\text{Highest ankle Doppler pressure}}{\text{Highest brachial Doppler pressure}}$$

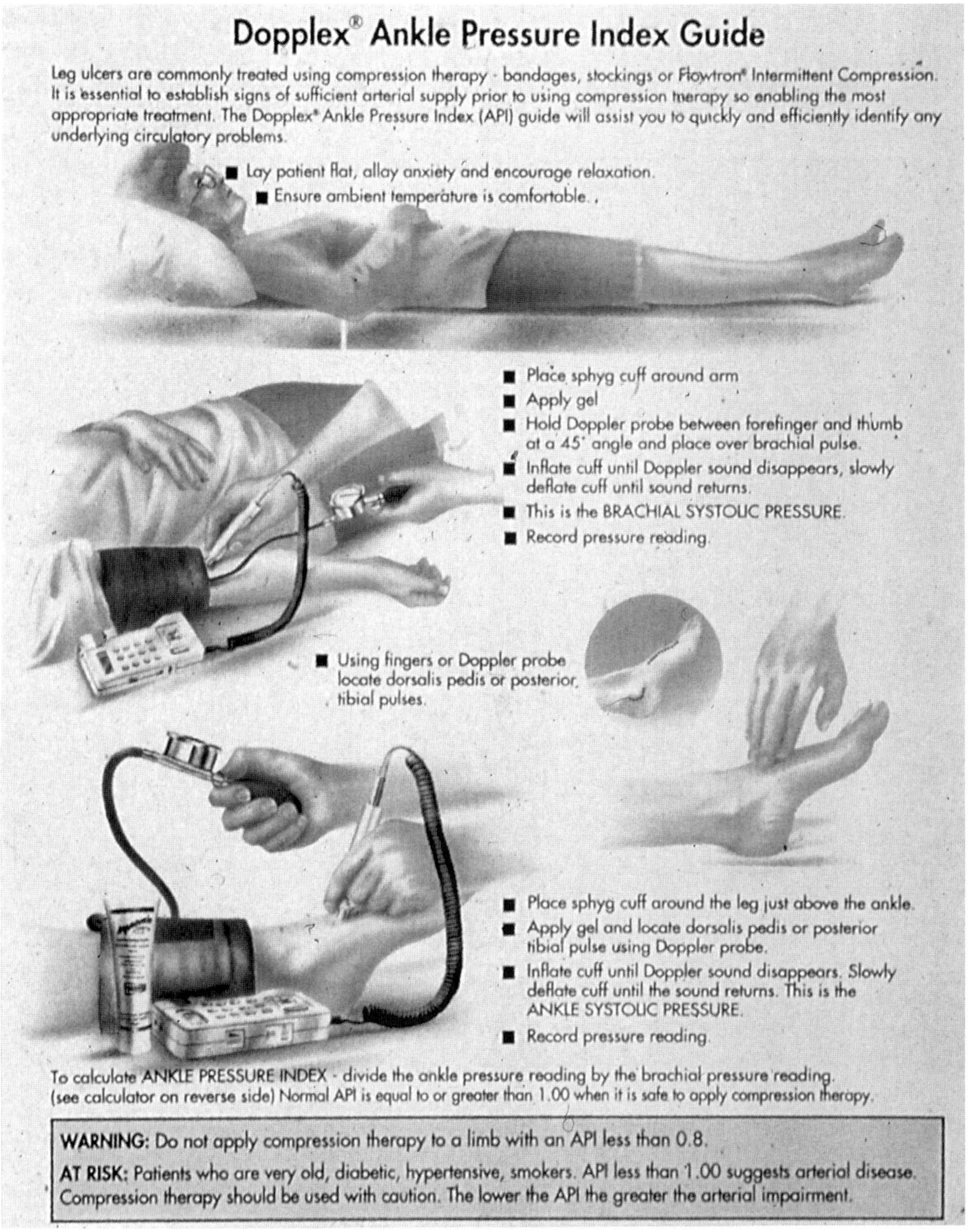

Figure 6–3 Procedure for performing ABI. *Source:* Reprinted with permission from C. Moffatt, The Charing Cross Approach to Venous Ulcers, *Nursing Standard,* Dec 12.5, No. 12, pp. 6–9, © 1990, Royal College of Nursing.

Table 6–1 Table of ABI Values

Dopplex® Ankle Pressure Index (API) Guide

Ankle Pressure (mmHg)

Brachial Pressure (mmHg)

B\A	30	35	40	45	50	55	60	65	70	75	80	85	90	95	100	105	110	115	120	125	130	135	140	145	150	155	160	165	170	175	180	185	190	195	200
180	.16	.19	.22	.25	.27	.30	.33	.36	.38	.41	.44	.47	.50	.52	.55	.58	.61	.63	.66	.69	.72	.75	.77	.80	.83	.86	.89	.92	.94	.97	1.00				
175	.17	.20	.22	.25	.28	.31	.34	.37	.40	.42	.45	.48	.51	.54	.57	.60	.62	.65	.68	.71	.74	.77	.80	.82	.85	.88	.92	.94	.97	1.00					
170	.17	.20	.23	.26	.29	.32	.35	.38	.41	.44	.47	.50	.52	.55	.58	.61	.64	.67	.70	.73	.76	.79	.82	.85	.89	.91	.94	.97	1.00						
165	.18	.21	.24	.27	.30	.33	.36	.39	.42	.45	.48	.51	.54	.57	.60	.63	.66	.69	.72	.75	.78	.81	.84	.87	.90	.94	.96	1.00							
160	.18	.21	.25	.28	.31	.34	.37	.40	.43	.46	.50	.53	.56	.59	.62	.65	.68	.71	.75	.78	.81	.84	.87	.90	.93	.96	1.00								
155	.19	.22	.25	.29	.32	.35	.38	.41	.45	.48	.51	.54	.58	.61	.64	.67	.70	.74	.76	.80	.83	.87	.90	.93	.96	1.00									
150	.20	.23	.26	.30	.33	.36	.40	.43	.46	.50	.53	.56	.60	.63	.66	.70	.73	.76	.80	.83	.86	.90	.93	.96	1.00										
145	.20	.24	.27	.31	.34	.37	.41	.44	.48	.51	.55	.58	.62	.65	.69	.72	.75	.79	.82	.86	.90	.93	.96	1.00											
140	.21	.25	.28	.32	.35	.39	.42	.46	.50	.53	.57	.60	.64	.67	.71	.75	.78	.82	.85	.89	.92	.96	1.00												
135	.22	.26	.29	.33	.37	.40	.44	.48	.51	.55	.59	.62	.66	.70	.74	.77	.81	.85	.88	.92	.96	1.00													
130	.23	.27	.30	.34	.38	.42	.46	.50	.53	.57	.61	.65	.69	.73	.77	.80	.84	.88	.92	.96	1.00														
125	.24	.28	.32	.36	.40	.44	.48	.52	.56	.60	.64	.68	.72	.76	.80	.84	.88	.92	.96	1.00															
120	.25	.29	.33	.37	.40	.45	.50	.54	.58	.62	.66	.70	.75	.79	.83	.87	.91	.95	1.00																
115	.26	.30	.34	.39	.43	.48	.52	.56	.60	.65	.69	.74	.78	.82	.86	.91	.95	1.00																	
110	.27	.31	.36	.40	.45	.50	.54	.59	.63	.68	.72	.77	.81	.86	.90	.95	1.00																		
105	.28	.33	.38	.42	.47	.52	.57	.61	.66	.71	.76	.80	.85	.90	.95	1.00																			
100	.30	.35	.40	.45	.50	.55	.60	.65	.70	.75	.80	.85	.90	.95	1.00																				

GREATER THAN 1.00

Huntleigh Healthcare, a world leading manufacturer of pocket Dopplers, offers an extensive range of bi-directional pocket Dopplers with visual flow and rate display, together with a wide range of interchangeable probes for both vascular and obstetric applications.

WARNING: False high readings may be obtained in patients with calcified arteries because the sphygmomanometer cuff cannot fully compress the hardened arteries. Calcified arteries may be present in patients with history of Diabetes, Arteriosclerosis and Atherosclerosis.

Courtesy of Huntleigh Diagnostics Ltd., Cardiff, United Kingdom.

Significance of Ankle-Brachial Index Values

API ≤0.5 Referral to vascular specialist (compression therapy contraindicated)

API = 0.5–0.8 Referral to vascular specialist. Intermittent claudicant indicating peripheral arterial occlusive disease (compression therapy contraindicated)

API = 0.8–1.00 Mild peripheral arterial occlusive disease (compression therapy with caution)

API = >1.00 Referral to vascular specialist. Indicates calcified vessels if diabetic

Clinical Wisdom: *Diabetic Patients*

The ankle-brachial index can be falsely elevated in patients with diabetes. This is due to the calcification of the inner layer of the artery, ie, the cuff is unable to compress calcified distal vessel(s). This phenomenon is referred to as *noncompressible vessels*. Instead of ABI, proceed with transcutaneous oxygen testing if available. Another option is to take toe pressures.

Patients sometimes present with different occlusive disease in the two legs. The following case study example describes such a situation.

Case Study: *Ankle-Brachial Index*

Systolic Doppler Pressures

	Brachial	Dorsalis Pedis	Posterior Tibial
RT	90	50	40
LT	100	0	100

Note: Always use the highest brachial pressure and the highest ankle pressure to calculate the ABI.

ABI = 50/100 =0.5 in the right lower extremity; the highest ankle pressure is 50. Using the highest brachial pressure (which is the left arm), divide the 50 by 100, which equals 0.5.

ABI = 100/100 = 1.0 in the left lower extremity; the highest ankle pressure is 100. Using the left arm pressure again, divide the 100 at the ankle into the 100 brachial pressure, which equals 1.0.

Additional Doppler Pressures

Further diagnostic information can be obtained by measuring the systolic Doppler pressures at different levels of the leg. Segmental Doppler pressures can identify the level of arterial obstruction. Blood pressure cuffs are placed at the high thigh, above the knee, below the knee, and above the ankle.

Systolic blood pressure measurements are then taken as previously described, by inflating the cuffs consecutively, starting at the ankle level. All pressure gradients should be less than 30 mm Hg between cuffs. The high thigh pressure should be greater than the brachial pressure. The segmental Doppler pressure study is usually performed in a vascular lab.

Digital Plethysmography

Digital plethysmography (toe pressures) is another study that is performed in a vascular lab with special equipment. Additional information can be obtained by measuring the systolic toe pressure. This study is very important in diabetic patients. Since the ABI can be unreliable in diabetic patients because of calcified vessels, this study can reliably assess the lower extremity circulation. The digital arteries are less likely to calcify and can be used to calculate a toe-brachial index. The normal toe pressure is approximately 80% to 99% of the brachial systolic pressure.

Transcutaneous Oxygen Measurements

Transcutaneous partial pressure of oxygen ($tcpO_2$) measures oxygen delivery to the skin tissue. This noninvasive measurement is very useful in predicting ulcer healing and amputation level. It is capable of documenting the hypoxemia characteristic of ischemic tissue. This study is very simple to perform and gives information that is very valuable in guiding the wound care management plan.

Performing the $tcpO_2$ Study

If a transcutaneous oxygen monitor is not available, this study can be performed in a vascular lab. The first step in performing the study is to calibrate the machine. There are different models, and the machines should be calibrated according to the manufacturer's instructions. The small $tcpO_2$ sensor is applied to the skin with an airtight self-adhesive fixation ring. At the end of the $tcpO_2$ electrode, there is a heating element. This element heats the skin temperature above 41°C, thus allowing oxygen transport from the capillary level to the skin surface. The sensor is left in place for 20 minutes and then the reading is taken from the machine.

Choosing the correct position for placement of the $tcpO_2$ electrode is a very important part of the study. The correct position depends on where the patient has the ulcer or wound that is being assessed. If the patient has a toe ulcer, the electrode is placed just proximal to the toe. Describe the area as "the base of the toes."

Significance of the $tcpO_2$ Finding

The significance of $tcpO_2$ readings is that if the $tcpO_2$ values are less than 20 mm Hg, the ulcer/wound will not heal. If the $tcpO_2$ value is greater than 30 mm Hg, healing will occur. If the $tcpO_2$ reading proximal to the toes (low dorsum) is greater than 30 mm Hg, then the wound can be safely debrided and dressing changes may proceed. If the patient has a gangrenous toe and it is being assessed for amputation healing, this toe amputation site would heal. If the $tcpO_2$ reading is less than 30 mm Hg at the low dorsum, do not debride the wound. Refer this patient to a vascular surgeon for further evaluation. If the patient has an ulcer higher up the leg, place the electrode around the wound edge. If the reading is greater than 30 mm Hg, debride the wound. If the patient does not have enough blood flow to heal a wound and the wound is still debrided, the wound will necrose again and probably become infected. The safe thing to do if there is any doubt is to refer the patient to a vascular lab or vascular surgeon for further evaluation.

If the vascular surgeon evaluates the patient and concludes that there is adequate blood flow to the extremity, wound care management can always be resumed for the patient. If vascular testing is performed and the patient has good circulation to the extremity but the wound will not heal, this patient needs to be referred to a vascular surgeon for evaluation. There may be an infection or malignancy that needs to be treated. Remember, when in doubt, refer the patient out!

Clinical Wisdom:
Accuracy of tcpO$_2$ Measurements

tcpO$_2$ measurements are not reliable in patients with swelling or infection! Do not test these patients. The patient can be tested when the infection is clear and the swelling is gone.

ADDITIONAL VASCULAR STUDIES

There are numerous additional vascular studies done in the vascular lab to assess the arterial circulation, some of which include duplex scanning and velocity waveform analysis. These studies complement the information obtained in the history and physical exam, but are not necessary in diagnosing the etiology of the patient's ulcer.

NONINVASIVE VENOUS TESTING

Venous evaluations are usually performed to rule out deep vein thrombosis (DVT). They are also used to evaluate for superficial and deep venous insufficiency in patients with severe varicose veins or venous ulcers. Venous Doppler ultrasonography is a noninvasive imaging study that is performed in a vascular lab. The ultrasound can visualize the veins within the leg, thus diagnosing incompetent venous valves or clot within the deep venous system (see Figure 6–4).

CONCLUSION

The noninvasive studies performed in addition to physical assessment can help determine the right choice for wound

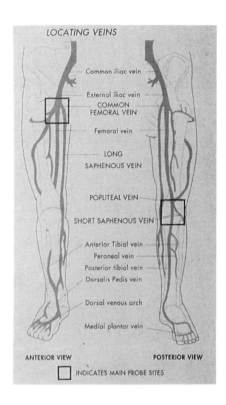

Figure 6–4 Locating veins. Courtesy of Huntleigh Diagnostics Ltd., Cardiff, United Kingdom.

---

care management and determine which patients need prompt referral to a vascular surgeon (see Figure 6–5).

REFERRAL CRITERIA

The following indicators guide referral to a vascular surgeon or the vascular lab:

- Ankle-brachial index greater than 1.0, tcpO$_2$ measurement greater than 30 mm Hg: semiurgent vascular appointment
- Gangrene present; urgent vascular appointment
- ABI:
  1. Greater than 0.8: routine vascular appointment
  2. Between 0.5 and 0.8: semiurgent vascular appointment
  3. Below 0.5: urgent vascular appointment

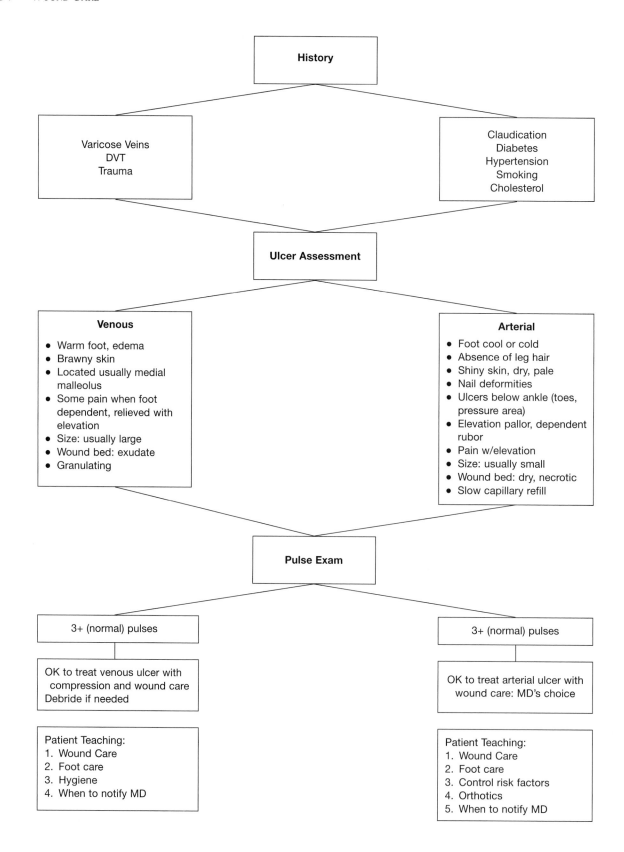

Figure 6–5 Vascular ulcers: algorithm for assessment and referral.

- Exposed bone or tendon at base of ulcer: urgent vascular appointment
- Gross infection or cellulitis: urgent vascular appointment
- Ankle-brachial index less than 1.0 with diminished or absent pulses: semiurgent vascular appointment
- Nonhealing wounds despite 3+ pulses and good wound care: semiurgent vascular appointment
- When in doubt, refer to vascular lab for further evaluation

SELF-CARE TEACHING GUIDELINES

The key to prevention of vascular diseases is patient education. Education is the key to preventing debilitating circulatory problems. Patients must learn the correct way to avoid added stress on their circulatory system and when to notify their physician if there is a problem.

Self-Care Teaching Guidelines Specific to Arterial Insufficiency

- Do not smoke! Even one cigarette a day can decrease circulation.
- Follow physician's directions for controlling blood pressure, diabetes, and high cholesterol.
- Inspect legs and feet daily and report any signs of redness, pain, or ulceration immediately. Be sure to inspect between toes.
- Wash and dry feet every day.
- Lubricate skin to avoid cracks.
- The first thing to go into the shoe in the morning should be a hand. Check to make sure there are no foreign objects that could injure the foot.
- Cut toenails straight across. If possible, have a podiatrist cut the toenails.

- Do not wear tight shoes.
- Test bath water with a hand or thermometer (<98°F) to avoid burns.
- Do not walk barefoot at any time, either inside or outside the home.
- Wear comfortable, wide-toed shoes that cause no pressure (orthotics if necessary).
- Do not wear constricting clothes.
- Wear clean cotton socks with smooth seams or without seams

Self-Care Teaching Guidelines Specific to Venous Insufficiency

- Do not smoke!
- Wear support stockings as prescribed.
- Avoid crossing legs.
- Elevate legs when sitting.
- Inspect legs and feet daily, and report any increased swelling, new or larger ulcers, increased pain, redness, or infection.
- Avoid trauma to legs, such as bumping or scratching.
- Keep legs and feet clean.
- Eat a well-balanced nutritional diet that is low in sodium.

REFERENCES

1. Fahey V. *Vascular Nursing.* 2nd ed. Philadelphia: WB Saunders; 1994:53–55, 63–66.
2. Young J, Graor R, Olin J, Bartholomew J. *Peripheral Vascular Diseases.* St. Louis, MO: Mosby-Yearbook; 1991:443–456.
3. Dickson C, ed. *Vascular Surgery Combat Manual.* Naperville, IL: WL Gore & Associates; 1996:4–11, 27–37.
4. Rutherford R. *Vascular Surgery.* 3rd ed. Philadelphia: WB Saunders; 1989:1:61–91.

Management by Wound Characteristics

Barbara M. Bates-Jensen

The Bates-Jensen rules for wound therapy are as follows: *If the wound is dirty, clean it. If there is leakage, manage it. If there is a hole, fill it. If it is flat, protect it. If it is healed, prevent it.*

Understanding the impact of wound characteristics on treatment options provides a template for intervention. Often the physical appearance of the wound is the driving force behind treatment options. Management of wound healing by examination of physical characteristics commonly observed in wounds is presented in Part II. The wound characteristics of necrotic tissue, exudate and infection, edema, and the clean, proliferating wound require specific interventions by the clinician.

Part II begins with a chapter on management of necrotic tissue. A description of the significance and pathophysiology of necrotic debris in the wound bed opens the discussion. Specific necrotic tissue characteristics of consistency, color, adherence, and amount are described. The characteristics of necrotic tissue in various wound types are described. The clinical presentation of the two types of necrosis, slough and eschar, is described.

Management of necrotic tissue involves wound debridement by one of four methods: mechanical, enzymatic, sharp, and autolytic. Each debridement method is presented with indications for use, contraindications, advantages, and disadvantages of the method and procedures for implementation. Outcome measures based on the color and amount of necrotic tissue in the wound are presented as tools to measure the effectiveness of debridement interventions. The chapter concludes with self-care teaching guidelines for other health care workers, family caregivers, and patients.

Chapter 8 reviews management of exudate and infection. The significance and pathophysiology of wound exudate are presented. Common wound exudate for various wound types

is discussed. The definition and significance of wound infection are presented. Misdiagnosis of wound infection occurs frequently in clinical practice. Differentiation of infection and colonization of the wound is not a simple task for most clinicians. Comparing characteristics of the infected wound with the inflamed wound reveals significant similarities as well as some key differences. One of the primary methods of differentiating between infection and inflammation is by wound culture. Bates-Jensen provides background and discussion on wound cultures with tissue biopsy, needle aspiration, and quantitative swab techniques. A procedure for each type of wound culture technique is included. The rising incidence of resistant organisms is presented with reference to methicillin-resistant *Staphylococcus aureus*. One method of management of exudate and infection is wound cleansing. Wound cleansing and irrigation are discussed in relationship to use of antimicrobial cleansers, and specific cleansing procedures for various wounds are presented. The use of topical antimicrobials (antibacterials, antifungals, and antiseptics) is presented, with discussion on management of exudate with moist wound dressings completing the management interventions. Outcome measures for evaluating exudate management in terms of amount and type of exudate are presented. The chapter ends with self-care teaching guidelines for use with other health care workers, family caregivers, and patients.

Chapter 9 focuses on the management of edema. Wiersema-Bryant presents discussion of the etiologies associated with edema and strategies directed toward the management of edema. Management of edema includes a description of the procedures for managing edema and the parameters to measure in determining outcomes of interventions. Edema assessment and measurement of edema and edema control are presented as two primary categories of quantitative and qualitative findings. Quantitatively, leg circumference and leg volume can be measured to give a reference range of leg size, and, with care, pitting edema can also be measured and quantified. Procedures and guidelines for determining leg circumference, leg volume, and pitting edema are included. Qualitative assessment includes general appearance of the skin and leg and patient statements about the edema.

Elimination and control of edema may be accomplished through leg elevation, exercise, and the use of compression therapy. Leg elevation facilitates the removal of fluid through utilization of gravity in assisting venous return. Compression therapy works with exercise to facilitate the movement of excess fluid from the lower extremity. Included as appropriate for edema management are leg elevation, elastic wraps, tubular bandages, paste bandages, graduated compression stockings, intermittent sequential compression devices, and exercise. A discussion of each method of edema management includes a definition of the method, the indications and contraindications for use, advantages and disadvantages of the method, and procedures for implementation of the method. Expected outcomes related to edema control with each method and helpful hints for using the method make these procedures very user friendly. The chapter concludes with several case studies emphasizing the principles of edema management and, finally, self-care teaching guidelines, including a sample patient contract.

The final chapter in Part II examines wound management of the clean wound. Geoffrey Sussman provides discussion of topical wound care products for moist wound healing. Discussion includes inert and passive products such as gauze, lint and fiber products, and modern moist wound dressings. The features of an "ideal" wound dressing are presented. Generic wound product categories of film dressings, foams, hydrocolloids, hydrogels, alginates, hydroactive dressings, and combination/miscellaneous dressings are then presented. Each wound category includes a definition of the products, the composition and properties of the dressing, indications and contraindications for use, procedures for application and removal of the dressings, and expected outcomes for each category. Discussion of wound cleansing and use of topical antimicrobials is presented in relation to the clean wound. The chapter concludes with a table of all dressing categories for easy reference by the clinician.

The chapters on wound management by wound characteristics in Part II all include tools such as procedures for specific interventions, self-care teaching guidelines, and guidelines for measuring outcomes. The procedures and guidelines included in these chapters provide the clinician with a "toolbox" for daily practice in wound management. Each chapter focuses on simplifying the often-complex task of determining which interventions are appropriate for the patient with a wound. As such, each follows the simple rules for therapy stated at the beginning of this part introduction. If the wound is dirty, if necrotic debris and infection are present, clean the wound. Debride the devitalized tissue and identify and treat infection. If the wound is leaking excess exudate or edema is present, manage the drainage. Control the edema and contain excess exudate. Provide for a moist wound environment, not a wet wound environment. If there is a hole, if significant tissue has been lost at the wound site, provide for tissue replacement with a wound dressing, or fill the hole. If the wound is flat, in the process of reepithelialization, protect it from external trauma. Finally, if the wound is healed, prevention of future wounds is critical.

CHAPTER 7

Management of Necrotic Tissue

Barbara M. Bates-Jensen

SIGNIFICANCE OF NECROTIC TISSUE

As tissues die, they change in color, consistency, and adherence to the wound bed. As necrotic tissue increases in severity, the color progresses from white/gray to tan or yellow and finally to brown or black. Consistency of the necrotic tissue changes as the tissues desiccate or dry. Initially consistency may be mucoid with a high water content. Later the material becomes more clumpy and stringy in nature. Eventually the tissues appear dry, leathery, and hard. The level of tissue death and the wound etiology influence the clinical appearance of the necrotic tissue. As subcutaneous fat tissues die, a collection of stringy, yellow slough is formed. As muscle tissues degenerate, the dead tissue may be more thick or tenacious. Histologic studies of human skin during pressure sore development demonstrate that as the insult to the tissue progresses the level of necrosis deepens.[1,2] Hard, black eschar represents full-thickness destruction, possibly occurring from prolonged ischemia and anoxemia or a sudden large vessel disruption from shearing forces.[2] Fat and dermal necrosis and the formation of a slough may be compounded by infection from previous contamination by normal skin flora.[1,3,4] The debris may appear as yellow slough or a mucoid substance.[4,5] Prolonged ischemia may cause necrosis of underlying tissues and manifest as a gray area, blueness of the skin, or white devitalized tissue.[1,5,6] Tissue color varies as necrosis worsens, from white/gray nonviable tissue to yellow slough and finally black eschar.

Consistency refers to the cohesiveness of debris (ie, is it thin or thick? stringy or clumpy?). Consistency also varies on a continuum as necrosis deepens. The terms *slough* and *eschar* refer to different levels of necrosis and are described according to color and consistency.[1–3] The term slough is described as yellow (or tan) and thin, mucinous, or stringy; eschar is described as brown or black, soft or hard, and representing full-thickness tissue destruction.[1,2] The more water content present in the necrotic debris, the less adherent the debris is to the wound bed. Adherence refers to the adhesiveness of the debris to the wound bed and the ease with which the two are separated. Necrotic tissue tends to become more adherent to the wound bed as the level of damage increases. Clinically, eschar is more firmly adherent than yellow slough. The boxed table on the following page refers to color plates for necrotic tissue assessment. Plate captions give more information.

The amount of necrotic tissue retards wound healing because it is a medium for bacterial growth and a physical barrier to epidermal resurfacing, contraction, or granulation.[7–9] The more necrotic tissue present in the wound bed, the more severe the insult to the tissue and the longer the time required to heal the wound.[1] In the process of treating the necrotic wound, the amount of necrotic tissue present leads to modification of treatment and debridement techniques. In addition, determining the severity of the tissue insult may be postponed if the amount of necrotic debris is sufficient to obscure visualization of the total wound. Necrotic tissue may be observed in chronic wounds with various etiologic factors.

Arterial/Ischemic Wounds

Necrotic debris in the ischemic wound may appear as dry gangrene. It may have a thick, dry, or desiccated, black/gray appearance. It is usually firmly adherent to the wound bed. It may be surrounded with an erythematous halo (see *Color Plates 45 and 47*).

Assessment of Necrotic Tissue Types—*Color Plates*				
Color	Black/brown eschar	Tan/yellow slough	Yellow fibrinous	White/gray
Moisture content	Hard	Soft/soggy	Soft/stringy	Mucinous
Adherence	Firmly attached base and edges	Attached base only	Loosely attached	Clumps
Color Plate(s)	7, 20, 21, 25, 29, 46	1, 30	3	27, 28, 30

Neurotrophic Wounds

Neurotrophic wounds usually do not present with necrosis but often have hyperkeratosis surrounding the wound. This hyperkeratosis looks like callus formation at the wound edges. The wound edges need to be decallused or saucerized frequently (see Chapter 15, Figures 15–9B, 15–9C, and 15–14).

Venous Disease Wounds

Venous disease wounds may have either eschar or slough present. Often venous wounds will appear with yellow fibrinous material covering the wound. Eschar may be attributed to desiccation of the wound and the necrotic debris (see *Color Plate 50*).

Pressure Sores

The necrotic debris that occurs in pressure sores relates to the amount of tissue destruction. In the early stage of pressure sore formation, the tissues may appear hard (indurated) with purple or black discoloration on intact skin. This is indicative of tissue death, and the necrosis appears as the wound demarcates. Exhibit 7–1 presents a critical thinking model, or guideline, for assessment of necrotic tissue and may be helpful in determining the best intervention choice.

INTERVENTIONS

The therapeutic intervention for necrotic tissue presenting in the wound is debridement. A variety of debridement choices are available to the clinician. Debridement choices often hinge on the wound appearance, the type of wound, and the type and amount of necrotic debris present in the wound. Some general guidelines may be helpful. Appendix 7–A presents debridement choices for a variety of wounds and necrotic tissue types. There are four main types of wound debridement: mechanical, enzymatic, sharp, and autolytic.

Discussion of advantages and disadvantages of each debridement intervention follows.

Mechanical Debridement

Mechanical debridement involves the use of some outside force to remove the dead tissue. The most common types of mechanical debridement are wet-to-dry gauze dressings, wound irrigation (using syringe and needle), and whirlpool (see Chapter 20). The advantages of mechanical debridement include the following:

- Mechanical debridement uses treatment options that are familiar to most health care professionals.
- Wound irrigation can effectively decrease the bacterial burden on the wound when done correctly, and it can be used in conjunction with other treatment options.

The disadvantages of mechanical debridement relate primarily to use of wet-to-dry gauze dressings and outweigh potential benefits; they include the following:

- Mechanical debridement is nonselective. It removes healthy tissue in addition to dead tissue.
- Wet-to-dry gauze dressings are rarely applied correctly.
- Wet-to-dry gauze dressings may cause pain on removal.
- Wet-to-dry gauze dressings may be more costly in terms of labor and supplies.

Procedures for each type of mechanical debridement are presented for reference and use.

Mechanical Debridement Procedures

Procedure: Wet-to-Dry Gauze Dressings

Equipment Needed:

- Sterile normal saline
- Gauze (rolled or 4 × 4-inch squares)

Exhibit 7–1 Necrotic Tissue Assessment Guideline

IDENTIFICATION OF NECROSIS
Is wound bed viable (pink or red)?

NO

YES
Wound clean, no necrosis
Refer to Chapter 10

PREDOMINANT COLOR OF WOUND?

Black/brown eschar   Tan/yellow slough   Yellow fibrinous   White/gray

MOISTURE CONTENT?

Hard   Soft/soggy   Soft/stringy   Mucinous

ADHERENCE?

Firmly attached base and edges   Attached base only   Loosely attached   Clumps

PERCENTAGE OF WOUND COVERED WITH NECROSIS?

100% Covered   50%–100% Covered   25%–50% Covered   <25% Covered

PREDOMINANT TYPE OF NECROSIS? (general characteristics of each type)

Eschar	*Slough*	*Fibrin*	*Hyperkeratosis*	*Gangrene*
Hard	Soft, soggy	Soft, soggy	Hard	Hard
Soft, soggy	Soft, stringy	Soft, stringy		Soft, soggy
	Mucinous	Mucinous		
Black/brown	Yellow/tan	Yellow/white	White/gray	Black/brown
Firmly attached	Firmly attached	Attached base	Firmly attached	Firmly attached
Attached base	Attached base	Loosely attached		Attached base
	Loosely attached	Clumps		
	Clumps			
100% Covered	100% Covered	50%–100% Covered	Surrounds wound edges	100% Covered
50%–100% Covered	50%–100% Covered	25%–50% Covered		50%–100% Covered
	25%–50% Covered			

- Cover/topper sponges
- Sterile gloves (one pair)
- Clean gloves (two pairs)
- Paper tape, trash bag

Frequency: Apply every 8 hours for wet-to-dry (see Chapter 10 for wet-to-moist gauze dressings).

Indications: Moist necrotic wounds (not effective on dry eschar).

Contraindications: Do not use on clean wounds because the healthy tissue will be "debrided."

Precaution: Patient may need premedication for pain at the time of dressing change.

Procedure:

1. Explain dressing and procedure to patient and caregiver.
2. Wash hands.
3. Prepare dressing supplies.
   a. Open gauze and moisten with normal saline.
   b. Open cover sponges.
   c. Tear tape.

4. Apply clean gloves (to protect from cross-contamination).
5. Remove dirty dressing and dispose of in trash bag.
6. Remove gloves and dispose of in trash bag (gloves have been contaminated with the dirty dressing).
7. Apply clean gloves (to protect from cross-contamination).
8. Evaluate wound (see Chapter 3 for more on wound evaluation).
9. Clean wound.
    a. Use 35-mL syringe and 19-gauge needle to apply wound cleanser directly into wound.
    b. Use normal saline or a nonionic surfactant wound cleanser.
    c. Antimicrobial solutions such as povidine-iodine destroy healthy wound tissues and should be used cautiously—*for short-term treatment, for appropriate bacterial flora only!* (See Chapter 8 for more on wound cleansers and infection.)
10. Remove gloves and apply sterile gloves (to prevent introduction of new bacteria into the wound). (When wound care is being carried out in the home or long-term care setting, the procedure may be performed using only clean gloves.)
11. Open the moistened gauze, fluff, and place in the wound loosely. Be sure to place some of the dressing in undermined or tunneled areas.
12. Cover the wound with the cover or topper sponges. Use one cover sponge for each gauze 4 × 4-inch square used in the wound or each 6 to 8 inches of roller gauze used in the wound.
13. Secure the dressing with paper tape, write the date and time, and initial the tape.
14. Dispose of the trash bag and wash hands.
15. Review procedure with patient and caregiver.

Procedure: Wound Irrigation

Equipment Needed:

- Sterile normal saline
- Goggles, if splashing is anticipated
- Clean gloves (one pair)
- 35-mL syringe and 19-gauge needle or angiographic catheter
- Irrigation tray
- Trash bag
- Gauze sponges (4 × 4-inch squares or Kerlix super sponges) *or* cover/topper sponges

Frequency: Apply with each dressing change.
Indications: All wounds.

Contraindications: Use "gentle" irrigation on clean wounds and more vigorous irrigations on necrotic wounds (see Chapter 8).
Procedure:

1. Explain procedure to patient and caregiver.
2. Wash hands.
3. Prepare supplies.
    a. Open gauze or cover sponges.
    b. Fill syringe with irrigant.
        (1) Use normal saline or a nonionic surfactant wound cleanser.
        (2) Antimicrobial solutions such as povidine-iodine destroy healthy wound tissues and should be used cautiously—*for short-term treatment, for appropriate bacterial flora only!* (See Chapter 8 for more on wound cleansers and infection.)
4. Apply goggles and clean gloves (to protect from splashing and cross-contamination).
5. Remove dirty dressing and dispose of in trash bag.
6. Remove gloves, dispose of in trash bag, and apply clean gloves (to protect from cross-contamination).
7. Evaluate wound (see Chapter 3 for more on wound evaluation).
8. Flush wound with irrigant. Hold needle/catheter 1 to 2 inches from wound bed.
    a. Irrigate forcefully to debride loose, necrotic tissue mechanically.
    b. May attach a 14-French straight catheter to irrigate tunnels and large undermined areas.
    c. Irrigate gently if wound is clean or free of necrotic debris.
9. Dry surrounding skin with gauze or cover sponges.
10. Apply prescribed dressing according to procedure for dressing.

Enzymatic Debridement

Enzymatic debridement involves the use of enzymatic ointments or solutions to remove the dead tissue. A physician's order is required, and manufacturer's guidelines should be followed. Enzymatic ointments are not active in dry environments and are not intended for use on dry eschar. Eschar must be cross-hatched with a scalpel and the wound surface kept moist for the preparations to be successful. The most common types of enzymatic preparations are shown in Appendix 7–B. The advantages are that enzymatic debridement is selective, working only on necrotic tissue, and is effective in combination with other debridement techniques, such as sequential sharp debridement and autolytic debridement. The disadvantages include the following:

- Often enzymatic use is prolonged more than necessary. It should be stopped when the wound is clean and free of necrotic tissue.
- Enzymatic debridement can be slow to achieve success: it may take from 14 to 30 days to achieve a clean wound bed.

Procedures for enzymatic debridement are included for reference and use.

Enzymatic Debridement Procedures

Procedure: Enzymatic Preparations

Equipment Needed:

- Enzymatic preparation
- Gauze (4 × 4-inch squares) or cover/topper sponges
- Cleansing solution
- Sterile gloves (one pair)
- Clean gloves (one pair)
- Paper tape, trash bag

Frequency: Follow manufacturer's guidelines.

Indications: All necrotic wounds; moist necrotic wounds are best. If the wound has dry eschar, *cross-hatch* the eschar to improve healing. It is useful to match type of necrotic tissue to actions of enzyme activity, but not essential. For example, a venous disease ulcer will have more fibrin associated with the necrosis, and an enzyme that works on fibrin might be more effective.

Contraindications: Do not use on clean wounds, dry gangrene, or dry ischemic wounds unless vascular consultation or ankle-brachial index (see Chapter 6) has been obtained and circulatory status determined.

Procedure:

1. Explain dressing and procedure to patient and caregiver.
2. Wash hands.
3. Prepare dressing supplies.
   a. Open gauze or cover/topper sponges and moisten with normal saline (most of the enzymatic ointments require a moist dressing for maximum effectiveness).
   b. Tear tape.
4. Apply clean gloves (to protect from cross-contamination).
5. Remove dirty dressing and dispose of in trash bag.

6. Remove gloves and dispose of in trash bag (gloves have been contaminated with the dirty dressing).
7. Apply clean gloves (to protect from cross-contamination).
8. Evaluate wound (see Chapter 3 for more on wound evaluation).
9. Clean wound (follow manufacturer's guidelines on use of cleaning solutions).
   a. Use 35-mL syringe and 19-gauge needle to apply wound cleanser directly into wound.
   b. Use normal saline or a nonionic surfactant wound cleanser.
   c. *Avoid* antimicrobial solutions such as povidine-iodine, which destroy enzymatic activity in the enzyme preparations.
10. Remove gloves and apply sterile gloves (to prevent introduction of new bacteria into the wound). (May use a dressing other than gauze or cover/topper sponges as appropriate topical therapy as the secondary dressing for the wound. When wound care is being carried out in the home or long-term care setting, the procedure may be performed using only clean gloves.)
11. Apply the enzymatic ointment with a tongue blade or cotton-tipped applicator to wound bed. As an alternative, the enzymatic ointment may be applied directly to the gauze dressing to be applied to the wound surface.
12. Open the moistened gauze, fluff, and place in the wound loosely. Be sure to place some of the dressing in undermined or tunneled areas. (May use a dressing other than gauze or cover/topper sponges as appropriate topical therapy as the secondary dressing for the wound.)
13. Cover the wound with the cover or topper sponges. Use one cover sponge for each gauze 4 × 4-inch square used in the wound or each 6 to 8 inches of roller gauze used in the wound. (May use a dressing other than gauze or cover/topper sponges as appropriate topical therapy as the secondary dressing for the wound.)
14. Secure the dressing with paper tape, write the date and time, and initial the tape.
15. Dispose of the trash bag and wash hands.
16. Review procedure with patient and caregiver.

Sharp Debridement

Sharp debridement may be performed as a one-time debridement or as sequential instrumental debridement. One-time surgical debridement is rapid and effective and may convert the chronic wound to an acute wound. Laser debridement may be considered a form of surgical debridement and may be effective on those patients who are not candidates for the operating room. Sequential instrumental debridement involves removal of loose avascular tissue with sterile instruments and may be performed by a variety of health care professionals. Both registered nurses and physical therapists may perform sharp debridement for wounds in most states. Check state practice acts before proceeding.

Clinical Wisdom: *Licensing Issues*

Registered nurses and physical therapists (PTs) may perform sharp debridement. Nurses must (and PTs should) complete an education course on wound debridement and competency validation of wound debridement skills. Competency validation involves performing debridement skills on a wound model such as a pig's foot and demonstration of debridement skills on patients with a qualified mentor to document competency. Some states do not allow nurses or PTs to perform sharp debridement, so it is wise to check with the state board of registered nursing, the state nursing practice act, and the PT licensing agency for validation of practice requirements for performing wound debridement.

Of course, the main advantage of sharp debridement is the speed of converting a necrotic wound to a clean wound. When sharp debridement is performed as a one-time operative procedure the chronic wound may convert to an acute wound with resultant wound closure. Sharp debridement is a selective form of debridement when performed properly. Sequential instrumental debridement is effective in combination with enzymatic, mechanical, and autolytic debridement and can speed the removal of necrotic debris when used in combination with other techniques. The disadvantages of sharp debridement include the following:

- Sharp debridement requires a level of experience or skill and specific education.
- There is often questionable reimbursement when sharp debridement is performed by nonphysicians (nurses). Reimbursement depends on individual state practice acts for nurses.

There are special indications for sharp debridement in relationship to pressure ulcers. Sharp debridement should be performed when gross necrotic tissue, sepsis, or advancing cellulitis is present. Ischemic wounds should not be debrided (by any means, but most certainly not with sharp de-

bridement) unless the clinician is certain of collateral circulation by vascular studies or an adequate ankle-brachial index is present. Pressure ulcers on heels that present with black hard eschar may be left intact provided they are inspected daily; if signs and symptoms of pathology develop (redness, sogginess, or mushy feel to the area or frank purulent drainage), they should be debrided immediately. Procedures for sharp debridement are presented for reference and use.

Clinical Wisdom: *Safe Sharp Debridement*

A key to successful, safe sharp debridement is knowledge of anatomy and assessment. The three-part *Sharp Debridement of Wounds* video series, *Introduction and Technique, Anatomy and Assessment of the Torso,* and *Anatomy and Assessment of the Lower Extremity,* is a training tool available to teach anatomy of common wound locations on the torso and lower extremities, assessment of necrotic tissue, instrument techniques, and procedures of sharp debridement.[10]

Sharp Debridement Procedure

Procedure: Sharp, Sequential Instrument Debridement

Equipment Needed:

- Silver nitrate sticks, Gelfoam, or hemostatic dressing (optional)
- Sterile normal saline
- Gauze or cover/topper sponges
- Instrument set
- No. 10 and No. 15 scalpel and blade
- Wound dressing of choice
- Clamp (Kelly or mosquito)
- Suture removal set
- Sterile gloves (one pair)
- Clean gloves (one pair)
- Paper tape, trash bag
- Cotton-tipped applicators
- Scissors (small, fine, serrated, and large with or without serrations)
- Forceps (Adson—with or without teeth—or Adson-Brown)

Frequency: Perform according to clinical judgment and physician's orders.

Indications: All necrotic wounds; moist necrotic wounds are best. If the wound has dry eschar, autolytic or enzymatic debridement may be used first to soften necrosis and facilitate sharp removal of debris.

Contraindications: Do not perform if you don't feel comfortable or don't know what you are cutting! Do not perform on clean wounds, dry gangrene, or dry ischemic wounds unless vascular consultation has been obtained and circulatory status determined.

Procedure:

1. Verify physician orders.
2. Explain procedure to patient and caregiver.
3. Premedicate patient for pain and relaxation.
   a. Topical: lidocaine (Xylocaine) spray or solution or benzocaine (Hurricane) spray. Lidocaine spray can be used as a gauze compress directly to the wound site for 10 minutes for effective topical anesthesia or may be locally injected.
   b. Systemic: oral, intramuscular, or intravenous as a preoperative/predebridement regimen. Administer approximately 30 minutes prior to therapy to increase patient tolerance and compliance with procedure.
4. Assemble equipment.
5. Arrange for an assistant.
6. Provide for adequate lighting.
7. Position patient.
8. Wash hands.
9. Prepare clean field and equipment.
10. Apply clean gloves (to protect from cross-contamination).
11. Remove dirty dressing and dispose of in trash bag.
12. Clean wound (follow manufacturer's guidelines on use of cleaning solutions). Warm solution to 96° to 100°F for patient comfort, if possible.
    a. Use 35-mL syringe and 19-gauge needle to apply wound cleanser directly into wound.
    b. Use normal saline or a nonionic surfactant wound cleanser.
13. Evaluate wound (see Chapter 3 for more on wound evaluation).
14. Remove gloves and dispose of in trash bag (gloves have been contaminated with the dirty dressing).
15. Apply sterile gloves (to prevent introduction of new bacteria into the wound). (When wound care is being carried out in the home or long-term care setting, the procedure may be performed using only clean gloves.)
16. Using the pickup forceps, lift the dead tissue or eschar that you are trying to debride and cut it with scalpel or scissors. Grasp dead tissue and hold it taut so that the line of demarcation is clearly visualized. Cut it with care and try to take it down in layers to prevent removal of healthy tissue. Pain and bleeding are signs of healthy tissue.

17. Remove as much nonviable tissue as possible, but limit procedure to 15 to 30 minutes.
    a. Request reevaluation when any of the following are present:
       (1) Elevated temperature or patient is on downhill course
       (2) No wound improvement over several weeks
       (3) Cellulitis *or* gross purulence/infection
       (4) Impending exposed bone or tendon
       (5) Abscessed area
       (6) Extensively undermined areas
    b. Aggressiveness of debridement should be guided by the following:
       (1) The amount of necrotic tissue present
       (2) Patient pain tolerance limits
       (3) Time schedule and limits to avoid patient and provider fatigue (15 to 30 minutes)
18. Stop debriding when the following occur:
    a. There is impending bone or tendon.
    b. You are close to a fascial plane or other named structure.
    c. You get nervous.
19. Provide postdebridement care.
    a. Cleanse wound with normal saline.
    b. Apply wound therapy of choice.
    c. Document procedure.
20. Secure the wound therapy with paper tape if necessary, write the date and time, and initial the tape.
21. Dispose of the trash bag and wash hands.
22. Review procedure with patient and caregiver. (See Exhibit 7–2 for more information on self-care teaching guidelines for wound care with necrotic tissue.)

Autolytic Debridement

Autolytic debridement refers to the breakdown of necrotic tissue provided by the body's own white blood cells. Autolysis may be accomplished by use of any moisture-retentive dressing. The moist wound surface promotes rehydration of the dead tissue, and the wound fluid contains white blood cells and enzymes that break down the necrotic tissue. Autolysis is facilitated by cross-hatching if the wound is covered with dry eschar. Autolysis is usually performed using one of the following dressing choices:

- Transparent film dressings (best for dry eschar; because they are nonabsorptive they rapidly create a fluid environment)
- Hydrocolloids (best for moist wounds with necrosis because they provide some asorptive capacity while maintaining a moist wound environment)
- Hydrogels (promote autolysis by maintaining a moist wound environment)

Exhibit 7–2 Self-Care Teaching Guidelines

Self-Care Guidelines Specific to Necrotic Tissue	Instructions Given (Date/Initials)	Demonstration or Review of Material (Date/Initials)	Return Demonstration or Verbalizes Understanding (Date/Initials)
1. Type of wound and reason for necrotic tissue			
2. Significance of necrosis			
3. Topical therapy care routine:			
a. Clean wound.			
b. Apply enzymatic preparation (if appropriate).			
c. Apply autolytic dressing—transparent film, hydrocolloid, or hydrogel.			
d. Apply secondary dressing if using enzymatic preparation.			
4. Frequency of dressing changes			
5. Expected change in wound appearance during debridement			
6. When to notify the health care provider:			
a. Signs and symptoms of infection			
b. Failure to improve			
c. Evidence of undermining			
d. Impending bone or joint involvement			
7. Importance of follow-up with health care provider			

The advantages of autolysis are that debridement is fast (there should be significant progress within 6 days), selective, low cost, and effective in combination with sharp debridement techniques. Disadvantages include the caregiver education required to prepare for the wound appearance with autolysis; the odor and exudate under the dressing also may be disturbing. Procedures for autolysis using several dressings are presented for reference and use.

Autolytic Debridement Procedures

Procedure: Autolytic Debridement—Transparent Film Dressing

Equipment Needed:

- Sterile normal saline
- Skin sealant
- Transparent film dressing

Frequency: Apply every 3 to 5 days. Always change dressing when drainage leaks out.

Indications: All necrotic wounds, but most beneficial for dry eschar; may cross-hatch eschar to facilitate autolysis.

Contraindications: Do not use for dry gangrene or dry ischemic wounds unless vascular consultation has been obtained and circulatory status determined.

Procedure:

1. Explain dressing and procedure to patient and caregiver.
2. Wash hands.
3. Prepare dressing supplies.
   a. Open transparent film dressing.
   b. Be sure dressing size is at least 2 inches larger than wound area to be covered.
4. Position patient off affected area.
5. Apply clean gloves (to protect from cross-contamination).

6. Remove dirty dressing and dispose of in trash bag. (There is likely to be an odor, and the wound drainage may appear quite disturbing.)

7. Remove gloves and dispose of in trash bag (gloves have been contaminated with the dirty dressing).

8. Apply clean gloves (to protect from cross-contamination).

9. Evaluate wound (see Chapter 3 for more on wound evaluation).

10. Clean wound (follow manufacturer's guidelines on use of cleaning solutions).
    a. Use 35-mL syringe and 19-gauge needle to apply wound cleanser directly into wound.
    b. Use normal saline or a nonionic surfactant wound cleanser.
    c. *Avoid* antimicrobial solutions such as povidine-iodine, which destroy healthy wound tissues and should be used cautiously—*for short-term treatment, for appropriate bacterial flora only!* (See Chapter 8 for more on wound cleansers and infection.)

11. Remove gloves and apply sterile gloves (to prevent introduction of new bacteria into the wound). (When wound care is being carried out in the home or long-term care setting, the procedure may be performed using only clean gloves.)

12. Apply skin sealant to skin surrounding the wound and allow to dry until skin looks shiny (skin sealant protects the skin surrounding the wound from maceration and stripping during dressing removal).

13. Apply the transparent film dressing according to manufacturer's guidelines.
    a. When treating lesions in the sacral/coccygeal area it is best to apply the dressing in a crisscross, overlapping fashion using strips of the dressing.
    b. Avoid tension and wrinkling of the dressing.

14. Secure the dressing, write the date and time, and initial the dressing.

15. Dispose of the trash bag and wash hands.

16. Review procedure with patient and caregiver.

Procedure: Autolytic Debridement—Hydrocolloid or Hydrogel Wafer Dressings

Equipment Needed:

- Sterile normal saline
- Hydrocolloid dressing or hydrogel wafer dressing
- Skin sealant (optional)
- Paper tape

Frequency: Apply every 3 to 5 days. Always change dressing when drainage leaks out.

Indications: All necrotic wounds. Dry eschar may benefit from cross-hatching to facilitate autolysis. This procedure is particularly effective in moist necrotic wounds with moderate amounts of exudate.

Contraindications: Do not use for cellulitis, documented wound infection, dry gangrene, or dry ischemic wounds unless vascular consultation has been obtained and circulatory status determined.

Procedure:

1. Explain dressing and procedure to patient and caregiver.

2. Wash hands.

3. Prepare dressing supplies.
    a. Open hydrocolloid/hydrogel dressing.
    b. Be sure dressing size is at least 2 inches larger than wound area to be covered.

4. Position patient off affected area.

5. Apply clean gloves (to protect from cross-contamination).

6. Remove dirty dressing and dispose of in trash bag. (There is likely to be an odor, and the wound drainage may appear quite disturbing.)

7. Remove gloves and dispose of in trash bag (gloves have been contaminated with the dirty dressing).

8. Apply clean gloves (to protect from cross-contamination).

9. Evaluate wound (see Chapter 3 for more on wound evaluation)

10. Clean wound (follow manufacturer's guidelines on use of cleaning solutions).
    a. Use 35-mL syringe and 19-gauge needle to apply wound cleanser directly into wound.
    b. Use normal saline or a nonionic surfactant wound cleanser.
    c. *Avoid* antimicrobial solutions such as povidine-iodine, which destroy healthy wound tissues and should be used cautiously—*for short-term treatment, for appropriate bacterial flora only!* (See Chapter 8 for more on wound cleansers and infection.)

11. Remove gloves and apply sterile gloves (to prevent introduction of new bacteria into the wound). (When wound care is being carried out in the home or long-term care setting, the procedure may be performed using only clean gloves.)

12. Peel backing off the hydrocolloid or hydrogel wafer dressing and apply according to manufacturer's guidelines.
    a. Apply strips of tape to the wafer edges in a picture-frame manner; use of a skin sealant under the tape is advised to protect from stripping.

b. Avoid use of skin sealants under hydrocolloid and hydrogel dressings.
13. Secure the dressing, write the date and time, and initial the dressing.
14. Dispose of the trash bag and wash hands.
15. Review procedure with patient and caregiver.

OUTCOME MEASURES

Outcome measures are tools used to evaluate the effectiveness of therapy. Three appropriate characteristics for evaluating the effectiveness of debridement taken from the Pressure Sore Status Tools[11,12] are the amount of necrotic tissue in the wound, the type of necrotic tissue in the wound, and the adherence of the necrotic tissue in the wound. The Sussman Wound Healing Tool uses the presence or absence of necrotic tissue as a predictor of healing and a way to monitor healing (see Chapter 5).[13] Changes in necrotic tissue are intermediate outcomes; the final outcome measure is healing.

Amount of Necrotic Tissue

The amount of necrotic tissue should diminish progressively in the wound if therapy is appropriate. The amount of necrotic tissue can be measured by linear measurements (measuring the length and width of the necrotic debris), by determining the percentage of the wound bed covered, and by photography. To determine the percentage of the wound bed covered use a transparent measuring device with concentric circles. Draw a horizontal and a vertical axis through the circles and use the device to help judge the percentage of the wound involved. A rating scale similar to the following may be used to quantify amount of necrotic tissue:

1 = None visible
2 = <25% of wound bed covered
3 = 25% to 50% of wound covered
4 = >50% and <75% of wound covered
5 = 75% to 100% of wound covered

Type of Necrotic Tissue

The type of necrotic tissue should change as the wound improves and heals. As the necrotic tissue is rehydrated, the appearance will change from a dry, desiccated eschar to a more soggy, soft slough, and finally to a mucinous, easily dislodged tissue. The color usually changes as the necrosis is debrided. The black/brown eschar gives way to yellow or tan slough. Usually eschar improves to slough material. Rating the type of necrotic tissue is best accomplished by the use of a scale similar to the following:

1 = None visible
2 = White/gray nonviable tissue and/or nonadherent yellow slough
3 = Loosely adherent yellow slough
4 = Adherent, soft black eschar
5 = Firmly adherent, hard black eschar

Adherence of Necrotic Tissue

Adherence of the necrosis should decrease as debridement proceeds. Initially the necrotic tissue may be firmly attached to the wound base and all wound edges. As debridement proceeds the necrosis begins lifting and loosens from the edges of the wound and eventually disengages from the base of the wound as well. Adherence is best evaluated using a rating scale similar to that for types of necrotic tissue.

General guidelines for length of time for debridement are presented in Table 7–1.

REFERRAL CRITERIA

Debridement in arterial/ischemic ulcers is contraindicated unless, and until, adequate circulatory status has been determined. If you don't feel comfortable or have limited or no experience in debridement, you may want to refer to a health care provider with more experience. The following patients may warrant referral to the physician or an advanced practice nurse:

- Dry gangrene or dry ischemic wounds should be routinely referred for vascular consultation for circulatory status determination.
- Patients with elevated temperature or those on a downhill course should be evaluated further.
- Patients with no wound improvement over several weeks should be evaluated further. In this case, the nurse may want to consult other health care practitioners (physical therapists, dietitians, wound care nurses, ET nurses, and physicians).
- Patients with evidence of cellulitis *or* gross purulence/infection.
- Patients with impending exposed bone or tendon present in the wound.
- Patients showing evidence of an abscessed area or patients with extensively undermined areas present in the wound should be evaluated further.

SELF-CARE TEACHING GUIDELINES

Patient and caregiver instruction in self-care must be individualized to the topical therapy care routine, the individual

Table 7-1 Debridement Time Frames

Necrotic Tissue Type	Debridement Choice	Expected Outcomes	Time Frame Guide	Notes
Eschar	Autolysis	1. Eschar nonadherent to wound edges 2. Necrotic tissue lifting from wound edges 3. Necrotic tissue soft and soggy 4. Color change from black/brown to yellow/tan	14 Days	Depending on type of dressing used for autolysis, may proceed at more rapid rate.
Eschar	Enzymatic preparations	1. Eschar nonadherent to wound edges 2. Necrotic tissue lifting from wound edges 3. Necrotic tissue soft and soggy 4. Color change from black/brown to yellow/tan 5. Change from eschar to slough	14 Days	Requires compliance on dressing changes in order to be effective.
Eschar	Sharp	1. Removal/elimination of eschar if done one time *or* significant change in amount and adherence if sequential	Immediate if one time, 7 days if sequential	If sequential sharp debridement used in conjunction with enzymatic preparation or autolysis, may expect clean wound base in 7 days.
Slough or fibrin	Autolysis *or* enzymatic preparations	1. Necrotic tissue lifting from wound base 2. Necrotic tissue stringy or mucinous 3. Tissue color yellow or white 4. Change in amount of wound covered—gradual decrease to wound predominantly clean	14 Days	Will require moderate amount of exudate absorption and protection of surrounding tissues from maceration.
Slough or fibrin	Sharp	1. Removal/elimination of necrotic slough if done one time *or* significant change in amount and adherence if sequential	Immediate if one time, 7 days if sequential	If sequential sharp debridement used in conjunction with enzymatic preparation or autolysis, may expect clean wound base in 7 days.

patient's wound, the individual patient's learning style and coping mechanisms, and the ability of the patient/caregiver to perform procedures. These general self-care teaching guidelines must be individualized for each patient and caregiver. Exhibit 7–2 presents self-care teaching guidelines related to necrotic tissue management.

REFERENCES

1. Shea D. Pressure sores: classification and management. *Clin Orthop.* 1975;112:89–100.

2. Witkowski JA, Parish LC. Histopathology of the decubitus ulcer. *J Am Acad Dermatol.* 1982;6:1014–1021.

3. Enis JG, Sarmiento A. The pathophysiology and management of pressure sores. *Orthop Rev.* October 1973;2:25–34.

4. Sather MR, Weber CE, George J. Pressure sores and the spinal cord injury patient. *Drug Intell Clin Pharm.* 1977;2:154–169.

5. Agris J, Spira M. Pressure ulcers: prevention and treatment. *Clin Symp.* 1979;31:2–14.

6. Edberg EL, Cerny K, Stauffer ES. Prevention and treatment of pressure sores. *Phys Ther.* 1973;53:246–252.

7. Alterescu V, Alterescu K. Etiology and treatment of pressure ulcers. *Decubitus.* 1988;1:28–35.

8. Winter G. Epidermal regeneration studied in the domestic pig. In: Hung TK, Dunphy JE, eds. *Fundamentals of Wound Management.* New York: Appleton-Century-Crofts; 1979:71–111.

9. Sapico FL, Ginunas VJ, Thornhill-Hoynes M, et al. Quantitative microbiology of pressure sores in different stages of healing. *Diag Biol Infect Dis.* 1986;5:31–38.

10. Sussman C, Fowler E, Wethe J. *Sharp Debridement of Wounds* (video series). Sussman Physical Therapy, Inc., Torrance, CA 90505.

11. Bates-Jensen BM, Vredevoe DL, Brecht ML. Validity and reliability of the Pressure Sore Status Tool. *Decubitus.* 1992;5(6):20–28.

12. Bates-Jensen BM. Indices to include in wound healing assessment. *Adv Wound Care.* 1995;8:25–33.

13. Sussman C, Swanson G. *The Utility of Sussman Wound Healing Tool in Predicting Wound Healing Outcomes Physical Therapy.* Fifth National Pressure Ulcer Advisory Panel Consensus Conference, Washington, DC; 1997.

ADDITIONAL RESOURCES AND REFERENCES FOR FURTHER STUDY

Black J, Black S. Surgical management of pressure ulcers. *Nurs Clin North Am.* 1987;22:429–438.

Bryant RA, ed. *Acute and Chronic Wounds: Nursing Management.* St. Louis, MO: Mosby-Year Book; 1992.

Davis JT. Enhancing wound-debridement skills through simulated practice. *Phys Ther.* 1986;66:1723–1724.

Fowler E. Instrument/sharp debridement of non-viable tissue in wounds. *Ostomy/Wound Manage.* 1992;38:26–33.

Haury B, Rodeheaver G. Debridement: an essential component of traumatic wound care. *Am J Surg.* 1978;135:238–242.

Knight DB, Scott H. Contracture and pressure necrosis. *Ostomy/Wound Manage.* 1990;26(1):60–67.

Mulder GD, Jeter KF, Fairchild PA. *Clinicians' Pocket Guide to Chronic Wound Repair.* Spartanburg, SC: Wound Healing Publications; 1992.

National Pressure Ulcer Advisory Panel. Pressure ulcers: incidence, economics, risk assessment. In: *Consensus Development Conference Statement.* West Dundee, IL: S-N Publications, Inc.; 1989:3–4.

Panel for the Prediction and Prevention of Pressure Ulcers in Adults. *Pressure Ulcers in Adults: Prediction and Prevention.* Clinical Practice Guideline Number 3. AHCPR Publication No. 92-0047. Rockville, MD: Agency for Health Care Policy and Research, US Public Health Service, US Department of Health and Human Services; May 1992.

Rodeheaver G, Baharestani M, Brabec ME, et al. Wound healing and wound management: focus on debridement. *Adv Wound Care.* 1994; 7:22–38.

Wound, Ostomy, Continence Nursing Society Standards Committee. *Standards of Care. Dermal Wounds: Pressure Sores.* Irvine, CA: Wound, Ostomy, and Continence Nursing Society, Inc.; 1992.

Appendix 7–A

Debridement Choices for Chronic Wounds

Wound Type	Tissue Type	Consistency	Adherence	Amount of Debris	Debridement Choices	Rationale and Notes
Pressure sores	Black/brown eschar	Hard	Firmly adherent, attached to all edges and base of wound	75%–100% Wound covered	1. *Autolytic*—best choice is transparent film dressing. May use hydrocolloid or hydrogel; score eschar with scalpel for more rapid results. 2. *Enzymatic ointment with secondary dressing*—must score eschar with scalpel.	1. Transparent film dressings trap fluid at the wound surface with no absorptive capabilities, providing for more rapid hydration of the eschar and facilitating autolysis. Hydrocolloid/hydrogel dressings have an absorptive capacity and may require more time for autolysis. 2. Enzymatic ointments effective against collagen and protein may be most effective.
	Black/brown eschar or Yellow/tan slough	Soft, soggy Soft, stringy	Adherent, attached to wound base, may or may not be attached to wound edges	50%–100% Wound covered	1. *Autolytic*—best choices are hydrocolloids and hydrogels; composite dressings may also be beneficial. 2. *Enzymatic ointment with secondary dressing*. 3. *Sharp, sequential, or one time*—may be used alone or in conjunction with any of the above methods.	1. Hydrocolloids and hydrogels provide for absorption of mild to moderate amounts of exudate while maintaining a moist wound environment to facilitate autolysis. 2. Enzymatic ointments effective against collagen and protein may be most effective. May need to protect intact skin from enzyme and excess exudate.
	Yellow/tan slough	Soft, stringy	Adherent, attached to wound base; may or may not be attached to wound edges or loosely adherent to wound base	Less than 50% wound covered	1. *Autolytic*—best choices are hydrocolloids and hydrogels. 2. *Enzymatic ointment with secondary dressing*. 3. *Sharp, sequential, or one time*—may be used alone or in conjunction with any of the above methods.	1. Hydrocolloids and hydrogels provide for absorption of mild to moderate amounts of exudate while maintaining a moist wound environment to facilitate autolysis.

continues

Wound Type	Tissue Type	Consistency	Adherence	Amount of Debris	Debridement Choices	Rationale and Notes
Pressure sores (cont.)						2. Enzymatic ointments effective against collagen and protein may be most effective. May need to protect intact skin from enzyme and excess exudate.
	Yellow slough	Mucinous	Loosely adherent to wound base, clumps scattered throughout wound	50%—100% Wound covered	1. *Autolytic*—best choices are hydrocolloids and hydrogels. 2. *Enzymatic ointment with secondary dressing.*	1. Hydrocolloids and hydrogels provide for absorption of mild to moderate amounts of exudate while maintaining a moist wound environment to facilitate autolysis. 2. Enzymatic ointments effective against collagen and protein may be most effective. May need to protect intact skin from enzyme and excess exudate. Should be discontinued when wound is *predominantly* clean.
Venous disease ulcers	Black/brown eschar	Hard	Firmly adherent, attached to all edges and base of wound	50%–100% Wound covered	1. *Autolytic*—best choices are hydrocolloids and hydrogels. 2. *Enzymatic ointment with secondary dressing.*	1. Hydrocolloids and hydrogel dressings have absorptive capacity, which helps prevent maceration of surrounding tissues and promotes autolysis. 2. Enzymatic ointments effective against fibrin may be most effective.

continues

Wound Type	Tissue Type	Consistency	Adherence	Amount of Debris	Debridement Choices	Rationale and Notes
Venous disease ulcers (cont.)	Yellow slough	Soft, soggy, or fibrinous	Firmly adherent, attached to all edges and base of wound	50%–100% Wound covered	1. *Autolytic*—best choice are hydrocolloids and hydrogels. 2. *Enzymatic ointment with secondary dressing.* 3. *Sharp, sequential, or one time*—may be used alone or in conjunction with any of the above methods.	1. Hydrocolloids and hydrogel dressings have absorptive capacity, which helps prevent maceration of surrounding tissues and promotes autolysis. 2. Enzymatic ointments effective against fibrin may be most effective. May need to protect intact skin from enzyme and excess exudate. Should be discontinued when wound is *predominantly* clean.
	Yellow slough	Fibrinous *or* Mucinous	Loosely adherent Clumps scattered throughout wound	Any amount of wound covered	1. *Autolytic*—best choices are hydrocolloids and hydrogels. 2. *Enzymatic ointment with secondary dressing.*	1. Hydrocolloids and hydrogel dressings have absorptive capacity, which helps prevent maceration of surrounding tissues and promotes autolysis. 2. Enzymatic ointments effective against fibrin may be most effective. May need to protect intact skin from enzyme and excess exudate. Should be discontinued when wound is *predominantly* clean.

continues

Wound Type	Tissue Type	Consistency	Adherence	Amount of Debris	Debridement Choices	Rationale and Notes
Arterial ischemic ulcers	Black/brown eschar	Hard	Firmly adherent, attached to all edges and base of wound	50%–100% Wound covered	1. Autolytic—best choices are hydrogels. 2. Enzymatic ointment with secondary dressing.	*Must be certain of circulatory status prior to initiating debridement.* 1. Hydrogel dressings have absorptive capacity, which helps prevent maceration of surrounding tissues and promotes autolysis. The amorphous hydrogels are nonadherent and require a secondary dressing. 2. Enzymatic ointments: may need to protect intact skin from enzyme and excess exudate. Should be discontinued when wound is *predominantly* clean.
		Soft, soggy	Adherent, attached to wound base; may or may not be attached to wound edges	50%–100% Wound covered	1. Autolytic—best choices are hydrogels. 2. Enzymatic ointment with secondary dressing. 3. Sharp, sequential, or one time.	1. Hydrogel dressings have absorptive capacity, which helps prevent maceration of surrounding tissues and promotes autolysis. The amorphous hydrogels are nonadherent and require a secondary dressing. 2. Enzymatic ointments effective against protein and collagen may be most effective. May need to protect intact skin from enzyme and excess exudate. Should be discontinued when wound is *predominantly* clean.

continues

Wound Type	Tissue Type	Consistency	Adherence	Amount of Debris	Debridement Choices	Rationale and Notes
Neurotrophic/ diabetic ulcers	White/gray	Hard	Hyperkeratosis, callus formation at wound edges	Involves all/ partial wound edges	1. *Sharp, sequential, or one time*—saucerization or callus removal. 2. *Autolytic*—best choices are hydrocolloids and hydrogels.	1. Saucerization may be required at each dressing change. 2. Hydrocolloids and hydrogels soften the callus formation, and this may facilitate removal as the dressing is removed.

Appendix 7–B

Enzymatic Preparations

Name	Action	Dose	Duration of Action	Notes
Elase and Elase-Chloromycetin (fibrinolysin and deoxyribonuclease)	Attacks DNA and fibrin of blood clots and fibrinous exudates	1–3 Times/day	6–8 Hours	• Hypersensitivity for people with bovine sensitivity. • Superinfection with chloromycetin. • More effective if applied more frequently rather than in thick layer. • Available in powder and can be used to pack wounds, but very expensive in this form. • Petroleum-based—remove completely before electrical stimulation.
Santyl (collagenase)	Digests collagen, lysis of collagen in necrotic tissue, and collagen fibers anchoring necrotic tissue to wound base	1 Time/day	24 Hours	• pH range is 6–8. • Can be used with triple antibiotic to treat infection. • Detergents, antiseptics, and heavy metals will inactivate the enzyme. • Petroleum-based—remove completely before electrical stimulation.
Panafil and Panafil-white (papain and urea; Panafil also contains chlorophyllin copper)	Enzyme debrider and emollient; keratolytic	1 Time/day	24 Hours	• pH range is 3–12. • Can be used under pressure dressings. • Hydrogen peroxide, detergents, antiseptics, and heavy metals will inactivate the enzyme. • May experience transient burning on application. • Petroleum-based—remove completely before electrical stimulation.
Granulex spray (trypsin 0.1 mg, balsam of Peru, castor oil)	Proteolytic pancreatic enzyme; capillary bed stimulant and emollient	2–3 Times/day	Variable	• Do not use on fresh arterial clots. • *External use only.* • May experience transient burning with initial application. • Petroleum-based—remove completely before electrical stimulation. • Not powerful enough to debride heavy amounts of debris.

CHAPTER 8

Management of Exudate and Infection

Barbara M. Bates-Jensen

Wound exudate (also known as wound fluid and wound drainage) is an important wound assessment feature because the characteristics of the exudate help the clinician diagnose wound infection, evaluate effectiveness of topical therapy, and monitor wound healing. Wound infection retards wound healing and must be treated. Proper assessment of wound exudate is also important because it affirms the body's brief, normal, inflammatory response to tissue injury. Thus, accurate assessment of wound exudate and diagnosis of infection are critical components of effective wound management.

SIGNIFICANCE OF EXUDATE

The healthy wound normally has some evidence of moisture on its surface. Healthy wound fluid contains enzymes and growth factors, which may play a role in promoting reepithelialization of the wound and provide needed growth factors for all phases of wound repair.[1] The moist environment produced by wound exudate allows efficient migration of epidermal cells and prevents wound desiccation and further injury.[2,3]

In acute wounds healing by primary intention, exudate on the incision line is normal during the first 48 to 72 hours. After that time, the presence of exudate is a sign of impaired healing. Infection and seroma are the two most likely causes. In chronic wounds, increased exudate is a response to the inflammatory process or infection. Increased capillary permeability causes leakage of fluids and substrates into the

injured tissue. When a wound is present, the tissue fluid leaks out of the open tissue. This fluid is serous or serosanguineous.

Evaluation of the wound type, the number and type of organisms present, and the condition of the patient are important in determining risk for infection. Evaluation of wound type includes assessment of acute versus chronic wounds and necrotic versus clean, nonhealing wounds. The number and type of organisms present in the wound are evaluated for burden on the wound, possible bacteria-produced toxins, and pathology of the organisms. Patient condition relates to immune function and local host defenses.

In the infected wound, the exudate may thicken, become purulent, and continue to be present in moderate to large amounts. An example of exudate character changes in infected wounds is the presence of *Pseudomonas* organisms, which produce a thick, malodorous, sweet-smelling, green drainage,[4] or *Proteus* infection, which may produce an ammonia odor. Wounds with foul-smelling drainage are generally infected or filled with necrotic debris, and healing time is prolonged as tissue destruction progresses.[5] Wounds with significant amounts of necrotic debris will often have a thick, tenacious, opaque, purulent, malodorous drainage in moderate to copious amounts. True wound exudate should be differentiated from necrotic tissue sloughing off the wound secondary to debridement efforts. Exudate from sloughing necrotic tissue is commonly attached to or connected with the necrotic debris. However, frequently the only method of differentiation is adequate debridement of necrotic tissue from the wound. The solubization of necrotic tissue occurs most often as a result of enzymatic or autolytic debridement. Often the removal of the necrotic tissue dramatically reduces the amount and changes the character of the exudate.

Wounds can become edematous when excessive amounts of plasma proteins leak from damaged capillaries and per-

Note: The contributions of **Nancy A. Stotts, MN, EdD,** Associate Professor, University of California, San Francisco, School of Nursing, Department of Physiological Nursing, to the section on quantitative wound culture are gratefully acknowledged.

vade the wound environment. The fluid of wound edema contains proteolytic enzymes, bacteria and bacterial toxins, prostaglandins, and necrotic debris, all of which contribute to prolonged chronic inflammation. Exudate also drains valuable and needed substrates, such as growth factors, from the wound bed and impairs the healing process. Excess exudate losses drain substrates and energy that could be used for wound healing processes.[4]

Assessment of Wound Exudate

Characteristics of exudate are color, consistency, adherence, distribution in the wound, the presence of odor, and the amount present.[6] The color and consistency of wound exudate may vary depending on the type of wound, degree of moisture in the wound, the wound recovery cycle, and the presence of organisms in the wound. Table 8–1 presents various types of wound exudate and associated characteristics. *Color Plate series 40 to 45* (reading the dressing and wound exudate characteristics) will help the clinician identify exudate types and make an appropriate assessment of significance.

Estimating the amount of exudate in the wound is difficult because of wound size variability and topical dressing types. Certain dressing types interact with or trap wound fluid to create or mimic certain characteristics of exudate, such as color and consistency of purulent drainage. For example, both hydrocolloid and alginate dressings mimic a purulent drainage upon removal of the dressing. Preparation of the wound site for appropriate exudate assessment involves removal of the wound dressing and cleansing to remove dressing debris in the wound bed. Then evaluate the wound for true exudate.

Cooper[6] suggests estimating the percentage of exudate in the wound by clinical observation. This approach works if the wound exudate is thick and can be observed in the wound bed. When wound exudate character is more serous in nature, clinical observation of the wound alone is insufficient to quantify the amount of drainage. For thinner wound exudate, the amount of drainage is estimated by noting the number of dressings saturated during a period of time. Although not part of exudate assessment, evaluation of the wound dressing provides the clinician with valuable data about the effectiveness of treatment. Evaluation of the percentage of the wound dressing involved with wound drainage during a specific time frame is helpful for clinical management that includes dressings beyond traditional gauze. In estimating the percentage of the dressing involved with the wound exudate, clinical judgment is quantified, as the clinician must put a number to visual assessment of the dressing. For example, the clinician might determine that 50% of the hydrocolloid dressing was involved with wound drainage over a 4-day wearing period. Based on the above data, the clinician might quantify judgment for this type of dressing, length of dressing wear time, and wound etiology as a "minimal" amount of exudate. Clinical judgment of amount of wound drainage requires some experience with expected wound exudate output in relation to phase of wound healing and type of wound and knowledge of absorptive capacity and normal wear time of topical dressings. One problem with assessment of exudate amount is the size of the wound. What might be considered a large amount of drainage for the smaller wound may be considered a small amount for the larger wound, making clinically meaningful assessment of exudate more difficult to obtain.

Table 8–1 Wound Exudate Characteristics

Exudate Type	Color	Consistency	Significance
Sanguineous/bloody	Red	Thin, watery	Indicates new blood vessel growth *or* disruption of blood vessels
Serosanguineous	Light red to pink	Thin, watery	Normal during inflammatory and proliferative phases of healing
Serous	Clear, light color	Thin, watery	Normal during inflammatory and proliferative phases of healing
Seropurulent	Cloudy, yellow to tan	Thin, watery	May be first signal of impending wound infection
Purulent/pus	Yellow, tan, or green	Thick, opaque	Signals wound infection; may be associated with odor

Appropriate wound exudate assessment requires consideration of wound etiology. Independent of exudate differences related to etiology of the wound, certain characteristics of exudate indicate wound degeneration and infection. If signs of cellulitis (erythema or skin discoloration, edema, pain, induration, and purulent drainage) are present at the wound site, the exudate amount may be copious and seropurulent or purulent in character. The amount of exudate remains high or increases in amount and character may change to frank purulence with further wound degeneration. Wound infection must be considered in these cases regardless of etiology.

Arterial/Ischemic Wounds

Exudate in the ischemic wound may vary in amount and character. Arterial/ischemic wounds are often dry or have only a scant to small amount of serous exudate present.

Neuropathic Wounds

Neuropathic wounds may present with very little exudate present. One possible reason for decreased exudate is a limited inflammation response due to concomitant vascular disease and immune status changes from diabetes. Generally, the exudate is minimal and usually serous or serosanguineous in character.

Venous Disease Wounds

Venous disease wounds usually are highly exudative both on initial presentation and throughout the course of healing.

As the venous ulcer heals, edema is lessened and the wound exudate increases. The excess fluid takes the path of least resistance, which in this case is the wound bed! Often venous wounds will appear with yellow fibrinous material covering the wound, which must be differentiated from true exudate.

Pressure Sores

Pressure sores present with a variety of wound exudate characteristics and amounts. In partial-thickness pressure sores the wound exudate is most likely to be serous or serosanguineous in nature and presents in minimal to moderate amounts. In clean full-thickness pressure sores the wound exudate is similar, with minimal to moderate amounts of serous to serosanguineous exudate. As healing progresses in the clean full-thickness pressure sore, the character of the exudate changes and may become bloody if the fragile capillary bed is disrupted and lessens in amount. For full-thickness pressure ulcers with necrotic debris, wound exudate is dependent on the presence or absence of infection and the type of therapy instituted. Exudate may appear moderate to large, but in fact be related to the amount of necrotic tissue present and the liquefaction of the debris in the wound. Typically, the necrotic full-thickness pressure ulcer presents with serous to seropurulent wound exudate in moderate to large amounts (Figures 8–1A and 8–1B). With appropriate treatment, the wound exudate amount may also temporarily increase, although the character gradually assumes a serous nature.

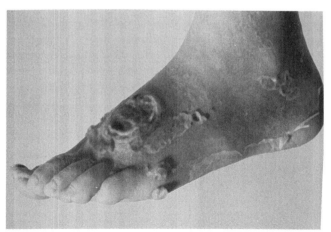

A

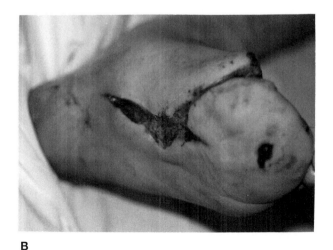

B

Figure 8–1 A and B, Obvious signs of infection.

SIGNIFICANCE OF INFECTION

Although bacteria colonize all chronic wounds, wound colonization by bacteria is not the same as infection. When host and wound conditions are favorable, infection can occur. Wound infection extends inflammatory response, delays collagen synthesis, retards epithelialization, and causes more injury to the tissues as the bacteria compete with fibroblasts and other cells for limited amounts of oxygen.[7]

Large acute wounds generally react to bacterial burden in a way different from that in small chronic ulcerative wounds. Acute wounds are more susceptible to bacterial invasion by skin flora, in particular those with prolonged inflammatory responses.[8] Wounds with loss of large amounts of surface area (15% of body surface area or greater) are also at a higher risk for bacterial invasion. Sufficient numbers of skin flora organisms will cause acute wounds like grafts and flaps to fail and, if untreated, lead to sepsis while a chronic leg ulcer may remain unchanged for months or years with no signs of infection or sepsis with the same or larger number of organisms present.[8] The same organisms that pose serious threat of infection and sepsis in some acute wounds present entirely different pictures in the small chronic wound, which may go on to heal despite the presence of these organisms. Chronic wounds are often contaminated with skin flora, such as *Enterococcus, Staphylococcus, Bacillus*, or occasionally gram-negative organisms.[8]

Distinguishing between contamination and infection in wounds is often difficult. The process of differentiating between a contaminated wound and an infected wound is important to better understand treatment choices. Colonization is the process of a group of organisms living together, whereas infection is the invasion of tissues by microorganisms, resulting in a systemic reaction. Most clinicians will agree that 10^4 to 10^5 organisms per gram of tissue indicate wound infection. Some laboratories use different references, so what may be considered colonization in one facility may be considered infection in another facility. In general, the overall condition of the patient also enters into the diagnosis process. Infection is signaled by a systemic reaction to the microorganisms, and contamination signals the presence of microorganisms in the wound.

High levels of bacteria are found in chronic wounds with necrotic debris. The number and density of aerobes and anaerobes are greater in necrotic wounds and those with undermining.[5] The presence of a foul odor is usually associated with anaerobic organisms. Sharp debridement of necrotic tissue virtually eliminates the anaerobic organisms (such as *Bacteroides, Streptococcus, Enterobacter*, and *Escherichia coli*) and decreases the aerobic organisms (such as *Staphylococcus aureus*) present in the wound.[5]

Methicillin-Resistant *Staphylococcus Aureus*

Methicillin-resistant *S aureus* (MRSA) presents special concerns for patients with wounds. *Staphylococcus aureus* is part of normal skin flora and is on the skin of approximately 20% to 50% of healthy adults and can persist in wounds.[9] Patients at highest risk for developing MRSA colonization and infection are those with a history of injection drug abuse, the presence of chronic disease, previous antimicrobial therapy, previous hospitalization, admission to an intensive care unit, or a prolonged stay in a health care institution.[10] All forms of *S aureus*, including MRSA, can quickly invade and infect breaks in skin integrity, making wounds one of the most common sites of *S aureus* infection and a site commonly colonized with *S aureus* or MRSA.

In the early 1940s, penicillin was found to be effective against *S aureus*; however, soon after its initial use, some strains of *S aureus* began to produce the enzyme penicillinase, which inactivates antimicrobials such as ampicillin, other penicillins, and cephalosporins. Methicillin was the first penicillinase-resistant semisynthetic penicillin and was (and is) used to treat *S aureus* infections. The late 1960s and early 1970s saw the emergence of MRSA with the first reports of outbreaks in both acute and long-term care facilities.[9] Infections caused by MRSA cause concern because resistance to methicillin is associated with resistance to other antimicrobials. A gene on the bacterial chromosome that codes for abnormal penicillin-binding protein (PBP) carries resistance to methicillin.[9] This abnormal PBP has a lower affinity for all penicillin, so very little methicillin binds to it. Therefore, all penicillins, which must bind to the PBP site in order to kill the bacteria, are ineffective. Some strains of MRSA mutate and become resistant to additional antimicrobials.

Of special concern is the recent finding of the potential for MRSA to acquire the gene-conferring vancomycin resistance from vancomycin-resistant enterococci (VRE), leading to vancomycin-resistant *S aureus*.[9] Since vancomycin is the drug of choice for treating MRSA, resistance to vancomycin would present critical problems. Treatment of an MRSA wound infection involves antimicrobial therapy and prevention of cross-contamination. Topical antimicrobial therapy specific for MRSA-infected or -colonized wounds must be used cautiously for routine wound infections so that the antimicrobial will be available if the patient develops MRSA. Mupirocin (Bactroban) is specific for MRSA and can be used topically for wounds infected with the organism. Prevention of cross-contamination between patients requires significant education of caregivers—at all levels— and patients in use of universal standard precautions and good hand-washing procedures. Care must be taken to prevent not only contamination of multiple patients with the organisms, but also multiple body systems within the same patient.

Wound Contamination versus Infection

Clean wounds are contaminated with bacteria but usually progress through wound healing uneventfully. The clinician should suspect bacterial overburden if healing does not occur in clean wounds with appropriate topical therapy. Failure of the wound to progress may indicate a "silent" infection with colony counts above 100,000 organisms per milliliter yet minimal outward signs of wound infection and superficial invasion of tissues.

Clinical Wisdom: *Bacterial Overburden*

The clinician should suspect high bioburden of bacteria in the clean wound if healing or improvement does not occur within a 2-week time frame and the patient is receiving appropriate topical therapy for the wound.

Wounds with continuing moderate to large amounts of seropurulent or purulent exudate and signs and symptoms of infection should be evaluated for infection. Local signs of wound infection include erythema or skin discoloration, edema, warmth, induration, increased pain, and purulent drainage with or without a foul odor. Systemic signs of infection include elevated temperature, white blood cell count, and confusion in the older adult. Table 8–2 gives local and systemic characteristics of wound infection.

Assessment of Wound Infection

Assessment of wound infection involves assessment of the patient's overall condition, observation of the wound and surrounding tissues to differentiate wound inflammation versus the infected wound, and wound cultures to determine colony count. Clinical signs of inflammation are often mistaken for infection. Table 8–3 presents clinical manifestations of both inflammation and infection for comparison. Immunocompromised patients may fail to demonstrate any signs of infection or the signs may be significantly diminished. For example, in older adults, confusion or agitation may be the first indicator of infection and elevated temperature occurs much later in the course of the illness. In some cases, the wound simply fails to progress without other obvious signs of infection. In the immunocompromised patient, identification of the organism may be critical to treatment, in that the responsible organism may be opportunistic in nature and not the typical culprit in wound infections.[11] Immunocompromised patients may also exhibit signs of infection when the bacterial burden is less than that required for producing infection in immunocompetent patients.

Clinical Wisdom: *Cellulitis and Wound Infection*

Advancing cellulitis indicates that the offending organism has invaded tissue surrounding the ulcer and is no longer localized. Advancing cellulitis begins as a small red or discolored area that is indurated, edematous, and warm to touch and progresses to involve more extensive tissues. Left uncontrolled and untreated, cellulitis can result in sepsis.

The common method of confirming clinical infection is by colony count. The clinician diagnoses the infection based on clinical signs and symptoms and obtains a culture to aid in determining the appropriate antibiotic therapy. For example, in outpatient clinics the usual sequence involves the clinician diagnosing the wound infection based on signs and symptoms present and obtaining a culture to confirm the correct selection of antibiotics for treatment. For inpatients diagnosed with infection, antibiotic therapy is generally initiated immediately and the culture reports are used to adjust or modify the antibiotic regimen. Colony counts higher than 100,000 (10^5) are considered indicative of infection. A heavy bioburden (bacterial contamination in the wound) or compromised host resistance (for example, immunocompromised or diabetic patients) can both result in bacterial colony counts higher than 100,000 (10^5) organisms/mL, which is considered confirmation of clinical infection. Chronic wounds do not have to be sterile in order to heal. However, when the bacterial burden in the wound is over 10^5 organisms per gram of tissue, wound healing is impaired or delayed.[5,12] Wounds colonized with β-hemolytic streptococcus can exhibit impaired healing with colony counts less than 100,000/mL.[7] There are also wounds that heal uneventfully in the presence of bacterial colony counts of greater than 100,000/mL.

It is clear that the determination of infection involves critical evaluation of the wound, the patient, and the pathogen.

Table 8–2 Characteristics of Wound Infection

Local Signs of Infection	*Systemic Signs of Infection*
Erythema or skin discoloration	Elevated temperature
Edema	Elevated white blood cell count
Warmth	Confusion or agitation in older adults
Induration	Red streaks from wound
Increased pain	
Purulent wound exudate with or without foul odor	

Table 8–3 Comparison of Wound Characteristics in Inflamed and Infected Wounds

Wound Characteristic	Inflamed Wounds	Infected Wounds
Erythema	Usually presents with well-defined borders. Not as intense in color. May be seen as skin discoloration in dark-skinned persons, such as a purple or gray hue to the skin or a deepening of normal ethnic color.	Edges of erythema or skin discoloration may be diffuse and indistinct. May present as very intense erythema or discoloration with well-demarcated and distinct borders. Red stripes or streaking up or down from the area indicates infection.
Elevated temperature	Usually noted as increase in temperature at wound site and surrounding tissues.	Systemic fever (may not be present in older adult populations).
Exudate: odor	Any odor present may be due to necrotic tissue in the wound, solubization of necrotic tissue, and the type of wound therapy in use, not necessarily infection.	Specific odors are related to some bacterial organisms, such as the sweet smell of *Pseudomonas* or the ammonia odor associated with *Proteus*.
Exudate: amount	Usually minimal; if injury is recent, should see gradual decrease in exudate amount over 3–5 days.	Usually moderate to large amounts; if injury is recent, will not see decrease in exudate amount—amount remains high or increases.
Exudate: character	Bleeding and serosanguineous to serous.	Serous and seropurulent to purulent.
Pain	Variable.	Pain is persistent and continues for an unusual amount of time. Must take wound etiology and subjective nature of pain into account when assessment is performed.
Edema and induration	May be slight swelling, firmness at wound edge.	May indicate infection if edema and induration are localized and accompanied by warmth.

Source: Adapted from J. Feedar, Wound Evaluation and Treatment Planning, *Topics in Geriatric Rehabilitation*, Vol. 9, No. 4, pp. 35–42, © 1994, Aspen Publishers, Inc.

Evaluation of the pathogen occurs by colony count and provides the documentation of infection. Documentation of infection is based on the amount of the bacteria present in the wound tissue.

The level of bacteria in the wound tissue is determined in order to document the presence of a wound infection. As traditionally performed, swab cultures detect only surface contaminants and may not reflect the organism causing the tissue infection.[13] Quantitative wound culture is recommended for determination of infection. According to Stotts,[14] if a standardized technique is used, a quantitative swab technique can accurately document the bacterial burden in wounds. The technique for obtaining the culture specimen should mirror bacteria in the wound tissue, not simply bacteria on the wound surface.

Quantitative Wound Culture

Tissue biopsy, needle aspiration, and the quantitative swab technique are the most frequently used methods of quantitative wound culture. Each has an important place in clinical practice.

Tissue Biopsy

Tissue biopsy is removal of a piece of tissue with a scalpel or by punch biopsy. Before performing a tissue biopsy for wound culture, the area is cleansed with sterile solution that does not contain antiseptic. The area may be treated with topical anesthetic or injected with local anesthetic. The biopsy is performed and pressure applied to the area to control bleeding. The biopsy tissue is promptly transported to the laboratory, where it is weighed, flamed to kill surface contaminants, ground and homogenized, and plated in various media in varying dilutions. Findings are expressed in number of organisms per gram of tissue.[15,16]

Needle Aspiration

Needle aspiration involves insertion of a needle into the tissue to aspirate fluid that contains organisms.[17] Intact skin next to the wound is disinfected with a substance such as povidone-iodine and allowed to dry. Using a 10-mL disposable syringe and a 22-gauge needle with 0.5 mL of air in the syringe, the needle is inserted through intact skin; suction is achieved by briskly withdrawing the plunger to the 10-mL mark. The needle is moved backward and forward at different angles for two to four explorations. The plunger is gently returned to the 0.5-mL mark, the needle is withdrawn and capped, and the specimen is transported to the laboratory. In the laboratory, the fluid aspirated is diluted in broth and plated. Data are expressed in colony-forming units (CFU) per volume of fluid. If tissue is extracted by this technique, the weighing and grinding described for tissue biopsy processing also need to be done and, in this case, the data generated are in number of organisms per gram of tissue.

Clinical Wisdom:
Performing Tissue Biopsy and Needle Aspiration

Physical therapists are not allowed by physical therapy practice acts to perform tissue biopsy or needle aspiration procedures. Physical therapists must work collaboratively with nursing to obtain these samples as required.

Quantitative Swab Technique

The swab technique often has been criticized as a method that produces information about colonization of the ulcer surface rather than in the tissue. One of the problems with the routine swab technique for culturing a wound is that it has been performed in a variety of ways, and therefore cannot be relied upon to address the issue of bioburden in the tissues. There is controversy on how to obtain a swab culture. Some recommend culturing the exudate in the wound prior to wound cleansing.[18,19] Others recommend that after cleansing of the wound is complete, the culture is obtained using a Z technique (side to side across the wound from one edge to the other).[20,21] Others suggest irrigation of the wound with sterile water or saline and pressing the swab against the wound margin or ulcer base to elicit fresh exudate.[22]

The recommended method of quantitative swab culture involves cleansing the wound with a solution that contains no antiseptic solution. The end of a sterile cotton-tipped applicator stick is rotated in a 1-cm^2 area of the open wound for 5 seconds.[22] Pressure is applied to the swab to cause tissue fluid to be absorbed in the cotton tip of the swab. The swab tip is inserted into a sterile tube containing transport medium and transported to the laboratory. The end of the applicator that is not sterile is not inserted into the tube for culture. Serial dilutions of the organisms are made on agar plates. A swab moistened with normal saline without preservative provides more precise data than use of a dry swab.[23] Results are expressed as organisms per swab or CFU per swab or in a semiquantitative manner, such as scant, small, moderate, and large (1+ to 4+) bacterial growths.

Tissue biopsy, needle inspiration, and the quantitative swab technique are used to evaluate the bacteria present in wound tissue rather than on the surface of the wound, in the exudate, or in necrotic tissue. They are used to examine tissue for aerobic and anaerobic organisms. They also can be used to obtain a specimen for Gram's stain, a method recognized as a rapid diagnostic technique of infection.[23,24] For a Gram's stain, the tissue fluid is placed on a slide, treated with various stains and viewed under the microscope. In wounds where swabs yielded less than 10^5 organisms, the Gram's stain is considered to show no bacteria.

Data show that the tissue biopsy, needle aspiration, and quantitative swab techniques are comparable in terms of sensitivity, specificity, and accuracy.[14] The following describes how the procedures are performed.

Procedures for Quantitative Wound Culture

Equipment Needed:

- Gloves (clean and sterile)
- Sterile saline (nonbacteriostatic)
- Container to transport specimen
- Lab requisition
- Appropriate dressing materials

Culture Technique–Specific Equipment Needed:

- Punch biopsy/scalpel
- Wound culture swab
- Anaerobic medium if required
- 10-mL syringe with 22-gauge needle
- Cork

Procedure Preparation—For All Methods

1. Wash hands. (Reduces transmission of microorganisms.)
2. Don clean gloves (gown if necessary). (Maintains universal precautions.)
3. Remove soiled dressings and discard in plastic bag. Then remove and discard gloves. (Prevents contamination and spread of microorganisms.)
4. Clean wound and surrounding skin with normal saline. (Cleaning removes contaminated debris.)

Procedure: Swab Method

1. Don sterile gloves and remove swab from culturette tube, taking care not to touch swab or inside of tube.

(Maintains universal precautions and aseptic technique.)

2. Swab wound area 1 cm^2 with sufficient pressure to obtain wound fluid. (Ensures collection of a good specimen.)

3. Use separate swabs if taking more than one specimen. Swab only a 1-cm^2 area of wound with each swab. (Ensures good culture specimen and prevents cross-contamination. Care must be taken to swab the wound instead of the wound edges to prevent contamination by skin flora and contaminated debris.)

4. Carefully place swab into culturette tube without touching swab, inside, outside, or top of container. (Prevents contamination and keeps those areas free of pathogens that could be spread to others who handle the tube.)

5. Crush ampule of medium in culturette and close securely, making sure swab is surrounded by medium. (Keeps specimen from drying out and provides supporting medium.)

Procedure: Anaerobic Swab Culture Method

1. If collecting a specimen for anaerobic culture, take care to keep anaerobic transport culture tube in an upright position to prevent carbon monoxide from escaping. Close container securely after swab is placed in tube. (Maintains anaerobic environment.)

Procedure: Syringe Method

1. Disinfect intact skin with antiseptic and allow skin to dry for 1 minute. (Anaerobic specimens are obtained from deep inside wounds.)

2. Place 0.5 mL of air in 10-mL disposable syringe with 22-gauge needle and insert needle into intact skin adjacent to wound. Withdraw plunger to achieve suction and move the needle back and forth at different angles. (Prevents contamination at needle withdrawal site.)

3. Return the plunger gently to the 0.5-mL mark; do not insert drainage into the tissues. (Ensures good specimen and prevents contamination from skin flora. Syringe method is used when large amounts of pus or drainage are present or for collecting tissue.)

4. Cork needle to send syringe/needle to laboratory as one unit-containing specimen. Do not recap or attempt to disconnect needle from syringe. (Maintains universal precautions. Prevents injury from needle stick and spread of microorganisms.)

Procedure: Tissue Biopsy

1. Don sterile gloves. Obtain a biopsy specimen using a 3- to 4-mm dermal punch or a scalpel. (Allows for determination of tissue level of microorganism contami-nation. Biopsy is usually performed by a physician or advanced practitioner.)

2. Place specimen in sterile container. (Prevents spread of microorganisms.)

Procedure: Final Steps—All Methods

1. Remove and discard gloves in plastic bag. (Reduces transmission of microorganisms.)

2. Wash hands.

3. Don sterile gloves and apply sterile dressing to the wound. (Dressing absorbs drainage and immobilizes and protects the wound.)

4. Label specimen container(s) with patient name, room number, date, time, and exact source of specimen. (Ensures proper identification of specimen. Proper source of specimen is important for laboratory to rule out normal flora from location.)

5. Place container in clean plastic bag, and have specimen transported to laboratory as soon as possible. (Plastic bag prevents spread of microorganisms. Immediate transport prevents overgrowth of microorganisms that can occur if specimen is left at room temperature for an extended length of time.)

6. Dispose of soiled equipment into appropriate receptacle. (Maintains universal precautions.)

7. Wash hands. (Reduces transmission of microorganisms.)

MANAGEMENT OF EXUDATE AND INFECTION

Management of exudate and infection includes wound cleansing; use of topical antimicrobials, antiseptics, and antifungals; and management of exudate with topical dressings.

Wound Cleansing

Effective wound cleansing removes debris that supports bacterial growth and delays wound healing. Wound cleansing delivers cleansing solution to the wound by mechanical force, aids with separation of necrotic tissue from healthy wound tissues, and removes bacteria and dressing residue from the wound surface. The process of wound cleansing involves selecting a cleansing solution and a method of delivering the solution to the wound. Exhibit 8–1 presents the Agency for Health Care Policy and Research (AHCPR) panel's recommended guidelines for pressure ulcer cleansing. Cleansing of all wounds can be performed using these principles.

The cleansing solution chosen must be effective and safe to the wound. Isotonic normal saline is preferred as a solution because it is physiologic, nontoxic, and inexpensive. Saline does not contain preservatives and must be discarded 24 to 48 hours after opening.[25] Commercial wound cleansers are available to assist in wound cleansing for wounds requiring more cleansing capacity to remove adherent debris from the wound surface. These wound cleansers contain surfactants that act to lower surface tension and to loosen matter from the wound surface.[25] Nonionic surfactant wound cleansers are recommended as safe to the healing wound.

Clinical Wisdom:
Normal Saline for Wound Cleansing

Two useful strategies for obtaining normal saline for wound care in the home setting:

1. Saline can be made at home by adding two teaspoons of table salt to 1 L of boiling water. Be sure to discard after 24 hours.
2. Another useful strategy is to use pressurized saline commonly used for contact lens wearers. This preserved saline may be used for a longer duration, and the pressure from the canister is not sufficient to cause wound trauma.

For healthy clean wounds, cleanse with normal saline and do not use antimicrobial solutions or skin cleansers. Clean wounds do not need to be cleansed with antimicrobial solutions as the goal of care is to clear low levels of contaminants from the wound. In fact, they are harmful. Solutions such as povidone-iodine, acetic acid, hydrogen peroxide, and sodium hypochlorite (Dakin's fluid) are toxic to fibroblasts. Use of antimicrobial agents is contraindicated in the healthy proliferative wound because of the damage to the healthy tissues.[13,26,27] In general, most skin cleansers are not appropriate wound cleansers as they have been developed for use externally, not internally, as is the case with a wound. What is appropriate for cleansing the skin is not appropriate for open wounds because an open wound lacks the protection of intact epidermis and provides direct access to internal body structures. For healthy clean wounds, cleanse with normal saline. For healthy wounds do not use antimicrobial solutions or skin cleansers.

For infected wounds, cleanse with normal saline or use a 10- to 14-day cleansing regimen with an antimicrobial solution. For infected wounds do not use skin cleansers and do not prolong the use of an antimicrobial solution. Antimicrobial agents may play a minor role in wound cleansing for infected wounds, wounds with large amounts of necrotic debris, or those with large amounts of exudate. Use of antimicrobial agents is best handled in a manner similar to that

Exhibit 8–1 AHCPR Recommended Guidelines for Pressure Ulcer Cleansing

---

1. Cleanse wounds initially and at each dressing change.
2. Use minimal mechanical force when cleansing ulcer with gauze, cloth, or sponges.
3. Do not clean wounds with skin cleansers or antiseptic agents (povidone-iodine, sodium hypochlorite solution, hydrogen peroxide, and acetic acid).
4. Use normal saline for cleansing most ulcers.
5. Use enough irrigation pressure to enhance wound cleansing without causing trauma to the wound bed. Safe and effective ulcer irrigation pressures range from 4 to 15 psi.
6. Consider whirlpool treatment for cleansing ulcers that contain thick exudate, slough, or necrotic tissue. Discontinue whirlpool when ulcer is clean.

Source: Reprinted from N. Bergstrom, M.A. Bennett, C.E. Carlson, et al., *Treatment of Pressure Ulcers,* Clinical Practice Guideline No. 15, December 1994, U.S. Department of Health and Human Services, Public Health Service, Agency for Health Care Policy and Research, AHCPR Publication No. 95-0652.

---

for antibiotic use, that is, for a short duration. Antimicrobial agents used as cleansing agents in the debris-filled wound should be used for 10 to 14 days and rinsed thoroughly from the wound with saline. Rinsing the wound with saline after cleansing with antimicrobial solutions decreases the cytotoxic effects in the wound. The antimicrobial cleanser should be discontinued after the course of therapy (10 to 14 days) or when the wound is clean and debris free.

Cleansing Method

There are several methods for cleansing the wound, including soaking, whirlpool, scrubbing, and irrigation. Soaking is a form of hydrotherapy (includes a variety of types from a bucket to a Hubbard tank) and may be useful for removal of gross contaminants and loosening necrotic tissue. The softening that occurs with the soaking helps to ease the separation of necrotic debris from healthy wound tissues. Wound soaking is appropriate only for wounds with large amounts of necrotic debris. Once a wound is clean and proliferating, whirlpool and wound soaking impede wound healing and thus generally are not appropriate.[13,25] Whirlpool may be useful for more than simply soaking and cleansing, as is the case with using whirlpool to increase perfusion to an area. (See Chapters 17 and 20 for information on pulsatile lavage and whirlpool.) Antimicrobial agents should not be used in the whirlpool or wound-soaking solution because of wound tissue toxicity.

Scrubbing the wound involves use of gauze or sponges in direct wound contact with mechanical force to enhance removal of debris and efficacy of cleansing solution used.[25] Scrubbing causes microabrasions in the wound and thus delays healing. Use of a nonionic surfactant cleansing solution will limit the damage inflicted with scrubbing to the healing wound tissues. Use of nonabrasive sponges will also help decrease the damage to the healing tissues. The more porous the sponge, the less damage inflicted on the wound surface.[25] Even use of nonionic surfactant cleansing solutions and non-abrasive porous sponges will injure the fragile wound tissue. Thus, no scrubbing is recommended.

Clinical Wisdom:
Shallow Wound Cleansing Procedure

Cleanse from the center of the wound in a circular motion, working toward the edge of the wound and the surrounding tissues. Do not return to the center of the wound after cleansing at the edge of the wound or the surrounding tissues, as this will recontaminate the clean wound center.

Wound irrigation can be performed using a variety of instruments and equipment. Wound irrigation is particularly appropriate for cleansing deep wounds with undermining or tunneling present. Use a catch basin and towels to absorb and accumulate waste materials and irrigant runoff. Repeat the irrigation procedure at each dressing change. Protect eyes, face, and clothing of the clinician by using universal precautions. Some newer irrigation devices include a splashguard to help protect the clinician.

Clinical Wisdom:
Deep Wound Cleansing Procedure

Use of a catheter or a syringe to irrigate wounds with undermining and tunneling will not injure the tissues and can effectively cleanse the tissues involved in the wound under the skin surface. Flush with copious amounts of irrigant solution, then gently massage the tissues above the tunneling to express the exudate accumulated in the tunnel. Repeat two or three times until the solution and fluids returned are clear (see Figure 8–2). After the wound cleansing the undermined spaces are usually packed loosely with packing materials such as roller gauze or alginate rope products to prevent infection from traveling up the tunnel (see Figure 8–3).

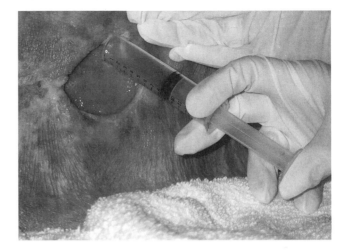

Figure 8–2 Irrigation of wound with syringe.

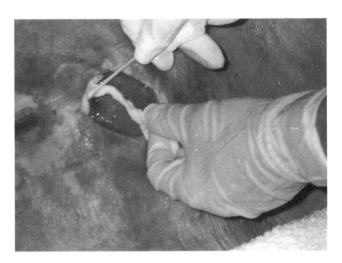

Figure 8–3 Packing wound with undermining.

The amount of pressure used for irrigation is determined by the desire not to harm the healing wound tissues and to cleanse the wound effectively. The pressure of delivering the irrigant is commonly described as low or high pressure. Pressure force is described in pounds per square inch (psi). Pressure force under 4 psi is commonly referred to as low pressure and can be obtained by use of bulb syringes or just pouring solution over the wound bed.[25] Pressure force between 4 and 15 psi is considered high pressure and can be achieved by using commercial devices, a 35-mL syringe attached to a 19-gauge needle or angiocatheter, pulsatile lavage, or whirlpool therapy. High-pressure irrigation using any of these forms is a method of debridement, loosening and softening necrotic tissue for easy separation from healthy tissue. Pressurized irrigation removes bacteria and debris more effectively than gravity or bulb syringe irrigation. As such, high-pressure irrigation is most effective with an inflammatory process. Use of high-pressure irrigation is not the method of choice for the healthy, proliferating wound, as this can damage fragile blood vessels and new tissue growth.

A number of available irrigation devices deliver solutions with too much pressure, thus driving bacteria and irrigant solution deeper into wound tissues. Pressures over 15 psi can cause trauma to the wound bed, forcing bacteria deeper into wound tissues. For example, use of a Water Pik at the middle and high settings provides 42 psi and more than 50 psi, respectfully, both of which are too high and will drive bacteria farther into the wound tissues. Irrigation pressures between 4 psi and 15 psi are recommended.

The clinical outcomes from wound cleansing are determined by the purpose of the cleansing and the wound assessment. For predominantly clean wounds with new tissue growth, cleansing is used only to remove dressing residue, and if any additional cleansing is needed, a low-pressure irrigation system should be used (such as pouring the solution over the wound or using a bulb syringe or piston syringe to deliver the irrigant). The goals of therapy with low-pressure irrigation are to dislodge wound dressing residue, reduce wound surface contaminants, and protect fragile new tissue growth. For wounds with necrotic tissue or debris, a high-pressure irrigation system should be used. Whirlpool therapy and pulsatile lavage are not always available or appropriate for all patients, and other devices such as the 35-mL syringe

and 19-gauge needle or angiocatheter may be the best choice. The goals of therapy are to loosen and soften the necrotic debris for easier separation from healthy tissues, reduce the bacterial burden, remove dressing remnants, and prevent undue wound trauma.

> **Research Wisdom:** *Wound Irrigation*
>
> Use of a 35-mL syringe with a 19-gauge angiocatheter or needle attached delivers saline at 8 psi and provides more effective removal of bacteria and debris than use of a bulb syringe.

Aseptic Technique

One of the continuing debates in wound management is what type of aseptic technique is necessary for wound care in various health care settings. Asepsis includes activities that prevent infection or break the chain of infection. It is generally divided into two types: surgical asepsis and medical asepsis. Surgical asepsis, or sterile technique, is the method used in surgery where all instruments and materials used are sterile and all health care providers involved wear sterile gloves, caps, masks, and gowns. Medical asepsis, or clean technique, involves procedures to reduce the number of pathogens and to decrease the transfer of pathogens. In surgical asepsis, the nurse prepares a sterile field, dons sterile gloves, and follows surgical aseptic techniques in caring for the wound. Sterile and clean techniques are compared in the following display.

Sterile Technique	Clean Technique
Preparation of a sterile field	Preparation of clean field
Clean gloves	Clean gloves
Decontamination of the wound and surrounding skin with an antimicrobial cleanser	Cleansing of the wound and surrounding skin
Change gloves: Sterile gloves	Change gloves: Clean gloves
Use sterile forceps, scalpel, and scissors	Use sterile forceps, scalpel, and scissors
Allow only "sterile to sterile" contact of instruments and materials used for the procedure	Prevent direct contamination of materials and supplies, but no "sterile to sterile" rules apply
Apply sterile dressing	Apply clean dressing

There are various viewpoints on which approach is most suitable for wound care patients. Some general guidelines may help to clarify use of an aseptic technique. Sterile technique is most appropriate in acute care hospital settings, for patients at high risk for infection (advanced age, immunocompromised, diabetic) and for certain care procedures such as sharp wound debridement. Clean technique is most appropriate for patients in long-term care settings, home care, and some clinic settings, and for patients not at high risk for infection and receiving routine wound care such as dressing changes. Further research is needed to determine outcomes with use of clean technique. Table 8–4 compares general guidelines for clean versus sterile technique choices for wound care patients.

Hand Washing and Infection Control

What is clear about infection management and wound care is the importance of hand washing by the health care practitioner. Hand washing is the single most important means for preventing spread of infection. Use of universal standard precautions and hand washing by the wound care clinician promote health maintenance for patients and caregivers and as such are critically important to include when instructing others in wound care programs. Along with hand washing, caregivers must be instructed in appropriate disposal of infectious waste products, such as used wound dressings, gauze used for wound cleansing, and instruments used in wound care. In institutional settings, such as hospitals and long-term care facilities, there are procedures for disposal of contaminated materials in bags clearly identified as infectious waste (eg, double bagging out of isolation rooms and use of red biohazard trash bags). In the home care arena, disposal of contaminated waste becomes more problematic and the wound care clinician must address disposal based on the area

served, local waste collection procedures, and agency protocols. In the home care setting, education of the caregiver regarding the procedures for waste disposal is essential for maintaining community health.

Topical Antimicrobials*

The use of antimicrobials is confusing for clinicians. Systemic antimicrobial drugs (those agents given orally or intravenously) are often superior to topical agents (ointments, creams, or solutions put directly on the wound surface) because of the better penetration of systemic agents. However, topical antimicrobials are often effective in limiting surface colonization so that tissue defenses can clean up without continual reinfection from superficial bacteria. Some superficial infections may respond better to topical agents and in some cases, it is wise to use topical agents to avoid sensitizing the patient or creating resistant microorganisms. Some topical antimicrobials can damage healthy tissues, exacerbating tissue destruction or damaging tissue defenses. The terms *antimicrobial, antibiotic, antibacterial,* and *antiseptic* are often used interchangeably; however, the definitions are slightly different according to the Food and Drug Administration (FDA). Exhibit 8–2 presents definitions of these terms for easy reference.

The three main classes of antimicrobials used for wounds include antibacterials, antiseptics, and antifungals. Understanding how antimicrobials are prescribed is helpful for

---

*This information is adapted with permission from G. Gilson, ed. *Topical Agents for Open Wounds: Antibacterials, Antiseptics, Antifungals.* Reviewed by G. Rodeheaver, J.W. Cooper, D.R. Nelson, and M. Meehan. Charleston, SC: Hill-Rom International, Inc.; 1991.

Table 8–4 Clean versus Sterile Technique General Guidelines

Factor	Sterile Technique	Clean Technique
Settings	Acute care hospitals Clinics in acute care facilities	Home care Long-term care facilities Community clinics Physician's office
Procedures	Invasive procedures Sharp debridement	Routine procedures Dressing changes
Patients	Immunocompromised Advanced age or very young age Diabetic	Patients NOT at high risk for infection

Exhibit 8–2 Definitions of Antimicrobial Terms

Term	Definition
Antimicrobial—	An agent that inhibits or kills microorganisms
Antiseptic—	A substance that prevents or arrests the *growth* by preventing multiplication (bacteriostatic) or *action* of microorganisms either by inhibiting their activity or by destroying or killing them (bactericidal). Applies to substances used on living tissues (eg, povidone-iodine)
Antibiotic—	An organic chemical substance produced by a microorganism that has the capacity in diluted solutions to destroy or inhibit the growth of bacteria and other microorganisms (eg, penicillin)
Antibacterial—	An agent that destroys or stops bacterial growth (eg, bacitracin)
Antifungal—	A wide variety of agents that inhibit or kill fungi (eg, nystatin)

Source: Adapted with permission from *Topical Agents for Open Wounds: Antibacterials, Antiseptics, Antifungals,* G. Gilson, ed., reviewed by G. Rodeheaver, J.W. Cooper, D.R. Nelson, and M. Meehan, © 1991, Hill-Rom International.

wound care clinicians. This is the process by which antimicrobials are ordered. The proper use of any antimicrobial requires determination of clinical infection in the wound, correct identification of the invading organism by culture and Gram's stain smears prior to beginning therapy, and consideration of pharmacology and toxicology when choosing the agent. If an agent must be chosen prior to receiving laboratory results, make the decision based on Gram's stain smears (either positive or negative), the most likely pathogens involved in the disease process (for example, *Escherichia coli* for a fecally incontinent patient with a sacral pressure sore), and the efficacy of the agent in similar situations.

Clinical Wisdom: *Factors Altering Response to Topical Antibacterials and Antiseptics*

Patient response to antibacterial and antiseptic agents may be altered by age, disease processes (such as diabetes), malignancy, neurologic disorders, immune dysfunction, pregnancy, allergy, or concomitant drug therapy.

Multiple factors influence the transcutaneous penetration of antimicrobial agents including physiochemical properties of the drug (polarity, stability, and solubility in base and lipids), nature of the pharmaceutical preparation (drug concentration, composition and properties of the base, and incompatible mixtures), method of application (inert delivery systems, time-released delivery systems, application in conjunction with occlusion, polar compounds to increase absorption, and substances that damage the stratum corneum to improve penetration), and nature of the skin (integrity of the epidermis, variability in skin thickness, and age). Problems

associated with topical antimicrobial use in wound care are related to absorption of chemicals into the body tissues through the wound bed. There are cases where absorption of certain chemicals contained in an antiseptic through the wound bed has caused systemic health problems. For example, iodine toxicity has occurred from use of povidone-iodine in open wounds.

Antibacterials

Antibacterial agents are chemicals that eliminate living organisms pathogenic to the host or patient. Some examples of antibacterials are bacitracin, gentamicin, metronidazole, mupirocin, and silver sulfadiazine. The use of antibacterials is common for most infections. In the elderly, the primary sites of infection in order of frequency are urinary tract, pulmonary system, and wounds.[28,29] Broad-spectrum antibacterials are useful for mixed infections when there is more than one pathogen present and quick identification of the organism is difficult. Antibacterial topical administration occurs in smaller drug doses, compared with systemic antibacterials, due to direct contact with the affected area.[29] The same or better results may be achieved without the risk of toxicity. Systemic agents may be used in combination with topical agents, as in the treatment of impetigo. Topically administered drugs are in more direct contact with organisms so that problems of absorption, distribution, and availability to the infected site are reduced. Frequently, topical agents are used in conjunction with one another to give broader coverage, thereby increasing the rate of bactericidal action against a large spectrum of bacteria.[30]

Topical antibacterials may be used prophylactically. When used properly, they can be effective chemical barriers that may impede the entrance of pathogenic organisms and diminish the local or systemic morbidity associated with infected wounds. When using topical antibacterials prophylactically, there is always a danger of overgrowth of resistant organisms; therefore, use of antibacterials for prevention requires good clinical judgment for optimal effectiveness.[30]

Clinical Wisdom:
Wound Healing and Antimicrobials

No antibacterial agent, whether bactericidal or bacteriostatic, will be curative when used in isolation. Attention to nutritional factors, management of underlying pathology, and relief of causative factors are also required.

Topical antibacterials used in a viscous vehicle provide a moist wound healing environment facilitating epithelial migration.[31] The indications for topical antibacterials include significant bacterial infection diagnosed or suspected, and an indication for prophylactic use due to the patient's underlying disease and/or the patient's increased risk of infection resulting from surgical procedures, viral or metabolic diseases, chemotherapy or radiation therapy, and prolonged corticosteroid administration. Contraindications relate to the excessive use of antibacterials for minor infections and for nonbacterial pathogens.[30] Inappropriate use of antibacterials subjects the patient to risk of drug toxicity, risk of allergy, superinfection with resistant organisms, and unnecessary costs.[30,32]

Clinical Wisdom:
Routine Use of Topical Antibacterials

Routine use of topical antibacterials is strongly discouraged because of the frequent development of resistant organisms. This is particularly true of mupirocin, as it is effective against methicillin-resistant *Staphylococcus aureus* (MRSA) and, if used inappropriately, will not be effective when most needed.

The base, or vehicle, is the form in which the antibacterial agent is available. In general, it is best to use a lotion or a paste for application to wet or weepy skin and wounds and a greasy ointment for application to dry, cracked skin. Creams are convenient since to some extent they can be used for wet or dry surfaces and are easier to use. Many ointments contain lanolin or wood alcohols, and patients can readily develop contact sensitivity to these substances. Creams less often contain lanolin, but usually contain a preservative or stabilizer such as parabens or ethylenediamine dihydrochlo-

ride, both of which are known to be occasional sensitizers. Ointments may be confused with creams, particularly with the introduction of synthetic bases that claim to have the properties of both creams and ointments. Lotions are preferable to greasy applications for areas that rub against each other, for example, groin areas and in between the toes. Lotions are usually less occlusive than ointments. Appendix A contains an index of antibacterial agents. The index provides a listing of commonly used antibacterials and individual entries for each antibacterial. Individual antibacterials are presented with a description of the agent, the action, indications for use, precautions, directions, and packaging information.

Antiseptics

Antiseptics are a group of widely differing chemical compounds possessing bactericidal (kills bacteria) or bacteriostatic (prevents bacterial multiplication) properties. Some examples of antiseptics are povidone-iodine, acetic acid, hydrogen peroxide, and hypochlorites. They are employed in medical practice with the object of preventing or combating bacterial infection of superficial tissues as well as for sterilization of instruments and infected material. Chemically, antiseptics may be inorganic or organic. Oxidizing disinfectants liberate oxygen when in contact with pus or organic substances. Different bacteria are sensitive to different antiseptics. For example, acetic acid is commonly used against infections caused by *Pseudomonas aeruginosa*. Antiseptic agents are applied directly to tissue to destroy microorganisms or inhibit their reproduction or metabolic activity. By reducing organisms, it is believed antiseptics may hasten wound healing and diminish local or systemic morbidity associated with wound infection.[33] However, many commonly used antiseptics are cytotoxic and actually inhibit wound healing; therefore, caution is recommended.[26] The major uses of antiseptics are as hand scrubs, cleansers, irrigants, and protective dressings. It is important to remember that the skin cannot be sterilized and that approximately 20% of the skin's normal resident flora are beyond the reach of antiseptics.[29] Excessive antiseptic use subjects the patient to risk of allergy, risk of drug toxicity, superinfection, unnecessary costs and pose significant public health concerns due to ecologic pressure favoring selection of bacteria resistant to antiseptics.[33] Antiseptics, regardless of type, damage the healthy wound and impair wound healing.[27] Appendix A contains an index to antiseptics. The index provides a listing of commonly used antiseptics and individual entries for each antiseptic. Individual antiseptics are presented with a description of the agent, the action, indications for use, adverse reactions (with special attention to effects on wound healing), dosage, and packaging information.

Antifungals

Fungi comprise five widely differing classes of primitive flora. Thus, antifungal agents include a wide variety of chemical types of a rather narrow antifungal spectrum. Some examples of antifungals include nystatin, ketoconazole, and miconazole nitrate. Not all antifungal agents are fungicidal; many are only fungistatic, and certain of them may owe their efficiency to a keratolytic action.

Broad-spectrum antifungal agents in general are toxic irritants, as expected from their nonselectivity; however, many of these have limited absorption through the epidermis and so may be used in dermatologic preparations.[29] The indications for an antifungal are a significant fungal infection diagnosed or strongly suspected and an indication for prophylactic antifungal use due to the patient's underlying disease or the patient's increased risk of fungal infection resulting from invasive procedures or environmental exposure (diarrhea, diaphoresis, poor hygiene, diabetes, etc). The major contraindication for antifungal use is known allergy to ingredients. Antifungals must be used for the prescribed time to eliminate the infection fully. Some areas are more difficult to treat and some fungi are more difficult to eliminate because of the patient's underlying disease process. External factors may affect the antifungal agent's ability to penetrate the skin, including temperature, ambient water vapor pressure, and drying agents such as powders, which reduce the excess moisture in the skin folds and may aid in efficacy of antifungals. Nonsporing anaerobes are a significant pathogen in ulcers with a foul smell and exposure to fecal contamination.[29] Metronidazole has been shown to be effective in eliminating or decreasing the odor associated with these wounds.[34–37] Appendix A contains an index of antifungal agents. The index provides a listing of commonly used antifungals and individual entries for each antifungal. Individual antifungals are presented with a description of the agent, the action, indications for use, precautions, available vehicle, dosage, and packaging information.

Research Wisdom:
Treatment of Malodorous Wounds

Topical metronidazole has been shown to be effective in resolving odor in foul-smelling wounds. Use of a 1% solution or 0.75% gel (Metrogel) applied twice daily reduced or eliminated odor in 80% to 90% of wounds in 4 to 7 days. Odor was significantly decreased in 2 days.[34–37]

Topical Dressings for Management of Exudate

Effective management of exudate requires knowledge of absorptive capacity of dressing materials and attention to fragile wound margins. Excess exudate on the wound edges can lead to maceration and destruction of the critical wound edge. Use of petrolatum products or other hydrophobic ointments around the wound can provide some protection for the wound edges. Use of a topical dressing that adequately absorbs the wound fluid will also protect the wound edges.

Clinical Wisdom: *Caution about Petrolatum Around Wound Edges*

If petrolatum products are being used and the patient is receiving physical therapy, nurses *must* notify the physical therapist. The therapist should be informed because petrolatum products interfere with PT technologies and are hard to remove from the patient's skin prior to PT interventions.

The choice of a dressing for a wound in many cases is dependent on the amount of drainage present in the wound and the expected drainage from the wound. For example, a wound that has been recently debrided of yellow necrotic tissue may have a history of moderate to large amounts of drainage; however, the amount of expected drainage postdebridement is less, usually minimal to moderate amounts. The topical dressing may also become not only the treatment but also the method of determining efficacy. For example, evaluation of the dressing upon removal from the wound allows the clinician to judge what percentage of the dressing material has interacted with wound drainage. Evaluation of the amount of dressing used by the wound exudate often determines whether treatment will continue with the same dressing or whether a new dressing will be applied. (See *Color Plate series* 40 to 45, reading the dressing, for determining the effectiveness of topical dressings in management of wound exudate and how to distinguish exudate from the wound versus material from wound fluid and dressing interaction.) Table 8–5 presents the generic product categories with notes about the absorptive ability of each dressing type. This information may be useful in choosing dressings for the exudative wound. How to choose a wound dressing to manage exudate is explained in detail in Chapter 10, Management of the Wound Environment.

The type of wound under treatment also affects the choice of dressing for exudate management. An example is the venous disease ulcer under appropriate management with compression therapy and topical dressings. For the venous

Table 8–5 Topical Treatment—Wound Dressings

Wound Dressings: Generic Categories	Not Absorbent	Low to Minimal Absorption	Minimal to Moderate Absorption	Moderate to Large Absorption
Skin sealants	X			
Composite dressings		X	X	
Transparent film dressings	X			
Gauze—woven		X		
Gauze—nonwoven			X	
Gauze—impregnated	X			
Calcium alginates			X	X
Exudate absorbers—beads, pastes, powders, flakes			X	X
Hydrocolloids—regular, thin, pastes, granules		X	X	X (when used with other forms of dressings)
Hydrogels—sheets, wafers, amborphous		X	X	
Lubricating stimulating agents	X			
Foams		X	X	
Hydrocolloid-hydrogel combinations			X	X

disease ulcer in the initial compression therapy stages, exudate amount will increase as edema in the extremities is being managed. Sometimes exudate amount will remain copious for several weeks as the edema is brought under control. In general, the exudate amount can be expected to remain large for 2 weeks.

The presence of large amounts of exudate on the patient is significant. The skin surrounding the wound can become macerated and, in some cases, a candidiasis or yeast infection may develop around the wound. The continual loss of proteins, fluids, and electrolytes in the wound exudate can cause fluid and electrolyte disturbances in severe cases; at a minimum, the loss of proteins and wound healing substrates can slow or impede the wound healing progress. Finally, the presence of a wound with large amounts of draining exudate takes a toll on the patient's daily quality of life, disrupting normal function.

OUTCOME MEASURES

Outcome measures are tools used to evaluate the results of therapy. Appropriate characteristics to assess in evaluating the results of exudate management are the amount of

exudate in the wound, the type of exudate in the wound, and the involvement of the wound dressing with the exudate present in the wound. Measurement of exudate is an intermediate outcome measure; healing is the final outcome.

Amount of Exudate

The amount of exudate should diminish progressively in the wound if therapy is appropriate. The amount of exudate can be measured by using clinical judgment to evaluate the distribution of moisture in the wound and the interaction of exudate with the wound dressing. A rating scale similar to the following may be used to quantify amount of exudate:

1 = None = wound tissues dry
2 = Scant = wound tissues moist, no measurable exudate
3 = Small = wound tissues wet, moisture evenly distributed in wound, drainage involved $\leq$25% of wound dressing
4 = Moderate = wound tissues saturated, drainage may or may not be evenly distributed in wound, drainage involved >25% to <75% of wound dressing

5 = Large = wound tissues bathed in fluid, drainage freely expressed, may or may not be evenly distributed in wound, drainage involved >75% of wound dressing

Type of Exudate

The type of exudate should change as the wound improves and heals. As the wound passes through the inflammatory phase of wound healing, serous drainage should become more serosanguineous and then sanguineous in nature. As infection or necrosis is resolved, the exudate type should also reflect improvement. Foul purulent drainage should become merely purulent and then seropurulent, and finally serous and serosanguineous in character. Measurement of type of exudate is best accomplished by the use of a rating scale. A scale similar to the following may be helpful:

Exhibit 8–3 Self-Care Teaching Guidelines

Self-Care Guidelines Specific to Exudate and Infection Management	Instructions Given (Date/Initials)	Demonstration *or* Review of Material (Date/Initials)	Return Demonstration *or* Verbalizes Understanding (Date/Initials)
1. Type of wound and reasons for exudate			
2. Significance of exudate and infection			
3. Topical therapy care routine: a. Clean wound.			
b. Apply absorptive dressing (note appearance of dressing when it interacts with wound drainage and on removal).			
c. Manage wound edges to prevent maceration.			
d. Apply secondary or topper dressing as appropriate.			
4. Frequency of dressing changes			
5. Expected change in wound drainage during healing			
6. When to notify the health care provider a. Signs and symptoms of infection			
b. Failure to improve			
c. Presence of odor			
d. Pus or purulent drainage			
e. Copious amounts of drainage			
f. Elevated temperature or signs of confusion in the older patient			
7. Universal precautions a. Hand washing			
b. Use of gloves during care procedures			
c. Disposal of contaminated materials			
8. Antibiotic regimen a. Oral medication use			
b. Topical medication use			
c. Antimicrobial cleanser use			
9. Importance of follow-up with health care provider			

1 = Bloody = thin, bright red

2 = Serosanguineous = thin, watery, pale red to pink

3 = Serous = thin, watery, clear

4 = Purulent = thin or thick, opaque tan to yellow

5 = Foul purulent = thick, opaque yellow to green with offensive odor

REFERRAL CRITERIA

Determining whether a patient is a candidate for wound management requires adequate assessment of the patient with attention to evaluation for possible referral. For example, the following patients would warrant referral to the physician and/or an advanced practice nurse for either a medical evaluation or immediate intervention or referral to another health care professional for consultation.

1. The person with a wound exudate that is copious, malodorous, and prolonged should be evaluated further for infection, cellulitis, abscess, or progressive degeneration. In this case the advanced practice nurse may choose to manage the patient initially. If the condition worsens or the patient fails to improve over a 2-week time frame, the physician should be consulted.
2. Patients with an elevated temperature or those on a downhill course should be evaluated further. Intervene as in No. 1.
3. Patients with no wound improvement over several weeks should be evaluated further. In this case the advanced practice nurse may want to consult other health care practitioners (physical therapists, dietitians, wound care nurses or ET nurses, and physicians).
4. Patients with evidence of cellulitis *or* gross purulence/infection should be evaluated further. Intervene as in No. 1.
5. Patients with impending exposed bone or tendon present in the wound should be evaluated further. Intervene as in No. 3.
6. Patients with evidence of an abscessed area should be evaluated further. Intervene as in No. 3.
7. Patients with extensively undermined areas present in the wound should be evaluated further. Intervene as in No. 3.

SELF-CARE TEACHING GUIDELINES

Patient and caregiver instruction in self-care must be individualized to the topical therapy care routine, the individual patient's wound, the individual patient's and caregiver's learning style and coping mechanisms, and the ability of the patient/caregiver to perform procedures. The general self-care teaching guidelines in Exhibit 8–3 provide a model of information to teach and should be individualized for each patient and caregiver.

REFERENCES

1. Wysocki AB. Wound fluids and the pathogenesis of chronic wounds. *J Wound Ostomy Continence Nurs.* 1996;23:283–290.
2. Winter GD. Formation of the scab and the rate of reepithelialization of superficial wounds in the skin of the young domestic pig. *Nature.* 1965;193:293–294.
3. Kerstein MD. Moist wound healing: the clinical perspective. *Ostomy Wound Manage.* 1995;41(supp 7A):37–45.
4. Stotts NA. Impaired wound healing. In: Carrieri-Kohlman VK, Lindsay AM, West CM, eds. *Pathophysiological Phenomenon in Nursing.* 2nd ed. Philadelphia: WB Saunders Company; 1993:343–366.
5. Sapico FL, Ginunas VJ, Thornhill-Hyones M, et al. Quantitative microbiology of pressure sores in different stages of healing. *Diagn Biol Infect Dis.* 1986;5:31–38.
6. Cooper DM. The physiology of wound healing: an overviw. In: Krasner D, ed. *Chronic Wound Care.* King of Prussia, PA: Health Management Publications, Inc; 1990:1–11.
7. Robson MC. Disturbances of wound healing. *Ann Emerg Med.* 1988;17:1274–1278.
8. Thomson PD, Smith DJ. What is infection? *Am J Surg.* 1994;167(supp 11A):7–11.
9. Pottinger JM. Methicillin-resistant *Staphylococcus aureus* in a sternal wound. In: Soule BM, Larson EL, Preston GA, eds. *Infections and Nursing Practice.* St. Louis, MO: Mosby–Year Book, Inc; 1995:240–245.
10. Boyce JM. Methicillin-resistant *Staphylococcus aureus*: detection, epidemiology, and control measures. *Infect Dis Clin North Am.* 1989;3:901–913.
11. Mosiello GC, Tufaro A, Kerstein MD. Wound healing and complications in the immunosuppressed patient. *Wounds.* 1994;6(3):83–87.
12. Daltrey DC, Rhodes B, Chattwood JG. Investigation into the microbial flora of healing and nonhealing decubitus ulcers. *J Clin Pathol.* 1981;34:701–705.
13. Bergstrom N, Bennett MA, Carlson CE, et al. *Treatment of Pressure Ulcers.* Clinical Practice Guideline No. 15. AHCPR Publication No. 95-0652. Rockville, MD: Agency for Health Care Policy and Research, U.S. Public Health Service, U.S. Department of Health and Human Services; December 1994:15–22.
14. Stotts NA. Determination of bacterial burden in wounds. *Adv Wound Care.* 1995;8:28–52.
15. Robson MC, Heggars JP. Bacterial quantification of open wounds. *Milit Med.* 1969;134:19–24.
16. Wood GL, Gutierrez Y. *Diagnostic Pathology of Infectious Diseases.* Philadelphia: Lea & Febiger; 1993.
17. Lee P, Turnidge J, McDonald PJ. Fine-needle aspiration biopsy in diagnosis of soft tissue infections. *J Clin Mibrobiol.* 1985;22:80–83.
18. Morrison MJ. *A Colour Guide to the Nursing Management of Wounds.* Oxford, England: Blackwell Scientific Publications; 1992.
19. Pagana KD, Pagana TJ. *Mosby's Diagnostic and Laboratory Test Reference.* St. Louis, MO: Mosby–Year Book; 1992.

20. Cuzzell JZ. The right way to culture a wound. *Am Nurs*. 1993;93:48–50.

21. Alvarez O, Rozint J, Meehan M. Principles of moist wound healing: Indications for chronic wounds. In: Krasner D, ed. *Chronic Wound Care*. King of Prussia, PA: Health Management Publications; 1990.

22. Levine NS, Lindberg RB, Mason AD, Pruitt BA. The quantitative swab culture and smear: a quick simple method for determining the number of viable aerobic bacteria on open wounds. *J Trauma*. 1976;16(2):89–94.

23. Georgiade NG, Lucas MC, O'Fallon WM, Osterhout S. A comparison of methods for the quantification of bacteria in burn wounds. *Am J Clin Pathol*. 1970;53:35–39.

24. Duke WF, Robson MC, Krizek TJ. Civilian wounds: their bacterial flora and rate of infection. *Surg Forum*. 1972;23:518–520.

25. Barr JE. Principles of wound cleansing. *Ostomy Wound Manage*. 1995;41(suppl 7A):155–225.

26. Lineaweaver W. Cellular and bacterial toxicities of topical antimicrobials. *Plast Reconstr Surg*. 1985;75:394–396.

27. Rodeheaver G. Topical wound management. *Ostomy Wound Manage*. 1988;20:59–68.

28. McConnell ES, Murphy AT. Nursing diagnoses related to physiological alterations: In: Matteson MA, McConnell ES, Linton AD, eds. *Gerontological Nursing: Concepts and Practice*. 2nd ed. Philadelphia: WB Saunders; 1997.

29. Gilman G, ed. *Topical Agents for Open Wounds: Antibacterials, Antiseptics, Antifungals*. Reviewed by Rodeheaver G, Cooper JW, Nelson DR, Meehan M. Charleston, SC: Hill-Rom International, Inc; 1991.

30. Cooper BW. Antimicrobial chemotherapeutics. In: Soule BM, Larson EL, Preston GA, eds. *Infections and Nursing Practice: Prevention and Control*. St. Louis, MO: Mosby; 1995.

31. Speight TM. *Avery's Drug Treatment: Principles and Practice of Clinical Pharmacology and Therapeutics,* 3rd ed. Baltimore: Williams & Wilkins; 1987.

32. Leaper DJ. Prophylactic and therapeutic role of antibiotics in wound care. *Am J Surg*. 1994;167(suppl 1A):158S–19S.

33. Crow S, Planchock NY, Hedrick E. Antisepsis, disinfection and sterilization. In: Soule BM, Larson EL, Preston GA, eds. *Infections and Nursing Practice: Prevention and Control*. St. Louis, MO: Mosby; 1995.

34. Poteete V. Case study: Eliminating odors from wounds. *Decubitus*. 1993;6(4):43–46.

35. McMullen D. Topical metronidazole, part II. *Ostomy Wound Manage*. 1992;38(3):42–48.

36. Jones P, Willis A, Ferguson I. Treatment of anaerobically infected pressure sores with topical metronidazole. *Lancet*. 1978;1:214.

37. Gomolin I, Brandt J. Topical therapy for pressure sores in geriatric patients. *J Am Geriatr Soc*. 1983;31:710–712.

CHAPTER 9

Management of Edema

Laurel A. Wiersema-Bryant

INTRODUCTION

In this chapter, the reader will find a discussion of the etiologies associated with edema and strategies directed toward the management of edema. Management of edema includes a description of the procedures for managing edema and parameters to measure in determining outcome. Emphasis is placed on the steps the client needs to take in order to care for himself or herself because the management and control of edema requires an investment of time, energy, and dedication on the part of the client. At the end of the chapter two case studies are discussed in an effort to apply the assessment, management plan, and outcome evaluation of the chapter content.

OVERVIEW OF THE PROBLEM

Venous disease with ulcers occurs in approximately 1% of the general population and 3.5% of persons over the age of 65 years. Edema in the client with venous disease occurs as a result of sustained increased venous pressure. This venous hypertension may occur primarily in the deep vein system (femoral, popliteal, and tibial veins) or the superficial system (the greater and lesser saphenous veins or the perforator veins that join the deep and superficial system). These problems may occur in isolation or in combination. Respecting the underlying pathology is critical in the management of these clients. Increased venous pressure may be a result of chronic venous insufficiency (as described above), cardiac disease, pelvic tumors that place increased pressure on or occlude venous and lymphatic return, or morbid obesity in which the weight of the abdomen may restrict venous and lymphatic return. In clients with edema secondary to cardiac disease, management of edema needs to be accomplished in concert with the cardiologist. A number of medications, especially the antihypertensive agents, may cause leg edema. These medications include calcium channel blockers, clonidine, minoxidil, guanethidine monosulfate, hydralazine, rauwolfia derivatives, methyldopa, and diazoxide.[1] Managing a client with morbid obesity requires the assistance of the team in directing the client to appropriate exercise and weight management strategies. Fitting these clients with compression therapy is a challenge; in these individuals we are asking for multiple lifestyle adjustments to be made to reduce the weight and manage the edema.

Increased interstitial volume is another reason for edema. These clients may suffer from a protein-losing enteropathy, liver cirrhosis, renal failure, and/or protein-calorie malnutrition. Care must be taken to manage the fragile skin, and edema management becomes a supportive therapy as the underlying medical problem is addressed. Another category of edema is that related to drug therapy with hormone replacement. Hormones in this category include corticosteroids, estrogen, testosterone, and progesterone. Clients experiencing edema secondary to hormone therapy generally respond well to leg elevation and exercise. If compression stockings are required, the low compression usually works well.

Clients with primary lymphedema require aggressive management and generally require compression at much higher levels than the individual with primary venous hypertension. Comprehensive management of lymphedema is not addressed in this chapter. The reader interested in this topic is encouraged to obtain information from the National Lymphedema Network or other sources available to them.[2]

TESTS AND MEASUREMENT

Measurement of edema and edema control can be divided into two primary categories of quantitative and qualitative findings. Quantitatively, leg circumference and leg volume can be measured to give a reference range of leg size; with care, pitting edema can also be measured and quantified. Measuring leg circumference is an easy tool for clinical use; measuring leg volume is less "friendly" clinically, but it is a good measure of leg volume. Leg circumference can be measured with a disposable tape, obtaining measures of the calf 10 cm below the inferior rim of the patella, at the visually largest portion of the calf (if different from the first measure), and 5 cm above the superior rim of the lateral malleolus. These measurements, plotted over time, provide a reference range for leg size and progress toward edema control. Leg volume measurement requires a large cylinder, which will hold the client's leg, and a basin to hold the water that is displaced. The cylinder or chamber is filled with water and the client's lower leg is placed in the chamber, allowing the excess water to be displaced over the top and contained in the reservoir. The volume of water is then measured; the amount displaced will decrease as leg volume (edema) is decreased. Leg circumference is measured weekly or with each clinic/nursing visit. Measurement of pitting edema is often descriptive; however, edema can be quantified by using a simple grading scale as outlined below:

0 to ¼-inch pitting	=	1+ (mild)
¼ to ½-inch pitting	=	2+ (moderate)
½ to 1-inch pitting	=	3+ (severe)
>1-inch pitting	=	4+ (very severe)

Clinical Wisdom:
Improper Bandaging of Edematous Foot

The foot shown in Figure 9–1 shows pitting at the arch where the bandage was wrapped. This indicates that the bandaging was started up too far on the foot. Bandage should have been started at the toes.

Qualitative measures to follow include the general appearance of the leg, the shininess of the skin, the amount of drainage from the ulcer(s), if present, and the client's sense of the heaviness or weight of the leg. It is also important to document the appearance of the leg when the wraps are removed, looking for areas of ridging and bulging between the layers or above the level of the wrapping. Clients may also identify changes in how their clothing and shoes feel.

MODES OF INTERVENTION AND PROCEDURES FOR INTERVENTION

Elimination and control of edema may be accomplished through leg elevation, exercise, and the use of compression

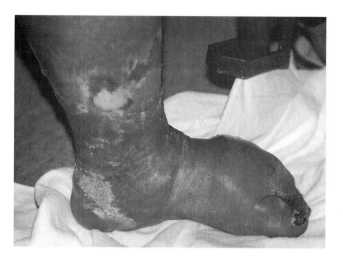

Figure 9–1 Pitting edema. *Source:* Reprinted with permission from R.B. Chambers and N. Elftman, Orthotic Management of the Neuropathic and Dysvascular Patient, in *Atlas of Orthoses and Assistive Devices,* 3rd. edition, B. Goldberg and J.D. Hsu, eds., p. 450, © 1997, Mosby-Year Book, Inc.

therapy. It is often necessary to utilize a combination of these therapies to achieve the desired control of edema in the affected limb(s). Clients should be encouraged to elevate their legs as often as possible and in general to avoid any length of time with their legs in a dependent position. Exercise that results in working the calf muscle pump should be encouraged while using the appropriate compression garment or wrap. Clients may also find that elevation of the foot of the bed to facilitate leg elevation while sleeping is helpful; however, this is not useful for the client with heart disease, such as congestive heart failure. It is not unusual to find clients requesting a diuretic or water pill to facilitate the removal of the edema. The health care provider is encouraged to see this as an opportunity to provide client education as to the futility of diuretics as a primary treatment for edema. It is true that diuretics may be useful as an adjuvant therapy, especially if a sequential compression pump is to be utilized for the client with compromised cardiac function; however, diuretics are not the long-term solution to edema management. Appropriate for edema management are leg elevation, elastic wraps, tubular bandages, paste bandages, graduated compression stockings, intermittent sequential compression devices, and exercise. A discussion of each of these follows.

Leg Elevation

Leg elevation facilitates the removal of fluid through utilization of gravity in assisting venous return. For leg elevation to be successful, the legs must be elevated higher than the heart. Simply placing the feet on a stool is of no benefit. To facilitate leg elevation, the client may find it helpful to place one or two bricks under the foot end of the bed, which results in the legs being elevated higher than the heart during sleep. It is helpful to demonstrate this with the client by utilizing the exam table or bed to elevate the legs while reclining on the surface. The client should be encouraged to exercise the feet and ankles while elevating the legs. It is important to stress that leg elevation can be intermittent and that total bed rest is not recommended. Intermittent leg elevation during the day for 20 to 30 minutes at a time for a total of at least 2 hours a day is a reasonable goal.

Compression Therapy

Compression therapy works with exercise to facilitate the movement of excess fluid from the lower extremity. Several options are available for vascular support during compression therapy, depending on need (Table 9–1). The level of compression needed for edema secondary to venous disease, for example, is approximately 40 mm Hg. It must be emphasized here that compression of 40 mm Hg is recommended for the client who is able to walk and work the calf muscles.

A client with dependent edema who is unable to work the calf muscles will not tolerate this level of compression and a lower level of compression, Class 1 or Class 2, should be considered. The four classes of compression used are as follows:

Class 1:	14–18 mm Hg
Class 2:	18–24 mm Hg
Class 3:	25–35 mm Hg
Class 4:	40–50 mm Hg

Research Wisdom: *Guidelines for Safe Compression*

Warning: *Do not* apply compression therapy to a limb with an ankle-brachial index (ABI) less than 0.8. Consult Chapter 6, Noninvasive Vascular Testing, for ABI testing and significance. An ABI less than 1.0 suggests arterial vascular disease.

Table 9–1 Vascular Support Options

Level of Support	Examples	Recommendations for Use
Light support (8–14 mm Hg)	• Fashion hosiery • Jobst • Sigvarus	• Edema prevention for persons engaged in activities/work that require standing/sitting without much activity; examples: beautician, cashier, factory worker, some nursing positions
Antiembolism stockings (16–18 mm Hg)	• Anti-EM/GP (Jobst) • TED stockings	• Deep vein thrombosis prophylaxis • Nonambulatory clients with edema
Low compression (18–24 mm Hg)	• Relief (Jobst) • Elastic wraps • Paste bandage	• Nonambulatory clients with edema failing 16–18 mm Hg stockings • Clients with dependent edema
Low to moderate compression (25–35 mm Hg)	• Fast-Fit (Jobst) • Custom Fit • Double reverse elastic wrap • Four-layer bandage	• Edema secondary to venous insufficiency • Edema in client able to participate in exercise rehab
Moderate compression (30–40 mm Hg)	• Ultimate (Jobst) • Custom stocking (Jobst, Sigvarus) • Sequential pump • Four-layer bandage (Profore, SurePress)	• Edema with/without ulceration • Edema that persists in spite of lower-level compression options • Ulcer that failed to heal after 6 months
High compression (40–50 mm Hg)	• Vairox (Jobst) • Custom stockings (Jobst, Sigvarus) • Sequential pump	• Edema secondary to lymphedema

Elastic bandages are relatively easy to apply, inexpensive, and easily removed. As with all compression garments/devices, it is best to apply the bandages within 20 minutes of waking and placing the feet below the level of the heart. Most compression wraps giving at least Class 2 compression are removed at night. Bandages do require practice to apply correctly and the skill needs to be taught to the client and caregiver. Manufacturer's guidelines should always be followed when applying the elastic bandage. The most common application technique is the spiral; an alternative is the figure-of-eight. Figure 9–5 shows the four-layer bandage being applied in spiral fashion. Several types of bandages are now available with printed rectangles that, when stretched to squares, apply the correct level of compression. These bandages facilitate correct wrapping of an extremity (see Figure 9–2).

Tubular Bandages

Tubular bandages are also available to provide light compression (Figure 9–3). One should be careful to select bandages that are tapered at the ankle. Straight tubular bandages provide compression that is higher at the calf than at the ankle; these are not as useful for the client with edema.

Paste Bandages

Paste bandages such as the Unna boot are widely used in the treatment of leg ulcers (such as that shown in Figure 9–4A) and as a result in the control of edema. The boot was developed in the 1880s by a German physician, Paul Gerson Unna, and consists of a fine gauze impregnated with

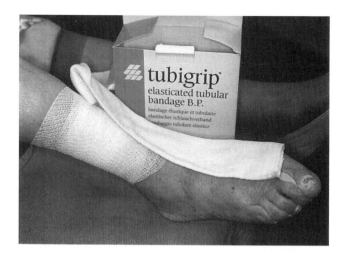

Figure 9–3 Tubular bandages. Courtesy of Convatec, Skillman, New Jersey.

zinc oxide, gelatin, and glycerin (some varieties also include calamine). The gauze is applied without tension in a circular fashion from the foot to just below the knee (Figure 9–4B). Paste bandages do not provide compression; however, as the boot dries and stiffens, the leg cannot continue to swell. Application of a compression wrap over the boot (Figure 9–4C) will enhance compression and protect the client's clothing from the moist paste of the boot. A paste bandage is routinely changed every 4 to 7 days.

Clinical Wisdom: *Dressing Application before Paste Bandage*

Venous ulcers are dressed before applying the compression bandages. They are often very large and exudative. Size may exceed that of standard dressings available. Two dressings such as the hydrocolloids illustrated in Figure 9–4B can be used and then covered with the paste boot.

Four-Layer Bandage

An alternative to the paste bandage is the four-layer bandage developed at Charing Cross Hospital in London. The four-layer bandage provides graduated, sustained compression through the application of a series of layers providing protection, padding, and compression (Figure 9–5). The dressing is removed weekly.

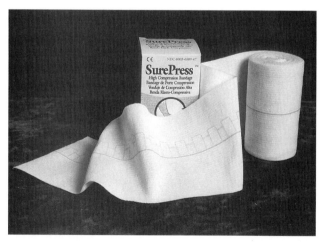

Figure 9–2 Short-stretch bandage. Courtesy of Convatec, Skillman, New Jersey.

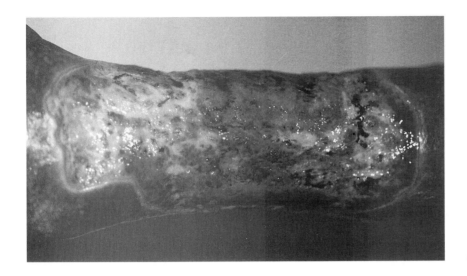

A

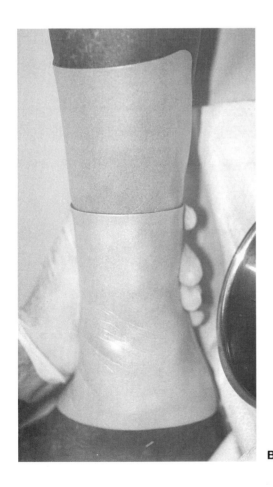

B

C

Figure 9–4 A, Large venous ulcer. **B,** Two overlapping dressings. **C,** Application of paste bandage over dressing.

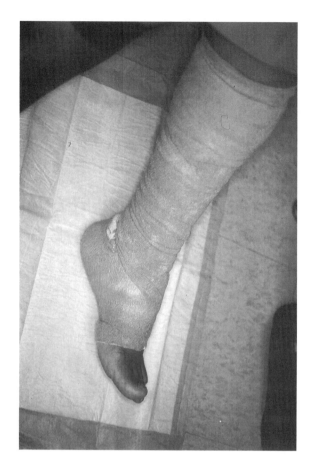

Figure 9–5 Four-layer bandage.

Graduated Compression Stockings

Graduated compression stockings assist venous return, thereby reducing edema (Figure 9–6). The client should be measured and fitted for compression stockings when the edema is absent or minimal. These stockings are then applied before the client has gotten out of bed or at least within 20 minutes of rising. Stockings may be difficult to get on, and devices are available to assist in donning. A nonambulatory client does not need moderate or high compression and will likely better tolerate a lower compression (18 to 24 mm Hg) stocking. Stockings do wear out and need to be replaced at the frequency recommended by the manufacturer. Many clients prefer to order two stockings (or two pairs) to prolong the life of the individual stocking and allow for laundering.

Clinical Wisdom: *Check Joint Range of Motion and Function at the Hip and Hands*

A joint range of motion and functional exam at both the hip and the hands should be performed to determine the patient's ability to don compression stockings.

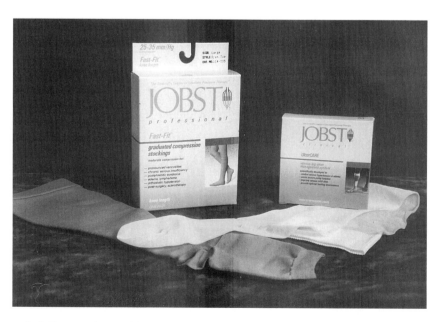

Figure 9–6 Compression stocking. Courtesy of Beiersdorf-Jobst, Inc., Charlotte, North Carolina.

Compression Pump Therapy

Sequential compression therapy has gained popularity for the management of lower extremity edema. The leg sleeve (either knee high or thigh high) is divided into a 3-, 5-, or 10-chamber style with peak pressures of 45 to 60 mm Hg at the ankle (Figure 9–7). The sleeve inflates first at the ankle, followed 2.5 seconds later at the calf chambers, and 3 seconds later at the thigh chambers. Each successive chamber inflates less, and the total inflation is sustained for approximately 5 seconds, followed by complete deflation. The cycle repeats every 7 to 8 seconds for the prescribed treatment period, which may range from 1 to 2 hours twice per day. Clients should be encouraged to follow treatment with either application of a fitted stocking or compression bandage to maintain edema control. Use of compression therapy at night while sleeping is not recommended. Clients with congestive heart disease should be monitored closely for tolerance of the extra intravascular fluid burden with compression therapy.

Medicare Guidelines for Sequential Compression Therapy

The following are the Medicare guidelines at the time of this publication. Check with durable medical equipment suppliers to make sure that the guidelines are still as listed.

- Types of lymphedema pumps
  1. 3-Chamber
  2. 5-Chamber
  3. 10-Chamber
- Qualifying diagnosis: refractory lymphedema
  1. Lymph node removal/surgery
  2. Postirradiation fibrosis
  3. Malignant spread to lymph nodes with obstruction
  4. Scarring of lymphatic channels
  5. Milroy's disease
  6. Congenital anomalies
- General qualifying criteria
  1. Treatment for edema with custom-fabricated pressure stockings used without success
  2. Scarring of lymphatic channels
     a. Significant ulceration of lower extremities
     b. Several unsuccessful treatments with elastic wraps or pressure stockings unsuccessful
     c. Ulcers that have failed to heal after 6 months of continuous treatment
- Authorization
  1. 3-Chamber: no ulcers
  2. 5-Chamber: ulcers present
  3. 10-Chamber: only after a 5-chamber has been used with minimal or no success or physician requests and documents condition accordingly

PROCEDURES FOR MANAGEMENT OF EDEMA

Leg Elevation and Exercise

Definition: The legs are elevated higher than the level of the heart, with or without foot and ankle exercise, to allow gravity to assist in the removal of fluid from the legs.

Advantages:

- No costs are associated with the procedure.
- Effective when used regularly in combination with other form(s) of compression bandaging or stockings.
- No special equipment is required.

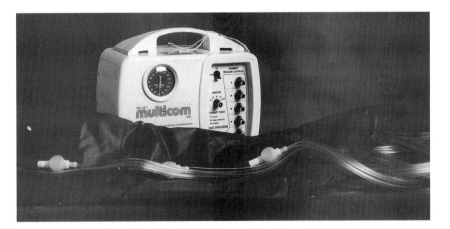

Figure 9–7 Compression pump and sleeve. Courtesy of Progressive Medical Technology, Inc., Lansing, Michigan.

- Involves client in active participation in edema reduction.

Disadvantages:

- Requires consistent performance in order to be of benefit.
- Some clients may be unable to elevate legs higher than the heart, such as those with morbid obesity, congestive heart failure, or orthopaedic limitations.
- Setting may not be conducive to reclining with legs elevated.
- May be ineffective in some forms of edema.

Equipment Needed:

- Clean surface upon which to recline
- Minute timer (optional)

Frequency: Elevate legs for 20 to 30 minutes every 2 to 3 hours during the day for a total of approximately 2 or more hours per day.

Indications: Edema of the lower extremities secondary to impaired venous return.

Contraindications:

- Morbid obesity
- Clients with arterial occlusive disease and ischemic pain with leg elevation
- Clients with congestive heart failure limiting ability to recline in a horizontal position
- Other medical conditions limiting client ability to recline in a horizontal position

Procedure: Leg Elevation and Exercise

1. Recline horizontally on a clean, comfortable surface.
2. Elevate legs approximately 30° so that the feet are higher than the heart. Rest feet against the wall or footboard of the bed.
3. Set timer for 20 to 30 minutes (optional).
4. With one leg at a time, flex and extend foot against wall or footboard, then make circles (rotate) the foot/ankle. Do 5 to 10 repetitions with each foot, then rest and repeat until timer goes off.
5. Remove compression bandage and rewrap leg if compression bandage is being used.

Expected Outcome: Edema and corresponding discomfort is relieved with leg elevation.

Clinical Wisdom: *Leg Exercise*

- Use of a kitchen-type minute timer is useful for ensuring an adequate amount of time.
- Encourage the client to work up to 20 to 30 minutes time if that is too much when starting out.
- Encourage the client to be creative at work in looking for opportunities to get the exercise in.

Compression Wraps (Elastic Bandages)

Definition: A compression wrap is a short-stretch elastic bandage that when applied to the leg applies sufficient external compression to cause movement of excess fluid from the extremity.

Advantages:

- Wraps are inexpensive.
- Wraps are readily available.
- Wraps are easily removed.
- Wraps involve clients in active participation of edema reduction.

Disadvantages:

- Requires practice to apply bandage correctly.
- Care must be taken to avoid uneven tension when wrapping.
- Wrap may telescope and fall down the leg with activity and will require reapplication.
- Client may be unable to comfortably reach the toes in order to wrap from the foot to below the knee.
- Client must be committed to application and wearing of the elastic bandage for it to work successfully.

Equipment Needed:

- Short-stretch elastic bandage(s), of a width to accommodate foot and leg size (3- or 4-inch bandages are the most common sizes selected)
- Cotton padding or combination ABD type dressings (optional)

Frequency: Apply wrap daily within 20 minutes of rising. Reapplication is required if wrap telescopes or slides down the leg.

Indications:

- Edema of the lower extremities secondary to impaired venous return
- Clients physically able to apply elastic bandages
- Clients who require edema reduction prior to fitting with compression stockings
- Clients who require low to moderate compression for the management of edema

Contraindications:

- Ankle-brachial index <0.8
- Clients unable to wrap legs independently and have no caregiver able to assist
- Allergy to any component in the elastic bandage (for example, latex)

Procedure: *Compression Wraps*

1. Wash lower leg and foot and dry thoroughly.
2. Apply topical agent if ordered.
3. Apply wrap.
   a. Begin wrapping the bandage at the base of the toes using two layers around the foot to anchor the bandage.
   b. Continue wrapping from toe to knee in a circular fashion by stretching the bandage approximately 50% of capacity or, if using imprinted bandages, until the rectangles become squares.
   c. If the leg is champagne bottle–shaped, pad the ankle area with cotton padding or ABD type dressing to minimize the shape disparity of the leg.
   d. With each turn around the leg, the wrap should overlap the previous layer by approximately 50%.
4. When the wrapping is complete, assess to make sure that wrap is not too tight by attempting to slide the index finger under one layer of the wrap. Assess skin under the anchoring clips (if used) to be certain the skin is not pinched.

Expected Outcome:

- Edema is decreased as evidenced by a decrease in circumference of the calf and ankle.
- Client/caregiver is able to provide a return demonstration correctly wrapping the leg.
- Client arrives at follow-up visit(s) with leg(s) correctly wrapped.

Clinical Wisdom: *Leg Bandaging*

- The index finger should be able to be slipped under the bandage if the dressing has been wrapped with the correct tension; if too tight, remove and rewrap.
- If the toes become numb and tingle, remove the bandage and rewrap.
- Encourage the client to walk for 30 to 60 minutes after wrapping, then remove and rewrap the bandage for correct compression.
- To maintain compression for a longer period, advise the client to walk after wrapping as above, then rewrap with a double-layer elastic bandage. Begin as above, holding the roll in the right hand, and wrap from toe to knee; then wrap again beginning with the roll in the left hand, wrapping from toe to knee. Layering anchors the wrap, and it stays in place for a longer period of time.

Paste Bandage

Definition: A paste bandage consists of a roll of gauze that has been impregnated with zinc oxide, gelatin, and glycerin (some have calamine added). The bandage is applied to the leg from the toe to the knee and left in place for 4 to 7 days. The bandage should be applied when the leg is without edema; as the bandage dries, it becomes resistant to additional swelling.

Advantages:

- It is useful for clients unable to comply with other modalities or contribute to self-care.
- It eliminates daily dressing changes.

Disadvantages:

- Client is unable to shower while bandage is in place.
- Client's ownership of the problem is transferred to the health care provider.
- Odor may be a factor when it is time to change the bandage.
- If the bandage is not wrapped correctly, new ulcerations may develop.

Equipment Needed:

- Pre-packaged paste bandage (review manufacturer's guidelines that accompany the bandage)

- Gauze (3- or 4-inch wide roll)
- Compression wrap (Coban or elastic bandage)
- Gloves (clean)
- Scissors
- Receptacle to contain old dressing
- Soap and water to wash leg
- Wound care supplies, if indicated

Frequency: Apply every 4 to 7 days; more frequent changes may be necessary if exudate is particularly heavy. Change immediately if the client experiences severe pain, excessive drainage, or foul odor.

Indications:

- Clients unable to comply with other modalities directed toward edema control
- Clients physically unable to wrap legs independently on a daily basis
- Clients awaiting custom-fitted compression garments who need interval assistance with edema control

Contraindications:

- Clients with poor personal hygiene
- Clients with significant arterial occlusive disease (ankle-brachial index < 0.8)
- Clients with frail, friable skin
- Clients with active cellulitis
- Clients with infected ulcers

Procedure: Paste Bandage

1. Apply gloves. Remove old bandage by unwrapping or carefully cutting with bandage scissors as boot is lifted from the skin.
2. Wash foot and lower leg well. Use a soft brush to remove dry scaly skin.
3. Dry foot and leg well (Figure 9–8A). A moisturizing cream may be applied.
4. Select paste bandage. Open all supplies.
5. Begin wrapping at the base of the toes (two revolutions) without applying tension (Figure 9–8B). Client should keep the foot and leg at a 90° angle.
6. Continue wrapping in a circular fashion around ankle and *enclosing* the heel (Figure 9–8C).
7. Overlap each turn by 50% as you continue to wrap up the leg to just below the knee (Figure 9–8D). A paste boot can and should be cut as often as necessary to avoid any folds, pleats, or wrinkles that may become pressure areas as the boot dries.
8. Strive for two to three layers of the bandage on the leg.

9. Smooth paste bandage and assess for wrinkles or folds, which should be removed.
10. Wrap from the toes to just below the knee with a single layer of gauze to facilitate drying and protection of clothing.
11. Remove gloves.
12. Apply an elastic bandage or short-stretch self-adherent wrap (Coban) from the base of the toes to the knee (Figures 9–8E and 9–8F). Overlap 50% with mild to moderate tension.

Expected Outcome:

- Wrap stays in place without complication for 7 days.
- Leg edema is controlled, as evidenced by measures of circumference.

Clinical Wisdom: *Paste Bandages*

- Client may wish to remove paste bandage immediately prior to clinic/nursing visit to allow time for showering. Leg must be elevated or an elastic bandage applied after showering if more than 20 minutes will elapse before new dressing can be applied.
- Some products recommend a figure-of-eight method of wrapping whereas others recommend a circular overlap; check the package insert.
- Cast padding may be used to absorb heavy drainage.
- If boot feels too tight after client has been up and active for several hours, encourage client to elevate legs higher than the heart for at least 30 minutes.
- Paste boot can and should be cut frequently during application to avoid pleats, folds, or wrinkles that may cause damage to the skin as the boot dries.
- Assess client for allergies prior to application. Clients allergic to calamine should use a calamine-free bandage.
- A client with a narrow ankle and large calf (champagne bottle) may need to have the ankle padded with ABD type dressings or cotton batting to avoid overpressurizing the calf.

Four-Layer Bandage

Definition: The four-layer bandage consists of a wound contact layer and four bandages for sequential application to the leg. Correctly applied, the four-layer bandage system provides 40 mm Hg pressure at the ankle, decreasing to 17 mm Hg at the calf.

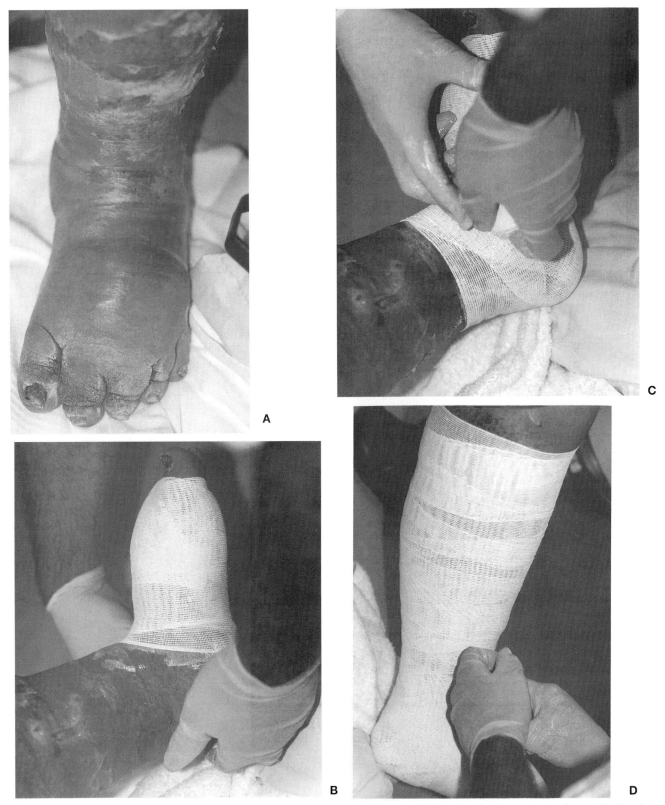

Figure 9–8 A to **F,** Procedure for putting on a paste bandage. *Source* for 9–8A, B, and F: Reprinted with permission from R.B. Chambers and N. Elftman, Orthotic Management of the Neuropathic and Dysvascular Patient, in *Atlas of Orthoses and Assistive Devices,* 3rd. edition, B. Goldberg and J.D. Hsu, eds., pp. 450, 451, © 1997, Mosby-Year Book, Inc.

Figure 9–8 continued

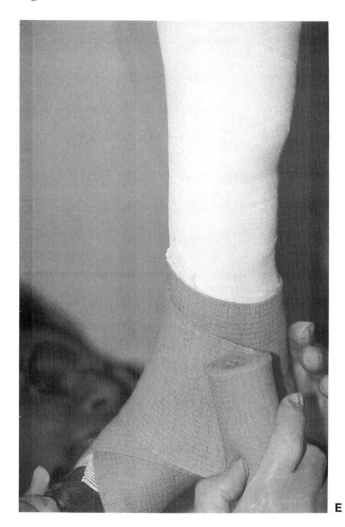

E

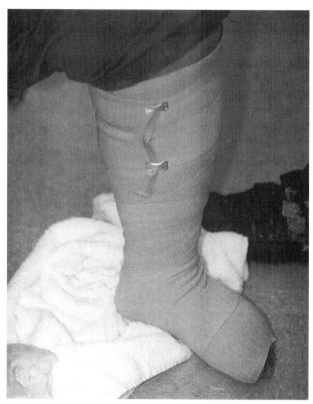

F

Advantages:

- It is useful for clients unable to comply with other modalities or contribute to self-care.
- It eliminates daily dressing changes.

Disadvantages:

- Client is unable to shower while bandage is in place.
- Client's ownership of the problem is transferred to the health care provider.
- Odor may be a factor when it is time to change the bandage.
- If the bandage is not wrapped correctly, new ulcerations may develop.

Equipment Needed:

- Four-layer bandage system (Profore)
- Gloves (clean)
- Scissors
- Receptacle to contain old dressing
- Soap and water to wash leg

Frequency: Apply every 4 to 7 days; more frequent changes may be necessary if exudate is particularly heavy. Change immediately if the client experiences severe pain, excessive drainage, or foul odor.

Indications:

- Clients unable to comply with other modalities directed toward edema control

- Clients physically unable to wrap legs independently on a daily basis
- Clients awaiting custom-fitted compression garments who need interval assistance with edema control

Contraindications:

- Clients with poor personal hygiene
- Clients with significant arterial occlusive disease (ankle-brachial index < 0.75)
- Clients with active cellulitis
- Clients with infected ulcers

Procedure: Four-Layer Bandage

1. Apply gloves. Remove old bandage by unwrapping or carefully cutting with bandage scissors as bandage is lifted from the skin.
2. Wash foot and lower leg well. Use a soft brush to remove dry scaly skin.
3. Dry foot and leg well. A moisturizing cream may be applied.
4. Measure ankle and calf circumference.
5. Open four-layer bandage system and prepare supplies. Review package insert for directions if not familiar with the system.
6. Cover wound (if present) with contact dressing.
7. Wrap cotton padding layer without tension from the toes to just below the knee (Figures 9–9A and 9–9B).
8. Wrap a light, conformable bandage over the cotton padding layer, again without tension (Figure 9–9C).
9. Wrap a light compression bandage. Wrap from toe to knee (Figure 9–9D).
10. Wrapping in the direction of the first two layers, wrap the cohesive compression bandage with 50% stretch from the toes to just below the knee using a figure of eight (Figures 9–9E and 9–9F).
11. Remove gloves and discard.

Expected Outcome:

- Wrap stays in place without complication for 7 days.
- Leg edema is controlled, as evidenced by measures of circumference.

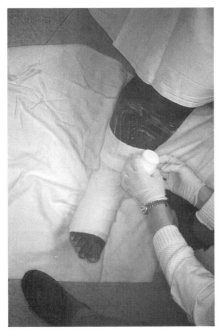 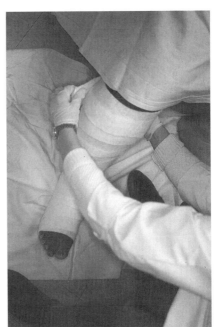

Figure 9–9 A and **B**, Padding under four-layer bandage.

Figure 9–9 continued

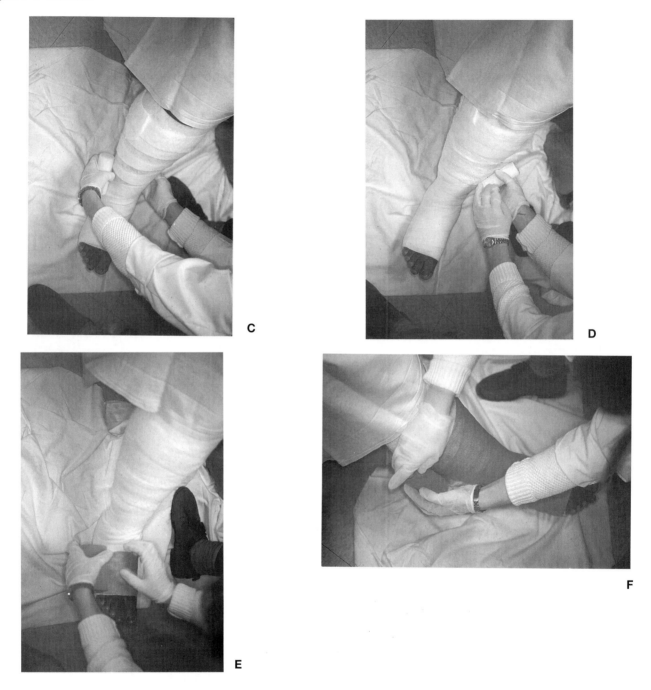

Figure 9–9 C, Light, conformable bandage covers padding without tension. **D**, The third layer is wrapped at 50% and in a figure of eight from the toes to just below the knee. **E** and **F**, The cohesive compression wrap is wrapped with moderate tension in direction of first two layers; wrap is from toes to below knee.

Clinical Wisdom: *Four-Layer Bandages*

- Client may wish to remove bandage immediately prior to clinic/nursing visit to allow time for showering. Leg must be elevated or an elastic bandage applied after showering if more than 20 minutes will elapse before new dressing can be applied.
- If bandage feels too tight after client has been up and active for several hours, encourage client to elevate legs higher than the heart for at least 30 minutes.
- A client with a narrow ankle and large calf (champagne bottle) may need to have the ankle more heavily padded with the cotton padding to avoid overpressurizing the calf.

Compression Stockings

Definition: Compression stockings are garments measured and fitted to the client that will provide external compression to the leg at a prescribed level. Stockings are available that will provide all levels of compression from light support to high compression. Individual needs can be met through special order and a wide variety of ready-fit garments. Stockings are available knee, thigh, and waist high.

Advantages:

- Stockings provide graded compression.
- Stockings last from 4 to 9 months, depending on the manufacturer.
- A variety of types is available, including custom made for the difficult-to-fit client.
- Stockings are cosmetically acceptable.

Disadvantages:

- Stockings may be difficult to get on clients who are disabled, have arthritis, or are elderly.
- The cost of stockings is not universally covered by insurance providers.
- The client must adopt a positive self-care attitude and be consistent with wearing the garment.
- Stockings are not recommended for clients with extensive leg ulcers or circumferential wounds.

Equipment Needed:

- Rubber gloves
- Stockings as ordered

Frequency: Stockings should be applied before getting out of bed in the morning and removed just before going to bed at night.

Indications:

- Venous disease
- Lymphedema

Contraindications:

- Clients with arterial occlusive disease with ankle-brachial index < 0.8 should use any stockings with caution.
- Clients with allergy to latex should not use stockings made with latex.

Procedure: Compression Stockings

1. Wash leg and foot and dry completely.
2. Measure ankle and calf circumference.
3. Apply lotion to the leg and foot if needed; refer to manufacturer's guideline for type of lotion, as many products break down the fibers in the stocking, shortening the stocking wear life.
4. Turn stocking inside out, holding the heel portion, so that the stocking is pulled back over the foot portion (Figure 9–10A).
5. Place stocking over the foot and place heel in the heel portion of the stocking (Figure 9–10B).
6. Pull stocking back in place over the foot and to below the knee (Figure 9–10C). (Procedure is the same for thigh-high stockings. Waist-high pantyhose type must be applied without inverting the stocking.)
7. Smooth stocking to eliminate wrinkles (Figure 9–10D).

Expected Outcome:

- Client/caregiver is able to apply stocking with minimal difficulty.
- Client arrives at office visits with stocking in place.
- Edema in leg is kept under control, as evidenced by clinical improvement and a decrease in leg circumference.

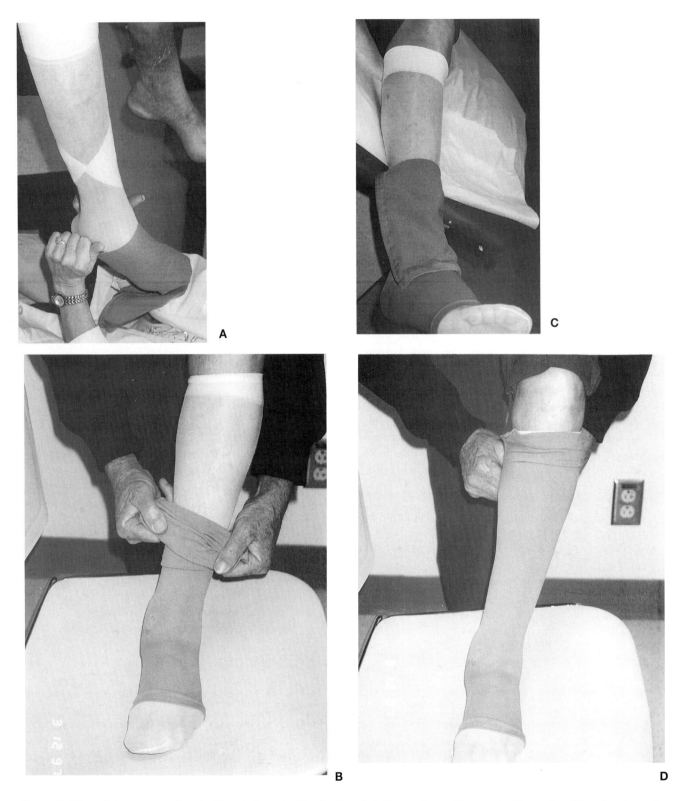

Figure 9–10 Applying compression stocking. **A,** Turn stocking inside out. A liner makes pulling on stocking easier. (Note dressing under the lining. The liner keeps the dressing positioned correctly). **B,** Work stocking gradually up leg, smoothing out all wrinkles. (Stockings are available with or without toes.) **C,** Knee-high stocking halfway up showing zipper rear closure. **D,** Stocking extended to below the bend on the knee. Patient is positioning stocking. *Source:* Copyright © Evonne Fowler, MN, RN, CETN.

- Clients should be measured for stockings when there is the least amount of edema in the leg—early morning or after using a sequential pump for 1 to 2 hours.
- Clients arriving for their appointment with stockings in a bag for you to put on do not understand the need for edema control.
- Review teaching.
- Inverting the stocking over the foot portion facilitates donning.
- Order two pairs at a time to allow one pair to be worn while the other is washed.
- Follow manufacturer's guidelines for washing.
- Stocking butlers are available as a device to assist a client in donning a stocking (see Figures 9–11A and 9–11B).
- Stockings are available in a variety of fabrics and colors. Cotton stockings are available from several manufacturers.

Clinical Wisdom: *Tubular Bandage as Alternative to Compression Stocking*

A tubular bandage may be used as an alternative to compression stockings (Figures 9–12A to 9–12C). For some patients it is easier to don than compression stockings.

Sequential Compression Pump

Definition: The sequential compression pump is a device that consists of a programmed pump and leg sleeves, which the client puts on. The pump is programmed to build and sustain compression from the lower leg/ankle to the thigh over a set period of time, then deflation occurs and after a brief rest the process starts all over again. Leg sleeves can be ordered for one or both legs.

Advantages:

- The pump provides true graded compression that "milks" the edema from the leg.
- The pump is used intermittently during the day.
- Studies have shown the therapy to be effective in clients with venous disease and ulcerations.
- The pump is easy to use.

Disadvantages:

- During pumping, the client is restricted to chair or bed.

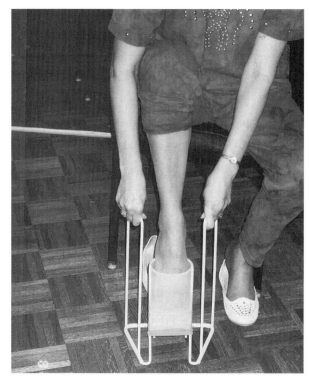

A

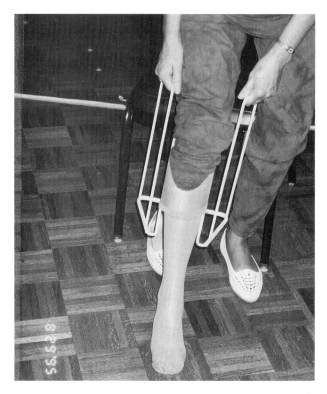

B

Figure 9–11 A and **B**, Using a stocking butler. *Source:* Copyright © Evonne Fowler, MN, RN, CETN.

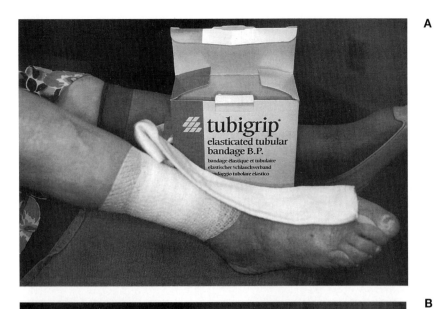

A

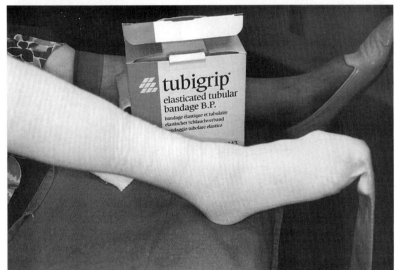

B

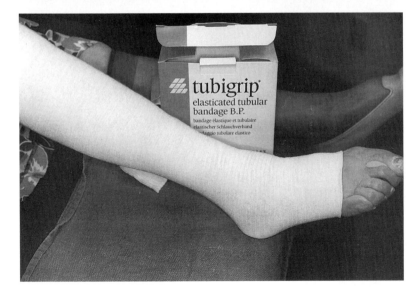

C

Figure 9–12 A to **C**, Using tubular bandage alternative. Courtesy of Convatec, Skillman, New Jersey.

- Pumping may be too aggressive for clients with congestive heart failure.
- The client will still need compression therapy of some type when not using the pump.

Equipment Needed:

- Sequential compression pump, as ordered by physician
- Sleeves for one or both legs

Frequency: Use for a 1- to 2-hour session twice during the day, preferably morning and late afternoon or evening.

Indications:

- 3-Chamber: edema, no ulcers
  1. Treated with custom pressure stockings without success
  2. Several treatments with elastic bandages without success
- 5-Chamber: edema, lower extremity ulcers
  1. Several treatments with elastic bandages without healing
  2. Treatment with custom pressure stockings unsuccessful
- 10-Chamber: only after 5-chamber used without success

Contraindications:

- Untreated congestive heart failure
- Inability to obtain sleeves that fit
- Cellulitis
- Active wound infection

Procedure: Sequential Compression Pump

1. Client should be in a comfortable reclining chair or in bed.
2. Pump should be plugged in with the controls (on/off) within easy reach of the client.
3. Remove stockings or elastic bandages (if possible).
4. Don and secure the sleeves.
5. Turn on pump. Most home units have an automatic "off" in 2 hours; if this feature is not on the pump, an alarm should be set for the prescribed time.
6. Remove sleeves when prescribed time interval has passed, reapply compression wraps or stockings.
7. Clean sleeves periodically according to manufacturer's recommendations.

Expected Outcome:

- Client tolerates procedure for 2 hours twice daily.
- Edema is relieved from extremity.

Clinical Wisdom: *Compression Pumping*

- If client is taking a diuretic, he or she should be advised to take it before pumping so that the peak effect will be realized as fluid is being pumped out of the leg(s).
- Clients who work may want to use the pump while at work. An extra pair of sleeves may be ordered so that only the pump travels back and forth, or a second pump may be obtained.

REFERRAL CRITERIA

When working with the client with peripheral edema, it is critical to know when to refer the client for additional evaluation and treatment. Knowing that there are many potential reasons for the edema and that many of these require a multifaceted approach to management, the practitioner needs to be aware of parameters that guide the making of referrals. The list below is to be considered as a guide only. In your practice, you may elect to accept, reject, or add additional parameters depending on the type of client seen and referral opportunities available.

- Physical assessment reveals indicators of arterial occlusive disease, including pain and cramping of the calf with walking, absent peripheral pulses, localized lack of hair growth, thickening of toenails, and delayed capillary refill.
- The client has persistent edema for 1 month despite compression wrapping, leg elevation, and exercise.
- The client develops new ulcerations or there is an increase in size of existing ulcer(s).
- The client has pain with leg elevation and exercise.

Where To Refer

Where and to whom the client should be referred needs to be established in conjunction with the medical director of the facility in which you practice. Some of the therapies require a physician's order (sequential compression pump) to receive reimbursement and therefore require that a physician see the client. Other circumstances are not quite so clear. It is also critical to take into consideration the client's insurance plan, as it may in fact dictate a particular path for the referral process. Some of the potential referral directions include the following:

- Internal medicine physician for general medical problems, including hypertension, congestive heart failure, and other conditions

- Dermatologist for venous dermatitis, ulcer with uncertain pathology, nonhealing ulcer, and other conditions
- Vascular surgeon for indicators of arterial occlusive disease
- Wound healing clinic/center for nonhealing wound, refractory edema, comprehensive evaluation, and the like
- Rehab specialist for a client with need for exercise therapy and rehabilitation
- Lymphedema network for a client with lymphedema and need for specialized management and care
- Bariatric specialist for a client with obesity complicating management of the edema
- Home health care for assistance with and tolerance of application of compression devices

SELF-CARE TEACHING GUIDELINES

Teaching the client with edema the techniques for self-management is critical to the management of edema. In most cases the edema does not represent a temporary, short-term problem. Therefore, management of edema requires that the client adopt lifestyle changes for a lifetime. It is important that the health care provider and the client respect that the problem of long-term edema management is owned by the client, not the practitioner. A client contract (Exhibit 9–1) may be of benefit in assisting the client to a position of ownership. For many clients, this may take some encouragement and effort because most clients come to the health care provider for a treatment and cure, not for the provider to instruct the client that he or she owns the problem and is key to its successful management.

In selecting a plan for managing the edema, ownership and responsibility need to be considered. Bandages/wraps that require the client to return for dressing changes, such as paste bandages and the four-layer system, may be a starting point for many. These systems, however, do not require active participation on the part of the client. Therefore, it is important to keep this in mind and move the client to an increasingly active role in his or her care as soon as possible. Several examples of edema management programs are illustrated by the two case studies that follow.

Exhibit 9–1 Sample Client Contract for Management of Venous Disease

Client name: _____

I.D. number: _____

Staff member: _____

Date of goal-setting interview: _____

Interval for reassessment:
___weekly   ___ monthly   ___ quarterly   ___ other

I, _____, understand that I have a problem with the veins in my leg(s). In order to take care of my leg(s), I understand that there are some things I must do. I agree to take care of my leg(s) as described below:

_____

_____

_____

_____

_____   _____
Client Signature/Date   Staff Member Signature/Date

Case Study 1: *A Case for Elastic Bandages*

R.A. is a 68-year-old man with a multiple-year history of swollen legs and ulcerations. The edema at the time of initial evaluation was severe with pitting (3+) to just inferior to the knee. A large irregular ulceration was present on the medial aspect of the left lower leg with irregular borders and minimal periwound erythema. R.A. reported a heavy drainage from the leg, which prompted him to "try again" to get help for the problem. His past medical history was significant for a deep vein thrombosis (DVT) 15 years prior to this evaluation. Now retired, client had worked in a position that required long periods of standing with little walking. Medications were felt to be noncontributory. The client's legs initially were wrapped with elastic bandages in a circular fashion. He was found to have the bandages wrapped correctly when returning for appointments; however, after 3 weeks, little progress had been made. A 5-chamber sequential compression pump was added to the regimen, with significant progress in edema management over the next month. The client was felt at this time to have minimal edema and was fitted with 40 mm Hg compression stockings, and sequential pumping was to continue twice daily. At a 1-month follow-up, the client was found to have increased edema with deterioration of the ulcer. The client felt that he did better with the wraps. The stockings were discontinued and R.A. resumed wrapping his legs with elastic bandages wrapped in a circular fashion, and a second layer counterclockwise to the first was added. He has continued to be followed every 3 months with this regimen and is doing well. R.A. wraps his legs daily and has decreased use of the pump to once per day. Edema has been kept under control with this combination, and the client is committed to the program.

Case Study 2: *Combination Therapy with Sequential Pump and Class 1 Stockings*

An 89-year-old woman presented to the clinic with more than an 18-year history of ulceration to the left lower extremity. Her history was significant for DVT in the left leg years earlier; the right leg was without significant change or edema. On assessment, the client's left leg was swollen, and the skin was shiny. There was a circumferential wound measuring 15 cm long anteriorly and 13 cm laterally; the drainage was clear yellow, and the wound edges were hypertrophic and scarred. The client is independent and refused home health nursing more frequently than twice per week. A sequential compression pump was ordered to be used for 1 hour twice daily, along with leg elevation every 2 hours. The client was able to do this herself and had been taking care of the wound without assistance. She had a family member raise the end of her bed with bricks. Wound care was directed toward keeping the area free of infection and the drainage contained. After 6 weeks of pumping, the leg was softer to the touch, but there was little change in the measurements. In collaboration with her internist, the client was given a diuretic and the pump interval was increased to 1½ hours twice daily. With this regimen, the edema began to resolve. Subsequently, the client was recommended Class 1 stockings, which she was able to apply herself between intervals on the pump. At present, the wound has shown progress toward healing, with a decrease in length by 1.5 cm on the lateral side and 1.2 cm on the anterior surface. The skin of her leg is less tense and shiny, and the circumference of her calf has decreased by 1.5 cm and the ankle by 2 cm. The mounded hyperkeratotic tissue has reduced in bulk and the client feels that her leg "has lost some weight." The client is able to continue this program and maintain her independence and church activities.

REFERENCES

1. Ciocon JO, Fernandez BB, Ciocon DG. Leg edema: clinical clues to the differential diagnosis. *Geriatrics.* 1993;48(5):34–45.

2. National Lymphedema Network, 2211 Post Street, Suite 404, San Francisco, CA 94115. (415) 921-1306; Fax (415) 921-4284; hotline (800) 541-3259.

SUGGESTED READINGS

Airaksinen O, Partanen K, Kolari PJ, Soimakallio S. Intermittent pneumatic compression therapy in posttraumatic lower limb edema. *Arch Phys Med Rehabil.* 1991;72:667–670.

Ciocon JO, Fernandez BB, Galindo-Ciocon D. Leg edema in the elderly: a practical diagnostic approach. *Compr Ther.* 1994;20:586–592.

Ciocon JO, Galindo-Ciocon D, Galindo DJ. Raised leg exercises for leg edema in the elderly. *Angiology.* 1995;46:19–25.

Dealey C. *The Care of Wounds.* Oxford, England: Blackwell Scientific Publications; 1994.

Gutnik LM, Lovrien FC. An algorithm for evaluating swollen extremities in a community hospital: recommendations and results. *South Dakota Med.*1995;48(3):93–94.

Liehr P, Todd B, Rossi M, Culligan M. Effect of venous support on edema and leg pain in patients after coronary artery bypass graft surgery. *Heart Lung.* 1992;21:6–11.

Lippmann HI, Fishman LM, Farrar RH, Bernstein RK, et al. Edema control in the management of disabling chronic venous insufficiency. *Arch Phys Med Rehabil.* 1994;75:436–441.

Moffatt CJ, Franks PJ, Oldroyd M, Bosanquet N, et al. Community clinics for leg ulcers and impact on healing. *Br Med J.* 1992;305:1389–1391.

Struckmann J. The pathophysiology of venous ulceration. *Scope Phlebol Lymphol.* 1995;2(3):12–16.

Zink M, Rousseau P, Holloway GA. Lower extremity ulcers. In: Bryant RA, ed. *Acute and Chronic Wounds: Nursing Management.* St. Louis, MO: Mosby-Year Book; 1992:164–212.

CHAPTER 10

Management of the Wound Environment

Geoffrey Sussman

INTRODUCTION

Dressings provide the appropriate environment for healing by both direct and indirect methods together with the prevention of skin breakdown. The history of the development and use of dressings has seen an evolution through many centuries from inert and passive products such as gauze, lint, and fiber products to a dazzling range of modern moist wound dressings.

INERT WOUND DRESSINGS

In examining the continued use of passive products as described by Turner,[1,2] particularly gauze, it is clear that there are a number of negative aspects in the use of gauze. Gauze, being a fibrous material, tends to shed very readily and as such will contaminate the wound. Gauze is highly absorbent and as a primary dressing will tend to dry the surface of the wound rapidly. Gauze is permeable to bacteria, and moist gauze tends to be an environment for the growth of bacteria. This would risk penetration and ultimate contamination of the wound. Gauze is also adherent and will traumatize the wound further on removal, risking damage to granulating tissue and pain.

In addition to gauze and lint, there are available other simple, modified absorbent pads covered with a perforated plastic film to prevent adherence to a wound, such as the trade name products Melolin and Telfa, which are used as both primary and secondary dressings. They are used in minor wounds and wounds with low exudation. Paraffin (petrolatum) gauze dressings were among the earliest modern dressings developed by Lumiere in the First World War. Many variations have been developed over the years by changing the loading of paraffin in the base and by the use of emulsified forms of paraffin such as Adaptic™. These dressings in general produce a waterproof paraffin cover over the wound, which may lead to maceration because fiber products, like gauze, may not allow water vapor and exudate to pass through and may be trapped within the wound. These products are permeable to bacteria and are known to adhere to the wound, causing trauma on removal. Their use is limited to simple, clean, superficial wounds and minor burns. They are also used over skin grafts. They need to be changed frequently to avoid drying out and always require a secondary dressing.[3]

IDEAL DRESSING

The properties of a good or ideal dressing have been described as follows[1]:

- Will remove excessive exudate from the wound but will not allow the wound to dry out so as to maintain a moist environment
- Will allow gaseous exchange so that oxygen, water vapor, and carbon dioxide can pass into and out of the dressing
- Will be thermally insulating so as to maintain the wound core temperature at approximately 37°C
- Will be impermeable to microorganisms to minimize contamination of the wound from outside the wound
- Will be free from either particulate or toxic contamination
- Will be nontraumatic and will not adhere to the wound so that on removal no damage is done to granulating tissue

In addition, the following properties should be considered when selecting the appropriate dressing:

- Will provide the environment for healing
- Will be user friendly (to ensure compliance)
- Will have ease of application and removal
- Will simplify treatment (minimal changes of dressing)
- Will be cost effective (ie, total management cost)
- Will be compatible with the wound
- Will have minimal need for secondary dressings
- May be suitable for combined use with compression therapy
- May be used in infected wounds
- Will remain in place

MODERN WOUND DRESSINGS

Film Dressings

Description and Effects

Film dressings are thin membranes coated with a layer of acrylic adhesive. They are moisture vapor permeable and oxygen permeable; these properties vary from brand to brand, but not significantly. They are impermeable to microorganisms and moisture. Film dressings are flexible and allow easy assessment of the wound because they are transparent. They do not have the ability to absorb any exudate. The latest films being developed, however, have a very high moisture vapor permeability and as such will allow their use on more highly exuding wounds. Film dressings are elastic and extensible.[4,5]

The effects that make these dressings useful include the following:

- Providing a moist environment
- Enabling autolytic debridement
- Providing protection from chemicals, friction, shear, and microbes
- Transmittal of oxygen into and carbon dioxide and water vapor out of the dressing
- Functioning as a secondary dressing

Indications for Use

Film dressings are indicated in the management of minor burns and simple injuries (eg, scalds, abrasions, and lacerations) and as a postoperative dressing over suture lines. They are also used as a protective layer over intravenous catheters and for the prevention and treatment of superficial pressure areas.[6,7] A film dressing enables autolytic debridement and provides a moist wound healing environment.

Indications for Discontinuation

An increased level of exudation that causes pooling under the dressing may lead to maceration of both the wound and the surrounding skin. The dressing also should be discontinued should the wound become clinically infected.

Method of Application

An appropriate size piece of film should be chosen to cover the wound and provide an overlap of at least 4 to 5 cm from the edge of the wound. It is important to ensure that the skin around the wound is dry and free from oils or cream, as these may reduce the capacity of the product to adhere to the skin. The bottom backing paper is removed, and the film dressing is carefully applied over the wound while maintaining light but firm stretching of the edges of the film to prevent it from sticking to itself. Once the dressing is in place the upper cover is removed.

Film dressings are also used as a secondary dressing over hydrogels and alginates and may be used as an alternative to tape for holding a dressing in place.

Removal

Film dressings may remain in place for 1 week or even longer. Changing of the dressing will depend on the position, type, and size of the wound. It is important to remove film dressings with care. The correct method is not to pull the dressing back across itself. This may cause a breakdown of intact skin particularly in the elderly and in those with fine and dry skin. The film should be carefully pulled away from itself while applying light pressure to the center of the film dressing until it has been entirely removed.

Precautions and Contraindications

Care should be exercised in applying film dressings to damaged or frail skin because of the risks of further damage on removal.

Film dressings are not recommended for use over deep cavity wounds, full-thickness burns, and wounds showing signs of clinical infection.

Outcomes Expected

Film dressings provide a transparent, flexible, waterproof, and breathing dressing that will protect simple wounds and encourage healing. They can be left in place for 1 week or more and are cost effective in that only one application of the dressing may be needed to manage the wound. When they are used postsurgery over sutures, they can remain in place until the sutures are removed.

COMPARISON OF MOISTURE VAPOR PERMEABILITY OF DIFFERENT WOUND DRESSINGS

Dressing Brand	Cup Upright g/m²/24 hours	Cup Inverted g/m²/24 hours
Opsite™	839	862
Bioclusive™	547	605
Ensure™	436	436
Opraflex™	456	477
Dermafilm™	422	472
Tegaderm™	794	846

The moisture vapor permeability test[5] is done under the conditions specified in the *British Pharmacopoeia 1980*. In this test, the cup is either placed upright so that any loss of fluid is by evaporation or is inverted so that the liquid comes in contact with the membrane. It should be noted that the loss of water vapor from intact skin is 240 to 1,920 g/m²/24 hours and the water vapor loss from an open wound is about 4,800 g/m²/24 hours.

Combination Film Dressings

Ventex™ combines a vented film dressing and an outer absorbent pad. The vented film is applied directly over the wound, allowing 2 to 3 cm greater than the wound size, and then the absorbent pad is stuck around the outer edge of the film. The pad remains in place until it is saturated with exudate. Then it is changed for a new pad without removing the vented film covering the wound. Viasorb™ also combines a vented film and absorbent pad, but they are not separate so the entire dressing is changed.

These dressings are indicated for use in exuding wound ulcers, pressure wounds, abrasions, and minor burns.

Foam Dressings

Description and Effects

Foam dressings are produced from polyurethane as soft, open cell sheets and may be single layer or multiple layers. They are also available impregnated with charcoal and with a waterproof backing.[4]

Foam dressings meet many of the standard requirements of the ideal dressings. They absorb exudate protecting the surrounding skin from maceration, and raise the core

temperature of the wound, maintaining a moist environment. They are useful as both primary and secondary dressings. The effects of foam dressings include the following:

- Providing a moist environment
- Providing high absorbency
- Conformability to body shape
- Providing protection and cushioning
- No production of residue
- Nonadherency
- Providing thermal insulation
- Transmitting moisture vapor out of the dressing
- Requiring no secondary dressings

FOAM DRESSINGS

Dressing Brand	Main Constituent	Form
Allevyn™	Polyurethane	Three layers Film/hydrophilic foam/plastic net
Curafoam™	Polyurethane	Single uniform structure
Hydrasorb™	Polyurethane	Single uniform structure
Lyofoam™	Polyurethane	Two layers Hydrophobic foam/hydrophilic contact layer
Lyofoam Extra	Polyurethane	Three layers Film/Hydrophobic foam/hydrophilic contact layer

Indications for Use

Foams are indicated for a wide range of minor and major wounds, including exuding wounds (both superficial and cavity types), leg ulcers, decubitus ulcers, and sutured wounds. They can be used over skin grafts, donor sites, and minor burns. They may also be used as a secondary dressing over amorphous hydrogels. Foams improve the functioning of amorphous hydrogels by removing excess exudate from the wound and raise the core temperature of the wound. This assists with autolysis. Foams may also be used around tracheostomy tubes and other drainage tubes and catheters.[8–10]

Indications for Discontinuation

Foam dressings should be discontinued when the level of exudation cannot be absorbed into the dressing in less than a 24-hour period.

Method of Application

The foam dressing is placed over the wound, allowing at least 3 to 4 cm greater than the size of the wound. The dressing should be kept in place with one of the following:

- In patients with fine or easily damaged skin
  1. Lightweight cohesive bandage
  2. Tubular bandage
- In other patients
  1. Adhesive tape (hypoallergenic)
  2. Tubular or lightweight cohesive bandage

The dressing can be used under compression bandaging and as a secondary dressing for amorphous hydrogels and alginates. In the case of a cavity device, select the appropriate size device to fit comfortably into the cavity and insert it into the wound. It may remain in place for 1 to 4 days or until saturated with exudate. A sheet foam dressing can remain in place for up to 7 days or until the exudate has saturated to the edge of the dressing.

Precautions

Foam dressings are of little value on dry wounds with a scab or eschar. Cavity dressings similarly should not be used on their own in a dry cavity, but they may be used with an amorphous hydrogel.

Contraindications

There are no specific contraindications for the use of foam dressings. The author has clinically experienced a local reaction causing erythema, but this may have been due to an allergic reaction or to the increased blood flow caused by the thermal effect of the dressing.

Outcomes Expected

Foam dressings provide a satisfactory primary and secondary dressing for a wide range of wounds. They will aid in the removal of exudate, raise the core temperature of the wound, and protect the wound from external irritation. They will also protect the healthy skin around the wound from becoming macerated by the wound exudate.

Hydrogels

Description and Effects

Hydrogels are a group of complex organic polymers having a high water content—from 30% to 90%. These broad classes of polymers are swollen extensively in water, but they do not dissolve.

Hydrogels are three-dimensional, water-swollen, cross-linked structures formed from hydrophilic homopolymers or copolymers. Hydrogels are of two types. The first type is amorphous, being a nonfixed, three-dimensional macrostructure consisting of hydrophilic polymers or copolymers. The polymers absorb water, progressively decreasing viscosity. They are free flowing and will easily fill a cavity space. These are amorphous gels. The second type is a fixed, three-dimensional macrostructure usually presented as a thin flexible sheet. These gels swell, increasing in size until the gel is saturated; they do not change their physical form as they absorb fluid. Many also contain propylene glycol, and all contain a high proportion of water—up to 90%.[4] The table below shows a comparison of water content of some amorphous hydrogel products.

Properties

Hydrogels are a moisture donor to a dry wound but are also able to absorb a certain amount of fluid. They have the following useful effects:

- Providing a moist environment
- Aiding in autolytic debridement
- Conformability to body shape
- Nonadherence
- Providing both moisture donors and moisture absorbers

WATER CONTENT OF SOME AMORPHOUS HYDROGEL PRODUCTS		
Dressing Brand	**Chemical Type**	**Water Content**
Carrasyn™ gel	Triethanolamine, carbomer 940, acemannan, sodium chloride	95%
DuoDerm™ gel	Sodium carboxymethylcellulose, pectin, propylene glycol	81.5%
Intrasite™ gel	Modified carboxymethylcellulose, propylene glycol	78%
Solugel™	Propylene glycol, saline	75%

Indications for Use

Amorphous hydrogels in general are indicated for dry and sloughy wounds to rehydrate the eschar and to enhance rapid debridement by autolysis. They are used on leg ulcers, pressure wounds, extravasation injuries, and necrotic wounds. They facilitate granulation and epithelialization by preventing the wound from drying out. They are used on simple and partial-thickness burns and on pressure wounds. Gels are used to prevent the drying out of tissue such as tendon. Gels are also a useful carrier of topical drugs to be applied to wounds, such as metronidazole and proteolytic enzymes. Hydrogels are suitable for use in infected wounds.

Amorphous hydrogels are also used for management of the lesions of chickenpox and shingles.[6,11–14]

Indications for Discontinuation

Amorphous hydrogels should be discontinued if the exudate from the wound is excessive. It is generally considered that sheet hydrogels should be stopped if the wound is clinically infected.

Method of Application

Amorphous hydrogel should be applied to a wound to a minimum thickness of 5 mm and covered with a secondary dressing. The choice of secondary material will depend on the type and position of the wound and availability and cost. The author has found that foams are the most satisfactory secondary dressings by virtue of their properties of absorption of exudate, thus maintaining the integrity of the gel for a longer time, protecting the surrounding skin from maceration, and raising the core temperature to aid in autolysis. Other products may be used such as film dressings, hydrocolloids, and simple nonadherent dressings. Gauze is also a suitable secondary dressing.

Hydrogels can remain in place with a clean wound for up to 3 days and then removed by irrigation with water or saline. When used for the lesions of chickenpox they should be applied four or five times a day.

The sheet hydrogels are placed over the wound with at least 3 to 4 cm coverage greater than the wound. They are held in place with either tape or a light cohesive bandage, depending on the skin of the patient. In difficult areas they should be held in place with a retention sheet such as Hypafix, Fixomull, or Medipore. The sheet hydrogels do not cause maceration of the surrounding tissue. The sheets are left in place, depending on the wound type and the amount of exudation, but generally should be removed after 3 to 4 days. For some superficial burns they may remain in place for up to 7 days. When removed they cause no discomfort and leave no residue on the skin.

Precautions

Sheet hydrogels should not be applied to wounds clinically infected without coverage with systemic antibiotics.

Contraindications

Amorphous hydrogels containing propylene glycol should not be used in patients known to be sensitive to propylene glycol. Sheet hydrogels should not be applied over small deep cavity wounds or clinically infected wounds. They should also not be used in highly exuding wounds.

Outcomes Expected

Hydrogels will aid in the rapid removal of necrotic tissue and rehydrate dry wounds, assisting in granulation and reepithelialization. In burns they reduce the heat and pain. The thicker sheet hydrogels, when used in the management of superficial pressure wounds, will also assist in the reduction of pressure by reducing friction and shear forces.

Hydrocolloids

Description and Effects

Hydrocolloids are a combination of gel-forming polymers with adhesives held in a fine suspension on a backing of film or foam. Hydrocolloid dressings are composed of a backing of either polyurethane foam or film and a mass containing in most cases sodium carboxymethylcellulose and other gel-forming agents such as pectin, gelatin, and elastomers. These form a self-adhesive mass.[4] These products are also available as granules, powder, and paste. When placed on a wound the exudate combines with the polymers to form a soft gel mass in the wound. They were originally introduced as Stomahesive to protect good skin around ileostomies and colostomies. They vary from being occlusive to being semipermeable. When removed, the gel remaining is yellow and malodorous but not infected. The presence of bacteria under hydrocolloid dressings does not retard healing.

When applied to an exuding wound the dressing absorbs exudate from the wound and forms a gel. This gel will vary in viscosity, depending on the brand of dressing. The dressing does not adhere to the wound itself, only to the intact skin around the wound. Hydrocolloids have the following effects[15,16]:

- Providing a moist environment
- Aiding in autolytic debridement of wounds
- Conformability to body shape
- Protection from microbial contamination
- Providing a waterproof surface
- Requiring no secondary dressing

The following table shows a comparison of some hydrocolloid products.

COMPARISON OF HYDROCOLLOID DRESSING PRODUCTS

Dressing Brand	Main Component	Backing	Forms
Comfeel™	Sodium carboxymethyl cellulose	Polyurethane film	Standard, thin
Duoderm™	Carboxymethyl cellulose	Polyurethane foam/film	Standard, thin
Tegasorb™	Polyisobutylene	Polyurethane film	Standard, thin

Indications for Use

Hydrocolloids are indicated in the management of superficial leg ulcers, burns, donor sites (when hemostasis has been obtained), and pressure wounds. They may be used in small cavity wounds in combination with hydrocolloid paste, powder, or granules. Thin versions of these dressings are indicated as dressings over sutures in both minor and major surgery.[6,9,17–19]

Indications for Discontinuation

Hydrocolloids should be discontinued on surface granulation of the wound or if hypergranulation occurs.

Method of Application

Hydrocolloids on a superficial wound should be applied to the wound with at least 3 to 4 cm of product greater than the wound size. The skin should be dry to ensure good adhesion, and it is preferable to place one third of the dressing above the wound and two thirds below the wound; this will prolong the wear time of the dressing. The dressing may remain in place for 5 to 7 days or until strikethrough has occurred, that is, exudate has migrated to the outside edge of the dressing. The dressing should be carefully removed and the wound irrigated with warm saline before applying a new dressing.

In the case of small cavity wounds, if relatively moist the cavity should be filled with hydrocolloid powder or granules and covered with a sheet of hydrocolloid dressing. With a low to moderately exuding cavity, hydrocolloid paste should be inserted carefully and the wound again covered with a sheet of hydrocolloid dressing. The dressing should be changed after 3 or 4 days by irrigation of the cavity with warm saline and gentle removal of any remaining product before applying the new dressing.

Thin hydrocolloid dressings are applied after suturing of a surgical wound, and in most cases, can remain in place and be removed at the time of suture, clip, or Steristrip removal. These dressings have the advantages of being flexible and waterproof. They require no secondary dressing, and help to appose wound edges by distribution of tension at the suture line across the surface area of the dressing.

Precautions and Contraindictions

Care should be taken in using these dressings on patients with thin and fragile skin, as they may cause further damage on removal.

There are no absolute contraindications for use of hydrocolloids. Hydrocolloids are not indicated for use in very heavily exuding wounds or in clinically infected wounds. They are also not considered suitable for deep cavity wounds.

Outcomes Expected

Hydrocolloids should help remove necrotic tissue and slough from the wound and encourage angiogenesis and granulation of the wound. The presence of colonized bacteria in the wound does not contraindicate the use of these dressings.

Alginates

Description and Effects

Alginates are the calcium or calcium/sodium salts of alginic acid and are composed of polymannuronic and guluronic acids obtained from seaweed—mainly the genus *Laminaria*. When applied to a wound the sodium ions present in the wound exchange for the calcium ions, producing a hydrophilic gel and providing calcium ions into the wound. This is part of the mechanism by which alginates act as a hemostat.

Alginates are gelling polysaccharides. They are presented as either calcium alginate, a mixture of sodium and calcium alginate in textile fiber sheets, or as a loose packing ribbon. Alginates combined with activated charcoal are also available. Alginates are combined with some hydrocolloid dressings to aid in the fluid handling properties.

Sodium alginate has the empirical formula $C_6H_7O_6Na$ with a molecular weight in the range of 32,000 to 200,000. Sodium alginate has a complex structure consisting essentially of two uronic acids, D-polymannuronic acid and L-guluronic acid. The ratio of these isomers will vary depending on the species of seaweed from which the alginate is extracted and the method of production. Gels rich in polymannuronic acid form soft amorphous gels that partially dissolve or disperse in solutions containing sodium ions. Alginates rich in guluronic acid tend to swell in the presence of sodium ions while retaining their basic structure.[4,20] Alginates have the following useful effects:

- Providing a moist environment
- Providing a high absorptive capacity
- Conformability to body shape
- Protection
- Providing hemostatis
- Nonadherence

The following table shows a comparison of the chemical composition of different alginate products.

COMPARISON OF ALGINATE CHEMICAL COMPOSITION

Dressing Brand	Guluronic Acid (%)	Polymannuronic Acid (%)	Calcium Alginate (%)	Sodium Alginate (%)
Algiderm™	58	42	100	
Curosorb™	68	32	100	
Kaltostat™	66	34	80	20
Kaltocarb™	66	34	80	20
Sorbsan™	34	63	100	
Tegagen HG™	40	60	80	20
Tegagen HI™	40	60	100	
Algosteril™	58	42	100	

Indications for Use

Alginates are used in exuding wounds such as leg ulcers, cavity wounds, and pressure wounds, and at donor sites as a hemostat postsurgically and other bleeding sites. They may be used in infected wounds.[6,10,21–24]

Indications for Discontinuation

Alginates should be discontinued if the level of exudation is insufficient to cause the fiber to gel. Alginates should not be premoistened with saline before application to a wound.

Method of Application

Sheet alginates should be placed in the wound to the shape of the wound and covered with a secondary dressing such as a foam, or a nonadherent dressing and held in place with tape or a light cohesive bandage, depending on the condition of the patient's skin. If the wound is highly exudative, an additional covering with a simple absorbent pad is appropriate. In the case of a cavity wound, rope or packing alginate material should be placed gently in the cavity, taking care not to pack the material tightly into the space. When used on a donor site, the sheet alginate should be applied to the donor area after harvesting of skin and covered with a film dressing or foam. This will aid in rapid hemostasis and provide the environment for reepithelialization of the skin. The dressing in general should remain in place in clean wounds for no longer than 7 days or when the gel loses its viscosity (this will vary depending on the level of exudation from the wound). Wounds clinically infected should be changed daily. The alginate is removed by simple irrigation of the wound or cavity with warm saline.

Precautions and Contraindications

Wounds clinically infected should be changed daily with consideration for the concurrent use of systemic antibiotics by the prescriber.

There are no known contraindications to the use of alginates. They are not suitable for use in dry wounds or wounds with thick black eschar.

Outcomes Expected

Alginates will absorb exudate and provide the moist environment for granulation. They are suitable for use in infected wounds and are very effective in the management of bleeding, in particular in postnasal surgery and when applied to donor sites. They will provide a comfortable dressing. Rapid healing of the skin is expected.

Combination Alginates

Manufacturers have combined alginates with other products to enhance effects of each.

Calcium/Sodium Alginate Combination

Kaltocarb.™ Kaltocarb™ is a combination of calcium and sodium alginate in a fiber sheet bonded to a layer of activated charcoal and an outer layer of viscose. This product is a highly absorbent dressing with the ability to absorb odor. It is indicated in infected malodorous wounds, fungating neoplasms and ulcers, and superficial pressure wounds.

The sheet should be applied to the surface of the wound, ensuring that the alginate white layer is in contact with the wound and the dark charcoal layer is on the outside. The product is covered with a secondary dressing and held in place with tape or a light cohesive bandage. The dressing should be changed every few days, depending on the level of exudate and the extent of infection. The use of systemic antibiotics in clinically infected wounds is indicated. The dressing is easily removed; removal may be assisted by irrigation with warm saline. This dressing, as with other alginates, is of no value in a dry wound with thick dark eschar.

Alginate/Hydrocolloid Combination

Curaderm™ and Comfeel Plus™. The combining of hydrocolloids and alginates in one dressing enhances the properties of the dressing and allows their use in more highly exuding wounds. They present in sheet form similar in appearance to standard hydrocolloid sheets. They are used in a manner similar to that for hydrocolloids; however, they can remain in place for a longer time because of the better absorptive properties.

Hydroactive Dressings

Description and Effects

Hydroactive dressings have some similarities to hydrocolloids; however, they are not gel-forming products. They act by absorbing exudate into the structure of the dressing, and swelling as the amount of exudate is absorbed. They maintain a moist environment at the interface of the wound.

Hydroactive dressings are multilayered dressings of highly absorbent polymer gel with an adhesive backing. These dressings are composed of an outer polyurethane film membrane combined with a polyurethane gel and other absorbents (eg, sodium polyacrylate). They are semipermeable and are adhesive to the skin. They are available in a number of forms, including cavity fillers, foam, and thin types.[4] Hydroactive dressings have the following useful effects:

- Providing a moist environment
- High absorbency
- Waterproof surface
- Regaining shape when stretched
- Aiding in autolysis
- Leaving no residue
- Semipermeability to moisture vapor

Indications for Use

Hydroactive dressings are indicated for use on exuding wounds including leg ulcers, pressure wounds, minor burns, and exuding cavity wounds. They are of particular use over joints such as the elbow, knee, fingers, toes, and ankle because of their ability to expand and contract without causing constriction.[25–27]

Indications for Discontinuation

Hydroactive dressings should be discontinued for the wound with little or no exudation or if the dressing is unable to absorb the level of exudate being produced by the wound.

Method of Application

The application of hydroactive dressings will vary depending on the type of dressings used. Tielle™ is placed over the wound so that the central island of dressing completely covers the wound. Allow 2 to 3 cm greater than the wound size, and then adhere to the surrounding skin. Cutinova™ is applied directly to the wound, allowing 3 to 4 cm of dressing greater than the wound size. It is preferable to warm the edges of the dressing slightly with the hand to aid in adhesion of the dressing. Cutinova Cavity™, because of its ability to absorb exudate and expand, should be placed carefully into the cavity, not occupying more than 33% of the space. The outer wound should be covered with a suitable dressing such as Cutinova Thin™ or Hydro™. These dressings may remain in place for up to 7 days depending of the level of exudation. Care should be taken on removal in patients with thin or easily damaged skin. When removed, they will leave no residue from the dressing; however, it may still be necessary to irrigate the wound with warm saline if there is exudate present on the surface of the wound before redressing.

Precautions and Contraindications

Hydroactive dressings are not considered suitable for use on clinically infected wounds or nonexuding wounds.

There are no known contraindications; however, care should be taken when using these products on fine and easily damaged skin.

Outcomes Expected

Hydroactive dressings will absorb exudate and provide a moist environment for granulation and epithelialization. They will provide a comfortable dressing that will remain in place and have a good wear time.

Miscellaneous Dressings

With constant research and development, new products have entered the market that do not fit into any of the standard groups mentioned. These products have properties resembling existing groups, but are composed of different materials.

Exu-dry™ is a nonadherent absorbent pad composed of an outer layer of perforated polyethylene-laminated rayon and an inner layer of absorbent rayon/polypropylene blend with a cellulose backing that wicks wound exudate and holds large quantities of fluid. It is indicated in highly exudative wounds and in particular in burns.[28]

AQUACEL™ is a nonwoven, 100% sodium carboxylmethyl-cellulose spun into fibers and manufactured into sheets and ribbon dressing. This product mirrors the properties and actions of alginate dressings; however, it differs in that it rapidly absorbs exudate vertically and can also absorb laterally. It retains fluid within the structure of the fiber. The sodium carboxymethylcellulose fibers swell and convert into a gel sheet. This product is indicated in heavily exuding wounds such as leg ulcers, pressure wounds, cavity wounds, minor burns, and donor sites.

The dressing is applied to the wound, allowing 2 to 3 cm greater than the wound size or wound cavity. The dressing will remain in place for 1 to 3 days depending on the exudate level and when the product is saturated.

CombiDerm is a multilayer absorbent pad combining a semipermeable hydrocolloid border with absorbent padding of hydrocolloid particles and a nonadherent cover against the wound. This product is highly absorbent and is able to hold the exudate within the dressing preventing maceration to the surrounding skin. It maintains a moist environment. It is indicated on highly exuding wounds, pressure wounds, leg ulcers, and surgical wounds. It may be used as a secondary dressing over cavity wounds.

DRESSING CHOICE

Wounds are dynamic and as such the choice of dressing will vary and change as the wound changes. The product you may commence treating the wound with initially will in many cases change as the wound itself changes. The choice should be based on the three major aspects of any wound: color, depth, and exudate (Table 10–1). The color will vary from pink (epithelializing), to red (granulating), to yellow (sloughy), to black (necrotic). The depth will include superficial, shallow, and deep cavity; the exudation will be none, minimal, moderate, or high.

The other aspects that will need to be considered are the presence of infection, the tissue surrounding the wound, the need also to apply graduated compression, the fragility of the skin, and any medical condition that may have an impact on the dressing choice.

Table 10–1 Dressing Choice

Wound Type (Color/Exudate)	Aim	Wound Depth	
		Superficial	Cavity
Black/low exudate	Rehydrate and loosen eschar. Enhance autolytic debridement.	Amorphous hydrogels Hydrocolloid sheets	
Yellow/high exudate	Remove slough and absorb exudate.	Hydrocolloids Alginates Enzymes Hydrofibre Hydroactive dressing	Hydrocolloids Hydrocolloids with paste Hydrocolloid granules or powder Hydrogels Enzymes Alginates Hydroactive cavity Hydrocolloid/Alginate Foam cavity dressing Hydrofibre
Yellow/low exudate	Remove slough, absorb exudate, and maintain a moist environment.	Amorphous hydrogels Sheet hydrogels Hydrocolloids Film dressings	Amorphous hydrogels Hydrocolloids with paste Hydrocolloid/Alginate
Red/high exudate	Maintain moist environment, absorb exudate, and promote granulation and epithelialization.	Foam Alginates Hydroactive Hydrofibre	Foam cavity dressing Alginates Hydrofibre Hydrocolloid/Alginate Hydrocolloid with paste Hydrocolloid powder or granules Hydroactive cavity
Red/low exudate	Maintain moist environment and promote granulation and epithelialization.	Hydrocolloids Foams Sheet hydrogels Films Zinc paste*	Hydrocolloids with paste Hydrocolloid powder or granules Amorphous hydrogels Foam cavity dressing
Pink/low exudate	Maintain moist environment, and protect and insulate.	Foams Films Hydrocolloids (thin) Hydroactive (thin) Nonadherent dressing. Zinc paste*	
Red unbroken skin	Prevent skin breakdown.	Hydrocolloids Films	

*See Chapter 9, Management of Edema.

SECONDARY DRESSINGS

The choice of secondary dressing will depend on the nature, position, and level of exudate. In general terms, film dressings and nonadherent dressings are suitable for low exudating wounds but not for high exudating wounds. Foam dressings are useful over amorphous hydrogels and alginates. The use of gauze as a secondary dressing is limited, especially over hydrogels or alginates, as the gauze will reduce the ability of the dressing to function at its optimum level. The other consideration is the method of dressing retention. If the surrounding skin is good, the dressing may be held in place with good-quality tape. If the skin is poor, a tubular bandage or a lightweight cohesive bandage is suitable. See Appendix B, Resources for Wound Care Products.

THE USE OF ANTISEPTICS IN WOUNDS

Antiseptics are an essential part of modern clinical practice. Their value as a hand-washing procedure prior to an aseptic procedure or for the preparation of the patient's skin prior to surgery is clearly documented. Studies have shown that the bacteria on the skin, whether resident or transient, are reduced by up to 95%. There is not, however, a considerable amount of research on the effects of antiseptics on open wounds. There will always be microorganisms present in a wound to a greater or lesser extent. It has been argued that one of the most prolific researchers and publishers in the area of antiseptics and healing has said that antiseptics for this purpose may in fact be harmful in that they damage healing tissue, thus allowing infection to gain a foothold.[29–33] It was Alexander Fleming in 1919 who said that it is essential in the estimation of the value of an antiseptic to study its effects on the tissues rather than its effect on bacteria. Unfortunately, Fleming's wise counsel of so many years ago has tended to be ignored in modern practice. It is known that the surface of open wounds does not need to be sterile for healing to take place. Equally, there is no evidence to support that dressing changes performed once or twice a day with antiseptics guarantee protection from invasive infection.

The concern with antiseptics is their toxicity. A number of studies, particularly with the hypochlorites, have shown major problems. Brennan and Leaper,[30] in their study of the effects of antiseptics on healing wounds, used a devised rabbit ear chamber that was irrigated with a number of products. The effect on microcirculation was measured using laser Doppler. This study clearly showed the effects of various antiseptics on the microcirculation. In particular, Eusol was shown to occlude permanently the microcirculation after a 1-minute exposure with no change in measured flow after 24 hours.[30]

Apart from the wound cell toxicity and the depression of collagen synthesis, hypochlorites may cause localized edema, hypernatremia, hyperthermia, and burns. It has also been reported that cases of renal failure associated with topical application of chlorinated solutions to pressure sores have occurred. This has been attributed to the release of a toxic lipid from bacteria, causing the bacteremia or endotoxic shock called Schwartzman's reaction.[34]

Hypochlorites as a chemical entity are chemically unstable, have a short shelf-life, are rapidly deactivated by organic material, and really are not cost effective, requiring frequent changes of dressing. And after all, sodium hypochlorite is a bleach. A further study by Brennan et al.[32] showed that in particular hypochlorite retards the deposition of collagen, an essential element in the matrix for the healing of wounds by secondary intention.

The commonly used antiseptics fall into the diguanide group, one example being chlorhexidine, which is a bactericidal agent with gram-positive and gram-negative activity. It is ineffective against acid-fast bacteria, bacterial spores, fungi, or viruses. Skin sensitivity is reported, and chlorhexidine is incompatible with soap; the presence of blood and organic material also will decrease its activity. Antimicrobial activity is best at neutral or slightly alkaline pH. Chlorhexidine is used mostly as a hand or skin disinfectant.

The second antiseptic group contains the quaternary ammonium compounds and there are a number of these, cetrimide being one example. Quaternary ammonium compounds are often used in combination with the chlorhexidine-type preparations, an example of which is Savlon. These are also bactericidal against gram-positive and gram-negative organisms. They are relatively ineffective against bacterial spores, viruses, or fungi, and some strains of *Pseudomonas aeruginosa* and *Mycobacterium tuberculosis* are resistant. They can also cause hypersensitivity.

The third most commonly used antiseptic is povidone-iodine, an organic complex of iodine with polymers. It is a polyvinylpyrrolidione. It is bactericidal and sporcidal and is active against fungi and viruses. Local irritation and sensitivity may occur, and it may cause burns if applied to denuded areas. It should not be used on patients with goiter. Its absorption may also interfere with thyroid function tests. It is incompatible with alkalis and is used as a skin preparation and as a disinfectant.

The topical application of an antiseptic will reduce the level of bacteria on the surface of the wound but will not penetrate into infected tissue.[35] If a wound is clinically infected, the use of systemic antibiotics should be considered as the most appropriate. Dr. Chris Lawrence considers that antiseptics and to some extent certain antibiotics, if used wisely, afford excellent antibacterial prophylaxis in a variety of skin wounds. Unwise use of antibacterial agents, however, especially antibiotics, can create further problems. Dr. Lawrence, as do a number of other investigators, considers that convincing comparative clinical trials concerning the possible value of antiseptics are lacking. There is, however, sufficient in vitro evidence that would indicate that a problem exists with the prolonged use of antiseptics in chronic wounds.[36]

In general the use of topical antiseptics in chronic wounds is considered to be of little benefit and may in fact be injurious to the tissue. The exceptions are patients with major arterial circulation deficiencies, such as diabetics and immunocompromised, neutropenic patients. A decision should be made for the individual patient, taking into account all the positive benefits and risks.

ANTISEPTICS AND ACUTE WOUNDS

The use of topical antiseptics and antibiotics for acute wounds is entirely different from that for chronic wounds. In a traumatic wound the risk of infection from contamination at the time of wounding is very high. Also, in the case of major burns, the presence of necrotic tissue is a focus for infection, and it is mandatory to use topical management. The aim of using antiseptics and antibiotics prophylactically is to reduce the level of bacteria in the wound and allow the body's own mechanisms to destroy the rest. The use of povidone-iodine, chlorhexidine, and chlorhexidine/cetrimide products is appropriate in the early management of acute traumatic wounds. The use of products such as silver sulfadiazine cream in burns is part of the early management of this type of wound.

ANTIBIOTICS

The use of topical antibiotics in chronic wounds should also be based on a general principle that topical use of antibiotics is not recommended because of the development of resistance and sensitization. However, in surface anaerobic contamination of some wounds, especially fungating wounds, the use of metronidazole gel is appropriate, and there have been cases of methicillin-resistant *Staphylococcus aureus* where topical mupirocin has been used. The other topical antibiotic used in clinical practice is silver sulfadiazine cream in some infected ulcers where *Pseudomonas* has been found to be present.[37–39] Appendix A has additional information on antiseptics and antibiotics.

WOUND CLEANSING

Cleansing of a wound at the time of dressing changes will depend on the nature of the wound. In general, if the wound is clean with little or no residue from the dressing, a simple irrigation with water or saline is the most appropriate. If there is dressing residue, slough, or dry or scaly tissue, then in addition to water or saline the use of a skin wash with surfactant properties will aid in the removal of the debris. The most important aspect is to minimize the direct contact with the granulating wound. It is considered best to use the cleansing materials at body temperature, as the application of a cold solution will reduce the temperature of the wound and may affect blood flow. The use of antiseptic cleansers is of little value in chronic wounds; however, they are of benefit in the initial cleaning of an acute wound.[40]

REFERENCES

1. Turner TD. Products and their development in wound management. *Plast Surg Dermatol Aspects*. 1979;75–84.

2. Turner TD. Surgical dressings in the drug tariff. *Wound Manage*. 1991;1:4–6.

3. Thomas S. Pain and wound management: community outlook. *Nurs Times*. 1989;85(suppl):11–15.

4. Thomas S. *Handbook of Wound Dressings*. London: Macmillan; 1994.

5. Thomas S, Loveless P, Hay NP. Comparative review of the properties of six semipermeable film dressings. *Pharm J*. June 18, 1988;240:785–788.

6. Golledge CL. Advances in wound management. *Mod Med Aust*. May 1993;42–47.

7. Myers JA. Ease of use of two semi-permeable adhesive membranes compared. *Pharm J*. December 1, 1984;233:685–686.

8. Loiterman DA, Byers PH. Effects of a hydrocellular polyurethane dressing on chronic venous ulcer healing. *Wounds*. September/October 1991;3:178–181.

9. Myers JA. Lyofoam: a versatile polyurethane foam surgical dressing. *Pharm J*. August 31, 1985;235:270.

10. Foster AVM, Greenhill MT, Edmonds ME. Comparing two dressings in the treatment of diabetic foot ulcers. *J Wound Care*. July 1994;3:224–228.

11. Sussman GM. Hydrogels: a review. *Primary Intention*. February 1994;2:6–9.

12. Smith RA, Rusbourne J. The use of Solugel in the closure of wounds by secondary intention. *Primary Intention*. May 1994;2:14–17.

13. Thomas S, Jones H. Clinical experiences with a new hydrogel dressing. *J Wound Care*. March 1996;5:132–133.

14. Thomas S. Comparing two dressings for wound debridement. *J Wound Care*. September 1993;2:272–274.

15. Thomas S, Loveless P. A comparative study of the properties of six hydrocolloid dressings. *Pharm J*. November 16, 1991;247:672–675.

16. Rousseau P, Niecestro RM. Comparison of the physicochemical properties of various hydrocolloid dressings. *Wounds*. January/February 1991;3:43–45.

17. Marshall PJ, Eyers A. The use of a hydrocolloid dressing (Comfeel transparent) as a wound closure dressing following lower bowel surgery. *Primary Intention*. August 1994;2:39–40.

18. Banks V, Bale SE, Harding KG. Comparing two dressings for exuding pressure sores in community patients. *J Wound Care.* June 1994;3:175–178.

19. Thomas SS, Lawrence JC, Thomas A. Evaluation of hydrocolloids and topical medication in minor burns. *J Wound Care.* May 1995;4:218–220.

20. Thomas S. Observations on the fluid handling properties of alginate dressings. *Pharm J.* June 27, 1992;248:850–851.

21. Sussman GM. Alginates: a review. *Primary Intention.* February 1996;4:33–37.

22. Miller L, Jones V, Bale S. The use of alginate packing in the management of deep sinuses. *J Wound Care.* September 1993;2:262–263.

23. Thomas S. Use of a calcium alginate dressing. *Pharm J.* August 10, 1985;235:188–190.

24. Thomas S. Alginates: a guide to the properties and uses of the different alginate dressings available today. *J Wound Care.* May/June 1992;1:29–32.

25. Williams C. Treating a patient's venous ulcer with a foamed gel dressing. *J Wound Care.* September 1993;2:264–265.

26. Achterberg VB, Welling C, Meyer-Ingold W. Hydroactive dressings and serum protein: an in vitro study. *J Wound Care.* February 1996;5:79–82.

27. Collier J. A moist odour-free environment. *Prof Nurse.* September 1992;804–807.

28. Brown-Etris M, Smith JA, Pasceri P, Punchello M. Case studies: considering dressing options. *Ostomy Wound Manage.* June 1994;40:5:46–52.

29. Sleigh JW, Linter SPK. Hazards of hydrogen peroxide. *Br Med J.* 1985;291:1706.

30. Brennan SS, Leaper DJ. The effects of antiseptics on the healing wound: a study using the rabbit ear chamber. *Br J Surg.* 1985;72:780–782.

31. Lawrence CJ. Dressings and wound infection. *Am J Surg.* 1994;167(suppl):21S–24S.

32. Brennan SS, Foster ME, Leaper DJ. Antiseptic toxicity in wounds: healed by secondary intention. *J Hosp Infect.* 1986;8:263–267.

33. Leaper DJ. Antiseptics and their effect on healing tissue. *Nurs Times.* May 1986;45–46.

34. Morgan DA. Chlorinated solutions: (E) useful or (e) useless. *Pharm J.* August 19, 1989;243:219–220.

35. Lawrence JC. The development of an in vitro wound model and its application to the use of topical antiseptics. In: *Proceedings of the First European Conference on Advances in Wound Management.* London: Macmillan; 1992:15–16.

36. Lawrence JC. Wound infection. *J Wound Care.* September 1993;2:277–280.

37. Leaper DJ, Brennan SS, Simpson RA, Foster ME. Experimental infection and hydrogel dressings. *J Hosp Infect.* 1984;5:69–73.

38. Young JB, Dobrzanski S. Pressure sores: epidemiology and current management concepts. *Drugs Aging.* 1992;2:42–57.

39. Brown CD, Zitelli JA. A review of topical agents for wounds and methods of wounding. *J Dermatol Surg Oncol.* 1993;19:732–737.

40. Dire JD, Welsh AP. A comparison of wound irrigation solution used in the emergency department. *Ann Emerg Med.* June 1990;704–707.

PART III

Management by Wound Etiology

Barbara M. Bates-Jensen

Determining the cause or etiology of a wound is a critical element in creating a comprehensive treatment plan for patients with wounds. The chapters in Part III focus on management by wound etiology. Specific attention to acute surgical wounds, pressure ulcers, vascular ulcers, and neuropathic ulcers is presented in the chapters in Part III. Emphasis is placed on understanding the pathophysiology involved in the wound type, assessment methods, and prevention and management of specific wound types. Improving and expanding knowledge of wound etiology empowers clinicians to provide quality comprehensive care in clinical practice.

In Chapter 11 Bates-Jensen and Wethe present management of the acute surgical wound. The chapter begins by defining the acute and chronic wound. When does an acute wound become a chronic wound? The easiest and perhaps the least controversial defining characteristic of the acute wound that becomes chronic is failure to follow the normal wound healing temporal sequence. Better understanding of acute wounds improves ability to monitor and treat all wounds. Types of surgical wound healing—primary intention, secondary intention, and tertiary intention—are presented. Extrinsic factors that affect wound healing during the preoperative, intraoperative, and postoperative time periods are described. Surgical wound classifications are presented and reviewed. Interventions for managing hypovolemia, thermoregulation strategies, and methods of optimizing tissue oxygen perfusion are described.

Intrinsic factors affecting healing of the acute surgical wound are those that influence the person systemically. Examples of intrinsic factors include age, concurrent conditions, nutritional status, and oxygenation and tissue perfusion. Each intrinsic factor is discussed with special attention to the patient with diabetes. Examination of the surgical in-

cision includes evaluation of wound characteristics such as incision location, length, presence of healing ridge, type and amount of exudate, type of wound closure materials, and approximation of wound edges. The incisional examination forms the basis of acute surgical wound assessment and is presented by phase of wound healing (inflammatory, proliferative, and remodeling).

Management of the surgical incision includes attention to factors that affect wound healing as addressed in Chapter 11, as well as dressing care. The surgical dressing includes the primary and secondary dressing. Discussion includes types of dressings used for primary and secondary dressings. Wound healing in secondary intention and tertiary intention wounds is discussed and contrasted with primary intention incisions.

Outcome measures for evaluating healing in incisional wounds following the phases of wound healing are presented and described. This section includes examples of appropriate documentation of the healing incision. Chapter 11 concludes with a case study for review of material and self-care teaching guidelines for use with other health care providers, family caregivers, and patients.

Chapters 12 and 13 describe issues related to management of pressure ulcers. Chapter 12 is devoted to pathophysiology and prevention of pressure ulcers. Pressure ulcers are areas of local tissue trauma that usually develop where soft tissues are compressed between bony prominences and any external surface for prolonged periods. Chapter 12 begins with a definition of pressure ulcers and an extensive review of the pathophysiology of pressure ulcer development. The relationship between time and pressure in the development of pressure ulcers is presented. Clinical presentation of pressure ulceration and the most prevalent locations for pressure ulcer development are covered. Specific information is included on assessment of the dark-skinned individual for risk of pressure ulceration.

Pressure ulcers are commonly classified according to grading or staging systems based on the depth of tissue destruction. The stage is determined on initial assessment by noting the deepest layer of tissue involved. The history of staging systems and the current system recommended by the Agency for Health Care Policy and Research and the National Pressure Ulcer Advisory Panel are described. The issue of pressure ulcer assessment and the use and misuse of staging classification systems are a subject of debate and controversy. Pressure ulcer development does not necessarily occur from one stage to the next, and there may be different etiologic factors for various stages. Chapter 12 reviews this issue. Discussion of pressure ulcer pathophysiology and etiology would not be complete without mention of other interacting factors. Pressure ulcers are physical evidence of multiple causative influences. Factors that contribute to pressure ulcer development can be thought of as those that affect the pressure force over the bony prominence and those that affect the tolerance of the tissues to pressure. Mobility, sensory loss, and activity level are related to the concept of increasing pressure. Extrinsic factors such as shear, friction, and moisture, as well as intrinsic factors such as nutrition, age, and arteriolar pressure relate to the concept of tissue tolerance. Each of the factors is presented and discussed. Particular attention is given to immobility or severely restricted mobility because it is the most important risk factor for all populations and a necessary condition for the development of pressure ulcers. The most common risk assessment tools, Braden's Scale for Predicting Pressure Sore Risk, Norton's scale, and Gosnell's scale, are all presented and discussed.

Prevention strategies are targeted at reducing risk factors present. Appropriate prevention interventions can be focused on eliminating specific risk factors. Thus, early intervention for pressure ulcers is risk factor–specific and prophylactic in nature. The prevention strategies are presented by risk factors, beginning with general information and ending with specific strategies for a particular risk factor. Chapter 12 includes specific information on the use of support surfaces with definitions of pressure-reducing and pressure-relieving devices, pillow bridging, and passive repositioning. Extensive discussion on nutrition interventions and management of incontinence is included. Skin hygiene interventions and skin maintenance interventions round out the prevention strategies. Chapter 12 concludes with outcome measures for evaluating the success of a pressure ulcer prevention program and extensive self-care teaching guidelines for other health care providers, family caregivers, and patients.

In Chapter 13, Rappl continues the discussion of support surfaces that began in Chapter 12. Rappl provides a look at therapeutic positioning for pressure ulcer prevention. Persons who become sitting dependent more than ambulatory and those who use the lying-down or the sitting position for the majority of their day are at high risk of skin breakdown. And for the patient with an existing pressure ulcer, proper positioning in the most active and functional position possible, both in sitting and in recumbent positions, improves the healing rate of the ulcer and minimizes the likelihood of developing new ulcers. Chapter 13 provides an overview of therapeutic positioning knowledge. The areas the clinician should examine in order to determine the need for intervention are presented and described. The basics of therapeutic positioning and a discussion of how therapeutic positioning affects body system impairments is presented. The chapter includes a table on functional diagnosis and relationship to prognosis, interventions, and outcomes related to therapeutic positioning. The ideal sitting position is described, and basic seating principles related to pelvic control, thigh control, seat depth, and footrest are discussed. Finally, specifics in positioning the patient with an existing ulcer both in sitting and in lying down are described. An extensive discussion of methods of determining appropriate wheelchairs and sitting position and procedures for recumbent positioning for patients is presented.

Donayre provides an in-depth analysis of the diagnosis and management of vascular ulcers in Chapter 14. The chapter begins with a review of general anatomy and physiology of the circulatory system and pathophysiology related to lower extremity ulcers. Thorough history and physical assessment are essential for the patient with a lower leg ulcer, and Donayre provides this information for each ulcer type; in addition, risk factors for arterial/ischemic, venous, and diabetic ulcers are discussed. Donayre describes presentation and assessment of common findings related to lower leg ulcers, such as intermittent claudication, rest pain, altered ankle-brachial index, edema, and tissue changes. Associated diagnostic tests for the lower leg are described. Differential diagnosis for leg ulcers is a key factor in determining appropriate treatment. Treatment that is appropriate for a venous ulcer may be contraindicated for an arterial/ischemic ulcer. The presenting clinical manifestations, diagnostic tests, and differential wound assessment are presented for each lower leg ulcer type. Medical and surgical management related to arterial/ischemic, venous disease, and diabetic ulcers is described. Special attention is given to diagnosing osteomyelitis in the diabetic and describing pathophysiology of edema related to venous disease with indications for clinical management.

Part III concludes with Elftman's presentation of the neuropathic foot. Chapter 15 opens with a discussion of the necessity of interdisciplinary collaboration in the management of neuropathic ulcers. The neuropathic patient often has dysvascular components that must be addressed by a medical team rather than one specialty. The trineuropathy assessment with attention to sensory, motor, and autonomic neuropathy is explained. Gradual and sudden-onset peripheral neuropathy are compared for easy differential diagnosis. Diabetic neuropathy is the major focal point of Chapter 15. Common infections and dermatologic changes are presented. The definitions of wet and dry gangrene are presented, and the two conditions are compared. Footwear assessment guidelines and interventions based on the Wagner ulcer grade is explained. Chapter 15 includes in-depth explanations of sensory, pressure, vibratory, and foot deformity evaluation. Charcot's deformity is explained and the method of assess-

ment described. Management with orthotic devices is explained. Specific instructions for procedures, such as how to make a foam toe separator are included. Interventions to decrease pressure, such as total-contact casting, use of splints and inserts, and neurowalkers are all discussed. The chapter concludes with self-care teaching guidelines for use with patients and family caregivers and documentation requirements for neuropathic ulcers.

Although similarities exist in the treatment of any wound, treatment approach varies depending on wound etiology. The chapters in Part III form a foundation on knowledge of wounds of various etiologies. This foundation should provide clinicians with a stronger and more individualized approach to the person with a wound.

CHAPTER 11

Acute Surgical Wound Management

Barbara M. Bates-Jensen and James Wethe

ACUTE SURGICAL WOUND DEFINITION

Acute wounds are defined as disruptions in the integrity of the skin and underlying tissues that progress through the healing process in a timely and uneventful manner. The acute elective surgical wound is an example of a healthy wound in which healing can be maximized. However, not all surgical wounds are uncomplicated, with maximal healing potential or the possibility of uneventful healing. For example, acute surgical wounds can occur in unhealthy tissues, in a compromised host, or as a result of unexpected or significant trauma. Surgical wounds may be allowed to heal by one of three methods: primary intention, secondary intention, and tertiary intention (Table 11–1). Wounds healing by primary intention are wounds with edges approximated and closed. Secondary wounds are wounds left open after surgery. Secondary healing wounds heal with scar tissue replacement in the tissue defect. Tertiary wound healing, or delayed primary closure, involves aspects of both primary and secondary wound healing. In tertiary wound healing the wound is left open initially and after a short period of time the edges are approximated and the wound is closed. Wound healing by secondary intention or dehisced wounds may not follow a timely and uneventful healing course and thus may be considered "chronic" wounds by some clinicians.[1] When does an acute wound become a chronic wound? The easiest and perhaps the least controversial defining characteristic of the acute wound that becomes chronic is failure to follow the normal wound healing temporal sequence. In general, the acute surgical wound should complete the proliferative phase of wound healing in 4 weeks. For example, the wound should have filled with granulation tissue and be resurfaced with epithelial tissue. Acute surgical wounds that progress at a slower pace or fail to progress can be considered chronic.

The surgical incision healing by primary intention might be described as the ideal wound for healing. The wound is controlled with attention to tissue handling and proper use of surgical instruments by the surgeon, and the wound edges are apposed and aligned immediately to decrease the risk of infection. The acute surgical incision wound healing by primary intention is the focus of this chapter.

FACTORS AFFECTING HEALING IN ACUTE WOUNDS

Healing in acute surgical wounds involves the interaction of extrinsic and intrinsic factors. Extrinsic factors relate to those agents outside the person, whereas intrinsic factors are those influencing the person internally or systemically.

Extrinsic Factors

The physical environment before and during surgery, the surgical preparation, the technique of the surgeon, and types of sutures are all examples of extrinsic factors affecting acute wound healing. Thus for the surgical wound, evaluation of the perioperative period is indicated, as it plays a role in the wound outcome. Wound infection is the major cause of surgical wounds' failure to progress through the healing process in a timely and uneventful manner. Operating room protocols, attention to instrumentation, and appropriate surgical technique are all means of decreasing the risk of infection and ensuring optimal healing from the outset for the surgical wound.

Table 11–1 Types of Surgical Wound Healing

Wound Healing Type	Definition
Primary intention	Wound edges approximated and closed at time of surgery
Secondary intention	Wound left open after surgery and allowed to heal with scar tissue replacing the tissue defect
Tertiary or delayed primary closure	After surgery, wound left open initially and after a short period of time the wound edges are approximated and the wound is closed

Preoperative Period

The length of time the patient spends in the hospital prior to surgery influences the rate of surgical wound infection. As the length of hospital time increases prior to surgery, the risk of wound infection increases.[2] Preparation of the operative site also influences the risk of wound infection. Showering immediately prior to surgery, using a hexachlorophene soap, has been shown to result in a decrease in infection rate, compared with not showering.[2] Shaving the operative area and the method used to shave the area have also been implicated in surgical wound infection.

Research Wisdom: *Operative Site Preparation*

Use of an electric razor, clipping hair, and not shaving the operative area are all associated with wound infection rates lower than those with use of a non-electric razor to shave the operative area.[2] Despite the research, however, most preparations still include non-electric shaving, most commonly performed in the operating room. The poor implementation of the research may be due to the absence of electric razors or clippers in the operating room.

Intraoperative Period

Limiting the infection rate intraoperatively is largely under the control of the surgeon. Sometimes infection control is hard to obtain. For example, the surgeon has limited power over the nature of the problem for which the surgery is performed, the operative site, and the general condition of the patient; all are more complicated factors that are not easily controlled. The type of surgical procedure influences the risk of infection. Surgical procedures are classified according to the risk of infection.[3] Table 11–2 presents wound classifications for surgery. Clean wounds are those nontraumatic injuries in which no inflammation is encountered during the procedure and there is no break in sterile technique. Clean-contaminated wounds are procedures wherein the gastrointestinal (GI) tract or respiratory tract is entered without significant contamination. A contaminated wound is one in which a major break in sterile technique or gross spillage from the gastrointestinal tract occurs. Procedures in which acute bacterial inflammation or pus is encountered with devitalized tissue or contamination are classified as dirty or infected wounds.

Increased length of time for the operative procedure increases the risk for wound infection significantly. One study found that the infection rate doubled each hour the surgical procedure continued.[2] Strict adherence by operating room personnel to a protocol has also resulted in decreased wound infection rates.[4]

The surgeon must be concerned with wound tension, vascular supply, and proper surgical technique. If the wound cannot be closed without a significant amount of tension or if the vascular supply is poor, there is increased risk of dehiscence and infection.[5] Suturing technique can assist with optimal wound healing outcomes. Use of buried sutures can improve primary wound healing by decreasing potential dead space underneath the incision, giving tensile support for 4 to 6 weeks while the wound is still weak, and decreasing tension on the apposed wound edges.[5] Surface sutures may provide additional concerns for optimal healing because they provide additional "wounds" to heal alongside the incision.

Postoperative Period

The stress response associated with surgery has also been implicated as a cause of impaired wound healing. The stress of surgery is known to stimulate the sympathetic nervous system with a resultant sympathetic nervous system–mediated vasoconstriction. The effect of high levels of circulating catecholamines in the immediate postoperative period causes the resulting vasoconstriction with factors leading to the trigger of the sympathetic nervous system, including hypoxia, hypothermia, pain, and hypovolemia.[6] In the immediate postoperative period measures of subcutaneous tissue/wound oxygenation are lower after major operations

Table 11–2 Surgical Wound Classifications

Wound Classification	Surgical Label	Definition
I	Clean	• Nontraumatic injuries • No inflammation found during procedure • No break in sterile technique
II	Clean-contaminated	• Procedures involving GI or respiratory tract • No significant contamination
III	Contaminated	• Major break in sterile technique • Gross spillage from GI tract
IV	Dirty or infected	• Acute bacterial inflammation found • Pus encountered • Devitalized tissue encountered

and correlate with extensive, more complex surgical procedures.[6] Attempts to restore tissue and wound oxygen deficits relate to minimizing the risks of hypothermia, pain, hypovolemia, and hypoxia simultaneously in the immediate postoperative period.

Clinical Wisdom: *Maximizing Wound Healing*

Critical measures to maximize wound healing in the immediate postoperative period include all of the following. Keep the patient

- Warm
- Well hydrated, intravenously or orally
- Pain free by use of patient-controlled analgesia if possible
- Well oxygenated by use of supplemental oxygen if needed

Thermoregulatory responses are diminished in the surgical patient because of the prolonged exposure to the cold operating room environment. Patients treated with active rewarming by use of heated blankets during the recovery period respond with a faster return of normal tissue/wound oxygen levels than do those allowed to return to normothermia without rewarming interventions.[6] Routine use of measures to warm the patient actively during the surgical procedure, such as warming blankets and the use of warmed intravenous fluids along with active monitoring during surgery, help prevent thermoregulatory problems. It is easier to prevent thermoregulatory problems than to remedy thermoregulatory problems.

Correcting hypovolemia with adequate fluid infusion prevents continuing vasoconstriction caused by hypovolemia. Fluid replacement occurs simultaneously with rewarming efforts. Assessment and management of pain and tissue perfusion are also recommended to ensure optimal wound healing.[6]

Additional factors crucial to optimal surgical wound healing in the postoperative period are intrinsic factors that can be controlled, which are discussed in the following section.

Intrinsic Factors

Intrinsic factors affecting healing of the acute surgical wound are those that influence the person systemically. Intrinsic factors include age, concurrent conditions, nutritional status, and oxygenation and tissue perfusion.

Age

The physiologic changes that occur with aging place the older individual at higher risk for poor wound healing outcomes. Decreased elastin in the skin and differences in collagen replacement influence healing in older adults.[7] A de-

---

Clinical Wisdom: *Risk of Delayed Wound Resurfacing in the Older Adult*

The delay in wound resurfacing puts the older patient at risk for wound infection. Daily wound assessments and use of topical dressings for protection are required for a longer period of time than necessary for younger patients.

---

creased rate of replacement of cells affects the rate of wound healing and, in particular, reepithelialization of the skin.[7]

Immune system function declines with age, and this may account for increased risk of infection in older adults. The microorganisms proliferate in the wound before they can be removed, due to the diminished immune response. Older adults present with chronic diseases, circulatory changes, and nutritional problems, which increase the risk for poor or delayed wound healing. Decreased motor coordination and diminished sensory function increase the potential for injury, wound complications, and repeated wounding at the same site.

Concurrent Conditions

The presence of certain diseases, conditions, or treatments can influence wound healing outcomes. Diabetes mellitus is one condition that interferes with wound healing. Diabetes is associated with small vessel disease, neuropathy, and problems specific to glucose control—all of which predispose the person to impaired wound healing. Diabetic wound healing problems include increased risk of infection, delayed epithelialization, impaired or delayed collagen synthesis, and slowed wound contraction and closure.[8] Hyperglycemia can affect the cellular response to wounding. There may be a delayed response or impaired functioning of the leukocyte and fibroblast cells, both of which are essential for wound repair.[8]

The effect of surgery on the diabetic patient can be dramatic. The diabetic responds to the stress of surgery by releasing a series of hormones: epinephrine, glucagon, cortisol, and growth hormone. The stress hormones reduce the amount of circulating insulin while increasing circulating glucose. Elevated glucose levels can reduce the effectiveness of neutrophils' phagocytotic function and alter the deposition of collagen by fibroblasts, leading to a decrease in wound tensile strength.[8] Elevated glucose levels can also lead to cellular malnutrition, as insulin is the key for allowing nutrient use in cells. Because glucose is not able to be used as energy, proteins and fats are used as fuel, depleting necessary substrates for wound healing. The ability to control the glucose level in the postoperative period is probably advantageous for positive wound healing outcomes in the diabetic. Maintaining serum glucose levels below 200 mg/dL is recommended for patients with wounds.[3] In the immediate postoperative period, close monitoring of blood glucose and insulin supplements as indicated are required for adequate wound healing. Careful attention to blood glucose levels can assist significantly in positive outcomes and prevent an acute surgical wound from becoming a chronic wound.

Clinical Wisdom: *Urine Glucose Levels*

Urine glucose levels are not sensitive enough to provide good glucose control because of the high renal threshold for glucose (approximately 180 mg/dL). The use of blood glucose monitoring for more definitive management is a critical assessment strategy.

Other conditions also affect wound healing. Cardiovascular disease presents risks for wound healing because of the associated perfusion alterations, impaired blood flow, and vascular disease. Atherosclerosis is a common cause of inadequate perfusion of wounds.[9] Immunocompromised patients are an additional group at risk for poor healing outcomes. The immune system plays a significant role in wound healing, and any impairment (eg, aging, malnutrition, and cancer) can have serious sequelae for the patient with a wound.

Treatments that affect wound healing include steroids, anti-inflammatory drugs, antimitotic drugs, and radiation therapy. Steroids inhibit all phases of wound healing, affecting phagocytosis, collagen synthesis, and angiogenesis. The effects of steroids can be reversed with the use of topical vitamin A. The vitamin A is applied directly to the wound and acts as an inflammatory agent. Vitamin A is appropriate to apply to open wound beds. Wounds healing by primary intention, closed with edges well approximated, may not be appropriate candidates for topical vitamin A.

Clinical Wisdom: *Vitamin A Use for Wounds*

The usual dose of topical vitamin A is 1,000 U applied three times a day to the open wound bed for 7 to 10 days.

Other anti-inflammatory drugs also inhibit wound healing, with effects seen predominantly in the inflammatory phase. Cancer therapies, antimitotic medications, and radiation therapy work by impeding the normal cell cycle in rapidly dividing cells. The antimitotic activity interferes with new tissue generation in the wound. In addition, radiation therapy has both acute effects on cellular function and long-term sequelae for healing. The long-term effects of radiation therapy on wound healing are caused by hypoperfusion of tissues in the irradiated field. Hypoperfusion induced by irradiation is due to damage, deterioriation, and fibrosis of the vasculature.[3]

Nutritional Status

Adequate nutrition is essential for wound healing. In the healthy surgical patient malnutrition may not be an issue. However, with the population aging and more procedures being performed on older adults, nutritional status is a concern for wound healing. Adequate amounts of calories, proteins, fats, carbohydrates, vitamins, and minerals are all required for wound repair. Inadequate amounts of any nutrients negatively influence wound healing.[10]

Proteins are needed for neovascularization, fibroblast proliferation, collagen synthesis, and wound remodeling. Amino acids are the structural components of proteins and are essential parts of deoxyribonucleic acid (DNA) and ribonucleic acid (RNA). DNA and RNA provide the pattern for cell mitosis and enzymes required for tissue generation. Protein malnutrition results in loss of body stores of amino acids and insufficient substrates for wound repair and new tissue growth.

Carbohydrates and fats provide necessary energy required for cellular function. When there are inadequate amounts of carbohydrates and fats (calorie malnutrition), the body uses catabolism to break down proteins in order to meet energy requirements. Glucose balance and available essential fatty acids are essential substrates for wound healing.

Vitamins and minerals play an important role in wound healing. Several vitamins and minerals have specific functions for wound healing. Vitamin A is a fat-soluble vitamin and is responsible for supporting epithelialization, angiogenesis, and collagen formation. It is also important for the inflammatory phase of wound healing. The water-soluble B vitamins are cofactors in enzymatic reactions. Vitamin C has been associated with wound healing. Vitamin C is essential for angiogenesis and collagen synethesis. Vitamin C also supports fibroblast function and is critical for leukocyte function. For patients with wounds, infection, or significant injury, supplemental vitamin C is often provided to assist in meeting the increased metabolic needs and wound healing needs. Consensus on specific guidelines for appropriate supplemental doses of vitamin C is not available; however, megadoses of vitamin C have not been proven beneficial. Vitamin C use and elimination increase with exercise, stress, injury, increases in metabolic rate, and smoking. Vitamin D is required for bone healing and absorption of calcium, which is important in enzyme systems. Vitamin K is necessary for coagulation and hemostasis. Vitamin E is used for fat metabolism; excess amounts are not beneficial to wound healing.

Clinical Wisdom: *Vitamin E and Wound Healing*

Many people think that vitamin E has healing properties. In fact, vitamin E delays healing and fibrosis.[10] It is the delay of fibrosis or scarring that may be responsible for decreased scar formation at the injury site.

Minerals also play a role in wound healing, *usually*; the minerals of concern are zinc and iron. Zinc plays an essential role in enzyme systems and immune system function and is a cofactor for collagen synethesis. Zinc deficiency contributes to disruption in granulation tissue formation, diminished tensile strength, dehiscence, and evisceration.[10] Low levels of zinc are found in older adults and low-income patients, with losses associated with diarrhea, renal failure, diuretic and laxative use, and parenteral and enteral nutrition.[11] Iron is a cofactor in collagen synthesis and acts to transport oxygen. Iron deficiency may be present in those with changes in eating habits, intestinal damage, or increased metabolic needs.

Oxygenation and Perfusion

Adequate wound oxygenation is essential for wound healing. The initial injury causes hypoxia, and the resultant growth factor release supports initial capillary budding. Oxygen is influential in angiogenesis, fibroblast function, epithelialization, and resistance to infection.[12–14] Tissue perfusion is intertwined with tissue oxygenation. Satisfactory tissue perfusion is essential for oxygenation. Ample circulating blood volume carries oxygen-rich hemoglobin to the tissues. Tissue perfusion alone, however, does not guarantee wound oxygenation. Problems related to tissue perfusion and oxygenation may be due to cardiovascular or pulmonary disease as well as other conditions such as hypovolemia. Thus, maintaining vascular volume is critical for ensuring adequate tissue perfusion. The clinician must balance fluid replacement to prevent both underhydration and overhydration. Excess hydration can lead to hypervolemia and edema, which may decrease tissue oxygenation. To optimize oxygenation in the presence of adequate tissue perfusion, use of pulmonary hygiene interventions, assessment and monitoring of tissue oxygen levels, and low-flow supplemental oxygen may be warranted.[15] Pulmonary hygiene, including incentive spirometry, deep breathing and coughing, and postural drainage, improves the pulmonary toilet and increases the likelihood of adequate oxygenation of the wound. Low-flow oxygen can saturate hemoglobin so that the supply to the tissue is ample. Promoting activity such as repositioning and early ambulation can also be beneficial for peripheral tissue perfusion and oxygenation.[15] Oxygenation and perfusion are vital to wound healing, and postoperative interventions to improve the circulatory and oxygen-carrying capacity of the tissues or blood (the oxygen saturation of tissues) can enhance wound healing.

ASSESSMENT OF THE ACUTE SURGICAL WOUND

Assessment of the acute surgical wound involves physical examination of the wound site and surrounding wound tissues in relation to the wound healing process (Figure 11–1). Physical examination of the wound and the surrounding tissues includes measurement of the incision; observation of the wound tissues with attention to epithelial resurfacing, wound closure, wound exudate, and surrounding wound tissues; and palpation of the incision with attention to collagen deposition and surrounding tissues. The linear measurement of the length of the incision and the anatomic location of the incision provide a baseline measure. Measure the length of the incision in centimeters.

Observation and palpation of the incision line provides insight to the healing process that occurs in the underlying tissues. Healing proceeds in the surgical incision as it does in other wounds with inflammation—proliferation of new tissues and remodeling. In the surgical incision the wound healing processes are not always visible. Thus, the standard for assessment of healing may be best based on time since the surgical injury. It is important for clinicians to track the amount of time postsurgery, since the healing progress of the wound can be measured against the standard time expectations for acute wound repair. Knowledge of the wound healing process provides a critical foundation for assessment of the acute surgical incision. During the inflammatory process, assessment focuses on identification of signs and symptoms of inflammation, evaluation of wound closure materials and wound dressings, and appraisal of epithelial resurfacing. The central point during the proliferation phase of wound healing is evaluation of collagen deposition, wound exudate, and tissues surrounding the incision. Assessment during the remodeling phase is directed toward examination of collagen remodeling at the incisional site.

Incisional Assessment during the Inflammatory Phase

The major assessment finding in the first 4 days postoperatively is the identification of inflammation. The surgical incision may feel warm to the touch, and there may be surrounding erythema and edema at the incision site. Signs of inflammation are expected and normal during the first 4 days postoperatively.

> **Clinical Wisdom:** *Signs of Inflammation*
>
> It is normal to observe signs of inflammation such as warmth, erythema or discoloration, pain, and edema at the incisional wound site during the first few days after surgery.

Patients with immune system compromise due to age, a disease process, or therapy (such as steroid treatments) may not be able to mount an effective inflammatory process, thus

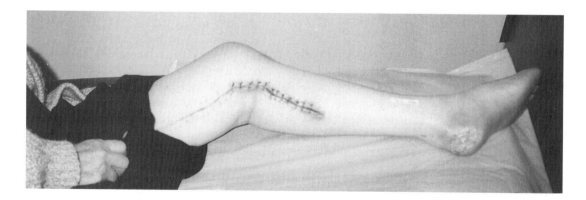

Figure 11–1 Surgical incision healing by primary intention. Note the lack of wound edge approximation and no healing ridge at the posterior half of the incision. Sutures remain present along the posterior incision. Courtesy of Evonne Fowler, MN, RN, CETN, Banning, California.

the signs of inflammation at the incision are not visible. The lack of inflammation at the incision site is an indication of immune system compromise. Thus, an abnormal finding during the first 4 days after surgery is an incision with no indication of inflammation. The process of epithelial resurfacing also occurs during the inflammatory phase of wound healing.

In the acute surgical incision, new epidermal tissues are generated quickly because of the presence of intact hair follicles and sebaceous and sweat glands and the short distance the epithelial cells must travel to resurface the incision. The surgical incision is resurfaced with epithelium within 72 hours postsurgery. The new epidermis provides a barrier to bacterial organisms and, to a small degree external trauma. The tensile strength of the incision is relatively weak and the incision is not able to withstand force.

The astute clinician can observe changes in the new incision indicating the presence of new epithelial tissue. The incision is evaluated for the close approximation of the wound edges and color of the incision line. Wound edges should appear well aligned with no tension observed.

Clinical Wisdom: *Incisional Color Changes*

As the new epithelial tissue migrates across the incision, the color of the incision may change from bright red to pink; although this is not observed in all patients, it is a useful clinical change that demonstrates maturing epithelial tissue.

A wound dressing is no longer necessary to prevent bacterial contamination of the incision once epithelial resurfacing has occurred. However, the wound dressing has other benefits at this point. Some clinicians suggest that the presence of the dressing at this point may be a reminder of the wound's presence and the need to use care in the wound area. The dressing provides a physical barrier to rough edges of clothing to limit local irritation, and the dressing can help the patient to include the wound in a new body image by allowing gradual viewing of the wound.

Wound closure materials are assessed for the reaction of the surrounding incisional tissues. The use of sutures, of any type, to approximate the wound edges creates small wounds alongside the incision wound. The wounds from the sutures increase the inflammation at the wound site and can cause ischemia if the sutures are pulled taut with increased tension, either from poor technique or wound edema postoperatively. The continued presence of sutures or staples provides additional tensile strength for the wound, but the sutures can also cause increased risk of infection and the potential for wound ischemia. Use of Steristrip tapes for wound closure or early removal of sutures with Steristrip tape replacement can decrease the problems associated with sutures. Removal of the wound sutures or staples in a timely manner is a proactive healing intervention. Removal of sutures in healthy surgical patients in 7 to 10 days postoperatively can be used as a general guideline depending on surgical site.

Incisional Assessment during the Proliferative Phase

Palpation of the surgical incision reveals the underlying process of collagen deposition. The new collagen tissues can be palpated as a firmness along the incision, extending 1 cm on either side of the incision.[4] This firmness to the tissues caused by new collagen deposition in the wound area is called the healing ridge. The healing ridge should be palpable along the entire length of the incision between day 5 and day 9 postoperatively.[4] If the healing ridge is not palpable within 5 to 9 days, the wound is at risk for dehiscence or infection.[4]

Evaluation of surgical incisional wound exudate requires knowledge of what wound exudate is expected in the course of healing. The character and the amount of the exudate changes as wound healing progresses. The wound exudate immediately after surgery is bloody. Within 48 hours the wound drainage becomes serosanguineous in nature and finally the exudate is serous. The amount of the wound exudate should gradually decrease throughout the healing period. An increase in wound exudate usually indicates compromised wound healing caused by infection. New drainage from a previously healed incision heralds wound dehiscence, infection, and in some cases fistula formation.

The tissues immediately surrounding the incision should be observed and palpated for the presence of edema and induration and for color changes. The presence of edema retards the wound healing process, as the excess fluids in the tissues provide an obstacle to angiogenesis and raise the potential for wound ischemia. Skin color changes may indicate the presence of bruising or hematoma formation caused by surgery. The skin color will appear dark red or purple. Skin color changes may also indicate impending infection. Signs of erythema, warmth, and edema and increased pain at the incision wound are indicators of possible wound infection. Evaluation of the healing ridge, wound exudate, and surrounding incisional tissues provides information on the progress of the proliferative phase of wound healing.

Incisional Assessment during the Remodeling Phase

The remodeling phase of wound healing is best assessed in the surgical incision by evaluation of the color of the incision. As the scar tissue is remodeled and organized structurally, the color of the tissue changes. The remodeling phase of wound healing can last 1 to 2 years. The incision color changes throughout the first year, gradually changing from bright red or pink to a silvery gray or white. The tensile strength of the wound gradually increases over the first year, eventually achieving approximately 80% of the original strength of the tissues. The main focus of interventions at this stage is to limit force on the wound site. Interventions to limit force and tension at the wound site include teaching the patient to avoid heavy lifting, bending, or straining at the site.

MANAGEMENT OF THE ACUTE SURGICAL WOUND

Management of the surgical incision includes attention to factors that affect wound healing as addressed earlier, as well as dressing care. The surgical dressing includes the primary and secondary dressing. The primary, or first, surgical dressing is the dressing in direct contact with the wound. The direct wound contact requires that the primary dressing be nontraumatic to the wound. The primary dressing provides absorption of drainage, maintains a sterile wound environment, and serves as a physical barrier to further wound trauma. The primary dressing should be nonadherent to the wound site. The traditional gauze dressing becomes adherent to the new incision and upon removal causes new tissue injury. Use of nonadherent absorptive dressings can facilitate wound healing because the nonharmful nature of the dressings allows wound healing to proceed.

The primary dressing absorbs wound exudate and wicks it away from the wound site, allowing the exudate to be absorbed into the secondary dressing. Secondary wound dressings provide increased absorptive capacity or hold the primary dressing in place. Secondary wound dressings are applied on top of the primary dressing and may be composed of the same materials as the primary dressing. The secondary dressing plays an important role for wounds when increased amounts of wound exudate are anticipated. The secondary dressing absorbs drainage from the primary dressing and wicks the exudate away from the wound bed and into the absorbent material of the dressing.

Clinical Wisdom: *Surgical Incisional Dressings*

The vast majority of primary intention surgical wound dressings continue to be gauze. Conversion to moist wound healing in the immediate postoperative period may facilitate wound healing and provide for patient comfort when changing dressings. Education of the surgeon on "better" primary wound dressings is also helpful.

Securing the wound dressing is usually done with the use of tape. Premature and frequent dressing changes can damage the tissues surrounding the incisional wound and negatively affect wound healing. Use of Montgomery straps, skin sealants, or hydrocolloid frames around the wound and underneath the tape can eliminate skin stripping around the incision wound from frequent dressing changes. Frequent dressing changes are more likely to be a problem with wounds healing by secondary intention, tertiary intention, or draining wounds.

SECONDARY AND TERTIARY INTENTION WOUND HEALING

Surgical wounds left open to heal by secondary or tertiary intention have a reparative trajectory similar to that of chronic wounds. Secondary intention healing is allowing wounds to heal without surgical closure. Wounds healing by secondary intention must heal by scar tissue replacement. The tissue defect at the wound site must fill with new collagen tissue during the proliferative phase of wound healing. The inflammatory phase of wound healing may be prolonged because of the contaminated nature of the wound.

Tertiary intention is a combination of both primary and secondary intention wound healing. The wound is allowed to heal secondarily and then primarily closed for final healing.[5] Tertiary wound healing is designed for specialized wounds in which primary intention is preferred but not possible at the time of wounding. The delay in primary closure may be to clear infection, allow some wound contracture, or create a healthy granulation base for a graft.[5]

Most surgical wounds left to heal by secondary or tertiary intention are those in which the risk of infection is increased or the tissue loss is such that the wound edges cannot be approximated without unacceptable tension on the incision. Reversal of both conditions—infection and extensive tissue loss—can be maximized in the early weeks following surgery. The administration of systemic antibiotics, when appropriate, and careful wound observation and care can lessen infection risk. The process of wound contraction and proliferation of granulation tissue occurs as the healing response attempts to decrease the total surface area of the wound[5] and to decrease the tissue loss.

The primary wound dressing takes critical importance in the wound healing by secondary or tertiary intention. Nonadherent, absorptive dressings optimize wound healing for secondary and tertiary intention wounds. Assessment of the wound for signs and symptoms of infection includes evaluation of the character and amount of wound exudate and examination of the wound and surrounding tissues for erythema, edema, induration, heat, and pain. Wounds healing by secondary or tertiary intention should be evaluated using the same parameters used for chronic wounds. Evaluate the wound size and depth, the presence or absence of necrotic tissue, the characteristics and amount of exudate, the condition of the surrounding tissues, and the presence of the healing characteristics of granulation and epithelialization.

OUTCOME MEASURES

Outcome measures for acute surgical incisions relate to healing progress according to time since injury. The outcome measures for incisional wounds are presented according to the time frame since surgery.

Postoperative Day 1 through Day 4

The following signs and symptoms represent measures of positive outcomes for acute surgical incision wounds. The presence of an inflammatory response, including erythema or skin discoloration, edema, pain, and increased temperature at the incision site during the first 4 days after surgery is a normal healing response. The lack of inflammation at the new surgical incision is a negative outcome. Wound exudate should be bloody in character initially, and toward day 3 and day 4 change to serosanguineous in nature. The amount of wound exudate should gradually decrease from a moderate amount to scant exudate by day 4. Many surgical wounds have no exudate past day 2 or 3, especially facial wounds. Failure of the wound exudate to decrease in amount and to change in character from bloody to serosanguineous is a negative indicator for healing. Epithelial resurfacing should be complete by day 4. The incision appears bright pink as opposed to the initial red color of the incision. Lack of epithelial resurfacing of the surgical incision indicates delayed healing and less than optimal outcomes.

One negative outcome that can occur at any time during the postoperative course of the patient is the development of a hematoma (swelling or mass of blood, usually clotted, confined in the tissues and caused by a break in a blood vessel). External evidence of hematoma formation includes swelling or edema at the site, a soft or boggy feel to the tissues initially, which may be followed by induration at the site, and color change of the skin (similar to bruising).

Postoperative Day 5 through Day 9

The major healing outcome in the surgical incision on days 5 through 9 is the presence of the healing ridge along the entire length of the incision. The healing ridge indicates new collagen deposition in the wound site. Lack of development or incomplete development of the healing ridge may be prodromal to wound dehiscence and wound infection. A defi-

---

Case Study:
Lack of Inflammatory Response Postoperatively

M.J., a 71-year-old Caucasian woman, was admitted for bowel surgery with resection of the descending colon and low anterior anastomosis. M.J.'s history included long-term steroid therapy for rheumatoid arthritis. On postoperative day 1 her midline incision primary dressing showed evidence of bright red bleeding. The wound edges were well approximated with staples as the closure material. Assessment of the incision on postoperative days 2 and 3 revealed no evidence of any edema, warmth, erythema, or discoloration at the incision site. Exudate was moderate and serosanguineous to seropurulent in nature. By postoperative day 4, the incision was not fully resurfaced with new epithelial tissue, and signs of inflammation, although now present, were diminished and the exudate remained seropurulent and moderate in amount. She showed signs of confusion and agitation (signs of infection in older adults); lab tests confirmed the presence of wound infection. In this case, the absent signs of inflammation were early warning signs of impaired healing and wound infection.

---

cient or nonexistent healing ridge is a negative outcome measure for wound healing. Wound exudate character should change from serosanguineous to serous and gradually disappear over days 4 to 6. The exudate amount should diminish from a minimal amount to none present. Any increase in the amount of wound exudate during days 5 through 9 should be viewed as a negative outcome and heralds probable wound infection.

The suture materials should begin to be removed from the incisional site during days 5 to 9. Adhesive tape strips or Steristrips may be used to provide additional wound tensile strength. Failure to remove any of the wound suture materials during days 5 through 9 may indicate a negative outcome for the wound.

Continued signs of inflammation at the incision site during days 5 through 9 are indicative of delayed wound healing. Signs of erythema or edema, extensive pain, or increased temperature at the incision wound during this time frame indicate that wound healing is not normal. Prolonged inflammation may occur as a result of underlying infection, immunocompromise, or continued trauma at the wound site. Documentation of all characteristics of the incision and healing are important for continuity of care throughout the wound recovery period but especially during this time frame, as the patient will likely be changing health care settings. For example, the surgical patient is often discharged from the acute care hospital to the home setting very soon after surgery.

Clinical Wisdom:
Documentation of Incisional Wound Healing

Documentation should include all of the following:

- Time since surgery in days
- Location
- Size in centimeters
- Closure materials present
- Color of the incision
- Type and amount of exudate
- Presence or absence of epithelial resurfacing
- Presence or absence of collagen deposition or healing ridge
- Actions taken for follow-up or referral as necessary
- Primary and secondary dressing as appropriate

Example: *Postop day 6 for a 12-cm midline abdominal incision with Steristrips present. Incision is completely reepithelialized with no exudate present. Incision is bright pink with healing ridge palpable along anterior 10 cm of incision. Posterior 2 cm of incision is soft and boggy to touch with no healing ridge palpable and erythema present. Physician notified of possible impaired healing. Dry gauze 2 × 2-inch dressing applied to posterior aspect of incision for protection of site.*

Postoperative Day 10 through Day 14

The major outcome measure for day 10 through day 14 is the removal of external incision suture materials. Internal or "buried" sutures remain in place. Failure to remove external suture materials during this time frame will prolong incision healing. Healing is delayed by increasing the risk of infection from the suture microwounds and the continued insult to the tissues by the presence of the foreign objects (the suture materials), prolonging the inflammatory response.

Postoperative Day 15 through 1 to 2 Years

During the end of the proliferative phase of wound healing and throughout the remodeling phase, attention is directed toward the changes in the incisional scar tissue. The collagen deposited alongside the incision is gradually realigned, restructured, and strengthened. The outcome measure for this time period is predominantly based on the changes in the incisional scar tissue color. The color of the incision changes from a bright pink after the initial epithelial resurfacing, gradually fading to pink and eventually turning a pearly gray or silvery white color. The noticeable induration and firmness associated with the healing ridge gradually softens during this time frame also. Negative outcomes include reinjury of the incisional line such as herniation of the wound site and complications associated with scarring such as keloid formation or hypertrophic scarring. Functional ability with the scar tissue becomes a key outcome measure for many surgical incisional wounds during this time frame.

A positive outcome measure at year 1 for the incisional wound includes lack of significant hypertrophic scarring or wound herniation, maximal functional ability with the new scar, and acceptable cosmetic results of healing with a silvery white or gray scar line. Tables 11–3 and 11–4 present the positive and negative outcome measures for time frames from the point of surgery to the end of remodeling.

CONCLUSION

There are many strategies clinicians use to optimize wound healing in the acute surgical incision. The astute and attentive clinician may diminish risk of complications, identify delayed or impaired healing, and provide for a supportive healing environment. The key to successful intervention for the patient with an acute surgical incision is knowledge of normal healing mechanisms and temporal expectations, knowledge of factors that impair wound healing, and vigilant attention to both. The case study at the end of this chapter helps to demonstrate the interaction between knowledge of normal healing and the time sequence associated with wound healing, and factors that interfere with normal healing.

REFERRAL CRITERIA

Watchful assessment of the patient with an acute surgical incision can influence prompt referral to the physician or advanced practice nurse for evaluation and intervention for complications of wound healing. The following criteria are helpful guidelines for referral of the patient to an-

Table 11–3 Positive Outcome Measures for Incisional Wound Healing

Outcome Measure	Days 1–4: Inflammation	Days 5–9: Proliferative	Days 10–14: Proliferative	Day 15–Years 1–2: Proliferative-Remodeling
Incision color	Red, edges approximated	Red, progressing to bright pink	Bright pink	Pale pink, progressing to white or silver in light-skinned patients; pale pink, progressing to darker than normal skin color in dark-skinned patients
Surrounding tissue inflammation	Edema, erythema, or skin discoloration; warmth, pain	None present	None present	None present
Exudate type	Bloody or sanguineous, progressing to serosanguineous and serous	None present	None present	None present
Exudate amount	Moderate to minimal	None present	None present	None present
Closure materials	Present, may be sutures or staples	Beginning to remove external sutures/staples	Sutures/staples removed, Steristrips or tape strips may be present	None present
Epithelial resurfacing	Present by day 4 along entire incision	Present along entire incision	Present	Present
Collagen deposition (healing ridge)	None present	Present by day 9 along entire incision	Present along entire incision	Present

other level of health care and to other specialties for their expertise:

- The patient with markedly increased bloody drainage during the immediate postoperative period may be at risk of hemorrhage from undetected leaking blood vessels in the surgical field.
- Patients who exhibit a change in exudate characteristics, from bloody or serosanguineous to purulent, should be evaluated for wound infection or abscess formation and treated with appropriate antimicrobial therapy.
- Any increase in amount of exudate after postoperative day 4 is indicative of wound infection or abscess formation and, as above, requires primary care provider evaluation and appropriate antimicrobial therapy.
- The absence of a healing ridge along the entire length of the incision wound by postoperative day 9 indicates

impaired healing and, often, abscess formation. Prompt referral to the primary care provider usually results in drainage of the abscess area, antimicrobial therapy, and a wound left to heal by secondary intention.
- The patient with the presence of signs and symptoms of wound infection, including erythema, edema, elevated temperature, and increased pain along the incision after day 4, *and/or* signs of systemic infection, including elevated temperature, elevated white blood cell count, or confusion in the older adult, requires evaluation. These signs and symptoms suggest a wound infection, and the primary care provider should evaluate and treat appropriately.
- The patient with a frank wound dehiscence or fistula formation requires evaluation by the primary care provider, usually the surgeon, and may need a referral to an enterostomal therapy (ET) nurse (specializing in management of draining wounds) for management.

Table 11–4 Negative Outcome Measures for Incisional Wound Healing

Outcome Measure	Days 1–4: Inflammation	Days 5–9: Proliferative	Days 10–14: Proliferative	Day 15–Years 1–2: Proliferative-Remodeling
Incision	Red, edges approximated but tension evident on incision line	Red, edges may not be well approximated; tension on incision line evident	May remain red, progressing to bright pink	Prolonged epithelial resurfacing, keloid or hypertrophic scar formation
Surrounding tissue inflammation	*No* signs of inflammation present: *no* edema, *no* erythema or skin discoloration, *no* warmth, and minimal pain at incision site; hematoma formation	Edema, erythema, or skin discoloration; warmth, pain at incision site; hematoma formation	Prolonged inflammatory response with edema, erythema, or skin discoloration; warmth and pain; hematoma formation	If healing by secondary intention, may be stalled at a plateau (chronic inflammation or proliferation), with no evidence of healing and continued signs of inflammation
Exudate type	Bloody or sanguineous, progressing to serosanguineous and serous	Serosanguineous and serous to seropurulent	Any type of exudate present	Any type of exudate present
Exudate amount	Moderate to minimal	Moderate to minimal	Any amount present	Any amount present
Closure materials	Present, may be sutures or staples	No removal of any external sutures/staples	Sutures/staples still present	For secondary intention healing, failure of wound contraction or edges not approximated
Epithelial resurfacing	Present by day 4 along entire incision	Not present along entire incision	Not present along entire incision, dehiscence evident	Not present *or* abnormal epithelialization, such as keloid or hypertrophic scarring
Collagen deposition (healing ridge)	None present	Not present along entire incision	Not present along entire incision, dehiscence evident	Abscess formation with wound left open to heal by secondary intention

SELF-CARE TEACHING GUIDELINES

The patient's and caregiver's instruction in self-care must be individualized to the type of surgical incision and the individual patient's wound, the specific incisional dressing management routine, the individual patient's learning style and coping mechanisms, and the ability of the patient/caregiver to perform procedures. The general self-care teaching guidelines in Exhibit 11–1 must be individualized for each patient and caregiver.

Case Study: *Incisional Wound Healing*

P.L., a 78-year-old African American man, was admitted for radical prostatectomy surgery for prostate cancer. P.L. has a history of diabetes mellitus, hypertension, obesity, and peripheral vascular disease. His diabetes is managed with oral hypoglycemic agents and an 1800-calorie diabetic diet (with which he is noncompliant). P.L. lives alone on a small pension and fixed income and is a smoker. He was admitted with a random blood sugar of 198 mg/dL.

Preoperatively

Assessment of P.L. revealed several risk factors for impaired healing: uncontrolled diabetes mellitus, obesity, advanced age, hypertension, and peripheral vascular disease. Control of blood sugar level was identified as a goal in the preoperative period, and P.L. was started on sliding-scale insulin therapy with blood glucose monitoring. P.L.'s history of hypertension and peripheral vascular disease put him at risk for poor tissue perfusion; thus, in the immediate postoperative period (days 1 and 2) he was put on supplemental oxygen per nasal cannula to optimize tissue oxygenation. Obesity is a risk factor for excess incision wound tension, which increases potential for poor perfusion of the incision wound due to the presence of excess subcutaneous fat.

Postoperative Day 4

P.L.'s 15-cm midline abdominal incision showed evidence of inflammation with edema, skin discoloration, and warmth at the site. There was evidence of epithelial resurfacing, and the incision line was bright pink. There was a continued minimal amount of serous drainage and staples remained in place. The primary gauze dressing was changed daily. Blood sugars ranged from 110 to 132 mg/dL on insulin therapy. Oxygen was administered the first 2 days postoperatively at 2 L per nasal cannula.

Postoperative Day 9

P.L. was discharged from the hospital to his home with home health care nursing follow-up. Upon discharge from the hospital, P.L.'s incision was bright pink with no exudate present. The incision was completely resurfaced with new epithelial tissue present along the entire incision, and half of the staples had been removed. A healing ridge was palpable along the anterior 13 cm of the wound but not palpable at the posterior aspect of the wound.

Postoperative Day 10

The home health nurse evaluated P.L.'s incision and found surrounding skin discoloration, increased pain, and edema present at the posterior aspect of the wound. No healing ridge was palpable at the posterior aspect of the wound, although collagen deposition was evident along the anterior 13 cm of the wound. Half of the original staples were still present in the incision line. The physician was notified, and P.L. was referred to the physician's office for evaluation of the incision.

Postoperative Day 12

The physician removed the remaining staples, performed an incision and drainage (I and D) of the posterior aspect of the incision in the office, started P.L. on systemic antibiotics, and left the posterior aspect of the wound open to heal by secondary intention, using moist saline gauze dressings.

Postoperative Day 15

P.L.'s posterior incision is 75% filled with granulation tissue and there is minimal serous exudate present. The anterior aspect of the incision is well healed and pale pink. P.L.'s incision wound went on to heal uneventfully by secondary intention over the next 10 days.

Exhibit 11–1 Self-Care Teaching Guidelines

Self-Care Guidelines Specific to Acute Surgical Incisions	Instructions Given (Date/Initials)	Demonstration *or* Review of Material (Date/Initials)	Return Demonstration *or* States Understanding (Date/Initials)
1. Type of incisional wound and specific cautions required a. No heavy lifting and other measures to prevent hernia formation			
b. Showering or bathing area			
c. Importance of adequate nutrition for wound healing			
2. Significance of wound exudate, incision wound tissue color, surrounding tissue condition, and presence of healing ridge			
3. Wound dressing care routine a. Wash hands, then remove old dressing and discard			
b. Clean wound with normal saline			
c. Apply primary dressing to wound			
d. Apply secondary dressing if appropriate			
e. Secure dressing with tape			
f. Universal precautions and dressing disposal			
g. Frequency of dressing changes			
4. Expected change in wound appearance during healing process a. Scheduled removal of closure materials			
b. Incision color change as wound heals (bright red or pink to pale pink and finally to silvery white or gray)			
5. When to notify the health care provider a. Signs and symptoms of wound infection (erythema, edema, pain, elevated temperature, change in exudate character or amount, discoloration in tissues surrounding incision wound)			
b. Absent or incomplete healing ridge along incision after postoperative day 9			
6. Importance of follow-up with health care provider			

REFERENCES

1. Lazarus GS, Cooper DM, Knighton DR, et al. Definitions and guidelines for assessment of wounds and evaluation of healing. *Arch Dermatol.* 1994;130:489–493.

2. Cruse PJE, Foord F. The epidemiology of wound infection: a ten-year prospective study of 62,939 wounds. *Surg Clin North Am.* 1980;60:27–40.

3. Stotts NA. Impaired wound healing. In: Carrieri-Kohlman VK, Lindsay AM, West CM, eds. *Pathophysiological Phenomena in Nursing: Human Responses to Illness.* 2nd ed. Philadelphia: W.B. Saunders Company; 1993:443–469.

4. Cooper DM. Acute surgical wounds. In: Bryant RA, ed. *Acute and Chronic Wounds: Nursing Management.* St. Louis, MO: Mosby–Year Book; 1992:91–104.

5. Moy LS. Management of acute wounds. *Dermatol Clin.* 1993; 11:759–766.

6. West JM. Wound healing in the surgical patient: influence of the perioperative stress response on perfusion. *AACN Clin Issues.* 1990;1:595–601.

7. Gerstein AD, Phillips TJ, Rogers GS, Gilchrest BA. Wound healing and aging. *Dermatol Clin.* 1993;11:749–757.

8. Rosenberg CS. Wound healing in the patient with diabetes mellitus. *Nurs Clin North Am.* 1990;25:247–261.

9. Weingarten MS. Obstacles to wound healing. *Wounds.* 1993;5:238–244.

10. Stotts NA, Washington DF. Nutrition: a critical component of wound healing. *AACN Clin Issues.* 1990;1:585–594.

11. Wagner PA. Zinc nutriture in the elderly. *Geriatrics.* 1985;40(3):111–125.

12. Jonsson K, Jensen JA, Goodson WH, Hunt TK. Wound healing in subcutaneous tissue of surgical patients in relation to oxygen availability. *Surg Forum.* 1986;37:86–89.

13. Pai MP, Hunt TK. Effect of varying oxygen tensions on healing of open wounds. *Surg Gynecol Obstet.* 1972;135:756–758.

14. Knighton DR, Silver IA, Hunt TK. Regulation of wound-healing angiogenesis: effect of oxygen gradients and inspired oxygen concentration. *Surgery.* 1981;90:262–269.

15. Whitney JD. The influence of tissue oxygen and perfusion on wound healing. *AACN Clin Issues.* 1990;1:578–584.

SUGGESTED READING

Bryant RA, ed. *Acute and Chronic Wounds: Nursing Management.* St. Louis, MO: Mosby–Year Book; 1992.

Mulder GD, Jeter KF, Fairchild PA. *Clinicians' Pocket Guide to Chronic Wound Repair.* Spartanburg, SC: Wound Healing Publications; 1992.

CHAPTER 12

Pressure Ulcers: Pathophysiology and Prevention

Barbara M. Bates-Jensen

PRESSURE ULCER DEFINITION

Pressure ulcers are areas of local tissue trauma usually developing where soft tissues are compressed between bony prominences and any external surface for prolonged time periods.[1,2] A pressure ulcer is a sign of local tissue necrosis and death. Pressure ulcers are most commonly found over bony prominences subject to external pressure. Pressure exerts the greatest force at the bony tissue interface; therefore, there may be significant muscle and subcutaneous fat tissue destruction underneath intact skin.

PRESSURE ULCER PATHOPHYSIOLOGY

Pressure ulcers are the result of mechanical injury to the skin and underlying tissues. The primary forces involved are pressure and shear.[3–7] Pressure is the perpendicular force or load exerted on a specific area, causing ischemia and hypoxia of the tissues. High pressure areas in the supine position are the occiput, sacrum, and heels. In the sitting position, the ischial tuberosities exert the highest pressure and the trochanters are affected in the side-lying position.[4,8]

As the amount of soft tissue available for compression decreases, the pressure gradient increases. Likewise, as the tissue available for compression increases, the pressure gradient decreases; thus most pressure ulcers occur over bony prominences where there is less tissue for compression and the pressure gradient within the vascular network is altered.[8] Figure 12–1 demonstrates this relationship.

The changes in the vascular network allow an increase in the interstitial fluid pressure, which exceeds the venous flow. This results in an additional increase in the pressure and impedes arteriolar circulation. The capillary vessels collapse and thrombosis occurs. Increased capillary arteriole pressure leads to fluid loss through the capillaries, tissue edema, and subsequent autolysis. Lymphatic flow is decreased, allowing further tissue edema and contributing to the tissue necrosis.[5,7,9–11]

Pressure, over time, occludes blood and lymphatic circulation, causing deficient tissue nutrition and buildup of waste products due to ischemia. If pressure is relieved before a critical time period is reached, a normal compensatory mechanism, reactive hyperemia, restores tissue nutrition and compensates for compromised circulation. If pressure is not relieved before the critical time period, the blood vessels collapse and thrombose. The tissues are deprived of oxygen, nutrients, and waste removal. In the absence of oxygen, cells use anaerobic pathways for metabolism and produce toxic byproducts. The toxic byproducts lead to tissue acidosis, increased cell membrane permeability, edema, and eventual cell death.[5,9]

Tissue damage may also be due to reperfusion and reoxygenation of the ischemic tissues or postischemic injury.[12,13] Oxygen is reintroduced into tissues during reperfusion following ischemia. This triggers oxygen-free radicals known as superoxide anion, hydroxyl radicals, and hydrogen peroxide, which induce endothelial damage and decrease microvascular integrity.

Time and Pressure

Ischemia and hypoxia of body tissues are produced when capillary blood flow is obstructed by localized pressure. How much pressure and what amount of time is necessary for ulceration to occur has been a subject of study for many years. In 1930 Landis,[14] using single-capillary microinjection techniques, determined normal hydrostatic pressure to be 32 mm

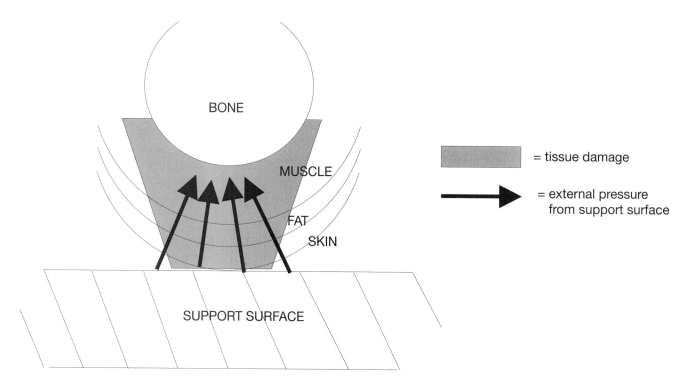

Figure 12–1 Pressure gradient at the bony prominence.

Hg at the arteriole end and 15 mm Hg at the venule end. His work has been the criterion for measuring occlusion of capillary blood flow. Generally, a range from 25 to 32 mm Hg is considered normal capillary blood flow and is used as the marker for adequate relief of pressure on the tissues.

Pressure is the greatest at the bony prominence and soft tissue interface and gradually lessens in a cone-shaped gradient to the periphery.[4,15,16] Thus, although tissue damage apparent on the skin surface may be minimal, the damage to the deeper structures can be severe. In addition, subcutaneous fat and muscle are more sensitive than the skin to ischemia. Muscle and fat tissues are more metabolically active and thus more vulnerable to hypoxia with increased susceptibility to pressure damage. The vulnerability of muscle and fat tissues to pressure forces explains pressure ulcers where large areas of muscle and fat tissue are damaged with undermining due to necrosis, yet the skin opening is relatively small.[10]

Intensity and Duration of Pressure

There is a relationship between intensity and duration of pressure in pressure ulcer development. Low pressures over a long period of time are as capable of producing tissue dam-

age as high pressures for shorter periods of time.[4] Tissues can tolerate higher cyclic pressures versus constant pressure.[17] Pressures differ in various body positions. Pressures are highest (70 mm Hg) on the buttocks in the lying position, and in the sitting position can be as high as 300 mm Hg over the ischial tuberosities.[4,8] These levels are well above the normal capillary closing pressure and are capable of causing tissue ischemia. When tissues have been compressed for prolonged periods of time, tissue damage continues to occur even after the pressure is relieved.[15] This continued tissue damage relates to changes at the cellular level that lead to difficulties with restoration of perfusion.

Figure 12–2 shows the relationship between time, pressure, and tissue destruction.

Four levels of skin breakdown occur depending on the amount of time exposed to unrelieved pressure.[18] Hyperemia can be observed within 30 minutes or less; it is manifested by redness of the skin and dissipates within 1 hour after pressure is relieved. Ischemia occurs after 2 to 6 hours of continuous pressure; the erythema is deeper in color and may take 36 hours or more to disappear after pressure is relieved. Necrosis is the third level and occurs after 6 hours of continuous pressure. The skin may take on a blue or gray color and become indurated. Damage that has progressed to this level disappears on an individual basis. Ulceration is the

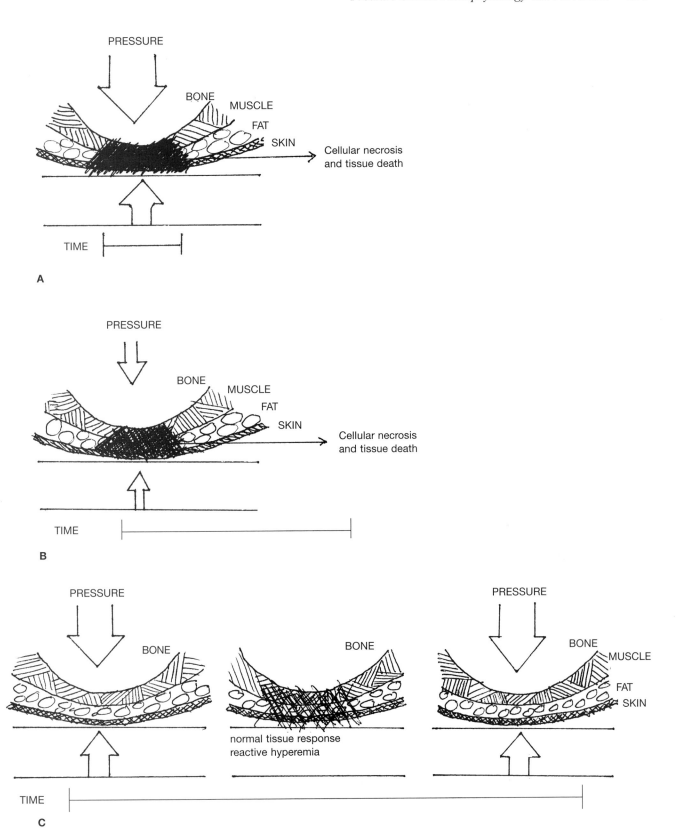

Figure 12–2 Relationship of time versus pressure. **A**, High pressures over a short period of time. **B**, Low pressures over a long period of time. **C**, Intermittent pressure.

fourth and final level and may occur within 2 weeks after necrosis with potential infection; it resolves on an individual basis.

In dark-skinned patients it is often difficult to discern redness or erythema of the skin. Redness and erythema may appear as a deepening of normal ethnic color or as a purple hue to the skin.[19,20] Other manifestations in dark-skinned patients are local changes in skin temperature and skin texture. The immediate response of inflammation of the tissues can be seen by an increase in skin temperature. As the tissues become more disturbed, the temperature decreases, signaling underlying tissue damage. Skin texture may feel hard and indurated, and observation of the skin may reveal heightened skin features or an orange peel appearance.[19,20] (See Chapter 3 for more information on assessment of the dark-skinned patient.)

CLINICAL PRESENTATION OF PRESSURE ULCERS

The clinical presentation of a pressure ulcer is a predictable cutaneous chain of events. The first clinical sign of pressure ulcer formation—blanchable erythema—presents as discoloration of a patch or flat, nonraised area of the skin larger than 1 cm. This discoloration presents as redness or erythema that varies in intensity from pink to bright red in light-skinned patients. In dark-skinned patients, the discoloration appears as a deepening of normal ethnic color or as a purple hue to the skin. Other characteristics include slight edema and increased temperature of the area. In light-skinned patients the severity of the tissue insult can be evaluated by testing for blanchability of tissues. After finger pressure is applied to the area, complete blanching occurs following by quick return of redness once the finger is removed. In dark-skinned patients, it is difficult to discern blanching. Use of temperature is a more valuable assessment of the severity of the tissue damage in the dark-skinned patient. Initial skin trauma and discoloration will exhibit an elevated skin temperature as compared with that of healthy tissues. The beginning clinical indicators of pressure ulceration all relate to the signs of inflammation in the tissues. At this beginning stage of damage, if the pressure is relieved the skin can return to normal in 24 hours.[21] If pressure is not relieved, the damage progresses.

Nonblanchable erythema involves more severe damage and is commonly the first stage of pressure ulceration. The color of the skin is more intense. It varies from dark red to purple or cyanotic in both light- and dark-skinned patients. Dark-skinned patients exhibit deepening of normal skin color, a purple or gray hue to the skin, and changes in skin texture with induration and an orange peel appearance.[19,20] Skin temperature is now cool, compared with healthy tissues, and the area may feel indurated. In light-skinned patients, nonblanchable erythema is detected by testing for blanching of tissues. The damage to tissues is more severe and is indicated by the inability of the tissues to blanch. This stage of tissue destruction is also reversible, although tissues may take 1 to 3 weeks to return to normal.[21]

The result of further deterioration in the tissues is evidenced as the epidermis is disrupted with subepidermal blisters, crusts, or scaling present. If properly treated the situation may resolve in 2 to 4 weeks.[21] The early pressure ulcer reflects continued tissue insult and progressive injury. The early ulcer is superficial with indistinct margins and a red shiny base. It is usually surrounded by nonblanchable erythema. If not dealt with aggressively, progression to a chronic, deep ulcer is inevitable. Superficial ulcers begin at the skin surface and progress to deeper layers. Deep ulcers do not originate at the skin surface; they begin at the bony prominence–soft tissue interface and spread to involve the skin structures.

The chronic deep ulcer usually has a dusky red wound base and does not bleed easily. It is surrounded by nonblanchable erythema or deepening of normal ethnic tone, induration, and warmth, and possibly is mottled. Undermining and tunneling may be present with a large necrotic cavity. Eschar formation may be a result of larger vessel damage from shearing force and may be the result of large vessel damage below skin level.[21] Eschar is the formation of an acellular dehydrated compressed area of necrosis, usually surrounded by an outer rind of blanchable erythema. Eschar formation indicates a full-thickness loss of skin.

Location

More than 95% of all pressure ulcers develop over five classic locations: sacral/coccygeal area, greater trochanter, ischial tuberosity, heel, and lateral malleolus.[6] Common pressure ulcer sites occur over bony prominences and depend on the patient's position; areas with large amounts of soft tissue between bone and skin are least susceptible to breakdown.[18] Meehan,[22] in a prevalence survey of 148 hospitals, found the sacrum the most common location of pressure ulcers and the trochanter the location of the most severe ulcers. Correct anatomic terminology is important in identification of the true location of the pressure ulcer. For example, many clinicians often document pressure ulcers as being located on the patient's hip. The hip, or iliac crest, is actually an uncommon location for pressure ulceration. The iliac crest is located on the front of the patient's body and rarely subject to pressure forces. The area most clinicians are referring to is correctly termed the greater trochanter. The greater trochanter is the bony prominence located on the side of the body, just above the proximal, lateral aspect of the thigh or "saddle-bag" area.

The majority of pressure ulcers occur on the lower half of the body. The location of the pressure ulcer may have an impact on clinical interventions. For example, the patient with a pressure ulcer on the sacral/coccygeal area with concomitant urinary incontinence will require treatments that address the incontinence problem. Ulcers in the sacral/coccygeal area are also more at risk for friction and shearing damage due the location of the wound. Figure 12–3 presents the usual locations of pressure ulcer development with correct anatomic terminology.

Pressure ulcers commonly occur over bony prominences, but ulcers can develop at any site where tissues have been compressed, causing tissue ischemia and hypoxia. Patients with contractures are at special risk for pressure ulcer development because of the internal pressure of the bony prominence and the abnormal alignment of the body and its extremities. (Refer to Chapter 13 on therapeutic positioning.)

Clinical Wisdom:
Contractures and Pressure Ulcer Formation

The compression of tissues may be greater in the presence of contractures, and the management of the contracture must be considered when assessing the patient for risk of pressure ulcer development.[23]

PRESSURE ULCER STAGING

Pressure ulcers are commonly classified according to grading or staging systems based on the depth of tissue destruction. The stage is determined on initial assessment by noting the deepest layer of tissue involved. The ulcer is not restaged

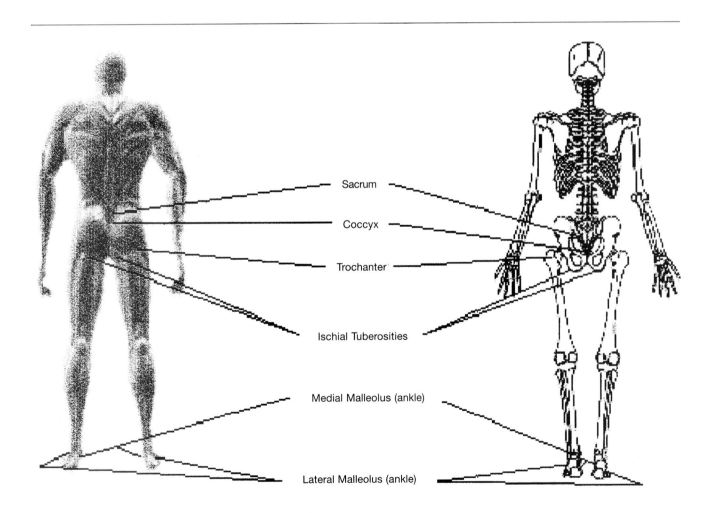

Sacrum

Coccyx

Trochanter

Ischial Tuberosities

Medial Malleolus (ankle)

Lateral Malleolus (ankle)

Figure 12–3 Anatomical locations. *Source:* Copyright © 1996, *Applied Health Science.*

unless deeper layers of tissue become exposed.[24] Historically, one problem in assessment was the lack of a universal staging system for classifying the severity of pressure ulcers. Many of the staging systems available are based on Shea's initial 1975 article[25] describing a method of classifying pressure sores. Shea believed that a pathology-based classification system would simplify communication for health care professionals, provide a mechanism for identification of pressure ulcers, and suggest a broad guide for determining whether operative care was needed. Shea defined each grade of pressure ulceration by the anatomic limit of soft tissue damage that could be observed. His numeric classification system suggested an orderly evolution of pressure ulceration. The National Pressure Ulcer Advisory Panel (NPUAP)[2] and the Agency for Health Care Policy and Research (AHCPR)[26] recommend use of a universal four-stage classification system to describe depth of tissue damage. The recommended system is similar to Shea's original system with the major exception being that of defining stage I lesions. Exhibit 12–1 shows the staging system recommended by the AHCPR and NPUAP.

The issue of pressure ulcer assessment and the use and misuse of staging classification systems is a subject of debate and controversy. Pressure ulcer development does not necessarily occur from one stage to the next, and there may be different etiologic factors for various stages. Ulcers do not heal by reverse staging. Staging systems measure only one characteristic of the wound and should not be viewed as a complete assessment independent of other indicators and should not be the sole criteria in determining treatment plans (see Chapter 3 on wound assessment). Staging classification systems do not assess for criteria in the healing process and hinder tracking of progress because of the inability of the staging system to demonstrate change over time. The staging system does not allow for movement within and between stages.[27] Many clinicians use the staging system as a measure of healing, despite the inherent difficulties associated with back staging or down staging (use of the stages in reverse order, for example, a wound moving from stage IV to stage II). Determining the stage of the pressure ulcer is a diagnostic tool for evaluating the level of tissues exposed. Once the stage of destruction is determined the stage should not change, even as the wound heals. In a full-thickness pressure ulcer (stage III or IV) the wound defect is filled with granulation tissue as the wound heals. The granulation tissue does not replace the structural layers of muscle, fat, and dermis that were present in the original tissues. Back staging of pressure ulcers is inappropriate use of the staging criteria and does not reflect physiologic healing phenomena.[27]

The terms *partial thickness* and *full thickness* are commonly used to describe wounds of various skin depths that heal by either regeneration or scar formation. Partial-thickness wounds involve only the epidermis and dermis. Full-thickness wounds involve complete destruction of the epidermis and dermis and extend into deeper tissues.

Exhibit 12–1 Pressure Ulcer Staging Criteria

Pressure Ulcer Stage	Definition
Stage I*	Nonblanchable erythema of intact skin; the heralding lesion of skin ulceration. In individuals with darker skin, discoloration of the skin, warmth, edema, induration, or hardness may also be indicators.
Stage II	Partial-thickness skin loss involving epidermis or dermis, or both. The ulcer is superficial and presents clinically as an abrasion, blister, or shallow crater.
Stage III	Full-thickness skin loss involving damage or necrosis of subcutaneous tissue, which may extend down to but not through underlying fascia. The ulcer presents clinically as a deep crater with or without undermining of adjacent tissue.
Stage IV	Full-thickness skin loss with extensive destruction, tissue necrosis, or damage to muscle bone or supporting structures (such as tendon, joint capsule).

* The National Pressure Ulcer Advisory Panel has recently considered an alternative definition of the stage I pressure ulcer. The definition under review is as follows: An observable pressure-related alteration of intact skin whose indicators, as compared to an adjacent or opposite area on the body, may include changes in skin color (red, blue, purple tones), skin temperature (warmth or coolness), skin stiffness (hardness, edema), and/or sensation (pain).

Superficial lesions involving the epidermis and dermis generally heal in days to weeks. Deeper lesions involving the subcutaneous tissues and muscle may require weeks to months to heal.[28] Tissue trauma extending to bone or joint structures may result in osteomyelitis and further prolong healing time. Ulcers involving the subcutaneous tissue layers may be obscured by necrosis or eschar and additionally may present as areas of both partial- and full-thickness tissue losses.

PRESSURE ULCER PREDICTION: RISK FACTOR ASSESSMENT

Discussion of pressure ulcer pathophysiology and etiology would not be complete without mention of other interacting factors. Pressure ulcers are physical evidence of multiple causative influences. Factors that contribute to pressure ulcer development can be thought of as those that affect the pressure force over the bony prominence and those that affect the tolerance of the tissues to pressure. The conceptual schema of Braden and Bergstrom[29] divides factors into categories according to the role played in eventual pressure ulcer development. Figure 12–4 illustrates Braden and Bergstrom's conceptual framework for pressure ulcer development.

Mobility, sensory loss, and activity level are related to the concept of increasing pressure. Extrinsic factors (shear, friction, and moisture) as well as intrinsic (nutrition, age, and arteriolar pressure) relate to the concept of tissue tolerance. Several additional areas may influence pressure ulcer development: emotional stress, temperature, smoking, and interstitial fluid flow.[30]

Pressure Factors

Immobility, inactivity, and decreased sensory perception all affect the duration and intensity of the pressure over the bony prominence. Immobility or severely restricted mobility is the most important risk factor for all populations and a necessary condition for the development of pressure ulcers. Mobility is the state of being movable. Thus the immobile patient cannot move, and facility or ease of movement is impaired. Exton-Smith and Sherwin[31] demonstrated that 90% of individuals with 20 or fewer spontaneous nocturnal body movements developed a pressure ulcer, while none of the persons with greater than 50 movements a night developed a pressure ulcer. Closely related to immobility is limited activity levels.

Research Wisdom: *Immobility*

Immobility or severely restricted mobility is the most important risk factor for all populations and a necessary condition for the development of pressure ulcers.

Activity is the production of energy or motion and implies an action. Activity is often clinically described by the ability of the individual to ambulate and move about. Those persons who are bed or chair bound, and thus inactive, are more at risk for pressure ulcer development.[26,32] A sudden change in activity level may signal significant change in health status and increased potential for pressure ulcer development. Sensory loss places patients at risk for compression of tissues and pressure ulcer development because the normal mechanism for translating pain messages from the tissues is dysfunctional.[24] Patients with intact nervous system pathways feel continuous local pressure, become uncomfortable, and change their position before tissue ischemia occurs. Patients with spinal cord injury have a higher incidence and prevalence of pressure ulcers.[33,34] Patients with paraplegia or quadriplegia are unable to sense increased pressure, and if their body weight is not shifted, pressure ulceration develops. Likewise, patients with changes in mental status functioning are at increased risk for pressure ulcer formation. They may not feel the discomfort from pressure, be alert enough to move spontaneously, remember to move, be too confused to respond to commands to move, or be physically unable to move.[24]

Extrinsic Factors

Shear

Extrinsic risk factors are those forces that make the tissues less tolerant of pressure. Extrinsic forces include shear, friction, and moisture. Shear is a parallel force. Whereas pressure acts perpendicularly to cause ischemia, shear causes ischemia by displacing blood vessels laterally and thus impeding blood flow to tissues.[35-37] Figure 12–5 shows the effect of shearing on the tissues.

Shear is caused by the interplay of gravity and friction. Shear is a parallel force that acts to stretch and twist tissues and blood vessels at the bony tissue interface and, as such, shear affects the deep blood vessels and deeper tissue structures. The most common circumstance for shear occurs in the bed patient in a semi-Fowler's position (semisitting position with knees flexed and supported by pillows on the bed or by elevation of the head of the bed; Figure 12–6). The

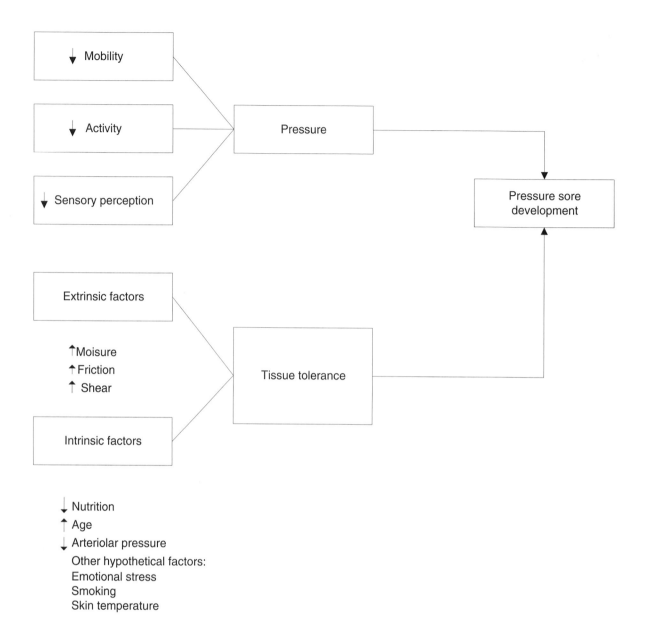

Figure 12–4 Factors contributing to the development of pressure ulcers. *Source:* Reprinted from *Rehabilitation Nursing, 12*(1), 9, with permission of the Association of Rehabilitation Nurses, 4700 W. Lake Avenue, Glenview, IL 60025-1485. Copyright © 1995. Association of Rehabilitation Nurses.

Bony Prominence
without Pressure

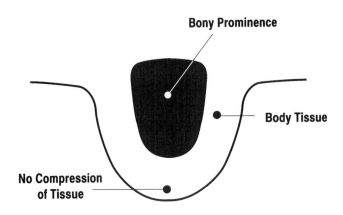

Bony Prominence
with Pressure

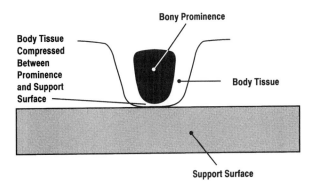

Bony Prominence
with Pressure plus Shear

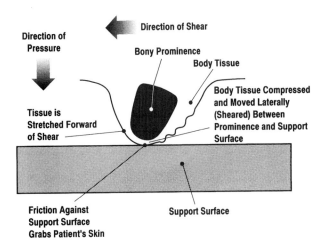

Figure 12–5 Effects of shearing and friction in conjunction with pressure on the skin. Courtesy of RIK Medical, Boulder, Colorado.

Shear Effect of Raising the Head of the Bed

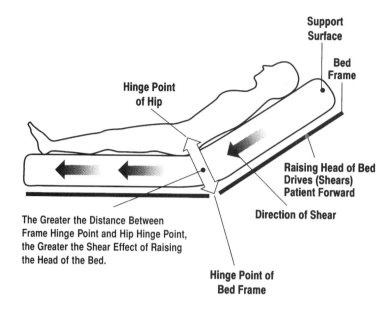

Support Surface

Bed Frame

Hinge Point of Hip

Raising Head of Bed Drives (Shears) Patient Forward

Direction of Shear

The Greater the Distance Between Frame Hinge Point and Hip Hinge Point, the Greater the Shear Effect of Raising the Head of the Bed.

Hinge Point of Bed Frame

Bottoming Out

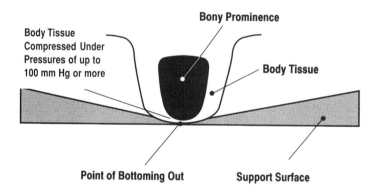

Bony Prominence

Body Tissue Compressed Under Pressures of up to 100 mm Hg or more

Body Tissue

Point of Bottoming Out

Support Surface

Figure 12–6 Semi-Fowler's position and shearing effect. Courtesy of RIK Medical, Boulder, Colorado.

patient's skeleton slides down toward the foot of the bed, but the sacral skin stays in place (with the help of friction against the bed linen). This produces stretching, pinching, and occlusion of the underlying vessels, producing ulcers with large areas of internal tissue damage and less damage at the skin surface.

Clinical Wisdom: *Shear Injury*

Shear is the reason many pressure ulcers are much larger than the bony prominence over which they occur. In clinical practice this explains, in part, pressure ulcers with large undermined areas.

Friction

Friction and moisture, although not direct factors in pressure ulcer development, have been identified as contributing to the problem by reducing tolerance of tissues to pressure.[37] Friction occurs when two surfaces move across one another (see Figure 12–5). Friction acts on the tissue tolerance to pressure by abrading and damaging the epidermal and upper dermal layers of the skin. Additionally, friction acts with gravity to cause shear. Friction abrades the epidermis, which may lead to pressure ulcer development by increasing the skin's susceptibility to pressure injury. Pressure combined with friction produces ulcerations at lower pressures than just pressure alone.[37] Friction acts in conjunction with shear to contribute to development of sacral/coccygeal pressure ulcers on patients in the semi-Fowler's position.

Moisture

Moisture contributes to pressure ulcer development by removing oils on the skin, making it more friable, as well as interacting with body support surface friction. Constant moisture on the skin leads to maceration of the tissues. The waterlogged tissues lead to softening of the skin's connective tissues. Macerated tissues are more prone to erosion, and once the epidermis is eroded there is increased likelihood of further tissue breakdown.[38] Moisture alters the resiliency of the epidermis to external forces. Both shearing force and friction increase in the presence of mild to moderate moisture. Excess moisture may be due to wound drainage, diaphoresis, and fecal or urinary incontinence.

Urinary and fecal incontinence are common risk factors associated with pressure ulcer development. Incontinence contributes to pressure ulcer formation by creating excess moisture on the skin and by chemical damage to the skin.

Fecal incontinence has an added detrimental effect: the presence of bacteria in the stool, which can contribute to infection as well as skin breakdown. Fecal incontinence is more significant as a risk factor for pressure ulceration because of the bacteria and enzymes in stool and the subsequent effects on the skin.[24,39] In the presence of both urinary and fecal incontinence, the pH in the perineal area is increased by the fecal enzymes' conversion of urea to ammonia. The elevated pH increases the activity of proteases and lipases found in stool, which in turn cause increased permeability of the skin, leading to irritation by other agents such as bile salts.[40–42] Inadequately managed incontinence poses a significant risk factor for pressure ulcer development, and fecal incontinence is highly correlated with pressure ulcer development.[32,43]

Intrinsic Risk Factors

Nutrition

There is some disagreement on the major intrinsic risk factors affecting tissue tolerance to pressure. However, most studies identify nutritional status as playing a role in development. Hypoalbuminemia, weight loss, cachexia, and malnutrition are all commonly identified as risk factors predisposing patients to pressure ulcer development.[44–47] Malnutrition is associated with pressure ulcer development.[44,46] Individuals with low serum albumin levels are associated with both having a pressure ulcer and developing a pressure ulcer.

Age

Age itself may be a risk factor for pressure ulcer development, with age-related changes in the skin and wound healing increasing the risk of pressure ulcer development.[48] The skin and support structures undergo changes in the aging process. There is a loss of muscle, a decrease in serum albumin levels, diminished inflammatory response, decreased elasticity, and reduced cohesion between the dermis and epidermis.[48,49] These changes combine with other changes related to aging to make the skin less tolerant of pressure forces, shear, and friction.[48]

Medical Conditions and Psychologic Factors

Certain medical conditions or disease states are also associated with pressure ulcer development. Orthopaedic injuries, altered mental status, and spinal cord injury are such conditions.[33,34,47,50,51] Others have examined psychologic factors that may affect risk for pressure ulcer development.[52,53] Self-concept, depression, and chronic emotional stress have been cited as factors in pressure ulcer development.

Risk Assessment Tools

For practitioners to intervene cost effectively, a method of screening for risk factors is necessary. There are several risk assessment instruments available to clinicians. Screening tools assist in prevention by distinguishing those persons who are at risk for pressure ulcer development from those who are not. The only purpose in identifying patients at risk for pressure ulcer development is to allow for appropriate use of resources for prevention. The use of a risk assessment tool allows for targeting of interventions to specific risk factors for individual patients. Selection of which risk assessment instrument to use is determined by reliability of the tool for the intended raters, predictive validity of the tool for the population, the sensitivity and specificity of the instrument under consideration, and the ease of use and time required for completion. The most common risk assessment tools are Norton's Scale, Gosnell's Scale, and Braden's Scale for Predicting Pressure Sore Risk.

Norton's Scale

The Norton tool is the oldest risk assessment instrument. Developed in 1961, it consists of five subscales: physical condition, mental state, activity, mobility, and incontinence.[54] Each parameter is rated on a scale of 1 to 4 with the sum of the ratings for all five parameters yielding a total score ranging from 5 to 20 (see Exhibit 12–2). Lower scores indicate increased risk, with a score of or below 16 indicating "onset of risk" and scores 12 and below indicating high risk for pressure ulcer formation.[55] Others have revised the Norton tool and developed additional tools for assessing risk such as the Gosnell tool.

Gosnell's Scale

Gosnell based her scale on further refinement of the Norton Scale. Gosnell kept the original categories on the Norton Scale, changed the general condition category to nutrition, and renamed the incontinence category continence.[56,57] She added skin appearance, medication, diet and fluid balance, and intervention categories to the tool, along with detailed instructions for use. Gosnell reversed the numerical scaling so that the higher the score the higher the risk of pressure ulcer development, so a Gosnell score of 5 is the lowest risk and a score of 20 is the highest risk (see Exhibit 12–3).

Braden's Scale for Predicting Pressure Sore Risk

The Braden Scale was developed in 1987 and is composed of six subscales that conceptually reflect degrees of sensory perception, moisture, activity, mobility, nutrition, and friction and shear.[29,30] All subscales are rated from 1 to 4 except for friction and shear, which is rated from 1 to 3. The subscales may be summed for a total score, with a range from 6 to 23 (see Exhibit 12–4).

Exhibit 12–2 Norton's Scale

NORTON RISK ASSESSMENT SCALE

		Physical Condition	Mental Condition	Activity	Mobility	Incontinent	TOTAL SCORE
		Good 4 Fair 3 Poor 2 V. bad 1	Alert 4 Apathetic 3 Confused 2 Stupor 1	Ambulant 4 Walk/help 3 Chairbound 2 Bed 1	Full 4 Sl. limited 3 V. limited 2 Immobile 1	Not 4 Occasional 3 Usually/Urine 2 Doubly 1	
Name	Date						

Source: Reprinted with permission from D. Norton, R. McLaren, and A.N. Exton-Smith, *An Investigation of Geriatric Nursing Problems in Hospitals* Re-issue © 1975, Churchill Livingstone.

Exhibit 12–3 Gosnell's Tool

GOSNELL SCALE—PRESSURE SORE RISK ASSESSMENT

I.D. _____   Medical Diagnosis:
Age _____ Sex _____   Primary _____
Height: _____ Weight: _____   Secondary _____
Date of Admission _____   Nursing Diagnosis:
Date of Discharge _____   _____

Instructions: Complete all categories within 24 hours of admission and every other day thereafter. Refer to the accompanying guidelines for specific rating details.

DATE	Mental Status	Continence	Mobility	Activity	Nutrition	TOTAL SCORE
	1. Alert 2. Apathetic 3. Confused 4. Stuporous 5. Unconscious	1. Fully Controlled 2. Usually Controlled 3. Minimally Controlled 4. Absence of Control	1. Full 2. Slightly Limited 3. Very Limited 4. Immobile	1. Ambulatory 2. Walks with Assistance 3. Chairfast 4. Bedfast	1. Good 2. Fair 3. Poor	

Date	Vital Signs				Diet	24-Hour Fluid Balance		COLOR	GENERAL SKIN APPEARANCE				Interventions		
	T	P	R	BP		Intake	Output	1. Pallor 2. Mottled 3. Pink 4. Ashen 5. Ruddy 6. Cyanotic 7. Jaundice 8. Other	**Moisture** 1. Dry 2. Damp 3. Oily 4. Other	**Temperature** 1. Cold 2. Cool 3. Warm 4. Hot	**Texture** 1. Smooth 2. Rough 3. Thin/ Transp 4. Scaly 5. Crusty 6. Other		No	Yes	Describe

PRESSURE SORE RISK ASSESSMENT MEDICATION PROFILE

Medication	Dosage	Frequency	Route	Date Begun	Date Discon.

GOSNELL SCALE—GUIDELINES FOR NUMERICAL RATING OF THE DEFINED CATEGORIES

Rating	1	2	3	4	5
Mental Status: An assessment of one's level of response to his environment.	**Alert:** Oriented to time, place, and person. Responsive to all stimuli, and understands explanations.	**Apathetic:** Lethargic, forgetful, drowsy, passive, and dull. Sluggish, depressed. Able to obey simple commands. Possibly disoriented to time.	**Confused:** Partial and/or intermittent disorientation to TPP. Purposeless response to stimuli. Restless, aggressive, irritable, anxious, and may require tranquilizers or sedatives.	**Stuporous:** Total disorientation. Does not respond to name, simple commands, or verbal stimuli.	**Unconscious:** Nonresponsive to painful stimuli.

continues

Exhibit 12–3 continued

Rating	1	2	3	4	5
Continence: The amount of bodily control of urination and defecation.	**Fully Controlled:** Total control of urine and feces.	**Usually Controlled:** Incontinent of urine and/or feces not more often than once q 48 hrs OR has Foley catheter and is incontinent of feces.	**Minimally Controlled:** Incontinent of urine or feces at least once q 24 hrs.	**Absence of Control:** Consistently incontinent of both urine and feces.	
Mobility: The amount and control of movement of one's body.	**Full:** Able to control and move all extremities at will. May require the use of a device but turns, lifts, pulls, balances, and attains sitting position at will.	**Slightly Limited:** Able to control and move all extremities but a degree of limitation is present. Requires assistance of another person to turn, pull, balance, and/or attain a sitting position at will but self-initiates movement or request for help to move.	**Very Limited:** Can assist another person who must initiate movement via turning, lifting, pulling, balancing, and/or attaining a sitting position (contractures, paralysis may be present).	**Immobile:** Does not assist self in any way to change position. Is unable to change position without assistance. Is completely dependent on others for movement.	
Activity: The ability of an individual to ambulate.	**Ambulatory:** Is able to walk unassisted. Rises from bed unassisted. With the use of a device such as cane or walker is able to ambulate without the assistance of another person.	**Walks with Help:** Able to ambulate with assistance of another person, braces, or crutches. May have limitation of stairs.	**Chairfast:** Ambulates only to a chair, requires assistance to do so OR is confined to a wheelchair.	**Bedfast:** Is confined to bed during entire 24 hours of the day.	
Nutrition: The process of food intake.	Eats some food from each basic food category every day and the majority of each meal served OR is on tube feeding.	Occasionally refuses a meal or frequently leaves at least half of a meal.	Seldom eats a complete meal and only a few bites of food at a meal.		

Vital signs:	The temperature, pulse, respiration, and blood pressure to be taken and recorded at the time of every assessment rating.
Skin appearance:	A description of observed skin characteristics: color, moisture, temperature, and texture.
Diet:	Record the specific diet order.
24-hour fluid balance:	The amount of fluid intake and output during the previous 24-hour period should be recorded.
Interventions:	List all devices, measures, and/or nursing care activity being used for the purpose of pressure sore prevention.
Medications:	List name, dosage, frequency, and route for all prescribed medications. If a PRN order, list the pattern for the period since last assessment.
Comments:	Use this space to add explanation or further detail regarding any of the previously recorded data, patient condition, etc. OR Describe anything which you believe to be of importance but not accounted for previously.

Source: Copyright © 1988, Davina Gosnell.

Exhibit 12–4 Braden Scale for Predicting Pressure Sore Risk

Patient's Name _____ Evaluator's Name _____ Date of Assessment _____

SENSORY PERCEPTION ability to respond meaningfully to pressure-related discount	**1. Completely Limited:** Unresponsive (does not moan, flinch, or grasp) to painful stimuli, due to diminished level of consciousness or sedation. OR limited ability to feel pain over most of body surface.	**2. Very Limited:** Responds only to painful stimuli. Cannot communicate discomfort except by moaning or restlessness. OR has a sensory impairment which limits the ability to feel pain or discomfort over 1/2 of body.	**3. Slightly Limited:** Responds to verbal commands, but cannot always communicate discomfort or need to be turned. OR has some sensory impairment which limits ability to feel pain or discomfort in 1 or 2 extremities.	**4. No Impairment:** Responds to verbal commands. Has no sensory deficit which would limit ability to feel or voice pain or discomfort.
MOISTURE degree to which skin is exposed to moisture	**1. Constantly Moist:** Skin is kept moist almost constantly by perspiration, urine, etc. Dampness is detected every time patient is moved or turned.	**2. Very Moist:** Skin is often, but not always moist. Linen must be changed at least once a shift.	**3. Occasionally Moist:** Skin is occasionally moist, requiring an extra linen change approximately once a day.	**4. Rarely Moist:** Skin is usually dry, linen only requires changing at routine intervals.
ACTIVITY degree of physical activity	**1. Bedfast:** Confined to bed.	**2. Chairfast:** Ability to walk severely limited or nonexistent. Cannot bear own weight and/or must be assisted into chair or wheelchair.	**3. Walks Occasionally:** Walks occasionally during day, but for very short distances, with or without assistance. Spends majority of each shift in bed or chair.	**4. Walks Frequently:** Walks outside the room at least twice a day and inside room at least once very 2 hours during waking hours.
MOBILITY ability to change and control body position	**1. Completely Immobile:** Does not make even slight changes in body or extremity position without assistance.	**2. Very Limited:** Makes occasional slight changes in body or extremity position but unable to make frequent or significant changes independently.	**3. Slightly Limited:** Makes frequent though slight changes in body or extremity position independently.	**4. No Limitations:** Makes major and frequent changes in position without assistance.

continues

Exhibit 12–4 continued

NUTRITION *usual* food intake pattern	1. Very Poor: Never eats a complete meal. Rarely eats more than 1/3 of any food offered. Eats 2 servings or less of protein (meat or dairy products) per day. Takes fluids poorly. Does not take a liquid dietary supplement. OR is NPO and/or maintained on clear liquids or IVs for more than 5 days.	2. Probably Inadequate: Rarely eats a complete meal and generally eats only about 1/2 of any food offered. Protein intake includes only 3 servings of meat or dairy products per day. Occasionally will take a dietary supplement. OR receives less than optimum amount of liquid diet or tube feeding.	3. Adequate: Eats over half of most meals. Eats a total of 4 servings of protein (meat, dairy products) each day. Occasionally will refuse a meal, but will usually take a supplement if offered. OR is on a tube feeding or TPN regimen which probably meets most of nutritional needs.	4. Excellent: Eats most of every meal. Never refuses a meal. Usually eats a total of 4 or more servings of meat and dairy products. Occasionally eats between meals. Does not require supplementation.	
FRICTION AND SHEAR	1. Problem: Requires moderate to maximum assistance in moving. Complete lifting without sliding against sheets is impossible. Frequently slides down in bed or chair, requiring frequent repositioning with maximum assistance. Spasticity, contractures, or agitation leads to almost constant friction.	2. Potential Problem: Moves feebly or requires minimum assistance. During a move skin probably slides to some extent against sheets, chair, restraints, or other devices. Maintains relatively good position in chair or bed most of the time but occasionally slides down.	3. No Apparent Problem: Moves in bed and in chair independently and has sufficient muscle strength to lift up completely during move. Maintains good position in bed or chair at all times.		
				Total Score	

Source: Copyright © 1988, Barbara J. Braden and Nancy Bergstrom.

Lower scores indicate lower function and higher risk for developing a pressure ulcer. The cutoff score for hospitalized adults is considered to be 16, with scores of 16 and below indicating at-risk status.[30] In older patients some have found cutoff scores of 17 or 18 better predictors of risk status.[46,58] Levels of risk are based on the predictive value of a positive test. Scores of 15 to 16 indicate mild risk, with a 50% to 60% chance of developing a stage I pressure ulcer; scores of 12 to 14 indicate moderate risk, with a 65% to 90% chance of developing a stage I or II lesion; and scores below 12 indicate high risk, with a 90% to 100% chance of developing a stage II or deeper pressure ulcer.[46,59] The Braden scale has been tested in acute care and long-term care settings with several levels of nurse raters and demonstrates high interrater reliability with registered nurses. Validity has been established by expert opinion, and predictive validity has been studied in several acute care settings with good sensitivity and specificity demonstrated.[30,46] Based on the current reliability and validity testing the AHCPR guidelines recommend the use of either the Braden Scale or the Norton Scale.[26]

Clinical Wisdom: *Quick Risk Assessment Screening*

The Braden scale activity subscale can be used as a quick screening tool. Those patients who receive a score of 1 or 2 (indicating patients who are not bed or chair bound) may be considered at low or no risk, and no further assessment is required. If patients are bed or chair bound, they should receive the full Braden Scale assessment, and prevention interventions should be instituted specific to level of risk and individual risk factors present.

Regardless of the instrument chosen to evaluate risk status, the clinical relevance is threefold. First, assessment for risk status must occur at frequent intervals. Monitor assessment at admission to the health care organization (within 24 hours), at predetermined intervals (usually weekly), and whenever a significant change occurs in the patient's general health and status. The second clinical implication is the targeting of specific prevention strategies to identified risk factors. The final clinical implication is for those patients in whom prevention is not successful. For patients with an actual pressure ulcer, the continued monitoring of risk status may prevent further tissue trauma at the wound site and may prevent development of additional wound sites. The prevention interventions presented are based on the Braden Scale Risk Assessment instrument items. Figure 12–7 presents an algorithm for determining when to perform risk assessment

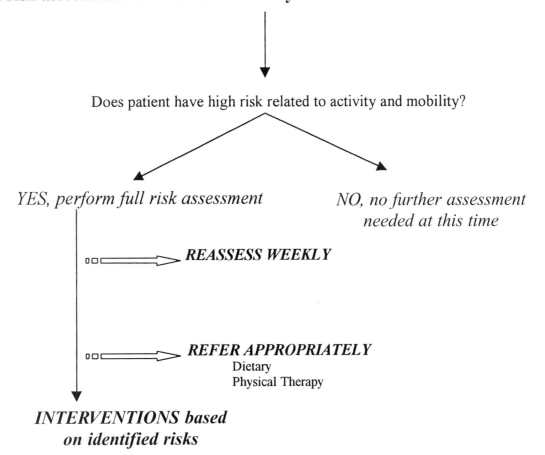

PATIENT ADMITTED TO ORGANIZATION
Perform risk assessment with focus on activity subscale score for Braden Scale

Does patient have high risk related to activity and mobility?

YES, perform full risk assessment   *NO, no further assessment needed at this time*

REASSESS WEEKLY

REFER APPROPRIATELY
Dietary
Physical Therapy

INTERVENTIONS based on identified risks

Figure 12–7 When to assess patients for risk of pressure ulcer development.

on patients and Exhibit 12–5 presents a flow diagram for determining prevention strategies based on risk factor assessment.

PRESSURE ULCER PREVENTION: EARLY INTERVENTIONS

Prevention strategies are targeted at reducing risk factors present. Appropriate prevention interventions can be focused on eliminating specific risk factors. Thus, early intervention for pressure ulcers is risk-factor specific and prophylactic in nature. The prevention strategies are presented by risk factors, beginning with general information and ending with specific strategies for a particular risk factor. The Braden Scale is the basis for these prevention interventions. Prevention interventions should be instituted that are appropriate to the patient's level of risk and specific to individual risk factors.[26] For example, the risk factor of immobility is managed very differently for the comatose patient versus the spinal cord–injured patient. The comatose patient requires caregiver education and caregiver-dependent repositioning. The spinal cord–injured patient requires self-care education and may be able to perform self-repositioning. Thus, the intervention for the risk factor of immobility is very different for these two patients.

Immobility, Inactivity, and Sensory Loss

Patients with impaired ability to reposition and who cannot independently change body positions must have local pressure alleviated by any of the following interventions.[24,26,59]

- Passive repositioning by the caregiver
- Pillow bridging
- Use of pressure-relief or pressure-reduction support surfaces for chair and bed

In addition, measures to increase mobility and activity and to decrease friction and shear should be instituted. Overhead bed frames with trapeze bars are helpful for patients with

---

Exhibit 12–5 Flow Diagram for Determining Prevention Strategies Based on Risk Factor Assessment

Presence of tissue trauma over bony prominence?
(usual locations: sacral/coccygeal, trochanter, ischial tuberosity, malleolus, heel)

NO   YES, provide for wound assessment and treatment plus prevention strategies

Patient NOT chair or bed bound and thus at no or low risk?
(patient scores a 1 or 2 on Braden Scale activity subscale)

NO, complete full risk assessment   YES, do not need further risk assessment

Pressure ulcer risk factors present?

Immobility	Inactivity	Decreased Sensory Perception	Nutrition	Friction and Shear	Moisture Urinary and Fecal Incontinence

Prevention interventions by risk factors:

Immobility, Inactivity, and Decreased Sensory Perception		Malnutrition	Friction and Shear	Moisture Incontinence
passive repositioning, pillow bridging, pressure-reducing/relieving support surfaces		provide nutrition supplement: protein, calorie, vitamin C, zinc, iron	cornstarch, lubricants, pad protectors, transparent film, thin hydrocolloid dressings, turning, and draw sheets	absorbent products, diagnosis of incontinence, general skin care

paraplegia, stroke patients with upper body strength, and obese patients and may increase mobility and independence with body repositioning. Wheelchair-bound patients with upper body strength can be taught and encouraged to do wheelchair pushups to relieve pressure and allow for reperfusion of the tissues in the ischial tuberosity region. For patients who are weak from prolonged inactivity, providing support and assistance for reconditioning and increasing strength and endurance will help prevent future debility.[24] Mobility plans for each patient should be individualized with the goal of attaining the highest level of mobility and activity individually possible. Mobility plans are the responsibility of nurses and physical therapists working together in all health care settings. It is essential that health care professionals train and observe home caregivers in the mobility plan and, in particular, passive repositioning techniques. Caregivers in the home are often left to fend for themselves for prevention interventions and may be frail and with health problems themselves. A return demonstration of a repositioning procedure can be very informative to the health care provider. The health care provider may need to coach, improvise, and think of creative strategies for caregivers to use in the home setting in order to meet the patient's need for movement and tissue reperfusion.

Passive Repositioning by Caregiver

Turning schedules and passive repositioning by caregivers is the normal response for patients with immobility risk factors. Typically, turning schedules are based on time or event. If time based, turning schedules are usually every 2 hours for full body change of position and more often for small shifts in position. Event-based schedules relate to typical events during the day, for example, turning the patient after each meal. Full body change of position involves turning the patient to a new lying position, for example, turning the patient from the right sidelying position to the left sidelying position or the supine position. When the sidelying position is used in bed, avoidance of direct pressure on the trochanter is essential. To avoid placing pressure on the trochanter, position the patient in a 30° laterally inclined position instead of the commonly used 90° sidelying position, which increases tissue compression over the trochanter.[60] The 30° laterally inclined position allows for distribution of pressure over a greater area (see Figure 12–8). Use of diagrams with clock faces and body position of patient are helpful in reminding staff when and how to position the patient[61] (see Figure 12–9).

Small shifts in position involve moving the patient but keeping the same lying position,[62] for example, changing the angle of the right sidelying position or changing the lower extremity position in the right sidelying position. Both strategies are helpful in achieving reperfusion of compressed tis-

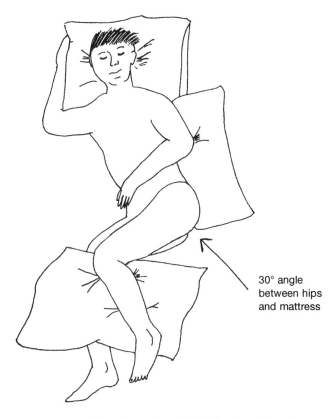

30° angle between hips and mattress

Figure 12–8 Thirty-degree laterally inclined position. *Source:* Copyright © Barbara M. Bates-Jensen and Lynette Merriman.

sues but *only full body change of position completely relieves pressure.*

There are techniques to make turning patients easier and less time consuming. Turning sheets, draw sheets, and pillows are essential for passive movement of patients in bed. Turning sheets are useful in repositioning the patient to a sidelying position, and draw sheets are used for pulling the patient up in bed and help prevent dragging the patient's skin over the bed surface. Two-person repositioning is a simple task with the turning sheet and can be accomplished in a very small amount of time with little risk of dragging the patient's skin across the bed linens:

1. Position one person on each side of the bed.
2. Bend the patient's knees and fold the patient's arms across the chest.
3. Roll up the draw sheet next to the patient's body and grasp firmly.
4. On a prearranged verbal cue, both persons lift the patient and move him or her up in bed.
5. Next, one person pulls on the turn sheet to roll the patient passively toward the side.
6. The person on the other side of the bed immediately places pillows behind the patient's back for support.

SUPINE
POSITION

RIGHT SIDELYING
POSITION

LEFT SIDELYING
POSITION

RIGHT SIDELYING
POSITION

LEFT SIDELYING
POSITION

SUPINE
POSITION

Figure 12–9 Clock method of determining turning schedule.

7. Additional pillows are then used for easing pressure on other bony prominences.

The recommended time interval for full change of position turning is every 2 hours, depending on the individual patient profile.

Similar approaches are useful for patients in chairs. Full body change of position involves standing the patient and resitting him or her in the chair. Small shifts in position for those in chairs might be changing lower extremity position. For the chair-bound patient, it is also helpful to use a footstool to help reduce the pressure on the ischial tuberosities and to distribute the pressure over a wider surface. Attention to proper alignment and posture is essential. Individuals at risk for pressure ulcer development should avoid uninterrupted sitting in chairs and should be repositioned every hour. The rationale behind the shorter time frame is the extremely high pressures generated on the ischial tuberosities in the seated position.[1] Those patients with upper body strength should be taught to shift weight every 15 minutes to allow

Clinical Wisdom: *One-Person Turning*

For one-person turning, the following procedure may be helpful:

1. First, remove the pillows previously used to position the patient.
2. Next align the patient's body in a central position.
3. Gently bend the right knee and position the right leg in a crossed position over the left leg.
4. Place the right arm across the body, as if the patient is reaching for the other side of the bed.
5. Using the turn sheet from the opposite side of the bed, gently pull the patient's body over to the left sidelying position.
6. Alternatively, from the same side of the bed, with hands on the shoulder and hip, gently push the patient's body over to the left sidelying position.
7. Position pillows at the patient's upper back area, between the knees, between the ankles, and under the feet if appropriate.

for tissue reperfusion. Again, pillows may be used to help position the patient in proper body alignment. Physical therapy and occupational therapy can assist in body alignment strategies with even the most contracted patient. (See Chapter 13 for further discussion on orthotic devices and seating therapeutics.)

Pillow Bridging

Pillow bridging involves the use of pillows to position patients with minimal tissue compression. The use of pillows can help prevent pressure ulcers from occurring on the medial knees, the medial malleolus, and the heels. Pillows should be placed between the knees, between the ankles, and under the heels.

Clinical Wisdom: *Positioning Pillows*

Five pillows can overcome repositioning pressure point difficulties. Use the pillows in the following positions:

Pillow 1:   under legs to elevate the heels
Pillow 2:   between the ankles
Pillow 3:   between the knees
Pillow 4:   behind the back
Pillow 5:   under the head

(Use a small pillow for comfort under the arm in sidelying position.)

Pillow use is especially important for reducing risk of development of heel ulcers regardless of the support surface in use.[26] The best prevention strategy for eliminating pressure ulcers on the heels is to keep the heels off the surface of the bed. Use of pillows under the lower extremities will keep the heel from making contact with the support surface of the bed. Pillows help to redistribute the pressure over a larger area, thus reducing high pressures in one specific area.

Research Wisdom: *Donut Pillow Devices*

One type of pillow device is not recommended for use. Use of a donut type or ring cushion device is contraindicated. Donut ring cushions cause venous congestion and edema and actually increase pressure to the area of concern.[26]

Use of Pressure-Relief or Pressure-Reduction Support Surfaces

There are specific guidelines for the use of support surfaces to prevent and manage pressure ulcers.[1,63,64] Regardless of the type of support surface in use with the patient, the need for written repositioning and turning schedules remains essential. The support surface serves as adjuncts to strategies for positioning and careful monitoring of patients. The type of support surface chosen is based on a multitude of factors, including clinical condition of the patient, type of care setting, ease of use, maintenance, cost, and characteristics of the support surface. The primary concern should be the therapeutic benefit associated with the surface. Table 12–1 categorizes the types of support surfaces available and their general performance characteristics[1]; Exhibit 12–6 presents ideal support surface characteristics. Table 12–1 and Exhibit 12–6 are presented as an overview to the remainder of this section. The information on support surfaces is organized in the following manner: first, information on tissue interface pressure is presented; second, information on pressure-reducing and pressure-relieving support surfaces is presented; finally, this section ends with information and guidelines on how to determine the appropriate surface for specific patients.

Tissue Interface Pressures. Tissue interface pressures are commonly evaluated by using capillary closing pressure (generally considered to be 12 to 32 mm Hg) as an indirect measure to label effectiveness of support surfaces. The use of capillary closing pressures implies that skin surface interface pressure is equal to capillary closing pressures. Further, as tissue interface (skin surface) pressures approach capillary closing pressures (12 to 32 mm Hg), the support surface is more effective and less likely to occlude blood vessels (less likely to cause pressure ulcer formation). One of the difficulties with the use of capillary closing pressures is the assumption that capillary closing pressures are absolute values. Capillary closing pressures may be more individualized than absolute values imply. Capillary closing pressures assume that skin interface pressures reflect pressure at the bony tissue interface. Some suggest that pressure on subcutaneous tissues may be three to five times higher than skin interface pressure. Interface pressure is a measurement obtained by placing a sensor between the skin and the resting support surface. It is usually obtained with some type of electropneumatic pressure sensor connected to an inflation system and gauge. Typically, three or more readings are obtained and the average of the readings is used as the reported value. Instrumentation (size of sensor, shape of sensor, and position of sensor) greatly affects values of pressure readings, so it is difficult if not impossible to make comparisons between studies.

Table 12–1 Selected Characteristics for Classes of Support Surfaces

Performance Characteristics	Air Fluidized (High Air Loss)	Low Air Loss	Alternating Air (Dynamic)	Static Flotation (Air or Water)	Foam	Standard Hospital Mattress
Increased support area	Yes	Yes	Yes	Yes	Yes	No
Low moisture retention	Yes	Yes	No	No	No	No
Reduced heat accumulation	Yes	Yes	No	No	No	No
Shear reduction	Yes	?	Yes	Yes	No	No
Pressure reduction	Yes	Yes	Yes	Yes	Yes	No
Dynamic	Yes	Yes	Yes	No	No	No
Cost per day	High	High	Moderate	Low	Low	Low

Source: Reprinted from N. Bergstrom, M.A. Bennett, C.E. Carlson, et al., *Treatment of Pressure Ulcers,* Clinical Practice Guideline No. 15, December, 1994, U.S. Department of Health and Human Services, Public Health Service, Agency for Health Care Policy and Research, AHCPR Publication No. 95-0652.

Exhibit 12–6 Ideal Support Surface Characteristics

- Reduces/relieves pressure under bony prominences
- Controls pressure gradient in tissue
- Provides stability
- No interference with weight shifts
- No interference with transfers
- Controls temperature at interface
- Controls moisture at skin surface
- Lightweight
- Low cost
- Durable

Source: Reprinted with permission from J. McLean, Pressure reduction or pressure relief: making the right choice, *Journal of ET Nursing,* Vol. 20, No. 5, pp. 211–215, © 1993, Mosby Year-Book, Inc.

Pressure-Reducing Support Surfaces. Pressure-reduction devices lower tissue interface pressures, but do not *consistently* maintain interface pressures below capillary closing pressures in all positions, on all body locations.[68] Pressure-reducing support surfaces are indicated for patients who are assessed to be at risk for pressure ulcer development, who can be turned, and who have skin breakdown involving *only one sleep surface.*[24,26] Patients with an existing pressure ulcer who are determined to be still at risk for development of further skin breakdown should be managed on a pressure-reducing support surface. Pressure-reduction devices can be classified as static or dynamic devices.

Static devices do not move; they reduce pressure by spreading the load over a larger area. The easy definition of a static support surface is a device that does not require electricity to function, usually a mattress overlay (lies on top of the standard hospital mattress). Examples of static devices are foam, air, or gel mattress overlays and water-filled mattresses. When considering the foam mattress overlays, the health care provider should consider stiffness of the foam and the density and thickness of the foam. Indentation load deflection (ILD) is a measure of the stiffness of the foam; generally, the ILD should be 25% for 30 lb. The density and thickness of the foam relate to the foam's ability to deflect the pressure and redistribute the pressure over a wider area. Typically, the density and thickness of a foam product should be 1.3 lb per cubic foot and 3 to 4 inches, respectively.[1] Foam devices have difficulties with retaining moisture and heat and not reducing shear. Air and water static devices also have difficulties associated with retaining moisture and heat.

Dynamic support surfaces move. The easy definition of dynamic support surfaces is that they require a motor or pump and electricity to operate. Examples are alternating pressure air mattresses. Most of these devices use an electric pump to alternately inflate and deflate air cells or air columns, thus the term *alternating* pressure air mattress. The key to determination of effectiveness is the length of time that cycles of inflation and deflation occur. Dynamic support surfaces may also have difficulties with moisture retention and heat accumulation.[1]

Pressure-reduction devices can also be categorized as overlays or replacement mattresses. Mattress overlays are devices that are applied on top of the standard mattress. Most overlays are pressure-reduction devices and require a one-time charge, setup fee, daily rental fee, or a combination of fees. Most are single-use items and may present environmental issues for disposal. When using mattress overlays, the height of the bed is increased, so transfers and linen fit may be complicated. Mattress overlays may be static or dynamic. Some provide air movement to reduce moisture buildup. Some examples include foam, gel, water, or air-filled mattress, alternating pressure pads, and low-air-loss overlays.

Research Wisdom:
Evaluating Studies Using Tissue Interface Pressures

- Look for interface pressures stated as a percentage against a standard surface, usually a hospital mattress. Standard hospital mattress interface pressures for sacrum = 36 to 48 mm Hg and for trochanter = 62 to 97 mm Hg.[65,66] For example, a support surface that reports tissue interface pressure readings of 25 mm Hg for the sacrum has approximately 30% lower pressures than the standard hospital mattress pressures for the sacrum (25 mm Hg/36 mm Hg × 100 = 69.44; 100 − 70 = 30% of hospital mattress pressures).
- Look for standard deviations (SD) reported in the study—95% of measurements lie within 2 SD of the mean (average). So the larger the standard deviation, the less reproducible the pressure measurements and the more variable the results with the product.[65,67] For example, a study reports *mean* tissue interface pressures of 25 mm Hg with *standard deviation* of 8.2. So 95% of all the measurements were between 8.6 and 41.4 mm Hg. This is not so bad at the 8.6 end, but what about the 41.4 mm Hg? That figure is far higher than capillary closing pressure of 32 mm Hg.
- To interpret the study results, consider these issues[67]:
  1. Range and number of pressure readings obtained for each site.
  2. Procedure used to acquire the pressure readings should be described.
  3. Who was tested?
  4. How were they tested?
  5. How often was equipment recalibrated?
  6. The equipment is fragile and subject to malfunction.

One additional concern when using mattress overlays is the bottoming out phenomenon. Bottoming out occurs when the patient's body sinks down, the support surface is compressed beyond function, and the patient's body lies directly on the hospital mattress. When bottoming out occurs there is no pressure reduction for the bony prominence of concern. Bottoming out typically happens when the patient is placed on a static air mattress overlay that is not appropriately filled with air or when the patient has been on a foam mattress for extended periods of time. The health care provider can monitor for bottoming out by inserting a flat, outstretched hand between the overlay and the patient's body part at risk. If the caregiver feels less than an inch of support material, the patient has bottomed out. It is important to check for bottoming out when the patient is in various body positions and to

check at various body sites. For example, when the patient is lying supine, check the sacral/coccygeal area and the heels; when the patient is sidelying, check the trochanter and lateral malleolus.[1] Use of a static support surface is warranted if the patient can turn off the pressure ulcer site without bottoming out.

Replacement mattresses are designed to reduce interface pressures and replace the standard hospital mattress. Most are made of foam and gel combinations. Some are air-filled chambers and foam structures. All are covered with a bacteriostatic cover that can be maintained with standard cleaning. These mattresses involve an initial significant expense, and there are minimal data on long-term effectiveness.

Pressure-Relieving Support Surfaces. Pressure relief devices *consistently* reduce tissue interface pressures to a level below capillary closing pressure, in any position and in most body locations.[68] Pressure-relief devices are indicated for patients who are assessed to be at high risk for pressure ulcer development and who cannot turn independently, or those who have skin breakdown involving more than one body surface. Most commonly, pressure-relief devices are grouped into low-air-loss therapy, fluidized air or high-air-loss therapy, and kinetic therapy.

Low-air-loss therapy is a bed frame with a series of connected air-filled pillows with surface fabrics of low-friction material. The amount of pressure in each pillow can be controlled and can be calibrated to provide maximum pressure relief for the individual patient. They provide pressure relief in any position, and most models have built-in scales.

Fluidized air or high-air-loss therapy consists of a bed frame containing silicone-coated glass beads and incorporates both air and fluid support. The beads become fluid when air is pumped through, making them behave as a liquid. High-air-loss therapy has bactericidal properties because of the alkalinity of the beads (pH 10), the temperature, and entrapment of microorganisms by the beads. High-air-loss therapy relieves pressure and reduces friction, shear, and moisture (due to the drying effect of the bed). It is difficult to transfer patients in these devices because of the bed frame. There is increased air flow, which can increase evaporative fluid loss, leading to dehydration. Finally, if the patient is able to sit up, a foam wedge may be required, thus limiting the beneficial effects of the bed on the upper back of the patient.

Kinetic therapy beds are designed to counter the effects of immobility by continuous passive motion. Kinetic therapy is believed to improve respiratory function and oxygenation, prevent urinary stasis, and reduce venous stasis. Multiple body systems are involved in the therapy, and generally the patient must have a stable spine. The beds usually are of two types: either the bed frame itself moves or the air cushions inflate or deflate, rotating the patient from side to side or pulsating. Pressure relief and low friction surface are provided with repositioning. Most models include built-in scales. Conscious patients may not tolerate the movement of the bed.

The last category of support surfaces includes those designed for obese accommodation. These support surfaces are designed to provide pressure reduction for the severely obese patient and can accommodate extreme loading, as is the case with the obese patient. Obese accommodation devices have features similar to the other support surfaces described. Generally, the bed frame is larger and many include the capability of raising the patient to a standing position while positioned in the bed. There are also chair devices for the obese patient.

Support Surface Selection. Determining which support surface is best for individual patients can be confusing. The primary concern must always be the effectiveness of the surface for the individual patient's needs. The AHCPR guidelines on prevention and prediction of pressure ulcers recommend the following criteria for determining how to manage tissue loading and support surface selection.[26]

- Assess all patients with existing pressure ulcers to determine their risk for developing additional pressure ulcers. If the patient remains at risk, use a pressure-reducing surface.
- Use a static support surface if the patient can assume a variety of positions without bearing weight on an existing pressure ulcer and without bottoming out.
- Use a dynamic support surface if the patient cannot assume a variety of positions without bearing weight on an existing pressure ulcer, if the patient fully compresses the static support surface, or if the pressure ulcer does not show evidence of healing.
- If a patient has large stage III or stage IV pressure ulcers on multiple turning surfaces, a low-air-loss bed or a fluidized air (high-air-loss) bed may be indicated.
- When excess moisture on intact skin is a potential source of maceration and skin breakdown, a support surface that provides air flow can be important in drying the skin and preventing additional pressure ulcers.
- Any individual assessed to be at risk for developing pressure ulcers should be placed on a static or dynamic pressure-reducing support surface.

Use of an algorithm can also be helpful in making clinical decisions. There are multiple decision trees and algorithms available. The algorithm recommended by the AHCPR guidelines (Figure 12–10) is offered as one example of a clinical decision-making tree or treatment algorithm.[1]

There are additional concerns in choosing a support surface. Criteria for choosing support surfaces can be classified as intrinsic and extrinsic. Intrinsic criteria include wound burden (tissue history—previous ulcers, surgical repair, stress, duration of pressure ulcer, number of pressure ulcers present), body build (obese, thin, contractures present), and the magnitude and distribution of interface pressures (location of highest pressures, etc).[65] The following case examples help illustrate how intrinsic criteria are used for determination of support surface: Patients who undergo specific surgical operative repair of the pressure ulcer may need to be placed on high-air-loss or fluidized air therapy postoperatively. Patients with multiple ulcers involving more than one turning surface also need to be placed on pressure-relieving devices such as low-air-loss therapy or high-air-loss therapy. Patients with severe contractures may not require a support surface that has good heel pressure readings (with contraction of the legs, the heels do not reach the bottom of the mattress). If the bony prominence of concern is the greater trochanter, then the support surface chosen must adequately reduce pressure over the trochanter. Although an algorithm is a helpful tool in choosing a support surface, as these case examples illustrate, the clinician must also evaluate the individual patient's needs.

Extrinsic criteria include all of the following:

- The number of hours spent on the support surface daily (Will product be needed for short- or long-term use?)
- Shear and friction effects
- Environment factors (temperature, humidity, continence, and moisture)
- Living arrangements (Will patient be in acute care, long-term care, or home care setting?)
- Self-care deficits (Is the risk of pressure ulcer development likely to increase or decrease?)
- Ease of transition and weaning to other products or other health care settings
- Ease of use and manageability
- Cost—reimbursement level
- Service and warranty
- Availability of product
- Scientific validity[64,65]

Evaluation of extrinsic criteria requires the clinician to review the goals for therapy. For example, the patient who uses the support surface only at night and spends most of the day in the chair will require an aggressive approach to seating support surfaces, and a lesser support surface can be chosen for the bed. If the patient spends most of the day in bed, the support surface chosen will be different. For agitated patients (particularly those with continual body motions), the support surface's ability to handle shearing and friction may be critical, and good choices may involve evaluation of the support surface covering. The external environment is also essential to include in choosing a support sur-

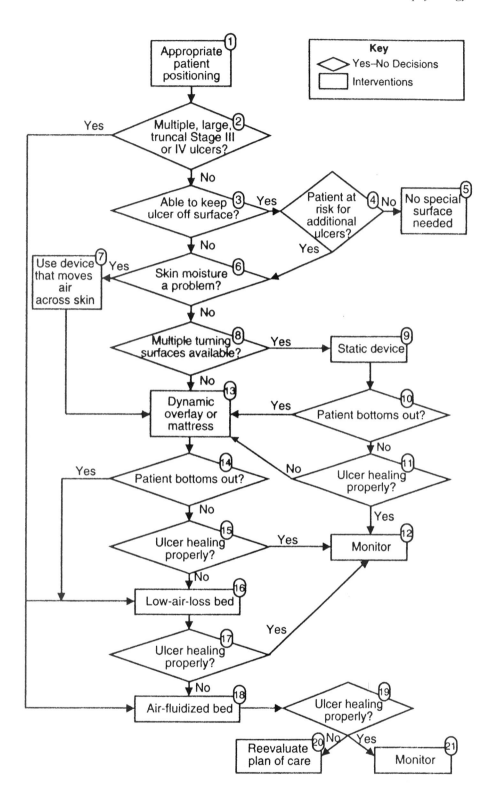

Figure 12–10 Management of tissue loads. *Source:* Reprinted from N. Bergstrom, M.A. Bennett, C.E. Carlson, et al., *Treatment of Pressure Ulcers,* Clinical Practice Guideline No. 15, December, 1994, U.S. Department of Health and Human Services, Public Health Service, Agency for Health Care Policy and Research, AHCPR Publication No. 95-0652.

face. If the patient is at home, with no air conditioning, is incontinent of urine, and lives in a humid environment, the breathability of the support surface and the ability to handle moisture are essential to positive outcomes. Likewise, evaluation of the patient's prognosis is helpful in support surface choice. Is the patient expected to recover and improve? If so, a pressure-reduction or lower-end support surface device may be very appropriate. However, if the patient is expected to decline in function, choosing a support surface that will meet future, as well as present, skin care needs may be prudent. Throughout the decision-making process one thought should prevail: it is important to promote patient independence, not patient dependent behavior. Encouraging patient movement out of bed and thus off the support surface is important for those patients who are able, and this must be considered by the clinician.

Clinical Wisdom:
Reimbursement of Support Surfaces

Support surfaces are reimbursed in home care under Medicare Part B benefits. Medicare requirements for reimbursement include the following:

- Must be stage III or IV pressure sore
- Must be located on trunk of body
- Must have current Medicare Part B coverage
- Must be in permanent residence (own home, long-term care facility, etc.)

Seating Support Surfaces. Support surfaces for chairs and wheelchairs can be categorized as the support surfaces for beds. In general, providing adequate pressure relief for chair-bound or wheelchair-bound patients is critical, as the patient at risk for pressure ulcer formation is at increased risk in the seated position because of the high pressures across the ischial tuberosities. Most pressure-reducing devices for chairs are static overlays, such as those made out of foam, gel, air, or some combination. Positioning chair-bound or wheelchair-bound individuals must include consideration of individual anatomy and body contours, postural alignment, distribution of weight, and balance and stability, in addition to pressure relief. Chapter 13 provides additional information on therapeutic positioning.

Evaluating Outcomes of Support Surfaces. In order to evaluate outcomes from the support surfaces chosen for a particular health care setting, *baseline data must be available on the prevalence and incidence of the condition in the setting. Prevalence is the number of all persons with the condition at one particular point in time.* Prevalence includes

---

Clinical Wisdom:
Teaching Wheelchair-Bound Patients

Wheelchair-bound patients with upper body strength can be taught and encouraged to do wheelchair pushups every 15 minutes to relieve pressure and allow for reperfusion of the tissues in the ischial tuberosity region. Use of a watch with a timer device may be a helpful reminder. The use of a chair support surface can help lessen the burden of wheelchair pushups, but does not eliminate the need for reperfusion of the tissues.

---

both facility acquired and those admitted with the condition. Prevalence studies can be done on one day (one point in time) and require a team to review all medical records and perform skin inspections of all patients in the organization on that day. *Incidence is the number of new cases developing over a period of time.* Incidence includes only facility-acquired conditions and, as such, reflects the effectiveness of the prevention program in the organization. Incidence studies are done over a period of time (a month, a quarter, a year) and require evaluation of all new patients with the condition (medical record review and skin inspection). The evaluation team reviews all patients (but counts only those with new conditions) at periodic intervals over the time period, for example, once a week for 4 weeks to determine monthly incidence. Many times prevalence and incidence studies are combined. The team performs a prevalence study on 1 day and then continues to evaluate the population over a period of time to evaluate the incidence also. Incidence is the most valuable of the two baseline studies because it reflects actual occurrence of pressure ulcer development in the facility. Over time, with an effective prevention program, including availability of the appropriate support surfaces, the incidence of pressure ulcer development in the facility should decline.

Choosing support surfaces for clients based on algorithms (see Figure 12–10) and predetermined criteria (factors chosen by the clinician, such as the support surface's ability to handle friction, cost, service, etc), use of a multidisciplinary team to finalize selections, and periodic reevaluation of products and patient/institution needs based on baseline prevalence and incidence data are the keys to effective support surface use.

Friction and Shear

Measures to reduce friction and shear relate to passive or active movement of the patient. To reduce friction several interventions are appropriate. Providing topical preparations to eliminate or reduce the surface tension between the skin and the bed linen or support surface will assist in reducing friction-related injury. Use of appropriate techniques in moving patients so that skin is never dragged across linens will lessen friction-induced skin breakdown. Patients who exhibit voluntary or involuntary repetitive body movements (particularly the heels or elbows) require stronger interventions. Use of a protective film such as a transparent film dressing or a skin sealant, a protective dressing such as a thin hydrocolloid, or protective padding will help eliminate the surface contact of the area and decrease the friction between the skin and the linens.[24] Even though heel, ankle, and elbow protectors do nothing to reduce or relieve pressure, they can be effective aids against friction.

Clinical Wisdom: *Reducing Friction*

Sprinkling cornstarch on the bed linen or use of skin lubricants is helpful in reducing overall friction.

Most shear injury can be eliminated by proper positioning such as avoidance of the semi-Fowler's position and limiting use of the upright position (positions over 30° inclined). Avoidance of positions greater than 30° inclined may prevent sliding and shear-related injury. Use of footboards and knee Gatches (or pillows under the lower leg) to prevent sliding and to maintain position are also helpful in reducing shear effects on the skin when in bed. Observation of the patient when sitting is also important, as the patient who slides out of the chair is at equally high risk for shear injury. Use of footstools and the foot pedals on wheelchairs and appropriate 90° flexion of the hip (may be achieved with pillows, special seat cushions, or orthotic devices) can help in preventing chair sliding.

Nutrition

Nutrition is an important element in maintaining healthy skin and tissues. There is a strong relationship between nutrition and pressure ulcer development.[44] The severity of pressure ulceration is also correlated with severity of nutritional deficits, especially low protein intake or low serum albumin levels.[44,46,47] The nutritional assessment is key in determining the appropriate interventions for the patient. A short nutritional assessment should be performed on all patients determined at risk for pressure ulcer formation at routine intervals.

Malnutrition can be diagnosed if serum albumin levels are below 3.5 mg/dL, total lymphocyte count is less than 1,800 mm,[3] or body weight decreases by more than 15%.[1] Exhibit 12–7 provides an example of a nutritional screening tool. Malnutrition impairs the immune system, and total lymphocyte counts are a reflection of immune competence. If the patient is diagnosed as malnourished, nutritional supplementation should be instituted to help achieve a positive nitrogen balance. Examples of oral supplements are assisted oral feedings, dietary supplements, or tube feedings. Oral assisted feedings and dietary supplements are the first option for intervention, and tube feedings should be tried after other methods have failed. The goal of care is to provide approximately 30 to 35 calories per kilogram of weight per day and 1.25 to 1.5 g of protein per kilogram of weight per day.[1] Patients should be encouraged to improve their own dietary habits, and education should focus on healthy nutrition with adequate caloric and protein intake. It may be difficult for a pressure ulcer patient or an at-risk patient to ingest enough protein and calories necessary to maintain skin and tissue health. Oral supplements can be very helpful in boosting calorie and protein intake. Liquid nutritional supplements are designed to be used as an adjunct to regular oral feedings.[69] Monitoring of nutritional indexes is essential to determine effectiveness of the care plan. Serum albumin, protein markers, body weight, and nutritional assessment should be performed at least every 3 months to monitor for changes in nutritional status.

Hypoalbuminemia (serum albumin levels below 3.5 mg/dL) may be associated with pressure ulceration,[44,47] although some have found no relationship and little prognostic value for pressure ulcer healing.[70–72] When protein intake is insufficient, the serum albumin decreases. Serum albumin contributes to the amino acid pool, and amino acids are essential building blocks for new tissue development. Serum albumin also maintains oncotic pressures within the vascular fluid compartment. Colloidal oncotic pressure is the total influence of proteins on the osmotic activity of plasma. When albumin levels decrease, there is a decrease in the oncotic pressure (fewer proteins in the plasma leading to increased osmotic activity from the vascular bed, as the blood vessels attempt to maintain homeostasis by allowing osmosis of water out of the vessels and into surrounding tissues), which leads to edema, further compromising tissue perfusion.[24] Ensuring adequate protein intake is a critical element in nutritional interventions for pressure ulcer patients and those at risk for pressure ulceration.

Dehydration may influence serum albumin levels and tissue health. Nutritional assessment should include assessment of fluid intake as well as dietary intake. Vitamin and mineral deficiencies may also be present in the patient at risk for pressure ulcer development. Vitamin C and zinc supplements may assist in wound healing when deficiencies exist. Use of a multivitamin for those with deficiencies and supplemental

Exhibit 12–7 Example of Nutritional Assessment Guide for Patients with Pressure Ulcers

Patient Name: _____ Date: _____ Time: _____

To be filled out for all patients at risk on initial evaluation and every 12 weeks thereafter, as indicated. Trends will document the efficacy of nutritional support therapy.

Protein Compartments

Somatic:

Current Weight (kg)　　　　　　　 _____
Previous Weight (kg)　　　　　　　 _____　　(_____ date)
Precent Change in Weight　　　　　 _____

Height (cm)　　　　　　　　　　　 _____
Height/Weight　　　　　　　　　　 _____
Current Body Mass Index (BMI)　　 _____　　(wt(ht)²]
Previous BMI　　　　　　　　　　 _____　　(_____ date)
Percent Change in BMI

Visceral:

Serum Albumin
(Normal ≥3.5 mg/dL)
Total Lymphocyte Count (TLC)　　 _____　　(optional)
　(White Blood Cell count × percent Lymphocytes/100)

Guide to TLC:

- Immune competence　　　　　 $\geq$ 1,800 mm^3
- Immunity partly impaired　　　 < 1,800 but ≥ 900 mm^3
- Anergy　　　　　　　　　　　 < 900 mm^3

State of Hydration

24-Hour Intake _____ mL　　　　　　　24-Hour Output _____ mL

Note:　Thirst, tongue dryness in non–mouth breathers, and tenting of cervical skin may indicate dehydration. Jugular vein distention may indicate overhydration.

Estimated Nutritional Requirement

Estimated Nonprotein Calories (NPC)　 _____/kg　　Estimated Protein　 _____ (g/kg)
Actual NPC　　　　　　　　　　　　 _____/kg　　Actual Protein　　 _____ (g/kg)

Recommendations/Plan

1.
2.
3.
4.

Source: Reprinted from N. Bergstrom, M.A. Bennett, C.E. Carlson, et al., *Treatment of Pressure Ulcers,* Clinical Practice Guideline No. 15, December, 1994, U.S. Department of Health and Human Services, Public Health Service, Agency for Health Care Policy and Research, AHCPR Publication No. 95-0652.

vitamin C, zinc, and iron (if indicated by anemia) can be supportive of skin and tissue health as well as beneficial for wound healing. Clearly, the area of nutrition intervention requires an interdisciplinary approach. Involvement of the dietitian during the early assessment of the patient is important to the overall success of the plan.

Clinical Wisdom: *When To Consult the Dietitian*

General parameters for consultation with the dietitian for a thorough nutritional assessment are:

- Inadequate dietary intake,
- Drop in body weight of 5%, *or*
- Serum albumin level below 3.5 mg/dL

Moisture

The preventive interventions related to moisture include general skin care, accurate diagnosis of incontinence type, and appropriate incontinence management.

General Skin Care

General skin care involves routine skin assessment, incontinence assessment and management, skin hygiene interventions, and measures to maintain skin health. Routine skin assessment involves observation of the patient's skin with particular attention to bony prominences. Reddened areas should not be massaged. Massage can further impair the perfusion to the tissues.[73] The skin should be evaluated for dryness and cracking. Older adults are at higher risk for dry skin, and dry skin may decrease tissue tolerance to external forces. Lack of moisture in the air may contribute to dry skin and can be counteracted by use of a humidifier in the room.[74] Attention should also be focused on gentle handling to prevent skin tears in older patients. The epidermis and dermis junction is lessened with age, making older patients at higher risk for skin tears. Other factors to include in a skin assessment include temperature, sensory ability, turgor, and texture.[75] Skin should normally be warm to touch. The dorsal aspect of the hand is more sensitive to temperature changes than the palm of the hand; thus clinicians should use the dorsal aspect of the hand to judge skin temperature. Two-point discrimination is used to evaluate skin sensation. Normally the patient should be able to distinguish sharp, dull, or pressure sensations against the skin surface. Diminished sensation may be generalized or localized to a specific area such as the lower extremities. Skin tone should be smooth and elastic. Edema causes the skin to appear taut and shiny, and dehydration is present if the skin is dry, wrinkled, and with-

ered. Observing the skin surface for texture and moisture may reveal signs of excessive moisture or dryness. Most factors in a skin assessment can be reviewed through observation and palpation skills. The information gathered through the simple act of inspection can form a basis for general skin care interventions and for pressure ulcer prevention interventions.

Incontinence Assessment and Management

Specifically related to moisture, the skin should be assessed for signs of perineal dermatitis. Evaluating perineal dermatitis requires understanding of the concepts of tissue tolerance, perineal environment, and toileting ability.[76] Objective signs of perineal dermatitis include erythema, swelling, vesiculation, oozing, crusting, and scaling with subjective symptoms of tingling, itching, burning, and pain.[76] The perineal region is broadly defined as the perineum (area between the vulva or scrotum and anus), buttocks, perianal area, coccyx, and upper/inner thigh regions.[77]

The clinical presentation is variable and may be dependent on the frequency of incontinence episode, rapidity and efficacy of postepisode hygiene, and duration of incontinence. Acute and chronic clinical manifestations of skin reactions in elderly nursing home patients have been described based on clinical experience.[78]

Skin reactions can be divided into acute reactions and chronic changes. Perineal dermatitis may present with acute episode characteristics or with more long-standing chronic skin changes apparent. In acute episodes, the skin characteristics most predominant are erythema, papulovesicular reaction, frank erosions and abrasions, and, in some cases, evidence of monilial infection due to the moist warm environment. In general, a diffuse blanchable erythema is present involving both buttocks, coccyx area, perineum, perianal area, and upper/inner thighs. The extent of the erythema varies and the intensity of the reaction may be muted in immunocompromised and some elderly patients. A papulovesicular rash is particularly evident in the groin and perineum areas (upper/inner thigh, vulva/scrotal area). Secondary skin changes include crusting and scaling and are usually evident at the fringes of the reaction. Erosions and frank denudation of the skin may be more common with incontinence associated with feces. The distribution of the dermatitis differs in men and women, as might be expected. Typically, the more severe damage in male patients occurs on the posterior aspect of the penile shaft and the anterior aspect of the scrotum. More damage is seen in the lower perineal regions such as the inner thighs and low buttocks than in the higher perineal regions such as the sacral/coccygeal area or groin. In women the skin damage usually involves the vulva and groin areas and spreads distally from those sites.

Chronic skin changes in elderly patients with long-standing incontinence include a thickened appearance of skin where moisture is allowed to maintain skin contact, and increased evidence of scaling and crusting. The thickened appearance of the skin is similar to the changes seen in peristomal skin of patients with urinary diversions or ileostomies who have pouches with too large an aperture, allowing the urine or fecal effluent to pool around the stoma. This skin is overhydrated and easily abraded with minimal friction. The reaction is notable at the coccyx, scrotum, and vulva. In a cognitively impaired nursing home sample[78] there was also evidence of excoriation from patients' scratching at the affected sites. This provides early clinical validation of the symptom of itching in perineal dermatitis.

In many cases partial-thickness ulcers are present over the sacral/coccygeal area and medial buttocks region, close to the gluteal fold. Although these lesions may present as typical pressure ulcers, the underlying etiology may be the effects of incontinence on the skin. There are some characteristics of these partial-thickness ulcers that assist in differentiating them from true pressure-induced skin trauma. First, the lesions tend to be multiple in nature. The ulcers are almost always partial-thickness or stage II lesions. The lesions may or may not be directly over a bony prominence and, finally, the lesions are typically surrounded by other characteristics of perineal dermatitis (eg, diffuse blanchable erythema). When caring for patients who are incontinent of urine and feces, health care providers are faced with the challenge of preventing perineal dermatitis and pressure ulceration as a result of the decreased tissue tolerance to trauma. True pressure ulcers result from compression of the soft tissue between the bony prominence and the external surface. When moisture, urine, and feces have caused maceration and overhydration of the epidermis, the skin and tissues are less tolerant of the pressure force. Stage II pressure ulcers and partial-thickness skin lesions such as abrasions are most commonly attributed to friction and shearing forces. It is likely that incontinence plays a critical role in the development of stage II pressure ulcers.[38]

Management of incontinence is a huge topic area, and volumes have been written about various management techniques. This discussion is meant to serve as a stepping stone to those resources available to clinicians on management of the incontinent patient. The discussion therefore by necessity is noninclusive of all management strategies and only briefly addresses several strategies most pertinent to the patient at high risk of developing a pressure ulcer and measures to protect the skin from wetness and irritants. Management of incontinence is dependent on assessment and diagnosis of the problem.

Incontinence Assessment. Assessment parameters to be addressed include history, physical examination, environmental assessment, voiding/defecation diary, laboratory studies, and other diagnostic studies.[79] The history is critical to assessing the problem accurately. History taking should elicit information on patterns of urinary/fecal elimination and past/current management program, patterns of incontinence, characteristics of the urinary stream/fecal mass, sensation of bladder/rectal filling, and a focused review of systems and medical-surgical history.[80] The physical examination is designed to gather specific information related to bladder/rectal functioning and thus is limited in scope. A limited neurologic examination should provide data on the mental status and motivation of the patient/caregiver, specific motor skills, and back and lower extremities. The genitalia and perineal skin are assessed for signs of estrogenization, pelvic descent, perineal skin lesions and perineal sensation, and bulbocavernosus response in women and penis/scrotal contents, rectal and prostate, and bulbocavernosus response in men.[79,81]

The enviromental assessment should include inspection of the patient's home or nursing home facility to evaluate for the presence of environmental barriers to continence. The voiding/defecation diary is the real tool for management of continence in patients without cognitive impairment. The diary provides baseline data on the problem and so provides a mechanism for determining therapy effectiveness for the future.[79] The diary may provide valuable information for diagnostic purposes. In cognitively impaired patients, the caregiver may complete the diary, and management strategies again can be identified from the baseline data.

Laboratory tests help to rule out infections and other pathology responsible for the incontinence. Some specialized studies are helpful in further evaluation of the condition. Urodynamic studies for urinary incontinence provide valuable data related to the pathology. Even in nursing home populations simple bedside urodynamics can be a useful clinical tool to elicit more specific data on urinary function.[81] Management strategies for incontinence are grouped into three main areas for this discussion: behavioral management, containment strategies, and skin protection guidelines.

Incontinence Management Strategies. Patients at risk for pressure ulcer developement are not candidates for all methods of behavioral management. The most successful behavioral management strategies for the frail cognitively impaired patient typically at risk of pressure ulcer development include prompted voiding and scheduled toileting programs. Both strategies are caregiver dependent and require a motivated caregiver to be successful. Scheduled intake of fluid is an important underlying factor for both strategies.

Scheduled toileting or habit training is toileting on a planned basis. The goal is to keep the person dry by assisting him or her to void at regular intervals. There can be attempts to match the interval to the individual patient's natural voiding schedule. There is no systematic effort to motivate patients to delay voiding or to resist the urge to void. Scheduled toileting may be based on the clock (toilet the patient every 2 hours) or based on activities (toilet the patient after meals and before transferring to bed). Several studies have demonstrated improvement in continence status in some patients.[80,82]

Prompted voiding has been shown to be effective in dependent and cognitively impaired nursing home incontinent patients.[83,84] Prompted voiding involves use of a toileting schedule (every 2 hours) similar to habit training or scheduled toileting. Prompted voiding supplements the routine with teaching the incontinent patient to discriminate their continence status and to request toileting assistance. The three major elements in prompted voiding include monitoring the incontinent patient routinely, prompting the patient to use the toilet, and praising the patient for maintenance of continence. Prompted voiding results in 40% to 50% reduction in frequency of daytime incontinence and between 25% and 33% of urinary incontinent patients in nursing homes respond to the therapy.[83,84] Both of these behavioral management strategies have the added benefit of moving the patient at routine intervals, which should relieve pressure over bony prominences and reduce the risk of pressure ulcer development by allowing reperfusion of the tissues.

Underpads and briefs may be used to protect the skin of patients who are incontinent of urine or stool. These products are designed to absorb moisture, wick the wetness away from the skin, and maintain a quick-drying interface with the skin.[26] Studies with both infants and adults demonstrate that products designed to present a quick-drying surface to the skin and to absorb moisture do keep the skin drier and are associated with a lower incidence of dermatitis.[41] It is important to note that the critical feature is the ability to absorb moisture and present a quick-drying surface, not whether the product is disposable or reusable. Regardless of the product chosen, containment strategies imply the need for a check and change schedule for the incontinent patient so wet linens and pads may be removed in a timely manner. Underpads are not as tight or constricting as briefs. Kemp[38] suggests alternating the use of underpads and briefs if the skin irritation is thought to be related to the occlusive nature of the brief. Her recommendations echo the early work of Willis[85] on warm water immersion syndrome, who found that the effects of water on the skin could be reversed and tempered by simply allowing the skin to dry out between wet periods. Use of briefs when the patient is up in a chair, ambulating, or visiting another department and use of underpads when the patient is in bed is one suggestion for combining the strengths of both products.[38]

External collection devices may be more effective with male patients. External catheters or condom catheters are devices applied to the shaft of the penis to direct the urine away from the body to a collection device. Newer models of external catheters are self-adhesive and easy to apply. For patients with a retracted penis, a special pouching system, similar to an ostomy pouch, is available—the retracted penis pouch.[86] A key concern with use of external collection devices is routine removal of the product and inspection and hygiene of the skin.

There are special containment devices for fecal incontinence as well. Fecal incontinence collectors consist of a self-adhesive skin barrier attached to a drainable pouch. Application of the device is somewhat dependent on the skill of the clinician, and the patient should be put on a routine for changing the pouch prior to leakage to facilitate success. The skin barrier provides a physical obstacle on the skin to the stool and helps prevent dermatitis and associated skin problems. In fact, skin barrier wafers without an attached pouch can be useful in protecting the skin from feces or urine.

The AHCPR panel on guidelines for the prevention and prediction of pressure ulcers in adults[26] recommends use of moisturizers for dry skin and use of lubricants for reduction in friction injuries. The panel also discusses the use of moisture barriers, to protect the skin from the effects of moisture. Although the recommendation is made to use products to provide a moisture barrier, the reader is cautioned that the recommendation is derived from usual practice and professional standards and it is not research based. The success of the particular product is linked to how it is formulated and the hydrophobic properties of the product.[38] Generally, pastes are thicker and more repellent of moisture than ointments. A quick evaluation is the ease with which the product can be removed with water during routine cleansing. If the product comes off the skin with just routine cleansing, it probably is not an effective barrier to moisture. Use of mineral oil for cleansing some of the heavier barrier products, such as zinc oxide paste, will ease removal from the skin.

The role of incontinence as a risk factor in predicting pressure ulcer formation is somewhat unclear. From a pathophysiologic perspective, creating a skin environment favorable to friction and abrasion makes incontinence a key risk factor for those persons with additional risk for pressure ulcer development. When caring for the incontinent patient, health care providers must address prevention by assessment and treatment of transient causes of the condition. Systematic assessment is the key to defining management strategies. Assessment includes the parameters of patient history, physical examination, environment, voiding/defecation diary, laboratory studies, and other diagnostic studies. Measures to manage incontinence include caregiver-dependent behavioral management therapies of scheduled toileting and prompted voiding, containment devices and products, and skin protection using barriers.

Skin Hygiene Interventions. Skin hygiene interventions involve daily skin hygiene and skin cleansing after fecal or urinary incontinent episodes. The older adults' skin is less tolerant of the drying effects of soap and hot water. Use of warm water and a mild soap (if any soap at all) can limit skin drying. Daily bathing is not necessary for skin health in most older adults. Use of a schedule of twice weekly or every other day bathing or showering is sufficient for most older adults. Daily cleansing of the feet, axilla, and perineal areas is appropriate, but daily showers or baths can be damaging to the skin. Use of solutions designed for incontinence care cleansing can be protective of the skin and can decrease the time and energy involved in postincontinent episode cleansing. These commercially available cleansers include surfactants as ingredients. The surfactants make the removal of urine and stool residue easier with less abrasiveness. Every attempt should be made to cleanse the perineal skin immediately after an incontinent episode to limit the amount of contact time between the urine and stool and the skin.

Skin Maintenance Interventions. Skin maintenance interventions involve actions to prevent skin breakdown and actions to promote healthy skin. Maintaining skin lubrication is an important skin maintenance intervention. Use of moisturizers on a routine basis can prevent skin drying and cracking. Application of moisturizers immediately after bathing or showering helps to remoisturize and lubricate the skin. There are three main types of moisturizers—lotions, creams, and ointments. Lotions have the highest water content and therefore must be reapplied more frequently to be effective. Creams are mixtures of oil and water and for best results should be applied four times a day. Ointments (generally lanolin or petrolatum bases) have the lowest water content, are the most occlusive, and have the longest duration of moisturizing action. Special attention to moisturizing the lower legs and feet is often needed to compensate for decreased perfusion and diminished skin health in these areas.

OUTCOME MEASURES

The most appropriate outcome measures to evaluate the effectiveness of prevention programs are incidence and prevalence rates. When a prevention program is successful, the organization's incidence of pressure ulcer development should decrease (if appropriate) or remain at a low level. If a patient already has a pressure ulcer, a successful outcome for pressure ulcer prevention is no further areas of skin breakdown.

REFERRAL CRITERIA

Referral criteria for pressure ulcer prevention programs relate to the need for a interdisciplinary approach to prevention of pressure ulcers. Referrals assist with appropriate management for particular risk factors for developing pressure ulcers. Use referral in the following circumstances:

- Nutritional consultation for patients determined at risk for malnutrition or with nutritional concerns
- Enterostomal therapy (ET) nurse (or clinical specialist in this area) consultation for patients with urinary or fecal incontinence
- Physical therapy for assistance with correct positioning in seated individuals

SELF-CARE TEACHING GUIDELINES

Patient's and caregiver's instruction in self-care must be individualized to specific pressure ulcer development risk factors, the individual patient's learning style and coping mechanisms, and the ability of the patient/caregiver to perform procedures. These general self-care teaching guidelines must be individualized for each patient and caregiver. In teaching prevention guidelines to caregivers it is particularly important to use return demonstration by the caregiver as evaluation of learning. Observing the caregiver perform turning manuevers, repositioning, managing incontinence, and providing general skin care can be enlightening and provides the context in which the clinician provides support and follow-up education. Exhibit 12–8 provides general self-care teaching guidelines.

Exhibit 12–8 Self-Care Teaching Guidelines

Self-Care Guidelines Specific to Pressure Ulcer Prevention	Instructions Given (Date/Initials)	Demonstration *or* Review of Material (Date/Initials)	Return Demonstration *or* States Understanding (Date/Initials)
1. Identification of specific risk factors for pressure ulcer development			
2. Immobility, inactivity, and decreased sensory perception strategies a. Passive repositioning			
(1) Demonstrates one-person turning			
(2) Demonstrates two-person turning			
(3) Frequency of turning/repositioning			
(4) Full shifts in position versus small shifts in position			
(5) Avoidance of 90° sidelying position, demonstrates 30° laterally inclined position			
(6) Passive range of motion exercises and frequency			
b. Pillow bridging			
(1) Use of pillows to protect heels			
(2) Pillows between bony prominences			
c. Pressure-reducing/relieving support surface			
(1) Management of support surface in use			
(2) Devices for sitting			
(3) Up in chair for _____ hour(s), _____ time(s) per day			
3. Nutrition strategies a. Provide adequate nutrition			
(1) Small frequent (six meals a day) high-calorie/high-protein meals			
(2) Nutritional supplements provided. Give _____ oz of _____ supplement _____ times per day.			
b. Provide adequate hydration (1) Eight 8-oz glasses of noncaffeine fluids per day unless contraindicated			
c. Provide vitamin/mineral supplements (1) Vitamin C, zinc, iron (Give as ordered.)			
4. Friction and shear strategies			
a. Use of turning and draw sheets			
b. Use of cornstarch, lubricants, pad protectors, thin film dressings, or hydrocolloid dressings over friction risk sites			
c. General skin care (1) Skin cleansing			
(2) Skin moisturizing (Use _____ product on _____ areas of skin, _____ times a day.)			

continues

Exhibit 12–8 continued

Self-Care Guidelines Specific to Pressure Ulcer Prevention	Instructions Given (Date/Initials)	Demonstration *or* Review of Material (Date/Initials)	Return Demonstration *or* States Understanding (Date/Initials)
5. Moisture—incontinence management strategies 　a. Use of absorbent products 　　(1) Pad when lying in bed			
(2) Brief or panty pad when up in chair or walking			
b. Use of ointments, creams, and skin barriers prophylactically in perineal and perianal areas (Use _____ product on perineal/perianal areas of skin, _____ times a day.)			
c. Use of behavioral management strategies for incontinence 　　(1) Scheduled toileting: toilet every _____ hours			
(2) Prompted voiding			
d. General skin care 　　(1) Skin cleansing 　　　(a) Cleanser: _____			
(b) Soap: _____			
(c) Frequency: _____			
(2) Skin moisturizing (Use _____ product(s) on _____ areas of skin, _____ times a day.)			
(3) Skin inspection daily			
6. Importance of follow-up with health care provider			

REFERENCES

1. Bergstrom N, Bennett MA, Carlson CE, et al. *Treatment of Pressure Ulcers.* Clinical Practice Guideline No. 15. AHCPR Publication No. 95-0652. Rockville, MD: Agency for Health Care Policy and Research, U.S. Public Health Service, U.S. Department of Health and Human Services; December 1994.

2. National Pressure Ulcer Advisory Panel. *Pressure Ulcers: Incidence, Economics, Risk Assessment. Consensus Development Conference Statement.* West Dundee, IL: S-N Publications, Inc; 1989:3–4.

3. Daniel RK, Priest DL, Wheatley DC. Etiologic factors in pressure sores: an experimental model. *Arch Phys Med Rehabil.* 1981;62(10):492–498.

4. Kosiak M. Etiology and pathology of ischemic ulcers. *Arch Phys Med Rehabil.* 1959;40:62–69.

5. Reuler JB, Cooney TG. The pressure sore: pathophysiology and principles of management. *Ann Intern Med.* 1981;94:661.

6. Seiler WD, Stahelin HB. Recent findings on decubitus ulcer pathology: implications for care. *Geriatrics.* 1986;41:47–60.

7. Witkowski JA, Parish LC. Histopathology of the decubitus ulcer. *J Am Acad Dermatol.* 1982;6:1014–1021.

8. Lindan O, Greenway RM, Piazza JM. Pressure distributor on the surface of the human body. *Arch Phys Med Rehabil.* 1965;46:378.

9. Scales JT. Pressure on the patient. In: Kenedi RN, Cowden JM, eds. *Bedsore Biomechanics.* Baltimore: University Park Press; 1976.

10. Parish, LC, Witkowski JA, Crissey JT. *The Decubitus Ulcer.* New York: Masson Publishing; 1983.

11. Slater H. *Pressure Ulcers in the Elderly.* Pittsburgh, PA: Synapse Publications; 1985.

12. Walker PM. Ischemial reperfusion injury in skeletal muscle. *Ann Vasc Surg.* 1991;5(4):399–402.

13. Hernandez-Maldonado JJ, Teehan E, Franco CD, Duran WN, Hobson RW. Superoxide anion production by leukocytes exposed to post-ischemic skeletal muscle. *J Cardiovasc Surg.* 1992;33:695–699.

14. Landis EM. Micro-injection studies of capillary blood pressure in human skin. *Heart.* 1930;15:209.

15. Husain T. An experimental study of some pressure effects on tissues, with reference to the bedsore problem. *J Pathol Bacteriol.* 1953;66:347–358.

16. Salcido R, et al. Histopathology of decubitus ulcers as a result of sequential pressure sessions in a computer-controlled fuzzy rat model. *Adv Wound Care.* 1993;7(5):40.

17. Kosiak M, Kubicek WG, Olsen M, Danz JN, Kottke FJ. Evaluation of pressure as a factor in the production of ischial ulcers. *Arch Phys Med Rehabil.* 1958;39:623.

18. Edberg EL, Cerny K, Stauffer ES. Prevention and treatment of pressure sores. *Phys Ther.* 1973;53:246–252.

19. Bennett MA. Report of the task force on the implications for darkly pigmented intact skin in the prediction and prevention of pressure ulcers. *Adv Wound Care.* 1995;8(6):34–35.

20. Graves DJ. Stage I in ebony complexion. *Decubitus.* 1990;3(4):4. Letter to the Editor.

21. Parish LC, Witkowski JA, Crissey JT, eds. *The Decubitis Ulcer in Clinical Practice.* Berlin, Germany: Springer-Verlag; 1997.

22. Meehan M. Multisite pressure ulcer prevalence survey. *Decubitus.* 1990;3(4):14–17.

23. Knight DB, Scott H. Contracture and pressure necrosis. *Ostomy Wound Manage.* 1990;26(1):60–67.

24. Maklebust J, Sieggreen M. *Pressure Ulcers: Guidelines for Prevention and Nursing Management.* 2nd ed. Springhouse, PA: Springhouse; 1996.

25. Shea JD. Pressures sores: classification and management. *Clin Orthop.* 1975;112:89–100.

26. Panel for the Prediction and Prevention of Pressure Ulcers. *Pressure Ulcers in Adults: Prediction and Prevention.* Clinical Practice Guideline No. 3. AHCPR Publication No. 92-0047. Rockville, MD: Agency for Health Care Policy and Research, U.S. Public Health Service, U.S. Department of Health and Human Services; 1992.

27. Maklebust J. Pressure ulcer staging systems: NPUAP Conference Proceedings. *Adv Wound Care.* 1995;8(4):28-11–28-14.

28. Allman RM. Pressure ulcers among the elderly. *N Engl J Med.* 1989;320:850.

29. Braden BJ, Bergstrom N. A conceptual schema for the study of etiology of pressure sores. *Rehabil Nurs.* 1987;12(1):8–12.

30. Bergstrom N, Demuth PJ, Braden BJ. A clinical trial of the Braden Scale for predicting pressure sore risk. *Nurs Clin North Am.* 1987;22:417–428.

31. Exton-Smith AN, Sherwin RW. The prevention of pressure sores: significance of spontaneous bodily movements. *Lancet.* 1961;2:1124–1126.

32. Allman RM, Goode PS, Patrick MM, et al. Pressure ulcer risk factors among hospitalized patients with activity limitations. *JAMA.* 1995;273:865–870.

33. Curry K, Casady L. The relationship between extended periods of immobility and decubitus ulcer formation in the acutely spinal cord injured individual. *J Neurosci Nurs.*1992;24:185–189.

34. Hammond MC, Bozzacco VA, Stiens SA, et al. Pressure ulcer incidence on a spinal cord injury unit. *Adv Wound Care.* 1994;7(6):57–60.

35. Reichel SM. Shearing force as a factor in decubitus ulcers in paraplegics. *JAMA.* 1958;166:762–763.

36. Bennett L, Kavner D, Lee BY, Trainor FS. Skin stress and blood flow in sitting paraplegic patients. *Arch Phys Med Rehabil.* 1984;65(4):186–190.

37. Dinsdale JM. Decubitus ulcers: role of pressure and friction in causation. *Arch Phys Med Rehabil.* 1974;55:147–153.

38. Kemp MG. Protecting the skin from moisture and associated irritants. *J Gerontol Nurs.* 1994;20(9):8–14.

39. Bates-Jensen B. Incontinence management. In: Parish LC, Witkowski JA, Crissey JT, eds. *The Decubitus Ulcer in Clinical Practice.* Berlin, Germany: Springer-Verlag;1997:189–199.

40. Berg RW, Milligan MC, Sarbaugh FC. Association of skin wetness and pH with diaper dermatitis. *Pediatr Dermatol.* 1994;11:18–20.

41. Zimmerer RE, Lawson KD, Calvert CJ. The effects of wearing diapers on skin. *Pediatr Dermatol.* 1986;3:95–101.

42. Buckingham KW, Berg RW. Etiologic factors in diaper dermatitis: the role of feces. *Pediatr Dermatol.* 1986;3:107–112.

43. Maklebust J, Magnan MA. Risk factors associated with having a pressure ulcer: a secondary data analysis. *Adv Wound Care.* 1994;7(6):25–42.

44. Pinchcovsky-Devin G, Kaminsky MV Jr. Correlation of pressure sores and nutritional status. *J Am Geriatr Soc.* 1986;34:435–440.

45. Bobel LM. Nutritional implications in the patient with pressure sores. *Nurs Clin North Am.* 1987;22:379–390.

46. Bergstrom N, Braden B. A prospective study of pressure sore risk among institutionalized elderly. *J Am Geriatr Soc.* 1992;40: 747–758.

47. Allman RM, Laprade CA, Noel LB, et al. Pressure sores among hospitalized patients. *Ann Intern Med.* 1986;105:337–342.

48. Jones PL, Millman A. Wound healing and the aged patient. *Nurs Clin North Am.* 1990;25:263–277.

49. Eaglestein WH. Wound healing and aging. *Clin Geriatr Med.* 1989;5:183.

50. Versluysen M. Pressure sores in elderly patients: the epidemiology related to hip operations. *J Bone Joint Surg Br.* 1985;67:10–13.

51. Shannon ML. Pressures sores. In: Norris CM, ed. *Concept Clarification in Nursing.* Gaithersburg, MD: Aspen Publishers, Inc; 1982.

52. Anderson TP, Andberg MM. Psychosocial factors associated with pressure sores. *Arch Phys Med Rehabil.* 1979;60:341–346.

53. Vidal J, Sarrias M. An analysis of the diverse factors concerned with the development of pressure sores in spinal cord patients. *Paraplegia.* 1991;29:261–267.

54. Norton D, McLaren R, Exton-Smith NA. *An Investigation of Geriatric Nursing Problems in Hospitals.* Edinburgh, Scotland: Churchill Livingstone; 1962.

55. Norton D. Calculating the risk: reflections on the Norton Scale. *Decubitus.* 1989;2(3):24–31.

56. Gosnell DJ. Pressure sore risk assessment: a critique, I: the Gosnell Scale. *Decubitus.* 1989;2(3):32–39.

57. Gosnell DJ. Pressure sore risk assessment: a critique, II: analysis of risk factors. *Decubitus.* 1989;2(3):40–43.

58. Braden B, Bergstrom N. Clinical utility of the Braden Scale for predicting pressure sore risk. *Decubitus.* 1989;2(3):44–51.

59. Bergstrom N, Braden BJ, Boynton P, Bruch S. Using a research-based assessment scale in clinical practice. *Nurs Clin North Am.* 1995;30:539.

60. Seiler WO, Allen S, Stahelin HB. Influence of the 30 degrees laterally inclined position and the "super soft" 3-piece mattress on skin oxygen tension on areas of maximum pressure: implications for pressure sores prevention. *Gerontology.* 1986;32: 158–166.

61. Lowthian PT. Practical nursing: turning clock system to prevent pressure sores. *Nurs Mirror.* 1979;148(21):30–31.

62. Smith AM, Malone JA. Preventing pressure ulcers in institutionalized elders: assessing the effects of small, unscheduled shifts in body position. *Decubitus.* 1990;3(4):20–24.

63. McLean J. Pressure reduction or pressure relief: making the right choice. *J ET Nurs.* 1993;20:211–215.

64. Krouskop TA, Garber SL, Cullen BB. Factors to consider in selecting a support surface. In: Krasner D, ed. *Chronic Wound Care.* King

of Prussia, PA: Health Management Publications, Inc; 1990: 135–141.

65. Garber SL, Krouskop TA, Cullen BB. The role of technology in pressure ulcer prevention. In: Krasner D, ed. *Chronic Wound Care.* King of Prussia, PA: Health Management Publications, Inc; 1990.

66. Krouskop TA, Garber SL. Interface pressure confusion. *Decubitus.* 1989;2:8.

67. Bryant RA, Shannon ML, Pieper B, et al. Pressure ulcers. In: Bryant RA, ed. *Acute and Chronic Wounds: Nursing Management.* St. Louis, MO: Mosby–Year Book; 1992.

68. International Association for Enterostomal Therapy (IAET). *Dermal Wounds: Pressure Sores. Standards of Care.* Irvine, CA: IAET; 1987.

69. Wroblewski JJ. Nutritional aspects of pressure ulcer care. In: Krasner D, ed. *Chronic Wound Care.* King of Prussia, PA: Health Management Publications, Inc; 1990:188–193.

70. Berlowitz D, Wilking S. The short term outcome of pressure sores. *J Am Geriatr Soc.* 1990;38:748–752.

71. Hill DP, Cooper DM, Robson MC. Serum albumin is a poor prognostic factor for pressure ulcer healing in controlled clinical trials. *Wounds.* 1994;6(5):174–178.

72. Stotts N. Nutritional parameters at hospital admission as predictors of pressure ulcer development in elective surgery. *J Parenter Enter Nutr.* 1987;11:298–301.

73. Olson B. The effects of massage for prevention of pressure ulcers. *Decubitus.* 1989;2(4):32–37.

74. Franz RA, Gardner S. Clinical concerns: management of dry skin. *Gerontol Nurs.* 1994;20(9):15–18, 45.

75. Gosnell DJ. Assessment and evaluation of pressure sores. *Nurs Clin North Am.* 1987;22:399–416.

76. Brown DS, Sears M. Perineal dermatitis: a conceptual framework. *Ostomy Wound Manage.* 1993;39(7):20–25.

77. Brown DS. Perineal dermatitis: can we measure it? *Ostomy Wound Manage.* 1993;39(7):28–31.

78. Schnelle JF, Adamson G, Cruise PA, et al. Skin disorders and moisture in incontinent nursing home residents: Intervention implications. (In Press).

79. Gray M. Assessment of patients with urinary incontinence. In: Doughty D, ed. *Urinary and Fecal Incontinence: Nursing Management.* St. Louis, MO: Mosby–Year Book; 1992:47–94.

80. Urinary Incontinence Guideline Panel. *Urinary Incontinence in Adults: Clinical Practice Guidelines.* AHCPR Publication No. 92-0038. Rockville, MD: Agency for Health Care Policy and Research, U.S. Public Health Service, U.S. Department of Health and Human Services; March 1992.

81. Kane RL, Ouslander JG, Abrass IB, eds. Incontinence. In: *Essentials of Clinical Geriatrics.* 2nd ed. New York: McGraw-Hill Information Services Company; 1989:139–190.

82. Schnelle JF, Newman DR, Fogarty T. Management of patient continence in long-term care nursing facilities. *Gerontologist.* 1990;30:373–376.

83. Schnelle JF. Treatment of urinary incontinence in nursing home patients by prompted voiding. *J Am Geriatr Soc.* 1990;38:356–360.

84. Ouslander JG, Schnelle JF, Uman G, et al. Predictors of successful prompted voiding among incontinent nursing home residents. *JAMA.* 1995;273:1366–1370.

85. Willis I. The effects of prolonged water exposure on human skin. *J Invest Dermatol.* 1973;60:166–171.

86. Jeter KF. The use of incontinence products. In: Jeter KF, Faller N, Norton C, eds. *Nursing for Continence.* Philadelphia: W.B. Saunders Company; 1990:209–220.

SUGGESTED READING

Bryant RA, ed. *Acute and Chronic Wounds: Nursing Management.* St. Louis: MO: Mosby–Year Book; 1992.

Jeter JF, Faller N, Norton C, eds. *Nursing for Continence.* Philadelphia: W.B. Saunders Company; 1990:223–240.

Krasner D, Kane D., eds. *Chronic Wound Care,* 2nd ed. King of Prussia, PA: Health Management Publications, Inc; 1996.

CHAPTER 13

Management of Pressure by Therapeutic Positioning

Laurie M. Rappl

INTRODUCTION

Therapeutic positioning is a dynamic and necessary part of the wound care management program of any person. Without properly positioning a person in bed or in a sitting position, skin management programs can be devastated by inappropriately high carrying loads on improper bony prominences. Persons who become sitting dependent more than ambulatory, and/or who use the lying down or the sitting position for the majority of the day, are at high risk of skin breakdown. And, for the patient with an existing pressure ulcer, proper positioning in the most active and functional position possible both in sitting and in recumbent positions will improve the healing rate of the ulcer and help minimize the likelihood of recurrence.

Advances in equipment to meet seating needs has, of necessity, elevated therapeutic positioning to a specialty within the therapist and technology supplier ranks. The specialty is as complex as the numbers of people it services, and it is beyond the scope of this chapter to cover all seating/positioning topics thoroughly. Information provided presents (1) an overview of the areas the clinician should examine in order to determine the need for intervention, (2) the basics of therapeutic positioning, (3) how therapeutic positioning affects body system impairments, and (4) some specifics in positioning the patient with an existing ulcer both sitting and lying down.

Just as pressure ulcers cross all ages, from pediatrics to young adults to middle age to older adults, so does the need for therapeutic positioning become appropriate for all age groups as well.

Although incidence rates of ulcers on specific bony prominences vary, it is conservative to estimate that 50% of all skin breakdown occurs on the sacrum and the ischial tuber-osities,[1,2] the major weight-bearing surfaces of the sitting-dependent person. It has also been estimated that 75% of the sitting-dependent population will experience the development of pressure ulcers. Of these, 75% will have a recurrence of that same breakdown.[3–5] Recent literature reports failure rates for flap surgeries of 76% to 91%.[3,4] In addition, it is standard procedure for the plastic surgeon to plan for five more donor sites for flaps on a patient before doing the first one! This confirms what is already known: treating the symptom does not effect a cure. Therapeutic positioning using correctly chosen equipment plays a direct and critical role in reducing these staggering numbers.

The human body requires support for proper balance both in the sitting position and in recumbent positions. Any person who depends on the sitting position for any part of the day or night should be evaluated to ensure that the optimal position is being attained. The more sitting dependent the person is, the more acute is the need for proper positioning interventions. However, although the full-time wheelchair user is often thought of as the only candidate for therapeutic positioning, the part-time user and the able-bodied who may only sit for relatively short periods of time each day are also candidates. Both full-time and part-time wheelchair users must be evaluated for appropriate support surfaces and positioning in recumbent postures.

THE DIAGNOSTIC PROCESS APPLIED TO THERAPEUTIC POSITIONING

The diagnostic process outlined in Chapter 1 begins with the reason for referral. The clinician should obtain a history of the patient before examination in order to determine the systems to review. The review of systems will determine the evaluations needed and will dictate the examination strategy. The clinician then collates the information gathered to determine a functional diagnosis that will guide selection of the equipment and positioning interventions required. A prognosis and predicted outcome complete the process.

History

The reason for referral will give the clinician the first clue to the positioning needs. The reason the family, the caregiver, or the person seeks positioning assistance will usually translate into the main goal for positioning, a goal that cannot be subordinate to the clinician's. The goal of the caregiver may be comfort in recumbent positions for a noncommunicative patient, whereas the clinician may want to pursue a more aggressive program to reverse contractures. The clinician's goal may be appropriate, but if the caregiver cannot devote the time or the financial resources to an aggressive program, the clinician may have to consider less aggressive positioning goals.

The medical history is significant for any past surgeries or conditions that would limit the ability of the patient to achieve the "ideal" position, or that may need accommodation to help the person maintain that position. Note any conditions that are progressive, such as multiple sclerosis, that would necessitate equipment that can be changed with the changing needs of the patient as the disease progresses and skills decrease. Conversely, conditions may improve with therapeutic positioning intervention, such as a decrease in abnormal muscle tone and a corresponding increase in postural muscle tone; this will also require modification to the seating intervention to match the patient's improvement. Orthopaedic interventions that have been performed that affect normal joint movement, or the normal functioning of the skeletal system, are of special note. For example, spinal fixation may limit range of motion in the trunk and pelvis, and may necessitate equipment that does not force the body to sit in level planes, but will accommodate and support a tilted pelvis or curved back posture.

The living situation and the person's level of independence will indicate the level of involvement the equipment can have. For example, a person in a solid, supportive home environment with a limited number of consistent caregivers may be able to handle more involved equipment than someone in a group living situation with multiple caregivers. The number of hours spent in sitting or in lying down will allude to the risk of breakdown; generally, increased time in sitting or lying down equates to higher risk of breakdown and more care in equipment selection and training.

Systems Review

Too often the wound management program fails to encompass system impairments leading to pressure ulcers, instead focusing on the support surface on the bed, and on the direct treatment of the wound through dressings and modalities that affect microcirculation. Impairments to be managed occur in the neuromuscular system, the musculoskeletal system, the cardiopulmonary and vascular systems, the integumentary system, and the psychosocial/cognitive system. Many impairments in all of these systems can be managed by therapeutic positioning in the bed or the chair. Some of these system impairments have been called the "hazards of immobility" and are well known. Therapeutic positioning is a powerful modality to effect changes in treatment programs involving all systems.

Neuromuscular System

Impairment of the central or peripheral nervous system will have profound effects on the development of pressure ulcers. If sensation is diminished, the bony prominences in the insensate areas of the body will have an undue susceptibility to pressure ulceration, especially those that will be weight bearing. Equipment selection and positioning must protect and unweight the skin over bony prominences in the impaired areas as much as possible. In sitting, these are the ischials, sacrum, and coccyx. It is well known that bed rest often leads to breakdown on several bony prominences, including heels, malleoli (ankles), and trochanters (hips). The choice of support surface and instruction in proper recumbent positioning are critical in protecting the insensate patient, especially one with poor self-repositioning abilities.

If there is an insult to the central nervous system, such as a stroke, brain injury, or spinal cord injury, or disease of the central nervous system, there may be a lack of reflex integrity or loss of motor control. A lack of reflex integrity will cause uncontrolled muscular movement patterns such as posturing or spasticity. A high level of spasticity or a loss of motor control requires equipment that offers more support to the body, as the equipment will give the person the ability to maintain a position. For example, excessive tone in extension will cause the hips to extend out of the ideal 90° position, and the hips will slide forward on the seat. Spasticity, with its uncontrolled, repetitive movements through specific ranges, causes shearing, a major factor in skin breakdown. If not inhibited with appropriate therapeutic positioning in the chair and the bed, spasticity can lead to the development of irreversible muscle and joint contractures. The equipment must support the body in reflex-inhibiting postures (neutral or flexion for extension tone, neutral or extension for flexion tone) in order to control involuntary movements and the development of contractures. With degenerative diseases of the central nervous system such as multiple sclerosis, the clinician must select equipment that can be modified as the disease progresses and that can be altered to provide more support.

Musculoskeletal System

The musculoskeletal system is responsible for motor function—strength, ergonomics, and activities of daily living. Impairment of the musculoskeletal system such as fixed or flexible contractures, limitations in range of motion and joint integrity, and skeletal deformities change strength and ability to perform activities of daily living. A loss of motor function or muscle strength, revealed in a manual muscle test and ergonomics or mobility assessment, will impair the person's ability to self-position and to maintain correct postures. Incorrect postures are unsafe for skin and will lead to breakdown and deformities unless accommodated for through positioning. The equipment may again be required to be more supportive than for a person with more intact motor abilities. The degree and location of muscular weakness will also have an impact on the choice of mobility base (wheelchair, scooter, recliner chair, etc.), as powered bases may be required for higher needs, or hemiheight chairs may be required for those who propel with their feet. A firm support surface that enhances mobility may be necessary to assist the person with musculoskeletal impairment in independent repositioning and thus enhances the safety of the skin.

The more activities of daily living that must be done sitting or lying down, the more positioning may be required to ensure proper body function and skin safety. For example, if the person eats in bed or in the mobility base, the positioning system must support safe swallowing. Impairments in range of motion and joint integrity will directly affect the ability of the body to maintain the ideal position and can result in the body's carrying uneven pressures, resulting in skin breakdown. For example, the person who cannot reach 90° of hip flexion will sacral sit and cause excessive pressures on the coccyx and the spinous processes. Equipment must accommodate for the limitations in range by supporting the body at the angle available at the hip with a reclining back and a supportive cushion and/or an angled seat. The person who has had a cerebrovascular accident (CVA), with one side of the body stronger than the other, will tend to sit unevenly, thus overweighting one ischium and putting skin in that location at high risk.

When considering skeletal deformities, consider both those induced by trauma (accident) and those induced by surgery (purposeful) and whether they are fixed or flexible. The deformity's effect on achieving the ideal position is the overriding concern. A common example of a purposeful skeletal deformity is a unilateral ischiectomy resulting in a flexible asymmetric pelvis and scoliosis. The ischiectomy causes the pelvis to sit unevenly on a cushion that works by weighting the ischials and can lead to scoliosis or to skin breakdown on the sitting surface of the lower side. A cushion that does not depend on ischial weight bearing, but rather on femoral weight bearing, will accommodate this patient better, as the cushion will not cause the pelvis to sit unevenly, despite the surgical procedure.

A flexible deformity is an impairment that can be corrected by the proper equipment, as described above. A fixed deformity, however, is a disability that must be accommodated by the equipment. Rather than attempting to correct a fixed deformity the equipment must conform to the deformity, and help hold it in the position as close to proper as possible.

Evaluation or reevaluation for seating needs must be done when significant weight loss is noted. Significant weight loss can make bony prominences that were once fairly protected much more vulnerable to the effects of pressure and shear.

Cardiopulmonary and Vascular Systems

Impairments in the cardiopulmonary and vascular systems directly affect the ability of the blood to carry oxygen and nutrients to the integumentary system. Medical diagnoses such as chronic obstructive pulmonary disease (COPD), emphysema, cardiomyopathy, arteriosclerotic vascular disease, and hypertension indicate impairment in these systems and in their ability to deliver oxygen to the tissues, increasing risk of ischemia and pressure ulceration to areas subject to compression of tissues by bony prominences. Therapeutic positioning of those areas of the body affected by the above diagnoses is of paramount importance in helping to avoid skin breakdown in the patient with impairments in these systems.

Inactivity and extended bed rest have several negative effects on these systems. Blood flow will be reduced throughout the body and, therefore, to any wound sites. Decreased total blood volume and decreased hemoglobin concentration, increased resting heart rate, and decreased maximum oxygen consumption ($\dot{V}o_2max$) have also been documented. Immobility promotes fluid stasis in the kidneys, which can lead to kidney stones and infection.[6] Nutrition intake can be impaired, as the recumbent and inactive positions reduce the appetite. Recumbency inhibits safe swallowing and facilitates aspiration of food, leading to pneumonia. Swallowing occurs 24 hours per day, not just at mealtime. The correct head and neck positions conducive to safe swallowing should be identified and attained in the chair and the bed; consultation with a speech/language pathologist may be necessary for success in this area.

Oxygenation of the blood may be impaired if the person carries any of the cardiopulmonary diagnoses. Proper upright positioning allows greater diaphragmatic expansion, improves breathing patterns and depth (thus improving oxygenation of the blood), and mobilizes pulmonary secretions.[7] Upright positioning in a functional and comfortable position will improve general circulation by placing the patient in a position that encourages activity and movement. Cardiac function is also improved in the upright position. Upright positioning with pressure eliminated on the bony prominences will improve circulation to the ulcer site by gravity, which pulls blood down to the ulcer site.

Clinical Wisdom: *Prone Positioning*

It has been suggested that, for the sitting-dependent person with breakdown on the sitting surfaces, the prone position with the wound uppermost actually inhibits circulation to the wound site by assisting blood to flow as a liquid will, away from the highest point.

Integumentary System

Skin is more susceptible to breakdown if it is dry, flaky, friable, aged, insensate, prone to excessive sweating, or subjected to incontinence, friction, or shear. Positioning can affect the integumentary system by protecting the skin over bony prominences on weight-bearing surfaces through correct use of the proper equipment to maintain safe postures and to unweight those bony prominences. For some people, an equalization of pressure is sufficient to protect skin from breakdown. For others, complete removal of pressure may be needed for protection, as their combination of risk factors makes them highly susceptible. For example, the skin over the coccyx is prone to breakdown because of the shape of the bone, lack of padding over the coccyx, and frequent use as a weight-bearing surface. Equipment that takes pressure off the coccyx in sitting, used correctly, can help avoid or treat this breakdown.

Persons who had pelvic irradiation prior to 1980 are at very high risk for skin breakown over the sacrum, coccyx, and buttocks areas due to the skin changes that the irradiation used at that time incited.

Psychosocial/Cognitive System

Often overlooked, but well-known, are the hazards of immobility as related to the psychosocial/cognitive system. Extended bed rest or loss of mobility leads to cognitive dysfunction. The recumbent position induces lethargy and inactivity. Often, a patient who refuses to follow prescribed treatments, including extended bed rest, is labeled "noncompliant." In many cases, however, he or she may simply be issuing a cry for help in changing the wound management program because, for the sitting-dependent person, bed rest is a sentence akin to imprisonment.

The patient with impaired cognitive abilities may be unsafe in self-mobility or in the ability to maintain safe postures independently. The equipment for someone with cognitive impairments will probably need to be more supportive than that for one with full abilities to reposition or to ask for assistance in maintaining safe postures. Cognitive and psychologic impairments are definitely affected by inactivity and poor positioning.

Summary

Wound management must be an interdisciplinary team effort. The total wound management program is a combination of the therapist's evaluation of the prominences, the body position, and body movement, along with evaluations by other clinicians with information on medications (eg, steroids), medical status, other health-related conditions (such as diabetes, cancer, and immunosuppressive disorders), nutrition, blood levels of serum albumin and protein, habits that increase risk (such as smoking), choices of clothing that negatively affect skin, excessive sweating, bed mobility, and incontinence.

FUNCTIONAL DIAGNOSTIC PROCESS

The clinician reviews the medical history and systems and then decides on the appropriate examination strategy for the patient. After the examinations are performed and the data collected, the information is reviewed and evaluated. The result of the evaluation is the functional diagnosis. The functional diagnosis will be based on the following:

- The impairments found in the examination that prevent the client from achieving the ideal position either sitting or lying down
- Identification of the client's preferred position(s)
- Identification of the client's alternative position(s)
- Specific interventions in the form of equipment choices and proper use of that equipment

Tables 13–1 and 13–2 list examples of medical and functional diagnoses relating to need for therapeutic positioning,

Table 13–1 Functional Diagnositic—Sitting Position

Medical Diagnosis— *Functional Diagnosis*	*Prognosis*	*Intervention*	*Outcome*
Kyphosis—Patient cannot maintain 90° hip flexion and keep face vertical due to thoracic kyphosis.	Patient will sit upright with face vertical and as close to 90° hip flexion as possible.	Reclining backrest with stabilizing seat cushion. May need antitippers.	Patient able to sit stabilized as close to 90° back/seat angle as possible with face vertical.
Scoliosis (fixed)—Patient cannot sit with shoulders and hips level due to fixed asymmetric spine or pelvis.	Patient will maintain sitting position with shoulders and hips as level as possible.	Cushion with buildup under higher ischium to accommodate asymmetry; back support to assist in comfortable trunk positioning.	Patient able to maintain upright sitting with shoulders and hips as close to level as possible.
Scoliosis (flexible)—Patient does not but can sit with shoulders and hips level.	Patient will maintain sitting position with level shoulders and hips without strain.	Cushion with pressure elimination at ischials and full femur support or cushion with buildup under lower ischium to raise that side of pelvis.	Patient able to maintain upright sitting with shoulders and hips level and spine straight.
<90° Hip flexion—Patient cannot sit at optimal 90° seat/back angle for maximal functional abilities and mobility.	Patient will maintain correct sitting position with hips on back of seat.	Positioning cushion to stabilize pelvis, with reclining backrest to approximate trunk/lower extremity (LE) angle allowed by range of motion limitations at hip.	Patient will maintain upright sitting as close to 90° as is allowed by range limitations.
<90° Knee flexion available—Patient unable to reach standard foot pedals for support.	Provide equipment that supports lower extremity at available range so that patient can maintain proper sitting position.	Elevating leg rest with full calf and foot support, set at full allowed knee flexion.	Patient will maintain upright sitting with hips on back of seat and LEs maintained at allowed knee flexion.
Foot propeller—Patient requires use of feet to mobilize chair; unable to reach floor to propel.	Provide equipment that allows efficient heelstrike on the floor.	Hemiheight chair with cushion or drop seat with cushion, so that total seat to floor height is 2 inches less than back of knee to floor measurement.	Patient will be self-mobile via foot propulsion while maintaining proper seating posture.
One-arm driver—Patient can use only one arm for self-mobility.	Provide equipment designed for propulsion with one arm.	One-arm-drive wheelchair.	Patient will be self-mobile using one arm while maintaining proper seating posture.
Above the knee (AK) amputee—Patient has limited femur length to support body weight; difficult to maintain posture in sitting; may lead to skin breakdown on ischials due to increased weight on ischials.	Provide firm flat support for femurs, and protection for ischials.	Stabilizing seat cushion; amputee adapters to move rear wheel axle backward from normal position; antitippers.	Patient will maintain upright sitting with full protection of ischials and full femur support.

continues

Table 13–1 continued

Medical Diagnosis—Functional Diagnosis	Prognosis	Intervention	Outcome
Skin breakdown on sitting surfaces (ischials, sacrum, or coccyx)—Patient cannot sit without pressure eliminated at ulcer site.	Pressure elimination on ulcer while maintaining correct postural alignment.	Cushion with selective pressure elimination.	Patient will maintain sitting schedule with pressure elimination provided at the site of breakdown.
Asymmetric tonic neck reflex (ATNR) influence—Patient has difficulty controlling direction with side-mounted joystick when head moves.	Change placement of joystick to decrease influence of ATNR.	Position joystick in center of lap tray.	Patient will drive safely and in control despite movement of head.
Hip fracture—Patient cannot sit with full 90° hip flexion; may lead to skin breakdown due to coccyx weight bearing.	Provide seating arrangement that allows <90° hip flexion with skin protection.	Seat cushion that provides ischeal/coccyx pressure reduction or elimination with positioning and can be customized with unilateral sloping to accommodate the lack of hip flexion on the involved side; reclining backrest with sacral protection; solid seat beneath cushion—may require cutout in board.	Patient will maintain upright sitting with maximum allowed hip flexion and no pressure on coccyx.
Trunk/hip extensor tone—Patient cannot maintain hips in proper position on seat due to uncontrolled hip extension; may lead to skin breakdown due to shearing.	Provide seating arrangement that decreases tone and helps maintain as close to 90° hip flexion as possible; antithrust seat assembly with preischial block.	Increase trunk/LE angle past 90°; firm contoured back support; 90° positioning belt.	Patient will maintain proper seated posture with hips on back of seat and trunk upright.

Source: Copyright © Laurie Rappl.

the prognosis, related interventions, and expected functional outcomes for the sitting-impaired and for the recumbent-impaired client.

Based on the functional diagnosis, the clinician will establish a prognosis and select interventions, with a targeted outcome for each intervention. Interventions include analysis of the most effective forms of equipment required, selection of appropriate equipment to achieve correct therapeutic position, analysis of the patient using the selected equipment, and education of patient and caregivers in correct use. Therapeutic exercise often is another important component of the total therapy plan of care.

RATIONALE FOR INTERVENTION IN THE SITTING POSITION

Sitting can be seen as either the cause of skin breakdown or as part of the solution. In a proactive environment, with an educated clinician with access to the right equipment and armed with techniques in therapeutic positioning, sitting can and should be a part of the healing of skin breakdown and part of a prevention program that can improve the quality of life for the person; it can also decrease medical costs over the course of time.

Table 13–2 Functional Diagnostic Process—Recumbent Position

Functional Diagnosis	Prognosis	Intervention	Outcome
Cardiorespiratory or gastrointestinal compromise requiring elevation of the head of the bed.	Patient will assume Fowler's position with proper positioning and skin protection devices to protect heels and sacrum.	Hip aligned at gatch of bed; sacrum protected by lifting under one hip with pillow or foam support; heel protection devices employed; frequent turning/repositioning schedule. Do not substitute elevated head of bed for upright sitting in a supportive chair.	Patient will tolerate head of bed elevated while maintaining safe postures with support devices.
Less than full hip or knee extension allowed due to joint integrity impairment at the knees. Undue susceptibility to pressure ulcers due to potential exposure of heel and sacrum.	Patient will assume supine position with foam support devices in place to accommodate hip/knee flexion requirements, and with protection of occiput, heels, and sacrum.	Foam positioning devices to protect occiput and heels, and to elevate lower extremities to accommodate flexion contractures. One side of pelvis elevated slightly with towel roll or foam to protect sacrum.	Patient will maintain supine position with support devices correctly placed.
Influence of the asymmetric tonic neck reflex (ATNR) causes involuntary movements into trunk extension, and inability to maintain sidelying position.	Patient will be positioned with strong side down and trunk and upper limbs fully supported. *Or* patient will be positioned with strong side up, body fully supported along full trunk, and the bed situated so that patient is not required to turn the face up to view the room.	Position with stronger side down and trunk fully supported from shoulder to pelvis. Bed is placed so that need for cervical movement is minimized, ie, against far wall, facing door of the room.	30° Foam wedge fully supporting trunk, pelvis, shoulders, and uppermost arm and leg supported away from midline in abduction; head supported in midline in both frontal and sagittal planes.
Venous ulcers on lower extremity with edema.	Patient will maintain supine or sidelying positions with lower extremity elevated above midline to reduce swelling, and with ulcer pressure free.	Foam device to support leg above the level of the heart in supine position and in 30° sidelying position.	Patient will maintain safe postures with limb elevated and sacrum protected.

Source: Copyright © Laurie Rappl.

When the sitting skeleton is viewed from the side, it is apparent that the ischial tuberosities (ITs) extend approximately 1.5 inches past the femurs, making the ITs the major weight-bearing points on the sitting surface. These points are also the most vulnerable to skin breakdown because of their conical shape and poor natural padding. As a person becomes more sitting dependent, atrophy causes the minimal natural padding to deteriorate, making that person even more vulnerable to skin breakdown. The ITs are the fulcrum point for the pelvis, and, when bearing weight, cause the pelvis to rock about a horizontal axis through the frontal plane that leads to anterior or posterior pelvic tilt. Most often, people tend to sit in a posterior tilt, or a slouched position. The act of moving into the slouch causes shearing forces on the ITs, and sacral sitting leads to the formation of pressure ulcers on the sacrum and coccyx as well.

The goal in seating a client is to help maintain a position that is as close to ideal as possible. Orthopaedic or neurologic limitations may prevent achievement of the ideal position as a realistic goal, but it is the benchmark position.

Ideal is the position that the body should be in to be anatomically aligned for muscle balance, to achieve proper alignment of the bones and joints according to their design, and to take advantage of the most load-tolerant areas of the body in handling pressure to keep the skin safe from breakdown. In the ideal position, viewed from the side, the client should have a 90° angle at the hip, knee, and ankle. The ear should be in line with the acromion process and the hip, and the foot should be positioned under the knee. The thigh should be parallel to the ground so that the hip and knee are in line with each other. The spine should be supported in its natural curves in the cervical, thoracic, and lumbar regions. The face should be vertical (see Figure 13–1). Viewed from the front, the trunk and head should be comfortably upright with shoulders and hips (pelvic crests) level, the thighs in neutral (not internally or externally rotated), feet pointed straight ahead, and arms supported so that the shoulders are not elevated or depressed when the elbows are resting on the armrests. Dignity issues clearly indicate the need for women to be positioned with their legs together rather than separated.

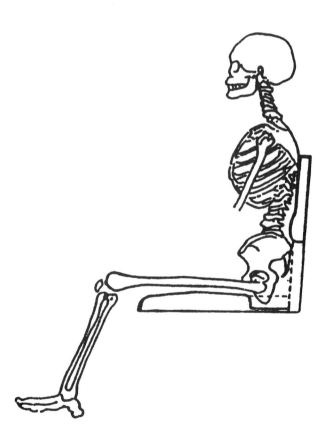

Figure 13–1 Ideal sitting position, side view. Courtesy of Span-America Medical Systems, Greenville, South Carolina.

Sitting Posture Examination and Evaluation

Knowing the ideal position, the clinician then evaluates the patient to determine how closely the patient can come to achieving the ideal position comfortably, what prevents the patient from attaining that position, and what equipment interventions can assist the patient in maintaining a position as close to ideal as is possible or functional.

Neuromuscular System

Reflex Integrity Examination. Nonintegrated primitive reflexes influence seating when central nervous system disorders make them more apparent than in the intact nervous system. One example of the influence of a primitive reflex on function and positioning involves the asymmetric tonic neck reflex (ATNR). This reflex causes the person to extend on the face side when the head is rotated. This can cause the person driving a side-mounted joystick to have difficulty controlling the device. A center-mounted joystick may solve this problem. The symmetrical tonic neck reflex (STNR) is influenced by head position; the STNR must be accommodated for by limiting the movement of the head so that voluntary control of the body is maintained. Extensor thrust is evident when the ball of the foot is stimulated, and causes extension throughout the body. Limiting contact with the ball of the foot on the foot pedal will help to relax extensor tone and help maintain an upright position. Hypertonicity, spasticity, and athetoid movements all demand stabilization of the body so that extraneous or involuntary movements will be minimized, and the person has some freedom to express voluntary movements.

Sensory Examination. The ability to detect both light and deep pressure must be assessed on all areas of the body that will be weight bearing or that may come in contact with equipment. The inability to detect pain or pressure may lead to skin breakdown. If the person is insensate in the skin over the sitting surfaces, he or she will not know when to shift weight to relieve undue pressure. For the insensate person, great care must be taken to search for and prescribe equipment that not only positions the body but also protects insensate skin (see the section on seat cushion categories).

Musculoskeletal System

Motor Function and Ergonomics Examination. Note how dependent or independent the patient is in self-mobility and what means is easiest for him or her to use. This will determine the mobility base (wheelchair, recliner chair, scooter, etc.) that is prescribed. If the patient does not have the physical, cognitive, or visual perceptive abilities to be safely independently mobile, a total support chair such as a recliner Geri-chair or recliner wheelchair may be needed;

either one may require additional support devices, such as a commercially available seat and back. If the patient has the cognitive and perceptive skills, but not the physical skills, then a powered base, either a power wheelchair or a scooter style, is chosen. If the person can self-propel, the therapist has a choice of a variety of manual chairs, depending on the body parts being used for mobility. The patient who needs one or both feet to propel will require a hemiheight wheelchair, one with a lower-than-standard seat-to-floor height so that the person can contact the ground firmly with the foot without having to scoot the pelvis forward on the chair. The most efficient foot propulsion can be accomplished if the patient can achieve a heel-toe pattern in forward propulsion. Foot propulsion can cause shearing forces on the skin over the ischials as the person pulls the body forward with the leg. The patient who can propel with only one arm will need a one-arm-drive chair. The patient who will use both arms is a candidate for a standard height wheelchair.

Shear and Friction Examination. While evaluating mobility capabilities, the clinician should pay attention to the quality of those capabilities, and assess them for the possibilities of friction and shear. These two causative factors in skin breakdown can become evident during propulsion or when postural changes happen while the patient is seated. Friction and shearing would be evidenced by irregular reddened areas on the weight-bearing surfaces. Proper equipment and positioning can limit trunk and pelvic movement to limit both friction and shearing.

Activities of Daily Living (ADL) Examination. The more functional activities done in the wheelchair, such as dressing, bathing, eating, and toileting, the more the equipment will have to accommodate beyond simple positioning. Waterproof materials will assist in toileting, and noncontoured seating may assist the caregivers in placing the person in many different positions to pull clothing on and off and to bathe the various body parts. Transfers, or the methods used to get the person into and out of the chair, are an important factor in determining seating equipment. Assess for the possibility of shear and friction during the transfer. Try to minimize the number of extra devices such as abductors and adductors. These tend to get in the way of independent transfers and are cumbersome for the caregivers in dependent transfers.

Clinical Wisdom: *Transfer Technique*

Poor transfer technique is a major contributor to skin breakdown, because the skin is dragged across surfaces, or is subjected to sudden overload when the person is set down suddenly.

Range of Motion and Joint Integrity Examination. The spinal curves should be in proper alignment; a fixed, exaggerated thoracic kyphosis will limit the person's ability to keep the face vertical. If hip flexion of 90° cannot be attained, the person cannot be accommodated in a chair with a 90° seat/back angle; the back will have to be reclined, and the seat cushion should provide enough pelvic stability to keep the hips from sliding forward. A seat that tilts up in the front may be helpful. If knee flexion is fixed at less than 90° from straight, or more than 90° from straight, the legs will have a tendency to pull the body forward from the back of the seat and out of position. Footrests that support the foot and allow the hip and knee to maintain as close to 90° as possible will be helpful in positioning the lower body.

Stabilizing the pelvis is critical to correct positioning. The pelvis must be evaluated in all planes of movement. The anterior/posterior rotation is assessed from the side. The anterior superior iliac spines (ASIS) should be roughly level with the posterior superior iliac spines (PSIS). A posterior tilt where the PSIS are lower than the ASIS will flatten the lumbar spine, decrease hip flexion from 90°, and cause the body to attain a "slouched" position. An anterior tilt will throw the body forward, making it difficult to attain upright sitting with arms free. A tilt to left or right in the frontal plane is termed a "pelvic obliquity." This obliquity must be defined as "fixed" or "flexible." To do this examination, place the person on a firm seat with knees at 90° and feet supported. Note whether one iliac crest is higher than the other, and note the presence of a lateral curvature of the trunk both with and without upper extremity support. Place a support under the ischium on the lower side of the pelvis to even the iliac crests. If the trunk curvature remains and the person becomes more unstable when the arms are raised, then the obliquity is fixed and should be accommodated for by building up the cushion under the opposite ischium. If the trunk curvature decreases and the person is more stable, the obliquity is flexible and can be accommodated for in one of two ways: (1) by putting the person on a firm cushion with both ischials unsupported and both femurs fully supported and at the same height, inducing a level pelvis, or (2) by building up the cushion under the lower, supported ischium to even the iliac crests. Pelvic rotation, a twist about a vertical axis, is noted if one iliac crest sits forward of the other.

Limitations in ankle dorsiflexion or plantarflexion or inversion/eversion will affect the support of the lower extremity on the foot pedal. If the ankle cannot be maintained in a neutral (right angle) position with 0° of inversion/eversion, a foot pedal that can change angulation will be needed to accommodate the position of the foot as closely to ideal as possible.

Limitations in the upper extremities are also important to note. A flaccid upper extremity can affect mobility, as that arm will not be useful for propulsion. A flaccid, unsupported arm can also affect positioning, potentially causing the body to sag toward the flaccid side and inducing excessive pressures on that side of the sitting surface. Reflex-inhibiting postures such as support in elbow flexion and shoulder protraction to break up severe extensor tone will help the client maintain a forward upright posture.

Skeletal Deformities Examination. Note any limitations in the range of motion that would affect the person's ability to sit upright easily. As previously discussed regarding the pelvis, these problems should be assigned a "fixed," that is, immovable, or "flexible," that is, movable or correctable, designation; "fixed" problems will need to be accommodated for as a disability, whereas "flexible" problems should be noted as places where the right equipment or positioning can help correct an impairment.

Integumentary Examination

The clinician must evaluate the status of all skin on the weight-bearing surfaces. The quality of the skin—dry, inelastic, friable, thin—must be noted. Use the bony prominences as anatomical locations under skin to see signs of impairment, that is, change in color (red, blue, purple) from adjacent continuity of skin color. Also record the anatomic locations of each area of breakdown, and include the size, date of occurrence, stage, history, and current plan of care of each. Note areas of previous breakdown and any previous surgeries to repair skin, as these areas are at high risk of reopening and must be protected at all costs.

Even if they have not experienced breakdown, any bony prominences on weight-bearing surfaces may be at risk, and palpation will reveal those at highest risk by showing which ones are most prominent, least protected, and bearing the most weight. Muscle atrophy or significant loss of body weight will make the ischium more prominent than usual, and may make protection from breakdown a primary need in the selection of seat cushions.

Interface Pressure Examination

With the advent of sophisticated mapping devices that determine interface pressures, many facilities and clinicians are using these measurements as the major factor in determining seat selection. Although pressure is one of the factors that cause breakdown, it is only one of several. The clinician should consider shearing, friction, heat/moisture buildup, and sitting instability as equally important, even though they are more difficult to measure than interface pressure. The clinician must use interface pressure measurements carefully, and be sure to look at the total picture of the patient and the equipment.

Pressure measurements can be taken with single-cell, hand-held devices, or larger, multiple-cell, computerized mapping devices. The hand-held, single-cell monitors are more portable and less expensive, but the single cell has a tendency to move during the inflation/deflation cycle. It also gives the reading over one small area, when the peak pressure may be somewhere far removed from the placement of the cell. The multiple-cell device gives a better overall picture of the pressures on the whole seating surface simultaneously, and prints those pressures out in numeric or pictorial form on a computer screen. These larger, computerized mapping devices are much more expensive and less portable, but they are valuable in that the whole sitting surface is read at the same time rather than just a single site.

Single-cell meters operate in one of two ways: inflate–placement–deflate–read, or deflate–placement–inflate–read. Accurate readings depend heavily on proper placement of the cell under the bony prominence while the person is sitting upright and stable. After taking the first reading, most clinicians will then remove the cell, replace it, and repeat the reading two times in order to get at least three readings per bony prominence. Some manufacturers recommend taking three readings and averaging the results. Make sure that the cell is not wrinkled during use; that the sitting surface is up to manufacturer's directions for inflation or support, placement on the chair, and support of extra pieces such as a solid base, a cover, or abductor/adductor/obliquity wedges; and that the sitting surface is smooth and free of wrinkles and excessive layers of padding.

The goal of pressure reading is to find out the location and the value of peak pressures on a particular client on a particular cushion. High pressures on the most vulnerable prominences (ischial, coccyx, sites of previous or current breakdown) may indicate that that cushion and client are not an appropriate match. It is preferred that the areas of highest risk (ie, ischials and coccyx) record lower pressures than those at lower risk, such as the femurs; the femurs are load tolerant, can support the majority of the weight, and can therefore tolerate higher pressures than the vulnerable ischials and coccyx.

Intervention Using the Principles of Seating

Therapeutic positioning[8–14] requires skill in evaluation and interpretation of the client's needs and in the matching of equipment to client. This has traditionally been considered the realm of physical therapy and/or occupational therapy; indeed, many physical therapists (PTs) and occupational therapists (OTs) are highly skilled in therapeutic positioning, and there are seating clinics staffed by therapists with a high level of specialization in positioning all ranges of client involvement. Unfortunately, many clinicians and patients do not have ready access to the skilled intervention of knowledgeable PTs and/or OTs. However, proper seating and positioning must be attended to by all clinicians or caregivers involved in health care, and the knowledge and application of the basic principles of seating will benefit the majority of patients. These basic principles of proper positioning can be learned and applied in the home setting as well as the nursing home and rehabilitation facility by all knowledgeable and willing clinical staff.

Clinical Wisdom: *Basic Seating Principles*

The basic seating principles include the following:

- Level cushion and seat upholstery to keep thighs horizontal to the ground; knees and hips even.
- Feet are supported so that the knees are even with the hips.
- Back is supported so that natural spinal curves are maintained; ideally the ear, shoulder, and hip should be in alignment.
- When the pelvis is properly positioned on the seat, the seat cushion ends 1½ inches from the back of the knee.

The clinician or caregiver should also identify when the basic seating principles will not or cannot help the patient, when equipment will have to accommodate a position that varies from these basic principles as stated in the text, and when referral to a skilled outside source is necessary.

Pelvic Control

Pelvic control is the cornerstone of seating. If the pelvis rolls out of position, the whole sitting posture will be difficult to control. Most seat products control the pelvis by putting some pressure on the most unstable aspect, the ischials, and attempting to control pelvic movement by padding all around the ischials. Others eliminate this unstable point as the control point and use the proximal femurs to control the pelvis. Any chosen cushion requires the assistance of a back support. The top of the back of the pelvis must be supported with the back support so that it cannot rock backward. The back support also fills in the lumbar curve for more supported and comfortable sitting and relieves stresses related to back pain by improving the seating ergonomics.

Thigh Control

Thighs should be parallel to the ground. The seat should be flat, with the hips and knees horizontally aligned. If the knees are lower than the hips, the weight of the legs pulls the body forward and pulls the pelvis into the posterior pelvic tilt the clinician is trying so hard to avoid, and the patient

slouches. This is the position most commonly seen in settings where generic chairs are used, and the footrests are lengthened as much as possible, or have been lost. Conversely, if the knees are higher than the hips as in the use of a wedge cushion, the lumbar lordosis is lost, the proximal femur along with the sacrum, coccyx, and ischials bear an inordinate amount of weight, and the patient is put at high risk of skin breakdown and back pain. These wedge type cushions are typically used in an attempt to keep the person from sliding out of the seat. Wedge cushions cause a number of problems, however, indicating that they should be prescribed with extreme caution, rather than as a general issue device. These problems can include skin breakdown on the sacrum and spine due to excessive body weight being forced on those prominences, discomfort in a flexed lumbar spine, difficulties in transferring, and loss of mobility and ADL skills.

Seat Depth

The seat depth should be about 1½ to 2 inches shorter than the distance from the seat back to the back of the knee. Seats with less depth than this do not take advantage of the weight bearing or the support that the posterior femur can give; greater depth than this and the seat will pull the body forward on the chair and out of position. Many people in fleet or institution chairs are sitting on very short seat depths, and, therefore, have a tendency to slide about on their chairs and slide out of position. Large recliner-style chairs have seat depths that are too deep, causing pressure on the lower legs and pulling the body forward on the seat.

Footrest

The footrest should support the leg so that the thigh is parallel to the ground. If the footrest is too high, the weight is unevenly distributed across the femur; if it is too low, the weight of the leg pulls the body out of position. To keep the thighs parallel to the ground, simply adjust the foot support, or provide a footstool or other support under the feet. Care should be taken to ensure that the individual wears the appropriate supportive footwear to protect the feet from trauma, to evenly distribute pressures across the whole foot, and to assist in decreasing dependent fluid buildup in the feet.

Clinical Wisdom: *Simple Tools*

A simple toolbox is a necessity and a relatively inexpensive investment when working with seating equipment. This should include a variety of screwdrivers, wrenches, and a lubrication agent. For example, a simple wrench is usually all that is needed to change the height of a footrest so that the footrest plate is the proper height for full foot support.

Wheelchair Measurement

Proper wheelchair seating requires that the seat/back angle accommodate the person as close to upright 90° as the person's body will allow. Proper measurements for a wheelchair include seat depth as described above, back height from seat cushion to the point on the back that gives needed support without hindering function, width from hip to hip and shoulder to shoulder kept as close as is comfortable so that the overall chair is as small as possible, and foot support placed so that the knee is even with the hip. This foot support will be the floor-to-seat height in hemi-style chairs, or footrest selection and setting in a manual or power-propelled chair. Measurements must include the cushion when measuring the backrest height, seat to floor, and footrest length (see Figure 13–2).

To choose equipment, match the needs of the client with the features of a product. The client's needs will be assessed in the evaluation; the features of the product are assessed with clinical skills, analytical skills, and common sense. Don't rely strictly on history or manufacturer's claims to determine what products to use; predetermine what features the product should have to fulfill the patient's needs before assessing the benefits of that product for the person.

Wheelchairs or Mobility Bases

The major piece of equipment in seating, the one carrying the highest price tag and acting as the basis for the rest of the seating system, is the chair, sometimes referred to as the mobility base. Figure 13–3 is an algorithm to guide the clinician through the decision-making process to determine mobility needs.

The appropriate mobility base must be determined along with the seating system. It is often impossible to make any seating system, even the appropriate one for the patient, work on an inappropriate seating base. For example, many people mobilize their chair by propelling with their feet. If the wheelchair seat is too high to allow the foot to reach the ground, all seat cushions will put the person even higher and further

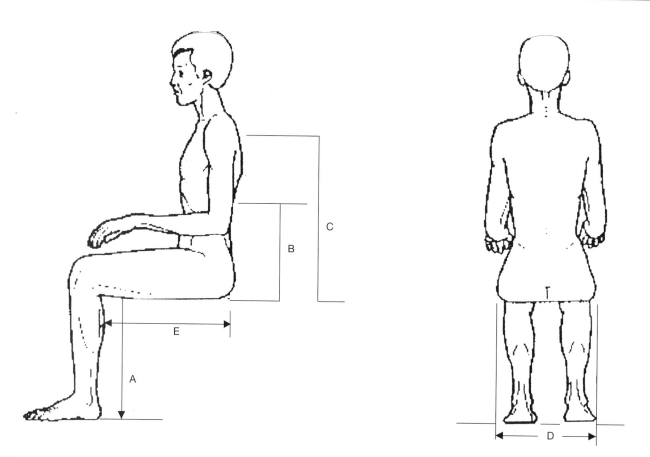

Figure 13–2 Measuring for a wheelchair. A = Seat to foot support height; B = seat to top of sacrum for placement of lumbar support; C = height of backrest needed for back support; D = seat width; E = seat depth, measured from backrest to popliteal fossa less 1.5 inches.

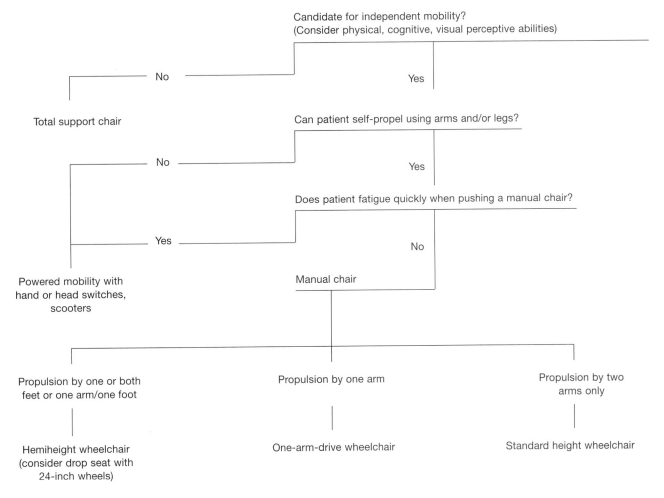

Figure 13–3 Algorithm: determining mobility base needs. *Source:* Copyright © Laurie Rappl.

reduce the mobility of the patient. "Quick fixes," such as a drop seat, are often only fair compromises at best. In the same way, using a seating system on a base it is not designed for will compromise the effect of the system. Reclining geri-atric or Geri-chairs offer little to no support and are not de-signed to accept most seating systems. However, sometimes these chairs are the only available alternative to bed rest; therefore, attempt to adapt this chair to fit the individual's needs by utilizing the appropriate back cushions, head sup-ports, lateral trunk or hip guides, seat cushions, and lower extremity support.

The standard wheelchair, a folding frame style with ad-justable or fixed armrests, a seat 18 inches wide by 16 inches deep, and elevating or adjustable footrests, is more for tem-porary transportation than for all-day everyday mobility and positioning usage. The vast majority of users require more support than these chairs can give. There are a multitude of variations on the standard theme:

- Hemiheight—The axle for the back wheel is fixed higher on the frame than standard, thereby lowering the height of the seat and allowing the user who foot propels to reach the floor with a heel-toe pattern, which is more functional and efficient.
- Sport or lightweight—These chairs are for the very ac-tive user who needs the lightest frame possible for trans-porting, and for maximum mobility. They can also as-sist the frail elderly to conserve energy, and can have a significant impact on overall endurance for activities of daily living.
- Rigid—This is a nonfolding frame style for the very active user; it is less prone to breaking and loosening.
- Pediatric-sized—These chairs are for the child or the child-sized adult.
- Reclining back chairs—These are adjusted by manual releases, hydraulic releases, ratchet-style fixation, or power. The seat to back angle can be changed to accom-

modate the person who cannot attain upright sitting or who needs to recline for some time during the day, but not necessarily out of the chair. Similarly, upholstered recliners such as Geri-chairs or living room reclining chairs allow the body to relax from upright. However, these chairs cause many positioning problems.

- Power chairs—These are available in wheelchair style or as scooters.

Seat Cushions

Seat cushions are commonly considered to be the primary intervention in positioning the client.[15–17] Products should be evaluated on how they control several physical and physiologic factors that cause skin and seating problems. These factors are pressure, shear, heat and moisture buildup, and postural control and stability.

Pressure. Pressure causes ischemia or loss of circulation to the cells under pressure. Pressure is considered the major

---

Clinical Wisdom: *Seat Cushions Are Not Mattresses in Miniature*

Understand that the seat cushion is not a mattress in miniature! Consider that a mattress has the advantage of the entire weight-bearing surface of the body over which to spread the load. There is more tissue in contact with the bed, so the goal of a mattress can be tissue support, that is, equalizing pressure across the bony prominences and plateaus such that pressures are not high enough to cause breakdown on any one point. Compare this with the seat cushion, which must bear 75% of the body weight on a small area, average size 18 × 16 inches. In seating, that body weight is concentrated on two prominences, the ischials, which are the lowermost skeletal points on the sitting surface. The ischials are small, pointed, and unprotected, and therefore less load tolerant than the large, flat, padded femurs. With this disparity in load tolerance in mind, it is imperative that the seat cushion be examined for the skeletal support it can provide to protect the skin over these at-risk areas, and shift the support to the load-tolerant areas. This is not equalization but load distribution consistent with tolerances. Equalizing the pressure over the sitting surface causes low-tolerance/high-risk prominences (the ischials) to bear the same weight as the high-tolerance/low-risk areas (the femurs). Skin management dictates that the ischials should bear less weight than the femurs, and should not bear any weight in the presence of skin breakdown or for those individuals who are identified as being at high risk for skin breakdown.

---

causative factor of skin breakdown on the sitting surfaces and has the greatest effect on bony prominences, where high forces are generated on small areas. Large, flat surfaces such as the posterior femurs seldom break down because they distribute forces over a larger area. It is generally acknowledged that the ischials can safely tolerate only one third to one half the amount of pressure that the femurs can. Also, beware that muscle tissue is affected by pressure before skin is. This is why pressure ulcers often show deep tissue destruction well before indications on the skin surface appear. "A little bit of breakdown" can be the tip of the iceberg.

Shear. Shear is the distortion force applied to the skin when bone movement pulls the skin one way, and the surface pulls the skin the opposite way. The result is a weakening or tearing of the skin and capillaries. Not only does shearing magnify the effects of pressure and cause skin damage, but it also makes it even more difficult to keep dressings on ulcers in place. To address shear, the seat cushion either must eliminate one of the two opposing forces at work on the skin (ie, the force coming from the surface onto the pressure-sensitive prominences) or must provide inherent movement with significant amplitude in individual cells that can shift with the body and decrease drag on the skin.

Heat and Moisture. On cushions that depend on immersion to equalize pressure, sweat and heat are contained around the ischials. This buildup causes maceration of the skin, which puts the skin at even more risk of breaking down. In addition, sweat and heat loosen the adherents that keep dressings in place. Cotton or air-exchange covers help, but cannot combat total contact around the ischium. A cushion should provide ventilation of the ischial area.

Postural Control and Stability. No product will help the patient fully if it does not address sitting stability and comfort. The patient must be supported in as close to an upright and aligned posture as possible. This will keep pressures on bony surfaces that can tolerate it (femurs) and off surfaces that cannot (ischials, coccyx, sacrum, spinous processes). As has been stated throughout this chapter, it also makes the person as functional as possible and helps prevent further complications such as contractures and internal organ compression.

It is commonly held that the pelvis is the cornerstone of positioning; stabilizing the pelvis is the foundation for stabilizing the entire body. However, the bases of this cornerstone, the ischials, are also the most vulnerable areas for skin breakdown and the pivot points for pelvic rotation. Most cushions, in equalizing pressure across the sitting surface, maintain pressure on the ischials and address pelvic stability by padding all around the ischials. An alternative way to keep the pelvis in place is to stop the fulcrum action of the ischials by eliminating pressure on them. The pelvis can be stabilized by stabilization of the femurs, because they are intimately connected to the pelvis and provide a larger surface area for the cushion to control. The cushion must match the posterior surface of the femurs with firm, flat support, especially the proximal femur closest to the pelvis. Stabilizing here controls rotation of the entire femur, and holds the pelvis on the back of the seat. Movement of the ischials and pelvis is contained within the elimination area (Figure 13–5).

Cushions can be divided into groups according to their features and abilities to meet various levels of patient need for both positioning and for skin breakdown risk or treatment. Here, cushions have been divided into four groups: simple pressure reduction, generically contoured, selective pressure elimination, and fully customized contouring.

Simple pressure-reduction cushions decrease pressure on the ischials and coccyx (compared with no cushion at all) and attempt to equalize that pressure across the entire sitting surface. They usually do little to address shearing forces, and may address heat/moisture via cover materials only. These cushions are for those at low risk for skin breakdown. Users may spend very little time sitting because they are partially ambulatory or may have sensation and the ability to shift weight, and have adequate nutrition and skin integrity. There are many cushions in many price levels that satisfy these basic requirements. Most of these cushions are in the lower price levels under $100. Some are priced very high, but still give only basic protection. The clinician must assess the pressure-relieving capabilities of the cushion without regard to price, and balance the capabilities of the product with the cost and the acuity of the patient's needs.

Generically contoured cushions are shaped with a depression area under the ischials to assist with pelvic placement, and troughing under the femurs to assist in neutral alignment or optimal lower extremity positioning. These cushions are more sophisticated than the simple cushions because they have some means of actively molding to the body to equalize pressure across the ischials and the femurs (air cells, gel or viscous fluids, viscoelastic foam, etc.) while offering contouring for body support. These products are for those who are at moderate risk for skin breakdown and/or for those who require more assistance with positioning than a noncontoured cushion can provide. Understand that the generic contour base is shaped to a muscled bottom, not to the atrophied bottoms of the sitting dependent, and so often do not hold the pelvis as securely as cushions more specifically contoured to fit individual bone structure. Many manufacturers have added the flexibility of providing optional components such as abductors, adductors, or hip guides that can customize the cushion to further control lower extremity positioning.

The third category, selective pressure elimination, is identified by an area that eliminates pressure on the ischials via a pocket that is sized to the user's ischial span—the measurement from the center point of one ischium to the center point of the other. It also offers flat support to the full length and width of the posterior femurs, thereby supporting the body on the femurs, not in the elimination area. This not only protects the skin over the ischials, but also protects the femurs by pressure distribution. Although appropriate for the moderate-risk patient as well, these products are often used for the highest-needs patients, who may be characterized by some of the following: sitting dependent, minimally ambulatory if at all, insensate, may have limited abilities to reposition themselves to relieve pressure, have existing or recurrent breakdown on the bony prominences of the sitting surfaces (ischials, sacrum, or coccyx), are in the granulation or re-modeling phases of wound healing, or have a history of skin breakdown on those sitting surfaces. Selective pressure elimination at the ischials, shearing elimination, and maximum ventilation puts the skin over the ischials in the healthiest possible environment. These requirements mirror and follow basic medical protocol for pressure ulcer treatment.[5,18–22] The benefits of this cushion design have been well documented.[8,14,17,23–29] This time-tested, fitted cushion design should never be confused with the donut design, which is specifically recommended against by the Agency for Health Care Policy and Research (AHCPR) guidelines. Unlike a true selective presure elimination cushion, which involves a full seating surface with a small relief area fitted to the user's bone structure, a donut cushion is simply a closed ring of material that cuts off circulation by inducing the tourniquet effect. In addition, the ring forces wieght bearing on the area around the ischials, rather than on the femurs, the anatomically load-tolerant areas. For these reasons, the donut cushion should never be used, especially by persons at high risk for, or with existing, breakdown.

As with any sitting-dependent person, especially those with skin breakdown, maintenance of the proper seated position is essential in order to enhance function and endurance and to protect the skin under other areas of the sitting surface from breaking down. The pressure elimination cushion positions the pelvis in two ways. First, the ischials are unweighted and cannot act as pivot points for pelvic rotation. Second, the body is controlled by fully supporting the femurs (both length and width) in a nonrotated position, and such that they are even with each other in the horizontal plane. This keeps the pelvis and the trunk level (rather than obliquely inclined), keeps the pelvis toward the back of the seat, and prevents the pelvis from falling into the cutout area. Third, the walls of the elimination area confine movement of the pelvis to a defined area and keep the ischials from sliding forward with an effective pre-ischial block. As with any cushion, the top of the back of the pelvis must also be supported with a back support so that it cannot rock backward. The back support also fills in the lumbar curve for more supported and comfortable sitting.

The fourth category, fully customized contouring, refers to one-of-a-kind cushions fashioned specifically for the individual client. These are usually prescribed for users with severe structural deformities that cannot be accommodated for by off-the-shelf products, or for those with excessive trunk and lower extremity tone that pulls them out of other products.

Other features to consider when evaluating cushions include urine-proof surface, stability of the sitting surface, cleanability, weight for portability, leakproof surface, low maintenance, easy to use correctly, cosmesis, durability, and slip resistance.

The algorithm in Figure 13–4 may help the clinician categorize seat cushion choices. A pictorial comparison of cushions that equalize pressure versus those that eliminate ischial pressure is shown in Figure 13–5.

Back Supports

A seat cushion is a key part, but only a part, of the seating system. To support a body adequately, the proper back support must also be prescribed. Most wheelchairs have a material back that allows the chair to fold. Unfortunately, this

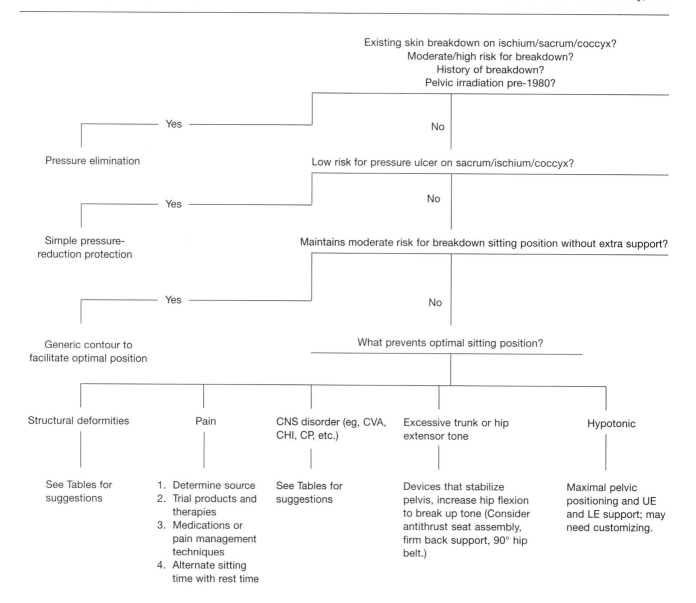

Figure 13–4 Algorithm: determining sitting surface. The surface must work with the mobility base to achieve optimal sitting height. CNS = Central nervous system; CHI = closed head injury; CP = cerebral palsy; UE = upper extremity; LE = lower extremity. *Source:* Copyright © Laurie Rappl.

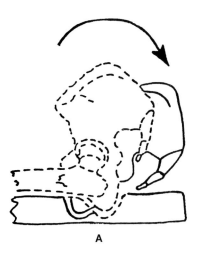 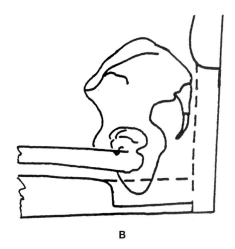 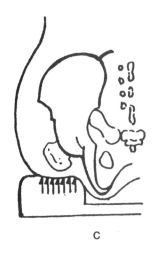

Figure 13–5 Pressure equalizing versus pressure eliminating. **A,** Side view of pressure equalizing cushion; loads the ischium which allows pelvic tilt. **B,** Side view of pressure eliminating cushion. Note pre-ischial bar limiting forward ischial movement. **C,** Rear view of pressure eliminating cushion. Note pressure distribution across full width of femur to support the load of the body. Courtesy of Span-America Medical Systems, Greenville, South Carolina.

material bows in the opposite direction that the back requires. Therefore, almost every patient sitting in a standard folding wheelchair will require some accessory back support as a means of accommodating the lumbar and thoracic curves. The complexity and expense of the back support depends on the needs of the client and the number of roles the back support must fill. The algorithm shown in Figure 13–6 may help the clinician categorize equipment when choosing a back support for a patient.

Skin breakdown on the sacrum will be one deciding factor in selecting a back support. Skin breakdown will require that the back support remove pressure from and ventilate the area. Postural support in an upright sitting position may require support on natural spinal curves, accommodation for fixed deformities, or correction of flexible deformities. None of these needs can be overlooked when positioning a patient with sacral skin breakdown in sitting. Look for a commercially available device that is designed to meet all of these goals for the patient.

The patient who can maintain the upright ideal position with little or no assistance may require only minimal back support, perhaps a firm contoured back that can be slid into the chair with attachment to the upholstery.

If the lumbar spine is flattened and hip range of motion is compromised so that it is less than 90°, a chair fixed at a 90° seat/back angle is inappropriate. This combination of physical factors, often found in the older adult population, can be accommodated by a reclining backrest with adjustments to the degree of recline. This allows the patient to be positioned with the hips all of the way back on the seat for full support, and the back to be supported at the appropriate degree of recline to facilitate safe swallowing, maximum mobility, and maximum function for the patient.

Those patients who have little inherent trunk support abilities will benefit from back supports that have the flexibility of lateral supports to help maintain the trunk in an upright position. Back supports can also be fully customized to fit the unique contours of an individual. These would be indicated for the patient with fixed trunk deformities or severe trunk weakness. Flexible thoracic or lumbar kyphosis or scoliosis can be handled by correcting the position of the pelvis and possibly using lateral supports on the trunk.

Accessories

The seat, back, and mobility base are the three key elements in a seating system. Many patients require the extra assistance of accessory products that include the following.

Head Supports. Head supports come in a variety of models, depending on the amount of support needed and the ability of the backrest to support the headrest. Models include flat (attach to the seat back uprights of manually reclining chairs), molded around the neck and occipital regions, adjustable in height and angle, and fixed.

Seat Cushion. Seat cushions have already been discussed. When cushions are placed on sagged seat upholstery, many of the positioning effects are negated. The seat support can be stiffened by adding a solid seat or board to the chair or

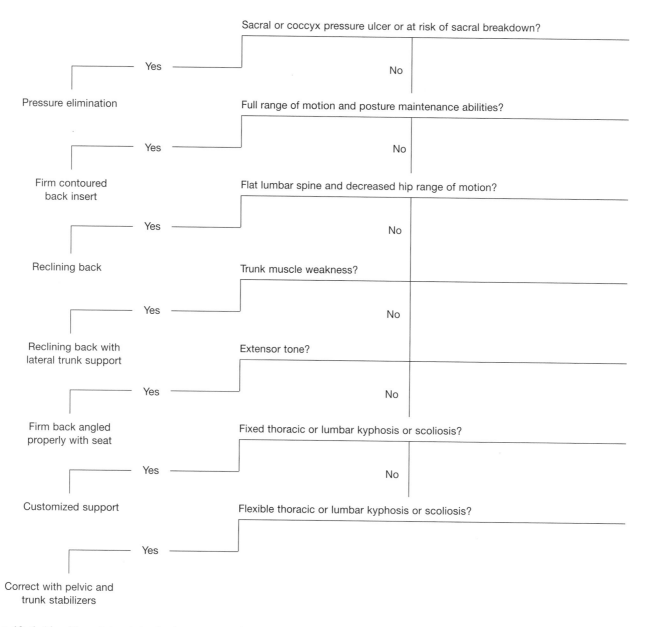

Figure 13–6 Algorithm: determining back support needs. Copyright © Laurie Rappl.

adding a drop seat that drops the seat pan beneath the level of the seat rails and lowers the patient closer to the floor. Consider adding a cutout seatboard under the seat cushion both to eliminate the sling of the upholstery and to distribute interface pressure away from the ischial tuberosities. Be aware that when a solid seat is added, this may increase the interface pressure over the ischial tuberosities if the cushion is inadequate in pressure distribution over time; in other words, if the cushion bottoms out, the ischial tuberosities will be pressing into a solid, unforgiving surface that could then contribute to the formation of a pressure ulcer.

Armrests. Armrests generally come in two styles: tubular with padding or standard with flat metal skirt guards. Either can be attached to the chair in a fixed position or can swing away or be removed for ease of transfers. Standard armrests come in full length, shortened desk length (allows the chair to be pulled up closer to a table or desk), and height adjustable to accommodate the needs of a wide range of patient heights.

Footrests. Footrests are critical pieces in the seating system. As a general rule, the footrests are adjusted so that the knee is even with the hip. Most footrests are adjustable in height, and some allow adjustment in the sagittal plane to change the angle of the ankle. The pedal or platform of the footrest can be ordered in various sizes to support as much of the foot as possible. Elevating height footrests, although thought useful for edema, often act to pull the body out of position and extend the turning radius of the chair, thus limiting mobility. The elevation has little effect on edema, as the extremity must be positioned above the level of the heart for passive edema control.

Back Wheels. The back wheels of wheelchairs are usually 24 or 26 inches in diameter and come in a variety of widths. The major choice to make is whether to order solid or inflated tires, and treaded or nontreaded tires. For everyday, general use, most people use an inflatable tire with moderate tread. There are now solid tires made with treads for those who do not want to deal with the possibility of flat tires. For mainly indoor use, consider a minimal tread. Hint: The height of the seat from the floor—a critical factor in the patient's mobility—can be affected by changing the diameter of the back wheel.

Front Wheels. The front wheels of the wheelchair (casters) come in almost as many varieties as the back wheels—solid or inflatable, and various widths and diameters. The standard caster is 8 inches in diameter, solid rubber, and minimally treaded if at all. Sport-type chairs are often seen with casters as small as roller blade wheels for increased turning abilities. Outdoor chairs have more substantial casters with larger diameters and widths, and often treads.

Ancillary Devices. Ancillary devices include the following:

- Lap belts—usually placed at a 45° angle to the seat/back angle, but often more effective when secured to the seat siderail a few inches in front of the seat/back junction and crossing the proximal femur at a 90° angle just below the trunk/leg crease.
- Lap trays—full or partial, clear or solid, padded or nonpadded, assist with upper extremity support. These should not be used as a restraint, but as an assist to daily living skills, including communication, for support to a flaccid arm or to help provide a point of stability for hypertonic extremities. Lap trays can also provide trunk support for those who may fatigue over time.
- Antitippers—small wheels that attach to the back of the wheelchair to keep it from tipping over backward, usually used as a safety factor. In everyday life, tipping backward is a necessary ability to lift the front of the wheelchair over small bumps and curbs, and antitippers may limit mobility while providing safety for the patient.

- Amputee adapters—allow the rear wheels to be moved posterior to the seat back upright to keep the user safe from tipping over backward.
- Residual limb support—holds the residual limb of the below-the-knee amputee.
- Chest straps—provide anterior support for the chest and upper trunk.

Working with Suppliers

The supplier is an important resource on the wound care team. A good supplier will help the clinician match equipment to individual needs. The supplier also should help the clinician keep abreast of new technology and new items on the market. Do not work with a supplier who limits access to equipment by offering only one or two lines of chairs and seating equipment. Look for suppliers who carry multiple lines and are proactive in assisting with this critical part of patient care—equipment selection. Ultimate accountability for the decision making resides with the clinician working with the patient.

Self-Care Treatment Guidelines

The patient and his or her caregivers must be taught as much as possible about the equipment that has been prescribed, including why each piece was chosen, how to use it properly, where it was ordered from for warranty repair, and how to care for it. The patient may need to follow a weaning-on schedule because new equipment may sit the patient differently or put loads on the skin in patterns different from those of the old equipment. A sample of a weaning-on schedule is as follows:

Day 1: 1 hour in morning and afternoon; assess skin response after each session.
Day 2: 1.5 hours in morning and afternoon; assess skin response after each session.
Day 3: 2.0 hours in morning and afternoon; assess skin response after each session.

Increase the sitting time gradually until a full day of sitting is achieved.

Positioning in the seated position requires constant learning, creativity, and patience. It is up to the responsible clinician to begin and continue the learning process by evaluating new technology as it is developed, determining the client needs, assessing the features of new products, and matching needs with features to benefit clients optimally. Since seating is a dynamic process, a reassessment date should be set so that the therapist can monitor the fit and functioning of the equipment and modify it to match the patient's needs.

RATIONALE FOR INTERVENTION IN THE RECUMBENT POSITION

The average person spends about one third of life in bed. The client who cannot maintain standing or sitting for normal hours spends increasing amounts of time recumbent. Just as with sitting, choosing the proper support surface and correctly positioning the person on the surface are necessary parts of humane treatment. The human body requires support for proper alignment in the recumbent positions. Technically, any person who depends on the recumbent position for any part of the day or night should be evaluated to ensure that the optimal positions are being attained. The more time spent in bed, the more need there is for positioning intervention. Certainly the person who has a musculoskeletal or neurologic insult that limits self-mobility, limits sensation to detect the need for position change, and/or makes the bony prominences more prominent and therefore at higher risk of breakdown is an uncontested candidate for therapeutic positioning.[30–34]

Bed rest puts many bony prominences of the body at risk of skin breakdown—occiput, shoulders, elbows, trochanters, sacrum, heels, and malleoli—hence the proliferation of "support surfaces" to protect the body in this relatively dangerous but needed environment. Statistics show that the sacrum and the heels are the most likely areas to break down, with references reporting incidence rates of up to 48% and 14%,[1] respectively.

Bed rest causes slowed circulation throughout the body and reduces the functioning of the respiration and elimination systems as well. Proper utilization of support surfaces, both through proper choice and correct and consistent positioning on the surface, can minimize contractures, minimize the effects of primitive reflexes released during central nervous system insult, affect the integrity of the skin, provide restful sleep, and maximize a person's independence in self-mobility.

Mattresses either equalize pressure by maximum distribution of pressure or alternately remove it from areas at even intervals. The clinician chooses the appropriate surface, determines the therapeutic positions for the patient, chooses the equipment to attain those positions, and instructs caregivers on use of the equipment.

Effects of Lying Down on Pressure Ulcer Formation

No matter how conforming the surface of the bed, when the many contours of the body are placed on a relatively flat bed, bony prominences are likely to endure high pressures and end up with skin breakdown. These prominences—the occiput, shoulder, elbow, lateral trochanter, sacrum/coccyx, fibular head, malleoli, and heels—must be protected when they are on the weight-bearing surface of the client. Supporting body parts so that the major joints are in positions of least stress and highest relaxation will decrease muscle stimulation, and therefore reduce spasticity and the formation of joint contractures. As with seating, the goal in positioning in the recumbent positions is to help maintain a position that is as close to ideal for tissue load management and muscle relaxation as is possible for the individual client.

In supine, the head and neck should be centered and the cervical and lumbar curves supported. The trunk should be aligned and straight. Anatomically, the resting position for the hips and knees is not fully extended or straight, but bent or flexed 25° to 30°.[30] Maintaining this slight flexion can put increased pressure on the sacrum and the heels. Therefore, these prominences must be watched carefully and provided with extra protection if the surface itself is not adequate. This protection may take the form of lifting one side of the pelvis so that the sacrum is not directly weight bearing. The heels may be protected by placing a pillow under the calves, or by using heel protection devices on the feet to unweight the heels (Figures 13–7 A and 13–7B). The ankles should be maintained close to 90° (a right angle) and the lower extremities should be maintained in a neutral position, with the knees and toes pointing straight up to the ceiling and about shoulder width apart. Protection in the form of pressure-reducing surfaces or ancillary positioners may be required for the at-risk areas of the occiput, thoracic spinous processes, and elbows.

Many people consider sidelying to be turning the body so that it is at 90° from supine. However, this is documented to put the greater trochanter at tremendous risk of breakdown, and recent documentation advocates the use of a 30° incline rather than a 90° incline. This position takes direct pressure off the pointed lateral trochanter and distributes weight across flatter areas of the posterolateral femur. In this position, the head and neck should be centrally aligned, with the cervical curve supported. Support will be needed behind the entire trunk and pelvis to maintain the 30° position (Figure 13–8). The uppermost leg tends to adduct and rest on the bed, but should be elevated with pillows or with foam positioners so that it is in a straight line with the trunk and maintained in a neutral rotation, with slight hip and knee flexion for comfort. The lowermost leg must be protected from pressure from the uppermost leg so that skin breakdown on the medial knee, malleolus, and foot can be avoided. Protection in the form of pressure-reducing surfaces or ancillary positioners may be required for the at-risk areas of the lowermost ear, shoulder, greater trochanter, lateral knee, lateral malleolus, and fifth metatarsal head, and the uppermost medial knee and medial malleolus. The uppermost arm must be given support as close to the neutral position of the shoulder (55° abduction with 30° horizontal adduction[30]) as can be achieved

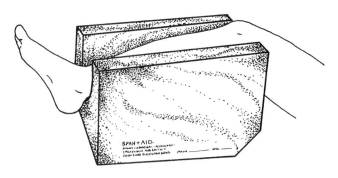

Figure 13–7 A, Limb elevator. Courtesy of Span-America Medical Systems, Greenville, South Carolina.

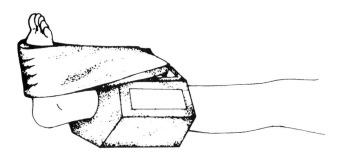

Figure 13–7 B, Footdrop stop. Courtesy of Span-America Medical Systems, Greenville, South Carolina.

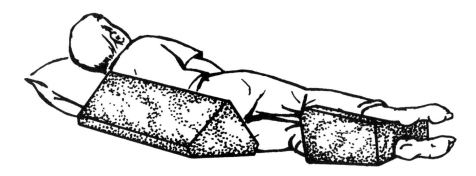

Figure 13–8 30° Wedge of body alignment in sidelying.

comfortably so that it does not fall forward across the body, or fall backward, pulling the trunk into a twisted position. The prone position requires full range of motion of the cervical, thoracic, and lumbar spine, and is not well tolerated by most patients. This position requires full extension at the hip and knee, and full external rotation of the shoulders. The trunk should be centrally aligned, with the head turned to the side. The hips should be in neutral rotation and slight abduction, and the ankles plantarflexed. The bony prominences at risk are the ears, patellas, and the dorsum of the feet. Not only does the prone position put the shoulder into its most stressful position of full external rotation with abduction, but it can also encourage footdrop due to the ankle position.

Examination and Evaluation

As with seating, the clinician must have an understanding of what the optimal or ideal positions are. During the examination, the clinician determines what prevents the patient from attaining ideal, recognizes what may be improved with therapy or other interventions, and accommodates for those factors that cannot be improved upon.

Neuromuscular System

Reflex Integrity Examination. Nonintegrated, primitive reflexes, released after neurologic insult, greatly affect recumbent mobility and positioning. A dominant ATNR will make maintaining a sidelying position very difficult. The strengthening of the face side will cause the client to rotate backward and extend the uppermost leg and arm. The trunk and uppermost side will need to be firmly supported in flexion in order to overcome the extension tendencies. Approaching the client so that he or she does not have to turn the face over the uppermost shoulder will also help combat this extension tendency. A dominant tonic labyrinthine reflex (TLR) will cause activation of flexion in prone and extension in supine. The prone position will cause breathing difficulties, and would be contraindicated without extreme caution to head and neck position. In supine, the TLR and extension tone in general may increase the risk of breakdown on the occiput and the heels, and should be broken up with head/cervical support, and flexion of the hips and lower extremities. In sidelying, the TLR causes extension on the weight-bearing side and flexion in the uppermost side; therefore, this is the preferred position for the client dominated by the TLR. Break up reflex postures as much as possible with support devices designed for controlling the body position. Usually, pillows are not stable enough to do this; an investment may have to be made in foam positioning aids specifically designed for certain positions and body parts. These may, on first glance, appear more expensive than pillows, but their effectiveness will outweigh cost (see Figures 13–7 and 13–8).

Sensory Examination. Neurologic insults often cause a lack of sensation in some part of the body. Those areas with loss of sensation are obviously at the highest risk of breakdown and will require the greatest care in positioning, support, and protection. Assess for the ability to detect both light and deep pressure and pain throughout the body, especially over the bony prominences. Those patients having a complete sensory, proprioceptive, and visual loss on one side of the body need attention to protect the involved limbs and to position for maximum environmental interaction. For example, position the individual so that he or she can visualize the entrance to the room with ease. This simple act will eliminate much fear and agitation. Caregivers should be instructed to approach from the noninvolved side first, and then move to the involved side as the patient learns to visually track to and beyond midline.

Musculoskeletal System

Motor Function and Ergonomics Examination. Assess for level of skill or assistance required to accomplish rolling right or left from supine, moving from sit to supine, supine to sit, sit to stand (exit from bed), stand to sit (enter into bed), move body toward head of bed, move body toward foot of bed, shift body side to side. Firmer, stable surfaces that do not move under the patient make bed mobility much easier to accomplish for all patients. Assess for the ability to perform transfers independently, dependently, or assisted in many combinations: bed to chair, chair to bed, commode to bed, bed to commode, sit to stand. The choice of support surface must directly and positively affect functional mobility to be considered a patient benefit and for eligibility for reimbursement of services and supplies. For the patient with skin breakdown, functional mobility occasionally may be compromised in favor of a less stable surface for improved tissue load management. Once the pressure ulcer is closed, a more stable support surface can be evaluated for both the functional mo-

bility of the patient on the surface and its efficiency in managing tissue loads.

Activities of Daily Living Examination. All ADLs done in bed, such as eating, bathing, and dressing, should be taken into account when determining the support surface and the recommended positions. Eating, especially, requires correct head elevation and cervical support for safe swallowing. The speech therapist should be consulted to determine the best head and neck positions for swallowing. This position may include aligning the ear over the acromioclavicular joint and the face in a vertical plane with the chest. Occupational therapy may be indicated to determine the upper extremity adaptations that can be utilized by the individual. Note that there are serious skin concerns in elevating the head of the bed for extended periods of time without protecting the sacrum or the heels. This position should not be used as a substitute for sitting in a chair properly positioned.

Range of Motion Examination. Note any surgeries that limit mobility, or that limit placing the client in the ideal posture in a given position. These would include orthopaedic surgeries that immobilize part of the body and therefore limit overall mobility. Note limitations in range of motion in the cervical, thoracic, and lumbar spines, hip extension, hip rotation, knee extension, ankle rotation, and plantar/dorsiflexion. Whether limitations are fixed or flexible, the limitations must be firmly supported as close to anatomically correct as possible to minimize progression of deformities. It is most important to note where limitations affect positioning. For example, a progression in spinal kyphosis will make the supine position dangerous to the skin over thoracic spinous processes and the sacrum/coccyx. One possible solution to this problem is to elevate the head of the bed just enough to accommodate for the kyphosis and to support the head and neck with or without the use of pillows. Gravity can then assist in at least maintaining the current degree of kyphosis without facilitating increased kyphosis. Consider managing tissue loads over the bony prominences with the effective use of support surfaces.

Another example of accommodation to limitations in range of motion deals with hip extension. Limitations in hip extension will necessitate support under the full lower extremity in supine to maintain the degree of hip extension allowed. This can be most easily accomplished with foam devices designed to position the leg (Figure 13–7A).

Integumentary System Examination

Pay special attention to surgeries and resulting incision or repair sites involving skin breakdown. Any area that has previously broken down or areas that have scar tissue are risk areas that require protection in the recumbent positions. All disciplines should note condition of the skin on weight-bearing surfaces—turgor, elasticity, hydration, edema, and thinness/brittleness. Note any sites with a past history of breakdown. Sites with current breakdown are obvious areas of primary concern in choosing surfaces and using therapeutic positioning. Where moist wound healing is being employed, the potential for low-air-loss or air-fluidized beds to dry out the wound should be considered. The patient should be positioned so that there is no weight bearing on areas of broken skin or on areas of scar tissue that are most vulnerable. If fecal or urinary incontinence is present, it is necessary to cleanse the skin with an appropriate acid-based (4.5 to 5.5 pH scale) skin cleanser, hydrated, and to protect the skin with a sealant. Be aware that every layer of incontinent liner that is used increases the interface pressure over that part of the body and inhibits the effectiveness of the support surface both in bed and in the chair.

Interface pressure measurements taken with either a single-cell monitor or a bed-sized computerized model may be helpful in determining areas at risk, and effectiveness of the chosen devices or positions. The procedure for performing interface pressure measurements is outlined in the seating section of this chapter. Record measurements at the bony prominences on the weight-bearing surfaces with body positioners in place in all of the positions that the patient will utilize. In sidelying, this includes the ear, shoulder, iliac crest, rib cage, trochanter, fibular head, lateral malleolus, fifth metatarsal, and first metatarsal of the uppermost foot. In supine, these include the occiput, scapulae, spinous processes, posterior iliac crest, rib cage, sacrum, coccyx, ischial tuberosities, and posterior heels. Assess pressures with the head both elevated and flat.

Cardiopulmonary/Gastrointestinal Systems

Involvement of the cardiopulmonary or gastrointestinal systems may require frequent position changes or may require elevation of the head of the bed. Note the reasons why the head of the bed must be elevated, to what degree, and for how long each day. Time in this position should be minimized; people tend to slide toward the foot of the bed when the head of the bed is elevated. This causes shearing forces on the skin, especially over the sacrum and the coccyx. Whenever the patient is in this position, line up the hip with the gatch angle of the bed to minimize sliding of the patient toward the foot of the bed. If this position is necessary for more than a half hour at a time, place a pillow or foam support under one femur, hip, and shoulder to tilt the patient slightly off the sacrum. Alternate the supported side at frequent and even time segments. Provide support under the plantar surface of the feet so that slipping down is minimized.

Assess for respiratory movements, level of breathing, and any oral secretions coming from the lungs. Take vital signs in the fully recumbent position and in the head-elevated position. Review the medical history for gastric reflux associated with hiatal hernias that require elevating the head of the bed. A patient taking oxygen probably cannot lie flat; extra care with positioning must be taken with these patients because of breathing difficulties and to ensure transport of oxygen to tissues.

Choosing Equipment

Many factors go into choosing bed support surfaces. Each of the categories detailing various surfaces of the skin have positive and negative features for maintaining position and maximizing mobility.

Overlays. Whether powered alternating surfaces, or contoured foam, all overlays raise the level of the bed surface. Sitting to standing is easier and safer to accomplish when the height of the surface of the bed is equal to the distance from popliteal fossa to the bottom of the foot. Overlays tend to raise this level, making ingress and egress more dangerous. However, overlays are inexpensive, and foam overlays with contoured, cross-cut cells (eg, Geo-Matt®) are extremely effective pressure distributors. If the level of the height of the bed can be changed, or if ingress or egress is not an issue, an overlay may be a cost-effective and appropriate choice.

Mattress Replacements. Most clinicians prefer a mattress replacement with a stable bolster edge for patient safety when sitting on the edge of the bed. A trapeze set-up will help the patient lift his or her body to move rather than sliding across the surface. This helps to limit shearing forces.

Static Mattress Replacements. These come in a variety of mediums: all foam, foam/air, foam/water, and foam/gel. These surfaces replace standard mattresses and offer better distribution of pressures than the standard mattress. They eliminate the extra height that an overlay entails and are often purchased as permanent equipment for the patient, rather than a rental item. However, they are more expensive than an overlay. Static surfaces generally offer a more stable surface to accomplish bed mobility and ingress or egress than alternating pressure or low-air-loss mattresses.

Powered Dynamic Mattress Replacements. These entail some means of moving air through the mattress to float the body, as in a low-air-loss mattress, or moving air through chambers in the mattress to alternately put pressure on and take pressure off of each area of the body at regular intervals. The air movement is accomplished by electrically powered motors. Although some clinicians feel that these surfaces are safer for the skin than static mattresses due to the constant changes in pressure on any one body part, the movement in the surface makes maintaining or changing a position more of a challenge than on a static surface. Surfaces that alternate under the patient may make transfers more dangerous as the bed surface is constantly shifting beneath the patient.

Nonpowered Dynamic Mattress Replacements. A new breed of mattress (eg, PressureGuard® CFT) offers the stability of the static mattress replacement for maintaining or changing position, along with the skin protection of a dynamic mattress. Dynamic air movement for self-adjustment to bony prominences is accomplished by elasticized reservoirs that accept air from and release air into the support tubes.

Air Fluidized. Although felt to be the best surfaces for equalizing pressures across the whole body, air-fluidized surfaces are extremely difficult to maintain therapeutic positions on, and independent ingress or egress is nearly impossible; maximal assist is usually required.

Positioning Supplies

All patients will require the use of positioning devices to help maintain therapeutic and anatomical body alignment, and protection of bony prominences. Pillows are an inexpensive support, but only minimally effective. They are puffy rectangles that do not naturally conform to body contours, have a tendency to slide on the surface when body pressure is applied, and are often not readily available for positioning if they have been confiscated for other purposes. Foam positioners are available that are shaped for supporting specific body contours, will not shift on the surface when pressure is applied, and will be less likely to be confiscated for other purposes. These devices are often inexpensive to purchase and more than pay for themselves in the quality of alignment, positioning, and protection they afford the patient. Table 13–3 describes the use and expected outcomes for commonly used and available positioning supplies.

Clinical Wisdom: *Photographs*

The use of photographs of the patient in position with the devices, displayed in a place easily seen by caregivers, is the most helpful way to describe positions and use of devices to all caregivers so that devices are used consistently and appropriately.

Table 13–3 Positioning Supplies

Device	Function	Action/Outcome
Abduction pillow	Maintains lower extremities in slight abduction, neutral rotation, and knee extension.	Supine—maintains lower extremities in neutral positions. Sidelying—maintains separation of LEs to protect medial knee and malleolus of upper leg.
30° Incline wedge (See Figure 13–8)	Supports trunk and pelvis in 30° sidelying position.	Sidelying—protects lower greater trochanter by maintaining 30° incline position.
Cradle Boot or Heel Protector	Keeps heel elevated off surface while maintaining right angle or neutral ankle dorsiflexion.	Supine—Protects heel from breakdown by suspending off surface. Should also protect malleoli, fifth metatarsal heads, and Achilles tendon. Sidelying—suspends lower malleoli and fifth metarsal head.

continues

Table 13–3 continued

Device	Function	Action/Outcome
Limb elevator (See Figure 13–7A)	Uses wedge with leg trough to put lower extremity in slight hip/knee flexion with ankle elevated above knee.	Supine—maintains neutral hip position with slight hip/knee flexion and foot elevation. Sidelying—is used with trough side down to cup the lower leg and maintain leg separation for skin protection.
Flexion/abduction pillow	Maintains slight knee flexion with separation of medial knee surfaces.	Supine—maintains hip/knee flexion while breaking up adduction tone.
Cervical pillow	Is shaped to support cervical curve while cradling occiput.	Maintains cervical curve in supine or sidelying.
Occipital pillow, head-neck cushion, Occi-Dish	Cradles posterior surface of skull to reduce or eliminate pressure on occiput.	Supine—protects occiput by pressure removal, supports cervical curve, inhibits tonic lab reflex. Sidelying—protects lower ear and supports cervical curve.

Source: Copyright © Laurie Rappl.

Case Study: *Therapeutic Positioning for Pressure Ulcer Healing*

History

The patient is a longtime resident in a nursing facility. Past medical history includes surgical removal of a benign brain tumor 10 years prior to therapy intervention. She has paralysis of the lower extremities and significant cognitive deficits (see Figures 13–9A and 13–9B).

Reasons for Referral

- Right ischial tuberosity pressure ulcer, stage III, increasing in length, width, and depth
- Abnormal extensor tone in trunk and hip musculature with mild flexion contractures in knees
- Sitting in wheelchair for 6 hours, two times per day, for a total of 12 hours daily
- Dependence in position changes in bed and sitting
- Dependence in all transfers, requiring a two-person lift
- Dependence in all ADL (feeding, wheelchair propulsion, personal hygiene, dressing)

Examinations

Neuromuscular

Reflex exam shows severe trunk and hip extensor tone present in recumbent and sitting positions.

Musculoskeletal

Motor Exam. Trunk strength is poor, upper extremity strength is fair. The patient has no volitional movement in lower extremities.

Joint Mobility Exam. All joint ranges of motion are within functional limits with the exception of knee flexion contractures, which measure 20° bilaterally. There is a flexible right pelvic obliquity, 2 inches lower on the right than on the left.

Postural Exam. The patient prefers full fetal positions with flexion of all major joints in sidelying when recumbent; in supine recumbent position, head and neck are hyperextended into the pillow and extensor tone dominates all other major joints. In sitting, she demonstrates trunk, hip, and knee extension with pelvis sliding forward on the seat and into posterior tilt, and the cervical spine is in hyperextension.

ADL. The patient is unable to move or change positions volitionally in the bed or wheelchair. She is dependent in all transfers, requiring total assistance of two persons to transfer, and in feeding, personal hygiene, wheelchair propulsion, and dressing.

continues

Case Study continued

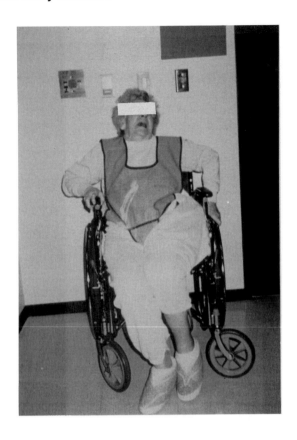

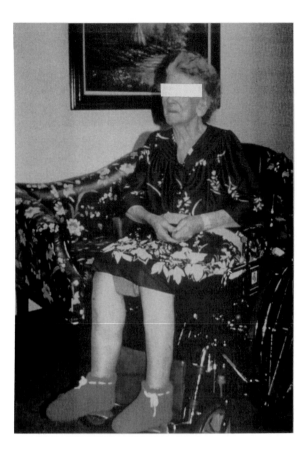

A

Figure 13–9 A, before. Note cervical and trunk hyperextension, pelvis/chest restraint, right pelvic obliquity, hips forward on seat, lower extremities unsupported. Courtesy of Debby Hagler, Cheyenne Mountain Rehabilitation.

B

Figure 13–9 B, after. Note that head and neck are in a safe and functional position, and lower extremities are supported. Courtesy of Debby Hagler, Cheyenne Mountain Rehabilitation.

Sensory

The patient is unable to detect deep or surface pressure on sitting surfaces and lower extremities.

Integumentary

The patient has a Braden Scale risk assessment score of 12. She presents with Stage III pressure ulcer on the right ischial tuberosity, measuring 3 cm × 3 cm × 1 cm deep. The pressure ulcer is 50% yellow slough and 50% granulation tissue. The surrounding skin is pale and the perimeter is macerated. Drainage is serosanguineous. No undermining or tunneling is present. Interface pressures over the sacrum, trochanter, heels, and shoulders in the supine and sidelying positions in bed were considered unsafe, as they ranged from 70 to greater than 100 mm Hg. Interface pressures over the right ischial tuberosity and the coccyx in the sitting position in the wheelchair were also considered unsafe, as they were greater than 100 mm Hg.

Evaluation

The patient has impairment of sensory, neuromuscular, and musculoskeletal systems, causing improper positioning and susceptibility to skin breakdown. There are impairments in musculoskeletal and neurologic systems that, in turn, affect the cardiopulmonary and circulatory

continues

Case Study: continued

system function to transport oxygenated blood to the wound site.

Functional Diagnosis

- There is functional impairment of volitional movement.
- There is functional impairment of reflex muscle tone resulting in dysfunctional body positions (postures) in sitting and in recumbent postures.
- The impairments of volitional movement and reflex muscle tone and dysfunctional body positions produce undue susceptibility to unsafe interface pressures on intolerant bony prominences: coccyx, ischial tuberosities, sacrum, heels, trochanter, and shoulders.
- The patient has risk factors of immobility, lack of sensation, joint integrity impairment of the knees, and abnormal extensor tone, which contribute to undue susceptibility to pressure ulceration.

Need for Physical Therapist Services

The patient needs intervention by a physical therapist to achieve the following goals:

1. Heal pressure ulcer
2. Correct impaired postural alignment
3. Position for redistribution of interface pressures from bony prominences to tolerant areas
4. Reduce risk of additional ulcerations

Prognosis

1. The ulcer will heal.
2. The risk of further pressure ulceration will be reduced by intervention with support surface and positioning equipment.
3. The patient will sit in a functional upright position in wheelchair with a 90° hip/back angle with a side-to-side wedged, pressure-eliminating seat cushion and a firm back cushion, with lower extremities supported and protected.
4. The sitting schedule will be 2 hours, three times per day for a total sitting time of 6 hours; the time up in the wheelchair will be coordinated with the meal schedule to facilitate safe swallowing and improved nutritional intake. Sitting time will be increased gradually according to a prescribed sitting schedule.
5. The patient will be positioned in functional positions in supine and 30° sidelying on a prescribed support surface in bed, with safe interface pres-

sure readings on all bony prominences in all positions.
6. Staff will demonstrate correct use of all equipment supplied and in therapeutically positioning this patient at all times, whether in bed or in the wheelchair.

Intervention: Therapeutic Positioning

- Analysis of patient for selection of adaptive seating equipment requirements. The following are recommeneded:
  1. Side-to-side 5- to 3-inch, side-to-side, wedged seat assembly with full pressure-relief pocket at ischials and coccyx, sized to distribute pressure fully over posterior trochanter and thighs.
  2. Firm back support to maintain 85° seat/back angle to inhibit extensor tone.
  3. A 90° positioning hip belt to facilitate 90° hip angle and keep pelvis in appropriate position.
  4. Padded lap tray to provide upper extremity and trunk support.
  5. Footrests, calf support, and protective footwear to protect and support lower extremities and to facilitate appropriate positioning.
  6. Hip abduction wedge to inhibit adductor and extensor tone and to facilitate positioning and pressure distribution on the seat assembly.
- Analysis of patient using adaptive equipment for appropriateness and safety
- Analysis of patient for recumbent positioning and pressure-relief devices. The following are recommended:
  1. A self-adjusting, dynamic air/foam mattress replacement to encourage mobility and allow skin protection
  2. Positioning in 30° sidelying to distribute interface pressure away from the trochanter and shoulder
  3. Utilization of wedges and a pillow between the knees to maintain the sidelying position
  4. In supine, utilization of a leg-positioning cushion to inhibit hip extensor tone, to accommodate for the knee flexion contractures, and to position heels off the bed
  5. Utilization of a head-positioning cushion to provide occipital and cervical spine support and to inhibit cervical extensor tone in supine
  6. Utilization of an over-the-bed trapeze and side rails to assist patient in self-mobility
- Analysis of patient using recumbent positioning and pressure-relief devices for safety and proper pressure relief
- Staff instruction: Instruction in appropriate usage of all seating and bed-positioning supplies and equip-

continues

Case Study continued

ment and in safe and effective position changes, transfers, and positioning in the bed and the wheelchair for two shifts of nursing personnel because of projected sitting schedule of 2 hours, three times per day, coordinated with the meal schedule. Increased sitting time according to a prescribed schedule as the patient's strength, endurance for sitting, and tolerance improve over time.

- Follow-up assessment of staff for appropriate and safe use of devices and components of the devices

Functional Outcomes

1. The patient is able to sit in a functional and safe position for a total of 9 hours per 24-hour period (3 hours, three times per day).
2. Interface pressure is eliminated on the ischial tuberosities and coccyx, and the flexible right pelvic obliquity is corrected.

3. Posture is corrected: The extensor tone in the neck, trunk, and hips is inhibited, and the abdominal musculature and cervical flexors are facilitated and strengthened, facilitating wheelchair self-propulsion, and self-feeding.
4. The patient is positioned in a safe and functional position in bed on a nonpowered dynamic air/foam mattress replacement with safe interface pressure on all bony prominences in all positions; in sidelying, using a wedge cushion behind the back, a wedge cushion under the bottom leg, and a pillow between the knees, and in supine, using a leg-positioning cushion and a head-positioning cushion.
5. The patient is able to assist in repositioning self from side to side, using the trapeze and the side rails. No additional ulcers have developed, providing a reduced pressure risk score.
6. The pressure ulcer on the ischial tuberosity is healed.

Note: Case study and pictures provided by Debby Hagler, Cheyenne Mountain Rehabilitation.

RESOURCES

The following is a representative listing of manufacturing sources for the categories of seat cushion products discussed in the text. Some manufacturers have products in multiple categories.

Simple Pressure Reduction

AliMed
Ken McRight Supplies; Bye-bye Decubiti
Maddak
Skil-Care
Span-America Medical; Geo-Matt®

Generic Countour

Cascade Designs; Varilite®
Crown Therapeutics; Roho® family
Flofit Medical; Flexseat®
Invacare; PinDot®
Jay Medical; Jay® family
Span-America Medical; Geo-Matt® Contour
Supracor

Selective Pressure Elimination

Span-America Medical; ISCH-DISH®

Customized Contour

Freedom Designs
Invacare

REFERENCES

1. Oot-Giromini B. Pressure ulcer prevalence, incidence and associated risk factors in the community. *Decubitus.* 1993;6(5):24–32.
2. Maklebust J, Sieggreen M. *Pressure Ulcers: Guidelines for Prevention and Nursing Management.* West Dundee, IL: S-N Publications; 1991.
3. Disa J, Carlton J, Goldberg N. Efficacy of operative care in pressure sore patients. *Plast Reconstr Surg.* 1992;89:272–278.
4. Evans G, et al. Surgical correction of pressure ulcers in an urban center: is it efficacious? *Adv Wound Care.* 1994;7(1):40–46.
5. Curtin I. Wound management: care and cost: an overview. *Nurse Manage.* 1984;15(2):22.
6. Ross J, Dean E. Integrating physiological principles into the comprehensive management of cardiopulmonary dysfunction. *Phys Ther.* 1989;69:255–259.
7. Gerhart K, Weitzenkamp D, Charlifue S. The old get older: changes over three years in aging SCI survivors. Report from Rehabilitation Research and Training Center on Aging with an SCI, Craig Hospital. *New Mobility.* June 1996;18–21.
8. Mooney V, et al. Comparison of pressure distribution qualities in seat cushions. *Bull Prosthet Res.* 1971;10(15):129–143.
9. Engstrom B. *Seating for Independence: Manual of Principles.* Waukesha, WI: ETAC USA; 1993.

10. Kreutz D. Seating and positioning for the newly injured. *Rehab Manage.* 1993;6:67–75.

11. Manser S, Boeker C. Seating considerations: spinal cord injury. *PT Magazine.* December 1993;47–51.

12. Presperin J. Postural considerations for seating the person with spinal cord injury. In: Proceedings from RESNA Seating Conference; June 6–11, 1992; Vancouver, BC.

13. Walpin LA. Posture: the process of body use: principles and determinants. In: Gelb H, ed. *New Concepts in Carniomandibular and Chronic Pain Management.* St. Louis, MO: Mosby–Year Book; 1994:13–76.

14. Zacharkow D. *Wheelchair Posture and Pressure Sores.* Springfield, IL: Charles C Thomas; 1984.

15. Rappl L. A conservative treatment for pressure ulcers. *Ostomy Wound Manage.* 1993;39(6):46–48, 50–55.

16. Garber S. Wheelchair cushions for spinal cord injured individuals. *Am J Occup Ther.* 1985;39:722–725.

17. Ferguson-Pell M. Seat cushion selection. *J Rehabil Res Dev.* 1990;(suppl 2):49–73.

18. Knight A. Medical management of pressure sores. *J Fam Pract.* 1988;27:95–100.

19. National Pressure Ulcer Advisory Panel. Pressure ulcers: prevalence, cost, and risk assessment: consensus development conference statement. *Decubitus.* 1989;2(2):24–28.

20. Noble PC. The prevention of pressure sores in persons with spinal cord injuries. In: *International Exchange of Information in Rehabilitation.* New York: World Rehabilitation Fund, Inc; 1981.

21. Stotts N. The physiology of wound healing. In: Stotts N, Cuzzell J, eds. *Proceedings from the AACCN National Teaching Institute.* Kansas City, MO: Marion Laboratories; 1988.

22. van Rijswijk L. Full thickness pressure ulcers: patient wound healing characteristics. *Decubitus.* 1991;6(1):16–21.

23. Ferguson-Pell MW, et al. Pressure sore prevention for the wheelchair-bound spinal injury patient. *Paraplegia.* 1980;18:42–51.

24. Key AG, Manley MT. Pressure redistribution in wheelchair cushion for paraplegics: its application and evaluation. *Paraplegia.* 1978–1979;16:403–412.

25. Perkash I, et al. Development and evaluation of a universal contoured cushion. *Paraplegia.* 1984;22:358–365.

26. Peterson M, Adkins H. Measurement and redistribution of excessive pressures during wheelchair sitting. *Phys Ther.* 1982;62:990–994.

27. Reswick JB, Rogers JE. Experience at Rancho Los Amigos Hospital with devices and techniques to prevent pressure sores. In: Kenedi RM, Cowden JM, Scales JT, eds. *Bedsore Biomechanics.* Baltimore: University Park Press; 1976:301–310.

28. Rogers J, Wilson L. Preventing recurrent tissue breakdowns after "pressure sore" closures. *Plast Reconstr Surg.* 1975;56:419–422.

29. Rappl L. Seating for skin and wound management. In: *Proceedings from Thirteenth International Seating Symposium.* Pittsburgh, PA, January 23–25, 1997.

30. Metzler D, Harr J. Positioning your patient properly. *Am J Nurs.* 1996;96:33–37.

31. Plautz R. Positioning can make the difference. *Nurs Homes Long Term Care Manage.* 1992;41:30–34.

32. Cantin JE. Proper positioning eliminates patient injury. *Today's OR Nurse.* 1989;11:18–21.

33. Kozier B, et al. *Fundamentals of Nursing: Concepts, Process and Practice.* 4th ed. Redwood City, CA: Addison-Wesley Publishing Co; 1991.

34. Magee D. *Orthopedic Physical Assessment.* Philadelphia: W.B. Saunders Company; 1992.

CHAPTER 14

Diagnosis and Management of Vascular Ulcers

Carlos E. Donayre

INTRODUCTION

When one takes into consideration what feet routinely accomplish, it is not hard to see why they develop so many problems. A man of average weight (160 to 170 lbs) walks 7.5 miles on an average day. This requires that each foot carry more than 500 tons a day! Women's lighter bodies place fewer demands on the feet than the usually heavier men's bodies, but fashionable footwear nullifies this weight advantage. High-heeled shoes put 75% more pressure on the balls of the feet than does going barefoot. The constant wear and tear that feet are submitted to daily takes its toll, and the older one gets the more likely one is to develop foot problems. At one time or another 85% of all Americans have foot problems serious enough to require professional attention. In nursing home patients this figure rises to nearly 100%.[1]

Most people afflicted with foot ailments fail to seek professional help promptly and rely on their self-diagnosis for treatment. The causes of foot problems are rarely obvious, and delays in correcting them give the underlying disorder more time to develop and worsen. Furthermore, when a serious disease is misdiagnosed as a minor foot malady, results are often drastic and costly. Dry skin, brittle nails, numbness, discoloration, and coolness are usually minor signs and symptoms of foot ailments, but they can also be the first indication of vascular insufficiency or diabetes.

VASCULAR ANATOMY OF THE LOWER EXTREMITIES

In order to have a clear understanding of the effects of altered circulation to the foot, a basic knowledge of vascular anatomy is needed. Neither the vascular system of the lower extremities nor the task it performs is terribly complicated.

The main role of arteries and veins is to provide a pulsatile flow of oxygen-rich blood to the foot and to return the oxygen-depleted blood back to the heart for restoration.

The aorta, the largest blood vessel in the body, divides into two large branches, the right and left common iliac arteries at the level of the umbilicus (see Figure 14–1). Each of these branches divides again into an external and internal iliac artery. The internal iliac artery, also known as hypogastric artery, supplies the pelvis via a variety of branches. The external iliac artery travels distally and becomes the common femoral artery when it crosses the inguinal ligament. This vessel again divides and gives rise to the superficial femoral and deep femoral arteries. The deep femoral artery, or profunda femoris, supplies the muscles of the thigh and is truly the workhorse of the leg. This vessel becomes a major collateral pathway to the lower extremity in the event that the superficial femoral artery becomes occluded due to atherosclerotic disease. The superficial femoral artery becomes the popliteal artery when it crosses the adductor canal, which is formed by the tendon of the adductor magnus muscle. This is the most common site of atherosclerotic disease in the lower extremity, and may be related to local vessel trauma caused by the constant pulsation of the superficial femoral artery against this hard tendinous structure.

The popliteal artery courses medially and divides below the knee to give rise to its first branch, the anterior tibial artery and the tibioperoneal trunk. This trunk divides into the peroneal and the posterior tibial arteries (see Figure 14–2). The peroneal artery terminates at the ankle, and only the anterior and posterior tibial arteries travel into the foot. The anterior tibial artery continues in the foot as the dorsalis pedis artery, but it is absent or terminates early in 2% of individuals. When this occurs the perforating branch of the peroneal artery can become the dorsalis pedis artery.

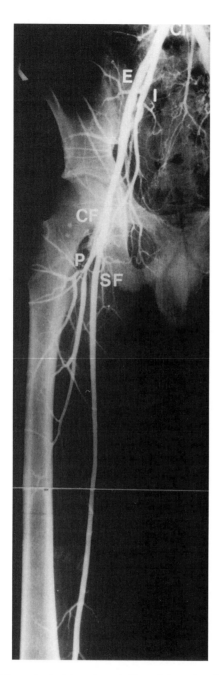

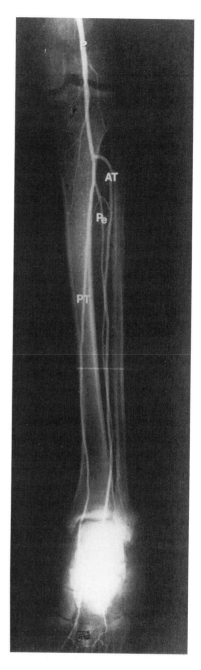

Figure 14–1 Normal arterial anatomy in the pelvic region. An angiogram demonstrates the usual course of the right iliac vessels: common iliac (*CI*), external iliac (*E*), and internal iliac (*I*) arteries. The external iliac artery becomes the common femoral artery (*CF*) when it crosses the inguinal ligament, and gives rise to the profunda femoris artery (*P*) and the superficial femoral artery (*SF*).

Figure 14–2 Normal arterial anatomy in the lower extremity. An angiogram of the left lower extremity demonstrates the usual course of the vessels. The superficial femoral artery traverses the adductor magnus canal to become the popliteal artery (*P*), which bifurcates into the anterior tibial artery (*AT*) and a tibioperoneal trunk. The tibioperoneal trunk also bifurcates to give rise to the posterior tibial (*PT*) and peroneal (*Pe*) arteries. The peroneal artery terminates at the ankle, and only the anterior and posterior tibial arteries travel into the foot. The anterior tibial artery continues in the foot as the dorsalis pedis artery, and the posterior tibial artery bifurcates into the medial and lateral plantar arteries.

In up to 5% of individuals the posterior tibial artery is either absent or terminates early. In this situation, the communicating branch of the peroneal artery gives rise to the plantar arches.[2] The plantar arch is formed by the lateral plantar artery, from the posterior tibial artery, and the deep plantar arch from the dorsalis pedis artery. The predominant blood supply to the plantar arch originates from the dorsalis pedis artery. In most individuals the dorsalis pedis artery and the deep plantar arch give rise to the dorsal and plantar metatarsal arteries, which go on to supply the toes.

The venous system to the lower extremity is in a sense more complex to describe because of the numerous vessels involved and the great number of anatomic variants. A short description will suffice to provide an adequate background to the discussion of chronic venous insufficiency that follows later. The veins of the lower extremity are divided into superficial, deep, and perforating veins (see Figure 14–3). The superficial veins are located in the subcutaneous tissues, superficial to the fascial envelope of the thigh and calf muscles. The deep veins accompany the above-mentioned arteries and lie deep to the fasciae and muscles. The perforating veins penetrate the deep fascial envelope to connect the superficial and deep venous systems. Venous flow is normally from the superficial to the deep veins and is directed by a system of one-way bicuspid valves, which are present in all three venous groups. These valves are more numerous in the deep venous system and in the distal veins.[3]

One comment about venous nomenclature needs to be made about the superficial femoral vein, which begins at the adductor hiatus as a continuation of the popliteal vein. It is joined by the deep femoral vein just below the inguinal ligament to form the common femoral vein, which receives the venous drainage from the longest vein of the body, the greater saphenous vein. The superficial femoral vein is not a superficial vein at all, and any evidence of thrombosis or reflux in this vessel must not be ignored.

OCCLUSIVE PERIPHERAL VASCULAR DISEASE—SIGNS AND SYMPTOMS

Intermittent Claudication

Ailments of the lower extremity can usually be diagnosed accurately by obtaining a careful history and performing a detailed physical examination. Intermittent claudication is the most common presenting complaint in patients with chronic arterial occlusion of the lower extremities. The first case of intermittent claudication in man was described by Charcot in 1858. The word *claudication* comes from the Latin word *claudicatio,* which means to limp, but the patient with claudication does not limp; he or she stops to rest. The pain due to intermittent claudication is characterized by a cramp-

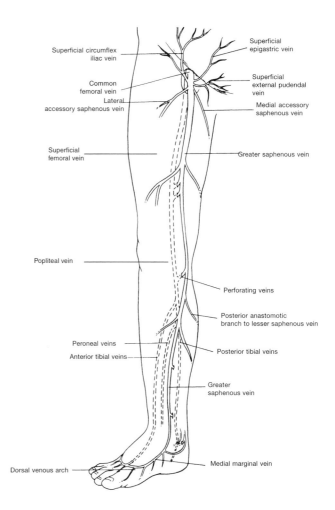

Figure 14–3 Normal venous anatomy. A schematic diagram demonstrates the veins of the lower extremity, which are divided into superficial, deep, and perforating veins.

ing or aching sensation, most often in the calf, that is associated with walking and is relieved by stopping without the need to sit down. Intermittent claudication most commonly occurs as pain in the calf area, but higher vascular obstruction, such as aortic or iliac occlusion, will cause pain in the buttocks and in the upper thigh, and is frequently accompanied by impotence in men. This is known as Leriche syndrome or aortoiliac occlusive disease.

The symptoms of intermittent claudication depend on the degree of ischemia that the muscles in the legs are submitted to. The distance a person can walk will vary from patient to patient, and intermittent claudication can occur after a short distance if a person is walking up a hill, is on a hard surface, or is walking fast. The distance a person walks will be longer if he or she walks more slowly and avoids inclines or hills. People with progressive intermittent claudication note that over time they are only able to walk shorter and shorter distances before discomfort develops.

Examination of the patient with intermittent claudication involving the calf muscle may reveal both a femoral and a pedal pulse but no popliteal pulse. In these patients after a brisk walk, the foot will become pale and pulseless because the blood flow bypasses the skin of the foot and tends to flow to the skeletal muscles of the calf instead. Intermittent claudication usually results from a single arterial blockage, which can be predicted accurately by a carefully performed pulse examination. If a femoral pulse is present but a popliteal pulse is diminished or absent, a stenosis or occlusion can be expected in the superficial femoral artery at the adductor canal. Intact pedal pulses in the presence of a popliteal pulse imply disease of the infrapopliteal vessels or trifurcation disease. Physical findings such as lack of hair growth on the dorsum of the foot, thickening of toenails, and delayed capillary filling should also be looked for because they point to chronic arterial insufficiency.

Another part of the physical examination that should be routinely performed on patients with suspected vascular insufficiency is the resting ankle-brachial pressure measurement or index. With the patient placed in a supine position, bilateral brachial and ankle (posterior tibial and dorsalis pedis arteries) pressures are measured by obliterating blood flow with a standard adult-size sphygmomanometer (blood pressure) cuff. The exact pressure at which there is cessation of arterial blood flow as determined by the use of a continuous-wave Doppler instrument placed over the area of maximum audible flow is recorded. Because systemic blood pressure may vary in patients, the absolute ankle pressure is usually normalized by expressing it as a ratio of the highest obtainable brachial pressure, or ankle-brachial index (ABI).[4] In the normal patient, the ankle pressure is usually greater than or equal to the brachial artery pressure, with an ABI greater than 1.0. An ABI equal to or less than 0.9 almost always represents some degree of arterial insufficiency. For each major arterial blockage that is present the ABI will usually be reduced by 0.3. Thus, in the patient afflicted with intermittent claudication the resting ABI will vary between 0.5 and 0.8 (see Exhibit 14–1).

Rest Pain

Rest pain is caused by nerve ischemia and is persistent in nature, with peaks of increasing intensity. It is worse at night and usually requires the use of narcotics for relief. Rest pain is decreased by dependency of the lower extremities but is aggravated by heat, elevation, and exercise. Because of the relief produced by dependency these patients often sleep in chairs, and the edema of the legs is secondary to constant dependency.

Exhibit 14–1 Noninvasive Evaluation of Arterial Insufficiency: Ankle-Brachial Index

Index	Clinical Description
>1.1	Calcified, noncompressible vessels must be suspected
0.9–1.1	Normal vessels
0.5–0.8	Intermittent claudication
<0.5	Rest pain; ulceration and tissue loss

Nocturnal pain is a form of ischemic neuritis that usually precedes rest pain. It occurs at night because during sleep the circulation is essentially of the core variety, with little perfusion to the lower extremity. The pain is classically described as occurring in the toes, across the base of the metatarsals, and in the plantar arches. The ischemic neuritis produced becomes intense at night and disrupts sleep. The patient gains relief by standing up, dangling the feet over the edge of the bed, or on occasion walking a few steps. This increases the cardiac output, leads to improved perfusion of the lower extremities, and results in relief of the ischemic neuritis. Thus, in patients with rest pain a chronically edematous, erythematous foot and ankle may reflect a reliance on dependence for relief of symptoms.

Rest pain usually indicates the presence of at least two hemodynamically significant arterial blocks. The ABI is reduced by 0.6 with two arterial blockages, and these patients usually have an ABI of less than 0.5. If the lesions that produce nocturnal and rest pain are not corrected by vascular surgery, tissue necrosis and gangrene almost always develop, necessitating amputation.

Ulceration and Gangrene

Ulceration and gangrene of the lower extremity represent the most advanced complications of arterial occlusive disease and are generally associated with diffuse, severe, multilevel arterial obstruction (see Figure 14–4). Ischemic ulcers generally occur on the distal portion of the foot, toe, or heel and are particularly painful. These ulcers generally do not bleed and often have a necrotic rim or crater; their associated pain may be relieved by dependency. Just as in patients with rest pain, the ABI is usually less than 0.5 in these patients. Arterial reconstruction, if feasible, must be undertaken in patients with ulceration to prevent limb loss.

Risk Factors

The importance of risk factors in patients with arterial occlusive disease and their order of appearance or develop-

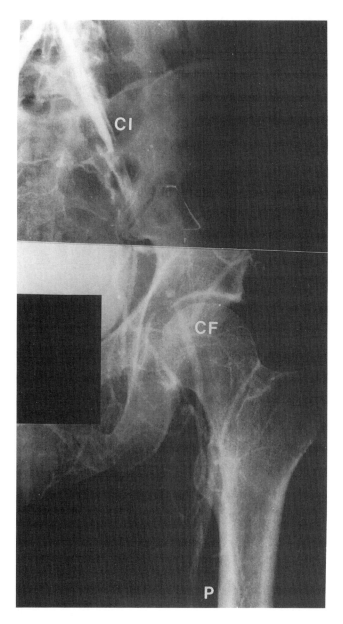

Figure 14–4 An angiogram reveals occlusion of left common iliac artery (*CI*), reconstitution of the common femoral (*CF*) and profunda femoris (*P*) arteries via collateral pathways, and occlusion of the superficial femoral artery. Multilevel atherosclerotic disease is consistent with failure of tissue healing and a decreased ABI. (See *Color Plate 49* for photos of the ulcer on this same patient.)

ment will vary widely from patient to patient. Genetic factors are extremely important risk factors, with premature atherosclerosis frequently seen in family groups with an age of onset of 40 years or older. However, it is not rare to find significant peripheral vascular disease before the age of 40 in the diabetic patient.

Another risk factor of importance is smoking. Clinical experience strongly confirms that patients who smoke and have chronic occlusive arterial disease affecting the extremities do not do well.[5] Among patients under the age of 50 years who quit smoking after they developed intermittent claudication, none progressed to rest pain, as opposed to those who continued to smoke. Smoking causes a decreased blood flow to the extremities and a decrease in the skin temperature of the digits. A single cigarette can cause spasms of the arteries and reduction of blood flow that may last as long as 1 hour or more. The mechanism by which smoking is atherogenic is unknown but may be related to intimal injury caused by increased levels of carboxyhemoglobin, or it may be caused by an effect on platelet function and an increased tendency toward thrombus formation.[6] Another effect of smoking is the influence it exerts on prostacyclin, an important prostaglandin produced by the endothelium of blood vessels that prevents platelet aggregation and promotes vasodilatation. Recent work has shown that cigarette smoking inhibits prostacyclin formation.[7]

Hypertension is another extremely important risk factor in the development of peripheral vascular disease. In the Framingham Study hypertension imposed a threefold increased risk of developing intermittent claudication during a follow-up period of 26 years.[8] The frequency of hypercholesterolemia and hypertriglyceridemia has also been found to be significant in most clinical diseases of the peripheral vascular system. It has been suggested that a high level of high-density lipoprotein (HDL) cholesterol does not protect the patient if the low-density lipoprotein (LDL) is also inordinately high. It is probably the ratio of HDL to LDL that determines the risk factor rather than the absolute level of each.

Patients presenting with signs and symptoms of arterial insufficiency should be counseled and educated about risk factor modification if disease progression is to be avoided.

DIABETES AND FOOT ULCERATION

Ulceration and other complications of the foot associated with diabetes are increasing problems of significant epidemiologic proportions. Nearly half of the major amputations performed each year are for patients suffering from diabetes.[9] Only 8% of the overall population in the United States, however, has diabetes at the present time. Each year 35,000 to 40,000 diabetic patients undergo major limb amputation at a cost of 1.2 billion dollars.[10] This figure does not include the costs of rehabilitation, prostheses, loss of time from work, loss of jobs, and welfare payments.

The amputation rate in people with diabetes is 15 times that of the nondiabetic population. The initial lesion in most of these cases is painless trauma occurring in a neuropathic, insensate foot. It is the presence of peripheral vascular disease, however, that prevents these lesions from healing. Impaired circulation is a major contributor to infection because the delivery of leukocytes and antibiotic agents is compromised by the lack of sufficient blood flow. The decreased delivery of oxygen to infected tissues further promotes the growth of highly destructive anaerobes. Studies have demonstrated that oxygen is necessary for macrophage mobility in wound debridement and the ingrowth of granulation tissue during wound healing.[11]

The function of some tissue growth factors is oxygen dependent. Furthermore, some antibiotics, principally the aminoglycosides, depend on oxygen for their function. The triopathy of neuropathy, vascular insufficiency, and an altered response to infection makes the diabetic patient uniquely susceptible to pedal complications. Not surprisingly, foot problems remain the most common indication for hospitalization in patients with diabetes mellitus.

Approximately 8% of non–insulin-dependent (type II) diabetic patients have evidence of peripheral vascular disease (PVD) at the time of diagnosis. The incidence of PVD rapidly increases with age and duration of diabetes. Nearly 45% of patients with diabetes over 20-year duration have evidence of PVD, and this percentage is much higher in those patients who smoke. Vascular disease affecting the lower extremity in diabetic patients has many similarities to that found in the nondiabetic patient. The changes in the vessel wall, in both the media and the intima (consisting of deposits of platelets, smooth muscle cells, lipids, cholesterol, and calcium), are qualitatively the same in both groups, although these changes are quantitatively greater in those with diabetes. There are, however, some important differences. The atherosclerotic process is more commonly seen in diabetic patients than in nondiabetic patients, occurs at an earlier age, advances more rapidly, and is almost as common in women as in men. Differences also exist with regard to the vessels that are involved and the extent of the involvement. The femoral, iliac, and aortic vessels appear to have a similar degree of atherosclerotic changes in diabetic and nondiabetic patients. The profunda femoris artery is affected with greater frequency and extent in diabetics, but the vessels most frequently involved in diabetes are those below the knee—the tibial and peroneal arteries and their smaller branches. In a diabetic patient multisegment occlusions can be seen with diffused mural changes proximally and distally, whereas in the nondiabetic subject the occlusions most often involve a single segment with a normal adjacent arterial tree. Once the process begins in the diabetic patient, both lower extremities are usually involved; in the nondiabetic patient the lesions are more likely to be unilateral. A summary of 485 patients in five studies showed that following the initial limb amputation, 42% of diabetics in the first 3 years and 56% in

3 to 5 years required a contralateral amputation (greater than 10% per year).[12]

Diabetes poses a special risk because diabetic individuals tend to have severely diffused vascular disease; therefore, the diabetic patient must pay particular attention to foot care to ward off ulceration and infection, which mandate an increase in blood flow that their vascular system cannot provide. A major risk factor that has always been considered important in the development of diabetic vascular disease is the control of blood sugar.[13] The Diabetes Control and Complications Trial Research Group in 1993 published a study of 1,444 patients followed for 6.5 years to assess the progression of retinopathy, nephropathy, and neuropathy. Clinical neuropathy was defined as abnormal neurologic examination findings consistent with peripheral neuropathy, plus either an abnormal nerve conduction test result in at least two peripheral nerves or unequivocal autonomic nerve testing. In this multicenter study patients were randomly assigned to standard insulin control or to an intensive therapy administered by either external insulin pump or by three or more daily injections of insulin, guided by frequent blood sugar monitoring. The developments of neuropathy and nephropathy were each significantly reduced by the strict monitoring of insulin levels. In patients assigned to an intensive management group, the incidence of retinopathy was reduced by 76% compared with that in patients receiving the usual twice-daily insulin injections. Equally impressive, a 69% reduction in the onset of neuropathy was reported. The findings represent the 3% incidence of neuropathy in those with intensive insulin management versus 10% development in those with the usual insulin management during this 5-year study. The results would support the theory that more stringent insulin management will reduce the onset and progression of neuropathy. The study did note, however, that there was a two- to threefold increase in severe hypoglycemic reactions, which required management in the strict control group. No fatalities and no serious complications were reported despite this complication. This and other studies support the need for optimum insulin control in diabetic patients. A therapy regimen designed to achieve blood glucose values as close to the normal range as possible would seem to prevent the onset and progression of diabetic complications. Thus, such monitoring should be part of optimum diabetic foot care.

In summary, the risk for developing peripheral vascular disease in the diabetic patient stems from a combination of factors. Heredity, age, and the duration of diabetes are factors that cannot be controlled. Nevertheless, the blood sugar level should be well controlled but balanced against the risk of hypoglycemia. Although each risk factor may have a variable degree of importance by itself, a combination of these factors can become very significant. Therefore, it is extremely important to control hypertension and reduce cholesterol and triglyceride levels. Needless to say, one of the strongest risk factors discussed above is smoking. It is critically important that diabetic patients and certainly all patients who have peripheral vascular disease do not smoke.

A common complaint of patients with peripheral vascular insufficiency is cold feet. It is the discomfort of cold feet that prompts the diabetic patient to resort to the use of hot water bottles, heating pads, or hot water soaks. This practice can result in severe burns to a foot that has become insensitive to heat because of a peripheral neuropathy. At an ambient foot temperature of approximately 70°F the patient requires 1 mL of blood flow per 100 g of tissue per minute. A patient with even moderate peripheral vascular disease can manage this. Soaking the foot in hot water can quickly raise the skin temperature to 104°F. This requires an increase of 10 times the flow of blood. A patient with peripheral vascular disease cannot achieve this. This results in blistering, ulceration, infection, and gangrene, which not infrequently may lead to an amputation. Another symptom that diabetics complain of is rest pain. In the diabetic patient, rest and nocturnal pain may be absent despite severe ischemia because neuropathy has destroyed sensory perception, stressing the need for a careful examination of these patients for vascular sufficiency at every clinic visit.

All of the modern advances in medicine, including sophistication of microbiologic analyses, new and more potent antibiotics with improved antimicrobial activity, advances in radiologic imaging of the foot and leg, and better education and understanding on the part of health care professionals and patients about the etiology and the therapy of the diabetic foot infections, should have reduced the major amputation rate in diabetic patients. Unfortunately, the major amputation rate for diabetic patients has not been significantly reduced. The triopathy of neuropathy, vascular insufficiency, and an altered response to infection makes the diabetic patient uniquely susceptible to foot problems. Diabetics live quite normally with all of these complications until minor trauma results in cutaneous ulceration and the development of an acute infection that may lead to hospitalization and limb loss. Neuropathy probably represents the greatest risk for ulcer development. Diminished or absent proprioception and sensation quite often delay early recognition and treatment of a seemingly benign problem. Autonomic nerve dysfunction characterized by dry skin, absent sweating, and increased capillary refill secondary to arteriovenous shunting leads to fissure, cracking, and a false sense of security about the circulation. Motor neuropathy leads to denervation of the intrinsic and skeletal muscles of the foot and leg, resulting in abnormal bone-related problems due to a compromised foot architecture that is susceptible to traumatic injury.

Ischemia may complicate up to one half of the diabetic foot ulcers; 40% of diabetic patients presenting with gangrene or severe limb threat infections will have palpable popliteal pulses. Aggressive vascular evaluation and treatment are essential for healing ischemic ulceration and must be considered for chronic ulcers that fail to respond to treatment. Diabetic patients tolerate infection poorly. Defects in the host defense include altered leukocyte function and wound repair. Most important is the fact that systemic signs and symptoms of a septic process often occur late, making unexplained and uncontrollable hyperglycemia the only reliable sign of a potentially serious limb and/or life-threatening infection. Less than one third of patients with pedal osteomyelitis have elevated temperature or white blood cell count. The lack of blood flow reduces oxygen to the afflicted tissue and contributes to the development of foot sepsis. Studies have demonstrated that oxygen is necessary for macrophage mobility in wound debridement and the ingrowth of granulation tissue during wound healing.

Restoration of blood flow with increased oxygen levels to ischemic tissue is of the utmost importance if limb salvage is going to be achieved.[14] The extent and severity of the infected diabetic foot ulcer determines the course of treatment. To determine the severity one must do a careful initial inspection of the wound, which because of neuropathy can usually be done at bedside. Sterile forceps, a probe, scissors, and a good light are all that are needed. The severity of tissue destruction and sepsis may not be totally apparent from just looking at the ulcer or infected callus, especially in those patients who continue to bear weight on a painless area or who do not have the visual acuity to recognize a problem. One must unroof all encrusted areas and, using a probe, inspect the wound to determine deep tissue destruction and possible bone or joint involvement. A determination can be made whether the ulcer is superficial so that treatment can be done at home, or whether there is any limb-threatening potential that requires immediate hospital admission. Patients with superficial ulceration and minimal (less than 2 cm) cellulitis may be treated on the outside initially if there is no evidence of systemic toxicity and the patient is compliant and reliable and has an adequate support system at home. Treatment requires that the patient be non–weight bearing to provide complete and total rest. Contact casting and other immobilization endeavors do not replace non–weight bearing and are used only in selected instances. The wound specimen is cultured at initial debridement and broad-spectrum oral antibiotics are begun, with changes made based on sensitivity reports and the response of the wound. Simple dressings appear to work best, with wet-to-dry dressings of either saline or diluted antiseptic solutions applied one or three times per day depending on the size and the area being treated. Dry, scaly skin is best treated with lubricated creams, and cracks and fissures are best managed with antibiotic oint-ment. Patients must be examined every 24 to 48 hours; if there is no improvement, hospitalization is recommended. Once healing is ensured, weight bearing is progressed in modified footwear to protect the high-risk areas. Simply al-lowing the patient to return to full activity or weight bearing may result in acute Charcot's foot or recurrent breakdown. Shoe modification and periodic follow-up are essential to all patients at risk. Patients with limb-threatening infections are managed with hospitalization. Again, inspection is es-sential because one cannot rely on systemic signs and symp-toms to ascertain severity. Indications for hospitalization are deep ulcers with bone or joint involvement, cellulitis greater than 2 cm, lymphangitis, and systemic toxicity. Initial man-agement includes immediate hospitalization, medical stabi-lization, control of blood sugar, and complete bed rest.

There is probably no greater controversy right now in the treatment of diabetic infection than the proper diagnosis and treatment of osteomyelitis. One thing is known for certain: inadequate diagnosis and treatment of osteomyelitis increase the risk for major amputation. Methods to diagnose osteo-myelitis include plain radiographs, bone scans, leukocyte scans, computed tomography scans, magnetic resonance imaging, and clinical evaluation. Proponents of each radio-logic test quote acceptable sensitivity and specificity but largely without confirmation by microbiologic or histopatho-logic proof. Whatever test one uses, it should not delay ur-gent or emergent surgical intervention. Cost is now also an important consideration, with fixed reimbursement the norm. These tests are costly; thus the use of a sterile probe to ex-amine the wound is very cost effective. If a sterile probe taps the bone or a joint, there is excellent sensitivity and speci-ficity that the area is involved with osteomyelitis. A plain radiograph should be obtained, with or without magnifica-tion views, to look for gas, foreign bodies, associated frac-tures, or other bony abnormalities. Antibiotics are adjunc-tive to good surgical debridement and management. At the time of debridement deep culture specimens are obtained, and bone or biopsy of deep tissue is sent whenever possible to ensure a reliable specimen. The majority of cultures from patients with limb-threatening disease grow gram-positive bacteria and 50% grow gram-negative enteric bacteria, and 50% to 70% of these patients also grow anaerobes. There-fore, antibiotic selection must take this into account, and broad-spectrum intravenous antibiotics or combination therapy to ensure maximum delivery to the infected site are recommended. Antibiotic changes are made only on the ba-sis of the sensitivity reports and the response of the wound.

Except in rare circumstances antibiotics do not cure os-teomyelitis. Studies supporting the use of antibiotics alone for curing osteomyelitis in general lack histopathologic or microbiologic proof and accept a major amputation rate of

almost 30% after treatment.[15] Opponents also note that bac-teremia, open wounds after treatment, gangrene, and ischemia are associated with poor outcome. Courses of antibiotics of 6 weeks or longer are also quite costly, even when delivered on an outpatient basis.

Infected limb-threatening ulcers are a surgical emergency. Surgical debridement and drainage of the infection should be carried out as expeditiously as possible. Diabetics do not tolerate undrained sepsis, and patients with systemic toxic-ity will not improve until this is done. A good monitor of accuracy of debridement is to follow the blood sugar levels and management, which should improve dramatically as in-fection is controlled. Incisions are carefully placed, ensur-ing adequate debridement and conserving as much healthy tissue as possible, such as small skin flaps that may later be used in reconstruction. Any viable area should be left and protected even if this means multiple trips to the operating room for infection control. Most of the debridement can be done with little or no anesthesia because of the presence of neuropathy.

The location of the ulcer, the extent of the infection and its control, and the adequacy of circulation will determine what the final result will be. It is important to remember that the more ischemic the lower extremity is, the more impor-tant it is to close an involved area primarily. A neuropathic foot with excellent circulation is managed differently than the same infection in an ischemic foot. Once sepsis is con-trolled, evaluation and treatment of the ischemia are the next most important options. The overwhelming success of sur-gical revascularization even to the pedal vessels supports an aggressive approach. Once circulation is reestablished, revi-sions or more definitive local surgical procedures can be performed. It is important to try to save as much of the weight-bearing part of the foot as possible, especially the first toe and its metatarsal head. Only with an aggressive control of diabetic sepsis and restoration of foot pulses by revascularization can the amputation rate be reduced in this challenging group of patients.

VENOUS STASIS ULCERS

Despite decades of clinical and laboratory research, the exact mechanisms by which patients develop venous stasis ulceration remains uncertain. There is little doubt that sus-tained venous hypertension remains the underlying etiologic factor common to all patients with venous stasis ulcers. Venous hypertension can occur primarily in the deep venous system or may be isolated to the superficial saphenous veins. These entities may also occur in combination. This has been associated with congenital or acquired valvular dysfunction within the deep veins, or with valvular incompetence located at the saphenofemoral junction or via incompetent perforators below the knee. Clearly, the underlying pathologic process must be determined in each individual patient prior to embarking on a specific treatment plan.

The Swollen Leg

One of the first complaints of patients with venous insufficiency is swelling of the legs, which on occasion is accompanied by discomfort and a heavy feeling in the lower extremities. As opposed to similar complaints in patients with arterial insufficiency, this complaint is readily relieved by leg elevation in the person afflicted by venous disease. A basic understanding of the function and structure of the venous system is needed in order to comprehend the pathophysiologic derangements that are responsible for the development of lower extremity edema.

The main and foremost task of the venous system is to return blood from the periphery to the heart. In addition it serves as a storage network intimately involved in blood volume regulation. It also facilitates the exchange of substances between tissue and blood in the capillary region. In order to carry out these functions and to maintain a vigorous flow of blood in a low-pressure system, the venous vessels have to rely on the elastic components of their walls (see *Color Plate 50*). The walls of veins consist of an intact endothelium that coats a thin basal membrane. An adjoining layer of fibrous connective tissue with strands of collagenous and muscle fibers helps to stabilize the walls of the veins and in conjuction with a delicate system of valves is responsible for the return of venous blood to the heart. The slightly helical structure of muscle fibers and collagenous strands enables healthy veins to return to their original position after undergoing distention of length and girth from increased blood volumes. Failure of this collagenous and muscular infrastructure results in veins that become wider, longer, and convoluted, giving rise to the formation of tortuous varices. Progressive venous dilatation can lead to valvular incompetence by interfering with the delicate apposition of venous valve leaflets, which is required for transport of blood up the leg and into the central circulation. Thus, the failure of proper venous valve closure may be the result and not the primary cause of blood vessel widening.

Venous congestion can also alter the delicate balance that exists between arterioles, venules, and the capillaries. About 20 L of fluid are filtered into the interstitial space by this complex system each day, with 18 L (90%) being reabsorbed by the venous branches of the capillary system. The remaining 2 L (10%) return to the circulatory system through lymph drainage. Hydrostatic and colloidal-osmotic forces work together in capillary filtration and reabsorption. Intracapillary pressure drops from 35 mm Hg in the arterial branches to 15 mm Hg in the venous branches. Higher pressure in the arterial side leads to outward filtration, which is counteracted on the venous side by a continuous reabsorption driven by colloidal and osmotic forces. A delicate balance is maintained as long as the amounts of filtered and reabsorbed fluid remain equal. Altered venous return due to increased venous dilatation and valvular deficiency results in perceptible increases in capillary hydrostatic pressure and permeability of the capillary endothelium. These two factors lead to an enhanced filtration of fluid into the interstitial space and the classic appearance of the signs and symptoms of peripheral edema.

As can be gleaned from the above discussion, the lymphatic system can also be involved in chronic venous insufficiency. Both the lymphatic and venous systems share an early embryologic development and an intimate anatomic relationship. The lymphatic channels course along the pathway of the lesser and greater saphenous veins to drain into the superficial inguinal lymph nodes. The deep lymphatic vessels of the lower extremity likewise accompany the deep vessels of the leg to the popliteal lymph nodes and then continue along the femoral vessels to reach the deep inguinal lymph nodes.

Congenital or acquired insufficiency of the lymphatic transport results in lymph stasis and the accumulation of protein-rich interstitial fluid. Chronic lymphedema, however, develops only if the collateral lymphatic circulation is inadequate or tissue macrophages (which aid in the removal of macromolecules from the interstitial space) are overwhelmed. Impaired lymphatic drainage results in significant structural changes in the lymphatic vessels themselves and the subcutaneous tissues they serve. This leads to fibroblast proliferation, sclerosis of the subcutaneous tissues, and increased vascularity, changes that are usually associated with chronic inflammation.[16] Secondary changes in lymph vessels due to lymph stasis include fibrosis of the wall with loss of permeability and lymph-concentrating ability. Furthermore, lymphatic valves, just as in the venous system, may also fibrose or become incompetent as a result of proximal lymphatic obstruction and distal vessel dilatation. The lymph vessel wall loses its intrinsic contractility, and the muscle pump is rendered ineffective. Lymph stasis favors the development of obstructive lymphangitis with further destruction of the main and collateral lymphatic channels.

Chronic venous insufficiency can lead to recurrent attacks of skin cellulitis, which may result in increased destruction of cutaneous lymphatic channels and subsequent obstructive lymphatic patterns.[17] This is strongly suggested by lymphoscintigraphy, a noninvasive imaging modality used to interpret the morphologic and functional alterations occurring in the lymphatic system. Lymphoscintigraphy has been used to show that the lymphatic system is often impaired in patients with chronic venous insufficiency. This impairment is reflected by the development of anatomic changes in lymphatic vessels as well as the presence of a delayed lymphatic flow. These changes ultimately may interfere with the absorption of interstitial fluid in the extremities of patients afflicted with chronic venous insufficiency and thus contribute to the increased clinical swelling that is seen in them.

Pathophysiology of Venous Ulceration

There are several mechanisms described in the literature that outline the pathophysiologic events leading to skin ulceration. The concept of fibrin cuffs developing at the capillary level was initially described by Browse and Burnand in 1982.[18] These authors suggested that sustained venous hypertension is transmitted to the superficial veins in the subcutaneous tissue and the overlying skin. This in turn causes widening of the capillary pores, thus allowing the escape of large macromolecules (including fibrinogen) into the interstitial space. Owing to associated defects in the fibrinolytic process, fibrin accumulates around these capillaries, thus forming a mechanical barrier to the transfer of oxygen and other nutrients. Ultimately, this leads to cellular dysfunction, which in turn leads to cell death and skin ulceration. Unfortunately, there is no published evidence that fibrin provides a barrier to oxygen diffusion.

In more recent years, additional physiologic changes have been noted in the microcirculation of patients with chronic venous hypertension. Specifically, this relates to an altered inflammatory mechanism in these patients. These changes have been linked to the accumulation of white blood cells at the capillary level, which has been termed the white blood cell–trapping hypothesis.[19,20] Transient elevations in venous pressures have been shown to decrease capillary blood flow, resulting in trapping of white blood cells at the capillary level. This occurs to a much greater degree in patients with long-standing venous hypertension and liposclerotic skin. These marginated white blood cells in turn plug capillary loops, resulting in areas of localized ischemia. These cells may also become activated at this level, which in turn causes release of various proteolytic enzymes as well as superoxide free radicals and chemotactic substances. These substances ultimately lead to direct tissue damage, thus leading to ulceration.[21]

Differential Diagnosis of Venous Stasis Ulcers

All that ulcerates is not venous in origin. The common feature of all ulcerations of the legs is an underlying systemic or local problem that complicates the healing of wounds, which are inevitably traumatic in origin. Once-minor trauma leads to a chronic, recalcitrant wound, which is a challenge to heal. Those ulcerations that are not venous, but may mimic or be confused with venous ulcers, are to be differentiated on the basis of a different historical evolution, the presence of other systemic or local disease processes, and often subtle but important different physical findings (see Exhibit 14–2).

Medical Treatment of Venous Stasis Ulcers

Definitive treatment of venous stasis ulcers is dependent on the operative repair of the underlying reason for venous incompetence of the affected extremity. This is seldom possible, however, and long-term success is rarely achieved. Excision and grafting of the ulcerated area and surrounding scar tissue, even when accompanied by local and regional subfascial ligation of perforating vessels, does not uniformly result in returning long-standing skin integrity. Therefore, there remain a great many patients whose venous stasis ulcers have to be managed nonoperatively.[22] Before attempting a medical management of a venous stasis ulcer, the diagnosis must be assured. Noninvasive measurements must eliminate a significant ischemic component to that etiology. The ABI must be at least greater than 0.5 and preferably greater than 0.75. If transcutaneous oxygen measurements are performed, the foot dorsal pressures should exceed 30 mm Hg. Hemoglobin electrophoresis should eliminate sickle cell disease and, if suspected, a biopsy should eliminate vasculitis as the cause of the ulcer.

To allow the ulcer to heal by secondary intention, the wound must be in bacterial balance and contain 10^5 or fewer bacteria per gram of tissue; it must not harbor β-hemolytic streptococci. If the biopsy shows the wound to be infected, bacterial balance is best reestablished by a topical antimicrobial. Systemically administered antibiotics do not lower the bacterial count in granulation tissue. However, systemic antibiotics are effective and indicated if the ulcer has an area of surrounding cellulitis. Another method of reestablishing bacterial balance is with the use of temporary biologic dressings, such as allograft skin. Once the ulcer is in bacterial balance, it can heal by secondary intention. The process of epithelialization is more important than the process of contraction for these ulcers.

Compression therapy is the cornerstone of effective nonoperative treatment of venous stasis ulcers. Many combination dressings, such as the time-honored Unna boot, have been reported to provide adequate compression if good patient compliance is achieved.[23] The Food and Drug Admin-

Exhibit 14–2 Differential Diagnosis of Lower Extremity Ulcers

	Ischemic	**Venous Stasis**	**Neuropathic**
Etiology	Arterial insufficiency	Chronic venous insufficiency	Diabetes
Usual location	Distal to medial malleolus; dorsum of foot or toes	Proximal to medial malleolus; lateral lower leg	Along pressure points; plantar aspect of metatarsal heads (first or fifth)
Pain	Severe; nocturnal, relieved by dependency	Mild; relieved by elevation	None
Bleeding	Little or none	Venous ooze	May be brisk
Lesion characteristics	Irregular edge; poor granulation tissue	Shallow, irregular shape; granulating base with rounded edges	Punched-out; callous edges with deep sinus
Associated findings	Trophic skin changes (dry skin, brittle nails, alopecia); absent pulses	Stasis dermatitis; hyperpigmentation; palpable pulses	Neuropathy; warm skin; pulses may be present or absent

Source: Modified from Rutherford RB. The vascular consultation. In: Rutherford RB, ed. *Vascular Surgery,* 4th ed. Philadelphia: W.B. Saunders Company, 1995, p. 9.

istration presently considers compression therapy to be the standard of care for venous stasis ulcers. *Color Plate 51* shows a patient with venous stasis ulceration. *Color Plate 52* shows an ulcer and associated signs of chronic venous insufficiency.

Recently, a variety of growth factors have been introduced for the treatment of venous stasis ulcers. The trial with transforming growth factor (TGF)-beta in a collagen sponge delivery system has given the most encouraging data of those trials that have been completed.[24] Interestingly, the topical antimicrobial silver sulfadiazine (Silvadene) has also shown beneficial results. It is thought that the base of this compound has properties that stimulate wound epithelialization. Contrary to previous experience, many patients who have healed during carefully controlled clinical trials have remained healed as long as they comply with compression therapy. Since the underlying etiology of the ulcer is not treated with medical therapy, such treatment can only be considered palliative. However, as more is learned about modulating the wound healing process, palliation may be extended for the life of the patient.

In order to evaluate properly the many therapeutic modalities that are being applied in the treatment of chronic venous disease the Ad Hoc Committee on Reporting Standards in Venous Disease of the Society of Vascular Surgery and the North American Chapter of the International Society for Car-

diovascular Surgery have recommended the use of a classification designed to allow such comparisons.[25] Limbs with chronic venous disease should thus be classified according to clinical signs (C), etiology (E), anatomic distribution (A), and pathophysiologic condition (P) (see Exhibit 14–3).

Any limb with possible chronic venous disease is first placed into one of seven clinical classes (C_{0-6}) according to objective clinical signs, and is further characterized as being asymptomatic ($C_{0-6,A}$) or symptomatic ($C_{0-6,S}$). Since therapy may alter the clinical category of chronic venous disease, limbs should be reclassified after any form of medical or surgical treatment. The venous dysfunction encountered is then to be classified according to one of three mutually exclusive categories: congenital (E_C), primary (E_P), or secondary (E_S). Next, the anatomic site or sites affected with venous disease are to be described as involving the superficial (A_S), deep (A_D), or perforating (A_P) veins. Finally, the pathophysiologic reason for the development of signs and symptoms of chronic venous disease are to be determined as being the result of reflux (P_R), obstruction (P_O), or both ($P_{R,O}$). Observance of this classification in the clinical arena will lead to an improvement in communications in the field of venous disorders and help in the evaluation and proper application of therapeutic regimens.

Exhibit 14–3 Chronic Lower Extremity Venous Disease

CLINICAL CLASSIFICATION

Class	Clinical Description
0	No visible signs of venous disease
1	Telangiectasias, reticular veins, malleolar flare
2	Varicose veins
3	Edema without skin changes
4	Skin changes ascribed to venous disease (eg, pigmentation, venous exzema, lipodermatosclerosis)
5	Skin changes as defined above with healed ulceration
6	Skin changes as defined above with active ulceration

ETIOLOGIC CLASSIFICATION

Etiology	Description
Congenital	Cause of chronic venous disease present since birth
Primary	Chronic venous disease of undetermined cause
Secondary	Chronic venous disease with an associated known cause (post-thrombotic, post-traumatic, other)

ANATOMIC CLASSIFICATION

Veins Involved	Description
Superficial	Telangiectasias/reticular veins and greater saphenous veins; lesser saphenous veins and nonsaphenous veins
Deep	Inferior vena cava, iliac, pelvis, gonadal, femoral, popliteal, tibial, and muscular veins
Perforating	Thigh and calf

PATHOPHYSIOLOGIC CLASSIFICATION

Type	Description
R	Reflex
O	Obstruction
R,O	Reflux and obstruction

Source: Adapted from Porter JM, Moneta GL, and International Consensus Committee on Chronic Venous Disease. Reporting standards in venous disease: an update. *Journal of Vascular Surgery,* Vol. 21, pp. 635–645, 1995.

REFERENCES

1. McGann MM, Robinson LR. *The Doctor's Sore Foot Book.* Avenel, NJ: Wing Books; 1994.

2. Kadir S. Arterial anatomy of the lower extremity. In: Kadir S, ed. *Atlas of Normal and Variant Angiographic Anatomy.* Philadelphia: W.B. Saunders Company; 1991:123–160.

3. Lundell C, Kadir S. Lower extremities and pelvis. In: Kadir S, ed. *Atlas of Normal and Variant Angiographic Anatomy.* Philadelphia: W.B. Saunders Company; 1991:203–225.

4. Strandness DE Jr, Summer DS. Application of ultrasound to the study of arteriosclerosis obliterans. *Angiology.* 1975;26:187–189.

5. Jonason T, Rinquist I. Factors of prognostic importance for subsequent rest pain in patients with intermittent claudication. *Acta Med Scand.* 1985;218:27–36.

6. Couch NP. On the arterial consequences of smoking. *J Vasc Surg.* 1986;3:807–812.

7. Hillis LD, Hirsch PD, Campbell WB, et al. Interaction of the arterial wall, plaque, and platelets in myocardial infarction. *Cardiovasc Clin.* 1983;14:31–44.

8. Kannel WB, McGee DL. Update on some epidemiologic features of intermittent claudication: The Framingham Study. *J Am Geriatr Soc.* 1985;33:13–21.

9. Reiber GE. Diabetic foot care. *Diabetes Care.* 1992;15:29–31.

10. Bransome ED Jr. Financing the care of diabetes mellitus in the United States. *Diabetes Care.* 1992;15:1–5.

11. Vogelberg KH, Konig M. Hypoxia of diabetic feet with abnormal arterial blood flow. *Clin Invest.* 1993;71:466–470.

12. Kucan JO, Robson MC. Diabetic foot infections: fate of the contralateral foot. *Plast Reconstr Surg.* 1986;77:439–441.

13. McDermott JE. *The Diabetic Foot.* Rosemont, IL: American Academy of Orthopaedic Surgeons; 1995.

14. LoGerfo FW, Gibbons GW, Pomposelli FB, et al. Evolving trends in management of the diabetic foot. *Arch Surg.* 1992; 127:617–621.

15. Bamberger DM, Daus GP, Gerding DN, et al. Osteomyelitis in the feet of diabetic patients: long-term results, prognostic factors and the role of antimicrobial therapy and surgical therapy. *Am J Med.* 1987;83(4):653–660.

16. Olszewski W. Pathophysiology and clinical observations of obstructive lymphedema of the limbs. In: Clodius L, ed. *Lymphedema.* Stuggart, Germany: Georg Thieme Verlag; 1977:79–102.

17. Hammond SL, Gomez ER, Coffey JA, et al. Involvement of the lymphatic system in chronic venous insufficiency. In: Bergan JJ, Yao JST, eds. *Venous Disorders.* Philadelphia: W.B. Saunders Company; 1991:333–343.

18. Browse NL, Burnand KG. The cause of venous ulceration. *Lancet.* 1982;2:243–245.

19. Thomas PRS, Nash GB, Dormandy JA. White cell accumulation in the dependent legs of patients with venous hypertension: a possible mechanism for trophic changes in the skin. *Br Med J.* 1988;296:1693–1695.

20. Butler CM, Coleridge-Smith PD. Microcirculatory aspects of venous ulceration. *Dermatol Surg Oncol.* 1994;20:474–480.

21. Coleridge-Smith PD, Thomas P, Scurr JH, et al. Causes of venous ulceration: a new hypothesis. *Br Med J.* 1988;296:1726–1772.

22. Robson MC. Medical treatment of venous stasis ulcers. Presented at American College of Surgeons Postgraduate Course 13: Current Treatment of Venous Stasis Ulcers; October 22–27, 1995; New Orleans, LA.

23. Villavicencio JL, Rich NM, Salander JM, et al. Leg ulcers of venous origin. In: Cameron JL, ed. *Current Surgical Therapy.* Toronto, Canada: BC Becker Inc; 1989:610–618.

24. Bishop JB, Phillips LG, Mustoe TA, et al. A prospective randomized evaluator-blinded trial of two potential wound healing agents for the treatment of venous stasis ulcers. *J Vasc Surg.* 1992;8:251–257.

25. Porter JM, Moneta GL, and International Consensus Committee on Chronic Venous Disease. Reporting standards in venous disease: an update. *J Vasc Surg.* 1995;21:635–645.

CHAPTER 15

Management of the Neuropathic Foot

Nancy Elftman

INTRODUCTION

Medical research has provided advancements in medication and technology that now extend the lives of patients with previously fatal diseases: the prognosis has changed from fatality to chronic complications.[1] The chronic disease complication addressed in this chapter is neuropathy. The objective of management of the problem is to control progression and reduce amputations conservatively.

The patient with neuropathy often has dysvascular components that must be addressed by a medical team rather than one specialty (see Chapter 14, Diagnosis and Management of Vascular Ulcers). With the team approach the limb can be evaluated, treated, and monitored through follow-up to provide continued ambulation for the patient.[2] The team goal is the prevention or delay of amputation and/or limb salvage of lower extremities. In the formation of clinical teams there has been a trend to include practitioners of several disciplines, including wound care nurse, advanced practice nurse, or enterostomal therapy (ET) nurse, diabetologist/endocrinologist, vascular surgeon, physical therapist, orthotist/pedorthist, orthopaedic surgeon/podiatrist, and dermatologist.

The multidisciplinary approach to treating foot problems is an optimum intervention for prevention of amputations. The disciplines playing the most important roles are nurse educators, who encourage high-risk patients to modify their behavior; orthotists, for recommendation of suitable footwear, stockings, and orthoses; and primary care providers, to remove calluses, treat minor trauma, and provide health care. Physical therapists will play a role in all of these aspects of care. Referrals should be available to vascular surgeons and other specialists when specified by a physician.[3]

The multidisciplinary clinic requires special training in treatment of chronic disabilities. Although the individual training programs of professionals include normal foot anatomy and biomechanics, few describe the neuropathic foot and associated complications, leading to inadequate medical advice or treatment.[4] In the clinical setting no initial problem is too small to address. The clinical team is important and must treat minor trauma immediately to prevent deterioration of the condition. There is a destructive chain of trauma surrounding the neuropathic foot, as follows:

1. Trauma
2. Inflammation
3. Ulceration
4. Infection
5. Absorption
6. Deformity
7. Disability

This chain can be broken with proper objective measurements, treatment, and patient education.[2]

The patient with neuropathy requires a consistent follow-up schedule relating to level of insensitivity, history of complications, and general physical condition. A patient with loss of protective sensation (10 g of force) and no history of ulceration will require less frequent follow-up than the patient with a chronic breakdown history. Records should reflect as many objective measurements as possible and a method of classification of patient types. Management of the neuropathic and dysvascular limb is a process of continuing evaluation. The process of history, examination, and charting details cannot be overemphasized. All clinical findings should be charted and relayed to the patient's primary care provider.[5]

Although neuropathy exists in many disease processes, there are concerns about the growing number requiring management. When breakdown occurs in one neuropathic limb, the contralateral limb is commonly involved within 18 to 36 months, so prophylactic measures are especially important. Many considerations must be addressed by the team treating the neuropathic and dysvascular limb before a treatment plan is developed. Once the plan is in place it is imperative to educate and involve the patient in the plan.

PATHOGENESIS

The neuropathic process is poorly understood and there are many theories regarding its etiology. When evaluating the neuropathic patient, the medical team encounters the following obstacles:

- Lack of clear definition of diabetic neuropathy
- Absence of single repeatable tests of neuropathy that are not dependent on either expensive technology or subjective clinical judgment
- Varied manifestations of neuropathy: distal symmetric, mononeuropathies, autonomic neuropathies
- Separation of diabetes from other potential etiologies of neuropathy

The neuropathic foot is affected by a trineuropathy, which consists of three phases that occur simultaneously; manifestations of two of these phases are shown in Figure 15–1.

1. Sensory neuropathy—loss of sensation, leaving patient incapable of sensing pain and pressure. The patient has no sense of identity with the feet.
2. Motor neuropathy—the loss of intrinsic muscles, resulting in clawed toes (Figure 15–2) and eventual footdrop. The ankle jerk reflex is absent.[6]
3. Autonomic neuropathy—the loss of autonomic system function, resulting in the absence of sweat and oil production and leaving skin dry and nonelastic.

Until recently, all forms of neuropathy were lumped together. It is now clear that there are different types, which develop differently. Peripheral neuropathy can be broken down into two major groups:

1. Gradual onset, those that develop gradually and are usually painless. The exact cause is unknown, but may be related to duration of diabetes and level of blood sugar control. Symptoms may include numbness, tingling, burning, and a pins-and-needles sensation.
2. Sudden onset and disappearance, those that develop suddenly (or acutely) and are almost always painful, then the pain disappears leaving sensory loss.

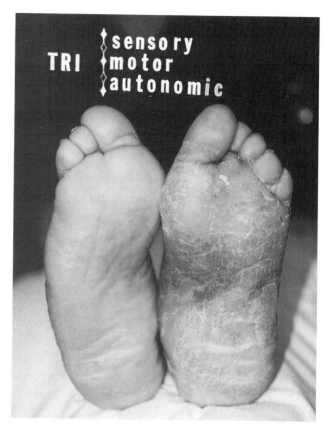

Figure 15–1 Feet of a patient with sensory, motor, and autonomic neuropathies. Manifestations of motor neuropathy (deformity, clawed toes, toe amputation, foot imbalance needing immediate intervention) and autonomic neuropathy (dry, cracked skin) are evident. Note the difference in trophic changes between the feet. *Source:* Reprinted with permission from N. Elftman, Clinical Management of the Neuropathic Limb, *Journal of Prosthetics and Orthotics,* Vol. 4, No. 1, pp. 1–12, Copyright © American Academy of Orthotists and Prosthetists.

Many believe that neuropathy is caused by hyperglycemia—high levels of glucose in the blood. Tight control may be the best prevention of severe neuropathy.[7]

MEDICAL HISTORY

The medical history is a useful way to identify potential neuropathy that may be present in many disease processes. The neuropathy may be isolated (nerve damage or entrapment), but for most chronic disease processes the effect is peripheral. The most common disease processes resulting in peripheral neuropathy are the following:

- Diabetes
- Spina bifida
- Hansen's disease

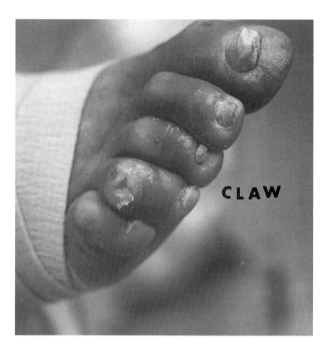

Figure 15–2 Clawed toes. Note the corn on the fourth toe caused by rubbing top of shoe.

- Systemic erythematosus lupus
- Acquired immunodeficiency syndrome (AIDS), human immunodeficiency virus infection, AIDS-related complex
- Cancer
- Vitamin B deficiency
- Multiple sclerosis
- Uremia
- Vascular disease
- Charcot-Marie-Tooth muscle disease

Toxins and toxic syndromes can also cause insensitivity in the limbs, including those related to overuse of or exposure to alcohol, arsenic, lead, steroids, gold, and isoniazid.

Many other chronic complications may result in neuropathy, but the above list indicates why all patients must be evaluated for neuropathy regardless of reported history. Congenital sensory loss, as in spina bifida, is important to the examiner because the patient has never experienced normal sensation and cannot evaluate his or her own sensory status.[8–10]

Diabetic Neuropathy

The most common disease process seen in neuropathy is diabetes, which results in true peripheral neuropathy. Statistics on diabetes are growing, and the medical cost related to diabetes in the United States is currently $14 billion per year. Included in this cost are 54,000 lower extremity amputations

per year, of which 50% to 70% could have been prevented by team management. It is estimated that 50% to 84% of the lower extremity amputations were preceded by a foot ulcer. More than 14 million Americans have diabetes (half are undiagnosed), with 700,000 cases diagnosed per year. In the general population, 1 in 20 has diabetes. Many diabetics are diagnosed when they present a nonhealing foot ulcer.[11–16] Of major concern is the mortality rate after amputation, which is 50% within 3 to 5 years. The rate of contralateral amputation is 50% within 4 years.[17]

Although there are several different divisions of diabetes, the two main categories are insulin-dependent diabetes mellitus (IDDM), or type I, and non–insulin-dependent diabetes mellitus (NIDDM), or type II. In IDDM the insulin deficiency is due to pancreas islet cell loss. It occurs at any age but is common in youth. NIDDM is more frequent in adults but occurs at any age. The majority of patients with NIDDM are overweight.[18]

The dysvascular patient may also be diabetic, which leads to impaired healing of a limb that cannot deliver antibiotics sufficiently to combat extremity infection (see Chapter 14). One limb may be severely insensitive, while the other is mildly affected (see Figure 15–1). The loss of vascularity caused by calcified arteries or a disease process is first referred to the vascular surgeon for possible correction or improvement.

The four types of stress that lead to ulceration and destruction of tissue in the neuropathic limb are as follows:

1. Ischemic necrosis is usually seen on the lateral side of the fifth metatarsal head and is due to wearing a shoe that is too narrow. The ischemia is caused by a very low level of pressure (2 to 3 psi) over a long period of time, causing death of the tissue.
2. Mechanical disruption occurs when a direct injury caused by high pressure (600+ psi) inflicts immediate damage to tissue. This can also be caused by heat or chemicals that damage the skin. Such injuries commonly occur by stepping on a foreign object.
3. Inflammatory destruction occurs with repetitive moderate pressures (40 to 60 psi). Inflammation develops and weakens the tissue, leading to callus formation and ulceration from thousands of repetitions per day.
4. Osteomyelitis (and other sepsis) destruction is the result of a moderate force in the presence of infection. Infection is spread as forces are applied by intermittent pressure.[19]

The highest incidence of ulceration occurs at sites of previous ulceration. The history should be reviewed carefully for previous ulcers or infection.[20] A newly healed ulcer is covered by thin skin that is likely to tear. In completely healed ulcer areas, scar tissue may adhere to underlying structures.

The healed areas are composed of tissues of different density and therefore compress uniquely, causing shear between opposing tissue durometers.[21,22]

The progression of breakdown continues at the metatarsal heads due to migration of fat pads, leaving bone and skin to absorb shock. The neuropathic limb has lost heat and cold sensation and reflex response. The incidence of ulceration is 71% on the forefoot, with the third metatarsal head most commonly affected, followed by the great toe and first and fifth metatarsal heads. Once breakdown has begun on the foot, 53% of the contralateral limbs follow the progression of breakdown within 4 years. Newly healed wounds need time to mature and become strong, yet there will always be a potential for breakdown in a previous area of ulceration. Scar compresses at a different rate than other tissue, and the area of adherence will be prone to shear stresses.[23]

Of all amputations, 86% could have been prevented by patient education and appropriate footwear.[3] The aging process alone will produce changes in appearance and alterations in sensitivity, joint motion, and muscle-force production, any of which can lead to dysfunction.[24] Improper nutrition can also delay healing.[25] The majority of amputations are due to gangrene (90%), followed by infection (71%) and nonhealing ulcers (65%).[26] The dry, dark ulcers of gangrene are usually found on toes or bony parts of the foot. Neuropathic ulcers are usually moist and draining.[15] Diabetic neuropathic ulcers occur in a foot with severe sensory impairment, yet they typically have adequate blood supply for healing.[24,27]

There are two types of gangrene: wet and dry. Dry gangrene is due to loss of nourishment to a part, followed by mummification. The area is dry, black, and shriveled and results in a well-defined line of demarcation with specific localization and self-amputation (autoamputation; Figure 15–3A). Wet gangrene is the necrosis of tissue followed by destruction caused by excessive moisture. Bacterial gases accumulate in the tissue. The line of demarcation is ill-defined and the limb is painful, purple, and swollen. Wet gangrene is common when infection exists.[28,29] Figure 15–3B shows wet gangrene of the fifth toe. *Do not* debride. The patient needs immediate referral to a surgeon.

SYSTEMS REVIEW AND EXAMINATION

A multisystems review and examination for the patient with neuropathy is required to determine the coimpairments that will affect wound healing and require management. Four systems to review for this patient population are the neuromuscular system, the vascular system, the musculoskeletal system, and the integumentary system.

Neuromuscular System

A foot with neuropathy is dry, with small fissures, has toes that are clawed, and is incapable of sensing trauma. The rigid anesthetic foot is more likely to break down than a flexible anesthetic foot.[30] The insensitive foot should be evaluated carefully and bilaterally. Any form of peripheral neuropathy can produce the discomfort of paresthesia: prickling, burning, and jabbing sensations.[31,32] The length of this period of discomfort is unknown; it varies among patients. Neuromuscular system examinations to assess for neurologic changes are the focus of the foot screening process and are described in detail later.

> **Research Wisdom:** *Interventions for Paresthesia*
>
> Paresthesia may be helped by use of a transcutaneous electronic nerve stimulator (TENS) unit, which generates small pulses of electricity similar to an electric massage. Another method of controlling the discomfort is with topical creams.[33,34]

Vascular System

Peripheral vascular disease (PVD) is a serious complication affecting millions of Americans. Of the 500,000 vascular-related ulcerations, 10% are arterial and 70% are venous ulcerations; some individuals have both venous and arterial diseases. Many patients with neuropathy also have PVD. Therefore, it is critical to review the vascular history before planning any intervention to identify strategies that are being used to manage vascular problems that will affect the prognosis and outcome for the patient. Some of the related circulatory systems diseases that usually accompany neuropathy and management recommendations are described here. Chapter 14 describes the pathogenesis and management of vascular problems in more detail.

Atherosclerosis is also known as hardening of the arteries. The interior wall of arteries is usually smooth, but with atherosclerosis platelets, calcium, and connective tissue deposit on the walls. In early stages the patient may experience intermittent claudication or cramping in the lower limb, which goes away with rest. As the disease progresses, symptoms appear when the patient is not walking (rest pain).[15] Arterial compromise can be noted by the loss of hair growth, shiny skin, atrophy, and cool skin over the toes.[35] Atherosclerosis leads to impaired circulation in the legs and is one of the most important causes of gangrene, leading to amputation.[36] Arterial ulcers are located on tips or between toes, heel,

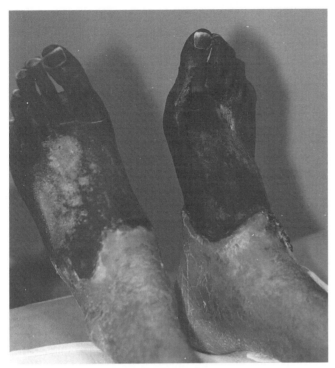

Figure 15–3A Dry gangrene. Such a lesion needs immediate referral to a surgeon. It should not be debrided.

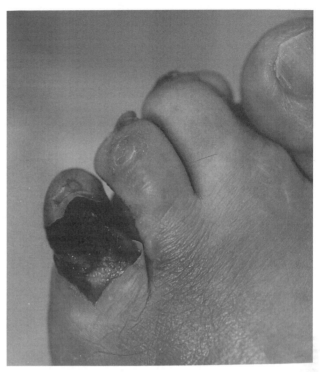

Figure 15–3B Wet gangrene. Such a lesion needs immediate referral to a surgeon. There is probable infection.

metatarsal heads, side or sole of foot, and above the lateral malleoli. The ulcer will look punched-out, with well-demarcated edges, and be nonbleeding (see *Color Plate 48*). The ulcer base may be deep and pale or black and necrotic. Treatment involves vascular reconstruction, bed rest, and immobilization. Arterial ulcers have a poor prognosis. Misdiagnosis of an arterial ulcer as a venous ulcer can lead to serious complications.

The venous stasis ulceration has a better prognosis for healing than the arterial ischemic ulceration. Veins are less elastic than arteries. The valves within veins no longer function to return blood to the heart against gravity, leaving blood to pool in the lower limb. The pooling does not allow new oxygenated blood into the area, and the cell walls of the veins begin to break down. The waste blood products begin to weep through the lower limb. Venous stasis ulcerations are commonly located in the anteromedial malleolus area and pretibial area. The ulcerations are irregular in shape, surrounded by bluish, brown skin. These ulcers are exudative and show evidence of bleeding.

Treatment of venous stasis ulcerations begins with leg elevation.[37] The limb must be treated with compression bandages or an Unna boot. The Unna boot is a semirigid dressing of gelatin and zinc oxide. Its application protects vulnerable skin from the weeping exudate, especially below the ulcer site. The Unna boot is applied wet. When it dries it forms a nonelastic, nonexpandable, nonshrinkable, porous mold that sticks to the skin. This treatment has been used on venous stasis for 100 years. It is a means of controlling edema when it is applied across a joint. The motion of the joint generates a pumping action.[1]

The chronic venous stasis lower limb without an open ulceration will show signs of edema that must be controlled. The presence of small water blisters or weeping will be a sign that compression should begin (see *Color Plates 53 and 54*). This limb should be treated with pressure-gradiated stockings as daily prevention; an Unna boot with Ace bandage wrap is required for severe edema or periods of breakdown. Pressure-gradiated stockings have a graduated pressure to facilitate pumping action and assist the venous system in removing fluids from the lower limb. Antiembolism stockings are not designed for the ambulatory patient and do not supply the pumping action required. Antiembolism compression is for the recumbent hospitalized patient.

Compression can be ordered to begin at the metatarsal heads and decrease pressure in the calf as a further assist to the venous system. Most patients do well with compression in the range of 30 to 40 mm Hg at the foot and ankle. When using these stockings for the neuropathic/dysvascular patient remember to avoid seams around bony prominences, and never place a zipper over the malleoli.

When venous stasis ulceration occurs on one limb, begin compression therapy on the contralateral side. The appearance of small water blisters or weeping is a sign that compression should begin. Chapter 9 describes procedures for management of edema.

Musculoskeletal System Examination

The musculoskeletal system examination includes examination of joint integrity, range of motion, skeletal deformity, and muscle strength. Motor neuropathy will distort skeletal alignment and Charcot joint will leave a foot deformed as shown in Figure 15–14. An analysis of abnormal gait should also be included. Beginning with the joint range of motion review, it is important that the foot has a dorsiflexion range of at least 10° to allow ambulation without harm to the great toe.[38] The forces on the plantar surface can peak to 275% of body weight when running and 80% when walking.[39] With limited motion in the joints the trauma can result in ulceration. It is important to test range of motion, as well as performing manual muscle testing.[2,40] There is an absence of the ankle jerk reflex when neuropathy is advanced to glove-and-stocking distribution.[41]

There is a constant concern with toe deformities that may result in ulceration. In the case of claw toe deformity, the toes are dorsiflexed at the metatarsal-phalangeal joints with flexion at the interphalangeal joints.[42] The great toe should be examined for deformity. A fibrous proximal joint can cause ulceration that is especially difficult to relieve. Great toe extension can be seen when weight bearing, as the patient will thrust the toe into extension when ambulating, causing calluses and discoloration on the distal tip near the nail from contacting the shoe. Great toe pronation is seen on the medial/plantar surface of the great toe. Hallux rigidus refers to limited range of motion in the proximal great toe metatarsal/phalangeal joint and requires a rigid rocker-bottom shoe to allow ambulation without excessive pressure on the great toe. Hallux valgus (bunion) is the increased valgus angle of the great toe in relation to the metatarsal, requiring a shoe that can be modified and molded to conform to the medial bunion formation.

Toe amputations may be for single or multiple toes (see Figure 15–1). The amputation may be a disarticulation or a resection (metatarsal shaft is removed). The distal end of the amputation site must be followed carefully and protected from trauma.

There are common complications to be addressed with the neuropathic limb. Bursa formation over the navicular prominence is due to the constant high forces and must be provided an area of pressure relief before ulceration occurs. A sinus tract formation will result when previous areas of ulceration heal over a pocket of bacteria instead of healing from internal to external tissues. The small pocket of bacteria will be moved anteriorly through the tissues, causing infection to spread.

A common complication of the neuropathic patient is severe foot deformity following neuropathic fractures or Charcot arthropathy including joint subluxation or dislocation (Figure 15–14). The presence of severe foot deformity has been shown to be predictive of prolonged healing time for patients treated with total-contact casting. Sinacore et al.[43] found that fixed foot deformity prolonged healing of ulcers with total-contact casting when located in the midfoot and rearfoot. Ulcers located in the midfoot healed in 73 ± 29 days, rearfoot ulcers 90 ± 19 days. Individuals without fixed deformities with chronic diabetes mellitus and those with forefoot ulcers healed in 41 days. Therefore, early detection during the musculoskeletal examination of a fixed foot deformity in a patient with an ulcer located in the midfoot or rearfoot can be used to determine a prognosis that healing time will be significantly longer when a total-contact cast is used as the treatment intervention.

Motor neuropathy produces common abnormal gait characteristics in the neuropathic population. The shoes are worn on the lateral side of the sole because of a varus deformity (see Figure 15–4A). This weakness often causes ankle injuries. After further deterioration, footdrop can occur. The stiffness in the complex joint structures leads to abnormal motion in the foot's function.

Clinical Wisdom:
Modification of a Standard-Depth Shoe

To compensate for varus gait abnormalities, shoes need to be modified. The modifications required are (1) a full, lateral-flare sole as shown in Figure 15–4B, (2) a strong counter to support the heel, and (3) a high top to support the ankle. A standard-depth shoe can be modified by an orthotist, or a shoe repairperson may be able to do the job if guided. While not all orthotists will agree to modify an existing shoe, others will. This will save the patient money.

Integumentary System Examination

Integumentary system examination of the foot includes the toenails. Toenail deformities are commonly seen in the neuropathic foot. Hypertrophic nails are caused by fungus and are common in the diabetic population. The nails tear

Figure 15–4A Shoe is worn on the lateral side due to a varus deformity. *Source:* Reprinted with permission from R.B. Chambers and N. Elftman, Orthotic Management of the Neuropathic and Dysvascular Patient, in *Atlas of Orthoses and Assistive Devices,* 3rd. edition, B. Goldberg and J.D. Hsu, eds., p. 443, © 1997, Mosby-Year Book, Inc.

Figure 15–4B Standard-depth shoe with sole modification. The shoe has a full-flare sole, a strong counter, and a high top to stablize the varus abnormality. *Source:* Reprinted with permission from R.B. Chambers and N. Elftman, Orthotic Management of the Neuropathic and Dysvascular Patient, in *Atlas of Orthoses and Assistive Devices,* 3rd. edition, B. Goldberg and J.D. Hsu, eds., p. 443, © 1997, Mosby-Year Book, Inc.

shoe lining and create areas of rough surface to abrade the toes (see Figure 15–5). Nail care for onychomycosis (fungus), ingrown toenails, and trimming must be performed by trained medical personnel to ensure injury is not inflicted. Soft corns are hyperkeratotic lesions found between toes (usually between the fourth and fifth toes) due to pressure of an opposing toe in a region that is moist.[29] Injury and maceration of the toes is commonly controlled by the use of lamb's wool between the toes or tube foam to space toes and prevent friction (Figures 15–6A and B). Buildup of callus is indicative of high pressures and stress of an isolated area that must be relieved. The thickening of the skin in the area of a callus is preceded by abnormal pressure or friction.[29,44] Areas of excess pressure require pressure redistribution in the clinic setting rather than scheduling additional appointments.

Dryness of the skin is the result of autonomic neuropathy in which the sweat and oil production is decreased and moisture must be replaced. Loss of hair growth may be indicative of vascular impairment. Ulcerations that are necrotic are debrided to allow healing to progress from internal to external tissues for optimum closure of the ulcer site.

Another common occurrence is burns, due to either heat or chemicals such as over-the-counter remedies. Soaking the foot in hot water is a specific cause of burns. A common wisdom is that neuropathic patients should *never soak* their feet. The insensitive foot cannot produce the warning signals necessary to prevent severe burns (see Chapter 4).

Dermatologic conditions can affect treatment programs until they are resolved. Necrobiosis can be confused with venous stasis disease but does not require or respond to extensive treatment. The round, firm plaques of reddish brown to yellow are seen three times more often in women.[45,46] These ulcerations are common along the tibia and require only protective dressings.

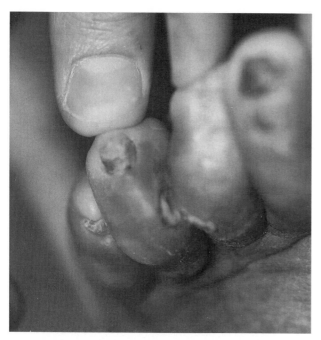

Figure 15–5 This foot has soft corns between toes, thickened toe-nails, and onychomycosis (fungal) infection.

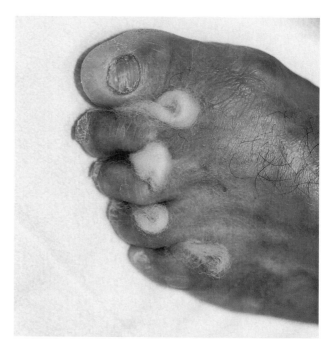

Figure 15–6A Lamb's wool pieces are placed between each toe to prevent maceration. They should be replaced after bathing. *Source:* Reprinted with permission from R.B. Chambers and N. Elftman, Orthotic Management of the Neuropathic and Dysvascular Patient, in *Atlas of Orthoses and Assistive Devices,* 3rd. edition, B. Goldberg and J.D. Hsu, eds., p. 441, © 1997, Mosby-Year Book, Inc.

Clinical Wisdom: *Tube Foam and Lamb's Wool for Quick Relief of Pressure on Toes*

Claw toes, hammer toes, calluses, corns, and small ulcerations can be relieved of pressure by inserts and shoe modifications and spaced with tube foam or lamb's wool separators to allow air flow. Separators prevent maceration and skin breakdown; they should be removed before and replaced after bathing. In addition, the custom tube foam separator serves as a toe separator, reduces shear from the shoe, cushions metatarsal heads, and can be used as a positioner for overlapping toes. Figure 15–6A shows lamb's wool pieces placed between toes. Figure 15–6B shows a tube foam toe separator in place. Figure 15–6C and Exhibit 15–1 illustrate and describe the diagram of steps to create a tube foam separator. The tube foam is available from podiatric supply companies.

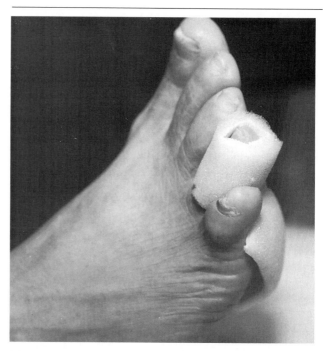

Figure 15–6B A custom tube foam toe separator. *Source:* Reprinted with permission from R.B. Chambers and N. Elftman, Orthotic Management of the Neuropathic and Dysvascular Patient, in *Atlas of Orthoses and Assistive Devices,* 3rd. edition, B. Goldberg and J.D. Hsu, eds., p. 431, © 1997, Mosby-Year Book, Inc.

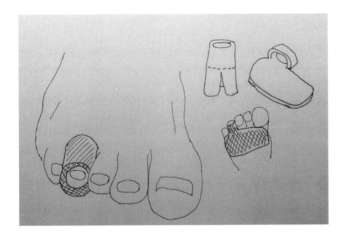

Figure 15–6C Diagram of construction of a tube foam separator.

Exhibit 15–1 Instructions To Make a Foam Toe Separator

Make a custom foam toe separator (Figures 15–6B and 15–6C) by the following steps:

1. Select a size of tube foam with a diameter that will not constrict the toe.
2. Cut a 2½- to 3-inch piece of the foam.
3. To make the toe cuff:
   a. Measure back ½ to ¾ inch from one end of the tube foam and mark.
   b. Cut across the diameter of the tube three fourths of the way through.
   c. Slit up the tube to the marking on the side that is cut to the diameter cut (see diagram)
   d. The foam will flatten out (see diagram).
   e. The tube will slip over the toe and the flat section will be located on the plantar surface of the foot.

Keratoderma plantaris, characterized by keratin cracks and ulcerations, is caused by the loss of sweat and oil elasticity in the skin (autonomic neuropathy). As keratin builds up it creates small fissures that allow entrance of bacteria, and infection begins. The entire sole around the margin of the heel will undergo diffuse thickening and develop painful fissures if the foot is sensate or go undetected if insensate (see Figure 15–7). Prevention includes reduction of keratin buildup and retention of skin moisture.[29] There are many forms of rashes and dermatological conditions that must be evaluated and treated in the neuropathic limb. These are usually discovered by inspection rather than patient discomfort. Typical skin conditions in the diabetic population include shin spots and diabetic bullae (with less frequency than necrobiosis).[45]

Infections are commonly seen in the neuropathic foot, including *Pseudomonas* infection, which is bacterial growth that occurs within a moist environment. Signs and symptoms of infection are usually absent in the neuropathic foot even though the infection is present and virulent due to impaired circulation and immunosuppression. Both are other common coimpairments of neuropathy. The problems of infection are identified during the integumentary system review. See Chapter 8, Management of Exudate and Infection, for strategies to assess and treat infection.

Dry gangrene is another finding that may be discovered during the integumentary system review. When dry gangrene is present, there is a line of demarcation at which the body will autoamputate the affected area. This process of autoamputation could take weeks to months;[42] it is nature's way of protecting the body from infection and should not be disturbed. Figure 15–3A (Wagner grade 5) is a photograph of a foot with dry gangrene. A patient with dry gangrene needs immediate referral to the surgeon.

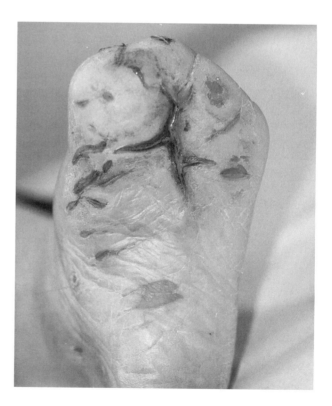

Figure 15–7 Typical neuropathic foot with keratoderma plantaris. Note the dry, cracked skin, dirt imbedded in the skin, open wounds, and the absence of dressing due to lack of awareness of the condition.

FURTHER VISUAL AND PHYSICAL ASSESSMENTS

Examination of the neuropathic limb includes further visual and physical examination to avoid future complications. The patient is never asked for his or her own foot evaluation. The shoes are removed to allow the practitioner to examine the foot. The neuropathic patient will not limp, even with a foot ulceration (see Figures 15–7 and 15–8). Inspection should be both weight bearing and non–weight bearing.

Footwear Assessment

The footwear must be examined for wear of orthosis and sock patterns indicating excessive pressure. The ends of the toes should be examined for injury caused by a short shoe. Figure 15–8 shows a toe wound caused by a short shoe. Notice the toe is to the end of the shoe insole. Figure 15–18 shows the alignment required when fitting a shoe for proper weight distribution and length measurement. The interventions section of this chapter describes orthotics and adaptive equipment and includes instructions in footwear interventions. Shoes should show a normal wear pattern on the lateral heel of the sole as contrasted with the pattern in Figure 15–4A. Shoes should be resoled on a regular basis to keep sides from wearing down. Inserts are replaced as required when relief modifications are no longer sufficient and shock absorption is decreased.

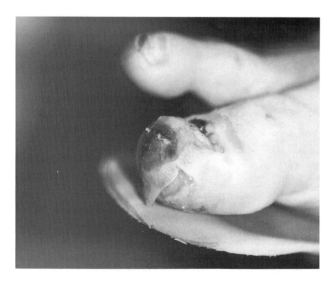

Figure 15–8 Short shoe. The toe extends to the end of the insole. *Source:* Reprinted with permission from N. Elftman, Clinical Management of the Neuropathic Limb, *Journal of Prosthetics and Orthotics,* Vol. 4, No. 1, pp. 1–12, Copyright © American Academy of Orthtists and Prosthetists.

Wound Assessment

The Wagner scale[47] for grading neuropathic ulcers classifies ulcer severity in six grades based on the depth of the ulcer and the presence of infection or necrosis. Ulcer grading is useful for prognosis and for selection of treatment intervention. In addition, the Wagner ulcer grading system is a uniform system that is used by health care practitioners of different disciplines to describe ulcers in neuropathic limbs. Ulcers with low grades are managed by conservative measures, whereas ulcers with higher grades are a direct threat to limb loss and require surgical management. The neuropathic limb often suffers from dysvascularity as well; therefore, the system is often used for both populations. The Wagner ulcer classification system differs from other grading systems by including a grade of 0, which describes preulcerative skin, healed ulcers, and the presence of a bony deformity where the skin is intact. Preulcerative areas include calluses located under the metatarsal heads or areas of weight bearing.[48] For continuity of documentation and communication the team must understand the Wagner scale of ulcer grading and use it consistently. Exhibit 15–2 shows the six Wagner ulcer grades. The preferred conservative method of treatment is guided by the Wagner grade. Exhibit 15–3 shows how the different grades dictate different treatment strategies.

Sensation Testing

When evaluated for insensitivity, most patients who had hypoesthesia could sense pinprick and cotton wisp applications. Patients with foot ulcers were observed to have less

Exhibit 15–2 Wagner Scale

Grade	Description
Grade 0	Skin intact (Figure 15–9A)
Grade 1	Superficial ulcer (Figure 15–9B)
Grade 2	Deeper ulcer to tendon or bone (Figure 15–9C)
Grade 3	Ulcer has abscess or osteomyelitis (Figure 15–9D)
Grade 4	Gangrene on forefoot (Figure 15–9E)
Grade 5	Gangrene over major portion of foot (Figure 15–9F)

Source: Reprinted with permission from F.E.W. Wagner, The Dysvascular Foot: A System for Diagnosis and Treatment, *Foot and Ankle,* 2:64-122, © 1981, Williams & Wilkins.

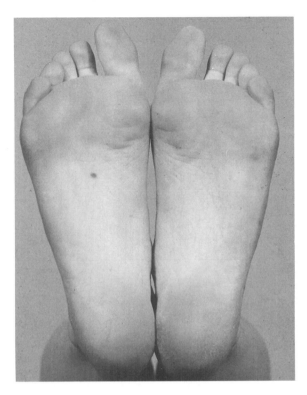

Figure 15–9A Skin intact, Wagner grade 0.

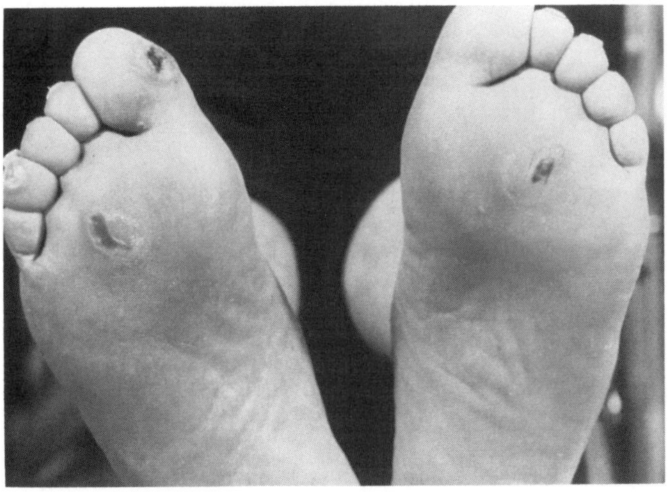

Figure 15–9B Superficial ulcer, Wagner grade 1.

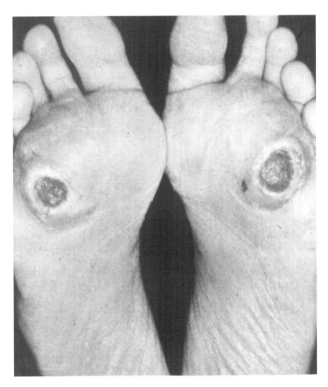

Figure 15–9C Deeper ulcer to tendon or bone, Wagner grade 2.

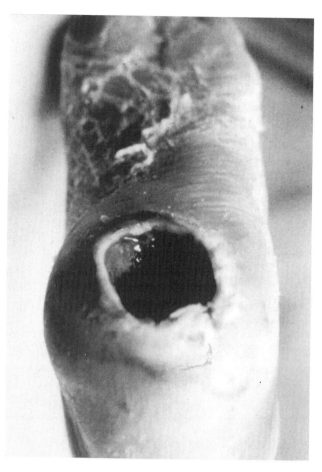

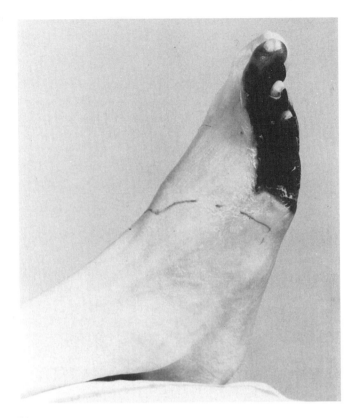

Figure 15–9E Gangrene on forefoot, Wagner grade 4.

Figure 15–9D Ulcer has abscess or osteomyelitis, Wagner grade 3.

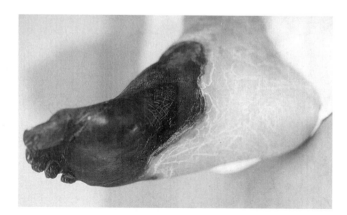

Figure 15–9F Gangrene over major portion of foot, Wagner grade 5.

pressure sensation than those without foot ulcers.[50] In 1898 von Frey attempted to standardize the stimuli for testing the subjective sense of light touch by using a series of horse hairs of varying thicknesses and stiffness. Wienstein used nylon monofilaments mounted on Lucite rods as substitutes for the hairs.[51] The Semmes-Wienstein monofilaments can be obtained commercially in elaborate sets for precise measurement, but research at Carville Hansen's Disease Center, Carville, Louisiana, has consolidated the testing to three sizes of monofilaments for grading the insensitive foot. The 4.17 monofilament supplies 1 g of force and is indicative of normal sensation. If the patient cannot feel the next monofilament (5.07), he or she does not have the protective sensation level of 10 g and cannot sense trauma to the foot to cease weight bearing. Failure to sense the 10-g monofilament is used as the determining factor for use of protective footwear and accommodative orthotics. No patient with protective sensation can ambulate on an ulcerated foot. A large percentage of patients do not feel the largest monofilament (6.10), which indicates a loss of sensation at 75 g. This largest-diameter monofilament indicates an insensate foot that must be accommodated and followed closely. Use of the monofilament is not to be confused with the testing for sharp/dull sensation. The sharp/dull test stimulates multiple nerves as opposed to a single-point perception test.

The monofilament is a single-point perception test and requires the examiner to place the monofilament on the skin, press until the monofilament bends (diameter of monofilament controls point of bend), and remove from the skin surface. The monofilaments are tested and determined to be reliable at the 95% confidence level.[52] The patient is to respond when he or she feels the pressure sensation. To avoid errors in testing, the monofilament is never used in areas of scarring, calluses, or necrotic tissue. The bilateral testing for sensation is especially important for the unilateral and bilateral amputee to determine areas of insensitivity and progression of the neuropathy. Figure 15–10 shows proper method for monofilament testing procedure. Note the bend of the monofilament. This must occur to measure correct pressure sensation.

Birke,[53] at Hansen's Disease Center, developed a risk classification system based on the loss of protective sensation. Loss of protective sensation, history of prior ulceration, and reduced circulatory perfusion are important factors in development of foot ulcers. A risk classification system based on these factors is useful in identifying patients who would benefit from different levels of intervention (Exhibit 15–3). Risk is classified by four grades: 0, no loss of protective sensation; 1, loss of protective sensation (no deformity or history of plantar ulceration); 2, loss of protective sensation and deformity or abnormal blood flow without history of plantar ulcer; and 3, history of plantar ulcer. Three interventions have proven effective in reducing risk of ulceration: protective footwear, patient education, and frequent clinic follow-up. For example, when a patient's ulcer is grade 0, preulceration, and the patient can sense the 10-g monofilament (has protective sensation), he or she will sense pain before damage occurs to the feet. Patients in this category

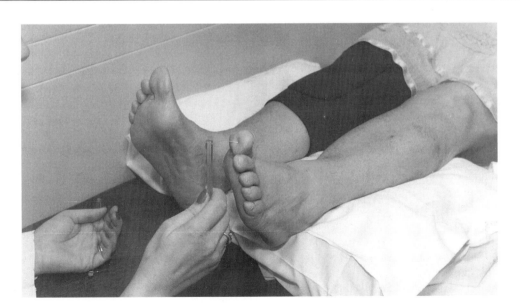

Figure 15–10 Monofilament testing. *Source:* Reprinted with permission from R.B. Chambers and N. Elftman, Orthotic Management of the Neuropathic and Dysvascular Patient, in *Atlas of Orthoses and Assistive Devices,* 3rd. edition, B. Goldberg and J.D. Hsu, eds., p. 433, © 1997, Mosby-Year Book, Inc.

Exhibit 15–3 Conservative Management by Wagner Ulcer Grade

Wagner Ulcer Grade and Recommended Treatment

Grade 0—may be treated with extra-depth shoe and insert
Grade 1—cast or Plastazote healing shoe, reducing weight to ulceration; antibiotic intervention as required[48]
Grade 2—debridement and cast; antibiotic intervention as required[48]
Grade 3—remove infected tissue and cast; antibiotic intervention as required[49]

Source: Data from M. Glugla and G. Mulder, The Diabetic Foot, in *Medical Management of Foot Ulcers in Chronic Wound Care: A Clinical Source Book for Healthcare Professionals,* D. Krasner, ed., pp. 223–239, © 1990, Mosby/Health Management Publications, Inc., and F.A. Wagner, *A Classification and Treatment Program for Diabetic, Neuropathic and Dysvascular Foot Problems,* pp. 1–47, © 1983.

---

usually do well with a standard shoe of correct sizing and a simple shock-absorbing pad.

The patient without protective sensation will not cease ambulating when damage begins to tissues. Patients with feet such as those in Figure 15–7 who walk into the clinic are insensate. They require extra-depth shoes with a total-contact accommodative insert to distribute pressure and reduce forces on areas of potential breakdown. The insert may be molded to the patient or fabricated on a cast. The cast does not have corrective forces added, only accommodation.

The accommodative insert does not apply correction; it fills only the spaces between the flat shoe and the foot contours. Any force added will receive full weight bearing and breakdown will occur. If the addition of metatarsal head (MTH) pads or scaphoid pads is requested, these pads must be of a soft durometer. Rigid pad additions will cause excess pressure and ulcerations. The MTH pads are placed proximal to the metatarsal heads to redistribute the weight from the heads to the metatarsal shafts.

Testing for vibratory sensation may be accomplished by using the bioesthesiometer. This instrument is essentially an electrical tuning fork that uses repetitive mechanical indentation of skin delivered at a prescribed frequency and amplitude.[54] The simple graduated tuning fork is a rapid means of sensory testing.[55,56] The purpose of all sensory testing equipment is to identify those at risk.[57]

Upper and lower extremity peripheral neuropathy is present when sensation testing reveals that the level of sensation loss is symmetric and equidistant from the spine in both arms and legs. The hands of these patients should be considered

in the evaluation process. Physical signs of upper extremity involvement include chaeroarthropathy (motor neuropathy in upper extremity), when the patient cannot touch his palms together in the prayer position. Another physical sign is atrophy of the web space between the thumb and first finger. This is the first sign of motor neuropathy in the hand. Consideration of the hand deficit must be taken into account for donning, doffing, and choice of closures for orthotics and footwear.[40] Little attention has been paid to the diabetic hand syndrome, or limited joint mobility (LJM), in which the joints of the fingers and wrists become limited. This condition occurs in 30% to 50% of people who have had type I diabetes for more than 15 years. One test for LJM is performed by having the patient place the hands flat on a table. Patients with severe LJM will not be able to flatten the fingers onto the table. The skin will also be thick and can be tented on the back of the metacarpophalangeal (MCP) joint[58] (see Figure 15–11).

Body Temperature Testing

Since Hippocrates, physicians have known that body temperature variations offer important clues for diagnosing disease. Diagnostic tools convert infrared radiation and display it on monitors with the use of thermography.[56] There are many

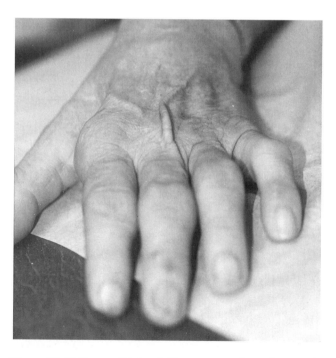

Figure 15–11 Neuropathic hand. Motor neuropathy testing reveals tenting on the back of the MCP joint, clawing of the fingers, and atrophy of the web space between the thumb and the first finger.

Objectives and Procedure for Taking Temperature

Objectives for taking temperature:

- To evaluate baseline temperature at sites of high incidence of ulceration
- To determine presence of inflammation
- To evaluate sites of baseline elevated temperature for decrease in temperature after intervention to relieve pressure

Procedure for taking and recording temperatures:

1. Expose the bare skin of the foot to the room temperature for 5–10 minutes before recording any temperature.
2. Take temperature at 10 locations on the sole of foot and toes (shown by circles on foot evaluation form Exhibit 15–3).
3. Follow steps for measuring temperature.
4. Record readings in degrees at each location on foot evaluation form and date.
5. Record readings at each location on successive evaluations below the initial reading and date.

Figure 15–12A Infrared scanner temperature display.

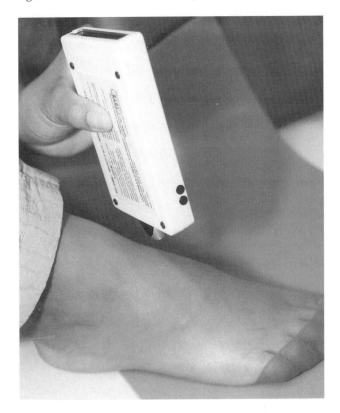

methods of acquiring surface temperatures. Thermistors or thermocouples are accurate recording devices that, when touched to the skin for 10 seconds, give a numeric display of temperature.[59] The infrared unit allows accurate immediate spot temperature reading and allows the feature of scanning the foot quickly. The use of temperature is valuable as an objective measurement of tissue damage and inflammation produced by repeated mechanical (pressure) trauma.[60] When evaluating the limb, the most distal aspects of extremities are cool. Muscular areas with good blood supply are warmer than bony regions. Arches are several degrees warmer than heels or toes.[59] Excessive heat in an area of the foot is a vascular response to trauma. The trauma may be due to external

---

Procedure for Use of an Infrared Scanner Thermometer

Follow these steps in measuring temperature with an infrared scanner thermometer:

1. Temperature testing may be done with or without contact of skin.
2. Read the first number seen.
3. Avoid pressure against the skin that causes ischemia.

Courtesy of Measurements Inc., New Orleans, Louisiana. (See Figures 15–12A and 15–12B.)

Figure 15–12B Placing the infrared scanner for temperature reading.

---

forces, infection, Charcot joint, or other internal complications. The examiner can feel the increased heat manually and determine where complications may reside, but without instrumentation to record actual numbers, there will not be objective documentation for follow-up and comparison. Using a surface-sensing temperature device (thermocouple or infrared), temperatures are recorded in predetermined areas, usually those related to common areas of breakdown. When there is one definite area whose temperature is 3°F higher than that of adjacent areas, it can be assumed an area of high pressure or stress. If there is no current breakdown, this area must be relieved of pressure and the pressure distributed over the remaining weight-bearing surfaces. Upon follow-up of this same patient the temperature differentiation should decrease as healing of tissue progresses. In a comparison of contralateral limbs, vascular impairment should be suspected when one limb is significantly colder, or distal portions of the foot show an extreme drop in temperature. A chronic hot spot points to the fact that there is a chronic stress or an underlying bone or joint problem. Increased temperature tells that there is a problem and where it is—not what it is![21]

Pressure Testing

A rubber mat was developed by R.I.Harris that would print light foot pressures in large light squares (formed by tall grid ridges) and heavier pressures in darker smaller squares (deep ridges).[2] The Harris mat will give a gridded analysis of pressure distribution at a relatively low cost per patient. The Harris mat can be used for static and dynamic assessment and provide permanent records. Figure 15–13 shows an imprint on a Harris mat. The darker areas are areas of high pressure.

Force plates have given us valuable information regarding peak pressures during ambulation, but represent a single step upon the plate. Attempts to place sensors in the shoes have been unreliable because of the sensor structure and attachment within the shoe.[61] The new age of computer-aided documentation provides color replicas of three-dimensional pressure recordings and illustrations that can be used for static or dynamic documentation. Although costs of the computer-aided devices are high, technology is advancing to provide

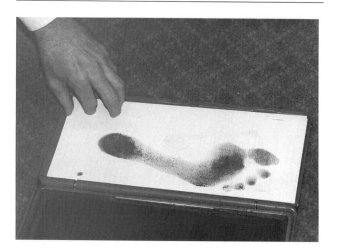

Figure 15–13 Harris mat pressure testing record. Darker areas represent higher pressure.

unrestricted data collection.[62] Progress is also being made to produce live scanning of the foot in order to produce a positive mold for orthotics as well as custom shoes.[63] Using computed three-dimensional digitizing computer graphics, a plastic sock may be molded to the patient and converted to a shoe cast.[64]

Charcot Joint Examination

Charcot joint (Charcot arthropathy) is a relatively painless, progressive, and degenerative arthropathy of single or multiple joints caused by underlying neuropathy. The neuropathy may be periosteal and not cutaneous. There are several theories behind the causes of Charcot joint, as follows:

- Multiple microtraumas to the joints cause microfractures. These fractures lead to relaxation of the ligaments and joint destruction.[65]
- There is increased blood flow (osteolysis) and bone reabsorption. Patients with Charcot joints have bounding pulses.
- Changes in the spinal cord lead to trophic changes in bones and joints.
- Osteoporosis is accompanied by an abnormal brittleness of the bones, leading to spontaneous fracture.[66]

In clinical observations, the limb is usually painless, swollen, and red. Unhealed painless fractures are often radiographically present. In advanced Charcot disease, there are multiple fractures accompanied by extensive bone demineralization and reabsorption. Later stages reveal architectural distortion of the foot with shortening and widening of the joint.[46] The foot joints most commonly affected are the following:

- tarsometatarsal (30%)
- metatarsophalangeal (30%)
- tarsus (24%)
- interphalangeal (4%)

Charcot joint is frequently misdiagnosed and mistreated, leaving the patient with deformities that require further medical intervention and/or expensive footwear (see Figure 15–14). The acute stage will show a foot that is 5° to 10° hotter than the contralateral limb in the same area. The red, hot, swollen foot will usually not have a skin opening or ulceration. Laboratory tests, including radiographs, may not

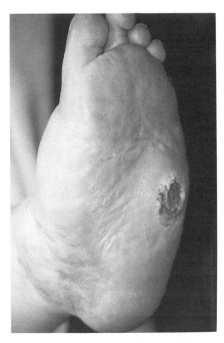

Figure 15–14 Classic Charcot rocker bottom foot deformity. Note ulceration over bony deformity surrounded by callus formation.

show changes in the acute stage to differentiate Charcot disease from other diagnoses.

The duration of the catastrophic destruction, dissociation, and eventual recalcification found with Charcot joint will vary with the individual, but the average healing time in a cast for the hindfoot is 12 months; for the midfoot, 9 months; and for the forefoot, 6 months. By evaluating with comparative temperature measurements of the contralateral foot, the stages can usually be verified by radiograph. As the involved foot temperature increases, the destruction and dissociation are taking place. The temperature gradually decreases as recalcification is in progress. A radiograph shows that recalcification is complete when temperatures bilaterally are within 3°F.

The treatment plan for acute Charcot joint is the total-contact cast. The cast must be changed in 1 week to accommodate volume changes. Following the period of volume changes, the cast should be changed every 2 to 3 weeks. When the temperature is equal to that of the other limb, the patient may be weaned gradually from the cast to a splint and then to shoes. Follow-up should continue to ensure that there is no recurrence of an episode of Charcot joint.

Case Study: *Charcot Arthropathy*

The patient was a 44-year-old woman with a 15-year history of non–insulin-dependent diabetes mellitus (NIDDM). She had neuropathic extremities to mid-calf bilaterally, loss of sensation and motor function demonstrated by bilateral drop foot. She had a right foot Charcot arthropathy post 4 years. The extremity was treated with a series of total-contact casts for 11 months and gradually weaned to ankle-foot orthotics with shoes. Contralateral side used ankle-foot orthosis to control drop foot.

The patient came to the clinic for an emergency checkup due to weekend traumatic injury to the left foot. She recalls twisting the left ankle and slight discomfort. Within an hour, there was swelling so she went to a local emergency department. The patient was told that she had possibly torn a ligament and was put in a precautionary plaster cast with a rubber walking pad.

When the patient came to the clinic two days later, she was in a great deal of discomfort and the plaster cast seemed to have absorbed exudate. The toes were left exposed in the cast and had swollen beyond the confines of the distal cast edge. When the cast was removed, it was observed that the walking pad had been forced through the plaster on the plantar surface and traumatized the entire plantar midfoot. The patient had Charcot arthropathy of the midfoot that was further destroyed by the nonreinforced walking pad. The edges of the plaster caused open abrasions to the exposed toes, leading to infection.

The patient was treated for abrasions and put into a total-contact cast. After 16 months, the Charcot episode was over but the foot was left with deformities that could not be accommodated in a standard shoe. A custom shoe was ordered for the left foot deformity.

Key Points

1. Immediate total-contact casting could have reduced the deformities and length of treatment.
2. A total-contact cast differs from a standard short leg cast and should be applied by a skilled technician.

Osteomyelitis Examination

The clinical observations for Charcot joint and osteomyelitis are very similar, and the patient should be monitored closely to verify the diagnosis. Laboratory tests will also be similar. The only exception would be the presence of an opening in the skin to allow an entrance for bacteria to infect the bone (see Figure 15–15A). Take the temperature over the best surrounding skin. Refer for immediate medical management. The recalcification would not occur radiographically as in Charcot disease (Figure 15–15B.) Verification may be made for osteomyelitis with a three-phase bone scan or biopsy.[20]

Diabetic patients with foot ulcers that expose bone should be treated for osteomyelitis, even if there is no evidence of inflammation.[67]

INTERVENTIONS

Orthotics and Adaptive Equipment

Treatment of the neuropathic foot requires accommodation, relief of pressure/shear forces, and shock absorption. Regardless of materials used for accommodative inserts, the combination of materials must be compressible by one half of original thickness to accommodate for pressure relief through the gait cycle.[21] It is important to evaluate the materials you will be utilizing in the manufacture of inserts. Cellular polyethylene foams such as Aliplast™, Plastazote™, and Pelite™ are composed of a mass of bubbles in a plastic and gas phase. The bubbles are cells with lines of intersection called ribs or strands and the walls are called windows. In closed-cell materials the gases do not pass freely; open-

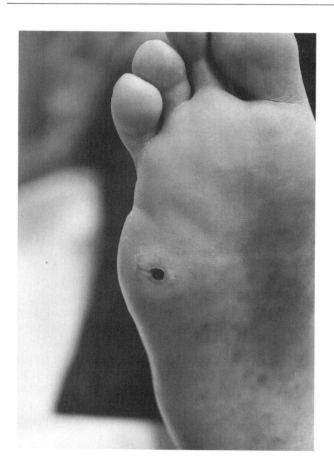

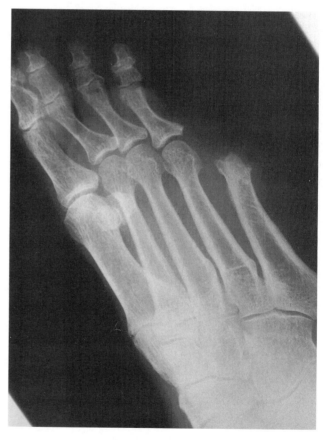

Figure 15–15A Osteomyelitis. Note puncture wound over the fifth metatarsal head, the site of the osteomyelitis. *Source:* Reprinted with permission from R.B. Chambers and N. Elftman, Orthotic Management of the Neuropathic and Dysvascular Patient, in *Atlas of Orthoses and Assistive Devices,* 3rd. edition, B. Goldberg and J.D. Hsu, eds., p. 439, © 1997, Mosby-Year Book, Inc.

Figure 15–15B Radiograph of same foot as in Figure 15–15A shows calcification changes at the head of the fifth metatarsal. *Source:* Reprinted with permission from R.B. Chambers and N. Elftman, Orthotic Management of the Neuropathic and Dysvascular Patient, in *Atlas of Orthoses and Assistive Devices,* 3rd. edition, B. Goldberg and J.D. Hsu, eds., p. 439, © 1997, Mosby-Year Book, Inc.

cell material has no windows, leaving many cells interconnected so that gas may pass between cells. Cell walls are not totally impermeable to the flow of gases. Under a sustained load (especially the heavy patient) gases are squeezed out; when the load is removed gases are drawn back into the cells.[68] These materials will bottom out from compaction of the materials as cells fracture under repetitive stress. The advantages are low-temperature molding, nontoxicity, water resistance, and washability without absorbency of fluid.[69] Plastazote has a limited effective period of about 2 days; Poron (PPT) remains effective for 6 to 9 months. The two materials can be combined for their attributes and perform well as a single unit.[70,71] There are different types of inserts, as follows:

- Soft: cushioning/accommodation, improves shock absorption
- Semirigid: some cushion/accommodation; affords pressure relief
- Rigid: hard, single layer of plastic; it controls abnormal foot and leg motion[72]

The Aliplast/Plastazote insert is an immediate preparation and can be provided within a clinic setting, but it has a relatively short life of compressibility (6 to 8 months). Plastazote is a closed-cell polyethylene foam that can be heated to 280°F and molded directly onto the patient's foot.[22] Care must be taken never to mold the toes or create ridges that the toes will ride over as the patient ambulates. By combining materials over a cast model of the foot, the composite type of insert can achieve all goals of the accommodative insert and provide a life of 1 year minimum.

An insert with a Plastazote surface in contact with the foot can be used as an excellent diagnostic tool for future follow-up. The self-molding properties of Plastazote reveal deep sock prints in areas of high pressure. These high-pressure areas should be noted and relieved in future insert design for the patient. By using temperature as a tool for evaluation, the areas of high trauma will be noted as increased temperature locations. After the patient has worn accommodative inserts, the temperature differentiation will decrease if the proper accommodation has been achieved. If the temperature has not decreased in the area, the relief may require enhancement, or there may be other underlying complications to be investigated. All relief areas are applied on the underlying surface in contact with the shoe, never in contact with the foot. The surface in contact with the foot is always a solid, uninterrupted surface that will not apply edges for the foot to receive shear forces. Figure 15–16 diagrams the fabrication of several different layers into an accommodative insert.

Shoes for the insensitive foot should be of soft leather that will conform to abnormalities on the dorsal surface and allow for the depth of an accommodative insert. Figure 15–17 shows modifications of the depth shoe appropriate for the insensitive foot.

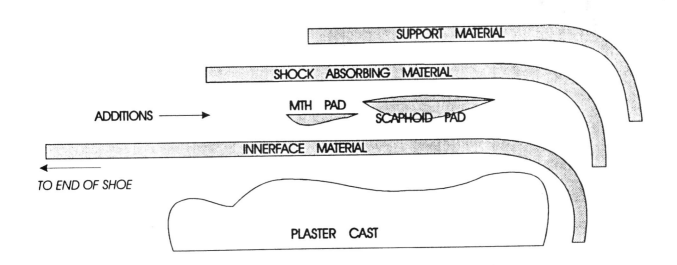

Figure 15–16 Diagram of accommodative insert fabrication. *Source:* Reprinted with permission from R.B. Chambers and N. Elftman, Orthotic Management of the Neuropathic and Dysvascular Patient, in *Atlas of Orthoses and Assistive Devices,* 3rd. edition, B. Goldberg and J.D. Hsu, eds., p. 444, © 1997, Mosby-Year Book, Inc.

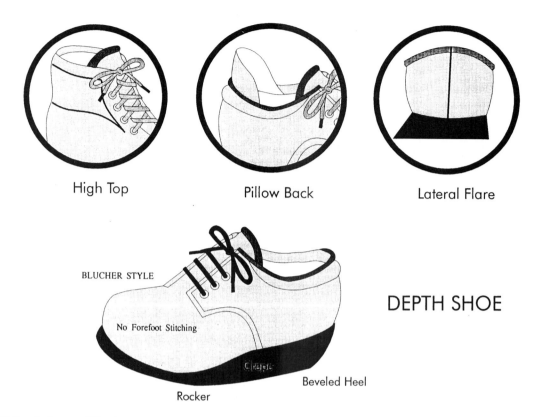

High Top   Pillow Back   Lateral Flare

BLUCHER STYLE

DEPTH SHOE

No Forefoot Stitching

Crepe

Beveled Heel

Rocker

Figure 15–17 Depth shoe modifications. *Source:* Reprinted with permission from R.B. Chambers and N. Elftman, Orthotic Management of the Neuropathic and Dysvascular Patient, in *Atlas of Orthoses and Assistive Devices,* 3rd. edition, B. Goldberg and J.D. Hsu, eds., p. 443, © 1997, Mosby-Year Book, Inc.

> ### Clinical Wisdom:
> *Choose Crepe Sole Shoes for Pressure Relief*
>
> Crepe soles, which are full of air cells, provide pressure relief to the plantar surface, whereas air or water "pillows," which are enclosed in an inflexible compartment, create pressure.

Leather gradually adapts to the slope of the foot and will retain shape between wearings. The leather will breathe and absorb perspiration.[69] The patient should not depend upon the "feel" of a shoe for correct size. The shoe must be full width and girth and allow ½- to ¾-inch space beyond the longest toe to prevent distal shoe contact through the gait cycle. Standard modifications of extra-depth shoes for the neuropathic patient include stretching of the soft toe box for clawed toes, flared lateral soles to discourage varus instability, and shank/rocker bottom for a partial foot, hallux rigidus, or decreased motion at the metatarsal heads. A rocker bottom should be added to the shoe when metatarsophalangeal extension is to be avoided.[22] When properly fit, the instep leather should not be taut. There are three tests to determine the proper fit of shoes (see Figure 15–18, how to measure for proper shoe fit):

1. *Length:* Allow ½ to ¾ inch of space in front of longest toe.
2. *Ball width:* With the patient weight bearing, grasp the vamp of the shoe and pinch the upper material, if leather cannot be pinched, it is too narrow. The ball should be in the widest part of the shoe.[73]
3. *Heel to ball length:* Measure the distance from the patient's heel to the first and fifth metatarsal heads. Bend the shoe to determine toe break, and repeat measurements on the shoe. They should be close to the same measurements.[74]

The simple addition of shoes instead of barefoot may correct many deformities.[75] Laced shoes will give the best control, but they must be broken in slowly, beginning with

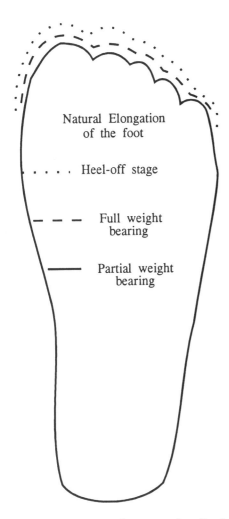

Figure 15–18 How to measure for proper shoe fit. *Source:* Reprinted with permission from R.B. Chambers and N. Elftman, Orthotic Management of the Neuropathic and Dysvascular Patient, in *Atlas of Orthoses and Assistive Devices,* 3rd. edition, B. Goldberg and J.D. Hsu, eds., p. 442, © 1997, Mosby-Year Book, Inc.

2 hours per day and slowly adding time.[22] Caution should be taken with cutout sandals for the possibility of irritation along the borders of the sandal and straps.[76] To evaluate pressures within a shoe, there is a pressure-sensitive sock that is coated with dye-filled wax capsules. The capsules fracture when a certain pressure threshold is exceeded, leaving dye stains in areas of high pressure.[69] To protect a healing area in which dressings will be applied, a healing shoe lined with Plastazote will allow greater circumference and volume adjustability.

Socks for the neuropathic limb should have no mended areas or seams over bony prominences. A cotton/acrylic blend will assist in the wicking of perspiration away from the foot.[77] The sock should be fully cushioned and have a nonrestric-

tive top. The partial foot requires a sock that will conform to the shape without distal prominent seams or excess material at the distal end. For the active patient, socks can be obtained with silicone over high-stress areas to prevent shear for full or partial feet.

The partial foot may require a block within the shoe for the area of amputation. The purpose of a block is to reduce migration of the partial foot and medial/lateral shear for the toe amputation. No block or "prosthetic toe" is to be used for a central digit amputation. The low pressures applied by a block to central digits cause ischemic ulcerations on opposing surfaces. Medial or lateral amputations (first and fifth toes) may require a block to hold the foot in the correct position within the shoe. The forefoot block holds the shoe leather away from the distal end of the foot and discourages distal migration of the foot. All forms of blocks must have space from the amputation site and be an integral part of the insert, not added to an existing orthotic. Forefoot blocks require a rigid rocker sole to prevent ulceration to distal end.

By utilizing state-of-the-art foams and room temperature vulcanized (RTV) silicone elastomers, shear can be reduced in areas of skin grafts, chronic ulcerations, and calcanectomies within more rigid orthotics. The viscoelastomer gel is a two-part gel that can be adjusted for durometer desired. The mixture can be used for shock absorption and shear reduction. Scar-adherent areas can benefit from a medium durometer mixture. The disadvantage is weight, so it should be used in small areas. Low-density foams can be designed into orthotics, such as toe breaks and forefoot blocks and reliefs. Reliefs for heel pain can be designed into the insert or shoe sole as a Sach heel. Sach heels use soft and medium durometer soling to simulate plantar flexion and provide shock absorption at heel strike.

Total-Contact Casting

The total-contact casting (TCC) method provides decreased plantar pressures by increasing weight bearing over the entire lower leg. It has been successful as a treatment for plantar ulcerations but requires careful application, close follow-up, and patient compliance with scheduled appointments to minimize complications.[78] Brand introduced the total-contact cast to the United States in the 1950s to redistribute walking pressures, prevent direct trauma to the wound, reduce edema, and provide immobilization to joints and soft tissue. The average healing time for ulcerations treated with the healing cast was 6 weeks.[76] This method has been used for patients with and without evidence of severe peripheral vascular disease.[79] The cast spreads weight evenly over the lower limb so that no part of the foot takes more than 5 psi. There is never a window cut in the cast or there may be localized swelling, shear stresses, and eventually a secondary wound[22] (see Figure 15–19).

Application methods of the total-contact healing cast vary with different institutions. The healing cast was originally designed with minimal padding, but padded variations are utilized. Although the steps for application of the Carville-type TCC are given, remember that it is most important to have the cast applied by a skilled technician, because harm can occur from improper application. Following are steps for fabrication of the Carville-type TCC:

1. The ulcer is covered with a thin layer of gauze.
2. Cotton is placed between the toes to prevent maceration.
3. A stockinette is applied.
4. A ⅛-inch piece of felt is placed over the malleoli and anterior tibia.
5. Foam padding is placed around toes.
6. A total-contact plaster shell is molded.

7. The shell is reinforced with plaster splints.
8. A walking heel is attached.
9. A fiberglass roll is applied around the plaster.

The patient is instructed to ambulate only 33% of usual activity. The cast is removed in 5 to 7 days and reapplied. New casts are applied every 2 to 3 weeks.[78] To allow thorough drying, the patient should not stand or walk on the cast for 24 hours.[76]

There have also been attempts to heal ulcers by using a healing cast shoe molded of plaster. This healing cast shoe must be changed in 3 days and then reapplied every 10 days. Results have reported healing of plantar ulcers in 39 days.[80] Contraindications for the use of a healing cast shoe include infection (redness, swelling, warmth, fever) and hypotrophic skin (thin, shiny appearance, marked dependent edema).[76]

> **Clinical Wisdom:** *Bathing While Wearing a TCC Is Simplified by Wearing a Seal Tight® Cast and Bandage Protector*
>
> This heavyweight plastic vinyl bag slips over the cast and forms a seal that is watertight. The product is convenient to use, durable, and has a sueded sole to minimize slippage in the shower.

Orthotic Dynamic System Splint

The orthotic dynamic system (ODS) splint was developed to take advantage of the casting method of a total-contact cast with the inclusion of a custom-molded insert that could be removed and reliefs modified. With all of the advantages of the total-contact cast, the advantages that were added with the ODS splint included the possibilities for daily inspection, regular cleaning/dressings/debridement, and adjustments to areas of excessive pressure and/or friction (see Figure 15–20).

The Plastazote/Aliplast insert is first molded to the patient's foot and trimmed to follow the plantar surface, with ¼-inch length added beyond toes. A stockinette is placed on the leg, the insert is positioned, and another stockinette is applied to hold the insert in place. A padded total-contact cast is applied, using fiberglass only. The cast is bivalved, straps are added, edges are finished, and the insert is removed, relieved, and replaced to deweight the area of ulceration. After insert modification, it is replaced within the splint, and the patient may ambulate with a rocker bottom cast shoe under the splint. The patient is instructed on volume control with sock thickness.

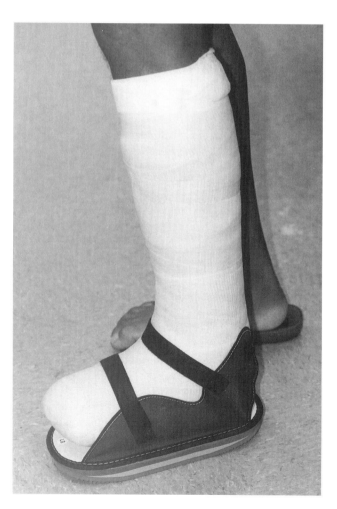

Figure 15–19 Total-contact cast.

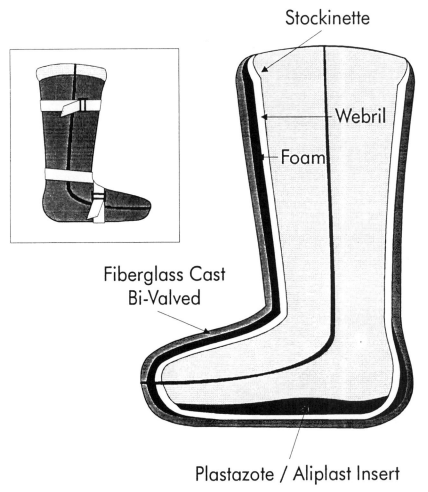

Stockinette

Webril

Foam

Fiberglass Cast
Bi-Valved

Plastazote / Aliplast Insert

Figure 15–20 Diagram of the ODS splint. *Source:* Reprinted with permission from R.B. Chambers and N. Elftman, Orthotic Management of the Neuropathic and Dysvascular Patient, in *Atlas of Orthoses and Assistive Devices,* 3rd. edition, B. Goldberg and J.D. Hsu, eds., p. 441, © 1997, Mosby-Year Book, Inc.

The disadvantage will lie with compliancy of the patient. The splint design allows donning and doffing by the patient, therefore allowing him or her to remove the cast. The total contact of a healing cast cannot be compared in its superiority, but the clinical experience of the author has found the daily inspection and relief adjustability to be a great asset in the treatment protocol.

Neuropathic Walker

The neuropathic walker is a combination of an ankle-foot orthosis (AFO) and a boot that is custom designed to be total contact for weight distribution. The ankle is locked to reduce force through the Lisfranc joint and/or ankle. The design is indicated for the patient with changes of Charcot joint in the tarsal and ankle joints, chronic recurrence of Char-

cot disease, and chronic ulcerations. The orthosis is easily donned and doffed and fabricated of a copolymer plastic with a closed-cell lining. The removable insert may be adjusted to reassign weight-bearing areas on the plantar surface. The insert may also be formed over chronic breakdown areas such as the malleoli, posterior heel, and bunions to reduce pressure. The rocker sole allows for easy ambulation, but the contralateral shoe must be adjusted for height.

When casting for the neuropathic walker, the patient's limb is wrapped and placed on a soft foam block until the plaster is set. The plantar surface will be accommodative without excessive pressures on bony prominences. Modifications of the positive model include smoothing the plantar surface but never removing plaster. Any area that has had plaster removed during modification will be an area of excess pressure in the finished orthosis. The distal end is built up at the medial and lateral metatarsal areas and the length extended ¾-inch to allow room for the toes and decrease the chances of maceration.

Fabrication is completed on the modified positive cast. The insert is first fabricated, finished, and placed in position. The posterior Plastazote lining is pulled over the insert, followed by the copolymer (plastic) vacuum-formed shell. The entire posterior section is finished and trimmed. The anterior Plastazote is positioned and the copolymer shell is applied over the entire posterior. There should be a ½- to 1-inch overlap of copolymer on the finished orthosis. The Velcro straps and rocker bottom are attached (apex of rocker proximal to MTH; Figure 15–21).

The patient must be instructed to check skin for redness and possible breakdown. The patient should be followed and temperatures of the plantar surface recorded for possible adjustment of insert pressures. Sock management will be very important to continue a snug fit of the orthosis and volume control.

Total-Contact Ankle-Foot Orthosis

Similar to the neuropathic walker, the total-contact AFO is utilized for the patient who has an area of trauma in the mid- or hindfoot. The orthosis includes a custom removable insert and is lined with Plastazote. This orthosis must be fit within a shoe, which may be difficult in standard shoes. The casting procedure is the same as that for the neuropathic walker. The toes are open, and the anterior shell terminates at midfoot.

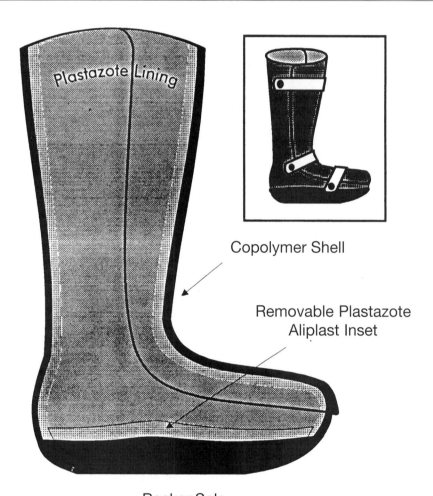

Figure 15–21 Diagram of the neuropathic walker. *Source:* Reprinted with permission from R.B. Chambers and N. Elftman, Orthotic Management of the Neuropathic and Dysvascular Patient, in *Atlas of Orthoses and Assistive Devices,* 3rd. edition, B. Goldberg and J.D. Hsu, eds., p. 448, © 1997, Mosby-Year Book, Inc.

Other Devices

Short leg walkers and orthopaedic walkers have been used by some clinics, but they compromise the total-contact feature. They are traditionally used for acute ligament/muscle and fracture immobilization.

Patellar tendon–bearing (axial resist) designs are intended to decrease forces on the plantar weight-bearing surface of the foot. With this design as a casting procedure, there have been attempts at its use in place of plaster cast immobilizations.[81] The design transmitted considerable axial forces from the knee region onto the cast, but it did not offer rotary stability. The results offered very little effectiveness in reducing the load off the lower leg.[82] The patellar tendon–bearing design AFO has been used successfully for the calcanectomy, plantar skin graft, and heel ulceration. This orthosis is contraindicated in the patient with vascular impairment because of the excess restriction in the popliteal area of arterial flow.

The prosthosis has been the orthotic replacement when the amputation case is complicated and the patient is not a candidate for prosthetic management. The prosthesis becomes a useful device for transfers and limb protection. This is always a creative design, with no two the same, unique to the individual and his or her needs.

Surgical Management

The most conservative treatment of foot infections will be utilized to rehabilitate, but antibiotic therapy alone is not always sufficient to treat aggressive virulent foot infections.[83] Surgical intervention may be in the best interest of the patient if conservative therapy is not an option or has proven ineffective. Options should be discussed with the patient and the family, and they should be involved in the final outcome when possible. Surgical debridement of all osteomyelitis and nonviable tissue must be completed.[84] The surgeon will preserve as much length and width as possible to balance the motor function.[9] The goal of amputation is ambulation and reconstruction. Typical locations of partial foot amputations are shown in Figure 15–22.

Metatarsal osteotomies can eliminate the intrinsic stresses caused by elongated or plantarflexed metatarsal joints in neuropathic limbs and decrease number of amputations.[85] Toe resections are the most distal amputation choices available. Expected outcomes of each toe resection are as follows:

- First toe—Interphalangeal disarticulation for an infected distal phalanx gives good balance. When possible a wafer of the proximal phalanx should be left to maintain the position of the sesamoids beneath the first metatarsal head.

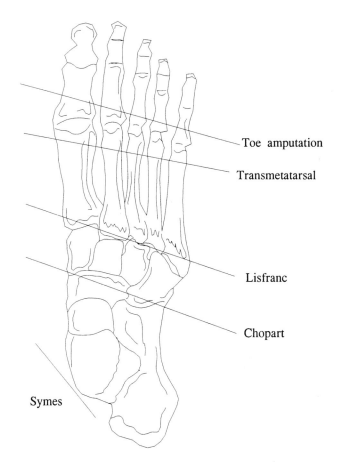

Figure 15–22 Typical locations of partial foot amputations. *Source:* Reprinted with permission from R.B. Chambers and N. Elftman, Orthotic Management of the Neuropathic and Dysvascular Patient, in *Atlas of Orthoses and Assistive Devices,* 3rd. edition, B. Goldberg and J.D. Hsu, eds., p. 432, © 1997, Mosby-Year Book, Inc.

- Second toe—Disarticulation results in loss of lateral support of the first toe. A second ray resection is usually better to avoid secondary hallux valgus.
- Third or fourth toes—The remaining toes will tend to shift to close the gap.
- All five toes—A long forefoot lever is left with good weight-bearing properties.[9]

The advantages of the partial foot amputation are the following:

- It preserves end weight-bearing function.
- It preserves proprioception.
- It provides for limited disruption of body image.
- It requires shoe modification/orthosis or limited prosthesis.

Limitations of the partial foot amputation are the loss of normal foot function related to loss of forefoot lever length and associated muscles, and the challenges presented in selecting appropriate adaptive equipment.

The Chopart amputation is selected when a patient retains sensation in the heel pad. Metatarsals and tarsals are removed, leaving a very short limb. It is difficult to suspend a shoe without the aid of an AFO or prosthesis.

The transmetatarsal/Lisfranc amputation is preferred for the resultant length of foot; amputation is through the metatarsals. The longest partial foot amputation is the distal metatarsal amputation in which the toes are amputated. This level will require a short shoe or forefoot block to prevent forward motion.

In all partial feet it is important to watch for an equinus deformity. The toes are no longer present, and visual inspection is more difficult without their reference.

Whether from trauma or chronic infection, the partial removal of the calcaneus is a follow-up challenge for the orthotist. Removing weight bearing from the heel is difficult, and the patient who has had a calcanectomy must be followed carefully.

The most successful methods of controlling future breakdown have involved the patellar tendon–bearing (axial resist) orthosis or the neuropathic walker. A soft RTV foam has been used to fill a void between the orthosis and the heel area. The same orthotic treatment is useful for chronic heel ulcers and plantar skin grafts that require reduction in weight-bearing and shear forces.

DOCUMENTATION

Documentation continuity is essential for all patients and requires a standard form to be used for assessment and future follow-up (Exhibit 15–3). Tracing the ulceration on transparent film will allow for accuracy of detailed healing progression. Providing the patient with a duplicate tracing can improve compliance as the patient can follow his or her own progress. Photographs of ulceration sites are important for noting improvement in depth and granulation of ulceration. Methods for making tracings and taking photos are described in Chapter 4.

SELF-CARE TEACHING GUIDELINES

Foot Inspection

The patient is the most important member of a clinical team approach to the treatment of his or her neuropathic limb. There is no complication too small to be addressed, and the patient must bring abnormalities to the team's attention. Self-

care begins with daily inspections of the feet with the help of mirrors, magnifying glasses, and family members when necessary. Examination includes footwear and orthotics for wear and foreign objects. The diabetic patient must understand that this examination may be complicated by other disease processes, including retinopathy, autonomic neuropathy (loss of smell and sensory signals), and decreased mobility of joints. These patients are handicapped by the lack of pain as a warning signal and require systematic instruction to educate them in the proper skills required for daily inspection and detection of impending trauma.

Precautions and Risk Reduction Methods

There are several precautions for the patient with a neuropathic limb. The skin is very susceptible to damage and infection and must be treated carefully. It is advised that the patient not soak the feet in water because the chance of burns is always present and the soaking will leave the skin moist and susceptible to fungal infection. Prolonged soaking can remove the natural protective barrier from the skin and lead to other infections. Feet should be washed with a nondrying soap and towel dried. After the foot wash, petroleum jelly can be applied to retain natural moisture and covered with socks. Care should be taken not to use creams with perfumes (alcohol) as they will further dehydrate the skin.

Dehydrated skin is especially susceptible to trauma. Adhesives of any form should never be applied directly to the skin of a neuropathic limb. Upon removal of the adhesive, there is a risk of loss of the outer layer of skin, leaving an area open to infection. The adhesives could be in the form of tape, a Band-Aid, or over-the-counter self-adhesive pads.

When the patient selects footwear he or she should choose not only the correct size and width, but also shoes with no stitching over the forefoot. The stitched areas will never mold to the foot, but instead will cause breakdown of the skin, especially over bony areas.

Keep current on recalled products. For example, one hair removal system published a product alert on its device because of problems occurring with diabetic patients. Small areas were bleeding after hair was removed, leaving an entrance for bacteria and possible infection! Over 50% of the over-the-counter foot care products should never be used by a patient with a neuropathic limb or diabetes. There are occasionally warnings, but in very fine print.

Care must be taken with exercise programs. When we walk, each step carries one and a half times our body weight; jogging increases the force to three times the body weight.[86] The patient with a neuropathic limb would be advised to choose an exercise program that includes aerobics, swimming, cycling, dance, or chair exercises. Even walking should include slow, short steps only; no jogging.[87]

Exhibit 15–3 Foot Evaluation Form

PATIENT _____ DIAGNOSIS _____

CODE _____ ORTHOTIST _____ DATE _____

INSENSITIVE FEET WITHOUT ULCERATION

CATEGORY	MONOFILIMENT RESPONSE		ULCER	DEFORMITY	FOLLOW-UP	INSERT
A	+5.07	(10 g)	No	Yes/No	12 Mo	Cushion
B	−5.07	(10 g)	No	No	6 Mo	Molded
C	−5.07	(10 g)	No	Yes	4 Mo	Molded
D	−5.07	(10 g)	Yes	Yes/No	3 Mo	Molded
E	−6.10	(75 g)	Yes/No	Yes/No	2 Mo	Molded

ULCER GRADE

0 Intact Skin
1 Superficial
2 Tendon or Bone
3 Abscess or Osteo
4 Forefoot Gangrene
5 Foot Gangrene

CHARCOT ARTHROPATHY

☐ Active ☐ Hx
L/R
___ Phalanges
___ Forefoot
___ Midfoot
___ Hindfoot
___ Other

FOOT DEFORMITY

___ Pes Cavus
___ Pes Planus
___ Valgus
___ Varus

TOE DEFORMITY

Claw Toe   Hallux
___ Mild   ___ Valgus
___ Severe ___ Rigidus
___ Rigid   ___ Extension

COMPLICATIONS

Proximal Neuropathy
☐ Calf
☐ Knee
☐ Thigh

Upper Ext. Neuropathy
☐ Fingers
☐ Hands
☐ Forearm

☐ Dialysis
☐ Vascular Impairment
☐ Venous Stasis
☐ Retinopathy
☐ Proprioception
☐ Dermatologic Breakdown
☐ Fungal Nail

Edema Control
☐ Full Foot
☐ Other

DORSAL

RIGHT   LEFT

Source: Reprinted with permission from R.B. Chambers and N. Elftman, Orthotic Management of the Neuropathic and Dysvascular Patient, in *Atlas of Orthoses and Assistive Devices,* 3rd. edition, B. Goldberg and J.D. Hsu, eds., p. 441, © 1997, Mosby-Year Book, Inc.

Exhibit 15–4 Self-Care Guidelines for the Patient with Neuropathic Foot

Self-Care Guidelines for Patient with Neuropathic Foot	*Instructions Given (Date/Initials)*	*Demonstration or Review of Material (Date/Initials)*	*Return Demonstration or States Understanding (Date/Initials)*
1. Foot Inspection Methods a. Use mirror to check feet b. Use magnifying glass to check feet c. If blind, family member performs foot inspection			
2. Foot Inspection Item a. Toe nails: check for broken, cracked, or sharp nails b. Broken skin: check between toes, along sides of feet, tops and ends of toes, sole of foot c. Soft toe corns: check between toes d. Callus: check for cracks e. Drainage: check for any drainage from a sore f. Odor: check for odor from any source on the foot			
3. Patient Understands a. Significance of findings of foot inspection: break in nails, skin, or callus b. When to notify health care provider if there is break in nails, skin, or callus c. To notify health care provider immediately if there is any injury to the feet			
4. Foot Care Routine a. Wash feet with nondrying soap and towel dry b. Apply coating of petroleum jelly to all skin surfaces of feet c. Cover coated feet with clean white socks			
5. Foot Care Precautions a. Never walk barefoot b. Never use adhesive tape products on the skin c. Never put feet in hot water or apply a heating pad or hot pack d. Never soak feet e. Never apply over-the-counter foot care products to remove corns or callus, or to treat nails			
6. Shoe Wear Orthotic Inspection a. Choose shoes that are correct size and width b. Make sure there is no stitching over the forefoot of shoe c. Check for wear: heels, soles, tops, inside, bottom, edges, counter d. Always check shoes, socks, and orthotics for foreign objects; remove objects before donning			
7. Exercise Precautions a. Never jog b. Walk with short slow steps			

continues

Exhibit 15–4 continued

Self-Care Guidelines for Patient with Neuropathic Foot	*Instructions Given (Date/Initials)*	*Demonstration or Review of Material (Date/Initials)*	*Return Demonstration or States Understanding (Date/Initials)*
8. Preferred Exercises a. Aerobic: low impact b. Swimming (wear soft bathing shoes in water to protect feet, dry feet thoroughly following) c. Cycling: protect feet and ankles from trauma d. Dancing e. Chair and mat exercises			
9. Importance of Follow-Up with Health Care Provider			

The patient with a neuropathic limb should never walk barefoot. Even in the pool or on the beach, water shoes should be worn. Hot sand can cause burns, and undetected objects in the sand can cause injury. Burns can be caused by the floorboard of an automobile, as well as any warmth-producing equipment. The interior of the shoe must be examined before every donning. Small objects can easily drop into a shoe.

Compliance Issues

The practitioner must understand compliance problems of patients with neuropathic limbs, and especially diabetic patients. They do not willfully neglect self-care activities but simply are not aware of the possible dangers and are not taught adequately or motivated sufficiently.[2] Diabetic patients may have other complications that the practitioner does not consider in the compliance of their activities. Many cannot see (retinopathy), feel (sensory neuropathy), or smell (autonomic neuropathy) when there is an infection or a potential problem. Those with vision impairments will need help from a family member or caregiver to perform self-care guidelines.

Patients with neuropathic and dysvascular limbs require knowledge and skills to administer self-examination and self-care. The medical community must educate the patients as well as the medical team to treat conservatively and accommodate the chronic complications that exist in a growing portion of the population. Exhibit 15–4 is a checklist of in-structional items with documentation to verify learning and understanding for the patient with neuropathic foot.

RESOURCES

Seal Tight® cast and bandage protector
Brown Medical Industries
481 South 8th Ave. East
Hartley, IA 51346
800-843-4395

Thermometer—Infra-red
Measurements, Inc.
2946 Ponce de Leon
New Orleans, LA 70119
504-949-1192, Fax 504-943-3489

Monofilament
North Coast Medical
187 Stouffer Blvd.
San Jose, CA 95125-1042
800-821-9319, Fax 408-277-6824

Harris Mat, Premade Foot Orthosis and Materials
Theradynamics
Division of National Pedorthic Services, Inc.
7283 W. Appleton Ave.
Milwaukee, WI 53216
800-803-7813, Fax 414-438-1051

REFERENCES

1. Brenner M. *Management of the Diabetic Foot*. Baltimore: Williams & Wilkins; 1987.

2. Shipley D. Clinical evaluation and care of the insensitive foot. *Phys Ther*. 1979;59:13–22.

3. Veves A, Boulton A. Commentary. *Diabetes Spectrum*. 1992;5:336–337.

4. Bowker J. Commentary. *Diabetes Spectrum*. 1992;5:335.

5. Brenner M. Management of the diabetic foot. *Podiatric Products*. May 1988:54–58.

6. Ellenberg M. Diabetic neuropathic ulcer. *J Mt Sinai Hosp*. 1968;35:585–594.

7. Green D, Waldhausl W. A forum on neuropathy. *Diabetes*. 1988:10.

8. Bowker J. Neurological aspects of prosthetic/orthotic practice. *J Prosthet Orthot*. 1993;5(2):52–54.

9. Bowker J. Partial foot and Syme amputations: an overview. *Clin Prosthet Orthot*. 1987;12:10–13.

10. Letts M. The orthotics of myelomeningocele. In: *Atlas of Orthotics*. St. Louis, MO: C.V. Mosby; 1985:300–306.

11. Weingarten M. Commentary. *Diabetes Spectrum*. 1992;5:342–343.

12. Pecoraro R, Reiber G, Burgess E. Pathways to diabetic limb amputation: basis for prevention. *Diabetes Care*. 1990;13:513–521.

13. Fylling C. Conclusions. *Diabetes Spectrum*. 1992;5:358–359.

14. Bamberger D, Stark K. Severe diabetic foot problems: avoiding amputation. *Emerg Decis*. 1987;3(8):21–34.

15. Olin J. Peripheral arterial disease. *Diabetes Forecast*. October 1992: 78–81.

16. Newman B. A diabetes camp for Native American adults. *Diabetes Spectrum*. 1993;6:166–202.

17. Harkness L, Lavery L. Diabetes foot care: a team approach. *Diabetes Spectrum*. 1992;5:136–137.

18. Robbins D. Office guide to diagnosis and classification of diabetes mellitus and other categories of glucose tolerance. *Diabetes Care*. 1991;14(suppl 2):3–4.

19. Brand P. Neuropathic ulceration. *The Star*. May/June 1983:1–4.

20. Ashbury A. Foot care in patients with diabetes mellitus. *Diabetes Care*. 1991;14(suppl 2):18–19.

21. Brand P. In: *Insensitive Feet—A Practical Handout on Foot Problems in Leprosy*. London, England: The Leprosy Mission; 1977.

22. Brand P. Management of sensory loss in the extremities: management of peripheral nerve problems. *J Rehab*. 1980;862–872.

23. Myerson M, Papa J, Eaton K. The total contact cast for management of neuropathic plantar ulceration of the foot. *Diabetes Spectrum*. 1992;5:352–353.

24. Edelstein J. Foot care for the aging. *Phys Ther*. 1988;68:1882–1886.

25. Utley R. Nutritional factors associated with wound healing in the elderly: the role of specific nutrients in the healing process. *Diabetes Spectrum*. 1992;5:354–355.

26. Knighton D, Fiegel V, Doucette M. Treating diabetic foot ulcers. *Diabetes Spectrum*. 1990;3:51–56.

27. Ellenberg M. Don't be fooled by peripheral neuropathy. *Diabetes Forecast*. January/February 1983.

28. Yale J. *Yale's Podiatric Medicine*. 3rd ed. Baltimore: Williams & Wilkins; 1980.

29. Cailliet R. *Foot and Ankle Pain*. Philadelphia: F.A. Davis; 1983: 181–189.

30. Jahss M. Shoes and shoe modifications. In: *Atlas of Orthotics*. St. Louis, MO: C.V. Mosby; 1985:267–279.

31. Tsairis P. Differential diagnosis of peripheral neuropathies. In: *Management of Peripheral Nerve Problems*. Rancho Los Amigos; 1980:712–725.

32. Thomas P. Clinical features and differential diagnosis. In: *Peripheral Neuropathy*. Philadelphia: W.B. Saunders Company; 1984;2:1169–1185.

33. Wakelee-Lynch J. Relieving pain with peppers. *Diabetes Forecast*. June 1992:35–37.

34. Dailey G. Effect of treatment with capsaicin on daily activities of patients with painful diabetic neuropathy. *Diabetes Care*. 1992;15:159–165.

35. *Diabetes Mellitus: Management and Complications*. New York: Churchill Livingstone; 1985:234–235, 277–293, 360–361.

36. Apelqvist J, Castenfors J, Larsson J. Prognostic value of systolic ankle and toe blood pressure levels in outcome of diabetic foot ulcer. *Diabetes Care*. 1989;12:373–378.

37. Cherry G, Ryan T, Cameron J. Blueprint for the treatment of leg ulcers and the prevention of recurrence. *Wounds*. 1992;3:1–15.

38. Perry J. Normal and pathological gait. In: *Atlas of Orthotics*. St. Louis, MO: C.V. Mosby; 1985:83–96.

39. Mann R. Biomechanics of the foot. In: *Atlas of Orthotics*. St. Louis, MO: C.V. Mosby; 1985:112–125.

40. Barber E. Strength and range-of-motion examination skills for the clinical orthotist. *J Prosthet Orthot*. 1993;5(2):49–51.

41. Thomas P, Eliasson S. Diabetic neuropathy. In: *Pheripheral Neuropathy*. Philadelphia: W.B. Saunders Company; 1984;2:1773–1801.

42. Oakley W, Catterall R, Martin M. Aetiology and management of lesions of the feet in diabetes. *Br Med J*. 1956;56:4999–5003.

43. Sinacore OR, Elsner R, Rubenow C. *Healing Rates of Diabetic Foot Ulcers in Subjects with Fixed Charcot Deformity*. Platform Presentation, Physical Therapy 1997 APTA Scientific Meeting and Exposition; San Diego, CA; May 30–June 4, 1997.

44. Tiberio D. Pathomechanics of structural foot deformities. *Phys Ther*. 1988;68:1840–1849.

45. Wilson J, Foster D. *Textbook of Endocrinology*. Philadelphia: W.B. Saunders Company; 1992:1294–1297.

46. Olefsky J, Sherman R. Diabetes. In: *Insensitive Feet—A Practical Handout on Foot Problems in Leprosy*. London, England: The Leprosy Mission; 1977.

47. Wagner FEW. The dysvascular foot: a system for diagnosis and treatment. *Foot Ankle*. 1981;2:64–122.

48. Glugla M, Mulder G. The diabetic foot. In: Krasner D, ed. *Medical Management of Foot Ulcers in Chronic Wound Care: A Clinical Source Book for Healthcare Professionals*. St. Louis, MO: Mosby/Health Management Publications, Inc; 1990:223–239.

49. Wagner F. A classification and treatment program for diabetic, neuropathic and dysvascular foot problems. *Foot Ankle*. 1983:1–47.

50. Sosenko J, Kato M, Soto R. Comparison of quantitative sensory threshold measures for their association with foot ulceration in diabetic patients. *Diabetes Care*. 1990;13:1057–1062.

51. Omer G. Sensibility testing. In: *Management of Peripheral Nerve Problems*. Philadelphia: W.B. Saunders; 1980:3–14.

52. Birke J, Sims D. Plantar sensory threshold in the ulcerative foot. *Br Lepr Relief Assoc*. 1986;57:261–267.

53. Birke J. Management of the diabetic foot. *Wound Care Manage.* 1995.

54. Ashbury A. Diabetic neuropathy. *Diabetes Care.* 1991;14(suppl 2):63–68.

55. Thivolet C, Farkh J, Petiot A. Measuring vibration sensations with graduated tuning fork. *Diabetes Care.* 1990;13:1077–1080.

56. National Aeronautics and Space Administration. Mission accomplished (thermography aids in the detection of neuromuscular problems). *NASA Tech Brief.* January 1993:92.

57. Apelqvist J, Larsson J, Agardh C. The influence of external precipitating factors and peripheral neuropathy on the development and outcome of diabetic foot ulcers. *J Diabetic Complications.* 1990;4:21–25.

58. Huntley A. Taking care of your hands. *Diabetes Forecast.* August 1991:11–12.

59. Bergtholdt H. Temperature assessment of the insensate. *Phys Ther.* 1979;59:18–22.

60. Chan A, MacFarlane I, Bowsher D. Contact thermomography of painful neuropathic foot. *Diabetes Care.* 1991;14:918–922.

61. Zhu H, Maalej N, Webster J. An umbilical data aquisition system for measuring pressures between foot and shoe. *IEEE Trans Biomed Eng.* 1990;37:908–911.

62. Wertsch J, Webster J, Tompkins W. A portable insole plantar measurement system. *J Rehabil Res Dev.* 1992;29:13–18.

63. Lord M. Clinical trial of a computer-aided system for orthopaedic shoe upper design. *Prosthet Orthot Int.* 1991;15:11–17.

64. McAllister D, Carver D, Devarajan R. An interactive computer graphics system for the design of molded and orthopedic shoe lasts. *J Rehabil Res Dev.* 1991;28:39–46.

65. Sims D, Cavanagh P, Ulbrecht J. Risk factors in the diabetic foot: recognition and management. *Phys Ther.* 1988;68:1887–1916.

66. DeJong R. *The Neurologic Examination.* New York: Harper & Row; 1969:742–743.

67. Newman L, Palestro C, Schwartz M. Unsuspected osteomyelitis in diabetic foot ulcers: diagnosis and monitoring by leukocyte scanning with indium in oxyquinoline. *Diabetes Spectrum.* 1992;5:346–347.

68. Kuncir E, Wirta R, Golbranson F. Load-bearing characteristics of polyethylene foam: an examination of structural and compression properties. *J Rehabil Res Dev.* 1990;27:229–238.

69. Levin M, O'Neal L. *The Diabetic Foot.* St. Louis, MO: C.V. Mosby; 1988.

70. Pratt D. Medium term comparison of shock attenuating insoles using a spectral analysis technique. *J Biomed Eng.* 1988;10:426–428.

71. Pratt D. Long term comparison of shock attenuating insoles. *Prosthet Orthot Int.* 1990;14:59–62.

72. Lockard M. Foot orthosis. *Phys Ther.* 1988;68:1866–1873.

73. Hack M. Fitting shoes. *Diabetes Forecast.* January 1989.

74. McPoil T. Footwear. *Phys Ther.* 1988;68:1857–1865.

75. McPoil T, Adrian M, Pidcoe P. Effects of foot orthoses on center-of-pressure patterns in women. *Phys Ther.* 1989;69:66–71.

76. Coleman W, Brasseau D. Methods of treating plantar ulcers. *Phys Ther.* 1991;71:116–122.

77. Dwyer G, Rust M. Shoe business. *Diabetes Forecast.* June 1988:60–63.

78. Mueller M, Diamond J, Sinacore D. Total contact casting in treatment of diabetic plantar ulcers. *Diabetes Care.* 1989;12:384–388.

79. Sinacore D, Mueller M, Diamond J. Diabetic plantar ulcers treated by total contact casting. *Phys Ther.* 1987;67:1543–1549.

80. Diamond J, Sinacore D, Mueller M. Molded double-rocker plaster shoe for healing a diabetic plantar ulcer. *Phys Ther.* 1987;67:1550–1552.

81. Birke J, Nawoczenski D. Orthopedic walkers: effect on plantar pressures. *Clin Prosthet Orthot.* 1988;12:74–80.

82. Lauridsen K, Sorensen C, Christiansen P. Measurements of pressure on the sole of the foot in plaster of paris casts on the lower leg. *J Int Soc Prosthet Orthot.* 1989;13:42–45.

83. McIntyre K. Control of infection in the diabetic foot: the role of microbiology, immunopathology, antibiotics, and guillotine amputation. *J Vasc Surg.* 1987;5:787–802.

84. Lai C, Lin S, Yang C. Limb salvage of infected diabetic foot ulcers with microsurgical free-muscle transfer. *Diabetic Spectrum.* 1992;5:356–357.

85. Tillow T, Habrshaw G, Chrzan J. Review of metatarsal osteotomies for the treatment of neuropathic ulcerations. *Diabetes Spectrum.* 1992;5:357–358.

86. Furman A. Give your feet a sporting chance. *Diabetes Forecast.* April 1989:17–22.

87. Graham C. Neuropathy made you stop. *Diabetes Forecast.* December 1992:47–49.

Management of Wound Healing with Physical Therapy Technologies

Carrie Sussman

INTRODUCTION

The management of wound healing with physical therapy technologies, including physical agents and electrotherapeutic modalities commonly used by physical therapists, is presented in Part IV. Physical agents and electrotherapeutic modalities are physical therapy technologies with long histories of clinical application and effectiveness. They are defined by the American Physical Therapy Association in the following way: "Physical agents use heat, sound, or light energy to increase the connective tissue extensibility, modulate pain, reduce or eliminate soft tissue inflammation and swelling caused by musculoskeletal injury or circulatory dysfunction, increase the healing rate of open wounds and soft tissue, remodel scar tissue or treat skin conditions."[1(p746)] These modalities include deep thermal modalities (eg, thermal ultrasound, pulsed short wave diathermy), nonthermal modalities, (eg, pulsed ultrasound, pulsed radio frequency energy), hydrotherapy (eg, whirlpool, pulsatile irrigation with suction).

"Electrotherapeutic modalities include . . . physical agents that use electricity to modulate or decrease pain, reduce or eliminate soft tissue inflammation caused by musculoskeletal . . . peripheral vascular or integumentary injury, disease, . . . or surgery . . . or increase the rate of healing in open wounds."[1(pp746–747)] These modalities include alternating, direct, and pulsed current (eg, high-voltage pulsed current, low-voltage pulsed current, and transcutaneous electrical nerve stimulation [TENS]).

Chapters 16 to 20 describe the rationale, device, application of, and case studies for six modalities: electrical stimulation, pulsatile lavage with suction, pulsed short wave diathermy, pulsed radio frequency stimulation, ultrasound, and whirlpool.

Interventions include the purposeful and skilled interaction of the skilled professional and the patient to produce changes in the patient's condition consistent with the diagnostic process. The diagnostic process described in Chapter 1 guides the physical therapist to select interventions that will promote the healing response. This process begins with the reason for referral, the history of the patient, and the wound. Interventions have three recognized components: direct intervention; patient-related instruction; and coordination, communication, and documentation. The physical therapy education curriculum includes instruction in the selection, protocols, and application of physical agents and electrotherapeutic modalities. Licensing examination includes testing of knowledge in appropriate, safe use; protocols; and interpretation of the results. Liability issues also suggest that physical therapists should be the health care professional responsible for treatment or instruction in the use of these interventions. Therefore, the physical therapist is the legally licensed and the most qualified practitioner to refer to for these interventions.

Nurses are usually the initial treatment provider and often initiate referral to the physical therapist, as well as serving as case managers and medical reviewers. Therefore, it is very important that nurses understand the candidacy, referral criteria, and clinical outcomes expected from the therapy. The chapters in Part IV have technical information that may be beyond the interest of most nurses, but there are also clinical decision-making sections that will guide the nurse through the rationale for treatment selection used by the physical therapist. Collaborative practice requires mutual understanding of the treatment recommended and the expected results. In addition, nurses, patients, or caregivers may be the individuals who deliver the direct treatment established by the physical therapist. Those modalities suited to self-care or care by a provider other than a physical therapist are explained in each chapter's section on self-care treatment guidelines.

CANDIDACY FOR THE INTERVENTION

Candidacy for application of physical agents and electrotherapeutic interventions follows a thorough diagnostic process described in Chapter 1 to determine those conditions that would benefit from or prevent use of the intervention and to determine that the body systems lack the ability to perform the necessary process of repair without intervention. The clinical decision-making process used for selecting each of the modalities is related to the system impairments it affects, as well as practical consideration. Candidates for physical therapy technologies include patients with observable acute inflammation of the tissues, including pain, chronicity of or absence of any phase of repair, circulatory compromise and edema, as well as impairments of different body organ systems such as the cardiopulmonary, musculoskeletal, neuromuscular, and integumentary systems. The mode of intervention best suited to the patient, the treatment setting, and the wound will be determined by the physical therapist.

As a guide, the patients should be referred to the physical therapist for intervention with a physical agent or electrotherapeutic modality when the additional following candidacy criteria are met:

- Medical comorbidities exist that predict that a wound needs extra help to heal (eg, insensitivity associated with spinal cord injury, diabetes).
- Healing will be speeded by the therapy.
- The wound has been recalcitrant to other methods.
- There is an acute wound in a patient with a coimpairment such as chronic obstructive pulmonary disease or impaired circulation, indicating a high probability of nonconforming healing.
- The acute traumatic wound(s) is associated with neuromuscular or musculoskeletal problems that may require immobilization.
- The wounds extend into subcutaneous tissue and deeper underlying structures and interfere with functional activities; eg, the patient is unable to sit up in a wheelchair because of the wounds over the ischial tuberosities or coccyx.
- The patient's functional status is impaired by slow wound healing; eg, gait will be helped if the wound is healed more rapidly, or patient may be able to return to work.

Reasons for Referral

The patient referred to the physical therapist for wound healing is usually an individual who has not shown signs of normal wound repair. Often other treatment interventions are being used or have been tried with limited or no success. Actually the very best time for intervening with physical agents or electrotherapeutic modalities is during the first 72 hours immediately after injury. Several recent studies show that intervention by a physical therapist soon after onset of the problem (eg, stroke,[2,3] acute musculoskeletal pain[4,5]) reduces cost. Appropriate early intervention by the physical therapist has a proven track record of significantly reducing the development of costly chronic health problems. A review of the research literature cited in the chapters on electrical stimulation, pulsed radio frequency, pulsed short wave diathermy, and ultrasound all cite research that demonstrates optimal effectiveness when the treatment intervention is applied early. However, since in reality more chronic wounds than acute wounds are referred to the physical therapist, other research cited in the chapters demonstrates efficacy of these technologies for healing of chronic wounds or to alter factors related to chronic wound healing such as circulation, oxygen uptake by cells, and edema. Expected outcomes should be based on the reason for the referral, the efficacy of the treatment intervention selected, and the chronicity of the wound.

Patients, caregivers, and physicians seek care for a wound for many reasons. Although it seems as if the obvious goal of treatment is healing, healing is not the highest priority for everyone with a wound, and that assumption should not be made. It is very important to ask the patient, family, physician, and payer the reason for the referral and base the intervention selected and expected outcomes on meeting those objectives. Most of the time the patient and family are looking for a simple functional outcome. For example, the patient with a foot ulcer secondary to pressure and insensitivity is fearful of amputation and loss of the ability to walk. The patient wants to know if the limb can be saved. The family of a debilitated nursing home patient wants their loved one with a pressure ulcer to be comfortable. They may realize that closure is not an option. Fear is a concern and creates a reluctance to come to therapy. All of these issues need to be addressed. The physical therapist's first intervention will be to learn as much about the patient and his or her goals and then begin education about the treatment options, effects of the treatment, and the expected outcomes.

Diagnosis

The diagnosis is the synthesis of the information gathered. Physical therapists use a functional diagnosis to describe an impairment, disability, or handicap of an associated body function. For example, the patient with a neuropathy as a consequence of alcoholism, diabetes, or spinal cord injury or the immobile or immobilized patient could all have a functional diagnosis of impaired sensation with undue susceptibility to ischemia, tissue anoxia, infection, and pressure ulceration. The impairment is decreased immunity, tissue anoxia, infection, and cell death. The disability is desensitized skin and risk for skin breakdown. The handicap is inability to maintain normal activity and mobility.

Patients with chronic wounds have an absence of progression through the phases of repair, that is, a functional impairment to wound healing at the cellular level or the tissue level. *Absence of inflammation and inability to progress to proliferation* is a functional diagnosis about functional impairment of the process at the cellular level or tissue level. This could be applied equally to a functional impairment of the proliferation phase: absence of proliferation or wound contraction with inability to progress to closure. Chronic wound edges do not produce functional epidermal cells to migrate across the wound to close it. *Absence of epithelialization due to impairment of epidermal cell activity* is a functional diagnosis for absence of wound progression to closure. A poorly healed wound or a minimally healed wound has a functional diagnosis of *absence of remodeling due to integumentary system impairment.*

Although traditionally patients with non-healing wounds are referred for physical therapy, patients with musculoskeletal injuries and soft tissue trauma should also be viewed as patients with a closed wound. Patients with wounds such as ligamentous tears, muscle strains, sprains, skin tears, hematomas, stage I pressure ulcers, stage 0 vascular ulcers, and abrasions that interfere with one's ability to walk, work, or compete in a sport should be viewed as candidates for intervention with physical agents and electrotherapeutic modalities including electrical stimulation, pulsed radio frequency stimulation, pulsed short wave diathermy, ultrasound, and whirlpool. In patients with metabolic diseases (eg, lupus or diabetes) who suffer wounding, acute wounds can, and often do, become chronic. Also, microtrauma resulting from excessive forces and repetition can also lead to closed wounds such as tendinitis and nerve entrapments. In these patients, the impairment is also a closed tissue wound. The disability is pain and usually limitation in range of motion. A handicap would result from prolonged disability and the resulting inability to work or participate in normal activities of daily living or recreation. Early and effective intervention to accelerate repair with the listed interventions should be considered.

In summary, a patient who has a functional diagnosis of impairment of a body system at the cellular, tissue, or organ level (or a combination) related to tissue repair should be considered a candidate for intervention with electrical stimulation, pulsed radio frequency stimulation, pulsed short wave diathermy, or ultrasound. In addition, patients with musculoskeletal injuries in need of accelerated repair should also be considered candidates for the same interventions used for closed wound healing.

Prognosis

The functional diagnosis is predictive of the need for the intervention. Intervention with physical agents and electrotherapeutic modalities must have a predicted outcome, or prognosis, that the intervention will reduce the impairment or alter the consequences of the disease associated with the functional diagnosis. A wound diagnosis of *absence of the inflammation phase*, for example, is predictive that the wound needs an inflammation phase followed by progression through the phases of healing to reach closure. The prognosis is *initiation of inflammation followed by progression of the wound through the phases of healing.* Part of a prognosis is the expected due date. There is enough information in the literature to evaluate the expected length of time to reach an outcome. The individual chapters in Part IV provide this information. Electrical stimulation, pulsed radio frequency stimulation, pulsed short wave diathermy, ultrasound, whirlpool, and pulsatile lavage with suction are all expected to reinitiate an inflammation phase followed by progression through the phases of healing. Another example of functional diagnosis is *impairment of sensation with undue susceptibility to pressure ulceration.* Reflexive neuronal mechanisms are impaired, and other methods must be used to stimulate circulatory responses; the prognosis for this functional diagnosis would be *adequate circulatory perfusion for delivery of oxygen and nutrients to tissues to progress through phases of repair.* Multiple functional diagnoses may be made that lead to multiple interventions, all of which will affect the outcome with the physical agent or electrotherapeutic modality intervention chosen for the wound. For instance, the patient with an impairment of sensation with undue susceptibility to pressure ulceration must be assessed for pressure risk. An intervention of pressure relief or elimination then must be included in the treatment plan so that the enhanced circulatory perfusion brought about by the selected intervention can reach the tissues. The physical therapist would apply this methodology to predict an outcome. The prognosis for repair of a closed tissue injury would be *accelerated absorption of hematoma, accelerated deposition of collagen, and restoration of normal ranges of motion, tissue extensibility, tissue strength for functional activities* (eg, self-care, work, leisure, or play).

Clinical research studies are very useful to guide the clinician in predicted outcomes and can function as a guide for a target due date. Clinical research studies should identify whether the wounds treated are acute or chronic. Because clinical research studies are usually carried out in ideal settings under optimal conditions, they should be considered only as guidelines that need to be tested in the individual clinical setting to determine the outcomes for the specific program. For example, the literature describes wound healing by closure or improvement. *Improvement* is less clearly defined and usually is described by reduction in depth of tissue loss or size and is listed as incompletely healed. Depth of tissue involvement (severity) will alter the expected length of time to closure. Partial-thickness wounds heal faster than full-thickness and deeper wounds.[6] Normal wound healing takes 3 to 4 weeks,[7] while the definition of chronicity is healing that has not occurred in the normal time frame. The concept of using physical agents and electrotherapeutic modalities is to initiate or accelerate the rate of repair of acute or chronic wounds. For example, Dyson and Young[8] found that application of low-intensity ultrasound during the early inflammatory phase accelerated the inflammatory phase of repair.

Choosing between Interventions

A frequently asked question is, How do I know which intervention to choose? There is no single answer to this question. The mechanisms of action on the biologic system are different, but the expected treatment outcomes of progression through the phases of healing are similar for each of the devices presented in Part IV. Some have optimal times for application, however. For instance, ultrasound is best delivered in the inflammatory phase—early proliferation[8] or to restart the inflammatory phase, but it is not effective for improvement of tensile strength if used in the later proliferative or epithelialization phase.[9] Figure IV–1 is an algorithm showing the phases of wound healing with a key to highlight which are the putative effects on the phase or factor of healing of the six physical therapy technologies described in Part IV. If one or more of the technologies affects the same biologic aspect of the phase, other criteria will be used to choose the modality. For instance, most devices described have the ability to increase tissue perfusion. What differs is the degree of tissue perfusion. The thermal modalities heat and increase circulation more vigorously than the nonthermal modalities. This effect may be suitable for some patients who need a vigorous attempt to enhance blood flow to reach ischemic tissues. The nonthermal devices affect the microcirculation but may not have a vigorous enough effect on circulation for all patients. Research is highly valued as the basis for selection of an intervention, and consequently the intervention with the most supporting research may be given the nod over less tested devices; however, clinical experience still must be valued. For example, whirlpool and pulsatile lavage with suction have no controlled clinical trials for efficacy of wound healing, yet clinical experience demonstrates that both have the ability to clean wounds of debris and exudate that leads to an outcome of wound healing. There are also practical considerations in choosing an intervention. These include the treatment setting, the treatment provider, the treatment payer, the treatment availability, medical contraindications, and adjunctive treatments (dressings, multiple technologies). If the treatment provider is to be other than a physical therapist or physical therapist assistant, the treatment must be safely applied by a person not trained in physical therapy. This would preclude use of pulsed short wave diathermy or ultrasound, for example. The treatment payer must be agreeable to paying for the physical therapy intervention selected. For example, Medicare contractors have an exclusion policy for payment of ultraviolet light to treat wounds. Treatment availability is as practical a reality as anything. If the preferred intervention is not available and cannot be obtained, then it is inaccessible and another choice will have to be made. Medical contraindications exist for all of the different technologies, but the medical contraindication that rules out the use of one will not necessarily rule out others. For example, a semicomatose patient should not be seen in the whirlpool, but wound cleansing with pulsatile lavage with suction at bedside would be an appropriate alternative. The following Case Study illustrates where thoughtful evaluation of the history and systems review narrowed down the choice of treatment intervention to one appropriate technology after considering all the factors.

Treatment Outcomes Management

Clinical managers have an obligation to review treatment outcomes systemically for wound patients referred to physical therapy. Most often the patient population referred are those individuals with complex wounds and comorbidities and many are also very debilitated. Careful screening and monitoring procedures are necessary to utilize treatment effectively. Sussman Physical Therapy, Inc. (SPT) is used to illustrate how a clinical program used a wound database to do program evaluation and quality improvement, and evaluate program outcomes. SPT treated a population of complex and debilitated nursing home patients. SPT developed and conformed to a self-imposed standard of 50% reduction in wound size within a 4-to-6 week period using Sussman's noninvasive, surgery-alternative treatment approach with physical therapy technologies and debridement. The first requirement was identification, for the patient's medical manager, wound stability, and the candidacy for surgical and other more costly interventions. SPT used paper-and-pencil instruments to record wound data information. The information was then transferred to bubble sheets and scanned into a computer database. Statistical analysis of the SPT wound database was performed by Swanson and Co., Inc.[10] Findings were that SPT had excellent success with chronic

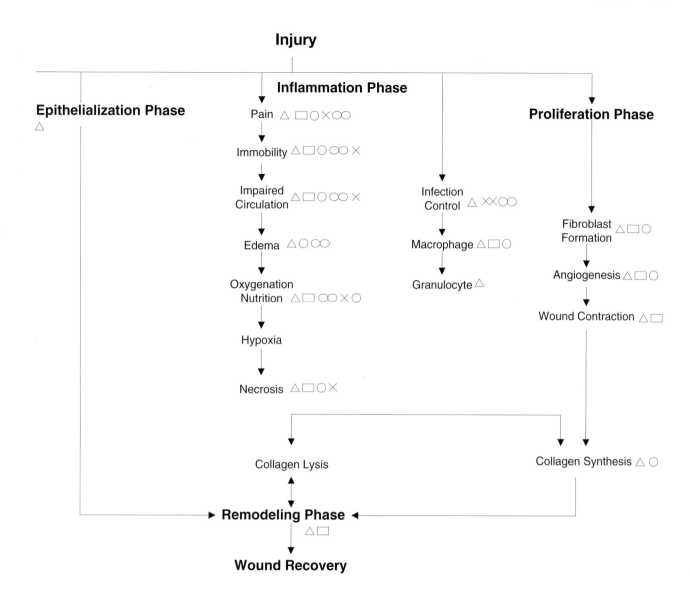

Injury

Inflammation Phase

Epithelialization Phase

Proliferation Phase

Pain

Immobility

Impaired Circulation

Edema

Oxygenation Nutrition

Hypoxia

Necrosis

Infection Control

Macrophage

Granulocyte

Fibroblast Formation

Angiogenesis

Wound Contraction

Collagen Lysis

Collagen Synthesis

Remodeling Phase

Wound Recovery

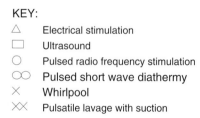

KEY:

△ Electrical stimulation

▢ Ultrasound

◯ Pulsed radio frequency stimulation

◯◯ Pulsed short wave diathermy

✕ Whirlpool

✕✕ Pulsatile lavage with suction

Figure IV–1 Putative Treatment Effects of Physical Therapy Technologies on Phases of Wound Healing. *Source:* Adapted with permission from Sussman CA. The role of physical therapy in wound care. In: Krasner D (ed), *Chronic Wound Care: A Clinical Source Book for Health Care Professsionals.* Wayne, PA: Health Management Publications, Inc., 1990, pp 327–367. Copyright © 1990, Health Management Publications, Inc., King of Prussia, PA.

Case Study: *Choosing the Appropriate Treatment Intervention*

A case example where multiple factors had to be considered when making a choice of intervention was required for E.F. E.F. An elderly lady, E.F. lived in a nursing home because of incompetence related to Alzheimer's disease. She had venous disease and a history of recurrent venous ulcers of the lower leg. A new episode of ulceration occurred and the patient was referred to the physical therapist. The patient had a pacemaker, would not stay in bed or in a wheelchair for 5 minutes, and would not tolerate dressings or compression devices. The venous disease diagnosis ruled out whirlpool. The pacemaker ruled out any form of diathermy. The low tolerance for compression ruled out compression devices. The inability to tolerate staying in one place more than 5 minutes and intolerance for dressings ruled out electrical stimulation. Pulsatile lavage with suction was not available and would not have been tolerated by the patient. The only choice remaining was ultrasound because she could be kept still and amused for the 5 minutes required for a periwound ultrasound treatment. This was also an appropriate choice because ultrasound is particularly effective during the acute inflammatory phase and effects absorption of hemorrhagic materials. This patient is included as one of the case histories in Chapter 19, Ultrasound. The results are viewed in *Color Plates 65 to 67.*

leg ulcers with its treatment approach. Patients were referred to SPT when other methods failed. The program evaluation demonstrated that more than two thirds of the chronic leg ulcers treated by the SPT method healed. This information was of value to the contract facility administrator, to the managed care contract payer, to the total quality assurance committee of the facility, and to the health department survey team. Furthermore, the information derived from the data analysis determined that the average length of stay for the patients in the healed group was 49 days. This information was then applied to do cost outcomes analysis as described below.[11]

Functional Wound Cost Outcomes Management

In 1992, the cost for treatment of pressure ulcers in all settings in the United States was $1.3 billion.[12] The average cost of treatment of a pressure ulcer in the United States,

based on 1990 data, is $2,000 to $30, 000. The typical cost for a medical approach to treatment of pressure ulcers by surgical debridement is at least $4,000.[13] How do costs for treatment with physical therapy technologies for wound healing compare? Based on data from Swanson,[14] Maver,[15] and Birke,[16] physical therapy technologies are competitive for certain wounds. Swanson[14] compared the costs of a course of wound care with hydrotherapy (whirlpool) with a high-voltage pulsed-current (HVPC) type of electrical stimulation and found that the course of 3 months (90 days) of care with hydrotherapy treatment (whirlpool) for necrotic wounds with an unknown outcome was $4,500 compared to $2,100 for a 7.5-week (52 days average) course of care with outcome of wound closure following treatment with high-voltage pulsed current electrical stimulation. Maver[15] compared the cost of conventional treatment for stage III pressure ulcers that did not heal during a course of care with a mean time of 34.62 weeks at a cost of $7,946.33, with 8.5 weeks course of care to healed status with Diapulse, pulsed radio frequency stimulation,[17] combined with conventional care cost of $2,929.62. The reported savings per ulcer in this study was $4,484. Birke[16] reported on numerous studies using total-contact casting (TCC) to heal plantar ulcers in patients with neuropathy. The average time to closure was 42 days. The average cost for a closed wound was $1,250. These cost savings do not include savings derived from reduced mortality, morbidity, and reduction in amputations. Comparative lengths of care and expected outcome for hydrotherapy, HVPC, and TCC are illustrated in Figure IV–2.

Cost comparison allows for a profile of wound cost outcomes and competitive analysis of the results of a course of care. Physical therapy is cost competitive for certain wounds (Figure IV–3). Physical therapist managers and program directors need to understand the information required to predict and manage cost for proper utilization management of services. The necessary information to predict cost and outcome are available from several sources: clinical trials, program evaluation reports, the facility's clinical database, the Agency for Health Care Policy and Research (AHCPR) standards, and payer data-based reports.

Does your clinic know your cost outcomes? Cost outcomes are differentiated from the technical outcome for the wound (eg, closure). Cost outcomes are what it costs to provide a course of care compared with the billed charges. That determines the cost to the provider as differentiated from the charges to the payer. The cost outcome is based on all the related costs for providing the service: labor cost, supply cost, and equipment cost. To determine the cost of treating a wound the clinical manager needs to predict the number of expected visits to achieve a predicted outcome. For example, if an

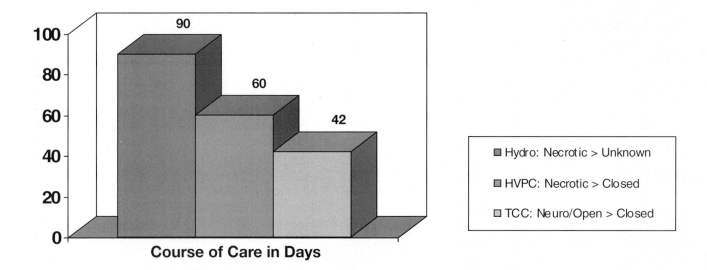

Figure IV–2 Length of stay dependent on wound type and procedure.

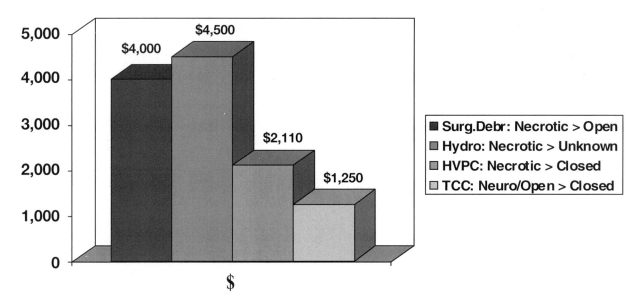

Figure IV–3 Cost comparison for different wound interventions and outcomes. Physical therapy is competitive for certain wounds.

outcome of closure is expected in 84 visits a cost analysis can be done as follows:

Labor cost at $30/visit × 84	=	$2,520
Supply cost at $6.25/visit × 84	=	$ 525
Equipment cost at 0.50 × 84	=	$ 42
Total cost	=	$3,087
Billed charges at $60/visit × 84	=	$5,040
Net profit	=	$1,953

The cost for a different outcome to convert the wound to clean and stable may take half the time to closure. Cost to the payer would be reduced by half to $2,520. The case manager for the payer may be more willing to authorize an interim step for a known cost than an unknown outcome at unmanaged cost.

Utilization and Cost Management

Utilization and cost outcomes management mean that continued ongoing evaluation of the patient candidacy be reviewed. Candidacy determined at the initial evaluation may change as the patient experiences a course of care (Figure IV–4). This would initiate a reevaluation to assess appropriateness for further treatment. The Sussman Wound Healing Tool, described in Chapter 5, was developed as a diagnostic tool to evaluate progression through the phases of healing when wounds were treated with physical therapy technologies. For example, reduction in wound depth is a finding of acute proliferation phase. Reduction in size is a measure of wound contraction and of epithelialization. If these benchmarks of healing are not occurring in an orderly manner, this may be due to a poor response to treatment or changes in medical status and should trigger a change in the treatment approach. The following are some examples of situations that trigger a change:

- *Failure to progress:* If the wound(s) are not progressing through the biologic sequence of repair after 2 weeks of treatment with high-voltage pulsed current (HVPC), for example, the entire wound management plan needs to be reviewed to determine whether it is the treatment with the HVPC or other factors that are responsible for failure to progress. Since all wounds have multiple associated interventions, including wound cleansing, topical treatments, dressings, and debridement, along with the HVPC, each intervention should be reviewed to determine whether continuation is appropriate or if there needs to be change in these interventions or with the HVPC protocol. It is standard wisdom that wounds should be progressing in the repair process during a 2-week interval or the treatment should be revised.[12]
- *Wound regression:* If the wound has gotten larger or deeper and is invading named structures or areas or has

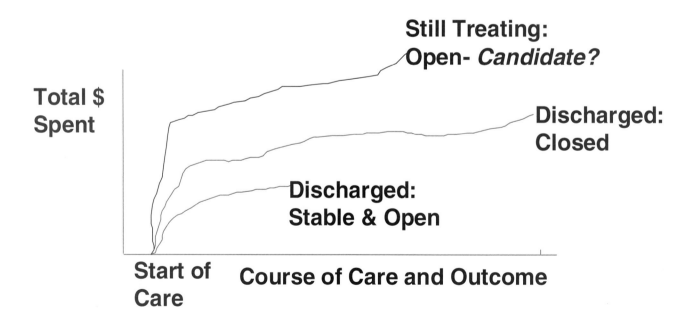

Figure IV–4 Monitor candidacy and outcome throughout course of care.

become infected, indicating that another management strategy is needed (eg, surgery for incision and drainage or antibiotics), this is referred to as wound regression. Although the physical therapist, physical therapist assistant, or nurse would not make the decision for the subsequent therapy, he or she should be able to recognize the signs and symptoms of disease and has responsibility to make a referral to the appropriate practitioner.

- *Medical instability:* If the patient has become medically unstable (eg, pneumonia, sepsis, renal failure), the body's ability to heal is impaired, and the situation requires a change in medical management before continuing with physical therapy. The physical therapist may determine that the physical therapy intervention may need to be put on hold until the medical condition is stabilized.

- *Other management required:* If the wound has progressed to a clean and stable wound in the proliferation phase, it may indicate that the wound is ready for grafting. It may be the best prognosis for the wound and/or for the patient and may have been the reason for referral, the objective of the patient, the family, the therapist, and the physician.

- *Wound needs less skilled care:* The wound is now at a phase of repair that demonstrates that the healing response is sustained and the wound is clean and stable. Now the patient/caregiver or nurse can provide standard wound care procedures to keep the wound clean and, if body systems support the process of healing, take it to closure.

- *Goals met:* Sometimes, the patient and family have reached their goals and do not wish to continue or become noncompliant with treatment. In other cases, the wound has healed to closure.

- *Closure and beyond:* Wound closure may be the intent of the treatment, but closure does not include remodeling. Wounds that are minimally closed are at very high risk for recurrence, especially when located over areas of friction, shear, and pressure, such as on the seating surface or plantar surface of the foot. Wounds in those areas of high risk would benefit from further stimulation of collagen synthesis by electrical stimulation until the minimally healed scar is acceptably healed.[18] Acceptable healing is achieved when there is a thickening of the scar formation and the color of the scar blanches from bright red or pink to light pink or white.

Plan of Care/Treatment

Part IV focuses primarily on the use of externally applied treatments for wound repair and does not address specific dressings and debridement, nor does it outline the specifics of an exercise program. It must be reinforced, however, that all of the described technologies are supplemental to the traditional wound management program of debridement, dressings, and medications. In addition to physical therapy technologies, every patient who is able to participate in exercise must be instructed in an appropriate exercise program. For some, traditional strengthening and conditioning exercises would be appropriate (eg, walking, running, stationary bike). In others it may be active range of motion of the extremities or isometric exercises. Every physical therapist must address the issues of immobilization and prevention of demineralization, atrophy, and contractures. In some cases, soft tissue mobilization techniques could be used around the wound. In all cases, the patients and caregivers must also be educated about hydration, nutrition, and a balanced lifestyle that addresses stress reduction and positive health. The physical therapist is usually the only team member who can manage the electrical stimulation program, the therapeutic exercises, and appropriate soft tissue mobilization procedures along with the wound care.

CONCLUSION

The rules for selection of treatment interventions includes consideration of the medical status of the patient, the status of the wound healing phase, and all treatments used to achieve the expected outcome. Wounds all receive multiple interventions. Treatment effects are additive. Therefore, all treatment interventions must be compatible with the patient, one another, and the wound. They will change during the progression of healing. The most universal treatment intervention is the wound dressing. Modern wound dressings have specific effects and times for reapplication. Because wounds need to be cleansed periodically, the wound cleanser is another common intervention. Topical agents from enzymes to antimicrobials are often added to the wound intervention regimen. Depending on the phase of wound healing, one or more of these interventions will be needed. The addition of a physical agent or an electrotherapeutic modality must be compatible with the other treatment interventions. This will require collaboration of the team members—nurse, physician, pharmacist, and physical therapist—to select interventions that are compatible and efficacious for wound healing. Exhibit IV–1 lists three rules of treatment selection, an example of how each is used, and a formula for selection of treatments to achieve a desire outcome in a prescribed period. The letters "A," "B," and "C," in the formula represent three treatment interventions. The number of treatments usually given is often three, but is not limited to three. Each chapter in Part IV will address the issue of treatment interactions and compatibility with other interventions.

Exhibit IV–1 Rules of Treatment Selection

1. **Medical assessment and tissue assessment determines the selection of treatment.**

   Example: Client has a venous stasis ulcer in inflammatory phase and has a cardiac pacemaker implant. Whirlpool, HVPC, PRFS and PSWD are contraindicated. Ultrasound would be a good choice for local application.

2. **Treatment changes during the progression of healing so as to affect the recovery process.**

   Example: Client has a necrotic hip ulcer with eschar. Treatment starts with whirlpool, enzymes, and occlusive dressing. Necrotic tissue is removed. Treatment changes.

3. **Each selected treatment is goal specific based on how it affects the predicted outcome.**

   Example: Client has a clean partial-thickness wound in the acute proliferation phase. Prognosis is wound closure. Treatment selected: clean with normal saline, use hydrogel impregnated gauze dressing, apply HVPC through dressing, and cover with secondary dressing.

   ———————

   Formula To Select Treatment

   Wound Healing Phase of Tissue + Treatment A + Treatment B + Treatment C = Wound Healing Phase of Tissue in X Period of Time

CHAPTER ORGANIZATION

Each chapter in Part IV covers the following information about each modality:

- Rrelated definitions and terminology
- The theory and science of the therapy
- Clinical trials when available
- Indications, contraindications, and precautions
- Expected outcomes and outcomes measures
- Equipment
- Procedures, including protocols and patient set-ups
- Clinical and research-related wisdom
- Self-care treatment guidelines, if appropriate
- Case study, using the functional outcome report

REFERENCES

1. American Physical Therapy Association. A guide to physical therapist practice, Vol 1: a description of patient management. *Phys Ther.* 1995;75:707–764.

2. General Accounting Office, U.S. Congress, reported in PT Bulletin. American Physical Therapy Association, Vol. 12, No. 10, March 7, 1997.

3. Hayes S, Carroll S. Early intervention care in the acute stroke patient. *Arch Phys Med Rehabil.* 1986;67:319–321.

4. Linton S, Hellsing A, Andersson D. A controlled study of the effects of early intervention on acute musculoskeletal pain problems. *Pain.* 1993;54(3):353–359.

5. American Physical Therapy Association. *Outcome Effectiveness of Physical Therapy: An Annotated Bibliography.* Alexandria, VA: APTA; 1993.

6. Ferrell BA, Osterweil D, Christenson P. A randomized trial of low-air-loss beds for treatment of pressure ulcers. *JAMA.* 1993;269: 494–497.

7. Harding K. Wound care: putting theory into clinical practice. In: Krasner D, ed. *Chronic Wound Care: A Clinical Source for Health Care Professionals.* King of Prussia, PA: Health Management Publications Inc; 1990:19–30.

8. Dyson M, Young S. Acceleration of tissue repair by low intensity ultrasound applied during the inflammatory phase, APTA/CPTA Joint Congress, Abstract No. R-186, presented Las Vegas, Nevada, June 1998.

9. Hart J. The effect of therapeutic ultrasound on dermal repair with emphasis on fibroblasts activity. PhD thesis, London: University of London, 1993.

10. Swanson G. *Sussman Physical Therapy 1991 Wound Database Report.* Long Beach, CA: Swanson and Co.

11. Sussman C. Functional wound cost outcomes. Presented at the American Physical Therapy Association Combined Sections Meeting, February 1996, Atlanta, GA.

12. Bergstrom N, Bennett MA, Carlson CE, et al. *Treatment of Pressure Ulcers.* Clinical Practice Guideline No. 15. AHCPR Publication No. 95-0652. Rockville, MD: Agency for Health Care Policy and Research, U.S. Public Health Service, U.S. Department of Health and Human Services; December 1994.

13. Wethe J. Sharp debridement of wounds instructional course. Wound Care Management Conference. October 1993.

14. Swanson G. Use of cost data, provider experience, and clinical guidelines in the transition to managed care. *J Ins Med.* 1991;23(1): 70–74.

15. Maver RW. An actuarial report on the cost effectiveness of a new medical technology. *J Ins Med.* 1991;23(2):120–123.

16. Birke J. Management of the diabetic foot instructional course. Wound Care Management Conference. November 1995.

17. Itoh M, et al. Accelerated wound healing of pressure ulcers by pulsed high peak power electromagnetic energy (Diapulse). *Decubitus.* 1991;4(1):24–34.

18. Lazarus G, et al. Definitions and guidelines for assessment of wounds and evaluation of healing. *Arch Dermatol.* 1994;130: 489–493.

CHAPTER 16

Electrical Stimulation for Wound Healing

Carrie Sussman and Nancy Byl

INTRODUCTION

Electrical stimulation (ES) for wound healing has achieved acknowledgment by the medical community, resulting in more referrals. All ES procedures are not alike, creating confusion about which one to use for wound healing. This chapter tries to straighten out some of the confusion. It begins with definitions and terminology used to discuss and distinguish electrical stimulation parameters. The second section details the science and theory of the therapy and relates back to the parameters. Clinical decision making applies the science and theory by considering the indications for the therapy, reasons for referral, medical history, and systems reviews that are part of the diagnostic process. This section is followed by description of the equipment and accessories used, the rationale for selection of protocols, the expected outcomes, and the patient set-up. Since ES is a treatment intervention that can be taught to patients or other caregivers, self-care teaching guidelines are included. Case studies applying the functional outcome report (FOR) to document the rationale for selection of electrical stimulation as the intervention followed by a discussion revealing the clinical decision-making process and the actual outcomes conclude the chapter.[1] Chapter 2 describes the FOR.

DEFINITIONS AND TERMINOLOGY

Electrical stimulation for wound healing is defined as the use of a capacitive coupled electrical current to transfer energy to a wound. The type of electricity that is transferred to the target tissue is controlled by the electrical source.[2]

Capacitive Coupling

Capacitively coupled ES involves the transfer of electric current through an applied surface electrode pad that is in wet (electrolytic) contact (capacitively coupled) with the external skin surface and/or wound bed. When capacitively coupled ES is used, at least two electrodes are required to complete the electric circuit. Electrodes are usually placed over wet conductive medium: (1) in the wound bed or on the skin a distance away from the wound—monopolar technique, or (2) straddling the wound—bipolar technique.

Amplitude and Voltage

Amplitude refers to either the voltage or the current intensity of an electric current. Voltage is a measure of the force of the flow of electrons and amperage is the measure of the rate of flow of the current. When voltage is turned up, the current will also go up, and vice versa. Some stimulators provide a readout of voltage and some a readout of current. The relationship between voltage and current is expressed as Ohm's law. The formula for this is current times resistance equals voltage [$V = IR$, where V is voltage, I is current, and R is resistance]. In general, low-voltage devices produce voltages of different ranges from 60 to 100 V. High-voltage devices range from 100 to 500 V. These are peak ranges.

Amperage

The unit of current is the ampere (A), which is defined as the rate at which electrons move past a certain point. A milliampere (mA) is one thousandth of an ampere, and a micro-ampere (μA) is one millionth of an ampere. Microamperage current is usually between 5 and 20 μA of current (less than 1.0 mA).

Charge

Electrical charge is the excess or deficiency of electrons or ions. An electrically neutral substance that loses electrons becomes positively charged, and if it gains electrons it becomes negatively charged. The unit of measure for charge is the coulomb. In biologic systems the charges are small and expressed in microcoulombs (μC).[3] A typical high-voltage stimulator, for example, has a maximum pulse charge of only 10 to 15 μC, which is very safe.[4(p65)] The charge density is the electrical charge per cross-sectional area of the electrodes. The larger the size of the electrode the smaller the charge density, and conversely.

Polarity

Polarity refers to the property of having two poles that are oppositely charged. The positive pole is called the anode and the negative pole the cathode. The positive pole lacks electrons and attracts electrons from the negative pole, or cathode. Polarity can be chosen or emphasized for biologic effects.

Waveforms

Different types of current have different characteristic waveforms. Waveforms are the graphic representations of a current on a current/time or voltage/time plot.[3] Waveforms are classified by the direction of current flow. Current flow is either unidirectional or bidirectional. Figures 16–1 to 16–6 show examples of direct current, monophasic square wave pulsed current, twin peaked pulsed monophasic current, alternating current, and balanced biphasic and asymmetric biphasic waveforms. Each waveform and related characteristics are described.

Direct Current

Unidirectional current is also called galvanic or direct current (Figure 16–1). Direct current (DC) is continuous, uninterrupted, unidirectional current. Direction of the flow is determined by the polarity selected. Direct current waveforms may be subdivided into pulsatile currents (PC).

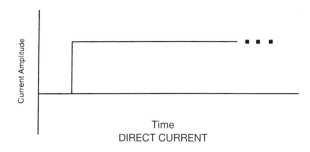

Figure 16–1 Graphic representation of the unidirectional flow of charged particles. *Source:* Reprinted with permission from *Electrotherapeutic Terminology in Physical Therapy,* p. 11, © 1990, Section on Clinical Electrophysiology and the American Physical Therapy Association.

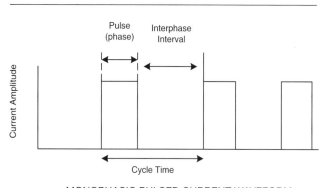

Note: In a monophasic waveform, phase and pulse are identical.

Figure 16–2 Graphic representation of monophasic pulses. *Source:* Reprinted with permission from *Electrotherapeutic Terminology in Physical Therapy,* p. 13, © 1990, Section on Clinical Electrophysiology and the Americal Physical Therapy Association.

Monophasic Pulsed Current

Pulsed current is phasic. Monophasic pulsed current is defined as pulsed direct current (PC) that deviates from baseline and returns to baseline after a designated time period. The monophasic pulsed current waveform may be either a square wave or the traditional twin peaked pulsed wave of the high-voltage pulsed current. Monophasic pulses and phases are identical (Figure 16–2). Monophasic waves are such that at one electrode the polarity is positive and the other is negative. This stays constant throughout the treatment unless changed by the clinician. Polarity appears to have specific effects on biologic responses.

Frequency or Pulse Rate

A pulse rate or frequency is the number of pulses delivered per unit of time. The *rate* of the off and on cycle is defined as pulses per second (pps). The range of pulses per second is usually from 0.1 Hz to 999 Hz. A pulse of 0.1 Hz is on for 10 seconds and a pulse of 999 Hz is on for 1 millisecond. The time between pulses when no electrical activity occurs is the interpulse interval (Figure 16–3). Pulsed electrical stimulation (PES) has a train of pulses that are repeated at regular intervals and are termed the pulse rate or pulse frequency. Pulsed current can be either unidirectional or bidirectional.

Pulse Duration

The on time during which current is flowing is the pulse duration. Pulse duration affects biologic responses. For example, direct current has a continuous duration and has the ability to raise tissue temperature and change the pH under the electrode. However, a short pulse duration, typical of high-voltage pulsed current, produces insignificant changes in both tissue pH and tissue temperature.[4–6] Such a current is therefore very safe but raises questions about the effect of

polarity when the pulse duration is so short. For purposes of muscle stimulation, the stimulation must be provided at an intensity and a duration that will stimulate a muscle contraction. If the goal is to keep the stimulation tolerable, the amplitude may be kept as low as possible, forcing the duration of the stimulus to be longer. Muscle is most sensitive to a stimulus from a negative electrode. When providing electrical stimulation to denervated muscle, some recommend that the stimulus be on for only 1 and 50 milliseconds.[7,8] Because high-voltage pulsed monophasic current has a shorter pulse duration it cannot be used to stimulate denervated muscle. For pain management and wound healing, the pulse duration and the amplitude of the current are variable. Some clinicians and researchers suggest that this current must be on for at least 1 second to produce strong polarity effects of the tissue under the electrodes.

Duty Cycle

The on/off ratio is the ratio of the time the current is on to the time the current is off. A duty cycle is the ratio of *on time* to the *total cycle time* including both the on and off time (Figure 16–2). A ratio is used to express the relative proportion of the on and off time and can be expressed as a percentage. For instance, if the total cycle is 60 microseconds, the on time is 20 microseconds, and the off time is 40 microseconds, there is a 1:2 on/off ratio and the duty cycle is a 1:3 ratio, or a 33% duty cycle.

High-Voltage Pulsed Current

High-voltage pulsed current (HVPC) typically has a twin peaked monophasic waveform (Figure 16–3). HVPC is a misnomer if galvanic is used with it. This current was named incorrectly by the manufacturers. The acronym HVPC does not have galvanic in the acronym. The pulse rate most frequently used for wound healing is 50 to 120 pps (0.83 to 1.25 milliseconds). Each peak or spike has an effective 5- to 20-microsecond phase duration. Voltage can be selected with intensity between 100 and 500 V. The amplitude selected for wound healing is usually between 80 and 200 V, and the polarity and pulse rate are varied. There is a long interpulse interval between pulses that makes a low average current. The high-voltage stimulation has a high peak current that means greater penetration into tissue, allowing for stimulation of deep motor points.[4(pp59–71)] On the skin surface, alkaline/acidity changes under the electrodes have not been measured.[5,6] Since HVPC is not galvanic, this explains why there is no alkaline/acidity effects. Absence of chemical changes under the electrodes has led to questions about how polarity effects can be the factor that stimulates cellular responses

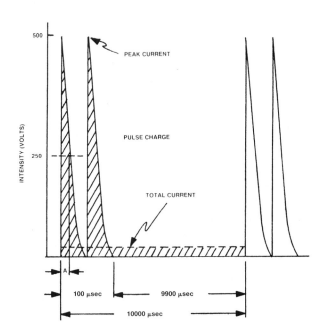

Figure 16–3 Typical pulse characteristics of a high-voltage stimulator. *Source:* Reprinted with permission from Alon G, De Domenico G. *High Voltage Stimulation: An Integrated Approach to Clinical Electrotherapy,* 1st ed., p. 62, © 1987, Hixton, TN: The Chattanooga Group.

when the duration of the HVPC pulse is so short. However, multiple studies demonstrate different effects under the anode and cathode using HVPC. Table 16–1 lists effects reported by various researchers using HVPC that are polarity dependent. For instance, one study showed that fibroblasts were attracted to the cathode of an HVPC stimulator, suggesting that there may be some cellular polarity effects under the electrode.[9] Although multiple studies show cellular effects and responses to HVPC, each study shows something different; therefore, corroborating research is needed to support the findings of these single studies.

Microcurrent Electrical Stimulation

A pulsed monophasic stimulus is referred to as monophasic low-voltage microcurrent electrical stimulation (MENS). This refers to a pulsed current at an intensity less than 1 mA (1 to 999 μA) and the voltage is less than 100 V. MENS is delivered at amplitudes that have minimal detectable sensation and are incapable of motor nerve stimulation. MENS typically has a single modified monophasic square waveform. The pulse duration of these devices ranges from 0.1 to 999 Hz, equivalent to on time of 10 seconds to 1 microsecond. The pulse duration is inversely related to the frequency. Microcurrent stimulation has a prolonged pulse duration at the lower frequencies, which will have a different tissue polarity effect than a shorter-duration pulse most typically used in high-voltage stimulation. For example, a low-voltage pulsed stimulus at 0.1 Hz is on for 10 seconds, whereas the high-voltage monophasic simulators are used at 80 to 120 pps and are on for only 0.83 to 1.25 milliseconds. Thus, pulsed low-voltage current of at least 1 pps can maintain the polarity effect delivered to the tissues under the electrode. The peak amplitude is usually 600 μA/60 V. The average amplitude commonly used is 200 to 300 μA for soft tissue[7] and 20 μA for bone healing in rabbits.[10] MENS current has been used in bone healing; however, in this clinical application, the amplitude recommended is 20 to 50 μA (bone healing research). When pulsed slowly, there are reported cellular and tissue polarity effects under the electrodes.[11] This type of current may be used to restore the normal bioelectrical resting current or reverse the injury current.[11] There is some concern that the voltage may be too low to push the current through the resistance of the skin and the subcutaneous tissues, but no specific studies could be found to confirm this.

Alternating Current

Bidirectional waveforms are referred to as faradic or alternating as well as biphasic or bipolar. British literature uses the term "faradic" for all alternating current, probably in reference to the scientist Faraday. In the United States, fa-

radic is no longer designed in ES units because it is very uncomfortable. Alternating current (AC) is uninterrupted bidirectional current flow (Figure 16–4). The waveforms may be symmetric, where the shape of the waveform is always balanced. Both the shape and size are the same. An asymmetric waveform can be balanced or unbalanced (see Figures 16–5A and 16–5B). One of the most common outputs from an electrical stimulator is balanced asymmetric. A balanced asymmetric waveform is typical of transcutaneous electrical nerve stimulation used for pain modulation (Figure 16–5). Biphasic waves are such that the polarity is constantly changing. They are opposite at any moment in time. But the waveform can be biased so that one polarity is emphasized. Several studies using this type of current for wound healing have been reported in the literature. The best wound healing effects seem to be achieved when a biphasic waveform is asymmetric and biased so that the polarity at one pole predominates. The effects of stimulation with this waveform on wound healing is discussed further in following sections.

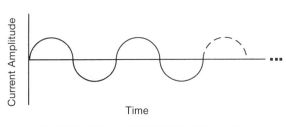

SYMMETRICAL ALTERNATING CURRENT

Figure 16–4 Symmetrical alternating (biphasic) waveform. *Source:* Reprinted with permission from *Electrotherapeutic Terminology in Physical Therapy,* p. 11, © 1990, Section on Clinical Electrophysiology and the American Physical Therapy Association.

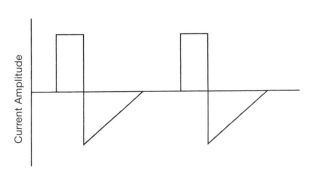

Time
BALANCED ASYMMETRICAL BIPHASIC WAVEFORM

Figure 16–5A Balanced asymmetrical alternating (biphasic) waveform. *Source:* Reprinted with permission from *Electrotherapeutic Terminology in Physical Therapy,* p. 12, © 1990, Section on Clinical Electrophysiology and the American Physical Therapy Association.

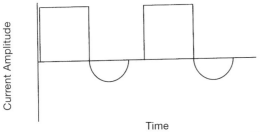

UNBALANCED ASYMMETRICAL BIPHASIC WAVEFORM

Figure 16–5B Unbalanced asymmetrical biphasic waveform. *Source:* Reprinted with permission from *Electrotherapeutic Terminology in Physical Therapy,* p. 15, © 1990, Section on Clinical Electrophysiology and the American Physical Therapy Association.

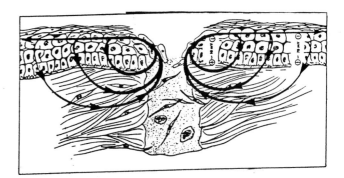

Figure 16–6 Current path in wounded section of skin. Disruption in epidermis has provided a return path for current driven by transepithelial potential. *Source:* Reprinted with permission from *Clinics in Dermatology,* Vol. 2, L.F. Jaffe and J.W. Vanable, Electric Fields and Wound Healing, pp. 34–44, 1984. Elsevier Science, Inc.

THEORY AND SCIENCE OF ELECTRICAL STIMULATION

Bioelectrical Systems

The body has its own bioelectrical system. This system influences wound healing by attracting the cells of repair, changing cell membrane permeability, enhancing cellular secretion through cell membranes, and orientating cell structures.

Sodium Current of Injury

The intact skin surface maintains an average constant electronegative charge of approximately –23 mV with respect to the deeper epidermal layers. The negative charge on the surface is created by negatively charged chloride ions (Cl^-), which stay on the surface after positively charged sodium ions (Na^+) are pumped into the inner layers of the epidermis by the sodium ion pump. Thus, the skin has electrical potentials across it and it acts as a battery. When there is a break in the skin surface, current can flow between the parts of the skin transmitted through the ionic fluids of the tissues between the outer and inner layers of the skin[12] (see Figure 16–6). Regenerating tissues show a distinct pattern of unidirectional current flow and polarity switching. As healing is completed, or *arrested*, these currents disappear. When ulcers become dry, the voltage gradient is eliminated and the current disappears.[11] This has been suggested as an explanation of why moist wounds heal better than dry wounds. One rationale for applying electrical stimulation is that it mimics the natural current of injury and will jump-start or accelerate the wound healing process.[13]

Galvanotaxis and Polarity

Unidirectional electrical current flow in the tissues attracts the cells of repair and is called galvanotaxis. There is a significant body of research that demonstrates that polarity

Clinical Wisdom: *Moist Wounds Promote the "Current of Injury"*

Keeping a wound moist with normal (0.9%) saline (sodium chloride) maintains the optimal bioelectric charge because it simulates the electrolytic concentration of wound fluid. Dressings such as amorphous hydrogels and occlusive dressings help promote the body's "current of injury" by keeping the wound environment moist.

influences healing in different ways at different phases. Table 16–1 summarizes the cellular effects by phase of wound healing. Table 16–2 summarizes the polarity effects on other aspects of biological systems related to wound healing.

Neutrophils, lymphocytes, platelets, and macrophages are early responders to injury and start the inflammatory response. The neutrophils are attracted to the negative pole if the wound is infected, to the positive pole if not infected.[14] Lymphocytes and platelets are attracted to the negative pole.[9] Macrophages are attracted to the positive pole.[15] These cells fight infection and produce chemotactic and growth-stimulating cytokines needed to repair or regenerate the tissue. Autolysis and phagocytosis are mediated by the macrophages and neutrophils. Thus, a suggested clinical application of electrical current that integrates these principles would be as follows: for a wound that is necrotic, but not infected, use a positive electrode over the wound to promote autolysis, and put the negative electrode over the wound if it is infected.[16] However, for the treatment of diabetic ulcers, Alon et al. used positive polarity with HVPC throughout the course of care.[17]

Fibroblasts are key cells in contraction and connective tissue formation. Fibroblasts are attracted by the negative pole

Table 16–1 Galvanotactic Effects on Cells by Phases of Healing

Effect	Cells	Pole	Type of Current	Researcher
Inflammation: autolysis and phagocytosis	Macrophages (–)	Anode	DC	Orida and Feldman[15]
	Neutrophils (±)	Anode/cathode	DC	Fukushima et al.[14]; Kloth[16]
	Mast cells (decreased) (–)	Anode		
			PES, 35 mA, 128 pps	Weiss et al.[22]; Gentzkow and Miller[12]
Proliferation: fibroplasia (collagen formation)	Fibroblasts (+)	Cathode	HVPC, 50 V, 100 pps	Bourguignon and Bourguignon[23]
			DC, 10–100 μV/cm	Canaday and Lee[24]; Erickson and Nuccitelli[25]
			DC, 1500 mV/cm	Yang et al.[26]
Wound contraction	Myofibroblasts (+)	Alternating	HVPC	Stromberg[19]
Epithelialization	Epidermal cells (–)	Anode	DC, 50 mV/mm	Cooper and Schliwa[27]

Table 16–2 Polarity Effects of Electrical Stimulation

Effect	Pole	Researcher	Type of Current
↑ Blood flow	Negative	Mohr et al.[28]	HVPC
		Politis et al.[29]	PES
		Pollack[30]	PES
		Gentzkow et al.[13]	PES
↓ Edema	Negative	Mendel and Fish[31]	HVPC
		Reed[32]	HVPC
		Ross and Segal[33]	HVPC
Debridement	Negative	Sawyer[34–36]	DC
Thrombolysis	Negative	Sawyer[34–36]	DC
Thrombosis	Positive	Williams and Carey[37]	DC
Oxygen	Anode	Byl et al.[38]	MENS, 100 μA low volt
Oxygen	Alternating	Baker et al.[39]	Asymmetric biphasic
Wound contraction	Alternating	Stromberg[19]	PES
Tendon repair	Positive	Owoeye et al.[40]	HVPC
Bacteriostatic effects	Both	Barranco et al.[41]	DC
		Rowley et al.[42]	DC
		Kincaid and Lavoie[43]	HVPC
		Szuminsky et al.[44]	HVPC

to proliferate and synthesize collagen and to contract the wound rapidly.[9] Protein and DNA synthesis are enhanced by negative stimulation. Under similar parameters, calcium ion (Ca^{2+}) or uptake by fibroblast cells is increased, which immediately produces an increased exposure of insulin receptors on the fibroblast cell surface. If insulin is available to bind, the additional receptors on the fibroblasts will significantly increase protein and DNA synthesis. If insulin is added after exposure to HVPC stimulation, further increase in Ca^{2+} uptake occurs and a twofold increase in protein and DNA synthesis. Therefore, timing of insulin delivery and HVPC treatment to diabetic patients with wounds may have a different outcome. Conversely, these same receptors are inhibited by Ca^{2+} channel blocker medications.[9] Slower healing can be expected in wounds if the patient is taking Ca^{2+} channel blocker medication. When the clinician is taking a medical history, the pharmaceutical history should be reviewed with these factors in mind. Drug effects could change the prognosis for healing.

The use of electrical stimulation to enhance the benefits of antibiotics is being researched.[18] Research to investigate timing of drug delivery and physical therapy modality treatment to enhance effects of both could open a new approach to interventions.

Research on rapid wound contraction can also provide clinical guidance for treatment selection. Stromberg[19] found that pulsed monophasic current, alternating polarity every 3 days, at 128 pps and amplitude at 35 mA, accelerated wound contraction during the first 4 weeks after injury. Conversely he found that constant polarity, either negative or positive, was less effective. Thoughtful application should be considered in areas where rapid wound contraction would not be desirable, such as in the hand or neck.

Epidermal cells have been reported as migrating toward the positive pole. Animal studies demonstrate that, in the early acute inflammatory phase of healing, the rate of epidermal cell migration in dermal wounds is enhanced by 3 days of stimulation with a negative pole, followed by stimulation with the positive pole for 4 days. Closure was achieved in 100% of the treatment group and only 87% of control group. Comparison of tensile strength and mitotic activity between treated and control groups was comparable.[20,21] This corresponds to a 0- to 3-day inflammatory phase and a 4- to 7-day repair phase of healing.

The goal of wound healing is a scar whose characteristics are most like the original skin. Mast cells regulate this process throughout the healing cycle. A large number of mast cells in the healing wound are associated with diseases of abnormal fibrotic healing such as keloid formation. After exposure to positive polarity current, a decrease in mast cells, decreased scar thickness, and better cosmetic results were observed in treated wounds.[22]

Refining the choice of polarity for specific effects has been the subject of many research studies (Tables 16–1 and 16–2). There will always be a need for additional research to explain and validate the efficacy of procedures and protocols. Meanwhile, reading and interpreting the current literature builds understanding and professional judgment. The physical therapist is the best-trained practitioner to understand and interpret the research pertaining to electrotherapeutic modalities. As such, the physical therapist has an obligation to understand the physiologic implications of each treatment intervention selected and to be responsible for accurately predicting outcomes.

In practice, the issues of polarity and wound healing are appropriate when referring to continuous or monophasic pulsed current. Even though the electrodes are marked as positive and negative for units that deliver AC, the imbalance of the charge of the electrodes is very small and not enough to affect the movement of the ions under the electrodes. When using continuous current, a change in polarity is a change in the direction of the current and a change in the flow of the ions under the electrode. The studies demonstrating these polarity effects have been done with continuous and pulsed currents, usually with the current on for more than 1 second. One of the concerns in wound healing research is whether the polarity effects of monophasic pulsed current predictably occur under the electrodes when the duration of the current is on for such a very short period of time. For example, with high-voltage stimulation, the monophasic waveform is on for less than 1 second (80 to 120 pps), and no measurable changes occur relative to alkalinity (H^+) or acidity (OH^-).[5] The question is whether some cell migration is still facilitated by the polarity of the electrodes at the wound site or whether some other factors explain the physiologic effectiveness of externally applied high-voltage, pulsed currents for healing wounds. More research is needed to show that high-voltage stimulation creates measurable polarity effects, or that other physiologic processes of healing are facilitated.

Although the effects of polarity and wound healing have focused primarily on the movement of ions under the electrodes, there are other issues about current flow that could facilitate healing. For example, Wolf's law[45,46] states that under conditions of repetitive stress, collagen is remodeled. One type of stress on a tissue is a mechanical force, such as weight bearing. This weight bearing facilitates the deposition of collagen in soft tissue and bone along the lines of the force on the tissue. Mechanical forces on the tissue can also be created when other types of energy are delivered to the tissue, such as ultrasound or electricity. When a sound wave pulsates or an electrical current pulsates, a force is created on the cell and it expands and contracts, creating a piezoelectric effect. It has been suggested that this piezoelectric effect accounts for the increased collagen deposition.[47,48] Thus, in pulsed current, it is possible that wound healing repair (collagen deposition) measurement is facilitated by this mechanism independent of the polarity effects of the electrode. If this is true, then biphasic current should have a piezoelectric effect. However, at this time, biphasic current is rarely used for wound healing. In the future, this may change given that recent results of several studies document significant healing effects with biphasic current.

Blood Flow and Edema

Several studies in the literature reported improved blood flow after treatment with electrical stimulation. Treatment with HVPC with negative polarity induced greater blood flow in rats than did positive polarity. The blood flow volume was increased nearly instantaneously at the pulse rates tested: 2, 20, 80, and 120 pps. In addition, blood flow was enhanced by increasing the amplitude of the current (up to stimulating muscle contraction). In a small number of cases, however, blood flow volume increased without visible muscle contraction. Blood flow velocity remained elevated from 4 to 20 minutes after treatment.[28] Necrosis of skin flaps and free full-thickness skin grafts are a major problem following plastic surgery. Several skin flap studies showed greater blood flow increases following electrical stimulation with a cathode in the treated flaps than that with untreated flaps.[29,30,49]

Alon and De Domenico[4] reviewed the literature on the effects of electrical stimulation on venous circulation. As yet electrical stimulation is not used extensively for management of venous circulation problems, but merits inclusion in this section for thoughtful application. There is no support for intervention in the acute phase of varicose hemorrhage or deep vein thrombosis, but electrical stimulation can effectively treat chronic conditions including deep vein thrombosis and venous stasis. When muscle groups in the calf and posterior thigh are stimulated to produce intermittent tetanic muscle contraction, there is very effective enhancement of venous return in cases of venous insufficiency or deep vein thrombosis. The required stimulation parameters are those needed to provide motor excitation leading to evoked intermittent tetanic muscle contraction. Augmentation of the venous return initiates a response of vasodilatation of the arterioles to bring blood flow to the muscles. Enhanced blood flow to tissues will support tissue demands for increased oxygen and nutrients required for healing. In the case of the patient with venous insufficiency, stimulation of enhanced blood flow will need to be evaluated and may require aftercare of compression to avoid pooling of blood at the ankles due to the incompetent valves (see Chapter 9). If the arterioles are severely occluded, the vasodilatation response may not occur and then electrically evoked muscle contraction may not be desired. In fact, the muscle contraction may cause

severe pain by curtailing limited blood flow to the area leading to ischemia. There is very limited clinical data to support specific protocols for this effect. Therefore, it is up to the physical therapist to evaluate the vascular impairments based on the diagnostic process and select a protocol to support the desired effect. The section on protocols and procedures provides an example for guidance.

Kaada[50,51] reported a causal relationship between transcutaneous electrical nerve stimulation (TENS) and mechanisms involved in widespread microvascular cutaneous vasodilatation. Results showed that a 15- to 30-minute period of TENS-induced vasodilatation produced a prolonged vascular response with a duration of several hours or longer, potentially indicating the release of a long-lasting neurohumoral substance or metabolite. Kaada attributed the effects to three possible modes of action: inhibition of the sympathetic fibers supplied to skin vessels, release of an active vasodilator substance, vasoactive intestinal polypeptide (VIP), or a segmental axon reflex responsible for affecting local circulation. The Kaada studies included reports of clinical results wherein patients served as their own controls of stimulation-promoted healing in cases of chronic ulceration of various etiologies.[51]

Edema reduction under the negative pole is attributed to a phenomenon called cataphoresis.[33] Cataphoresis is the movement of nondissociated colloid molecules, such as droplets of fat, albumin, particles of starch, blood cells, bacteria, and other single cells, all of which have an electrical charge due to the absorption of ions, under the influence of a direct current toward the cathode. Ross and Segal[33] claimed benefit in treating postoperative edema, healing, and pain with HVPC. Effects of direct current on edema were attributed to cataphoresis based on the effects of direct current. They formulated a protocol based on the use of the cathode to reduce edema. Albumin is a colloidal protein found in blood and is negatively charged and is repelled by negative polarity, causing a fluid shift and thereby a reduction of edema. Several attempts have been made to learn whether the same effect occurs with HVPC.[12,32] Reed[32] reported reduction of posttraumatic edema in hamsters following HVPC and attributed the effect to reduced microvessel leakage. Posttraumatic edema was curbed in frogs treated with HVPC when the cathode was used. There was no effect if the anode was applied. Treatment effect was significant from the end of the first treatment session until the end of data recording 17 hours later.[31] A similar study using HVPC on rat hind paws found significant treatment effects after the second 20-minute treatment with the cathode.[28] More investigation is needed to verify this phenomenon in humans.

Debridement and Thrombosis

Review of the research is a guide for the clinician and provides evidence to support a protocol for wound healing initiated with the negative pole at the wound site. Debridement is facilitated if the tissue is solubilized or liquefied such as occurs with enzymatic debriding agents or autolysis. For example, necrotic tissues are made up of coalesced blood elements. ES using negative current can solubilize this clotted blood.[34–36]

Reperfusion of tissues is rapidly followed by autolytic debridement. Increased blood flow, stimulated by electrical stimulation at the negative pole, has been attributed to having this effect. When the clinical studies are compared, it becomes clear that the negative pole has been used to initiate treatment in all reported controlled clinical studies. Many of the wounds in the treatment groups included necrotic wounds.

The positive electrode has been found to induce clumping of leukocytes and forming of thromboses in the small vessels. These clumping and thrombotic effects can be reversed with the negative electrode.[13] This may explain a clinical observation, where hematoma and hemorrhaging at the wound margin or on granulation tissue are dissolved and reabsorbed following application of HVPC with the negative pole. Hemorrhagic material goes on to necrosis if not dissolved and reabsorbed quickly. Perhaps continuous use of positive polarity produces the clumping of leukocytes and also explains why a protocol of intermittently changing polarity restarts the healing process. These are critical issues that need to be researched.

Antibacterial Effects

Because infection is a contributing factor in chronic wound healing, methods to control infection are of clinical importance. Bactericidal effects have been attributed to electrical stimulation. Research suggests that there is evidence to support this theory. In vitro and in vivo studies applying direct current have both been shown to inhibit bacterial growth rates for organisms commonly found in chronic wounds at the cathode.[41,42] Passage of positive current (anode) through silver wire electrodes was found to be bactericidal to gram-negative bacteria in wounds and inhibitory to gram-positive wound bacteria.[52] At low levels of amplitude, 0.4 to 4 μA, there were negligible bactericidal effects.[41] Kincaid and Lavoie[43] tested in vitro stimulation, using HVPC at the cathode and anode, and Szuminsky et al.[44] tested HVPC in vitro at the cathode. Both studies found inhibition of *Staphylococcus aureus*, *Escherichia coli*, and *Pseudomonas aeruginosa*. However, the amplitude of the stimulation reported by Kincaid and Lavoie was at an amplitude of 250 V, and Szuminsky et al. reported 500 V. Patients would likely find this voltage amplitude intolerable. Since there is inconsistency in these findings and since there are no chemical changes (acidity or alkalinity) measured under the electrodes of high-voltage pulsed current, it is not clear whether the

antibacterial effects are due to polarity or another mechanism. For example, increased subcutaneous oxygen was found under the anode when a microamperage current (0.3 Hz) was passed through the electrode.[38] It is possible that the oxygen rather than the polarity is the variable that is responsible for the bactericidal effects on pathogens.

Oxygen

Oxygen is critical for wound healing. Constant delivery of oxygen is required to meet high metabolic demands of the tissues, oxidative killing of infectious organisms, protein and collagen synthesis, and hydroxylation of proline to make useful collagen. Blood flow is the mechanism of oxygen transport to the tissues. Treatment interventions that increase blood flow consequently will enhance oxygen delivery to the tissues and improve healing. Electrical stimulation may be one way of enhancing oxygen and nutrient enrichment to the tissues. Increasing oxygenation could be an important reason to use ES. Lack of adequate oxygen could be a partial explanation for difficulty in healing diabetic ulcers.[53] Baker et al.[54,55] measured oxygen enrichment to the cells of wound repair in a study of age-matched older normal adults and diabetic subjects. Oximetry readings of the partial pressure of transcutaneous oxygen (tcpO$_2$) were taken 30 minutes prior to stimulation, during 30 minutes of stimulation, and 30 minutes after stimulation. The electrical stimulation waveforms used were monophasic paired spikes with negative polarity and a compensated monophasic waveform. Both waveforms were introduced with the cathode over the wound. The older normal adults also showed higher tcpO$_2$ levels at the end of 30 minutes of stimulation regardless of waveform used. However, there were differences in response time for the diabetics. The normal adults showed increased oxygen levels earlier in the treatment period than did the diabetics. Diabetic subjects showed measurable but not significant increases in tcpO$_2$ at the end of the 30 minutes of stimulation but did show significant increases 30 minutes after cessation of the stimulation. Increases occurred with both waveforms, but no change occurred when submotor or trace muscle contraction was elicited with the compensated monophasic waveform. For some reason the trace muscle contraction blunted the tcpO$_2$ response in the diabetics. The same effects were found for both waveforms and with stimulation by either the positive or the negative pole.

In another study of diabetics, Baker et al.[39] compared the effects of a monophasic paired spike waveform using both negative and positive polarity with a symmetric biphasic waveform. Transcutaneous oxygen pressure from baseline 30 minutes prior to stimulation, during 30 minutes of stimulation, and 30 minutes after treatment were compared. The findings showed that the tcpO$_2$ levels were significantly increased regardless of waveform or polarity. Increases were present at the end of the stimulation period and continued to rise during the next 30 minutes after stimulation. Therefore, Baker et al.[39] concluded that the mechanism of action of ES on increasing transcutaneous oxygen was unrelated to polarity and did not require any net ion flow. Byl et al.[56] found that when supplemental oxygen was given by mask prior to and during microamperage stimulation (100 μA for 45 minutes), there were significant increases in subcutaneous oxygen measured. Maximal oxygen saturation may be necessary prior to and during ES in order to facilitate the dissociation of oxygen from the hemoglobin.[56]

In transferring technology from the lab bench to the bed, the physical therapist could take the information from these three research studies and formulate and test a protocol for wound healing for diabetics. For example, nasal supplementation of oxygen could be provided during ES treatment for patients with diabetes to accelerate the oxygen uptake. A trial to evaluate the difference in wound healing outcomes for diabetics treated with ES while breathing room air or supplemental oxygen could yield useful clinical data from these types of studies. The results would be development of a new clinical protocol for treating diabetic wounds.

Pain

Noninvasive electrical stimulators that stimulate sensory nerves can be classified as TENS.[57] A large body of literature supports the use of TENS for both acute and chronic pain management. Techniques for pain modulation can be used along with the wound healing protocols. For example, one electrode may be placed on the painful area, which includes the wound and adjacent tissues, and the indifferent electrode over the related spinal nerve. The electrodes can also be bracketed proximal and distal to the areas of pain around the wound, such as with a bipolar technique described later in this chapter.[58] Pain management would be a good reason to use electrodes of equal size so that there would be sufficient current density at the dispersive electrode.

Scar Formation

In animal and human studies, flaps and grafts treated with monophasic pulsed current electrical stimulation heal without ischemia and result in flatter, thinner scars than in controls.[19,22]

CLINICAL STUDIES

Since the 1960s a series of clinical trials has been undertaken to evaluate the effect of electrical stimulation on wound healing. The early studies are classics in this field.

Low Voltage Pulsed Microamperage Direct Current Studies

Direct current was used in three clinical studies. Wolcott et al.[53], Gault and Gatens[59], and Carley and Wainapel[60] treated ischemic and indolent ulcers. In all three studies a positive (anode) polarity was used after a period of 3 or more days at the cathode. The polarity was reversed every day or every 3 days if wound healing did not progress. Rationale for cathode application was the solubilization of necrotic tissue[16] and bactericidal effects.[41,42] The first two studies used an amplitude of 200 to 800 μA and the later study 300 to 700 μA. Duration of treatment was very long: 2 hours, two or three times per day, or 42 hours per week for the first two studies, and 20 hours per week for the later study. A combined total of 163 patients were treated and 29 served as controls. In most cases the patient served as his or her own control. Mean healing times reported were 9.6 weeks, 4.7 weeks, and 5.0, respectively, for the three studies. The difference in healing time between these three studies is not clear. Perhaps in the Wolcott et al. study the wounds were more extensive.

Microcurrent stimulation has been studied in animal models in which current was applied only one or two times per day for 30 minutes for 1 to 2 weeks; no significant clinical effects were demonstrated on wound healing.[38,62] In another study, there were significant increases in subcutaneous oxygen measurements when supplemental oxygen was given by mask during the MENS stimulation.[56] There was no acceleration in healing.

Modified Biphasic Stimulation Study

Barron et al.[61] reported a study of six patients with pressure ulcers who were treated three times a week for 3 weeks for a total of nine treatments with microcurrent stimulation. The waveform was a modified biphasic square wave. The treatment characteristics were 600 μA, 50 V, and 0.5 Hz. The electrode probes were placed 2 cm away from the edge of the ulcer and then moved circumferentially around the ulcer. Each successive placement of the probes was 2 cm from the prior placement. In this small study, two ulcers healed 100%, three healed 99%, and one decreased in size 55%.

High-Voltage Pulsed Current Studies

Three controlled clinical studies have been reported by Kloth and Feedar,[63] Griffin et al.,[64] and Unger et al.[65] In the study by Kloth and Feedar,[63] wounds had a mean healing time of 7.3 weeks, and 100% of the treatment group healed. Unger et al.[65] reported on a controlled study of nine subjects in the treatment group and eight controls. The average wound size in the treatment group was 460 mm^2, compared with the control group whose average wound size was 118.5 mm^2. Mean healing time was 7.3 weeks for the treatment group, with 88.9% completely healed. Griffin et al.[64] had demonstrated an 80% reduction in size in 4 weeks, but ulcers were not treated until healed. Unger[66] reported an uncontrolled study using HVPC treatment for 223 wounds. The mean healing times for the 223 wounds in the uncontrolled study was 10.9 weeks. In all studies, the treatment frequency was five to seven times per week for 45 to 60 minutes. All treatment protocols began with negative polarity. After the wounds were clean of infection, polarity was changed to positive except in the study by Griffin et al.,[64] where the polarity was kept at negative for the 4-week study period (Table 16–3).

Two additional published uncontrolled studies included 30 patients. Alon et al.[17] used positive polarity and stimulated wounds three times a week for 1 hour; 12 of the 15 or 80% of the ulcers treated healed. One patient died, one did not respond, and the ulcer in one decreased significantly in size but did not heal in 21.6 weeks. Akers and Gabrielson[67] published a study that compared (1) HVPC direct application to the wound; (2) application of HVPC using the whirlpool as a large electrode; and (3) whirlpool alone. The direct application of the active electrode to the wound site had the best outcome, followed by HVPC using the whirlpool as an electrode. Whirlpool alone was the least effective.

Low-Voltage Pulsed Electrical Current Studies

Two controlled clinical trials with low-voltage pulsed current, labeled PES, were located in the literature. Gentzkow et al.[13] reported a study of 40 ulcers in 37 patients. Nineteen pressure ulcers were stimulated and 21 were sham stimulated. The trial lasted for 4 weeks. The treated ulcers healed

Clinical Wisdom:
Best Method for Effective HVPC Treatment

Apply HVPC directly to the wound for best expected outcome. Conducting current to the tissues during whirlpool is not recommended because it is less effective, and some clinicians report that stimulator leads have become entangled in the agitator. There have even been stories of stimulators falling into the water.

more than twice as much as the sham-stimulated ulcers (49.8% versus 23.4%), healing at a rate of 12.5% per week compared with 5.8% for the sham-stimulated group. Crossover results for 15 of the 19 sham-treated ulcers showed a fourfold greater healing during the 4 weeks of stimulation compared to 4 weeks of sham treatment. This difference was statistically significant.[13] Feedar et al.[68] published a study on pressure ulcers. The 61 patients served as their own controls. The treatment phase of the study was preceded by a 4-week control phase of optimal nonelectrically stimulated wound care. Only the stage III or IV ulcers with need of surgical debridement, necrotic/purulent drainage, or exudate seropurulent drainage that did not improve during the control phase went on to the treatment phase. After 4 weeks of treatment 58.8% of the wounds had improved. After an average of 8.4 weeks, 23% completely healed and 82% improved significantly.

Biphasic Stimulation Studies

There are reports in the literature by Kaada,[51] Lundeberg et al.,[69] Stefanovska et al.[70] and Baker et al.[71,72] of clinical trials of wound healing with biphasic waveforms. Kaada[51] and Lundeberg et al.[69] each used biphasic symmetric wave-

Table 16–3 HVPC Clinical Studies

Researchers	No. of Patients	% Healed	Mean Time to Heal
Alon et al.[17]	15 Treated, 0 controls (diabetic)	80%	2.6 Months (10.4 weeks)
Kloth and Feedar[63]	9 Treated, 7 controls, 3 crossovers (mixed wound etiology)	100%	7.3 Weeks
Griffin et al.[64]	8 Treated, 9 controls (pressure ulcers)	80% Reduction in size	4-Week treatment period
Unger[66]	223 Treated, 0 controls	89.7%	10.85 Weeks (54.25 days)
Unger et al.[65]	9 Treated, 8 controls (pressure ulcers)	88.9%	7.3 Weeks (51.2 days)

forms with significant improvement in both ulcer area and healed ulcers. Kaada[51] reported results of TENS on 10 subjects, who served as their own controls, with recalcitrant ulcers of different etiologies. Stimulation was provided indirectly over the web of the thumb daily during three 30-minute sessions with rests of 45 minutes between for a total of 1½ hours stimulation. Stimulation was below visible muscle contraction. Lundeberg et al.[69] performed a controlled study on 64 patients with chronic diabetic ulcers due to venous stasis. All patients received standard treatment with paste bandage in addition to the sham or TENS treatment. Asymmetric biphasic stimulation was determined to produce significant wound healing effects, whereas the other waveforms did not increase the healing rate. The study by Stefanovska et al.[70] compared direct current and asymmetric biphasic current. In another study, Baker et al. compared asymmetric biphasic, symmetric biphasic, and microcurrent (DC). The asymmetric biphasic waveform has a potential for some polar effect that should not be discounted. The polar effect may explain why it was more effective than the symmetric biphasic waveform. However, another likely explanation of the effects are stimulation of neural mechanisms that effect healing.[71] In all of the studies except Kaada, stimulation was delivered to the skin at the wound perimeter rather than into the wound bed. An advantage of the perimeter stimulation was less disruption of the wound bed, less cross-contamination of the wound, and less interference with the dressing. Benefits were found in patients with spinal cord injury who had pressure ulcers[70,71] and patients with diabetic ulcers including those with peripheral neuropathy[72] and venous stasis.[69] Table 16–5 shows protocols used in these studies.

Summary

Electrical stimulation studies have varied from continuous waveform application with direct current to pulsed short-duration monophasic pulses to biphasic pulses. What is known and acknowledged is that electrical stimulation seems to have positive effects on wound healing or on the components necessary for wound healing (eg, blood flow and oxygen uptake, DNA and protein synthesis), but there is still ambiguity about the type of electrical stimulation characteristics that are most important or critical. For instance, polarity has played an important role in protocols used even though the likelihood of polarity effects of currents with pulses of very short duration is questionable. One possible reason for the wound healing effects of electrical stimulation with any type of current may result from the effect of low-level sensory stimulation on the peripheral nerves, which is not wholly dependent on the polar nature of electrical current. Kaada[50] describes effects that include inhibition of sympathetic in-

put to superficial vessels, release of an active vasodilator, and axon-reflex stimulation.

CHOOSING AN INTERVENTION: CLINICAL REASONING

Applying Theory and Science to Clinical Decision Making

The previous section evaluated the efficacy of electrical stimulation on many components of healing, as well as clinical trials of wound healing. The studies basically looked at four components:

1. Galvanotaxis and effect at the cellular level
2. Circulatory effects
3. Effects on pain
4. Effects on repair, regeneration, and completeness of healing

The clinician should consider these variables when selecting ES intervention and choosing a protocol.

The specific medical diagnosis may not be a significant factor in selecting ES for wound healing. The medical diagnosis of patients in the studies included burns, pressure ulcers, diabetic ulcers (vascular and neuropathic), vascular ulcers, and vasculitic ulcers. The surgical wounds included in the studies were skin flaps, donor sites, and dehiscence. Acute wounds were also included. Electrical stimulation had demonstrated efficacy for wound healing across diagnosis and pathogenesis. Reported effects were related to the stimulation of the mechanisms of healing at the cellular, tissue, and/or systems level. Healing follows a predictable pattern regardless of etiology; what affects the outcome are the intrinsic, extrinsic, and iatrogenic factors that alter healing described in Chapter 2. The physical therapist intervenes in wound management specifically to facilitate the functional mechanisms of healing. Electrical stimulation is just one of the interventions that can be used.

Wound attributes that have positively responded to electrical stimulation were necrotic tissue, inflammation, wound contraction, infection, and wound resurfacing. Wounds of all depths from partial thickness to full thickness and deeper have been successfully treated with electrical stimulation (eg, stage II to stage IV pressure ulcers). Wounds have traditionally been classified by medical diagnosis, by depth of tissue disruption, and/or by phase of wound healing. Depth of tissue disruption is a description of the tissue loss and function that is broader and more generic than that in the medical diagnosis system. The depth of tissue disruption system can be used for wounds regardless of the wound etiology. Classification by phase of wound healing is also independent of the medical diagnosis. Change in wound phase is an outcome of the process of wound healing.

The typical subjects selected for clinical trials with electrical stimulation had nonconforming wound healing with long chronicity. The chronic wounds were the reason for referral for electrical stimulation. There is significant scientific evidence to support that early intervention with externally applied electrical currents will also accelerate healing for the acute healthy wound. Early intervention with electrical stimulation could be a useful method to prevent chronicity and return the individual earlier to a functional status. This is consistent with other areas of physical therapy practice, such as stroke and low back rehabilitation, where early intervention can reduce the development of costly chronic health problems.

In summary, selection of ES for wound healing is not dependent on the medical diagnosis. Select ES intervention and treatment characteristics when there are impairments to the systems that interfere with healing at one or more levels: cellular, tissue, or organ. Functional loss at any of these levels suggests that the wound will not or has not healed with the current level of intervention. The reason for referral to the physical therapist is for the development of another strategy to facilitate healing. The use of externally applied currents is one such strategy. The type of stimulation that has been most consistently evaluated clinically and found to be efficacious is high-voltage pulsed current (see Table 16–4).

Table 16–4 Appropriate Wound Descriptors for High-Voltage Electrical Stimulation

Wound Classification	HVPC
Level of tissue disruption	Superficial, partial thickness, full thickness, subcutaneous and deep tissues
Etiologies/diagnostic groups	Burns, neuropathic ulcers, pressure ulcers, surgical wounds, vascular ulcers
Wound phase diagnosis	Inflammation phase: acute, chronic, absent Proliferation phase: acute, chronic, absent Epithelialization phase: acute, chronic, absent Remodeling phase: collagen organization
Age	Older than 3 years

Precautions

Signs of adverse effects using electrical stimulation for wound healing were evaluated in the various clinical trials. The only two adverse signs were some skin irritation or tingling under the electrodes in a few cases and pain in some other cases. Patients with severe peripheral vascular occlusive disease, particularly in the lower extremity, may experience some increased pain with electrical stimulations, usually described as throbbing. An alternative acupuncture protocol has been suggested in these cases: placing the active electrode on the web space of the hand between the thumb and first finger instead of over the ulcer located on the leg.[50,51] Young children under the age of 3 years should not be considered candidates for intervention with ES. Healing mechanisms for this group are not well understood and, although there are no known adverse effects, the benefits are not defined.

Contraindications

Contraindications for the use of electrical stimulation as described are from various sources and fall into the following categories: (1) when stimulation of cell proliferation is contraindicated (eg, malignancy); (2) where there is evidence of osteomyelitis; (3) where there are metal ions; (4) where the placement of electrodes for treatment with electrical stimulation could adversely affect a reflex center; or (5) where electrical current could affect the function of an electronic implant.[16,58] Carefully evaluate the medical history and review body systems when considering candidates for use of this intervention.

Presence of Malignancy

When there is a malignancy in the area to be treated, electrical stimulation should not be used (eg, malignant melanoma, basal cell carcinoma). Electrical stimulation stimulates cell proliferation and could lead to uncontrolled cell growth. If the malignancy is distant from the wound (eg, breast cancer in a patient with a pressure ulcer on an ankle), however, local use of electrical stimulation would be a precaution, but not a contraindication, although this is not consistent with required manufacturer labeling.

Active Osteomyelitis

Stimulation of tissue growth with electrical stimulation may cause superficial covering of an area of osteomyelitis. This could blind the site from observation. If the medical record documents a history of a bone infection that should trigger an investigation of the current status of the infection. It is not unusual for the osteomyelitis to be resolved but not to be noted in the medical record.

Clinical Wisdom: *Identification of Osteomyelitis*

If a wound penetrates to the bone, as determined by inserting a probe, it must be assumed that osteomyelitis is present and the patient should not be treated with electrical stimulation. An immediate referral to a surgeon for evaluation[73] must be initiated.

Topical Substances Containing Metal Ions

Topical substances containing metal ions (eg, povidone-iodine, zinc, Mercurochrome, and silver sulfadiazine that may be used as part of the wound treatment regimen) should be removed before the application of ES. Direct-current electrical stimulation has the ability to transfer ions into the tissues by iontophoresesis. Heavy metal ions may have toxic properties when introduced into the body. If removal of the topical substance is not appropriate, however, electrical stimulation could be used on other areas of the skin where the topical agent has not been applied.

Electronic Implants

Demand type cardiac pacemakers and other electrical implants raise concerns regarding the use of electrical current. Electrical stimulation is contraindicated *over* electrical implants because the current and electromagnetic fields could disrupt the function of the implant. Safe application of TENS in 10 patients with 20 different cardiac pacemakers at four sites (lumbar area, cervical spine, left leg, and lower arm area ipsilateral to the pacemaker) without ill effects was reported by Rasmussen et al.[74] Therefore, using electrical stimulation locally in an area away from the implant could be done safely, since it is unlikely to transmit to the electronic implant.

Natural Reflexes

There are areas of the body that are particularly sensitive to any stimulation (eg, carotid sinus, heart, parasympathetic nerves, ganglion, laryngeal muscles, phrenic nerve). Sensory levels of electrical stimulation might create a vasospasm or some type of vasoconstriction that could lead to a vasovagal response and other neural responses that could interfere with the function of vital centers and be harmful to the patient. Thus, ES is contraindicated to run current through the upper chest and anterior neck.

Equipment

Regulatory Approval

Under what is called premarket approval (PMA), manufacturing companies are allowed to make claims of effectiveness and safety about medical devices. PMA requires extensive clinical trials, typically 2,000 to 3,000 cases for approval. "Off label" means treatment not approved by the Food and Drug Administration (FDA). No electrical stimulators have received PMA by the FDA for wound healing. Externally applied currents for wound healing are considered as "off label" use at this time. Off label use for medical devices is an accepted and common practice in medicine as innovative therapy, as long as the participants are not closely associated with the manufacturer.[75] For example, the "on label" uses for neuromuscular stimulators, such as HVPC, include application for increased circulation, relaxation of muscle spasms, and muscle reeducation. The on label use for TENS is pain management.

Expect to find an FDA-mandated instruction manual accompanying each electrical stimulator. Listed in the manual are labeled indications, contraindications, warnings, and precautions (Exhibit 16–1). The FDA indications and contraindications do not exactly match what is described in the previous text. The physical therapist must be aware of these limitations when selecting a protocol with electrical stimulation and use thoughtful clinical judgment.

Exhibit 16–1 FDA Indications and Contraindications for Electrical Stimulation

---

FDA Indications for Electrical Stimulation

- Relaxation of muscle spasms
- Prevention or retardation of disuse atrophy
- Increasing local blood circulation
- Muscle reeducation
- Immediate postsurgical stimulation of calf muscles to prevent venous thrombosis
- Maintaining or increasing range of motion
- Pain

FDA Contraindications for Electrical Stimulation

- Should not be used on patients with demand type cardiac pacemakers
- Should not be used on persons known to have cancerous lesions
- Should not be used for symptomatic pain relief unless etiology is established or unless a pain syndrome has been diagnosed
- Should not be used over pregnant uterus
- Electrode placements must be avoided that apply current to the carotid sinus region (anterior neck) or transcerebrally (through the head)

Devices

Electrical stimulators have three basic components: a source of power, an oscillator circuit, and an output amplifier. There are two size ranges: clinical models and portable models. The latter may be as small as a beeper. Two basic power sources are used: batteries and house line current. Batteries are used in portable stimulators. House line current is usually used in the clinic setting. Batteries need to be fully charged to deliver the output expected. A spare battery should be kept on hand. Rechargeable batteries may be more cost effective than single-use types. House line current is usually available.

Many electrical stimulators now use microprocessors with a choice of several waveforms and pulse rates and even include preset protocols for wound treatment. The clinician should not assume that this is the "correct" protocol for the wound. It is the clinician's responsibility to know the rationale for protocol characteristics and what the settings are on the chosen stimulator. Most programs allow clinicians to override the preset programs.

Select a stimulator based on the available waveform, pulse characteristic, and ability to adjust intensity and polarity. A desirable stimulator should allow for flexibility to set up and deliver a variety of protocols based on changes dictated by clinical trials and current concepts of physiologic rationale. Manufacturers are an important source of helpful information about the characteristics of their devices.

Testing Equipment

Meters are very useful to the clinician to check on the current flow between two electrodes. Use the device meter if available; if no meter is available on the stimulator, go to other options. Patient sensation is always a good indicator, if the patient can give a report. The use of electrical stimulation for wound healing is usually done at a sensory level, but many of the patients are insensate or unable to communicate, or the wounds are deep and below the level of sensation and the patient will not be able to indicate if the current is not felt. Another test method is to position the dispersive/indifferent electrode over a muscle motor point to see whether there is a muscle twitch or tingling under the electrode. The electrode pads can be checked by the physical therapist by placing a wet contact on both positive and negative electrodes and then resting the forearms on each electrode pad. Ask a colleague to turn up the device until a sensation of prickling is felt.

Electrical stimulation equipment should have regular calibration checks. In between checks, a multimeter can be used for periodic spot checking to see that the equipment is functioning properly. Multimeters, which are a combination of volt-ohm-milliammeter, have the ability to determine current flow. They are inexpensive, easy to use, and readily available. A broken lead wire, weak battery, or resistant electrode may not be apparent because the stimulation in the wound bed is below the level of sensation or the patient is insensate or cognitively impaired and cannot report changes in sensation. Checking for good electrical conduction is the responsibility of the clinician.

Electrodes

Electrode Materials

The electrode is the contact point between the electrical circuit and the body. The electrode must be a good conductor and provide very little resistance to the current. All metals are good conductors of electricity. Aluminum foil is an excellent conductor to use for electrodes (Figures 16–7A and 16–7B). It is nontoxic, inexpensive, disposable, and conformable and can be sized as needed. Carbon-impregnated electrodes are sold to go with most electrotherapeutic devices. They are designed for multiple uses and are relatively inexpensive, but they need to be disinfected between use even if restricted to a single patient. They are nonconformable and will become resistive over time as they lose carbon and accumulate body oils and cleaning products.

Electrode Arrangements

Size and Shape of Electrodes. Size, shape, and arrangement of electrodes affect the current density and depth. Current density is the amount of current flow per unit area. Current density is a measure of the quantity of charged ions moving through a specific cross-sectional area of body tissue. The unit of measurement is milliamperes per square centimeter. This measure will affect the reaction of the tissues being stimulated. In general, the greater the current density the greater the effect on the tissue biology. Two determinants of current density are *size* of the electrode and the *amplitude* of the current applied.[76] Small electrodes concentrate the current for local effects more than larger electrodes, which tend to disperse the charge. Also, the farther apart the electrodes, the deeper the current penetrates.

Active and Dispersive Electrode. The small electrode is commonly referred to as the active electrode and the large electrode as the dispersive electrode. If the two are nearly equal size or have equal current, the current will be divided between the two, with the current density at the two treatment sites the same. If the two are not of equal size, the larger electrode will have less current density than the smaller electrode. A rule of thumb is that the combined area of the active electrodes should not exceed the overall area of the dispersive electrode. Brown[77] found that the effects of ES extends and affects events 2 to 3 cm beyond the edge of the elec-

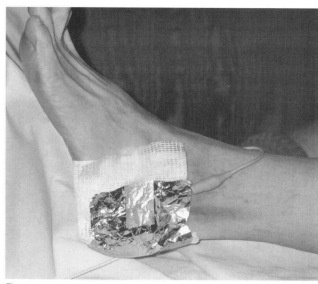

A

B

Figure 16–7 A and **B,** Aluminum foil electrode with alligator clip.

trodes. Therefore, avoid placement of the active and dispersive electrodes so that they touch each other. Allow at least 4 to 5 cm spacing between them to avoid the possibility that the wound is receiving stimulation from both poles (Figure 16–9A).

In clinical practice, at times it is necessary to treat multiple wound sites with a single electrical circuit using one or two bifurcated lead wires (Figure 16–8). The advantage of bifurcation is that more sites can be treated simultaneously. A disadvantage is that although the same current passes through all the bifurcated leads, the physiologic responses may vary significantly because the subliminal stimulation is perceived under one electrode and the sensory stimulation under the other. Another disadvantage is that if there is a difference in the total surface area of the electrode(s) connected to one lead compared with the other, the stimulation will be stronger under the electrode with the smaller total surface area because there will be greater current density under that electrode. Often, the wound sites are different sizes. The depth and undermining may make the effective electrode size of a small wound larger than the surface area appears. The physical therapist must consider these physical properties when planning treatment and correct them. At this time it is not known what is the optimal current density or the best electrode size to choose.[57] It may be prudent to use a stimulator with two channels or have two treatment sessions if there are multiple wounds with a large discrepancy in wound sizes.

Dispersive Pad Placement. Attempts have been made to apply scientific findings to electrode placement. Most

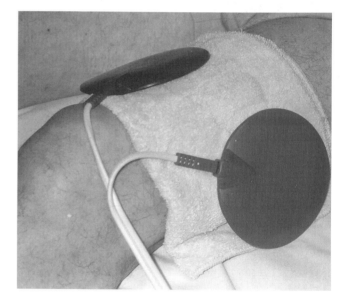

Figure 16–8 Bifurcated leads.

studies use the active electrode for direct application (Figure 16–9A) to the site,[63–66] but some use the bipolar technique (Figure 16–9B), at the wound edges.[69–72] The dispersive electrode placement has more variation. For example, in two similar studies, the dispersive electrode was placed differently. In one study,[63] it was placed cephalad on the neural axis, while in the second study it was placed 30.5 cm from the wound.[68] One study on spinal cord–injured patients

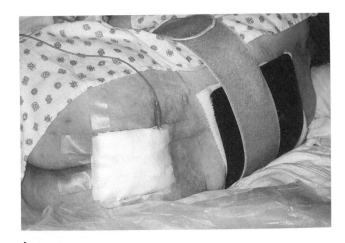

A

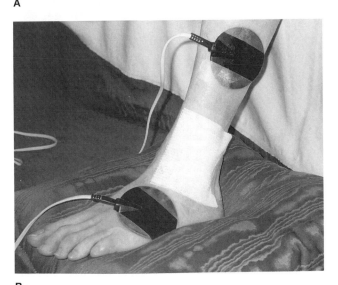

B

Figure 16–9 A, Monopolar technique. **B,** Bipolar technique.

with pressure ulcers in the pelvic region used a protocol where the dispersive was always placed on the thigh. Another method is to place the dispersive proximal to the wound.[65,66] Current thinking suggests that the dispersive should be moved around the wound to induce the current to enter the wound from different sides. At this time there is not an established proven method that has been shown to change the effect of the treatment. All reported treatment methods had statistically significant treatment results.

Monopolar Technique

With the monopolar technique, an electrode is placed to control the polarity at the wound site. Usually, one active electrode is placed on a wet conductive medium in the wound bed and the dispersive electrode, in a wet conductive medium at a distance from the wound site, is placed on the in-

tact skin (Figure 16–9A). Polarity for the two electrodes will be opposite. Current will flow through the intervening tissues between the two electrode poles. The current under the active electrode is the polarity selected on the stimulator. As stated before, the farther apart the two electrode poles the deeper the current will flow into the intervening tissues. Current will flow through the tissues by following the path with the lowest resistance, which is usually through the muscles and nerves and deeper tissues. Increasing the distance between the electrodes is a good position choice if wounds are deep and extend into underlying tissues, such as stage III and stage IV pressure ulcers, and/or having tunneling and undermined spaces.

The electrodes can be arranged to target the stimulation to specific tissue sites. Remember to visualize the path of the current flow when placing the dispersive pad. The poles are usually set up in parallel fashion enabling current to flow between the positive and negative electrodes no matter how many electrodes are used at either pole. When the surface area of the electrodes is unequal, the current density will not be the same under the two sites. Current density may also vary according to the impedance of the intervening tissues and the size of the electrodes. Impedance is the opposition to current flow within the circuit. Different body tissues have different impedances to current flow. Skin, bone, and fat have high impedance and are poor electrical conductors. When there is a break in the skin, however, there is a significant lowering of the skin impedance to current. Techniques to reduce skin impedance include abrasion of the skin surface to remove the hard layers of keratin on the surface, tissue warming, and hydration. High-voltage currents of approximately 100 V have the demonstrated ability to cause sudden, spontaneous breakdown in skin impedance.[76] Because of the fluid in muscles and blood vessels, these tissues are good electrical conductors, and it can be expected that current will flow directly through them with little impedance.

It is important to understand these principles of tissue impedance and current flow and then apply them correctly to derive the optimal benefits from treatment with electrical stimulation. For example, if the dispersive electrode is to be placed on the back, place it *below* the scapula to avoid the impedance to current flow by the bone. Patients with thick layers of callus on the feet will have high impedance to current. Paring the callus should precede ES treatment, or find another placement where the electrode does not lie on callus. A good placement for the dispersive electrode when treating wounds of the lower leg or foot is the muscular tissue of the thigh. One suggestion is to switch the dispersive electrode for each treatment so that the current flows into the wound from each side of the wound through different surrounding tissues and through a different wound edge.[77,78] Not only the active electrodes can be bifurcated. The dispersive electrode can also be bifurcated. This allows use of smaller electrode pads that can be made to conform to smaller body parts such as an arm or a lower leg (see Figure 16–8).

Clinical Wisdom:
Enlarging the Dispersive Electrode

If the dispersive electrode area size needs to be increased, this can be accomplished by using a wet washcloth wrapped around a limb or extending a wet washcloth out from the edges of the dispersive electrode to cover a larger skin area. If the wound area size is nearly as large as or larger than the skin area under the dispersive electrode, it will be more comfortable for the patient but the intensity of the current or the treatment time may need to be increased to deliver the same total amount of current, but at a lower current density.

Bipolar Technique

The definition of bipolar technique is the placement of the two leads with their respective electrodes on either side of the target area. This confines the stimulation to the area associated with the clinical problem.[57] For instance, the two electrodes with opposite polarity may both be placed on the intact skin adjacent to the wound site so that the current passes between the electrodes through the wound tissue. The closer together the more superficial the effect; this is a reasonable choice for superficial or partial-thickness wound disruptions. The bipolar technique is used with either monophasic or biphasic waveforms. An application of the bipolar technique is to place the electrodes on either side of the wound, or place the treatment electrode in the wound and use four bifurcated dispersive leads connected to electrodes placed around the wound so that current will flow through the wound from all sides at once. Finally, one active electrode could be placed in the middle of the wound and a dispersive electrode fashioned like a donut, made from aluminum foil, slipped over the treatment electrode with an intervening space between so that stimulation would flow into the wound bed from all sides of the wound edges simultaneously. The foil electrode would connect to the dispersive lead with an alligator clip just like the active leads (see Figure 16–9B).

WOUND HEALING PROTOCOL SELECTION FOR ELECTRICAL STIMULATION

Aspects

There are many different ES protocols for wound healing. This section first describes some of the aspects of the protocols described, including electrode polarity, rationale, frequency, and amplitude as described by the researchers.

Polarity

Polarity must be considered when using galvanic and monophasic pulsed current. Electrode polarity varies depending on the protocol selected. Most researchers studying electrical stimulation for wound healing start their protocols with the negative pole as the active electrode and then change the polarity after a period of treatment. Griffin et al.[64] maintained negative polarity to the wound site throughout the assessment period of 4 weeks. The other researchers recommend using negative polarity for 3 to 7 days and then changing polarity. Another recommendation is to use negative polarity until the wound is cleansed of necrotic tissue and drainage is serosanguineous, then continue with the negative polarity for 3 additional days or change to the positive pole.[65,66] Some researchers suggest that the polarity should be changed back to negative for 3 days when the wound plateaus. Another method is to change the polarity every 3 days until the wound is healed to a partial-thickness depth. Once that outcome is achieved, change the polarity by alternating daily until the wound is closed. Several animal studies demonstrate better healing when polarity is initiated at the negative pole and then switched to positive.[20,21,79] See earlier sections on theory and science for additional rationale for selecting polarity.

Rationale

Usually the negative electrode is used as the active electrode when infection is suspected. The polarity is often switched back and forth during the course of healing. Electrode polarity switching accommodates the variability in the skin battery potentials that occurs during the course of healing. Thus, electrode polarity may need to be alternated during treatment to achieve an optimal rate of healing. Additional research is needed to ascertain whether wound healing with electrical stimulation is dependent on matching treatment electrode polarity with fluctuations in wound injury potential polarity.[63] So far, studies have not reported on this important issue. Still, the idea of polarity switching has some demonstrated merit.

Biphasic Protocols

Protocols demonstrating significant benefit for wound healing with biphasic current are now appearing regularly in the literature.[59,69–72] The five studies reported in this chapter have similar protocols, except that the two studies by the Baker et al.[71,72] research group found that the best outcome was achieved when the biphasic waveform was asymmetric and biased toward the negative pole. Biphasic treatment protocols are shown in Table 16–5.

Table 16–5 Biphasic Treatment Protocols

Parameters	Kaada[51]	Lundeberg et al.[69]	Stefanovska et al.[70]	Baker et al.[71,72]
Phase duration	Not reported	1 msec	0.25	100 µsec
Pulse rate	100 Hz	80 Hz	40 Hz	50 Hz
Waveform	Symmetrical	Symmetrical	Asymmetrical, charge balanced	Asymmetrical
Amplitude	15–30 mA below contraction	15–25 mA below contraction	Below contraction	Below contraction
Frequency and duration	Daily; three 30-min sessions (off 45 min between sessions)	Twice daily for 20 min	Daily for 2 hours	Daily; three 30-min sessions (off between sessions)
Location	Web between 1st and 2nd metacarpal bones	Wound edge	Wound edge	Less than 1 cm from edge; proximal and distal to ulcer
Patient population	Multiple diagnoses	Diabetics with venous stasis ulcers	Spinal cord injury with pressure ulcers	Spinal cord injury with pressure ulcers Diabetic ulcers

Frequency

Frequency or pulse rate is another variable that varies from study to study without much explanation. Several studies used a pulse rate of 100 to 128 pps for treatment with HVPC.[63,64] One investigator starts treatment at 50 pps.[65,66] Sussman uses 30 pps. Rationale is based on the effect of HVPC on blood flow. In some research studies, lower pulse rates produced higher mean blood flow velocity after HVPC than higher pulse rates and had a longer mean recovery time following cessation of HVPC compared to control levels.[28] Frequency switching is also not well understood. For example, in one study the rationale given for reducing the pulse rate from 128 pps to 64 pps was "because we believed the higher pulse frequency might be harmful to the newly healed tissue."[68(p648)] This concern is probably due to the higher pulse charge delivered to the tissue at the higher pulse rate.

Amplitude

Wound healing protocols for amplitude are usually constant, repeated in either milliamperes or voltage. The HVPC protocols all report amplitudes of 100 to 200 V, the low-voltage direct-current protocols call for a 35-mA amplitude, and the low-voltage microamperage stimulation units have an amplitude less than 1 mA. The ability of the patient to tolerate high-intensity current will depend on the sensory per-ception of the individual. For example, in superficial or partial-thickness tissue disruption if there is intact sensation, an amplitude above 100 V may be very uncomfortable. In deeper wounds or in cases of impaired sensation, these higher amplitudes are well tolerated. Adjust the amplitude to patient comfort. It has been suggested to test the amplitude by stimulating until there is a visible muscle contraction under the electrode. This is not practical if the active electrode is located in a wound within a muscle because the sensory nerves will not be stimulated. If the dispersive electrode is secure over a large body area, the intensity of the stimulation required to cause a muscle contraction will be very high and probably uncomfortable, and may not be visible to the physical therapist.

Conclusion

Clearly, more investigation is needed to achieve an optimal treatment protocol with electrical stimulation. In the meantime, the protocols presented in this chapter are for use with low- and high-voltage monophasic and biphasic wave forms, which represent these authors' interpretation of the literature and the application to clinical treatment. The authors have used these protocols for several years with good clinical results. Protocols are listed for wound healing for the three phases of repair and for the treatment of an edematous limb where the edema extends beyond the wound area. Protocols change for each phase of repair and have expected outcomes for each. Expected outcomes are based on the literature and clinical experience.

Selecting the Device and Treatment Protocol

The physical therapist is now ready to select the electrical stimulator for treatment. Depending on the stimulator selected, the protocol for treatment will vary. In some cases, the characteristics of electrical stimulation for different current type may not always be based on the wound healing phases. For example, asymmetric biphasic stimulation parameters are not varied during the progression through the phases of healing.[71,72]

The most common stimulator used for wound healing today is the high-voltage pulsed current neuromuscular stimulator. This may change in the future. The protocols presented below are based on use of the high-voltage pulsed current

stimulator. Since the protocol given mimics the studies done with low-voltage pulsed electrical current,[68] the protocol would also be appropriate to use with those stimulators. The protocols are based initially on the wound healing phase diagnosis, and there are changes in polarity and pulse rate as the wounds progress through the phases of healing.

Sussman Wound Healing Protocol

Sussman uses a wound healing protocol for HVPC based on the completed diagnostic process (see Chapter 1). Table 16–6 lists the Sussman Wound Healing Protocols for HVPC for all four phases of wound healing and edema control. In using this method, the clinician initiates an HVPC treatment protocol based on the assessed wound healing phase diagnosis, and predicts an expected outcome for that protocol. Since the polarity of the healing wound changes during the phases of healing, different treatment characteristics are used as wound healing progresses. In the protocol given be-

Table 16–6 Protocols for HVPC Treatment

Parameters	Edema	Inflammation	Proliferation	Epithelialization	Remodeling	Venous Return[4]
Polarity	Negative	Negative	Alternate negative/ positive every 3 days	Alternate daily	Alternate daily	Not critical; adjust for patient comfort
Pulse rate (frequency)	30–50 pps	30 pps	100–128 pps	60–64 pps	60–64 pps	40–60 pps
Intensity	150 V or less depending on patient tolerance	100–150 V	100–150 V	100–150 V	100–150 V	Surge mode, on time, 3–15 sec; off time, 9–40 sec (1:3 on/off ratio) to motor excitation
Duration	60 min	60 min	60 min	60 min	60 min	5–10 min, progress to 20–30 min
Treatment frequency	5–7 times/ week for first week, then 3 times/week for 1 week	5–7 times/ week, once daily	5–7 times/ week, once daily	3–5 times/ week, once daily	3 times/week, once daily	Daily; modify to biweekly

low, the stimulation selected for treatment is a monophasic current and monopolar technique used with HVPC. For wounds in the acute inflammation phase, with an absence of inflammation phase, or in a chronic inflammation phase, the therapist would start treatment with characteristics to stimulate circulation and cellular responses to healing that are listed under the inflammation phase. The protocol calls for change of characteristics as the wound healing phases progress. Likewise, for a wound healing phase, diagnosis of the repair (proliferation) phase, and a wound in the remodeling phase, the therapist would start treatment using a different set of characteristics as outlined.

Predictable Outcomes with Sussman Wound Healing Protocol

Predictable outcomes are expected for each protocol, which are equivalent to a change in the wound phase characteristics. For example, if the wound healing phase diagnosis is *acute inflammation phase* the *expected outcomes* are hemorrhage free, necrosis free, erythema free, edema free, exudate free, red granulation, and progression to the next phase—the proliferation phase. If there is absence of inflammation or chronic inflammation, an acute inflammation phase needs to be initiated if possible. Expected outcomes would indicate change to an acute inflammation phase, described as increased erythema (change in skin color), edema, and warmth. The phase change outcome predicted is *initiation of acute inflammation phase*. Each wound healing phase has its own diagnosis and expected outcomes that are independent of wound etiology.

When the wound healing phase diagnosis is *acute proliferation phase* the *expected outcomes* are reduction in size (eg, open area, depth, undermining/tunneling), red granulation tissue–filled wound bed, minimal serous or serosanguineous wound exudate, odor free, adherence of wound edges, and at the end of the phase a change in wound healing phase to the epithelialization phase. When the wound healing phase diagnosis is absence of or chronic proliferation, the predicted outcome must be acute proliferation: reduction in depth, reduction in open area size, and closing of tunnels or undermining. Chronic proliferation may be due to infection of the granulation tissue. There would be clinical signs of infection, including purulent exudate, malodor, and change in appearance of the granulation tissue from beefy red to dull pink. The additional expected outcome for a chronic proliferation phase then would enable the wound to become infection free and to restart the proliferation phase.

A wound healing phase diagnosis of *acute epithelialization phase* has the *expected outcome* of resurfacing and a change in wound healing phase to *remodeling*. A wound in the remodeling phase has an immature scar formation that lacks optimal healing and could benefit from continued

---

> **Clinical Wisdom:** *Ultraviolet Light Stimulation To Restart Epithelialization Phase*
>
> One method suggested to restart the epithelialization phase is to use ultraviolet C light stimulation to create an erythema of the wound edges.[81] By using a dosage that produces a second-degree burn, there is a burning back of the leading edge of the cells that have stopped migration. The erythema response to ultraviolet light may lead to shedding of the outer layer of the skin, followed by a mild inflammatory response that includes vasodilatation and capillary permeability and reinitiates the epithelialization process. Ultraviolet light also has the benefit of being bactericidal.[81] Another approach is use of topical or oral vitamin A to stimulate an erythema in the tissues. Treatment with electrical stimulation should cease if a method to restart the epithelialization process is not also attempted.

stimulation with electrical stimulation to enhance the migration of the epidermal cells and the maturation of the vascular system of the scar tissue. Absence of an epithelialization phase may result from a drying out of the wound tissues due to either a poor dressing choice or an absence of dressing. Epidermal cells require a moist environment to migrate across the wound surface. Correction of the inadequate wound treatment would be a necessary part of the plan of care. Chronic epithelialization is associated with rolled wound edges that have become fibrotic and stuck without resurfacing the wound. Other adjunctive measures may be required to reinitiate an inflammatory response in the wound edges that in turn will reinitiate the epithelialization process.

Once closure is achieved, the patient is usually discharged from a treatment protocol, including electrical stimulation. However, the remodeling phase is often overlooked as a point at which treatment with electrical stimulation can be beneficial in reducing the risk of immature scar breakdown. The remodeling phase is the longest of all the phases of healing, lasting from 6 months to 2 years. A scar that is thicker, better vascularized, softer, and flatter is more resistant to stress from shearing, friction, and pressure, all of which account for a high incidence of recurrence of ulceration on the seating surface or plantar surface of the foot. Electrical stimulation enhances the remodeling of the scar. Of course, other methods also need to be considered to protect the new scar tissue, including pressure-relief devices and dressings. The physical therapist also would include a program of stretching, exercise, and soft tissue mobilization techniques to enhance the elasticity of the mature scar. *Color Plates 1 to 6* illustrate a case taken through the four phases of healing with electrical stimulation.

Procedures for High-Voltage Pulsed Current

The procedure section of this chapter is outlined in a stepwise fashion to help the physical therapist (PT) and physical therapist assistant deliver the treatment intervention with electrical stimulation in a systematic and time-efficient way for both the patient and the clinician. Unfortunately, treatment with electrical stimulation requires a number of supply items and steps. First of all, consider having a physical therapist aide set up the treatment station where the equipment and supplies are available (see list of equipment and supplies needed). The same set of instructions would be useful to give to a patient or caregiver for home treatment. The PT aide can also be responsible to see that the supplies are ordered and available in the department. Always have enough supplies on hand so that treatment is not delayed while someone is running around chasing down the needed equipment.

Protocol for Wound Healing

Equipment Needed:

- Normal saline (0.9%)
- Clean gloves
- Irrigation syringe, 35-mL with 19-gauge needle or angiocatheter
- Clean gauze pads
- Aluminum foil electrode or carbon electrode
- Alligator clips or electrode lead
- Bandage tape
- Nylon stretch strap
- Wet washcloth
- Dispersive pad
- HVPC machine leads
- Infectious waste bag

Instructions for Patient and Caregiver:

1. Explain the procedure, the reason for treatment, and how long it will last. Explain that a mild tingling will be felt and where it will be felt.
2. Advise the patient not to handle, replace, or remove electrodes during the treatment. Patients who cannot understand these directions or will not cooperate need to be monitored closely.
3. Give patient a call light to use.

Setting Up the Patient for HVPC Wound Treatment:

1. Have supplies ready before undressing the wound.
2. Position the patient for ease of access by staff and for the comfort of both.
3. Remove the dressing and place in infectious waste bag (usually a red bag).

Clinical Wisdom: *Suggestions for Set-up To Maximize Treatment Effectiveness and Efficiency*

- Assemble the setup supplies into kits before the start of the treatment day to make the delivery of service more time efficient.
- Precut and shape the aluminum foil electrodes. Size and shape should be close to the size of the wounds. Round is preferable to rectangular.
- To make an electrode, cut a strip of household aluminum foil the width of the electrode. Fold the strip in half and turn in the edges to make a smooth pad.
- To make a packing strip from gauze, open a gauze pad and pull on the bias or diagonal and twist to make a spaghetti strip, or use stretch gauze strips.
- Warm saline or a package of amorphous hydrogel by placing bottle between a folded hot pack before use to avoid chilling the wound tissue and slowing mitotic activity. Check the temperature with a digital thermometer. The temperature should not be greater than 100°F to avoid burns. Myer[81] reported keeping the wound care products, including a 16-oz bottle of saline, warm for 3 to 4 hours. She observed that warming of the wound care products before electrical stimulation treatment resulted in brighter redness of granulation tissue and contributed to reduction of pain.[81]

Clinical Wisdom: *Irrigation Devices*

Spray bottles and bulb syringes may not deliver enough pressure (2.0 psi or less) to cleanse wounds adequately. The Water Pik at middle to high settings may cause trauma to the wound tissue and drive bacteria into wounds; it is not recommended for cleansing soft tissue wounds. Use a cleanser delivery device such as syringe with a 19-gauge catheter to deliver water at 4 to 8 psi. Warm the solution before application.[82]

Clinical Wisdom: *Perform Sharp Debridement before HVPC Treatment*

Complete sharp debridement procedure before setting the patient up for HVPC treatment so that the wound packing will act as a pressure dressing to control any bleeding and so that the wound environment will not have to be disturbed again after HVPC treatment.

4. Cleanse wound thoroughly to remove slough, exudate, and any petrolatum products.
5. Sharply debride necrotic tissue, if required, before HVPC treatment.
6. Open gauze pads and fluff, then soak to moisten in normal saline solution; squeeze out excess liquid before applying.
7. Fill the wound cavity with gauze, including any undermined/tunneled spaces. Gauze pad can be opened to full size and then pulled diagonally to form a thin "spaghetti" strip. Insert into undermined/tunneled spaces like roller gauze. Pack gently.
8. Place electrode over the gauze packing; cover with a dry gauze pad and hold in place with bandage tape.
9. Connect an alligator clip to the foil.
10. Connect to the stimulator lead and to output device.
11. Place the dispersive electrode.
    a. The dispersive electrode is usually placed proximal to the wound (see section on electrode placement for alternative locations).
    b. Place over soft tissues; avoid bony prominences.
    c. Place a moist washcloth over the dispersive electrode.
    d. Place a washcloth against the skin and hold it in good contact at all edges with a nylon elasticized strap. (Covering the wet dispersive set-up with a plastic sheet to separate it from the bed and the patient's clothing to keep them dry will be appreciated by the patient and the nursing staff.)
    e. If placed on the back, the weight of the body plus the strap can be used to achieve good contact at the edges.
    f. Dispersive pad should be larger than the sum of the areas of the active electrodes and wound packing.
    g. The greater the separation between the active and dispersive electrode the deeper the current path. Use greater separation for deep and undermined wounds
    h. Dispersive and active electrodes should be 4 to 5 cm apart and **should not touch**. Current flow will be shallow. Use HVPC for shallow, partial-thickness wounds.

Additional Treatment Methods:

• Up to four wounds can be set up with a single-channel stimulator using double bifurcated leads from the stimulator to the electrodes. However, this will not provide maximum current density at the treatment sites. For a patient with multiple wounds, it is not practical to run several series of treatments. An alternative is to use two HVPC stimulators, if available. Electrode placement will require careful planning so that the current flows through target tissues. For example, if there is a wound on the right hip, coccyx, left foot, and right heel, the dispersive electrode should be placed on either the right or left thigh. The thigh has a good blood supply and good conductivity. This set up will send the current flowing through the deep tissues to the feet, the hip, and the coccyx.

• Alternate placement of the dispersive electrode for each treatment, if possible, to direct current flow to opposite sides of the wound has been suggested.[78] This will be more difficult when wounds are located in the feet.

• If a limb is involved, the circumference may be too small to wrap with the large dispersive electrode and maintain good contact. An alternative is to use bifurcated leads, which are available to use with the dispersive cable for some stimulators. When using this set-up, attach two round carbon-impregnated electrodes to make the surface area of the dispersive electrode larger than the active electrode. Place the electrodes on either side of the limb. It is easier to conform the two pads to a small limb segment than the large rectangular dispersive electrode standard with most stimulators. Use wet gauze under the electrodes; if a greater conductive surface is required, extend the wet gauze out from the edges of the electrode over the surrounding skin. Hold the dispersive electrode in place with nylon elasticized straps. If the patient complains of excessive tingling under the dispersive set-up, check for good contact and see whether the size can be increased further. (See Figure 16–8, which shows bifurcated leads spread out on a washcloth for dispersive electrode.)

Alternative Methods of Conducting Current to the Wound. Alternative methods of conducting current to the wound using dressing products have been of interest for a number of years. A recent study of conductivity of different wound dressings reported that: (1) transparent films are poor conductors, (2) fully saturated hydrocolloids will conduct current, and (3) hydrogel amorphous gels and sheet forms are good conductors because of their high water content.[83] An animal study using pigs with burn wounds demonstrated that use of a hydrogel dressing with pulsed electrical stimulation delivered through the dressing increased the levels of collagenase during the critical period of epithelialization initiation. Collagenase enhancement may be one mechanism by which the electrical stimulation accelerated the wound healing of these burns.[84] See Chapter 10 for a description of amorphous and sheet hydrogel characteristics.

Use an amorphous hydrogel–impregnated gauze to conduct current. This type of dressing is used for partial-thickness, full-thickness, and subcutaneous lesions extending into deep tissue wounds. Hydrogels can be left in the wound for up to 3 days. This product class can benefit the wound management by:

- Conducting electrical current when covered with an electrode.
- Promoting the "sodium current of injury."
- Absorbing light to moderate wound exudate.
- Maintaining a moist wound environment.
- Gradually absorbing wound moisture and is also a moisture donor to the wound.
- Retaining the cell growth factors in the wound bed.
- Reducing trauma and cooling of the wound through less handling.
- Reducing product and labor costs by serving a dual purpose.

Hydrogel sheets also have high water content and can also be used to conduct current when placed under the electrode.[83] They have benefits similar to the amorphous hydrogels except that they should not be left on an infected wound. They are used for lightly exudating wounds and are best used for superficial partial-thickness wounds such as donor sites after skin grafting.

Amorphous hydrogel–impregnated gauze or a hydrogel sheet can be used as the wet contact coupler under an electrode. Although manufacturers say that all that is required is to clip the alligator clips to the dressing to conduct current, Alon[85] explained that this will focus the current at one small area of the dressing and not disperse it throughout the wound area unless the entire dressing surface is covered with an electrode. Follow the setup steps described above, but substitute the saline-soaked gauze with the amorphous hydrogel–impregnated gauze or hydrogel sheet. Dressings may be left in place for up to 3 days. The amorphous hydrogel should be warmed before application, but be careful not to overheat the product and cause burns. Check temperature with a digital thermometer. Temperature should not be greater than 100°F. If wound conditions permit, cover with a moisture/vapor-permeable transparent film or another dressing to retain moisture without maceration and maintain body warmth. For amorphous hydrogel–impregnated gauze, on the second day, lift the secondary dressing and slip an aluminum foil electrode underneath; connect an alligator clip lead to the

---

Clinical Wisdom:
Remove Petrolatum before Stimulation

All petrolatum products, including enzymatic debriding agents such as collagenase (Santyl), and fibrinolysin (Elase), which are petrolatum-based products, must be removed before treatment or current will not be conducted into the wound tissues.

---

dressing and the stimulator. Replace secondary dressing. Repeat on the third day. The same approach would apply to the hydrogel sheet.

Protocol for Treatment of Edema

Soft tissue trauma and a closed or minimally open wound would benefit from electrical stimulation to control, eliminate, or reduce edema formation. Edema stimulates pain receptors because of the tension in the tissues, blocks off circulation inflow to the tissues, and impairs mobility. Edema eliminated, controlled, or reduced would be the expected outcome from this intervention. Table 16–6 shows a protocol for treatment for edema reduction using high-voltage pulsed current stimulation. There are limited reports and no clinical trials to support this treatment.[31–35]

Setting Up the Patient for Treatment of Edema:

1. Use the method for setting up the wound described under protocol for wound healing.
2. Elevate the limb and support it on a pillow or foam wedge, above the heart if possible.
3. Use three or four electrodes.
4. Place one electrode over the wound and arrange the other electrodes over the vascular areas of the limb.
   a. If the wound is in lower leg, place the second electrode over the medial aspect of the foot and the third over the popliteal area.
   b. If the edema is in the foot distal to the wound, a "foot sandwich" can be made by surrounding the foot with a foil electrode that wraps around the top and bottom of the foot.

Note: Apply the same clinical reasoning for the upper extremity.

Protocol for Infection Control and Disinfection

A clean technique is recommended for treatment of chronic wounds. The use of aluminum foil electrodes is a good method of controlling infection and eliminates the need for disinfection of the electrode pads. If carbon electrodes or electrodes with sponges are used over the wound, they need to be disinfected between each use even if used for a single patient. A cold disinfection solution, such as Cydex+, will disinfect for all organisms within 10 minutes according to the material data sheet. Cydex+ comes with an activating solution that is added to the main solution when the bottle is opened. The activated solution can be reusable for up to 28 days. The product is available in quart and gallon sizes. Unless large quantities of electrodes are going to be disinfected at one time, the quart solution has been found to be most cost effective.[86]

Another cold disinfectant, Milkro-Quat, at the dilution of 18.6 g (⅔ oz) in 3.8 L (1 gal) of water, has been tested for disinfection of electrodes and electrode sponges after treatment of colonized wounds. The electrodes and sponges were soaked in the disinfecting solution for 20 minutes and then tested for bacterial counts. Both the efficacy of the disinfectant and the protocol for disinfection were evaluated. Samples taken from 92% of the post-treatment electrode sponges after they were disinfected contained no bacterial growth. The remaining 8% contained two or fewer colonies. The results were the same for samples cultured anaerobically.[85] The dispersive pad, which is placed on intact skin, should be cleaned between uses with soap and water or wiped with an alcohol-soaked pad. Alligator clips that come in contact with wound contaminants should be disinfected between uses. One company furnishes alligator clips with packs of hydrogel-impregnated gauze that can be kept for single patient use. Over time, the carbon electrodes will absorb oil and detergent products and become resistant to current flow. A periodic check (eg, every 30 days) of the conductivity of the electrodes is highly recommended.

Clinical Wisdom:
Benefits of Aluminum Foil Electrodes

Aluminum foil electrodes are very cost effective and time efficient for treatment of open wounds. They are easily made, are good conductors, can be molded to fit the body part, can be sized for maximum current density to the wound, and are disposable. Saline-soaked gauze packed in the wound and covered with an electrode is also cost efficient and is particularly good on deep lesions.

Aftercare. After the electrical stimulation treatment is complete, slip the electrode out from between the wet and dry gauze. The wound can be left undisturbed. If saline-soaked gauze is the conductive medium, it should be changed before it dries or be covered with an occlusive dressing. If additional topical treatments are required, such as enzymatic debriding agents or antibiotics, the packing will need to be removed. Frequent dressing changes are being discouraged because it disturbs the wound healing environment by removing important substances in wound exudate and cooling the wound. It takes 3 hours for a chilled wound to rewarm and slows leukocytic and mitotic activity.[87,88]

Protocol for Treatment of Chronic Venous Insufficiency or Chronic Deep Vein Thrombosis

---

This protocol from Alon and De Domenico[4(pp155–160)] is based on using HVPC to elicit the pumping action of skeletal muscles (see Table 16–6 showing HVPC protocols). The best muscle-pumping action is achieved from active exercise, but for some patients this is not an option or is inadequate to facilitate the venous pump mechanisms. Therefore, electrical stimulation can be used as an intermittent method for stimulation of muscle pump action. Patients with chronic lymphedema may also benefit.

Setting Up the Patient:

1. A bipolar technique is usually used.
2. Place both electrodes over the plantarflexors, one proximal and one over the muscle bellies.
3. Use a surge or interrupted mode with an on time of 3 to 15 seconds and an off time of 9 to 40 seconds. This 1:3 on/off ratio is essential to avoid muscle fatigue.
4. Begin with shorter on/off time and then increase the stimulation time as patient accommodates.
5. Polarity is not critical and can be adjusted for patient comfort.
6. Pulse rate is between 40 and 60 pps and can be adjusted for patient comfort.
7. Intensity that will produce intermittent, moderate *tetanic* muscle contraction is required. Increase intensity gradually for patient comfort and compliance.
8. Expect that a few treatment sessions will be required to reach the desired level of muscle contraction.
9. Treatment time is pathology dependent.
   a. Chronic thrombophlebitis: 30 to 60 minutes biweekly
   b. Venous stasis: commence 5 to 10 minutes daily; progress to 20 to 30 minutes biweekly
10. Precaution: Plantarflexors have a tendency to cramp; proceed slowly to avoid cramping. Such cramping must be avoided. To avoid cramping, place the feet against a footboard that limits full range of plantar flexion.
11. Expected outcome: enhanced venous return measured by reduced edema. May facilitate healing of venous ulceration.

Selecting the Candidate for Self-Care. HVPC stimulation and TENS are very safe and easy-to-apply treatments that a patient or caregiver can be taught for self-treatment at home. HVPC stimulators, as described, are available as portable, battery-pack units. Some units come with compliance meters. TENS are also portable. This is a simple treatment, but it requires several steps and clear instructions. Review the procedures with the person who will deliver the care to ensure that adequate care will be given to achieve the predicted outcomes. If the physical therapist does not believe that the person is able to be taught safe, appropriate procedures, this should be documented and may be a rationale for skilled services or another intervention.

To achieve success in a self-care program, psychosocial concerns need to be addressed before establishing the program. Select the patient and/or caregiver who is alert, motivated, and able to learn the directions for application. It will require clinician support and encouragement to convince the patient/caregiver to accept the responsibility for self-care. Patients and caregivers are accustomed to receiving medical care at the clinic or by a home care practitioner rather than doing self-care. The concept of sharing the problem between patient and clinician is new to many people. It takes a step-by-step process to gain patient cooperation. Begin in the clinic or at the home visit by encouraging and teaching the patient and/or the caregiver to participate in the setup process. Many people are repulsed by the sight of a dirty, smelly, ugly wound. That is often the first hurdle. Take it slowly, with patience and understanding of these feelings. Explain in simple language why the wound is dirty, smelly, and ugly and how the treatment will improve the problem. Wound measurements and pictures can be used as motivation to encourage continued participation. Before-and-after pictures of other cases treated this way are particularly effective ways of showing the patient/caregiver how other wounds improved. Move the patient or caregiver increasingly into the role of treatment provider as soon as possible. Observe, instruct, and offer words of support and praise.

Instructions. Independence in the treatment routine must be established before dismissing the patient with an electrical stimulator for self-care at home. While it may seem overwhelming to give five steps of instructions for a single treatment protocol, understanding the five steps of instructions listed here will ensure that the patient or caregiver is able to achieve the goal of independence in the treatment routine. Keep instructions as simple as possible so the responsible party will not be overwhelmed. Because of the number of steps required, prepared instruction sheets listing the five steps would be helpful. Stick-figure drawings can be helpful in teaching the proper placement of the electrodes. Don't assume that the patient will know where to place the electrodes or how to put on the dressing when he or she arrives home. Two or three visits with the physical therapist may be necessary to complete the instruction. Schedule regular follow-up assessments.

The Five Steps of Instruction Are As Follows:

1. The list of needed supplies: Make sure that the patient can acquire all the necessary items or help make arrangements to acquire those that are needed (eg, a por-

table HVPC stimulator with dispersive pad and nylon stretch strap).

2. Set-up of the patient and the wound for treatment, including all the steps listed: Review what is on paper and then do a demonstration and return demonstration to confirm understanding.

3. The treatment protocol: Review the treatment protocol by dialing in the characteristics for the selected protocols on the stimulator to be used. The dials can be left at the correct setting to help the patient, but they may be moved and should be rechecked at each treatment session. Give *only* the treatment protocol for the current wound healing phase. Tell the patient or caregiver what outcomes to expect and what findings should be reported promptly. Change instructions as the wound heals.

4. The aftercare procedures: Aftercare procedure instructions should include how to apply the prescribed dressing product and disposal of the disposable waste products from the treatment in the home setting (see Chapter 10). It is important to make sure that the patient or caregiver understands the proper use of the prescribed aftercare dressing products. Damage to the wound and failure to achieve predicted outcomes can be avoided by instruction in use of products. Again, practice and a return demonstration are proven methods of teaching new techniques.

5. A list of expected signs and symptoms: The patient and the caregiver need to be aware of the importance of any expected changes in signs and symptoms related to the treatment and know when to report any undesirable results.

DOCUMENTATION

Documentation validates the treatment intervention. Documentation is required to show treatment characteristics, and to track responses to treatment such as described in Chapter 4, Wound Measurements, and Chapter 5, Tools To Measure Wound Healing. Following are two case studies using the documentation methodology described in the functional outcomes report. The functional outcomes report explains the physical therapist's rationale for selecting the intervention based on the patient evaluation and wound diagnosis, and the target outcomes expected from the intervention as shown in Chapter 1, The Diagnostic Process. Data obtained during documentation about treatment outcomes should be done in a systematic manner; they can then be entered into a database to evaluate the program in the clinic, report success of the therapy, and predict outcomes and management costs.

Case Study 1: Pressure Ulcer Treated with ES

Patient ID: A.S.   Age: 85   Onset: May

Initial Assessment: Brief Medical History and Systems Review

Reason for Referral

The patient has developed pressure ulceration along the lateral border of her left foot. She is not a candidate for surgical intervention because of multiple comorbidities.

Medical History

The patient is an 85-year-old woman who is unresponsive, with fetal posture and fixed contractures of all four extremities. She has a history of multiple cerebrovascular accidents. She does not reposition herself in bed and cannot sit up in a wheelchair. She is on nasogastric tube feeding for nutrition; a Foley catheter is in place to control incontinence of urine. The wound onset was 2 weeks prior to referral to physical therapy. The wound has deteriorated and become necrotized. The nursing staff has been using enzymatic and autolytic debridement methods.

Systems Review

Circulatory System. The patient has systemically impaired circulation due to arteriosclerotic vascular disease. The circulation to the lower extremity is further impaired as a result of contractures of the hips and knees.

Respiratory System. The patient has shallow, impaired respiration due to inactivity and her bed-bound status.

Musculoskeletal System. The patient has impaired joint mobility due to contractures, resulting in severe disability of the musculoskeletal system.

Neuromuscular System. The patient lacks the ability to respond to the need for self-repositioning and is cognitively unaware.

Examinations Indicated and Derived Data

Vascular Examination

Palpation of pulses indicates a weak dorsal pedal pulse. Determination of the ankle-brachial index is not possible due to contractures at the elbow. Pulse oximetry of the great toe shows an oxygen saturation of 96%.

Musculoskeletal Examination

There is limited passive range of motion (less than 90° at either the hips, knees, or elbows). There is no active motor movement.

Integumentary Examination

The surrounding skin is erythematous, seen as red glow under darkly pigmented skin. The tissue is edematous. The temperature of the wound is elevated compared with surrounding tissues. There are hemorrhagic areas along the wound margin, and necrotic tissue covers the wound surface.

Evaluation of the Examination Findings and Relationship to Function

The specific dysfunction that generated a referral for the services of the physical therapist is loss of wound healing capacity. The patient's loss of function is due to generalized impairments (circulatory, cardiopulmonary, musculoskeletal, and neuromuscular). Limited bed mobility and limited cognitive ability further complicate the ability to heal without physical therapy intervention for integumentary management.

Diagnosis

Musculoskeletal Disability

Impaired flexibility and strength leads to increased susceptibility to pressure ulceration of the feet.

Neuromuscular Disability

The patient has neuromuscular disability associated with insensitivity and inability to reposition and make needs known.

Wound Healing Impairment

The signs and symptoms identified by the wound assessment, including edema, erythema, heat, and the pres-

continues

Case Study 1 continued

ence of necrotic tissue, indicate that the wound healing phase diagnosis is *a chronic inflammation phase of healing* and impaired wound healing associated with a chronically inflamed wound.

Functional Diagnosis

- Undue susceptibility to pressure ulceration on the feet
- Impaired wound healing
- Chronic inflammation phase
- Insensitivity to need for position change

Need for Skilled Services: The Therapy Problem

The patient has failed to respond to interventions with dressing changes for the last 2 weeks. She now requires the following four interventions:

1. Debridement of the necrotic tissue from the wound bed to determine level of tissue impairment and to initiate the healing process
2. *HVPC to enhance circulation to the foot, facilitate debridement, and restart the process of repair*
3. Therapeutic positioning to remove pressure trauma on the foot
4. Range-of-motion exercises to all four extremities to maintain tissue extensibility and increase circulation

Prognosis

Healing is not expected without intervention; however, the prognosis is good for a clean, stable wound. Initiation of the acute inflammation phase with electrical stimulation is expected in 2 weeks with progression to a proliferation phase in 4 weeks, and a clean, stable wound in 6 weeks.

Treatment Plan

- Instruction will be given to nurses' aides in range-of-motion needs of the patient; it will include initial and follow-up for two different shifts (four visits).
- Instruction will be given to the nursing staff in therapeutic positioning; it will include initial instruction and follow-up for two different shifts (three visits).
- HVPC parameters:
  1. The active electrode will be placed on the wound site.

2. The dispersive electrode will be placed on the thigh.
3. Polarity initially will be negative, then alternated between positive and negative, as described under the Sussman Wound Healing Protocol, as the wound changes phases.
4. The pulse rate will be changed from 30 pps to 120 pps to 64 pps as phases change.
5. The current intensity will be set at 150 V throughout.
6. HVPC will be of a 60-minute duration, seven times a week.
- Debridement will be achieved by HVPC, enzymes, and sharp instruments daily as needed to remove necrotic tissue.

Interventions

Passive Range-of-Motion Exercises

Passive range-of-motion exercises will be performed to all four extremities, ranged twice daily by the restorative nurses' aide as instructed by the physical therapist.

Targeted Outcome. The nurses' aide will be able to provide the optimal amount of range of motion for all four extremities; increase tissue extensibility at elbows, hips, and knees; and increase perfusion to the lower extremities; *due date:* 2 weeks.

Healing Pressure Relief

Therapeutic positioning with adaptive equipment will be used to keep feet off the bed, and a pressure-relief mattress replacement will be provided.

Targeted Outcome. The nursing staff will be able to use therapeutic positions to reduce the risk of pressure ulcer formation on the feet, including elimination of pressure on the lateral border of the foot with pressure ulcer; *due date:* 1 week.

Electrical Stimulation with HVPC 7 Days per Week

Targeted Outcome. The intervention will stimulate perfusion and cellular responses of the inflammatory phase, and wound debridement will progress to the acute inflammation phase followed by progression to the proliferation phase; *due date:* 6 weeks.

continues

Case Study 1 continued

Debridement

Sharp debridement will be used for nonviable tissue; enzymatic debridement will be used to solubilize the necrotic tissue between sharp debridement sessions.

Targeted Outcome. The wound will be necrosis free; *due date:* 4 weeks.

Discharge Outcome

Within 4 weeks the wound was clean, granulating wound edges were contracting, and epithelialization was starting. Because it was now evident that there was potential for wound closure, the prognosis was changed to healed wound from clean and stable; HVPC treatment was continued, and at 12 weeks the wound was fully epithelialized and closed.

Case Study 2: Vascular Ulcer Treated with ES

Patient: C.Z.   Age: 80
(Color photos of the case are *Color Plates 55 and 56.*)

Initial Assessment

Reason for Referral

The patient came to the physical therapist because a vascular ulcer on the posterior right calf would not heal. The patient and his wife reported that they had been caring for the ulcer for more than 6 months, and they wanted it to heal so they could resume their usual activities in the community.

Medical History

The patient has a history of severe arterial vascular occlusive disease of the lower extremities. Old World War II burn scarring covered the surrounding area of the calf, with hyperketotic scarring that kept breaking down. The recurrent skin breakdown on his leg resulted in protracted periods of healing (eg, more than 1 year). One ulcer had healed in 6 months after a course of care using electrical stimulation (HVPC). The previous ulcer took more than a year and did not heal. The patient was ambulatory and alert, with mild confusion. His wife reported that any moisture left on the surrounding skin caused maceration and skin breakdown. A femoral angioplasty had been done the week before the patient was seen in the outpatient clinic.

Functional Diagnosis and Targeted Outcomes

Integumentary Examination

Adjacent Skin. Hyperketotic; scar tissue; flaky, friable, dry skin; and pallor are present.

Functional Diagnosis. The patient has loss of functional mobility due to integumentary impairment.

Targeted Outcome. The patient will have improved skin texture and integrity; *due date:* 6 weeks.

Wound Tissue Examination

The wound edges are poorly defined. There is necrotic tissue along the margins. There is a small island of skin in the middle of the wound bed. The wound has partial-thickness skin loss with moderate exudate. The wound is about 200 cm^2.

Functional Diagnosis. There is absence of an inflammation phase.
Targeted Outcome: Acute inflammation will be achieved; *due date:* 2 weeks.

Associated Impairment. Necrotic tissue is present.
Targeted Outcome: A clean wound bed will be achieved; *due date:* 4 weeks.

Functional Diagnosis. There is absence of a proliferation phase.
Targeted Outcome: The wound will exhibit granulation tissue and be ready for grafting; *due date*: 6 weeks.

Vascular Examination

Medical Diagnosis. The patient has severe arterial vascular occlusive disease, status postangioplasty.

Functional Diagnosis. The patient has vascular impairment contributing to impaired healing.

Targeted Outcome: Perfusion will be enhanced; *due date:* 2 weeks.

continues

Case Study 2 continued

The patient's loss of function in these systems is responsible for the undue susceptibility to skin breakdown on the legs and inability to heal without integumentary intervention. The patient has improvement potential. The wound will heal partially, and the wound bed will be prepared for grafting following intervention.

Need for Skilled Services

The patient has failed to respond to treatment with wound dressings and conservative management of the leg ulcer. It requires debridement of necrotic tissue to initiate the healing process and HVPC to initiate the healing phases and to enhance perfusion so that the wound bed is prepared for grafting.

Treatment Plan

- The patient and wife will be instructed to perform HVPC as a daily home treatment program with a portable HVPC rental unit.
- Wound debridement will be performed to remove necrotic tissues; methods will include autolysis, sharp debridement, and enhanced perfusion with the use of HVPC.
- The wife will be instructed in wound dressing changes with alginate to absorb moderate exudate, including how to cut the dressing to fit the wound to avoid maceration.

Discharge Outcomes

- The patient started care in mid-December.
- The wound was necrosis free.
- The wound phase changed to both proliferation and epithelialization. The wound size was reduced to less than half the original area.
- The wound was grafted at the end of February.
- The wound graft was successful. A smaller graft was needed than originally expected because of the epithelialization. Surrounding integumentary integrity was improved: the skin was softer and smoother, and no new hyperkeratosis developed in the scar tissue area.

General Comments

The patient and his wife were very compliant with the home treatment regimen. The femoral angioplasty apparently opened the vessels enough to permit the enhanced perfusion from the HVPC to reach the tissues. Grafting was the best option for this couple because it provided faster closure and allowed them to live more functional lives without having wound care duties. It also provided a better covering with healthier skin from the opposite thigh to cover the open area. New scar tissue was better-quality tissue than that surrounding older scars, possibly due to the improved collagen organization and vascularization associated with the HVPC.

REFERENCES

1. Swanson G. Functional outcomes report: the next generation in physical therapy reporting. In: Stewart DL, Abeln SH, eds. *Documenting Functional Outcomes in Physical Therapy.* St Louis, MO: Mosby–Year Book; 1993.

2. Bergstrom N, Bennett MA, Carlson CE, et al. *Treatment of Pressure Ulcers.* Clinical Practice Guideline No. 15. AHCPR Publication No. 95-0652. Rockville, MD: Agency for Health Care Policy and Research, U.S. Department of Health and Human Services; December 1994.

3. Kloth L, et al. *Electrotherapeutic Terminology in Physical Therapy.* Alexandria, VA: Section on Clinical Electrophysiology, American Physical Therapy Association; 1990.

4. Alon G, De Domenico G. *High Voltage Stimulation: An Integrated Approach to Clinical Electrotherapy.* Hixton, TN: The Chattanooga Group; 1987.

5. Newton RA, Karsellis TC. Skin pH following high voltage pulsed galvanic stimulation. *Phys Ther.* 1983;63:1593–1596.

6. Newton RA. High-voltage pulsed current: theoretical bases and clinical applications. In: Nelson R, Currier D, eds. *Clinical Electrotherapy.* Norwalk, CT: Appleton & Lange; 1991:201–220.

7. Gersh M. Microcurrent electrical stimulation: putting it in perspective. *Clin Manage.* 1989;9(4):51–54.

8. Nelson R, Nestor D. Electrophysiological evaluation: an overview. In: Nelson R, Currier D, eds. *Clinical Electrotherapy.* Norwalk, CT: Appleton & Lange; 1991:331–360.

9. Bourguignon CJ, Bourguignon LYW. Electric stimulation of human fibroblasts causes an increase in Ca^{2+} and the exposure of additional insulin receptors. *J Cell Physiol.* 1989;140:379–385.

10. Friedenberg ZB, Andrews ET, et al. Bone reaction to varying amounts of direct current. *Surg Gynecol Obstet.* 1970;131:894–899.

11. Jaffe LS, Vanable JW. Electric fields and wound healing. *Clin Dermatol.* 1984;3:34.

12. Gentzkow G, Miller K. Electrical stimulation for dermal wound healing. *Clin Podiatr Med Surg.* 1991;8:827–841.

13. Gentzkow GD, Pollack SV, et al. Improved healing of pressure ulcers using Dermapulse, a new electrical stimulation device. *Wounds.* 1991;3:158–160.

14. Fukushima K, Sends N, et al. Studies of galvantotaxis of leukocytes. *Med J Osaka Univ.* 1953;4:195–208.

15. Orida N, Feldman J. Directional protrusive pseudopodial activity and motility in macrophages induced by extracellular electric fields. *Cell Motil.* 1982;2:243–255.

16. Kloth LC. Electrical stimulation in tissue repair. In: McCulloch J, Kloth L, Feedar J, eds. *Wound Healing Alternatives in Management.* 2nd ed. Philadelphia: F.A. Davis; 1995:275–310.

17. Alon G, Azaria M, Stein H. Diabetic ulcer healing using high voltage TENS. *Phys Ther.* 1986;66:77. Abstract.

18. Alon G. Antibiotics enhancement by transcutaneous electrical stimulation. Presented at Symposia, "Future Directions in Wound Healing"; American Physical Therapy Association Scientific Meeting; June 1997; San Diego, CA.

19. Stromberg BV. Effects of electrical currents on wound contraction. *Ann Plast Surg.* 1988;21(2):121–123.

20. Brown M, McDonnell M, Menton DN. Polarity effects on wound healing using electrical stimulation in rabbits. *Arch Phys Med Rehabil.* 1989;70:624–627.

21. Alvarez O. The healing of superficial skin wounds is stimulated by external electrical current. *J Invest Derm.* 1983;81(2):144–148.

22. Weiss D, Eaglestein W, Falanga V. Exogenous electric current can reduce the formation of hypertrophic scars. *J Dermatol Surg Oncol.* 1989;15:1272–1275.

23. Bourguignon CJ, Bourguignon LYW. Electrical stimulation of protein and DNA synthesis in human fibroblasts. *FASEB J.* 1987;1:398–402.

24. Canaday DJ, Lee RC. Scientific basis for clinical application of electric fields in soft tissue repair. In: Brighton CT, Pollack SR, eds. *Electromagnetics in Biology and Medicine.* San Francisco: San Francisco Press; 1991.

25. Erickson CA, Nuccitelli R. Embryonic fibroblast motility and orientation can be influenced by physiological electrical fields. *J Cell Biol.* 1984;98:296–307.

26. Yang W, et al. Response of C3H/10T1/2 fibroblasts to an external steady electric field stimulation. *Exp Cell Res.* 1984;155:92–104.

27. Cooper MS, Schliwa M. Electrical and ionic controls of tissue cell locomotion in DC electrical fields. *J Cell Physiol.* 1985;103:363–370.

28. Mohr T, Akers T, Wessman HC. Effect of high voltage stimulation on blood flow in the rat hind limb. *Phys Ther.* 1987;67:526–533.

29. Politis MJ, Zankis MF, Miller JE. Enhanced survival of full-thickness skin grafts following the application of DC electrical fields. *Plast Reconstr Surg.* 1989;84(2):67–72.

30. Pollack S. The effects of pulsed electrical stimulation on failing skin flaps in Yorkshire pigs. Paper presented at the Meeting of the Bioelectrical Repair and Growth Society; 1989; Cleveland, OH.

31. Mendel F, Fish D. New perspectives in edema control via electrical stimulation. *J Athlet Train.* 1993;28:63–74.

32. Reed BV. Effect of high voltage pulsed electrical stimulation on microvascular permeability to plasma proteins: a possible mechanism in minimizing edema. *Phys Ther.* 1988;68:491–495.

33. Ross C, Segal D. HVPC as an aid to post-operative healing. *Curr Podiatry.* May 1981.

34. Sawyer PN. Bioelectric phenomena and intravascular thrombosis: the first 12 years. *Surgery.* 1964;56:1020–1026.

35. Sawyer PN, Deutch B. The experimental use of oriented electrical fields to delay and prevent intravascular thrombosis. *Surg Forum.* 1955;5:163–168.

36. Sawyer PN, Deutch B. Use of electrical currents to delay intravascular thrombosis in experimental animals. *Am J Physiol.* 1956;187:473–478.

37. Williams RD, Carey LC. Studies in the production of "standard" venous thrombosis. *Ann Surg.* 1959;149:381–387.

38. Byl N, McKenzie A, et al. Pulsed microamperage stimulation: a controlled study of healing of surgically induced wounds in Yucatan pigs. *Phys Ther.* 1994;74:201–218.

39. Baker L, Dogen P, Johnson B, Chambers R. The effects of electrical stimulation on cutaneous oxygen supply in diabetic older adults. *Phys Ther.* 1987;67:793.

40. Owoeye I, Spielholtz NI, Fetto J, et al. Low intensity pulsed galvanic current and the healing of tenotomized rat Achilles tendons: preliminary report using lead to break measurements. *Arch Phys Med Rehabil.* 1987;68:415–418.

41. Barranco J, Spadaro J, et al. In vitro effect of weak direct current on *Staphylococcus aureus. Clin Orthop.* 1974;100:250–255.

42. Rowley B, McKenna J, Chase GR. The influence of electrical current on an infecting microorganism in wounds. *Ann NY Acad Sci.* 1974;238:543–551.

43. Kincaid C, Lavoie K. Inhibition of bacterial growth in vitro following stimulation with high voltage, monophasic, pulsed current. *Phys Ther.* 1989;69:29–33.

44. Szuminsky NJ, et al. Effect of narrow, pulsed high voltages on bacterial viability. *Phys Ther.* 1994;74:660–667.

45. Wolf J. *Das Gesetz der Transformatin der Knochen.* Berlin, Germany: Hirschwald; 1897.

46. Forrester JC, et al. Wolf's law in relation to the healing of skin wound. *J Trauma.* 1970;10:770–778.

47. Byl NN, McKenzie A, Wong T, West J, Hunt TK. Incisional wound healing: a controlled study of low- and high-dose ultrasound. *JOSPT.* 1993;18(5):619–627.

48. Byl NN, McKenzie A, West JM, Whitney JD, Hunt TK, Scheuenstuhl HA. Low-dose ultrasound effects on ultrasound healing: a controlled study with Yucatan pigs. *Arch Phys Med Rehabil.* 1992;73:656–664.

49. Lundeberg T, Kjartansson J, Samuelsson U. Effect of electrical nerve stimulation on healing of ischemic skin flaps. *Lancet.* 1988;2:712–714.

50. Kaada B. Vasodilation induced by transcutaneous nerve stimulation in peripheral ischemia (Reynaud's phenomena and diabetic polyneuropathy). *Eur Heart J.* 1982;3(4):303–314.

51. Kaada B. Promoted healing of chronic ulceration by transcutaneous nerve stimulation (TNS). *Vasa.* 1983;12:262–269.

52. Kloth LC. Bactericidal effect of passing an electrical current through a silver wire [poster presentation]. Presented at the Symposium on Advanced Wound Care; April 1996; Atlanta, GA.

53. Wolcott L, Wheeler P, Hardwicke H, et al. Accelerated healing of skin ulcers by electrotherapy: preliminary clinical results. *South Med J.* 1969;62:795–801.

54. Baker LL. The effect of electrical stimulation on cutaneous oxygen supply. *Rehabil Res Dev Prog Rep.* 1988;176.

55. Baker LL, Chamber R, et al. The effects of electrical stimulation on cutaneous oxygen supply in normal older adults and diabetic patients. *Phys Ther.* 1986;66:749.

56. Byl N, McKenzie A, et al. Microamperage stimulation: effects on subcutaneous oxygen (II). Presented at the Annual Conference of the California Chapter of the American Physical Therapy Association; 1990; San Diego, CA.

57. Alon G. Principles of electrical stimulation. In: Nelson R, Currier D, eds. *Clinical Electrotherapy.* Norwalk, CT: Appleton & Lange; 1991:35–103.

58. Barr JO. Transcutaneous electric nerve stimulation for pain management. In: Nelson R, Currier D, eds. *Clinical Electrotherapy.* Norwalk, CT: Appleton & Lange; 1991:280.

59. Gault W, Gatens P Jr. Use of low intensity direct current in management of ischemic skin ulcers. *Phys Ther.* 1976;56:265–269.

60. Carley PJ, Wainapel SF. Electrotherapy of acceleration of wound healing: low intensity direct current. *Arch Phys Med Rehabil.* 1985;66:443–446.

61. Barron JJ, Jacobson WE, Tidd T. Treatment of decubitus ulcers. *Minn Med.* 1985;68(2):103–106.

62. Leffmann DJ, Arnall DA, Holmgren PR. Effect of microamperage stimulation on the rate of wound healing in rats: a histological study. *Phys Ther.* 1994;74:195–200.

63. Kloth LC, Feedar J. Acceleration of wound healing with high voltage, monophasic, pulsed current. *Phys Ther.* 1988;68:503–508.

64. Griffin J, et al. Efficacy of high voltage pulsed current for healing of pressure ulcers in patients with spinal cord injury. *Phys Ther.* 1991;71:433–444.

65. Unger P, Eddy J, Raimastry S. A controlled study of the effect of high voltage pulsed current (HVPC) on wound healing. *Phys Ther.* 1991;71(suppl):S119.

66. Unger PC. A randomized clinical trial of the effect of HVPC on wound healing. *Phys Ther.* 1991;71(suppl):S118.

67. Akers T, Gabrielson A. The effect of high voltage galvanic stimulation on the rate of healing of decubitus ulcers. *Biomed Sci Instrum J.* 1984;20:99–100.

68. Feedar JA, Kloth LC, Gentzkow GD. Chronic dermal ulcer healing enhanced with monophasic pulsed electrical stimulation. *Phys Ther.* 1991;71:639–649.

69. Lundeberg TCM, Eriksson SV, Mats M. Electrical nerve stimulation improves healing of diabetic ulcers. *Ann Plast Surg.* 1992;29(4):328–330.

70. Stefanovska A, Vodovnik L, et al. Treatment of chronic wounds by means of electrical and electromagnetic fields, 2: value of FES parameters for pressure sore treatment. *Med Biol Eng Comput.* 1993;31:213–220.

71. Baker LL, Rubayi S, et al. Effect of electrical stimulation waveform on healing of ulcers in human beings with spinal cord injury. *Wound Rep Reg.* 1996;4:21–28.

72. Baker LL, Chambers R, et al. Effects of electrical stimulation on wound healing in patients with diabetic ulcers. *Diabetes Care.* 1997;20(3):1–8.

73. Donayre C. Diagnosis and management of vascular ulcers: arterial, venous and diabetic. Presented at Wound Care Management 96; Torrance, CA; October 1996.

74. Rasmussen MJ, Hayes DL, et al. Can transcutaneous electrical nerve stimulation be safely used in patients with permanent cardiac pacemakers? *Mayo Clin Proc.* 1988;63:443–445.

75. Eaglstein W. Off-label uses in wound care. Paper presented at the Symposium on Advanced Wound Care; Atlanta, GA; April 1996.

76. Cook T, Barr JO. Instrumentation. In: Nelson R, Currier D, eds. *Clinical Electrotherapy.* Norwalk, CT: Appleton & Lange; 1991:11–33.

77. Brown M. Electrical stimulation for wound management. In: Gogia PP, ed. *Clinical Wound Management.* Thorofare, NJ: Slack, Inc; 1995;176–183.

78. Kloth LC. Electrical stimulation for wound healing. Exhibitor presentation at American Physical Therapy Association Conference; Minneapolis, MN; June 1996.

79. Davis S. The effect of pulsed electrical stimulation on epidermal wound healing. *J Invest Dermatol.* 1988;90:555.

80. Cummings J, Kloth LC. Role of light, heat and electromagnetic energy in wound healing. In: McCulloch J, Kloth L, Feedar J, eds. *Wound Healing Alternatives in Management.* 2nd ed. Philadelphia: F.A. Davis; 1995:275–314.

81. Myer A. Observable effects on granulation tissue using warmed wound care products. Presented at Symposia, "Future Directions in Wound Healing"; American Physical Therapy Association Scientific Meeting; June 1997; San Diego, CA.

82. Beltran, KA, Thacker JG, et al. Impact pressures generated by commercial wound irrigation devices. Unpublished research report. Charlottesville, VA: University of Virginia Health Science Center; 1994.

83. Bourguignon GL, et al. Occlusive wound dressings suitable for use with electrical stimulation. *Wounds.* 1991;3(3):127.

84. Agren MS, Mertz MA. Collagenase during burn wound healing: influence of a hydrogel dressing and pulsed electrical stimulation. *Plast Reconstr Surg.* 1993;94:518–524.

85. Alon G. Panel discussion. Symposia, "Future Directions in Wound Healing"; American Physical Therapy Association Scientific Meeting; June 1997; San Diego, CA.

86. Kalinowski DP, Brogan MS, Sleeper MD. A practical technique for disinfecting electrical stimulation apparatuses used in wound treatment. *Phys Ther.* 1996;12:1340–1347.

87. Lock PM. The effect of temperature on mitotis at the edge of experimental wounds. In: Lundgren A, Sover AB, eds. *Symposia on Wound Healing: Plastic, Surgical and Dermatologic Aspects.* Sweden: Molndal; 1980.

88. Myers JA. Wound healing and the use of modern surgical dressing. *Pharm J.* 1982;229:103–104.

CHAPTER 17

Pulsatile Lavage with Concurrent Suction

Harriett Baugh Loehne

DEFINITION

Pulsatile lavage with concurrent suction is a method of wound care that provides cleansing and debridement with pulsed irrigation combined with suction. It thus provides negative pressure to remove the irrigant and debris to help reduce infection and to enhance granulation. This ultimately provides an improved foundation for wound healing.

Both console and battery-powered units are available, along with a selection of tips for cleansing and debridement of different wound configurations. Physicians have used these systems in the operating room since the early 1980s for irrigation in surgical procedures and to clean wounds of debris. Physical therapists (PTs) have used the systems since the late 1980s for irrigation and debridement to enhance healing of soft tissue wounds.

THEORY AND SCIENCE OF THE THERAPY

Whirlpools traditionally have been the most common choice for hydrotherapy, with jet lavage and bulb syringes also being used. Just as with whirlpool, there is limited research to support the use of pulsatile lavage with suction for wound healing. There are numerous anecdotal reports and case studies of benefits.[1,2] Haynes et al.[1] reported that the rate of granulation tissue formation was 12.2% per week for wounds treated with pulsatile lavage with suction and 4.8% per week for those treated with whirlpool. Other scientific and theoretic rationales for use of the therapy are as follows:

- It cleanses via gentle pulsatile lavage to stronger irrigation and debridement.

- It reduces bacteria and infection.
- It promotes granulation and epithelialization.
- Theory: the negative pressure of the suction stimulates granulation of clean wounds.

Management of Infection

Wound infection is a major concern in management of wounds. Dead and dying tissue, debris, clotted blood, and foreign bodies are predisposing conditions to wound infection. Rapid removal of these contaminants has been demonstrated to speed healing. Studies in the literature report that high-pressure pulsating irrigation decreases the presence of these contaminants and results in a lower incidence of wound infection.

Debridement and irrigation are important methods for controlling infection in wounds. Different methods are described for irrigation of wounds, including bulb syringe, Water Pik, shower spray, spray bottles, and pulsatile irrigation/lavage. Irrigation pressures vary with use of these different devices. If the pressure used to deliver the irrigation solution is too low, below 4 pounds per square inch (PSI), the lavage will not cleanse effectively. Safe, effective irrigation pressures range from 4 to 15 PSI. Exhibit 17–1 indicates the irrigation pressures obtained with these commonly used clinical devices.[3(p52)] A pressure of 8 PSI has been found to be significantly effective in removing bacteria and infection.[4] Irrigation at 13 PSI has attributed to reduction of inflammation in traumatic wounds. Irrigation pressures exceeding 15 PSI may traumatize tissue and drive bacteria into the wound tissues.[5,6] Stevenson et al.[4] reportedly calculated and tested combinations of syringe and needle sizes to determine wound irrigating pressure. The pressure produced

Exhibit 17–1 Irrigation Pressures Delivered by Various Devices

Device	Irrigation Impact Pressure (PSI)
Spray bottle—Ultra Klenz	1.2
Bulb syringe	2.0
Piston irrigation syringe (60 mL) with catheter tip	4.2
Saline squeeze bottle (250 mL) with irrigation cap	4.5
Water Pik at lowest setting (1)	6.0
Irrijet DS syringe with tip	7.6
35-mL syringe with 19-gauge needle or angiocatheter	8.0
Water Pik at middle setting (3)	42
Water Pik at highest setting (5)	>50
Pressurized cannister—Dey-Wash	>50

Source: Reprinted from N. Bergstrom, M.A. Bennett, C.E. Carlson, et al., *Treatment of Pressure Ulcers,* Clinical Practice Guideline No. 15, December, 1994, U.S. Department of Health and Human Services, Public Health Service, Agency for Health Care Policy and Research, AHCPR Publication No. 95-0652.

by a 35-mL syringe and a 19-gauge needle combination produced 8 PSI. Irrigation pressure of a bulb syringe is 2 PSI, which is not adequate to cleanse a wound.[3] The Water Pik ranges from 6 to more than 50 PSI, which may cause trauma to a wound and drive bacteria into it.[5]

Comparison studies among gravity flow irrigation, bulb syringe, and jet lavage on removal of bacteria and foreign bodies in wounds showed that the number of bacteria in the jet lavage group was comparable to the 10^5 levels attributed to the body's ability to manage infection.[7] The pulsatile lavage systems, described later in this chapter, allow the PSI to be adjusted. The PSI treatment setting chosen will depend upon the amount of necrotic tissue/exudate, the location of the wound, and the patient's comfort. Pulse rate, as well as PSI, has been demonstrated clinically to effect granulation formation and epithelialization of clean wounds.[2]

The medical community has been concerned that high-pressure irrigation may drive bacteria and contaminants into a wound and adjacent tissues. Bierbaum reviewed several studies that looked at this problem.[7] A high pressure of 70 PSI delivered 3 cm from the surface in moderately contaminated wounds was found to spread the fluid laterally rather than beneath the wound surface; however, it also impaired tissue defenses. In heavily contaminated wounds there was a 100-fold reduction in bacterial count after high-pressure irrigation. Part of clinical decision making involves weighing the risk-benefit ratio. Sometimes multiple risks have to be considered when selecting a treatment intervention. For example, will the benefit of high-pressure cleansing of a highly contaminated wound outweigh the known risk of tissue trauma and have a better outcome than an inadequate response? Physical therapists would not use high-pressure irrigation unless under the direct supervision of a physician. If the assessment indicates that high-pressure irrigation needs to be considered, it is a criterion for referral to the physician.

Pulsed jet lavage has been used for treatment of traumatic wounds in operating rooms and in the military for decades.[8] Delivery of vancomycin-, streptomycin-, and tetracycline-water solutions with pulsating jet lavage eliminated or reduced bacteria as early as the second day, with earlier healing, less tissue loss, and reduced scarring. Diabetic foot lesions treated with pulsatile lavage and topical antibiotics had infection controlled, and the wounds were able to be closed surgically with grafts or flaps. Reduced inflammation has been reported following pulsed lavage treatment and was correlated to the extent of foreign material remaining in the tissues. Early cleansing with this therapy accelerated wound healing.[7]

Mechanical Debridement

Irrigation is an effective mechanical debridement method to loosen and flush out debris and bacteria from contaminated wounds. Fluid dynamics plays an important role in expelling the loosened debris with the high-flowing irrigation stream. The incidence of wound infection is decreased as the amount of irrigation fluid increases.[7]

Pulsed stimulation of the tissue is also thought to affect wound debridement. The pulse phase rapidly compresses the tissue and then, during the interpulse phase, the tissue decompresses. This may be a mechanism for mechanically loosening debris. There is increased ease of sharp debridement after the treatment due to the loosened and softened necrotic tissue.

Negative Pressure

Concurrent suction with pulsatile lavage appears to stimulate production of granulation tissue in "clean" wounds as a result of the negative pressure.[9] Negative pressure applies noncompressive mechanical forces to the tissues and dilates arterioles. Dilatation allows increased blood flow and transcutaneous oxygen delivery to the tissues.[10] Suction also removes debris, bacteria, and irrigant.

INDICATIONS FOR THERAPY

The author's clinical experience includes use of pulsatile lavage with suction for both clean and infected wounds of

Exhibit 17–2 Wound Groups Indicated for Pulsatile Irrigation

Ulcers	Traumatic	Dermatology
Pressure	Multiple—eg, from motor vehicle accident	Pyoderma gangrenosum
Diabetic	Gunshot	
Venous insufficiency	Stab	
Arterial	Burn	
Arthritic/sclerotic	Abrasion	
	Puncture	
	Bite—insect, animal, human	
	Chemical	

Surgical and Dehisced	Infection	Other
Sternotomy	Necrotizing fasciitis	Intravenous (IV) site
Extremity bypass graft	Abscess	Drain site
Bypass graft donor site	Peritonitis	Maceration
Failed skin graft	Elephantiasis	Perineal
Failed flap	Lymphangitis	
Donor site	HIV/AIDS	
Fasciotomy	Hidradenitis	
Panniculectomy	Cellulitis	
Amputation site		
Tumor excision—with physician's order if malignant		

many etiologies. Wounds that have benefited from this therapy are included in the list shown in Exhibit 17–2.

Benefits to the Patient

There are many benefits to the patient with treatment by pulsatile lavage with suction. Frequently the patient can be treated by the physical therapist instead of the physician in the operating room, with significant cost savings. Treatment has contributed to the salvage of limbs.[2] There is improved safety with no transfers into/out of the whirlpool, as well as improved comfort with no change in temperature and the ability to control the pressure of the fluid on the wound. Periwound maceration is avoided with site-specific treatment. Benefits to the patient are summarized as follows:

- Pulsatile lavage with suction offers cost savings if operating room is not needed.
- It has contributed to salvage of limbs.
- It has improved safety.
- It offers improved comfort.
- Periwound maceration is avoided.

- It can be used for treatment of tunnels and undermining.
- Treatment is possible if whirlpool treatment is contraindicated.
- Treatment is possible if whirlpool treatment is inaccessible.

Clinical Wisdom:
Irrigation and Debridement of Tunnels

Pulsatile irrigation is an excellent choice for irrigation and debridement of tunnels and/or undermining.

Patients who would benefit from hydrotherapy but are contraindicated for whirlpool should be considered for pulsatile lavage, such as those who are unresponsive, those with cardiopulmonary compromise or venous insufficiency, and those who are febrile or incontinent. Pulsatile lavage also can be offered to patients who cannot be placed in the whirlpool because of contractures; ostomies; incisions with intact sutures; IV placement; skeletal traction; casted extremities; obesity; confinement to the intensive care unit (ICU), intermediate care unit (IMCU), burn unit, or isolation (negative pressure room); or combativeness/restraints.

Treatment is possible for the following conditions if whirlpool treatment is contraindicated:

- Unresponsiveness
- Cardiopulmonary compromise
- Venous insufficiency
- Fever
- Incontinence if body whirlpool is required.

Treatment is possible in the following circumstances if whirlpool treatment is inaccessible:

- Contractures—difficult body placement
- Ostomies
- Closed incisions with sutures intact
- IV placement
- Skeletal traction
- Casted extremities
- Obesity exceeding weight limit for stretcher/whirlpool
- Patient combative/restrained
- Patient in ICU, IMCU, burn unit, or isolation (negative pressure room).

Benefits to the Physical Therapist

The physical therapist is able to use time more efficiently and effectively when performing pulsatile lavage with suction compared to whirlpool. For instance, a pulsatile lavage treatment takes 15 to 30 minutes compared to 45 to 60 minutes of the therapist's time for a whirlpool treatment. It is convenient since there is no need to fill, drain, and clean a whirlpool. Cleanup is minimized since all supplies are disposable. This makes it possible for the PT to schedule more treatment visits. The design of the devices used for pulsatile lavage with suction provides the PT with the ability to control the intensity of the treatment, in pounds per square inch, and to select the correct tip for specific effects, leading to optimal results while safeguarding tissue. Some units allow greater control than others. Therefore, it is important for the PT to be aware of parameters and the limitations of the available equipment. Sharp debridement is significantly easier after pulsatile lavage with suction treatment because of the presence of loosened, softened debris and necrotic tissue. Benefits to the physical therapist are summarized as follows:

- There is no destruction of granulation tissue.
- There is increased efficiency with increased productivity.

- The PT has the ability to control PSI.
- Ease of sharp debridement is increased after treatment.
- Treatment is convenient.
- Cleanup is minimized.

Benefits to the Facility

In an acute care facility, pulsatile lavage with suction contributes to a decreased length of stay because of the rapid rate of granulation and epithelialization. Physician and staff time is saved if the patient does not have to be taken to the operating room for treatment. Cross-contamination is virtually eliminated, since all supplies are disposable. This is especially important with infection control issues for blood-borne pathogens (BBP) and the spread of methicillin-resistant *Staphylococcus aureus* (MRSA) and vancomycin-resistant enterococci (VRE). There are cost savings with no need to buy whirlpools, the disinfectant to clean them, the water and the power to heat the water, and the staff to maintain them. Benefits to the facility are summarized as follows:

- The length of stay is decreased because of the rapid rate of granulation and epithelialization.
- Physician and operating room staff time is saved.
- Cross-contamination is eliminated.
- Cost savings are gained with elimination of whirlpools.

PRECAUTIONS

The most important three words to remember when treating a patient with pulsatile lavage with suction are: ***know your anatomy!*** As with any method of debridement it is imperative to have a strong anatomy background, enhanced by cadaver dissection, and to have an illustrated textbook in close proximity. Just as important is awareness of the possibility of anomalies. When unsure of specific anatomy, it is recommended that the patient's surgeon be contacted for edification as to exposed and nearby structures. This is especially true when irrigating tracts and undermining.

There are no absolute contraindications to treatment with pulsatile lavage with suction. As with any wound care treatment, however, certain precautions should be observed. These precautions apply to treatment of the following:

- Insensate patients
- Those taking anticoagulant medication
- Those with wounds with tunnels and/or undermining.

Experienced therapists will treat wounds that require extra attention to the entire procedure (see *Color Plate 59*). These include the following:

- Wounds near major vessels (eg, in the groin or axilla)
- Wounds near a cavity lining (eg, pericardium or perito-neum)
- Bypass graft sites, anastomoses
- Exposed vessel, nerve, tendon, bone
- Grafts, flaps
- Facial wounds

Certain wounds should be assessed carefully before being treated in a facility or home where a physician and emergency medical aide is not immediately available. Careful decision making is needed before treating wounds near major vessels, cavity linings, and bypass graft sites outside of an acute care hospital or hospital outpatient setting.

OUTCOME MEASURES

Clinical decision making involves evaluation of intervention choices to achieve a desired outcome. Pulsatile lavage with concurrent suction is a very versatile treatment choice. As discussed earlier, it can be used for most wounds where the expected functional outcome is infection free, necrosis free, inflammation free, exudate free, and good granulation base, in preparation for closure by secondary intention or surgery.

Wound closure by secondary intention or preparation for surgical closure and limb salvage with an intention of pulsatile lavage with suction are reported in case studies.[2,7] Surrounding skin is protected from maceration. Because there are no controlled clinical trials of this therapy to compare, they cannot be used as a guide to length of time to achieve an expected outcome. Clinical judgment of the author suggests that the clinician should expect a decrease in necrotic tissue in 1 week and an increase in granulation/epithelialization in 1 week (see *Color Plates 58 and 59*). Following are some additional expected clinical outcomes:

- Odor and exudate free: 3 to 7 days
- Necrosis free: 2 weeks
- Progression from chronic inflammation phase to acute inflammation phase: 1 week
- Progression from acute inflammation phase to proliferation phase: 2 weeks

Clinical outcomes are one type of expected outcome. Another type of outcome to be considered is cost outcome. The cost of an outcome includes many factors, such as labor, supplies, and length of stay. For example, the average treatment time with pulsatile irrigation is 15 to 30 minutes, compared with 45 to 60 minutes for a whirlpool treatment. Infection control costs are minimal because of single-use, disposable components. Cross-contamination is virtually eliminated. These are very important cost-management factors in facilities that must work continuously to control contamination with BBP, MRSA, and VRE. Debridement with pulsatile irrigation with concurrent suction can be performed as a physical therapy procedure rather than a surgical procedure. This reduces surgeon and operating room costs.

Patient and caregiver satisfaction surveys monitor perceptions of how patients feel about the treatment they received and how it has affected function. Patients want to feel safe, secure, and comfortable during the treatment procedure. They may be scared about the consequences of failure to heal. Some are unable to attend a therapy session in the PT department. Treatment with pulsatile lavage can be given at the bedside with no need for lifts and transfers. Because of its portability and disposable components, it is an ideal modality for home treatment.

FREQUENCY AND DURATION

Patients are usually treated once a day. If the wound has more than 50% necrotic/nonviable tissue with purulent drainage/foul odor, and especially if sepsis is present, treatment twice a day is reasonable. Treatment two or three times a week is recommended if there is a full granulation base, no odor, and no purulent drainage. If the wound is being treated with the vacuum-assisted closure device (VAC), pulsatile lavage with suction is used with each VAC change, usually three times a week (VAC is described further below, under Vacuum Assisted Closure). Pulsatile lavage with suction should be discontinued when the wound is closed, there is no increase in granulation/epithelialization in 1 week, or there is no decrease in necrotic tissue in 1 week (Exhibit 17–3).

CAUTIONS

Treatment should be stopped if the patient complains of increased pain or is unable to tolerate treatment because of pain. A premedication order may be needed from the patient's physician. With an arterial bleeder, treatment must be stopped immediately and the physician called STAT (immediately). Any other bleeding not stopped with pressure within 10 minutes requires a physician consultation. If an abscess other than the one being treated is opened or a bone/joint disarticulation occurs, the physician also should be notified. Cautions are summarized as follows:

- Stop treatment when the following occurs:
  1. Patient complains of increased pain.
  2. Patient is unable to tolerate treatment because of pain.

Exhibit 17–3 Frequency and Duration of Treatment

Frequency	Daily	Twice Daily	Three Times per Week	Discontinue
Most wounds	X			
>50% Necrotic		X		
Purulent drainage		X		
Sepsis		X		
Full granulation base			X	
VAC being used			X	
Duration				
No increased granulation for 1 week				X
No decreased necrotic tissue for 1 week				X
Wound closed				X

Clinical Wisdom: *Prevent Disruption of Clot following Pressure To Stop Bleeding*

After applying pressure over gauze packing to stop bleeding and bleeding has stopped, leave the bottom layer of gauze in place to avoid disruption of the clot and restarting the bleeding. Cover with the prescribed dressing.

- Stop and call physician in any of the following circumstances:
  1. Patient has an arterial bleeder: notify physician STAT.
  2. Bleeding has not stopped after 10 minutes of pressure.
  3. Abscess is opened.
  4. Joint is disarticulated.

VACUUM ASSISTED CLOSURE

Kinetic Concepts' VAC is a device that uses a pump, attached by tubing to a sponge placed in the wound, to create a vacuum to remove fluid. The negative pressure on the wound helps reduce edema, increase blood supply, and decrease bacterial colonization. The procedure increases tension among the surrounding cells, which encourages cell growth and division, drawing the edges of the wound to the center and assisting wound closure. It provides a moist wound environment to promote more effective cellular activity and also helps prevent contamination of the wound site from outside bacteria.

Indications for use are pressure ulcers, chronic open wounds, and meshed grafts and flaps. The VAC is contraindicated in the presence of fistulas to organs or body cavities, osteomyelitis, and malignancy in the wound. Precautions are observed when there is active bleeding, patients are taking anticoagulants, and wound hemostasis is difficult.

The sponge is not changed for meshed grafts. It is changed every 12 hours with an infected wound and every 48 hours with a chronic open wound. After the sponge is removed, pulsatile lavage with suction is indicated to irrigate and debride the wound, including tunnels and undermining, before a new sponge is placed and secured with an adherent, occlusive dressing. The combination of the VAC and pulsed lavage has healed wounds four times faster than nontreated wounds, producing extraordinary cost savings.

PERFORMANCE OF PULSATILE LAVAGE WITH SUCTION (Figure 17–1)

Procedures for Pulsatile Lavage with Suction

Procedure Set-Up

Most patients ideally are treated on a high-low stretcher, bed, or treatment table adjusted to a height that ensures the therapist's proper body mechanics. Treatment may be delivered in the physical therapy department or at bedside in the patient's room. A fluid-proof or fluid-resistant pad is placed under the body part with the wound, and towels are strategically placed around the wound and covering adjacent body parts. A sterile field is set up with treatment and dressing supplies in easy reach. A strong light source is important during pulsatile lavage and during debridement.

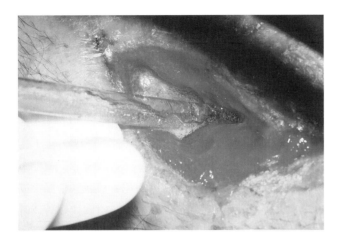

Figure 17–1 Gunshot wound with tunnel.

Outpatients with foot wounds can be treated seated in a wheelchair with an elevating footrest, with towels padding the footrest. The therapist sits on low footstool in front of the patient and in easy reach of the sterile field set-up of treatment and dressing supplies. A basin may be placed under the foot to catch any overflow of irrigant.

An aide is invaluable for efficiency and assistance with difficult body placement in treatment of some wounds. Duties vary depending on the system used. Connecting the tubing to the power source and suction source, spiking the bags of fluid, turning the unit off and on, adjusting the PSI at the therapist's direction, and emptying and replacing the filled suction canisters and new fluid bags are common procedures that can be done by the aide, saving the therapist time and from having to change gloves during treatment. After the treatment is completed, the aide also can dispose of the personal protective equipment, old dressings, and disposables while the therapist completes the documentation.

Infection Control

Universal Precautions. Protocols should adhere to each facility's policy. The patient should be treated in an enclosed area, separate from other patients. If at the bedside, ask all visitors to leave the room during treatment. If in a semiprivate room, curtains must be drawn around the patient being treated. Call housekeeping to change the curtains if they are visibly soiled after the treatment. If a home treatment, ask the family members/visitors to leave the room during treatment; otherwise personal protective equipment must be worn as discussed below.

All exposed linen used to control splash should be placed in a clear plastic biohazard bag after treatment for transport to the laundry. Clean the stretcher/wheelchair after each treatment if it is used to transport and treat the patient. Do not use a mattress or cushion with tears in the protective cover-

ing. Use basins to contain the irrigant overflow with treatment of extremity wounds. Disinfect the basin after each use. Clean the dressing cart with an approved disinfectant solution after each use. Dispose of all disposables in the appropriate waste stream per Occupational Safety and Health Administration (OSHA) guidelines.

Personal Protective Equipment. Secondary to mist and splashing, all staff present during treatment must wear personal protective equipment, consisting of the following (see Figure 17–2):

- Face shields or goggles and masks
- Fluid-proof gowns
- Fluid-resistant knee-high boots
- Nonsterile/sterile gloves
- Hair covers

Single-Use Only. All disposables except one discussed below are marked single-use only, Food and Drug Adminis-

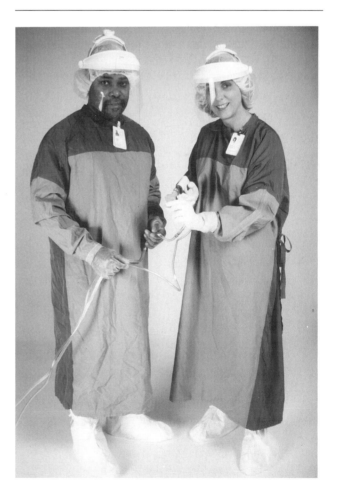

Figure 17–2 Personal protective equipment for hydrotherapy treatment.

tration and OSHA mandate compliance. In fact, if used more than one time, Medicare and other payers consider the occurrence investigational and not reimbursable. Legal liability is possible if disposables are reused.

Davol has a suction diverter tip that allows the same hand piece to be used multiple times with the *same* patient. Otherwise, units cannot be cleaned without damaging the product or being assured that all contaminants and/or disinfection material is removed.

Latex Content

The latex content of the product used (see Exhibit 17–4) is important for latex-sensitive and latex-allergic patients, especially those with myelodysplasia, who must be treated in a latex-free environment.[12]

Equipment Needed

Power Unit

Units are available powered by three sources (Exhibit 17–5). A machine console unit is electrically driven and is attached to a mobile operating room base and stand or a mobile wound care cart. Another product is driven by nitrogen or medical air tanks, which can be attached to a wound care cart. All product manufacturers have a battery unit that is completely disposable.

Sterile debridement tips include a fan spray/shower head for soft tissue debridement and general irrigation, and open tract tips for undermining tracts, and tunnels (Exhibit 17–6). Multiple other tips are available, depending on the manufac-

Exhibit 17–4 Latex Content of Products

Latex	Davol	Stryker	Zimmer
Present	Simpulse Plus	N/A	Pulsavac
Not present	VariCare Simpulse Solo	SurgiLav	Pulsavac III Var-A-Pulse

Exhibit 17–5 Products Available and Power Sources

Power Source	Davol	Stryker	Zimmer
Electrically driven console	None	None	Pulsavac Pulsavac III
Medical air/nitrogen tanks	Simpulse Plus	None	None
Batteries—unit disposable	Simpulse Solo VariCare	SurgiLav Plus	Var-a-Pulse

Exhibit 17–6 Most Often Used Tips for Soft Tissue Wound Care

Tip	Davol	Stryker	Zimmer
Fan spray with splash shield	Yes—small	Yes—large	Yes—small
Retractable splash shield	Yes	No	No
Open tract	Yes	Yes	Yes
Narrow open tract	Yes (no suction)	No	Yes
Retractable splash shield	No	No	Yes
Flexible, narrow open tract	Yes	No	No

turer, with new tips in product development. A small, rather than large, splash shield placed in total contact with the tissue is recommended to obtain adequate suction for negative pressure. Figure 17–3 shows a wound view with an irrigation tip.

All products have hand controls and tubing for spiking the saline bag (see Figure 17–4).

Irrigation Fluid

Normal saline (0.9% sodium chloride) is preferred. Antibiotics can be added with a physician's order. Water is not recommended because it is not physiologic. Antiseptic agents or skin cleansers (povidone-iodine, iodophor, sodium hypochlorite, hydrogen peroxide, acetic acid) should not be used due to cytotoxicity to normal and/or wound tissue.[5]

Saline bags should be warmed in hot tap water. The number of bags used depends on the number and size of the wounds, the amount of necrotic tissue and exudate, and the patient's tolerance of the procedure.

Suction

Either a wall suction or portable pump is necessary for this modality. Equipment includes canisters, a regulator, and connecting tubing, which is required with the Stryker product and with the others if the suction source is too far away from the wound with the tubing provided.

The suction removes debris, bacteria, and the irrigant, and provides negative pressure to increase the rate of granulation tissue.[3] Parameters are usually 60 to 100 mm Hg of continuous suction. It should be decreased if there is bleeding, the wound is near a vessel or cavity, or the patient complains of pain.

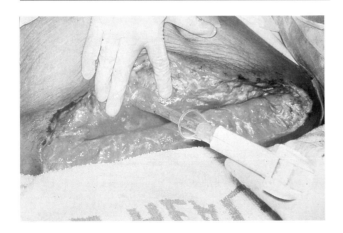

Figure 17–3 Wound view with a tip. Courtesy of Zimmer, Inc., Dover, Ohio.

Figure 17–4 Hand controls and tubing pack. Courtesy of Zimmer, Inc., Dover, Ohio.

Pressure

> **Clinical Wisdom:** *Importance of Impact Pressure*
>
> It is very important for the therapist to control and to know the impact pressure at all times during the treatment.

Pressure is measured in pounds per square inch (PSI). If the pressure is too high, bacteria and foreign matter can be forced into viable tissue, and granulation and epithelial tissues can be damaged. The Agency for Health Care Policy and Research (AHCPR) guidelines recommend a treatment range of 4 to 15 PSI.[3]

Initiation of treatment is usually 2 to 4 PSI, with a typical range of 4 to 8 PSI. A setting of 2 to 4 PSI is advised for tracts and undermining due to inability to visualize the wound base and nearby structures. Treatment with greater than 15 PSI should be undertaken only if the physician is present and with a specific written order (Exhibit 17–7).

During treatment PSI should be increased in the presence of tough eschar and excessive necrotic tissue. It should be decreased if the patient complains of pain, bleeding occurs, or the tip is near a major or exposed vessel, nerve, tendon, or cavity lining. Exhibit 17–8 gives the pressure range and control available on various pressure products.

HOW TO USE DIFFERENT EQUIPMENT MODELS

> **Davol Simpulse Plus Procedure**

Begin Treatment.

1. Attach the suction canister to the regulator on suction source.

Exhibit 17–7 Pressure Used

PSI	2–4 PSI	4 PSI	4–8 PSI	15 PSI	16+ PSI
Pulsatile Lavage with Suction					
Initiation	X				
Tracts/undermining	X				
Minimum effective		X			
Typical range			X		
Maximum—PT				X	
With physician present					X

Exhibit 17–8 Pressure Range and Control Available (On/Off Control on All Hand Pieces)

Product	PSI Range	Gauge on Power Source	Digital Readout LED	Adjust at Source	Vary at Hand Control
Davol Simpulse Plus	3.6–12.3 PSI (Flexible Open tract tip 1.3–5.1 PSI)	Yes	No	Source gauge	Yes
Simpulse Solo	0–12.3 PSI (Open tract tip 0–11.5 PSI)	N/A	No	No	Yes
VariCare	3–11.3 PSI (Open tract tip 1.7–11.5 PSI)	N/A	No	Dial control— three settings	Yes
Stryker SurgiLav	0.8–6.8 PSI (Varies with tip used)	N/A	No	No	Switch with two settings
Zimmer Pulsavac	0–60 PSI	Yes	No	Dial control	Yes
Pulsavac III	0–60 PSI 0–30 PSI switch	Yes	Yes	Dial control	Yes
Var-A-Pulse	0–60 PSI	N/A	No	Dial control— six settings	Yes

2. Adjust suction to the appropriate mm Hg continuous.
3. Hang the saline bag(s) on an IV pole or place on any surface.
4. Remove the hand piece, tubing, tip, and dual spike adapter from the package; place on sterile field.
5. Connect the dual spike adapter to the pump spike if desired.
6. Remove the blue lock pin on the hand piece to release the trigger, and the blue retaining ring if the tip with the large splash shield is used. Discard blue items.
7. Insert the tip.
8. Attach the suction tubing onto the suction tubing connector and suction canister.
9. Spike the irrigation bag.
10. Prime the unit by squeezing the trigger until irrigant exits the tip. The bag may be squeezed to facilitate priming.
11. With the gas source (nitrogen or medical air) pressure at zero, insert the gas connector into a Schrader style connector until a click is heard.
12. Set the source pressure to the desired pounds per square inch. Do not exceed 80 PSI source pressure for open tract tips or 60 PSI for the splash shield, so as not to exceed 15 PSI impact pressure. Pressure may be adjusted from 2 to 15 PSI.
13. Place the tip in/on the wound.
14. Squeeze the hand piece trigger to irrigate.
15. The trigger lock button may be used to lock at maximum flow. While squeezing the trigger, push the lock button to engage; to release, squeeze the trigger.

When Treatment Is Completed.

1. Reduce the pressure regulator to 0 PSI at the gas source.
2. Detach the unit from the source.
3. Turn off suction and remove the tubing from the suction source.
4. Dispose of all equipment in a white biohazard bag.
5. Empty the suction canister into a hopper or commode.
6. If disposable, place the empty canister in a white biohazard bag. If glass, place in a clear biohazard bag to be sent for resterilization.

Davol Simpulse Solo/Simpulse VariCare Procedure

Begin Treatment.

1. Attach the suction canister to the regulator on suction source.

2. Adjust suction to the appropriate mm Hg continuous.
3. Hang the saline bag(s) on an IV pole or place on any surface.
4. Remove the hand piece and the tip from the package; place on sterile field.
5. Attach the tip to the hand piece.
6. Spike the irrigation bag; a dual spike adapter is available.
7. Connect the tubing to the suction connection on the hand piece and to the suction source.
8. Remove the blue lock pin on the hand piece to release the trigger, and the blue retaining ring if the tip with the large splash shield is used; discard blue items.
9. With the hand piece at a 45° angle, squeeze the trigger to fill the tubing with solution. The bag may be squeezed to facilitate priming.
10. Place the tip in/on the wound and pull the trigger. The delivered pressure varies with the amount of pressure on the trigger.

When Treatment Is Completed.

1. Turn off suction and remove the tubing from the suction source.
2. Release the latch on the bottom of the hand piece, pull out the battery compartment, and remove the batteries. Batteries can be recycled if not contaminated.
3. Dispose of all other equipment in a white biohazard bag.
4. Empty the suction canister into a hopper or commode.
5. If disposable, place the empty canister in a white biohazard bag. If glass, place in a clear biohazard bag to be sent for resterilization.

Stryker SurgiLav Plus Procedure

Begin Treatment.

1. Attach the suction canister to the regulator on suction source.
2. Adjust suction to the appropriate mm Hg continuous.
3. Hang the bag of saline on an IV pole.
4. Remove the hand piece and the tip from the package; place on sterile field. Place extension tubing on the field.
5. Insert the tip into the hand piece.
6. Spike the bag of saline.
7. Attach the extension tubing, one end to the hand piece and other end to the suction canister.
8. Squeeze the trigger to fill the tip with solution.

9. Place the tip in/on the wound and pull the trigger.
10. Adjust speed for desired PSI—varies with the tip; only two pressures are available with each tip.

When Treatment Is Completed.

1. Turn off suction and remove the tubing from the suction source.
2. Break open the hand piece to remove the batteries (can be recycled if not contaminated).
3. Dispose of all other equipment in a white biohazard bag.
4. Empty the suction canister into a hopper or commode.
5. If disposable, place the empty canister in a white biohazard bag. If glass, place in a clear biohazard bag to be sent for resterilization.

Zimmer Pulsavac Procedure

Begin Treatment.

1. Attach the suction canister to the regulator on suction source.
2. Adjust suction to the appropriate mm Hg continuous.
3. Hang the saline bag(s) on the suspension support on the solution support pole.
4. Remove the hand piece, tubing, and tip from the package; place on sterile field.
5. Attach the tip to the hand piece.
6. Connect the hand control suction tube to the wall suction canister.
7. Insert the fluid pump; close and secure the door to the unit.
8. Push the transducer connector onto the barbed fitting on the side of the unit.
9. Push the tubing into the retainer clip.
10. Move the clamps to "Y" and close.
11. Spike the irrigation bag; the unit is dual spike capable.
12. Remove the dust covers from the tubing and connect the hand control to the fluid set.
13. Plug in the unit with the power switch in the *off* position and the pressure control at zero setting.
14. Depress the power switch to the *on* position.
15. Rotate the pressure control setting to 10 to prime; return to the appropriate setting for desired PSI.
16. Place the tip in/on the wound.
17. Pull on or push on the trigger available to turn the unit on.

When Treatment Is Completed.

1. Reduce the pressure control to zero.
2. Turn off suction and remove the tubing from the suction source.

3. Remove the tubing from the retainer clip and the transducer connector from the barbed fitting.
4. Open the door to the unit and remove the fluid pump.
5. Dispose of all equipment in a white biohazard bag.
6. Empty the suction canister into a hopper or commode.
7. If disposable, place the empty canister in a white biohazard bag. If glass, place in a clear biohazard bag to be sent for resterilization.

Zimmer Pulsavac III Procedure

Begin Treatment.

1. Attach the suction canister to the regulator on suction source.
2. Adjust suction to the appropriate mm Hg continuous.
3. Hang the saline bag(s) on the IV hanger on top of the Pulsavac III console.
4. Empty the sterile packages of Pulsavac supplies onto a sterile field.
5. Attach the appropriate tip to the hand control.
6. Plug the console into the electricity source.
7. Turn the machine to *on*.
8. Depress the *load/unload* switch; the cassette platform will recede into the unit.
9. Securely snap the blue fluid pump cassette onto the platform, pressing gently *one* time until clicks are heard; the platform will slide out automatically.
10. Move the clamps to "Y" and close.
11. Connect the suction tube, and the connecting tubing if needed, to the suction canister.
12. Spike the irrigation bag.
13. With the hand control in the *on* position, open the clamp compressing the spike tubing.
14. To prime the fluid, depress the *run/stop* switch and turn the pressure setting to maximum PSI until fluid flows freely. The half-power switch, located on the back of the console, should be used.
15. Decrease the pounds per square inch setting to the desired pressure.
16. Place the tip in/on the wound.
17. Pull on or push on the trigger.

When Treatment Is Completed.

1. Depress the *run/stop* switch.
2. Depress the *load/unload* switch; the plate will slide in.
3. Remove the tubing and the hand control by removing the cassette, squeezing on the concave sides of the cassette body, and then lifting up.

4. Depress the *on/off* switch to the *off* position.
5. Turn off suction and remove the tubing from the suction source.
6. Dispose of all equipment in a white biohazard bag.
7. Empty the suction canister into a hopper or commode.
8. If disposable, place the empty canister in a white biohazard bag. If glass, place in a clear biohazard bag to be sent for resterilization.

Zimmer Var-A-Pulse Procedure

Begin Treatment.

1. Attach the suction canister to the regulator on suction source.
2. Adjust the suction to the appropriate mm Hg continuous.
3. Hang the saline bag(s) on an IV pole.
4. Remove the hand piece, tubing, and tip from the package; place on sterile field.
5. Attach the tip to the hand piece.
6. Spike the irrigation bag; a dual spike is available.
7. Connect the tubing to the suction source.

8. Set the dial at the hand piece's base for the desired PSI.
9. Place the tip in/on the wound and turn the hand piece on.

When Treatment Is Completed.

1. Turn off suction and remove the tubing from the suction source.
2. Open the latch at the base to separate the handle to remove the batteries (can be recycled if not contaminated).
3. Dispose of the entire unit in a white biohazard bag.
4. Empty the suction canister into a hopper or commode.
5. If disposable, place the empty canister in a white biohazard bag. If glass, place in a clear biohazard bag to be sent for resterilization.

DOCUMENTATION

The following case study uses the diagnostic process described in Chapter 1, The Diagnostic Process, to document the need for skilled PT intervention using pulsatile lavage with suction. The methodology of the functional outcome report is provided.[11]

Case Study: Gunshot Wound Treated with Pulsatile Lavage with Suction

Patient ID: W.S.   Age: 29   Onset: January 2

Initial Assessment

Reason for Referral

The patient was referred for a blasted shoulder wound with buckshot, necrotic tissue, tunnels, and undermining in the wound.

Medical History and Systems Review

The patient, previously fully functionally independent with no prior medical history, suffered a self-inflicted gunshot wound to the left shoulder. On the day of the injury and admission to the hospital, January 2, 1995, he had surgical exploration of the blasted shoulder wound. The humeral head was resected; fragments were resected from the laterally pulverized clavicle. There was no injury to the brachial plexus or axillary vasculature. The left upper extremity was placed in traction with pins. He had subsequent surgical incisions and drainage of the wound in the operating room on January 3, 4, 5, and 6, with closure of the shoulder capsule on January 6 (see Figure 17–3).

Evaluation

The patient was admitted to the burn unit after the initial surgery because of the severity of the wounds and the complicated dressing changes required. The presence of necrotic tissue, purulent exudate, buckshot, and numerous tunnels and undermining were indications for treatment with pulsatile lavage with concurrent suction.

Examination—January 13

Joint Integrity

The left humeral head has been resected. The left upper extremity is in skeletal traction with pins, with shoulder abducted to 90°. The lateral clavicle is pulverized.

Circulation

There is no injury to the axillary vasculature; there is edema in the left upper extremity.

Sensation

There is no injury to the brachial plexus.

Mobility

The patient is restricted to the supine position.

Integumentary

The left shoulder has a through-and-through wound, with the shotgun entrance wound on the anterior and the exit wound on the posterior.

Size.

- Anterior border—118.75-cm surface open area
- Posterior border—50.0-cm surface open area
- Medial depth—2.0 cm
- Lateral depth—1.75 cm
- Tunneling and undermining cannot be measured because of proximity of vessels.

Tissue Assessment. The wound has red granulation with scattered areas of yellow and brown necrotic tissue; there is buckshot present. The periwound tissue is erythematous and edematous.

Wound Healing Phase. The wound is in acute inflammation phase.

Functional Diagnosis

- Soft tissue injury
  1. Absence of proliferation phase
  2. Absence of epithelialization phase
  3. Undue susceptibility to infection caused by debris in wound
- Functional loss of mobility associated with shoulder injury leading to inability to perform self care and undue susceptibility to pressure ulcers.

Need for Skilled Services

Pulsatile lavage with suction by physical therapist is indicated in an attempt to avoid another surgical incision and drainage and to prepare the wound for a subsequent skin graft. Increased mobility will be allowed with an accelerated healing process. Therapeutic positioning is necessary to avoid pressure ulcers.

Targeted Outcomes

- The wound bed will be clean, including tunnels and undermining.
- The wound will progress through the phases of healing from inflammation to epithelialization.
- The patient will be properly positioned to remove pressure.

Treatment Plan

- Irrigate and mechanically debride the wound with the Pulsavac System, including tunnels and undermining. Remove the buckshot. Treat with 1 L of normal saline, 4 to 12 PSI, 80 mm Hg suction.
- Perform sharp debridement of necrotic tissue with forceps and scissors.

- Maintain moist wound bed and obliterate dead space with dressing changes of wet to damp Dakin's solution–soaked gauze; cover with a 5 × 9-inch gauze pad and secure with dry gauze and paper tape. Tunnels and undermining will be loosely packed.
- Perform therapeutic positioning.

Prognosis

There will be no necrotic tissue and no debris. The wound will have a red granulation base and be ready for skin grafting by the physician.

Target Date. Two weeks.

Frequency. Once a day, 6 days per week.

Reexamination by Physical Therapy on January 20

Size.

- Anterior wound—68.25-cm surface open area
- Posterior wound—28.75-cm surface open area
- Medial depth—1.5 cm
- Lateral depth—1.0 cm

Tissue Assessment. The wound has no necrotic tissue. There is a full red granulation base and increased epithelialization. There is no periwound erythema. Tunneling and undermining are present only in the proximal portion of the anterior wound.

Wound Healing Phase. Proliferation phase.

Intervention

Physical Therapy. Six treatments of pulsatile lavage with suction, followed by sharp debridement as needed.

Physical Therapy and Nursing. Dressing changes.

Physicians. On January 19 the pins are removed and traction is discontinued. The patient is transferred from the burn unit to a regular room.

Revised Prognosis

Closure of the wound by secondary intention.

Discharge Outcome

The patient's wounds not only required no further surgical incisions and drainage, but also had a significant increase in granulation and epithelialization with no necrotic tissue present. Anterior and posterior wounds had a decreased surface open area of 42%. Medial depth decreased 25% and lateral depth decreased 43% within 7 days. The physicians decided to allow the wound to close by secondary intention rather than a skin graft. The patient was discharged home January 21, to continue dressing changes by his mother. Future surgical procedures were anticipated to replace the shoulder joint. He was lost to follow-up.

REFERENCES

1. Haynes LJ, et al. Comparison of Pulsavac and sterile whirlpool regarding the promotion of tissue granulation. Lubbock TX: University Medical Center and Methodist Hospital; 1994.

2. Loehne HB. Enhanced wound care using Pulsavac System: case studies. *Acute Care Perspect.* 1995 Summer; 9:13–15.

3. U.S. Department of Health and Human Services. Treatment of pressure ulcers. *AHCPR Clinical Practice Guideline.* 1994;15:50–53.

4. Stevenson TR, Thacker JG, Rodeheaver GT, Bacchetta C, Edgerton MT, Edlich RF. Cleansing the traumatic wound by high pressure syringe irrigation. *JACEP.* 1976 Jan;5(1):17–21.

5. Bhaskar SN, Cutright DT, Gross A. Effect of water lavage on infected wounds in the rat. *J Periodontol.* 1969;40:671.

6. Wheeler CB, Rodeheaver GT, Thacker JG, Edgerton MT, Edlich RF. Side effects of high pressure irrigation. *Surg Gynecol Obstet.* 1976; 143:775–778.

7. Bierbaum B. *High Pressure, Pulsatile Lavage in Wound Management: A Literature Review.* Cranston, RI: Davol, Inc.; 1986.

8. Bhaskar SN, Cutright DE, Hunsuck EE, Gross A. Pulsating water jet devices in debridement of combat wounds. *Milit Med.* 1971;136:264–266.

9. Morykwas MJ, Argenta LC. Use of negative pressure to increase the rate of granulation tissue formation in chronic open wounds. Presented at the annual meeting of the Federation of American Societies of Experimental Biology; March 28–April 1, 1993; New Orleans, LA.

10. Argenta LC, Morykwas M, Rouchard R. The use of negative pressure to promote healing of pressure ulcers and chronic wounds. Presented at the joint meeting of the Wound Healing Society and the European Tissue Repair Society; August 22–25, 1993; Amsterdam, Netherlands.

11. Swanson G. Functional outcome report: the next generation in physical therapy reporting. In: *Documenting PT Outcomes.* St. Louis, MO: Mosby-Year Book; 1993.

12. US Food and Drug Administration. Allergic reactions to latex-containing medical devices. *FDA Medical Bulletin.* 1991, July 2–3.

CHAPTER 18

Pulsed Short Wave Diathermy and Pulsed Radio Frequency Stimulation

Carrie Sussman

INTRODUCTION

Short wave diathermy was introduced in Germany in 1907 and spread throughout Europe and the United States.[1] In the next decades diathermy was used to treat all types of illnesses and injuries. The stimulator used electromagnetic short waves from the short wave radio portion of the spectrum and was called continuous short wave diathermy (CSWD). The word *diathermy* was used to describe the relatively uniform heating that was produced by conversion of high-frequency electrical currents into heat.[1] CSWD was an application of electromagnetic energy to medicine. CSWD became popular because it was then possible to target deep tissue structures and produce subcutaneous tissue heating rather than superficial heating with hot packs and infrared, where heat is rapidly dissipated by the superficial vasculature.

DEFINITIONS AND TERMINOLOGY

Electromagnetic Fields

CSWD, pulsed short wave diathermy (PSWD), and pulsed radio frequency stimulation (PRFS) medical equipment operates in one small portion of the electromagnetic spectrum (sometimes referred to as the radio, radiation, or frequency spectrum). The entire spectrum goes from below power transmission waves (very-low frequency) to above cosmic rays (very-high frequency) and includes radio waves, visible light, and X-rays. All frequencies within the spectrum have certain characteristics in common. For example, they all travel

at the speed of light, which is 300,000 km (186,000 miles) per second. They all travel unimpeded through a vacuum. They all consist of two parts, a magnetic field and an electrostatic field, traveling at right angles to each other. One of many important differences between waves from different portions of the spectrum is what happens when they encounter an object. Are they adsorbed (like heat waves)? Do they have some other effect on the object? Are they reflected (like light waves striking a mirror)? Or do they ignore the object (like cosmic rays passing through the earth)?

It should be noted that electromagnetic waves discussed here are not sound, or ultrasonic waves, which require a physical medium through which to travel. They are "pure energy" and do not have any mass. Also, the equipment and techniques for using the equipment discussed in this chapter are not the same as the high- or low-voltage electrical stimulation equipment, which operates on pulsed direct current (DC), not the 27.12 MHz of the typical CSWD or PRFS equipment discussed in this chapter. At the 27.12 MHz used by short wave diathermy and pulsed radio frequency medical equipment, some of the energy will pass through a patient's body, some will be reflected from a patient's skin, some will be absorbed by the tissue and converted to heat, and some will cause the tissue cells within the patient's body to react in a certain way. How to best use heating and tissue reaction is the subject of this chapter. Exhibit 18–1 is a reference list of the devices discussed and their acronyms.

Units of Measurement

There are several units of measurement associated with electromagnetic fields of which the reader should be aware. The frequency of a wave may be expressed in two manners: first, as a frequency, or how many cycles occur within a

Note: The contributions of **Robert J. Sussman, MSEE, and Marko S. Markov, PhD**, are gratefully acknowledged.

Exhibit 18–1 List of Devices and Their Acronyms

Acronym	Device
CSWD	Continous Short Wave Diathermy
PSWD	Pulsed Short Wave Diathermy
PRFS	Pulsed Radio Frequency Stimulation

1-second period (eg, 27.12 million for a 27.12-MHz wave); second, the same frequency may be expressed as a wave length, which is how far the wave has traveled (while moving at the speed of light) during one cycle. For our 27.12-MHz example this would be 11 m. Signal (or wave) strength is measured in volts per meter (V/m). This unit represents how much voltage would be induced by the magnetic flux portion of the wave while traveling through free space and going through a 1-m long wire.

Carrier Frequency and Waveforms

In studying diathermy equipment there are two frequencies of which one must be aware: the carrier frequency and the waveform or modulation frequency. The carrier frequency is the basic radio frequency (ie, the radio station frequency) that the equipment operates (ie, 27.12 MHz); for CSWD equipment it is the only frequency involved. The waveform or modulation frequency is the frequency at which the carrier frequency is modulated (ie, the music from the radio station). For PSWD and PRFS equipment, modulation frequency is the rate at which the carrier frequency is turned on and off (ie, 600 pulses per second [pps]). For the pulsed high-voltage equipment of Chapter 16, the waveform is monophasic pulsed current. The waveform frequency may be the same as that used for PRFS equipment.

When radio frequency is transmitted as a continuous wave (or signal), enough energy can be absorbed by the body to cause noticeable heating (eg, the microwave oven effect). To control these heating effects and still maintain the tissue-stimulation benefits of the electromagnetic field stimulation, several manufacturers developed a pulsed short wave radio frequency generator that delivers bursts or trains of radio frequency pulses.

Diathermy equipment, including CSWD, PSWD, and PRFS, operate at frequency specified by the Federal Communications Commission (FCC), which allows use of radio frequencies of 13.56, 27.12, and 40.68 MHz for these medical devices. Typically, PSWD and PFRS use 27.12 MHz. Signals at these frequencies can travel through the body relatively uninterrupted, without contact between the applicator and the body. This is an important attribute for treatment.

Radio frequency waves transport electromagnetic energy through air or a vacuum without the need for a conductive medium such as water or air. The energy delivered to the tissues is reduced, however, as the air gap between the tissues and the applicator head increases because a portion of the energy is dispersed away from the target. For example, a clinical application is to increase the air gap between the applicator head and the tissues to reduce the heating effects of PSWD for patients with heat sensitivity or where mild heating is required. When using PRFS the distance should be *small*, 0.5 cm, so as *not* to significantly reduce energy delivered. Radio waves can interact and influence matter with which they contact, because matter contains electrical charges affected by electromagnetic waves.

Clinical Wisdom:
Using the Air Gap To Modify Heating Effects

Increase the air gap when using PSWD for patients with heat sensitivity or where mild heating effects are desired.

**Greater Pulse Frequency and Width ⇨
More Energy ⇨ More Heat**

Pulse Rate and Pulse Duration (Width)

PSWD and PRFS use radio waves that are interrupted (eg, pulsed) at regular intervals. The pulse rates for PSWD vary from 1 to 7,000 pps. The pulse duration (or width) varies from 65 to 400 microseconds (μs; 1 μs is 10^{-6} seconds). While the pulse is on, the signal is generated. For example, during a 65-μs pulse period, some 1,763 waves of 27.12-MHz energy are generated. During the intervals between pulses no energy is generated.

Longer pulse duration coupled with greater pulse frequency delivers more energy to the tissues and has more thermal effect. With high pulse rates (which results in short interpulse intervals) heat builds up in the tissues because the short interpulse interval does not allow heat to dissipate. Conversely, a low-frequency pulse rate along with a short pulse duration (which means a long interpulse interval) produces insignificant tissue heating because the interpulse interval is long enough to allow heat dissipation.

Nonthermal PRFS medical devices generally have a fixed pulse duration of 65 μs (of the basic 27.12-MHz wave) with pulse rates that can vary from 80 to 600 pps. They are classified as low frequency. This type of signal does not have adequate intensity to heat tissues.

It is very important for the physical therapist to be familiar with the device to be used. Some devices offer a large range of variability of pulse rates and pulse durations from which to choose. Treatment effects will be different depending on the parameters selected. Read and understand the instruction manual that comes with the device and choose parameters that provide the physiologic response required. For example, the Megapulse (PTI Corporation, Topeka, Kansas) specification sheet says that a pulse mode of less than 200 μs and less than 200 Hz is nonthermal and, conversely, greater pulse rate and duration are thermal. Three pulse modes are offered with the device on: off cycles consisting of one third on time and two thirds off time; two thirds on time and one third off time; and continuous. The pulse durations and frequency can be changed during those three modes. When longer on time and shorter off time are selected there will be more thermal effects. Shorter on and longer off time will be less thermal, and the effects will be stimulation of the cells rather than heating.

Clinical Wisdom: *Testing Thermal and Nonthermal Effects at Different Settings*

Try the different combinations of on/off time and different pulse rates on normal subjects over superficial tissues. Evaluate by measuring the surface temperature changes of the skin with a liquid crystal skin thermometer or deeper tissue with infrared scanner before and after the treatment at different time intervals to determine heating effects.

Duty Cycle

The duty cycle is the ratio of on time to total cycle time, which includes both the on and off time. As an example, at a pulse duration having an on time of 65 μs and a pulse rate of 600 pps, each complete period lasts 1/600, or 1,667 μs. The interpulse interval, or off time, is then $1,667 - 65 = 1,602$ μs. At 600 pps the duty cycle is 65 μs/1,667 μs = 3.9%.[2] This means that in a 30-minute treatment (30×60 seconds × 3.9%) only 70 seconds of energy is delivered.[3]

Intensity

Historically, power was the way in which the intensity of the generated field was measured, but this has nothing to do with what is delivered to the tissues. For example, 1,000 W of generated power is transferred to the drum applicator,

where it undergoes significant transformation to the electromagnetic field that is then delivered to the patient. Until the transformation into an electromagnetic field, it is appropriate to speak of power, but at the last step it is more correct to speak of the amplitude of the electromagnetic field delivered to the tissues. The electric or magnetic field itself can be measured, but it is not yet possible to measure the intensity received by the tissues.

Manufacturers include tables in their instruction manuals listing the approximate values of average output power in watts at different pulse rates and widths. This information should be used only as a guide not as a definite amount of power delivered to the tissues.

Comparison of PSWD and PRFS Equipment

Both PSWD and PRFS apply radio waves from the short wave range of the spectrum at 27.12 MHz. Both modulate the 27.12-MHz carrier frequency with square or pulse bidirectional waveforms (see earlier discussion under Carrier Frequency and Waveforms). Like all radio wave signals, the 27.12-MHz signal travels through air and is not impeded by nonmetallic structures (eg, otherwise your radio will not play indoors). Heating effects are adjusted by changing pulse rate and intensity. Higher pulse rates are thermal. Low pulse rates in the 90 to 200 pps range produce mild heating and are nonthermal at lower rates. Both transmit radiation from a coil contained in the drum head to the target tissues. The separation of the drum from the tissues can be used to modify the heating effect of PSWD by dissipating some of the energy into the air. Minimal separation is recommended for PRFS so that the low energy level is targeted at the tissues and not dissipated into the air. This method of energy transfer to the tissues is called induction. An electrical current is induced in the tissues as described above. Both types of stimulation penetrate deeply into the tissues and most affect those tissues with good conductivity. Since they are so similar, it is easy to equate them; however, they are not synonymous and the effects are based on two different physiologic phenomena. PSWD has the ability to heat the tissues, whereas PRFS affects the tissues at the cellular level. Further investigation may find that PSWD has cellular effects also. Because PSWD energy penetrates deeply it heats from the inside out, as when cooking food in the microwave the center is heated first. Heating effects may continue even after the stimulation is removed. Delayed response to stimulation is an important concept to remember, because the patient may not report heating right away because the skin is not heated first such as when a hot pack is applied. Follow the guidelines listed in the protocols for treatment parameters to use.

Since both PSWD and PRFS deliver a signal at 27.12 MHz to the tissues, this signal has equal ability to penetrate tissues. The depth of penetration of the magnetic field decreases approximately by the square of the distance as it moves away from the surface of the applicator. Guy et al.[1] measured thermal changes in the tissues at a depth of 5 to 6 cm up to 15 cm from the applicator. Markov[3] found that the magnetic field of 27.12 MHz radio waves is 30% of the initial value at 5 cm distance from the applicator, 10% at 10 cm, and 3% to 5% at 15 cm. As already described, treatment effect would be expected to be altered by the distance of the applicator from the target tissues.

Distance from Applicator	Magnetic Field Value
Surface	100%
5 cm	30%
10 cm	10%
15 cm	3% to 5%

Comparison of PRFS and HVPC Fields

PRFS induces electrical currents in the body through the action of an electromagnetic or a radio field. As such it has no positive or negative poles and the current goes in concentric circles (see Figure 18–1).[4] This induced alternating current is not related to intervening tissue but is related to the

distance from the coil, with the current intensity being greatest just beneath the coil edges.

For treatment purposes, high-voltage pulsed current (HVPC) has, in general, the same amplitude as does PSWD/PRFS. HVPC, however, has a unidirectional flow, with a specific polarity (Figure 18–2),[5] whereas the electromagnetically generated current is a circular flow of current without polarity as shown in Figure 18–1. The mechanism of action for PSWD/PRFS is a direct effect of magnetic field and induced electric current on the cells. HVPC, on the other hand, has a negligible magnetic field and the method of cellular stimulation is by electric current. The direct effect of magnetic and electrical fields in the tissues cannot be distinguished because they come together with high frequency fields. Methods of delivery are different. PSWD/PRFS is delivered without skin contact, through the air (Exhibit 18–2). HVPC is delivered by capacitive coupling from an electrode, through a wet contact medium to the skin. HVPC has a negligible magnetic field. This stimulation is mainly by electric current. PRFS delivers a more uniform and predictable signal to the tissues than capacitive coupled electrodes.[3]

Attributes of PSWD and PRFS stimulation that make them useful for treatment of wounds are as follows. (1) The penetration of the magnetic field into the tissues is not restricted by impedance from intervening structures such as skin, bone, or plaster. However, metal (eg, rings) will alter penetration and/or localized heating (see Safety Issues, later). (2) The stimulation at the skin level is not sufficient to depolarize the pain nerve endings in the skin and is painless. (3) Another important aspect of PRFS is that it is nondisruptive; treatment may be made over a bandaged wound, thus the dressing need not be changed just because of the PRFS treatment. This decreases the possibility of infection and tissue cooling.

Figure 18–1 A PSWD or PRFS coil placed over the anterior thigh showing the exciting current (solid line) and the resultant induced current (broken line). *Source:* Reprinted with permission from R. Kellogg, Magnetotherapy: Potential Clinical and Therapeutic Applications, in *Clinical Electrotherapy*, D.P. Currier and R.M. Nelson, eds., pp. 390–391, © 1991, Appleton & Lange.

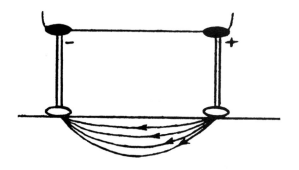

Figure 18–2 A pair of direct contact electrodes like used for HVPC placed over the skin showing the resultant current flow through the skin. *Source:* Reprinted with permission from R. Kellogg, Magnetotherapy: Potential Clinical and Therapeutic Applications, in *Clinical Electrotherapy*, D.P. Currier and R.M. Nelson, eds., pp. 390–391, © 1991, Appleton & Lange.

Exhibit 18–2 PSWD/PRFS Characteristics

- 27.12-MHz radio waves
- Modulation waveform square or pulse bidirectional
- Signal travels through air
- Not impeded by nonmetallic structures
- Pulse rates: 1 to 7,000 pps maximum;
  PR = maximum average intensity
- 200 pps ⇨ moderate to vigorous heating
- 90 to 200 pps ⇨ mild heat
- <90 pps ⇨ nonthermal
- Applicator: wire coil covered by housing
- Uniform magnetic field
- Induce electric current in tissues
- Deep penetration 5 to 6 cm up to 15 cm (MF value decreased by approximately the square of the distance)

Clinical Wisdom:
Implications for Wound Healing with PSWD/PRFS

- Perfusion of tissues is increased either directly or indirectly.
- Deep tissue heating with PSWD allows heating within deep wounds and tunnels including areas with abscess or infection.
- PSWD raises tissue temperatures.
- Painful wounds and associated soft tissue can be treated without direct contact.
- Provides analgesia of pain endings.
- Produces edema reduction.
- PRFS stimulates cellular activity and cell wall permeability.
- PRFS stimulation can take place over clothing, wound dressings, elastic wraps, and casting materials.
- No disruption of the wound healing environment is needed with PRFS.
- Stimulation of deep structures with PSWD, including nerves and blood vessels, can effect physiologic changes.

THEORY AND SCIENCE OF THE THERAPY

Both PSWD and PRFS send electromagnetic field signals to the tissues, but they are not considered synonymous therapies. Both are classified as diathermy by the Food and Drug Administration (FDA) but in two separate classes: thermal and nonthermal. The cellular effects of PSWD have not been reported in the literature; however, there are numerous reports about PRFS cellular effects. This is not to say that PSWD does not have similar effects on cells that as yet are uninvestigated.

Basic Science of PRFS (Nonthermal)

The electromagnetic field (EMF) has been identified as the signal to the tissues that is the therapeutic factor with the ability to modulate biologic phenomena.[3] Cellular activity can be modified by induced changes in the electrical status of the cell, the cell membrane, and the cell-to-cell communications. Cell-to-cell communications via electrically conducting gap junctions increase the electromagnetic field sensitivity by several orders of magnitude versus a single cell exposed to the same EMF source.[3] Understanding the mechanisms of action induced by applying PRFS to tissues has generated interest in the effects on different cellular systems. This section presents a synopsis of the effect of PRFS on some cellular systems studied.

Basic science research findings show that by applying nonthermal PRFS to cells the energy modulates Ca^{2+} binding kinetics, stimulates all types of cell proliferation, affects the cell membrane diffusion and/or permeability, and moves negatively charged plasma proteins toward lymph capillaries. Cellular changes following treatment with PRFS have been observed to alter processes that are essential to tissue repair, including proliferation of parenchymal and connective tissue cells, synthesis of extracellular matrix proteins, collagenization, and acquisition of wound strength.[3] Because an electrical field is induced, it has been proposed that PRFS energy probably affects the body's bioelectric system. One theory is that the sodium ions in the cell build up during the inflammatory phase, and the action of the sodium pump is reduced. This results in a decrease in the cell's negative charge that in effect reduces the action of the sodium pump. Under the influence of the electromagnetic field from the PRFS energy source, the sodium pump is reactivated and the cell's ionic balance can be restored.[6]

Hematoma Absorption

Rupture of small or large vessels accompanies both surgical and traumatic wounding and produces hematoma in the tissues. Hematoma is normally absorbed slowly. Fenn[7] found that hematoma absorption in rabbit ears was accelerated compared to the control group and the acceleration became statistically significant on the sixth day after initiation of treatment with Diapulse PRFS. The FDA has allowed pulsed short wave diathermy to list hematoma as an indication for application although no support for this claim could be found in the literature.

One nonthermal phenomenon observed after application of PRFS with Diapulse was called a pearl chain phenomenon. When fat globules in milk were exposed to PRFS, the fat globules aligned into an order array of pearl chains and remained in that formation until the energy was removed. A second test using thermal energy caused agglomeration of the fat particles that was irreversible. This pearl chain phenomenon is also reproducible with blood and lymph cells.[8] Cameron[9] looked at wound healing in 20 dogs, comparing a control group of untreated animals with a Diapulse PRFS–treated group. He took specimens from 24 hours to 10 days after wounding and studied the tissues under the microscope. At 48 hours the hematoma had been absorbed and replaced by fat that was arranged in strands migrating toward the ends of the wound. By comparison the control animals had minimal fat activity by day four postwounding.

Sambasivan[10] treated four cases of extradural hematomas with Diapulse PRFS. Treatment was applied twice daily for 10 days at a maximum pulse rate of 600 pps and a 65-µs duration for 30 minutes per session, alternating right and left sides of the head. The treated cases showed clearance of hematoma. If the results are reproducible, this could have tremendous potential for shortening healing times. Clinicians can begin gathering data about wounds that are treated in the clinic that have hemorrhagic areas and that are treated with PRFS. Rapid reabsorption of clotted blood could be a way to prevent tissue death.

Edema

Ionescu et al.[11] observed successful prevention of edema formation, pain, and reduction in local symptoms after burns by application of PRFS. These observations led to further investigation to understand the mechanisms involved and to demonstrate objective proofs. Local skin enzymatic activity was chosen as an indicator of the viability of the tissue. Samples of proteins and some principle enzymes in normal and burned tissue were compared before and after PRFS therapy. The enzymatic activities of the skin decreases when traumatized or burned. The data showed that, compared with normal skin, the enzymatic activity was significantly modified after the treatment. The earlier the application of treatment the sooner the normal enzymatic activities are restored.

Studies on nerve regeneration with Diapulse have shown that nerve tissue regeneration can be accelerated and that there will be less pain and scar tissue.[12]

Blood Flow and Oxygen

Increased blood flow benefits wound healing by autolytic debridement of necrotic tissue, delivering critically needed oxygen and nutrients, and removing metabolites. Local application of heat causes vasodilation of the vasculature and allows for increased blood flow. Infection rates are inversely proportional to blood flow. All of the processes of wound healing are oxygen dependent, including collagen deposition. Heat is a simple and effective method to enhance blood flow.[5,13] For example, if blood flow can increase to the lower extremities without elevating body heat and if it can be maintained, it can then be applied as a helpful treatment of vasospastic peripheral vascular disease and could be beneficial in controlling infection. Treatment interventions that can increase perfusion to the tissues are important tools. The following studies report on the effects of CSWD, PSWD, and nonthermal PRFS on blood flow to the extremities.

Continuous Short Wave Diathermy

The primary benefits of CSWD are attributed to the heating effects and its subsequent effect on physiology. Early experimental and clinical research was focused on the effects associated with tissue heating that can occur when tissue temperatures are raised to 41° to 45°C in the deep tissue structures. Continuous and pulsed short wave diathermy can be used to raise deep tissue temperature 5°C for therapeutic effects.[14] This was determined to be a safe tissue temperature range when the body could respond to pain stimuli and there was sufficient reservoir of blood with adequate cooling capacity to dissipate the heating through blood flow. Where circulatory occlusion is present, however, heating is contraindicated because in limited circulatory systems there is poor heat dissipation and subsequent high risk for burns.[15] Early CSWD did not have a pulsed option and was therefore contraindicated for impaired circulatory conditions. In response, there was an effort to reduce the effects of continuous heating by developing pulsed short wave equipment. The equipment developed allowed adjustment of the pulse rate, the interpulse interval, and the energy output so that the heat created in the tissues during the on time would dissipate during the off time. Because the signal was pulsed it was called pulsed short wave diathermy and was described in early literature as "athermal." Despite use of the term *athermal* that appears in the literature, this is not scientifically accurate. A better description is to use the term *nonthermal* because the movement of atoms and molecules in all bodies produces some heat.

Pulsed Short Wave Diathermy

As described, PSWD is a thermal agent that can heat both deep and superficial tissues. Silverman and Pendleton,[16] in the first study, and Santoro et al.,[17] in the second study, wanted to know if indirect tissue heating in the abdomen and lumbosacral areas would raise the distal tissue temperature in the foot and the calf. PSWD, CSWD, and placebo were used to treat young adults by placing the treatment head over the lower abdomen. Silverman and Pendleton's treatment protocol lasted 20 minutes at a high average power setting of 65 W and low average power of 15 W for both treatment machines. To achieve the high power, the pulse rate was 2,400 pps and the low power pulse rate was 600 pps. Peripheral circulation was then measured in the calf and in the foot. The result was that the change in circulation was most prominent in the foot and only occurred with high average power. The mean increase was 165% with pulsed high power and 195% with continuous high power. No circulatory effects were found in the foot with low power of either type. Temperatures were recorded under the treatment head. The mean increase in skin temperature was 5.3°C with continuous treatment and 5.8°C with pulsed treatment. The foot temperature increased 1.9°C and 2.2°C, respectively. Local heating occurred on the abdomen of the subjects who received low power, with mean changes of 3.1°C and 3.4°C for continuous and pulsed. Subjects reported a comfortable sensation under the treatment heads. These are statistically significant changes in temperature and blood flow, but not between the pulsed and continuous generators, confirming the ability of a PSWD generator to heat tissue.

In Santoro's study,[17] 10 patients with moderate to severe arterial peripheral vascular disease (PVD) were treated with PSWD 5 days a week for 20 days spread over the period of 1 month. The treatment consisted of a 30-minute two-part protocol. The first 20 minutes the treatment was at maximum intensity for the unit, which is a high-dose heating level. The parameters were 95 μs at a rate of 7,000 pps. The last 10 minutes the intensity was reduced to a low heating level. The parameters were 95 μs at a rate of 700 pps. This was called the "cooling phase." Two applicator heads were used, with one placed over the plantar surface of the foot and the second over the area of the anterior thigh. In cases where both limbs were affected, both applicators were placed over the plantar surfaces of the feet. Variables measured included surface temperature, transcutaneous partial pressure of oxygen (tcpO$_2$), segmental Doppler blood pressure, and superficial blood flow measured with a laser Doppler flowmeter and patient perceptions. Findings were that temperature peaked at the end of the 20 minutes of high heat, then gradually reduced. The tcpO$_2$ readings increased in the treated and the untreated limbs. They were insignificant in the treated limbs but significant in the untreated limbs, possibly because of reflex vasodilatation from the warm circulating blood and sympathetic nervous system activity. Sixty percent of the patients reported subjectively that they felt that the treatment had improved their quality of life. No adverse effects were reported[17] (Exhibit 18–3).

Exhibit 18–3 Summary of Effects of PSWD

↑ Perfusion
↑ Local tissue tcpO$_2$
↑ Tissue metabolism
↑ Antibiotic delivery to tissue
↑ O$_2$ antimicrobial effect

Nonthermal Pulsed Radio Frequency Stimulation

Pulsing the radio waves did not solve all the problems of creating a device that was really nonthermal. The next modification was to change the signal so that the signal was pulsed at lower rates and longer intervals. In the late 1950s a device was developed that was actually nonthermal and did not produce significant tissue heating. PRFS, which is nonthermal, was introduced in the late 1950s just as use of diathermy was waning. The first device that was approved by the FDA for medical use and appeared on the market was the Diapulse®. The FDA allows the Diapulse Corporation to market the device as a short wave diathermy class III device. Diathermy class III devices that are currently being marketed are described under "Equipment" later in the chapter. What needs to be clear is that, although there are similarities between PSWD and PRFS (nonthermal), they are not synonymous (Table 18–1).

Several studies applying nonthermal PRFS are reviewed. They represent studies using two available commercial PRFS devices, Diapulse® and MRT sofPulse®. The way in which these two manufacturers handle the technical specifications for their devices is the way in which the outputs are reported. Diapulse is constructed with vacuum tubes. MRT sofPulse is a solid-state analog of Diapulse. These devices use fixed pulse duration, 65 μs, pulse rate adjustable from 80 to 600 pps at the maximum generated power. When pulsed at the maximum rate, power is applied only 3.9% of the time. This equipment was designed to allow for dissipation of heat and to reduce its accumulation.

Erdman[18] studied the effect of the Diapulse PRFS device, with the inductive head placed over the epigastrium, in a study measuring changes in blood flow to the feet of 20 normal young adults. The findings were mean increase in foot temperature of 2.0°C and an average volume increase of 1.75-fold at the maximum generated power. Rectal temperatures did not change, nor did pulse rates. Furthermore, in all 20 cases increased blood flow was directly proportional to the energy applied at the three highest settings. A short period of effect followed cessation of the treatment.

Table 18–1 Comparison of CSWD, PSWD, and PRFS Characteristics

Device	Signal	Pulse Rate	Effect
Continuous short wave diathermy	27.12 MHz	Continuous	No heat dissipation
Pulsed short wave diathermy	27.12 MHz	High repetition rate, moderate repetition rate	Limited heat dissipation, moderate heat dissipation
Pulsed radio frequency stimulation	27.12 MHz	Low repetition rate	Heat dissipation, cellular effects

Mayrovitz and Larsen[19] reported that treatment with PRFS increased skin blood perfusion in the treated region. PRFS stimulation with the MRT sofPulse at 65 µs at a pulse rate of 600 pps and peak power, applied for 40 minutes on the forearm skin of nine healthy men and women, produced enhanced microvascular perfusion, averaging 30% compared with pretest levels. Skin temperature was increased by an average of 1.8°C but the rise occurred ahead of the measured increased perfusion. This is similar to the study by Erdman.[18] The mechanisms of action are not readily understood.

Mayrovitz and Larsen[20] conducted another study using the MRT sofPulse, also to study effects on perfusion. Laser Doppler red blood cell (RBC) perfusion, volume, velocity, and skin temperatures were evaluated for the effects of PRFS on 15 subjects, each of whom had had diabetes for at least 5 years and each of whom had an ulcer on the foot or toe of one limb. Ulcer duration was a minimum of 8 weeks. The contralateral limb was intact and served as the control. Nine subjects had peripheral vascular disease as confirmed by noninvasive vascular testing. Baseline data were collected for the multiple variables. The ulcerated limb had pretreatment perfusion and volume much greater than the control limb. A single treatment was administered at the periulcer site. The result was an increase in laser Doppler perfusion and skin temperature due to PRFS treatment. These preliminary findings may suggest that, if the resting perfusion is marginally inadequate for healing, giving this small boost in perfusion may be sufficient to aid the healing of the ulcer. Parameters of the stimulation were 65 µs, 600 pps, at peak power with the head 1.5 cm above the surface of the ulcer.[20] Table 18–2 summarizes changes in tissue temperature after application of PSWD/PRFS.

Edema and Pain Reduction

Reduction of soft tissue edema resulting from trauma has been reported following treatment with PRFS for 20 to 30 minutes and has persisted for several hours after treatment. The mechanism by which it is postulated that this occurs is that the PRFS affects sympathetic nervous system outflows to induce vasoconstriction and restriction of blood flow from blood vessels to the interstitial areas around the wound site.[3]

Some PSWD devices can be set at a protocol that is thermal or nonthermal. The Magnatherm is such a device. A study on 25 podiatric surgical patients was conducted by Santiesteban and Grant[21] at a dosage of 700 pps and a power setting of 12 or approximately 120 W. This intensity, however, is now called mildly thermal but was reported in the study as athermal. A control group of 25 did not receive this treatment. Two electrodes were used, one over the plantar aspect of the postoperative foot and the other on the inguinal region. If both feet were operated upon, the electrodes were placed over the plantar aspects of both feet. Two treatment sessions were given. One was given as soon after surgery as possible and the other 4 hours later. Nurses noted the number and types of pain medications used and the length of the hospital stay, measured in hours. There were significant dif-

Table 18–2 PSWD/PRFS Change in Tissue Temperature

Device	Area Stimulated	Pulse Rate	Intensity	Tissue Temperature
PSWD	Abdomen	2,400 pps	High dose	↑ 2.2°C at foot[18]
PRFS	Abdomen	600 pps	Peak power	↑ 2.0°C at foot[20]
PRFS	Arm (normal subjects)	600 pps	Peak power	↑ 1.8°C[21]
PRFS	Foot (diabetics)	600 pps	Peak power	↑ 0.5°C[22]

ferences between the treatment group and the control group. The former had an 8-hour shorter length of stay and used less strong analgesic medication.

Early intervention with PRFS (Diapulse) in the treatment of hand injuries was studied by Barclay et al.[22] to compare the effects on edema, pain, and improvement of function. Sixty matched pairs of patients who had hand injuries within 36 hours of admission for treatment were evaluated. In the treated group, with the exception of two cases, there was a complete resolution of edema by the third day, compared with the controls, in whom swelling greatly increased. The 17 patients in the treated group were symptom free by the third day and by day 7 only one in the treated group had slight loss of function; the 29 other patients had been discharged. By contrast, in the control group of 30 patients, 3 had been discharged and the remaining 27 were still symptomatic with edema, pain, and loss of function.[22]

Acute ankle sprains have a rapid onset of edema and pain and are common injuries in athletes and in the military. Pennington et al.[23] studied the effect of PRFS (Diapulse) on 50 patients with grade I and II ankle sprains at 1 to 24 hours, 25 to 48 hours, and 49 to 72 hours after injury and found a statistically significant decrease in the edema (0.95% versus 4.7%) and pain in the treatment group. Reduced pain was reported for 64% of the treated patients, compared with 33% for the control group. Because of the small sample size in the three different time-elapsed groups no analysis was performed on this component, but overall, those patients who were treated within the 72-hour time frame had a statistically significant effect, including a significant decrease in the time lost from military training.

Early intervention during the inflammatory phase of healing was attributed to the successful outcomes of reduced swelling and pain and early return to functional activities in the studies by Barclay et al.,[22] Pennington et al.,[23] and Ionescu et al.[11] Research information such as this can be used as a clinical guide for referral to the physical therapist (PT) for evaluation of the appropriateness of this treatment following acute trauma. Then it is up to the PT to evaluate the treatment outcomes and compare them with the research studies.

Research Wisdom:
Early Intervention with PRFS Hastens Recovery

Intervention during the acute inflammatory phase—the first 72 hours postinjury (eg, trauma including burns, pressure, etc)—with PRFS has demonstrated reduction of edema, pain, and enhanced perfusion of the tissues with resulting acceleration through the phases of repair and early return to work.[23]

Clinical Studies

There are no controlled clinical trials on the effects of wound healing with PSWD and the studies on wound healing with PRFS have small sample size with limited reported results. Although the support for these interventions is weak, they are presented here for thoughtful consideration.

Medium-Thickness Split-Skin Grafts

A controlled clinical trial by Goldin[24] used Diapulse PRFS to study the effects on healing and pain on medium-thickness split-skin grafts. The patients were randomized into two groups. The parameter for the treatment group was peak output frequency, 400 pps. The average pulse was fixed at 65 µs. Mean energy output was nonthermal, 25.3 W. Treatment was given preoperatively and postoperatively every 6 hours for 7 days. Two variables were evaluated: the stage of healing and the degree of pain during the healing phase. Healing rates on day 7 were 90% or greater healing for 59% of the treatment group and 29% of the sham-treated group. Mechanisms of healing are not clear. The theories to explain the results include increased blood flow and reduced incidence of edema. The stimulation of cells of repair and repolarization of the depolarized cell membranes of damaged cells that reversed the "injury potential" and the electrical field were thought to be the mechanisms of action.[24]

Pressure Ulcers

Pressure as the wound etiology was the criteria for participation in the following two studies. Itoh et al.[25] studied effect of PRFS on stage II, partial-thickness, and stage III, full-thickness ulcers. Comorbidities included cerebrovascular accidents, multiple sclerosis, organic brain syndrome, spinal cord tumor, diabetes, spinal cord injury, and spinal stenosis. Conventional treatments of dressings and topical agents were continued. In all, 22 patients were included during the 9-month study. All ulcers healed. Stage II ulcers healed in 1 to 6 weeks (mean 2.33 weeks) and all stage III ulcers healed in 1 to 22 weeks (mean 8.85 weeks). Treatment was provided using the Diapulse PRFS device at a setting of 600 pps pulse frequency and a setting of 6 (peak power) for 30 minutes twice daily. Treatment sessions were scheduled at approximately 8-hour intervals.[25] Fifty patients with recalcitrant pressure ulcers (25 stage II, 11 stage III, and 14 stage IV) received Diapulse stimulation in a study reported by Wilson.[26] Significant healing was observed in the most difficult ulcers in 3 to 7 days. The ulcers of all but one patient healed, and that one improved but the patient died before healing was complete.

Salzberg et al.[27] studied 20 patients with spinal cord injuries, 10 of whom had stage II pressure ulcers and 10 had stage III pressure ulcers. The group was randomized to 10 treated and 10 sham-treated groups. Again the device tested was the Diapulse. Although the study did not list the treatment parameters, an inquiry to the principal author and the Diapulse Corporation provided the information that the settings were 600 pps pulse frequency and 6, peak power. The treatment lasted for 30 minutes twice daily for 12 weeks or until the ulcers healed. Results were that the active treatment group with stage II ulcers had a shorter mean time to complete healing than did the control group (13.0 days vs. 31.5 days). The stage III ulcers also healed faster than the controls, but the size of the group was very limited. The study authors' conclusion was that the treatment significantly improved healing.[27]

Postsurgical Wounds

Postsurgical wounds were treated with Diapulse over the wound site and over the hepatic area. Fifteen were selected for treatment and 10 served as the control group. The local application was at 600 pps at maximum power output for 20 minutes and the hepatic application at 400 pps at a power setting of 4 for 10 minutes. Treatment started on the second postoperative day and continued for five days. Comorosan et al.[28] reported that the results of this protocol were evaluated by looking at the clinical criteria for wound healing, including the disappearance of edema, hematoma, and parietal seroma; the lack of inflammatory and infectious processes; the suppleness and presence or absence of keloids in the scar; and the degree of postoperative sensitivity. All showed clear-cut improvement in these parameters. An additional analysis of the effects of the hepatic stimulation showed increased fibronecton levels in the treated patients and lower fibronecton levels in the controls. This is another measure of healing.

CHOOSING AN INTERVENTION: CLINICAL REASONING

Applying Theory and Science to Clinical Decision Making

The prior section evaluated the scientific studies of the mechanisms and efficacy of PSWD and PRFS on components related to and in clinical trials of wound healing. PRFS studies reported effects on the cells' and the body's bioelectric system. PSWD studies described the heating effects of this type of therapy on the body. PSWD effects are attributed to changes in the circulatory system and the nervous system, whereas the effects of PRFS are attributed to changes in the cellular activity of the tissues and mechanisms that control blood flow that are not heat related. Both devices showed that they can increase blood flow, which increases oxygen transport essential to support the metabolic demands of the tissues. Both affect pain and edema during the inflammation phase. Since the treatment outcomes desired are edema free and pain free and these are benefited by enhanced circulation, it is logical to choose a treatment approach with demonstrated outcomes for these aspects of the inflammation phase. If the circulatory effects desired require vigorous stimulation, the PSWD is probably the first choice. A protocol for PSWD is given that is based on the circulatory effect on acute, subacute, and chronic inflammation. The effects on the inflammation phase of healing are well established, but information about the effect on phases of healing following inflammation until closure is very limited. Enhanced circulation and oxygen are requirements of all the phases of healing, so continuation during all phases appears appropriate. If the patient is not a candidate for PSWD and if less vigorous blood flow is desired, PRFS is a good alternative. PRFS is the preferred choice if the objective is to stimulate at the cellular level, over a dressing, cast, or bandage, or the patient has a medical history that rules out heat (see Selection of Candidates, later). Treatment effects should be seen within hours for acute wounds and within 2 weeks from the start of the protocol for chronic wounds. Progress through the phases of healing should continue throughout the episode of care.

Summary

PWSD and PRFS are similar but not identical. They both are radio wave signals from the short wave spectrum. PSWD has the ability to heat tissue; PRFS does not. Application of both have reported increased perfusion and blood flow. Cellular changes are reported for stimulation with PRFS but not for PSWD. Exhibit 18–2 and Tables 18–1 and 18–2 show a summary of the characteristics of each; Table 18–4 shows a summary of precautions to be taken when using PSWD and PRFS equipment.

The studies reviewed are limited and several are older. Although the results presented look promising, more new studies are needed to answer questions about the effects of PSWD and PRFS on wound healing. There are still many unknowns about mechanisms of action. However, that does not mean that the use of PSWD or PRFS is experimental. Positive outcomes have been reported for both in controlled clinical trials. The cellular effects of PSWD have not been reported, but they should be investigated. To summarize, the studies looked at seven components that the physical therapist should consider when selecting this intervention.

1. PRFS stimulates cellular activity and cell permeability.
2. PRFS affects the body's bioelectric system.
3. PSWD and PRFS affect edema formation, but possibly through different processes.
4. PSWD and PRFS prevent or modulate pain.
5. PSWD and PRFS affect circulation as measured by increased blood flow and tcpO$_2$, but through different processes.
6. PRFS promotes absorption of hematoma.
7. PSWD heats tissue, PRFS does not.

Patients who were treated in the studies had pressure ulcers or PVD, or were postsurgery or post-trauma. The wounds were either partial- or full-thickness tissue disruption extending into deeper tissues (eg, stage III and stage IV pressure ulcers; Table 18–3). None of the effects of treatment described are dependent on the medical diagnosis or the depth of the wound. However, wounds that are deeper and more severe will probably heal faster with one of these interventions.

Selection of Candidates

A comprehensive patient history, systems review, and examination are very important in making a clinical decision to choose either PSWD or PRFS. Review the history and systems for information about sensation, circulation, edema, metal and electronic implants, acute osteomyelitis, cancer, and pregnancy. According to the manufacturer's labeling requirements, PSWD is contraindicated for all conditions for which heat is contraindicated. PSWD should not be used over areas of insensitivity that prevent the patient from reporting sensation of heating. One way to mitigate the heating effect is to leave a greater air gap or more toweling between the applicator and the tissues. Check pulses and perform other visual examinations to detect circulatory deficits. If findings show diminished circulation, noninvasive vascular testing may be required. Do not use PSWD over ischemic tissue (eg, an ankle-brachial index [ABI] of less than 0.8) because the body requires adequate perfusion to regulate tissue temperature. If circulatory perfusion is obstructed, it may not allow for the heat to dissipate and result in burning. However, consider indirect heating with PSWD or PRFS over the lumbar area or the abdomen that will produce reflex vasodilatation in areas remote from the site of heating, for example, the foot.[18,20] This is also suggested for patients with vasospasm. Do not use PSWD over metal, including surgical metal hardware; foreign bodies such as shrapnel, bullets, or metallic sutures; and interuterine devices. The metal may become heated and reflect high levels of energy that will cause burns. Do not use PSWD if the patient has electronic implants or is connected to electrical or electronic equipment because the electromagnetic field of the PSWD may cause interference with these electronic devices. PSWD is contraindicated over any area where there is primary or metastatic malignant tissue growth or over organs or tissues containing high fluid volumes (eg, the heart, edematous extremity, and over the abdomen and lumbar areas during pregnancy). Treatment over an area with acute osteomyelitis without adequate drainage or before drainage has been established is contraindicated. A diagnosis of active tuberculosis would be a contraindication for PSWD. Review the patient's vital signs. Patients who are febrile should not be treated with additional heat. Check the pharmacy history for blood-thinning medications and tendency for hemorrhage. Patients during the first 24 to 48 hours after traumatic injury should not be selected for treatment with PSWD because the treatment may increase bleeding and edema. Hemorrhaging tendency, including heavy menstruation, is a precaution for use of PSWD. Changing the parameters of the treatment would be indicated to modify the amount of heating. If wound examination findings are acute inflammation, direct heating should be avoided, but indirect heating could be useful (eg, inflammation in the foot can be treated with PSWD or PRFS applied over the

Table 18–3 Wound Classification and Characteristics

Wound Classification	*PSWD/PRFS*
Level of tissue disruption	Superficial, partial thickness, full thickness, subcutaneous and deep tissues
Etiologies/diagnostic groups	Burns, neuropathic ulcers, pressure ulcers, surgical wounds, vascular ulcers
Wound phases	*Inflammation phase:* necrosis, exudate, edema, pain *Proliferation phase:* Granulation, contraction, collagen synthesis, angiogenesis *Epithelialization phase:* epidermal migration *Remodeling:* collagen organization

abdomen). Examination for wound drainage is important. Wounds that have a heavy amount of wound exudate would require special handling to absorb all moisture to avoid burns.[2,29]

Age should be considered when selecting candidates for PRFS or PSWD. Application of PRFS or PSWD over growth plates is probably not harmful because of the short duration of the wound healing treatment application, compared with the lengthy period of stimulation required to alter bone formation in bone healing studies using pulsed electromagnetic fields. Children have growth plates until about 16 years of age, depending on race, sex, and the bone involved (use over immature bone is a listed contraindication). Children usually do not have the underlying comorbidities that lead to chronic wounding, but forced immobility due to pain would be detrimental to a child. Some of the most common wounds in children are burns. A child with burn wounds would benefit from PRFS early intervention to normalize skin enzymes and to eliminate edema and pain, resulting in less scarring and quicker return to play and school activities. Sometimes the risk is insignificant compared with the benefit. For example, children were treated for subdural hematoma with PRFS without complications and had more rapid resolution of edema and hematoma than controls who were not treated.[10] If the benefit of accelerated wound healing outweighs the small risk of interference with a bone plate, prudent judgment should be used. Adults older than age 60 years can expect slower healing because of physiologic changes in the mechanisms of repair. Heat applications must always be applied carefully because of impairments of circulatory system functions and changes in sensory perceptions.

PRFS has fewer precautions and contraindications because it does not heat tissues (Table 18–4). Key information to check in the medical history is the presence of electronic or metal implants (including intrauterine devices), osteomyelitis, cancer, or pregnancy. Avoid using this intervention in the presence of any of these conditions.[2,30] Metals reflect radio frequency energy common to both PSWD and PRFS, so application over metal implants will reflect the energy back into the tissues, creating more intense energy levels in the tissues over the implant than usual, or the energy may be blocked from reaching the target tissues. Location of the metal should guide the physical therapist to consider an alternative method of application, such as moving the applicator head above or below the area of metal, whichever is closest to the wound, to treat the surrounding wound tissues. Con-

Table 18–4 FDA Contraindications, Warnings, and Cautions for PSWD and PRFS

PSWD	PRFS
• Do not treat over ischemic tissue with inadequate blood flow	• Do not use as a substitute for treatment of internal organs
• Do not treat over or near metallic implants	• Do not use over metal implants
• Do not use with patients with cardiac pacemakers	• Do not use with patients with cardiac pacemakers
• Do not treat in any region where presence of primary or metastatic malignant growth is known or suspected	• Do not use with patients who are pregnant
• Do not treat over immature bone	• Do not treat over immature bone
• Do not treat over acute osteomyelitis without adequate drainage or before adequate drainage has been established	
• Do not treat patients who have a tendency to hemorrhage (including menses)	
• Do not treat over pelvic or abdominal region or lower back during pregnancy	
• Do not treat transcerebrally	
• Do not use over anesthetized areas	
• Avoid situations that could concentrate the field, including moist dressings, perspiration, adhesives	
• Use caution when treating patients with heat sensitivity	
• Use caution when treating patients with inflammatory processes	

Source: Data from International Medical Electronics, *Magnatherm® Model 1000 Instruction Manual* and Electropharmacology, *MRT® sofPulse™ User's Manual.*

trary to the recommendation to wait until the acute hemorrhaging or acute inflammation have passed to treat with PSWD, PRFS should be applied early after wounding. As described, studies have shown that application of PRFS during the first 72 hours reduces pain, post-traumatic edema, and, in burn patients, the enzymes associated with trauma.

Safety Issues

PSWD

Contact with any metal (eg, jewelry, zippers, bra fasteners, and bra underwires) should be avoided when using PSWD because of the risk of burns. Also avoid contact with metal furniture or parts (eg, mattress springs). PSWD should not be used over synthetic materials that may melt and cause burns.[1] Electronic devices (eg, hearing aids, watches) should not be worn during treatment with these devices because the EMF may cause disruption of the device. Hearing aids may produce annoying noise feedback.

PRFS

Electronic devices (eg, hearing aids, watches) should not be worn during treatment with PRFS devices for the same reasons cited above. Do not administer PRFS directly over metal (eg, jewelry, zippers) because the energy will be reflected and not reach the target tissues.

Personnel Safety

Many sources of EMFs are present in the environment and most do not affect the human body. By the nature of the PSWD and PRFS devices described in this chapter, the EMFs do not pass 100% of the energy into the tissues being treated. Some energy is dissipated into the area close to the equipment. Operators and persons close to the equipment will absorb a small amount of EMFs. EMFs from PSWD, at distances of 0.5 m from the cables and 0.2 m from inductive applicators, are low at low and medium pulse settings. A study of PT work habits found that most remain at least 1 m from the applicator and 0.5 m from the cables during the operation of PSWD equipment. At those distances, there is little danger of excess absorption.[31] However, some older model PSWDs may not have shielded cables. The device should be checked for leakage of EMF energy. For personnel working with this equipment who have electronic implants, however, it would be prudent not to be exposed to the EMF because the stray radiation can affect the operation of those devices. The same holds true for other patients or family members occupying the same treatment areas. A timer is usually part of the equipment and it will turn the equipment off automatically, but if the patient needs to be assisted during the

treatment the staff member can approach the console without standing close to the tables. Several studies have attempted to measure the effects of EMFs on personnel working in areas where frequent exposure to SWD occurs. An epidemiologic study looked at the risk of birth defects, perinatal deaths, and late spontaneous abortions affecting fetuses of female therapists working with SWD. The result of this retrospective study showed that the risk of a miscarriage was not associated with reported use of SWD.[32] Patients, except as mentioned, have no measurable risk from the EMF associated with this equipment, and the benefits probably outweigh any negative effects.

EQUIPMENT

Regulatory Approval

The PSWD generators are classified as Class II short wave diathermy devices used for therapeutic deep heating for purposes of treatment of pain, muscle spasms, and joint contractures. PRFS generators are classified as Class III, short wave diathermy for all other uses (except treatment of malignancy), intended to treat medical conditions by means other than deep heating as nonthermal units, and are sold to control pain and edema.[33] State licensing agencies regulate what is physical therapy. Medicare guidelines say that the use of diathermy should always be by or under the supervision of a licensed physical therapist. Table 18–4 lists FDA contraindications and Table 18–5 lists FDA indications.

Devices

Pulsed Short Wave Diathermy

A PSWD generator uses a coil, mounted within a case (called a head) as the radiating element. This coil is driven by a crystal-controlled amplifier contained within the main chassis of the unit. The output of this head is an electromagnetic field with a radio frequency of 27.12 MHz. The head is mounted on a movable adjustable arm. Depending on the

Table 18–5 FDA Indications

PSWD	PRFS
Improved blood flow	Relief of pain and edema
Improved oxygenation	
Increased metabolic rate	
Inflammatory conditions	
Relief of pain and edema	

unit design, the head may be rectangular or round. Some devices allow the frequency to be delivered continuous or pulsed. The range of heating and nonthermal effects will depend on the pulse rate and duration. A PSWD device that can be operated at a broad range of pulse rates and pulse durations will have the most potential clinical applications. Heating effects are the principle action of the device at high pulse rates of long duration and nonthermal effects at the low pulse rates and short duration. At the nonthermal settings, the PSWD may have effects equivalent to those of the PRFS devices, which are limited to this range. PSWD devices are on the market, including the Magnatherm™ and the Megapulse® (International Medical Electronics, 6700 SW Topeka Boulevard, Forbes Field, Building 281-G, Topeka, KS 66619).

Pulsed Radio Frequency Stimulators

PRFS generators, like PSWD generators, consist of a radiating treatment head or applicator and an electronic console. The output of this head is also an electromagnetic field with a radio frequency of 27.12 MHz. The devices on the market, which are deemed by the FDA as equivalents, include the Diapulse® (Diapulse Corporation of America, 321 East Shore Road, Great Neck, NY 11023), the MRT sofPulse® (Electropharmacology Inc., 2301 NW 33rd Court, Pompano Beach, FL 33069), and the Curapulse® (Henley International, 120 Industrial Park Road, Sugarland, TX 77478). Electromagnetic effects at the cellular level are the actions to expect from these devices, not heating.[2] They are considered equivalent; however, there are differences in available pulse rates and pulse duration, and average outputs. Also, the Curapulse is available with either one or two electrodes that can be operated with different protocols. For example, the pulse rate and the duration of treatment must remain constant for both heads, but the other parameters can be set separately for each.

Two models are also available: model 403 has a pulse duration from 65 to 400 seconds and a frequency of 26 to 400 pps, and model 419 has a fixed pulse duration of 400 seconds and a frequency of 15 to 200 pps. Maximum outputs are also different. Table 18–6 shows the available parameters for these different models.

PROCEDURES

Protocols

Protocols are established to achieve a predictable outcome. PSWD is a thermal agent and as such has predictable effects on tissue temperature and blood flow. Normal resting body temperature is between 36.3°C and 37.5°C. PSWD at thermal levels has the ability to raise deep tissue temperature to 45°C. Vigorous heating is defined as raising tissue temperature to between 40°C and 45°C.[14] This is estimated to be the maximum safe upper limit to raise tissue temperature and corresponds to the pain threshold of the skin. Maintaining the tissue temperature of 45°C for a sufficiently long period will result in irreversible tissue damage. Three factors influence the maximum tissue temperature reached: the square of the intensity, the tissue impedance, and the length of time the tissue is heated. Also, tissue perfusion determines how quickly the blood flow will dissipate the heat.[2] The observable effect of heating is hyperemia due to increased blood flow. This is a mild inflammatory response initiating the biologic cascade associated with the process of inflammation (see Chapter 2). Vasodilatation occurs, along with increased capillary hydrostatic pressure and vessel permeability. This promotes movement of fluid from the vessels into the interstitial spaces. Symptoms associated with this process are *edema, pain*, and *warmth*. Raising the tissue temperature within a 5- to 15-minute period will raise the tissue tempera-

Table 18–6 Typical Equipment Parameters

Device	Operating Frequency (MHz)	Pulse Rates (pps)	Pulse Widths (µs)	Generated Power (W)
Magnatherm™	27.12	700–7,000	95 Fixed	0.2–100% (1,000 peak)
Megapulse®	27.12	50–800	20–400	150 Peak, 5–40 average
Nonthermal mode		< 200	< 200	
Thermal mode		> 200	> 100	
Curapulse®				
Model 419	27.12	15–200	400 Fixed	1,000 Peak, 80 average
Model 403	27.12	26–400	65–400	200 Peak, 32 average
Diapulse®	27.12	80–600	65 Fixed	293–975 Peak, 1.5–38 average
MRT sofPulse,® model 912	27.12	80–600	65 Fixed	174–373

ture to the maximum range. The resulting vasodilatation will produce a marked increase in blood flow that will then dissipate the heat and decrease the temperature by several degrees. A total exposure period of 20 to 30 minutes is described in the literature as the required time for the optimal therapeutic benefits of heating to occur. Studies show that this can be achieved with inductive coupling using PSWD while avoiding excessive heating of the superficial tissues and subcutaneous fat.[1] Tissue heating below 40°C temperature is considered mild.[5]

PRFS protocols used in the reported studies have a single set of parameters regardless of whether perfusion or reduction of edema or pain was the outcome. It is not currently known, however, what may be the optimal parameters of dosage that affect different levels of tissues at different stages of repair. This requires further research to be determined. In the current situation, the experimental protocols have validity and reliability and can be used safely. These are listed below under the Setup for Treatment sections.

Expected Outcomes

A change in temperature is not a functional outcome, just as a change in range of motion is not a functional outcome because in neither case are the effects of the measured change related to a change in an impairment. The change in temperature measures the change in tissue perfusion after the treatment. How the tissue responds functionally to the enhanced perfusion is the functional outcome (eg, progression to the proliferation phase). The sequence of predictable biologic events occurs during the process of healing. This sequence progresses from an initial phase of healing (inflammation) to a later phase of healing (epithelialization or contraction). The steps of the progression are outcome measures for measuring and predicting wound healing. See Chapter 1 for possible wound outcomes and prognoses. The expected outcome for a chronic wound treated with a physical agent such as PSWD or PRFS should progress from one phase to the next phase in a 2- to 4-week period. The mean time for healing in one study was 8.5 weeks with PRFS (Diapulse®). The healing time will be at the end of the range for patients with the factors that affect healing, such as older age, immobility, comorbidities, and depth of tissue involvement. If the reassessment does not confirm the predicted outcomes, treatment must change. Change can be a change in protocol (eg, mild heating change to vigorous heating), an increased length of treatment time, a change in frequency from three times per week to daily, or a change in dressing or topical agent. Any or all of the above are ways to consider changing the treatment to affect the wound status to reach a predictable outcome. Below are expected outcomes for the protocols for both PSWD and PRFS.

Wound Healing Phase Diagnosis: Acute or Chronic Inflammation

Expected Outcome Protocol for Acute or Chronic Inflammation

- Hyperemia: change in skin color to red, blue, or purplish depending on color of surrounding skin
- Temperature: increased temperature due to increased tissue perfusion
- Edema: hardness, tightness of tissues, and shiny skin
- Wound progression to the proliferation phase

Wound Healing Phase Diagnosis: Subacute Inflammation

Expected Outcome Protocol for Subacute Inflammation

- Skin color: change to that of surrounding skin
- Temperature: change to that of adjacent tissues or same area on corresponding opposite side of the body
- Edema: free
- Necrosis: free
- Wound progression to the proliferation phase

Protocols for PSWD

Kloth and Ziskin[2] devised a protocol for using PSWD based on the definitions of Lehman and deLateur[14] of vigorous and mild heating to write a protocol for the acute, subacute, and chronic inflammation phases of healing. The power level of the PSWD unit is divided into four levels. The four levels range from quarter power, which has a sensory effect below sensation of heat, to full power, which is vigorous heating. Table 18–7 shows the PSWD dosages and effects and the aspect of the inflammation phase of healing to be treated at that level. Table 18–8 shows the dosage, level, duration, frequency, and expected temperature changes in the tissues.

Magnatherm™ PSWD Protocol

The protocol used by Sussman and reported in Case Study 1 at the end of this chapter was for treatment of a patient with a pressure ulcer and parameters were proposed by the manufacturer (International Medical Electronics) for the Magnatherm™. This protocol called for a short initial phase (5 minutes) of heating at a high pulse rate and intensity followed by a reduction in the pulse rate to the lowest level, which also reduced the heating effect (see Table 18–9). The lower level was maintained for 25 minutes. The total treatment time was 30 minutes. The rationale was that

Table 18–7 PSWD Power, Effects, and Application

Dose	Level	Effect	Phase of Healing
I (¼ power)	Lowest	Below sensation of heat	Acute inflammation
II (½ power)	Low	Mild heat sensation	Subacute, resolving inflammation
III (¾ power)	Medium	Moderate, comfortable heat sensation	Subacute, resolving inflammation
IV (full power)	Heavy	Vigorous heating, well tolerated; reduce to just below maximum tolerance	Chronic conditions

Source: Reprinted with permission from L. Kloth and M. Ziskin, Diathermy and Pulsed Radio Frequency Radiation, in *Thermal Agents in Rehabilitation*, 3rd ed, S. Michlovitz, ed., © 1996, F.A. Davis Company Publishers.

Table 18–8 PSWD Dosage, Duration, and Outcomes

Dose	Duration*	Outcome
I	15 Minutes one or two times daily for 1–2 weeks	Temperature ↑ 37.5–38.5°C
II	15 Minutes daily for 1–2 weeks	Temperature ↑ 38.5–40.0°C
III	15–30 Minutes daily for 1–2 weeks	Temperature ↑ 40.0–42.0°C
IV	15–30 Minutes daily or two times per week for 1 week to 1 month	Temperature ↑ 42.0–44.0°C

*Continue for 2 weeks. If outcomes are achieved through the phases of healing, continue.

Source: Reprinted with permission from L. Kloth and M. Ziskin, Diathermy and Pulsed Radio Frequency Radiation, in *Thermal Agents in Rehabilitation*, 3rd ed, S. Michlovitz, ed., © 1996, F.A. Davis Company Publishers.

Table 18–9 Magnatherm Protocol Used by Sussman for Case Study 1

Magnatherm™ Settings	Duration	Effect
PR 5,000 pps Power level 12 (thermal)	5 Minutes	Vigorous heating—warm up
PR 700 pps Power level 12 (nonthermal)	25 Minutes	No perceived sensation of heat

the effects of the high-dose heating treatment would rapidly raise the tissue temperature and cause vasodilatation. The lower pulse rate produced mild heating and the longer interpulse interval would allow for heat dissipation. Additional rationale for this setting was that this would sustain the vasodilatation effects of the high heating phase throughout the duration of the treatment. The biologic regulatory effects attributable to the PRFS portion of the treatment were not taken into consideration.

Change Moist Dressing during PSWD Treatment

According to the PSWD instruction manual, it is necessary to remove wound dressings before PSWD.[29] To avoid burns of wound tissue during treatment with PSWD, replace any moist wound dressing with a dry sterile gauze pad. Check the gauze pad during the treatment when there is much wound exudate observed during the set-up. If dressing is moist, remove and replace with another dry gauze.

There are anecdotal clinical reports that the use of PSWD over wound dressings does not have harmful effects. Also, clinical practice for wound management has changed since the PSWD instruction cautions were first issued in 1981. Further evaluation of the effects of PSWD on wound fluids and dressing adhesives is needed to update this position.

Set-Up for Treatment with Pulsed Short Wave Diathermy

1. Explain the procedure to the patient and caregiver.
2. Inspect and remove all metal items, including jewelry, wristwatches, bras with metal fasteners, and clothing with zippers.

3. Remove hearing aids and external electronic devices.
4. Place the patient on a nonmetal surface.
5. Avoid contact with synthetic materials, including pillows.
6. Remove clothing from body area.
7. Position the patient for comfort in a position that can be maintained for 30 minutes.
8. Remove the wound dressing and absorb excess exudate; cover with dry gauze.
9. Cleanse the wound of debris, metallic and petrolatum-based products; blot dry.
10. Cover the wound and surrounding skin with ½-inch thickness of toweling.
11. Cover the drum with a disposable surgical head cap or terry towel for hygiene.
12. Place the drum 0.5 to 1 cm above the terry cloth.
13. Set the protocol and treatment duration. Start.

Patient Monitoring

- Never leave a patient who is confused or disoriented alone and unsupervised while receiving treatment.
- When using PSWD, remember that pain is a warning that excessive heating is occurring. Give the patient a call light and pay immediate attention to a call. Reduce intensity. Increase air space.
- Check skin before application for unguents that may have been applied (eg, oil of wintergreen, Ben-Gay); clean thoroughly, and dry.

Aftercare for Pulsed Short Wave Diathermy

Because the dressing is always removed before this treatment, it is important that the wound be dressed with the appropriate dressing as soon as possible after conclusion of the treatment. A dressing should be selected that will match the frequency of the PSWD treatment and other components of the wound healing. Rapid redressing of the wound safeguards against wound contamination and desiccation of the wound tissues, sustains the warmth of the wound that has occurred from the increased profusion, and promotes optimal cell regeneration.

Clinical Wisdom: *Tissue Perfusion*

When tissue perfusion is the treatment effect the wound will be warmed, and the cells will proliferate faster in the warm environment. Therefore, dress the wound *immediately after* PSWD and *before* PRFS.

PSWD (Magnatherm™) for Venous Disease

Patients with venous disease do not tolerate high heating and subsequent effects of vasodilatation. Two phases are used. For the first phase of treatment, energy is adjusted to deliver a pulse rate of 1,600 pps for 15 minutes. This is followed by a second phase at 700 pps for a 15-minute period. Power levels are kept at power level 12.[34]

Pulsed Radio Frequency Stimulation Protocol

The protocol suggested for PRFS is based on the parameters used in the two clinical trials with the Diapulse (Diapulse Corporation) described earlier. These are nonthermal parameters but have a demonstrated ability to enhance tissue perfusion. Mechanisms of action may be different. Consider this therapy intervention if heating is contraindicated, if wound dressing is to be left intact during the treatment, or if the wound is inside a cast (Exhibit 18–4).

Set-Up Treatment with Pulsed Radio Frequency Stimulation

1. Explain the procedure to the patient and caregiver.
2. Position the patient for comfort, with the treatment site accessible, so that it can be maintained for 30 minutes.
3. Cover the drum with a disposable surgical head cap or terry towel for hygiene.
4. Place the drum 0.5 to 1 cm above the terry cloth over the wound site.
5. Leave the dressings in place unless there is strike-through or it is time to change dressing.
6. Set the protocol and treatment duration. Start.

Exhibit 18–4 Protocol for PRFS

Pulse rate: 600 pps
Intensity: peak power
Duration: 30–60 minutes
Frequency: twice daily or every day three to seven times per week

---

Clinical Wisdom:

Use PSWD or PRFS over Painful Wounds

Use either PSWD or PRFS over open wounds of all depths of tissue involvement, where contact would be painful, for edema reduction and pain relief (eg, surgical wounds, both primary intention and tertiary intention).

Adjunctive Treatments

PSWD and PRFS can be used in conjunction with the other adjunctive treatments such as hydrotherapy or pulsatile lavage with suction and possibly enhance results. It may be preferable to treat with the PSWD before and PRFS and immediately after the other interventions after the wound is dressed. The treatment effect will be to add perfusion to the area, and providing it after the wound is dressed will keep the wound warm and protected. Benefits of multiple treatments with different physical agents and electrotherapeutic modalities have not been proven. The physical therapist should assess whether the addition of another of these interventions is needed, and support it with a rationale. This is an area that merits further research for best utilization management of services and best efficacy for the patient.

Another adjunctive treatment with well-established effect on circulation is exercise. Exercise following PSWD or PRFS would use the muscle pump for exchange of nutrients and oxygen brought to the tissue by the PSWD or PRFS treatment and removal of waste products as well as to help dissipate the effects of heating and avoid burning. Exercise encourages movement of fluids from the venous system into the lymphatics and is a way to avoid stasis in the area of heating. For those patients who are unable to exercise actively, assisted or passive range of motion would encourage change in fluid dynamics in the effected area. Therapeutic positioning should also be considered as an adjunctive treatment because improper positioning may have blood flowing away from the target tissues or applying pressure to the area that is to be perfused.

SELF-CARE TEACHING GUIDELINES

Both PSWD and PRFS labels state "federal law restricts the sale and use of this equipment to a licensed health practitioner."[9,30] Therefore, self care is not a recommended option for these technologies.

DOCUMENTATION

The functional outcome report (FOR) described in Chapter 1 is an accepted method to meet Medicare and third-party payer guidelines for documentation of the need for physical therapy intervention for wound healing. The two cases presented as examples of the use of PSWD and PRFS are documented by using the FOR method. A sample form and case are found in Chapter 1. Also, try to apply the method to wound cases in the clinic.[35] Data collected about treatment outcomes in a systematic manner can be of great value to report the success of the therapy and to predict outcomes.

Case Study 1: Pressure Ulcer Treated with Pulsed Short Wave Diathermy

Patient ID: S.D.   Age: 86

Functional Outcome Report: Initial Assessment

Reason for Referral

The patient is minimally mobile and has developed a pressure ulcer on the left heel and fifth metatarsal head. She is alert but lacks the ability to reposition. Autolytic debridement with occlusive dressing has not been successful.

Medical History and Systems Review

The patient experienced a left fractured hip with open reduction and internal fixation 3 years ago. She never regained the ability to ambulate after the hip fracture. She also has a history of multiple cerebrovascular accidents that shows that her circulatory system is impaired. She is placed in a wheelchair for a few hours a day. She takes food orally and eats most of the diet offered. There has been no recent loss of weight. She is incontinent of bowel and bladder and has a Foley catheter in place.

Evaluation

The patient has an impaired healing response that is due to impairment of the circulatory system and the musculoskeletal system. This functional loss causes the inability to progress through the phases of repair without intervention. The patient has improvement potential for the wounds but will remain at risk for future pressure ulceration. The following examinations are indicated:

- Joint integrity
- Mobility
- Circulatory function
- Integumentary system: surrounding skin and wound

Examination Data

Joint Integrity. The patient has a fixed varus deformity of the leg, and no active mobility of the left hip joint exists. There is minimal mobility of the left knee, and a knee flexion contracture at 75° limits function of the left leg. The hip and knee deformities have created a positioning problem, with the left ankle crossing over the right leg and the lateral aspect of the foot, from toes to heel, in a position that is subject to pressure. Ankle joint mobility is also severely impaired.

Mobility. The patient is immobile. She does not attempt to self-reposition in either bed or wheelchair.

Circulation. There is edema of the left foot extending to the ankle. The foot is warm (98.6°F), with 1+ palpable pulses. No dependent rubor is noted when the patient is seated in a wheelchair.

Integumentary System. There is an ulcer on the left lateral heel; it has eschar necrosis, inflammation signs of changes in skin color (red), warmth (98.6°F), and local edema. The whole foot to the ankle is edematous. There is an ulcer on the left fifth metatarsal head with eschar necrosis, signs of mild inflammation, no pain, changes in skin color (red), and warmth (98.6°F) and edema. It is 6.9 cm². (See *Color Plates 60 and 61* for pictures of the wounds.)

Functional Diagnosis

- Undue susceptibility to pressure ulceration on the feet
- Both wounds chronic inflammation phase
- Initial associated impairment status eschar

Need for Skilled Services: The Therapy Problem

The patient has failed to respond to interventions with dressing changes for the last 2 weeks. She now requires debridement of the eschar from both wounds to determine the extent of tissue impairment and to initiate the healing process; PSWD to enhance circulation to the foot, facilitate debridement, and restart the process of repair; and therapeutic positioning to avoid trauma from pressure to the foot.

Targeted Outcomes.

- The wound bed will be clean.
- There will be an enhanced inflammatory response: erythema, edema, and warmth.
- The patient will progress through the phases of healing from inflammation to epithelialization.
- The patient will be properly positioned to remove pressure from the left foot.

Treatment Plan

Debridement Strategy

Score eschar and use an enzymatic debriding agent and occlusion for autolysis. Sharply debride when eschar is softened. Apply PSWD for perfusion.

Prognosis. Clean wound bed; *due date:* 21 days.

continues

Case Study 1 continued

PSWD

Apply PSWD for increased circulation to the foot, using the protocol of one applicator over the abdomen and the second applicator over the plantar surface of the foot. Use the device at the vigorous heating setting for 5 minutes followed by mild heating (nonthermal) for 25 minutes.

Prognosis.

- Acute inflammation; *due date:* 14 days.
- Progression through phases to closure; *due date:* 8 weeks.

Frequency. Apply PSWD daily seven times per week, twice daily for 30 minutes.

Therapeutic Positioning

Use therapeutic positioning with pillows to keep pressure from the left foot; instruct nurses' aides in proper positioning.

Discharge Outcome

The wound on the fifth metatarsal head was healed by day 15. The wound on left heel had full-thickness skin loss after removal of eschar and necrotic tissue. The wound had a clean bed by week 4. Closure was achieved by week 7. (See *Color Plate 62*.)

Discussion

The use of PSWD was selected to bring enhanced perfusion to the left leg. Care had to be taken to position the applicator head at a distance away from the metal internal fixation devices at the hip. The patient was not a candidate for whirlpool to soften the eschar because the hip deformity made it difficult to position her in the whirlpool. Electrical stimulation was ruled out because more vigorous perfusion to the foot was desired. Debridement by several methods was selected for the fastest relief of the wound bioburden (see Chapter 7). Immobility limits blood flow to the area and increases risk of ischemia from pressure. Therapeutic positioning for pressure elimination was essential to avoid repetitive trauma from pressure to the wounded areas and to allow the wound to heal (see Chapter 13).

Case Study 2: Surgical Wound Treated with Pulsed Radio Frequency Stimulation

Patient ID: L.W.   Age: 85   Onset: July 26

Functional Outcome Report: Initial Assessment

Reason for Referral

The patient had an above-the-knee amputation of the left leg secondary to arterial occlusion and infected ulcers of the left leg and foot. The surgical wound had sutures placed in the tissues and was left open to close by delayed primary intention. The incision dehisced and the stump became very edematous and painful over a period of a few days after discharge from the hospital. The patient was referred to the physical therapist for relief of the pain and edema associated with the surgical procedure and for mobility training in bed and for transfers.

Medical History and Systems Review

At the time of admission to the acute hospital both legs of the patient were severely edematous. There is a longstanding history of congestive heart failure (CHF) and pulmonary emboli. She had been on anticoagulation therapy with Coumadin. Lasix was used to treat the CHF. She had a long-standing chronic renal failure. She was

hugely obese, very weak, and unable to stand or walk. Examinations performed in the hospital included vascular evaluation with findings of no distal pulses palpable or detected by Doppler ultrasound in either foot. The patient complained of severe pain in the left foot. The wound became more necrotic, and the infection failed to respond to antibiotic therapy while in the hospital; surgical above-the-knee amputation was the treatment of choice. The history revealed replacement of both hips and lumbar laminectomy. The patient tolerated the amputation well. She was afebrile, and the wound drainage was negligible. She had a Hemovac drain removed on July 28, 2 days after surgery. At this time she was transferred from the hospital to a subacute unit for rehabilitation and nursing care of the wound using normal saline wet-to-dry dressings. In the subacute unit she has needed continuous oxygen by nasal cannula from a concentrator. The course of healing of the wound changed with increased severe edema, increased drainage, and pain.

Evaluation

The specific functional item that caused the patient's need for the services of the physical therapist is loss of wound healing capacity. The patient's loss of function is

continues

Case Study 2 continued

due to generalized impairment (circulatory impairment, cardiopulmonary impairment, renal impairment) and motor impairment (limited bed mobility and ability to transfer out of bed). The loss of function causes inability to heal without integumentary intervention.

Examination

The following examinations are indicated:

- Integumentary: surrounding skin, wound tissues
- Mobility
- Circulatory

Examination Findings

Integumentary Examination. Surrounding skin shows erythema along the wound edges; there is 2+ edema with induration. The patient has constant pain requiring Tylenol #3. The wound has moderate exudate, and there is yellow slough in the wound bed (see *Color Plate 63*). The wound is held together with four sutures. Wound open area size: 24 cm × 2 cm = 48 cm². Depth: >0.2 cm, undermining 0.

Functional diagnosis: dehiscence of wound, exacerbation of inflammation phase

Targeted outcome: edema free, exudate free, erythema free, pain free, inflammation free, progression to proliferation phase

Mobility Examination. The patient is unable to reposition self in bed and is unable to do supine to sit or transfer out of bed.

Functional diagnosis: lacks bed mobility, lacks transfer mobility, undue susceptibility to pressure ulceration

Targeted outcome: able to reposition without assistance, reduce risk of pressure ulceration

Circulatory Examination. There is a palpable left femoral pulse.

Functional diagnosis: functional circulation for healing

Need For Skilled Services: The Therapy Problem

The wound has failed to respond to treatment interventions of wet-to-dry dressings and has regressed, demonstrating loss of functional healing capacity. Lack of bed mobility causes undue susceptibility to pressure ulcers on the sacrum and coccyx as well as the right heel. Immobility causes loss of function of muscle pump for circulation and inability of the wound to heal without intervention. The wound is very large. The patient requires moist wound healing; PRFS to reduce pain and edema, enhance circulation, and stimulate cells of repair; and establishment of a bed mobility training and transfer training program.

Treatment Plan

- Apply wet-to-dry dressings four times daily.
- Use PRFS for 30 minutes twice daily at maximum intensity and pulse rate. (*Note:* The device used for this case study was the MRT sofPulse.)
- Begin bed mobility training with an overhead trapeze.
- Provide a support surface to relieve pressure for bed and wheelchair.

Treatment Frequency. PRFS twice daily seven times per week; *due date:* 6 weeks

Discharge Outcome

The wound progressed from the acute inflammatory phase to the proliferation phase within 2 weeks from start of treatment. The wound was closed and resurfaced by week 4. Further surgery, as had been originally planned, was not needed to close the wound. (See *Color Plate 64* for progression of the wound.)

Discussion

The clinical decision making for this patient considered the following factors. Instead of progression from the inflammation phase to the proliferation phase the wound had regressed to an acute exacerbation of the inflammation phase. The tissues surrounding the wound were very edematous and painful, and the wound size was enlarged from admission to subacute from acute care. A direct contact treatment such as ultrasound or pulsatile lavage with suction would not have been tolerated because of severe pain. Electrical stimulation (ES) was ruled out as an option for two reasons: (1) the electrode for the ES would have been about the same size as the dispersive electrode, with low-current density to the wound site, and (2) the capacitive coupling would have required handling the painful tissues. Whirlpool was contraindicated because of the congestive heart failure and the respiratory impairment. PSWD was ruled out because of the severe peripheral vascular disease (PVD). Therefore, PRFS was the treatment of choice. It could be applied directly over the wound dressing. Therefore, nurses could provide the dressing changes four times daily and timing of dressing changes and PRFS treatment was not a problem. The surgeon would allow only saline wet-to-dry dressings four times daily as the wound dressing. Because of the large PRFS applicator head, it could be positioned to cover the entire length of the wound opening without physical contact. It would enhance circulation but less aggressively than PSWD, which was contraindicated over the wound because of the PVD. Pressure relief and bed mobility training were essential components of the treatment plan.

REFERENCES

1. Guy A, Lehmann J, Stonebridge J. Therapeutic applications of electromagnetic power. *Proc IEEE.* January 1974:55–75.

2. Kloth L, Ziskin M. Diathermy and pulsed radio frequency radiation. In: Michlovitz SL, ed. *Thermal Agents in Rehabilitation.* Philadelphia: F.A. Davis; 1996:213–254.

3. Markov MS, Pilla A. Electromagnetic field stimulation of soft tissues: pulsed radio frequency treatment of postoperative pain and edema. *Wounds.* 1995;7(4):143–151.

4. Kellog R. Magnetotherapy: potential clinical and therapeutic applications. In: Nelson R, Currier D, eds. *Clinical Electrotherapy.* Norwalk, CT: Appleton & Lange; 1991:390–391.

5. Rabkin J, Hunt TK. Local heat increases blood flow and oxygen tension in wounds. *Arch Surg.* 1987;122:221–225.

6. Sanservino EG. Membrane phenomena and cellular processes under action of pulsating magnetic fields. Presented at the Second International Congress for Magneto Medicine; November 1980; Rome, Italy.

7. Fenn JE. Effect of pulsed electromagnetic energy (Diapulse) on experimental hematomas. *Can Med Assoc J.* 1969;100:251.

8. Ginsberg AJ. Pearl chain phenomenon. Presented at the 35th Annual Meeting of the American Congress of Physical Medicine and Rehabilitation; 1958;36:112–115. Abstract.

9. Cameron BM. Experimental acceleration of wound healing. *Am J Orthop.* November 1961:336–343.

10. Sambasivan M. Pulsed electromagnetic field in management of head injuries. *Neurol India.* 1993;41(suppl):56–59.

11. Ionescu A, Ionescu D, et al. Study of efficiency of Diapulse therapy on the dynamics of enzymes in burned wound. Presented at the Sixth International Congress on Burns; August 31, 1982; San Francisco.

12. Ross J. Evolution, prevention and relief of acute and chronic pain with the application of Diapulse® therapy (pulsed high peak power electromagnetic energy). *Schmerz.* 1984;1:9–16.

13. Jonsson K, Jensen J, et al. Tissue oxygenation, anemia, and perfusion in relation to wound healing in surgical patients. *Ann Surg.* 1991;214(5):605–613.

14. Lehman JF, deLateur BJ. Therapeutic heat. In: Lehmann JF, ed. *Therapeutic Heat and Cold.* 4th ed. Baltimore: Williams & Wilkins; 1990.

15. Brown G. Diathermy: a renewed interest in a proven therapy. *Phys Ther Today.* Spring 1993:78–80.

16. Silverman D, Pendleton L. A comparison of the effects of continuous and pulsed short-wave diathermy on peripheral circulation. *Arch Phys Med Rehabil.* 1968;49:429–436.

17. Santoro D, et al. Inductive 27.12 MHz: diathermy in arterial peripheral vascular disease. 16th International IEEE/EMBS Conference; October 1994; Montreal, Canada.

18. Erdman W. Peripheral blood flow measurements during application of pulsed high frequency currents. *Orthopedics.* 1960;2:196–197.

19. Mayrovitz H, Larsen P. Effects of pulsed electromagnetic fields on skin microvascular blood perfusion. *Wounds.* 1992;4(5):197–202.

20. Mayrovitz H, Larsen P. A preliminary study to evaluate the effect of pulsed radio frequency field treatment on lower extremity periulcer skin microcirculation of diabetic patients. *Wounds.* 1995;7(3):90–93.

21. Santiesteban J, Grant C. Post-surgical effect of pulsed shortwave therapy. *J Am Podiatr Med Assoc.* 1979;75:306–309.

22. Barclay V, Collier R, Jones A. Treatment of various hand injuries by pulsed electromagnetic energy (Diapulse). *Physiotherapy.* 1983;69(6):186–188.

23. Pennington G, Daily D, Sumko M. Pulsed, non-thermal, high-frequency electromagnetic energy (Diapulse) in the treatment of grade I and grade II ankle sprains. *Mil Med.* 1993;158:101–104.

24. Goldin JH, Broadbent JD, et al. The effects of Diapulse on the healing of wounds: a double-blind randomised controlled trial in man. *Br J Plastic Surg.* 1981;34:267–270.

25. Itoh M, et al. Accelerated wound healing of pressure ulcers by pulsed high peak power electromagnetic energy (Diapulse). *Decubitus.* 1991;4(1):24–34.

26. Wilson C. Clinical effects of Diapulse® technology in treatment of recalcitrant pressure ulcers. Poster Presentation, Clinical Symposium on Pressure Ulcer and Wound Management; September 1992; Orlando, FL.

27. Salzberg A, et al. The effects of non-thermal pulsed electromagnetic energy (Diapulse®) on wound healing of pressure ulcers in spinal cord-injured patients: a randomized, double-blind study. *Wounds.* 1995;7(1):11–16.

28. Comorosan S, Paslaru L, Popovici Z. The stimulation of wound healing processes by pulsed electromagnetic energy. *Wounds.* 1992;4(1):31–32.

29. International Medical Electronics. *Megatherm® (Model 1000) Short Wave Therapy Unit Instruction Manual.* Kansas City, MO: International Medical Electronics LTD;1981.

30. Electropharmacology. *MRT® SofPulse™ User's Manual.* Pompano Beach, FL: Electropharmacology, Inc.

31. Martin CJ, McCallum HM, et al. Electromagnetic fields from therapeutic diathermy equipment: a review of hazards and precautions. *Physiotherapy.* 1991;77:3–7.

32. Ourllet-Hellstrom R, Stewart. Miscarriages among female physical therapists who report using radio- and microwave-frequency electromagnetic radiation. *Am J Epidemiol.* 1993;138:775–786.

33. 21 CFR Ch. 1 (4-1-93 Edition). Device described in paragraph (BX1) see section 890.3, 48 FR 53047, Nov. 23, 1983, as amended in 52 FR 17742, May 11, 1987, Document No. A779269.

34. Frankenberger L, personal communication.

35. Swanson G. Functional outcomes report: the next generation in physical therapy reporting. In: Stewart DL, Abeln SH, eds. *Documenting Functional Outcomes in Physical Therapy.* St. Louis, MO: Mosby–Year Book; 1993.

CHAPTER 19

Therapeutic and Diagnostic Ultrasound

Carrie Sussman and Mary Dyson

INTRODUCTION

Ultrasound (US) has been used for treatment of soft tissue trauma for decades. This chapter compares and contrasts megahertz (MHz) and kilohertz (kHz) US, demonstrating how their physical properties and biologic effects can be employed to accelerate the healing of skin and other forms of tissue repair. For therapeutic US, the therapist is provided with sufficient information to select the most appropriate method of treatment for injuries of different types and in different locations. For high-resolution diagnostic ultrasound, this chapter describes recent advances in the use of this modality, coupled with fractal analysis, to monitor the extent of soft tissue injury and its repair in a quantitative, objective manner.

DEFINITIONS AND TERMINOLOGY

Ultrasound

Ultrasound is a mechanical vibration transmitted at a frequency above the upper limit of human hearing (ie, above 20 kHz, where 1 hertz [Hz] = 1 cycle per second and 1 kHz = 1,000 cycles per second). It causes the molecules of media that can transmit it (eg, biologic tissues) to oscillate or vibrate, and can be used therapeutically to accelerate wound healing and diagnostically to assess the extent of soft tissue injuries and to monitor their repair in a quantitative manner.

Megahertz US, typically between 0.5 and 3 MHz (ie, 0.5 and 3 MHz, or 0.5 and 3 million cycles per second [ie, 500,000 and 3 million Hz]) has been used for more than 40 years to stimulate healing. During the last 5 years, 30 and 50 kHz US, also known as long-wave US, has been demonstrated

to have therapeutic effects; this new form of therapeutic US is growing rapidly in use.

Frequency

Many of the clinically relevant properties of US are related to its *frequency*. This is the number of times per second that a molecule displaced by the US completes a cycle of movement and returns to its original position. Frequencies (*f*) are expressed in hertz, where 1 Hz = one cycle per second. The time taken to complete a cycle is termed a *period* (*T*).

Attenuation

Attenuation refers to the lessening of the force of the US wave as the sound energy is absorbed into, scattered, or reflected by the tissues. At higher frequencies, more of the energy is absorbed at the surface than penetrates into deeper structures. For example, US units offering 3 MHz are now becoming widely available and are used for wound healing when superficial tissues are to be treated. For decades, 1-MHz US has been useful for deep penetration into tissues. This additional option provides opportunities to select devices with higher and lower frequencies for different treatment protocols and applications.

Half-Value Thickness

When US is transmitted through tissue, its intensity gradually decreases as a result of absorption, scattering, and reflection. The thickness of tissue necessary for the intensity applied to it to be reduced to one-half of the level applied to it is termed the half-value thickness. The intensity available at any depth within the tissue is inversely proportional to the depth of penetration (ie, the greater the depth, the less the remaining available intensity). For example, if 1 W/cm² of 1-MHz US is applied to the skin at a depth of 5 cm, only 0.25 W/cm² would be available; at a depth of 10 cm, only 0.25 W/cm² would be available. Absorption, which is a major cause of attenuation (eg, loss of intensity), is frequency dependent. The greater the frequency, the shorter the wavelength; the shorter the wavelength, the greater the absorption. For a US beam of 3 MHz, the wavelength is shorter than that at 1 MHz, and therefore absorption occurs more readily than at 1 MHz, reducing the half-value thickness by 3. Thus, in the example above, the half-value thickness would be 5/3 = 1.7 cm. A frequency of 3 MHz is an efficient one to use to treat superficial regions, such as injured skin, but lower frequencies are indicated for deeper targets, such as injured muscle or bone.

The amount of absorption varies with the composition of the tissues as well as with the wavelength, which, as described above, is inversely related to frequency. Bone is more absorptive than highly proteinaceous tissues (eg, dermis and muscle); protein is more absorptive than fat (eg, adipose tissue); and fat is more absorptive than water-rich materials (eg, plasma, edematous tissues). Because of this, the half-value thickness of bone is less than that of muscle, which is less than that of fat, which is less than that of edematous soft connective tissue. US can therefore penetrate skin, fat, and edematous tissues to reach a deeply located injury in, for example, a joint capsule or a muscle.

Clinical Wisdom: *Use the US Unit Available*

If a 3-MHz US unit is not available, good results can be had with a 1-MHz unit. Part of the US wave will still be absorbed by the superficial tissues, just a lesser amount. As 3-MHz units become more widely available in the clinic, the options for treatment will be enhanced. In the meantime, do not hesitate to use what is available, but for best results start as soon as possible after injury.

Wavelength

The *wavelength* (λ) is the shortest distance, measured parallel to the direction of wave propagation, between molecules that are at equivalent points of vibration in the repeated cycle of movement, which constitutes a wave. It is related to the frequency and *velocity* (*c*) of the wave by the following equa-

tion: $\lambda = c/f$. The velocity of US in water, blood, interstitial fluid, and soft tissues is approximately 1,500 m/s. The higher the frequency, the shorter the wavelength. This is important diagnostically, because the shorter the wavelength, the greater the degree of resolution. The frequency of 20 MHz that is used by the prototype soft tissue scanner currently being developed at Guy's Hospital, London, England, and being tested at West Jersey and West Hudson Wound Healing Centers, produces a wavelength that is sufficiently short to allow collagen fiber bundles and other acoustically different components of intact and damaged soft connective tissues to be distinguished. High frequencies are more readily absorbed by tissues than low frequencies, and produce a greater thermal effect in the tissues. Lower frequencies produce cavitation and the microstreaming associated with it more readily than do higher frequencies; there is evidence that many of the biologic effects produced by therapeutic US are caused by cavitation and microstreaming.[1]

Equipment for Generation of Ultrasound

The equipment used to produce therapeutic levels of megahertz US typically consists of a microcomputer-controlled high-frequency generator linked by a coaxial cable to an applicator or treatment head. The treatment head contains a disc of a piezoelectric material, such as lead zirconate titanate (PZT), which acts as a transducer to change one form of energy into another, in this case into *ultrasound*. When an alternating voltage is applied across such a disc, it expands and contracts at the same frequency as the oscillation, transducing electrical energy into US. A similar system is made use of for kilohertz US, but the frequency of vibration is much lower, and the transducers have a different coposition and mode of operation.

The Ultrasonic Field

The ultrasonic pressure field generated by the transducer depends on the size and shape of the transducer and on how it is mounted in the applicator. The pressure varies across the surface of the applicator and also with the distance from it. The pressure changes experienced by the tissues being treated, therefore, depend in part on their position relative to the applicator. Ultrasound is emitted from a disc-shaped transducer of the type used with megahertz therapeutic US as a beam, which is at first cylindric; this region is termed the *near field* or *Fresnel zone*, and the energy distribution in it is extremely variable. Beyond this, the beam starts to diverge and the energy distribution with it becomes more regular; this region is termed the *far field* or *Fraunhofer zone*. The distance (*d*) from the transducer to the beginning of the far field is related to the radius (*a*) of the transducer and the wavelength (λ) of the ultrasound: *d* = *a*²/λ.

Unless the part to be treated is immersed in a water bath in which the transducer and target tissue can be separated by a distance sufficient for the target tissues to be in the far field, US therapy usually involves treatment of tissue in the nonuniform near field. The *beam nonuniformity ratio* (BNR) is a measure of this nonuniformity, and is the ratio of the spatial peak intensity (I[SP]) to the spatial average intensity (I[SA]). These terms are defined below. Applicators with low BNRs give more *predictable* results and are *safer* than those with higher BNRs, since the higher spatial peak intensities of the latter are potentially damaging.[2(p141)]

Intensity

Intensity (I) is the amount of energy (in watts) per unit area per unit time. Applicators typically have an *effective radiating area* (ERA) of a few square centimeters. The I can be averaged in space over the face of the applicator (termed *spatial average* [SA]) or in time (termed *temporal average* [TA]). When pulsed US is used, pulse average (PA) intensity (this is the temporal average during the period of the pulse) should be noted and also the temporal average during the full pulse repetition cycle. The type of intensity should be specified as either I(SATA) if continuous or both I(SATA) and I(SAPA) if pulsed.

Thermal and Nonthermal Effects

A medium-intensity range required to elevate tissue temperature to a range of 40° to 45°C is 1.0 to 2.0 W/cm² continuously for 5 to 10 minutes.[2(p145)] This is acceptable only in inadequately vascularized tissues. Temperatures above this cause thermal *necrosis* and *must be avoided*. Thermal effects occur with both 1-MHz and 3-MHz US when continuous wave US is applied, but at different tissue depth. At a frequency of 3 MHz, energy absorption occurs mainly in superficial tissues (1 to 2 cm beneath the surface). At a frequency of 1 MHz, less energy is absorbed by the superficial tissues provided that there is an adequate output from the transducer. This frequency also penetrates into deeper tissues, with effective energy levels being available up to 5 cm below the surface. Nonthermal effects are reduced by pulsing the wave, since this reduces the temporal average intensity. Whenever US is absorbed, heat is produced, but if the temperature increases less than 1°C this is not considered to be physiologically relevant; therapeutic effects are due primarily to nonthermal mechanisms.

Because many wounds occur in ischemic tissues, care must be used when applying thermal US in the presence of arte-

rial occlusive disease. In these areas, there is reduced ability to dissipate heat, and burns can result. Ultrasound is contraindicated in the presence of arterial occlusion. Nonthermal application is safer over areas of impaired circulation.

Stable Cavitation and Microstreaming

Nonthermal effects of US occur at a low spacial average intensity, which can be achieved by pulsing at, for example, a 20% duty cycle and are attributed to two different mechanisms: *cavitation* and *acoustic streaming*. Cavitation involves the production and vibration of micron-sized bubbles within the coupling medium and fluids within the tissues. The US beam affects small, gaseous bubbles that move within the tissue fluids. As the bubbles collect and condense, they are compressed before moving on to the next area. The movement and compression of the bubbles can cause changes in the cellular activities of the tissues subjected to US. Stable cavitation occurs when the bubbles in the field do not change much in size. The effect of stable cavitation can result in diffusional changes along cell membranes and thereby alter cell function. Stable cavitation is potentially beneficial to influence cellular changes within the tissues. Unstable or transient cavitation refers to collapse of the bubbles mentioned above. Transient bubbles implode, causing local mechanical damage and free radical formation. This is potentially very hazardous. It occurs at high intensities, particularly when the sound head is not moved during treatment and standing waves develop.

A second nonthermal effect of US is acoustic streaming. This is defined as the movement of fluids along the acoustic boundaries (eg, bubbles or cell membranes) as a result of the mechanical pressure wave associated with the US beam.[2(p147)] Outcomes attributable to this effect include increased cell membrane and vascular wall permeability and increased protein synthesis.

It is suggested that stable cavitation and microstreaming are responsible for the stimulatory effects of low-intensity US, acting as a stimulus which reversibly modifies plasma membrane permeability and thus modulates cellular activity. Transient cavitation and standing wave formation are potentially damaging but are readily avoided by using low intensities and keeping the applicator moving during treatment.

HIGH-RESOLUTION DIAGNOSTIC ULTRASOUND

Ultrasound, a mechanical vibration transmitted at a frequency above the limit of human hearing, that is, in excess of 20 kHz (20 thousand cycles of vibration per second), is widely used as both a diagnostic and therapeutic agent. The US is generated by the electrical stimulation of a piezoelectric material termed a transducer. Ultrasound has an excellent safety record and is considered sufficiently safe to use to image sensitive structures, such as the developing fetus.

Imaging

Ultrasound imaging depends on the principle that different tissue components reflect and absorb the waves of US to varying degrees, depending on their acoustic properties, which in turn depend upon their structure. For example, tissues rich in fat absorb less US than do tissues rich in protein. Reflection occurs at the interface between materials that differ in their acoustic properties, specifically in their acoustic impedance. Piezoelectric materials not only transduce electrical signals into mechanical vibrations, but also transduce mechanical vibrations into electrical signals. In US imaging, the reflected US is detected by the same transducer that produced it during the short intervals between the pulses of US emitted by the transducer. The transducer converts the reflected mechanical vibrations into electrical signals, which are used to visualize structures deep to the surface by converting the digitized data from consecutive A-scans (scans of echo amplitude) into a two-dimensional image, termed a B-scan or brightness scan. Movement of the transducer allows a series of scans produced consecutively to be used to form an image analogous to that of a multielement transducer. The reflections or echoes received at each beam position are displayed as spots on the display screen of the scanner, the brightness of each spot being related to the echo amplitude as a gray-scale display. The position of the spots is determined by the orientation of the beam and the time of arrival of the echoes. The gray scale can be replaced by different colors to assist in visual interpretation of the image, the colors representing differing levels of echogenicity from different tissue components. These components, and hence the pattern and brightness of the reflections from them, vary with the tissue and are modified by injury and during repair. The resultant image, which superficially resembles a histologic section, can be thought of as a noninvasive biopsy, produced in a nontraumatic, painless manner with no damage to the tissues that interact with the low-intensity US.

Visual Details

The detail that can be visualized ultrasonically is dependent upon the resolution of the imaging equipment used, and this depends mainly on the wavelength of the US, which is determined by the frequency; the higher the frequency, the shorter the wavelength and therefore the greater the resolution. There is an inverse relationship between frequency and depth of penetration, higher frequencies being less penetra-

tive than lower frequencies. In 1991, US at a frequency of 5 MHz (that is, 5 million cycles of vibration per second) was described as providing "high resolution"[3] and was considered to be adequate to view, for example, the plantaris tendon provided that this was at least 2 mm thick, when the aim was merely to demonstrate whether it was present and whether it was thick enough to be used as a graft. Plantaris is a vestigial muscle; its elongated tendon is an excellent source of tendon graft, being long enough to be used for a wide range of tendon and ligament reconstructions. However, cadaveric studies, cited by Simpson et al.,[3] have shown that it is absent from 7% to 20% of human legs, and if absent from one leg, there is only a one in three chance that it will be present on the contralateral side; in some other limbs it may be too small to be surgically useful. Ultrasound imaging is thus of clinical value in determining in a non-invasive manner whether the plantaris is present and whether it is of a suitable thickness for use as a graft.

More recently, improved instrumentation, coupled with the use of higher frequencies and image analysis, has resulted in the effective use of US to visualize noninvasive changes in tissue associated with the presence of injury or its development, and with its repair. In 1993, O'Reilly and Massouh[4] published a pictorial essay in which they compared the ultrasonic appearance of normal and damaged Achilles tendons using a real-time scanner equipped with a 7.5-MHz linear transducer and a 5.0-MHz sector transducer. They were able to detect and distinguish between tenosynovitis, acute and chronic tendinitis, peritendinitis, nodular tendinitis, and partial or complete tendon rupture on the basis of differences in echogenecity and measurements of tendon thickness, the changes detected ultrasonographically being confirmed invasively by fine-needle aspiration and histologic examination.

Higher frequencies, permitting greater resolution, can be used for more superficial structures such as the components of skin, where less depth of penetration is required. In 1994, 20-MHz ultrasound was used by Karim et al.[5] to image skin from various parts of the body, and it was demonstrated that mathematical algorithms could be used to characterize and classify the dermal monograms as to their site of origin. Two analytic techniques were investigated, fractal analysis and fast Fourier transform, the aim being to develop image analysis techniques sensitive enough to detect minute changes in the pattern of the ultrasonically produced images and to avoid interobserver differences in interpretation of these images.

Fractals

Fractals are a language of geometry, fractal structures being those that have a characteristic form that remains constant over a range of magnifications. A dichotomously branching tree is an example of a fractal structure, maintaining a self-similarity independent of the scale at which it is viewed. The fractal texture analysis program operates by first representing the region of interest selected as a three-dimensional landscape, with lateral and axial dimensions on the horizontal plane and the intensity of the reflections that comprise the image on the vertical axis. The program then calculates the area of the landscape.[6] The area of the image is measured at different resolutions from 1 to 20 pixels. At a given resolution, the rate of change of this area with respect to resolution is related to the estimated fractal dimension at that resolution. This set of fractal dimensions defines the fractal signature. It describes the manner in which any pattern varies from a fully fractal pattern, the fractal signature of which would be a horizontal line, since true fractals have a constant fractal dimension at all resolutions; the fractal signatures of partially fractal structures are complex curves, any horizontal region indicating the range of resolutions at which the structure is fractal. B-scans of skin from different regions of the body have different fractal signatures, as do scans of damaged and repairing dermis. Williams et al.[7] and Karim et al.[5] found that Fournier analysis, which models the ultrasonic image by mathematically decomposing it into a series of periodic functions (sine waves) of different frequencies and phases from which the original can be reconstructed, was somewhat less consistent than fractal analysis in distinguishing between scans of dermis from different regions of the body. Fourier analysis has not yet been used to analyze damaged and repairing dermis, although its ability to do this should be investigated.

Dyson Diagnostic US Scanner

Most recently, a new generation of high-resolution diagnostic US equipment has been developed at the United Medical and Dental Schools of Guy's and St. Thomas' Hospitals, London, England. This is currently being made available as research prototypes to institutions wishing to use it in a controlled manner to investigate its value in monitoring changes in soft connective tissues associated with damage and its repair. A patent was applied for to cover this equipment in 1995, the final version of the patent being provided by Dyson et al. in 1996. The prototype is portable and is fitted with a polyvinylidene difluoride piezoelectric polymer transducer, incorporated into a handset filled with distilled water. It can emit a single cycle pulse at a frequency of between 10 and 50 MHz, although it is generally used at a frequency of the order of 20 MHz. This allows the production of images of the interfaces between acoustically different materials with a resolution such that structures separated by approximately

65 µm in the direction of US transmission can be distinguished. The transducer is moved within the probe by a stepper motor, producing pulses of US with a repetition frequency of 1 millisecond. The system has been designed to emit an ultrafast rise and fall time pulse of duration of less than 50 nanoseconds. These sharp pulses allow excellent detection of reflected signals, which, after transduction, pass through a preamplifying unit in the probe before passing to the main unit. As with other US imaging devices, including those operating at lower frequencies, time-gain compensation is used to control for the attenuation that occurs as the US is reflected back to the transducer. Digitization of the reflected signals produces data that can be stored and used for statistical analysis.[8,9] A digital scan converter stores information in the US scan format and displays it in the video format.

Practical Implications

Practically, the system allows the epidermis to be distinguished from the dermis; differences in the pattern of the reflections distinguish the papillary from the reticular layers of the dermis; and blood vessels, tendon sheaths, tendons, ligaments, and adipose tissue can be identified, as can the interfaces between soft tissue and calcified tissue. Cross-sectional images of the skin produced by this high-resolution, B-mode, 20-MHz ultrasound scanner have a very characteristic appearance. The epidermal/dermal interface is clearly identifiable as a hypoechoic zone, deep to which is a highly reflective band followed by the highly echogenic dermis,[10] the pattern of echoes varying from a speckled appearance in the papillary zone of the dermis to a linear appearance in its deeper reticular zone where the collagen fiber bundles are thicker. Fluid-containing spaces within the dermis appear to be less echogenic, as does subcutaneous fat, although this produces some thin linear echoes that may represent strands of collagenous fibrous connective tissue. The scanner allows changes in soft tissue associated with the development of injury and its repair to be monitored and subjected to fractal analysis, producing fractal signatures that can be compared, as did earlier, less informative and versatile instrumentation.[11,12] Most recently it has been used to detect dermal changes associated with exposure to pressure[13] and as a means of quantifying the irritant response.[14] Its ability to detect, and possibly quantify, muscle inflammation remains to be investigated; in 1990 Van Holsbeek and Introcaso[15] demonstrated echogenic differences between normal and inflamed muscle with the less sensitive instrumentation then available.

Other uses are as a means of monitoring changes in the thickness of the epidermis and of underlying soft connective tissues, and in detecting lesions such as melanomas, potentially when as small as approximately 70 µm in thickness. As long ago as 1984, Shafir et al.[16] indicated that what were then considered to be high-resolution US scanners could measure precisely the thickness of melanomas. Accurate measurement of thickness can provide useful prognostic information, as this dimension is directly related to metastatic potential.[17] Also of importance is the potential of fractal analysis of these high-quality images to provide quantitative data for comparison and assessment of the effectiveness of various therapies in the treatment of injured tissues. Fractal analysis of the images may also be an aid to the diagnosis of a variety of skin pathologies, but this possibility remains to be examined critically.

The clinical future for high-frequency, high-resolution, diagnostic US is of considerable importance and will grow as more uses are demonstrated for it. What is now required is more research of a high quality; this is now being organized internationally.

THEORY AND SCIENCE OF ULTRASOUND ON WOUND HEALING

Cells close to stable bubbles are subject to bubble-associated microstreaming that has been shown to increase their plasma membrane permeability to calcium ions temporarily acting as a stimulus to cell activity (eg, cell migration, proliferation, synthesis of intracellular and extracellular materials), and synthesis and release of growth factors. All these activities would be expected to accelerate wound healing. In cells treated in suspension, the suppression of cavitation also suppresses this stimulation of cellular activity. It should be noted that the ultrasonic stimulus is perceived by the cells and transduced by them; an amplified response then occurs, of a type that varies according to the cell type involved.

Effect on the Phases of Healing

Wound recovery occurs as a series of overlapping biochemical responses to injury. Recovery normally concludes in approximately 21 days. Inflammation occurs in the first 72 hours. In these early hours, epithelial cells begin migration and reproduction to restore the skin integrity and protect the body from infection or admission of foreign substances.

Inflammatory Phase

In normal wounding, the acute inflammatory state occurs following an initial clotting response that initiates a vascular response involving the arterial and venous systems. This in turn leads to vasodilatation and invasion of the area by a large number of white blood cells that release growth factors necessary to initiate repair. (See Chapter 2 regarding biology of wound healing.) These white blood cells include macrophages, polymorphonuclear leukocytes, and mast cells. The mast cells degranulate, releasing histamine hyaluronic acid and other proteoglycans that bind with the watery wound fluid to create a gel. Coagulated wound gel will later be replaced by a dense, binding scar. The massive vascular incursion into the periwound tissues produces the symptoms associated with the inflammatory phase: calor, dolor, rubor, and turgor. This is a critical period of repair. Ultrasound delivered at this time stimulates the release of growth factors from platelets, mast cells, and macrophages, which in turn are chemotactic to the fibroblasts and endothelial cells that later form collagen-containing vascular granulation tissue. Early intervention with US accelerates the inflammation phase, leading to more rapid entry into the proliferative phase of repair. It is not anti-inflammatory. Therefore, US treatment should begin as soon as possible, that is, during acute inflammation.

Research and Clinical Wisdom:
Use US To Restart the Inflammation Phase

- Use US as soon as possible after injury to accelerate the inflammation phase, leading to more rapid entry into the proliferative phase of repair.
- A single thermal treatment with US has been shown to induce the inflammatory phase in chronic wounds.
- In the clinic, chronic diabetic foot ulcer and pressure wounds that have a diagnosis of "absence of inflammation phase" (see Chapter 3 for information about diagnosis of absence of inflammation phase) responded with restarting of inflammation, including periwound erythema, and a gel-like serous exudate within 2 to 3 days after this application of US. In the next 2 to 3 weeks there were measurable decreases in wound size, depth, and undermining, indicating an increase in fibroplasia and wound contraction. No adverse reactions occurred. This is a topic for further research. The protocol used involved 1 MHz, 0.5 W/cm² (SA, TP), 20% duty cycle, daily for 5 minutes to periwound area.[18]

Proliferation Phase

Following the acute inflammation phase, the proliferation phase begins about 72 hours after injury and overlaps the late inflammation phase. Proliferation is divided into two stages: fibroplasia and contraction. New tissue has a pink granular appearance and is called granulation tissue. Granulation tissue builds on the collagen matrix laid down by the fibroblasts. Granulation tissue will remodel into tissue with mechanical properties similar to those of the uninjured tissue. Ultrasound stimulates fibroblast migration and proliferation. Dyson[19] reports that fibroblasts exposed to therapeutic levels of US *in vivo* were stimulated to synthesize more of the type of collagen that gives soft connective tissue most of its tensile strength. Endothelial cells, responsible for vascularization of the granulation tissue, are also affected by US at this stage to produce more prolific growth. Under histologic examination more angiogenesis is seen in granulation tissue that has been sonated at 0.75 MHz and 0.1 W/cm² than untreated tissue.[1,19,20]

The late phase of proliferation is wound contraction. During this process the wound is pulled together by the centripetal movement of the surrounding tissue. This results in less scar tissue formation. Fibroblasts transform into specialized contractile cells called myofibroblasts for this process. Myofibroblasts at this phase resemble smooth muscle cells. In some experiments, smooth muscle cells are reported to contract when treated with therapeutic levels of US. It is postulated that myofibroblasts are similarly affected. US applied during the inflammatory and early proliferative phases may accelerate wound contraction by causing those cells to develop earlier and increasing their efficiency. At this time, however, the mechanisms by which this occurs are not fully understood. Dyson states that no reports have been found of excessive pathologic contraction (ie, contracture) following treatment with therapeutic US.[1,19] Therefore, intervention with low-intensity, nonthermal US within 72 hours following injury can be used to promote wound contraction, which results in a reduction in size of the resulting scar.[21]

Clinical Wisdom: *Ultrasound and High-Voltage Pulsed Current for Dual Purpose*

Ultrasound has been useful in the clinic to treat over periwound tissue above undermined and tunneled areas because 1 MHz can penetrate up to 5 cm. This treatment has been given in conjunction with high-voltage pulsed current to the wound bed. Response has been decreased size of depth and undermining measurements within the first 2 weeks from start of this treatment. No adverse reactions occurred. This is a topic for further research. Protocol used involved 1 MHz, 0.5 W/cm² (SA, TP), 20% duty cycle, daily for 5 minutes to periwound area for 2 to 3 weeks.[18]

Epithelialization Phase

Epithelialization begins concurrently with inflammation and proliferation. The epithelial cells begin moving and reproducing within a few hours of injury. These cells require an environment that is warm, moist, and free of infection and a supply of nutrients and oxygen in order to move and to multiply.[22–24]

Ultrasound stimulates the release of growth factors necessary for regeneration of the epithelial cells. Ultrasound has the capability of increasing the vascularity of the tissue and may therefore improve nutrient and oxygen delivery. Ultrasound, therefore, appears to stimulate epithelialization and hasten it, associated with granulation, by application to the periwound areas.

Remodeling/Maturation Phase

This phase is *only* affected by low-intensity US *if* treatment is commenced in the inflammatory phase. If so, the effects are more rapid entry into the remodeling phase, increased wound tensile strength, increased capacity to absorb energy without mechanical damage, increased elasticity, and deposition of collagen fibers in a pattern closer to that of intact tissue. Several researchers have reported the application of thermal US during the remodeling phase to affect collagen extensibility and enzyme activity mechanically. Frieder et al.[25] reported improved collagen organization, and Jackson et al.[26] reported improved tensile strength in tendon repairs of US-treated animals. Hart[21] demonstrated that treatment with low-intensity nonthermal US in the early inflammatory phase influences the outcome of the scar collagen density and organization. Later treatment is less effective.

Pain and Edema

Pain threshold has been raised with thermal application of therapeutic US due to a rise in the nerve conduction velocity of the C fibers.[27] Pain is a symptom associated with the inflammatory phase due to the influx of blood, the release of chemicals such as histamine, prostaglandins, and bradykinin, and the associated pressure from post-traumatic edema on surrounding nerve endings. Reduction of pain is an essential part of wound healing, resulting in reduced muscle guarding and increased activity that in turn enhances circulation to the area of wounding. Pain also stimulates the sympathetic nervous system, producing a reactive hyperemia. The result is an increased area of inflammation. This enhances the metabolic requirements of the surrounding tissue for more nutrients and oxygen. Pain relief can reduce the area of involvement and decrease the bioburden.

Enhanced blood flow creates greater capillary pressure and fluid shift into the interstitial tissues and this creates edema. Acoustic streaming described earlier may affect the vascular permeability and help control periwound edema. Edema- and pain-free outcomes are highly desirable because they accelerate and decrease the duration of the inflammatory process.[2]

Circulation

Transcutaneous partial pressure of oxygen ($tcpO_2$) can be measured before and after treatment as a method of monitoring changes in blood flow. (See Chapter 4 for taking $tcpO_2$ measurements.) Byl and Hopf[28] found that following pulsed low-intensity, 0.5 W/cm², 1-MHz ultrasound, little increase in tissue temperature or oxygen transport occurred unless the individual was both well hydrated (three to four glasses of water) and receiving supplemental oxygen by nasal cannula. Those subjects then had an increase in subcutaneous oxygen four times higher than that measured when the same subjects were breathing room air. Thermal application with high-dose 1.0 W/cm², low-frequency, 1-MHz US produced vasodilatation and raised tissue oxygen levels and temperature significantly. Care must be taken to avoid excessive thermal effects whereby circulation is diminished and heat cannot be dissipated rapidly.[28] Increased circulation brings nutrients and oxygen to the tissues and also removes waste products that can impede healing. Because increased circulation and oxygen are such critical components of wound healing and are dose dependent, this needs to be considered in the use of protocols for healing.

Bruising/Hematoma

Ultrasound has been described as increasing dispersal of hemorrhagic material associated with bruising.[30] Ultrasound treatment may increase the efficiency of the phagocytic cells, which remove this material by modifying membrane permeability.

Hemorrhagic materials in the tissues can lead to tissue death from hypoxia and ischemia in the surrounding tissues, leading to ulceration following a tissue trauma (eg, a stage I pressure ulcer). Unassisted, the body can take several weeks to clear this material from the tissues. US can accelerate the absorption. *Color Plates 65 through 70* show case examples of absorption of hemorrhagic material following the use of US. In both cases *no* other treatment intervention was given.

Clinical Wisdom: *US and Absorption of Hematoma*

Stage I pressure ulcers are histologically the rupture of small capillaries and venules, producing a hematoma in the tissue.[31] Treatment with US promotes absorption of hematoma after two to four treatments. Depending on depth of tissue involvement and size of the area, the hematoma resolves in about 2 weeks without ulceration. Protocol: 1 MHz, 0.5 W/cm² (SA, TP), pulsed 20% for 5 to 10 minutes depending on size of area sonated. Apply with conductive gel/lotion five to seven times per week for 1 to 2 weeks or until color returns to that of surrounding skin.[18]

Clinical Studies

Ultrasound was used as a periwound treatment for a controlled trial for patients with chronic varicose ulcers by Dyson et al.[32] Two groups received either sonation or sham sonation three times per week for 4 weeks. Treatment parameters for the US treatment were 3 MHz, 1.0 W/cm² (SA, TP), pulse duration 2 milliseconds was delivered to the tissues every 10 milliseconds for up to 10 minutes. The treatment technique involved moving the head of the device over the skin immediately adjacent to the ulcer. At the end of 4 weeks, the experimental, sonated group had statistically significant reduction in wound size compared with the control group (experimental group 66.4 ± 8.8%; control group 91.6 ± 8.9%). No adverse effects of treatment were found.[32]

Based on the scientific evidence that therapeutic US affects the biologic processes of repair through stable cavitation and/or acoustic streaming described above, a study was undertaken by McDiarmid et al.[33] to determine whether these nonthermal therapeutic effects could be used to treat soft tissue wounds. Patients with partial-thickness skin loss caused by pressure ulcers but not extending beyond the dermis were selected. Forty patients were entered into the study and randomized into a US treatment and a sham US treatment group. Treatment parameters for the US treatment were 3 MHz, 0.8 W/cm² (SA, TP), pulse duration 2 milliseconds, duty cycle 20%, SATA intensity, 0.16 W/cm², effective radiating surface area 5.2 cm². Treatment duration was a minimum of 5 minutes for all pressure ulcers up to 3 cm². One additional minute was added for each 0.5-cm² area for a maximum of 10 minutes. Frequency was three times per week. The insonated ulcers tended to heal more quickly, but the difference was not statistically significant. However, when

comparing clean ulcers with infected ulcers, the mean healing time for the clean ulcers was 30 days versus 40 days for the infected ulcers. This was a healing rate ratio of 2.7, suggesting that the clean sores healed nearly three times more quickly than the infected sores. This result is statistically significant, implying that the major factor influencing healing is whether the ulcer is clean or infected. The effect of healing in the US-treated group of clean sores was not statistically significant. However, there appeared to be a significant effect of US on the healing of the infected sores.

Dosimetry for treatment with US is an area that lacks consensus. To learn more about dosage and wound healing, Byl et al.[34] made incisional wounds in miniature Yucatan pigs and treatment was applied at different doses for different lengths of time. The tensile strength of wounds treated with different intensities, called high- and low-dose US, was tested. Two variables were evaluated: the breaking strength of the incision and the deposition of hydroxyproline, which is a measure of collagen deposition. High-dose US was classified as 1.5 W/cm², continuous mode. Low-dose US was 0.5 W/cm², pulsed mode, 20% duty cycle. Both treatment groups received a frequency of 1 MHz for 5 minutes. The wounds were sonated approximately 1.25 min/cm of incisional length, beginning 24 hours after surgery. The wounds were covered with a moisture- and vapor-permeable adhesive dressing (Tegaderm, 3M Medical-Surgical Division, St. Paul, Minnesota) that was left in place for up to 1 week. The dressing was found to permit transmission of US energy and could be left in place avoiding disruption of the wound between treatment sessions. Forty-eight wounds were made and the wounds were divided into three groups: 12 for control, and 18 each for high-dose US and low-dose US. The groups were subdivided into two groups of 12 that received low dose or high dose for 5 days and two groups of six that received high dose or low dose for 10 days. Results were that the tensile strength for all treatment groups was significantly higher than that of the controls, but there was no difference in hydroxyproline deposition. A significant interaction was found between the number of days of treatment and the US dose. Hydroxyproline deposition was significantly higher and the breaking strength was higher for the low-dose group compared with the high-dose group after 10 days of treatment. During the first week the study findings suggest that either a low or a high dose will enhance wound breaking strength, but to facilitate collagen deposition and wound strength low-dose US should be used if treatment is to continue for 2 weeks or more.[34]

Nussbaum et al.[35] conducted a comparison study of nursing care alone, nursing care with laser, and nursing care with an alternating protocol of US and ultraviolet C (UVC) was carried out on 20 spinal cord–injured patients with 22 pressure ulcers. Of the initial group four subjects dropped out, leaving 16 with 18 wounds who were considered for the analysis. Nursing care consisted of moist dressings and continuous pressure relief. The laser regimen was provided three times per week. The US/UVC regimen consisted of US treatment five times weekly, alternating the US and UVC daily 5 days per week. If the ulcer had purulent drainage, the UVC was used three times per week; if not, US was used three times per week. US protocol was frequency 3 MHz, and an intensity (SATA) of 0.2 W/cm² (1:4 pulse ratio) for 5 minutes per 5 cm² of wound area delivered to the periwound area. Results showed that the US/UVC treatment had a greater effect on wound healing than did the other treatment regimens. The mean treatment time to wound closure was 4.1 weeks. The trend was for ulcers to heal faster in sites where wound contraction was the primary mode of closure (eg, over the coccyx). The conclusion was that this regimen of US/UVC may decrease the healing time for spinal cord–injured patients with pressure ulcers. This was a small study and combined two interventions. Further study would determine whether the combination was essential and the effects of each.

Pressure ulcers were the subject of another study using US by ter Riet et al.[36] Eighty-eight subjects were randomized into two groups, 45 for the treatment group and 43 for the control group. The trials lasted 12 weeks. Sixteen ulcers were stage IV, extending into muscle tissue; 72 had less depth of tissue involvement. Treatment was given directly to the wound surface and to an extended radius 0.75 cm beyond the wound edge. Treatment parameters were frequency 3.28 MHz, pulse duration 2 milliseconds, SATA, 0.1 W/cm², BNR <4. Minimum treatment duration was 3 minutes, 45 seconds. Wounds with treatment areas larger than 5 cm² were treated longer. A wound with an area of 10 cm² was treated for 7½ minutes. Four wound characteristics (color of surrounding skin, necrotic tissue, granulation tissue, and deepest tissue involved) were each marked on a four-point scale with grading, from 1 = bad to 10 = excellent. Two outcome variables were end points: surface area reduction in square centimeters and wound closure (yes or no). After 12 weeks, 40% of the ulcers (18/45) in the US group and 44% of the ulcer (19/43) in the sham US group were closed. The results showed a tendency for the US to be more effective in small wounds than in larger wounds, which could not be explained.[36]

CHOOSING AN INTERVENTION: CLINICAL REASONING

The prior section of this chapter evaluates the efficacy of US on the phases of wound recovery and in clinical trials. To summarize, the studies looked at seven important physiologic effects of US therapy that the physical therapist should consider when selecting US intervention. Ultrasound has the following effects:

- It affects all phases of wound recovery at the cellular level if applied during the inflammation phase.
- It accelerates the rate of progression through the phases of repair.
- It affects different tissue types differently according to the tissues' ability to absorb energy. More tissue absorption requires lower-intensity application.
- It promotes absorption of hemorrhagic materials.
- It increases circulation and tcpO₂ if the patient is well hydrated and oxygenated.
- It raises the threshold of pain.
- It enables noninvasive, nontraumatic treatment of deep or superficial tissue, depending on frequency.

Information about the effects of US on wound healing is less clear because of the limited number of clinical trials, the different parameters used for each study, the small sample sizes, and perhaps because the intervention was not appropriately applied; for example, it was applied to chronic wounds at intensities that would not restart the inflammatory phase of healing leading to progression through the phases of repair. One study included two interventions, US and UVC, with good outcomes. Two studies included subjects who had pressure ulcers; one study included patients with venous ulcers. The biologic effects described are independent of the wound etiology. The pressure ulcers ranged from partial thickness to full thickness extending to muscle levels of tissue involvement. Partial-thickness ulcers heal by reepithelialization, deep ulcers by contraction. The results for infected ulcers were better than those for clean ulcers. Infected ulcers are usually in an inflammatory phase of healing, which is when US is known to be most effective. Would a different protocol be better for a different phase of healing and would that affect the outcome? More evaluation of the dosimetry parameters on the efficacy of US are still required. In the meantime, US may be the treatment of choice for some patients. Two examples are described in the case studies at the end of this chapter.

Candidacy for the Intervention

With any interactive treatment, the benefit to the patient must outweigh any possible risk. The physical therapist must therefore be able to assess both benefit and risk. The potential benefits have been described above. Knowledge of the mechanisms by which US interacts with tissue aids the physical therapist in risk assessment. There is a long list of contraindications in the literature,[1] and the excellent safety record of US owes much to the constraints on treatment that these have engendered (Exhibit 19–1). However, not all contraindications listed have been verified experimentally, and it is possible that some patients who could have benefited from US treatment have been denied it. To ensure continued safe use, basic precautions must be considered (Exhibit 19–2).

Basic precautions start by selection of the right candidates for the treatment. The medical history of the patient, the onset date, location of the injury, depth of the injury, and size of the area to be treated will all guide the physical therapist in the selection of US. For example, review the medical history for information about the circulatory system. Look for information about arteriosclerotic vessels, ischemia, and occlusion from reports of vascular studies, or plan to do a noninvasive vascular examination. Uultrasound is not recommended over deep vein thrombosis or thombophlebitis because of the risk of dislodging thrombi. Likewise, hemophiliacs should not be treated with US because of the risk of disturbing clot formation. (See Chapter 6 for noninvasive vascular testing.) Check for information about diabetes mellitus, type I or type II; patients with type I diabetes are likely to have vascular impairments and sensory impairments. Diabetes is an impairment to the repair process; expect slower healing. Ultrasound should be used in the pulsed mode over areas of poor circulation. Loss of sensation due to many pathologic causes (eg, spinal cord injury and alcoholic neu-

Exhibit 19–1 Contraindications for US[1]

DO NOT USE US	
Over the uterus during pregnancy	
Over the gonads	
Over malignancies and precancerous lesions	
Over tissues previously treated with deep X-ray or irradiation	
On patients with vascular abnormalities	
	Deep vein thrombosis
	Emboli
	Severe atherosclerosis
Over the cardiac area in advanced heart disease	
Over the eye	
Over the stellate ganglion	
For hemophiliacs not covered by factor replacement	
Over the spinal cord after laminectomy	

Exhibit 19–2 Precautions for Use of US[1]

EXERCISE CAUTION IN USE OF US
In acute infections
Over subcutaneous bony prominences
Over epiphyseal plates
Over subcutaneous major nerves
Over the cranium
Over anesthetic areas

ropathy; see Chapter 15 for a more complete list) means that the patient is not a candidate for thermal US. Treatment over anesthetic areas is a risk because malfunction of the equipment could lead to exposure to intensities that would normally induce pain and be indicative of tissue damage. The insensate patient will not be able to indicate pain during the treatment; therefore, pulsed low-dose US should be used for those cases. If the patient has a history of spinal laminectomy, do not treat with US over that area because of effects on the spinal cord that have not yet been determined but may be harmful. A history of malignant or precancerous lesions or tumors in the area to be treated would be a contraindication because therapeutic levels of US could stimulate cellular proliferation. Sometimes injuries occur around the eye, but this is a location that should *not* be treated with US because the sensitive retina may be affected by it. Metal implants, including foreign objects, are often described in the medical history or by the patient. Use only kilohertz US over metal implants. Do not treat over the uterus during pregnancy, to ensure that no embryo or fetus is exposed to the intensities used in therapeutic US, which are higher than those used diagnostically. Do not treat over the gonads. After a thorough review, consider whether US therapy is indicated. If in doubt, do not irradiate.

PROCEDURES

Protocol Considerations

Review the history for onset of the wound and prior treatment interventions. This will determine both the candidacy and the appropriate treatment parameters. If the wound is acute, make use of the nonthermal effects of US. If chronic, use a protocol of one upper-medium-intensity treatment and subsequently treat at lower intensity. If the wound is located over a bony prominence, the physical therapist must consider a method of sonation that will avoid increasing periosteal temperature. There are several ways to accomplish this objective: (1) select a high frequency (3 MHz), which is absorbed in the more superficial tissues; (2) move the treatment head continuously to avoid standing waves; (3) treat through water for a more uniform far field; or (4) for deeper wounds, select a lower frequency, 1 MHz. If the local circulation is poor, use pulsed US to avoid excessive heating because it will take longer for heat to be dissipated from the area. Assess the size of the area to be treated. Use this assessment to determine the duration of the treatment and the size of the applicator to select. Note that an applicator with a larger ERA will allow treatment of a large wound more rapidly than if an applicator with a smaller ERA is used. Small applicators, however, are very useful for being more selective in treating specific tissues. Select the coupling medium depending on whether the skin is intact or broken. Coupling media are described later. Intensity selection for acute conditions is the upper end of the low range; for chronic conditions, the middle range (see later). The anatomic location of the wound is a very important consideration when using US. For example, be aware of the location of major subcutaneous nerves, which absorb US energy very well and can become overheated, and epiphyseal plates, if treating young people prior to the termination of growth of the plate concerned. This varies with the bone and with the sex. There are also racial differences.

To ensure the continued safe use of US, the following basic precautions are recommended:

- Use US only if adequately trained to do so.
- Use US only to treat patients with conditions known to respond favorably to US therapy, unless it is being used experimentally with the understanding and approval of the patient, his or her medical advisors, and the local medical ethics committee.
- Use the lowest intensity that produces the required effect, since higher intensities may be damaging. Burns, for example, occur when the intensity is too high or the frequency is low, but the treatment head is not moved continuously or is moved too slowly.
- Move the applicator constantly throughout treatment, to avoid the damaging effects of standing waves and of high-intensity regions when treating in the nonuniform near field.
- Make sure that there is adequate couplant and that it is free of air bubbles.
- Make sure that the equipment is calibrated regularly. A broken crystal, for instance, may occur if the applicator head is dropped. Staff must report any dropping of the applicator head so that it can be tested before reuse. A faulty piece of equipment can result in inadequate treatment for the patient or can produce shear waves and standing waves that can cause burns or other harmful effects.[1]

Expected Outcomes

Ultrasound is most effective when treating in the acute inflammatory phase of healing. During this phase expect an acceleration of the inflammation and early progression to the proliferation and epithelialization phases of healing (Exhibit 19–3). In chronic wounds the first outcomes to treatment will be increased perfusion, observed as warmth, edema, and darkening of tissue color compared to adjacent skin color tones (Exhibit 19–4). In necrotic wounds, expect to see autolysis of the necrotic tissue; the outcome will be a clean wound bed. Wounds in two clinical trials progressed to closure in a mean time of 4 to 6 weeks.[33,35] These times could be longer for patients with intrinsic and extrinsic factors that limit healing. Published research is a valuable guide to the clinician in prediction of outcomes, but it must be supported by the experience of the program where the treatment is used.

Reassessment should confirm the predicted outcomes. If the wound does not change phase and/or reduce the size of surface area or overall size estimate within 2 to 4 weeks, the treatment regimen must change. There are several changes to US treatment to consider: enhance the inflammation phase

Exhibit 19–3 Outcomes: Acute Wound

Wound healing phase diagnosis: acute inflammation

Expected outcome:
Skin color: change to that of surrounding skin
Temperature: change to that of adjacent tissues or same area on corresponding opposite side of the body
Edema free
Necrosis free
Wound progressed to proliferation phase

Exhibit 19–4 Outcomes: Chronic Wound

Wound healing phase diagnosis: chronic inflammation

Expected outcome:
Hyperemia: change in skin color to reddish blue or purplish depending on color of surrounding skin
Temperature: increased temperature of tissue due to enhanced perfusion
Edema: hardness, tightness, and shiny skin
Wound progressed to proliferation phase

or restart it with the protocol for chronic wounds; change the frequency of the transducer; use a different size transducer for better ERA, or increase the treatment time; or recalculate the area if the wound has been debrided and wound is larger than initial size.

Dyson Protocol

Acute Wounds

Onset. Begin as soon as possible, ideally within a few hours of injury, but always during the inflammatory phase of healing, when treatment with megahertz US has been shown to result in the liberation of stimulatory growth factors from platelets, mast cells, and macrophages with the result that inflammation is accelerated, the proliferative and remodeling phases occur earlier, and the scar tissue is stronger than that of controls (Exhibit 19–5). If treatment is delayed beyond the inflammatory phase, the strength of the scar tissue is not affected.[21]

Duration. Duration is usually based empirically on the surface area to be treated. The area is divided into zones, each 1.5 times the area of the ERA of the applicator, with 1 to 2 minutes being allowed for treating each zone. Some physical therapists recommend 1 min/cm². For the sake of the therapist, the maximum treatment time should be no longer than 15 minutes. If the wound is large, two sessions per day, one to each section of the wound, would be preferable. Three treatments per week have been found to be effective.

Intensity. In the interests of safety, the lowest I(SATA) should be used. This is usually near the upper end of the low range (see Table 19–1). Note that to obtain a significant increase in temperature an I(SATA) of at least 0.5 W/cm² is required, but that primarily nonthermal effects can be obtained with lower SATA intensities, obtained by pulsing I(SATP) 0.5 W/cm² at, for example, 2 milliseconds on, 8

Exhibit 19–5 Nonthermal US Protocol: Acute Inflammation

Frequency	1 or 3 MHz
Pulsed duty cycle	20%–50%
Intensity	0.1–0.2 W/cm² (SATA)
Treatment frequency	3 times per week
Time	1 min/cm², max 15 min total

Table 19–1 Intensity Levels for Therapeutic Ultrasound[1]

Intensity Levels	Range	Area
Low	<0.3	W/cm²
Medium	0.3–1.2	W/cm²
High	>1.2–3.0	W/cm²

---

milliseconds off. Treatments should be pulsed if the local circulation is compromised and might be unable to dissipate heat efficiently.

Chronic Wounds

Onset. Begin as soon as possible.

Duration. Duration is the same as for acute wounds.

Intensity. I(SATA) at approximately the middle of the medium range is generally recommended (eg, 0.5 to 1.0 W/cm² SA, TP). Pulsing should be used. Repair can be initiated by using *one* treatment at the upper end of the medium range (eg, 1.2 W/cm²), after which lower intensities in the medium range are used, as described above. It is suggested that the higher intensity may produce acute trauma followed by local inflammation, which is necessary to initiate healing in any postnatal wound. Note that this is a hypothesis that requires testing.

Frequency Selection

The physical therapist should consider the following when selecting a frequency for treatment:

- If the lesion is superficial, a higher frequency is appropriate because high-frequency US is absorbed superficially.
- Although it is not readily available in many clinics, kilohertz US is another frequency that may be considered more in the near future. Differences between kilohertz and megahertz US are that kilohertz US is less attenuated, but less readily absorbed, than megahertz, and there is little or no reflection from metal implants or from bone; however, sufficient absorption must occur to produce a stimulatory effect if it is to be of value.
- High frequencies (more than 1 MHz) are more appropriate than lower frequencies if thermal changes are required in the tissues.
- Lower frequencies (1 MHz or less) are more appropriate than higher frequencies if primarily nonthermal effects such as stable cavitation and/or microstreaming are required in the tissues. Equipment now on the market allows more flexibility to choose US frequencies

and provide additional choices for the physical therapist. The physical therapist must know what each frequency is best suited to treat.

Coupling Media

Megahertz US requires a coupling medium that displaces air. This is essential because megahertz US is reflected from air/water or air/tissue interfaces. The greater the difference in *acoustic impedance* (z) between the two materials forming the interface, the greater the amount of energy reflected. The acoustic impedance of a medium is the product of its density (p) and the velocity of US through it (c). With megahertz US, only 0.2% reflection occurs at the interface between soft tissue and water, more than 50% between soft tissue and bone, and virtually complete reflection (99.9%) between soft tissue and air. Reflection reduces the amount of energy reaching the target tissues; if this falls below the stimulatory threshold (approximately 0.2 W/cm² I[SATA]), the US will be ineffective. The ideal coupling medium would

- Have the same acoustic impedance as skin
- Also act as a wound dressing
- Be sterile, thixotropic, nonstaining, nonirritant, and chemically inert
- Be slow to be absorbed and to evaporate
- Be free from gas bubbles and other inclusions
- Not break down when the US energy is transmitted through it
- Be inexpensive

Examples of suitable coupling media that displace air and that can be used over wounds are commercially available US transmitting gel (if separated from the wound by a sterile film dressing) and sterile, transparent, US-transmitting wound dressings with a high water content (eg, Geliperm [Geistlich Pharmaceuticals], Hydroscan [Echo Ultrasound], and Tegaderm [3M]). Hydroscan is not labeled for use as a dressing but is used for diagnostic US transmission and is an excellent transmitter of US energy. Geliperm is available in Europe but not the United States at this time. Tegaderm was tested for transmission of US energy and found to transmit 69% of the acoustic energy.[34] Tests of the results of US stimulation on tcpO₂ measurements when energy was transmitted through Tegaderm showed no significant differences in the measurements with or without the Tegaderm.[28] Tegaderm and similar transparent film dressings are useful for treating full-thickness wounds because the film will stretch down into the wound bed under the pressure of the US head. Make sure that the size of the film dressing is larger than the wound so that the stress of the stretching doesn't pull the adhesive away from the skin. Using US transmission gel on the surface of

the film makes gliding of the head easier. The method to use hydrogel sheets for transmission is as follows:

1. Place the dressing over the superficial to full-thickness open area, ensuring that no air is trapped beneath the dressing.
2. Coat the surface of the dressing lightly with US transmission gel or lotion to ease the movement of the applicator head over the dressing surface (Figures 19–1A and 19–1B).

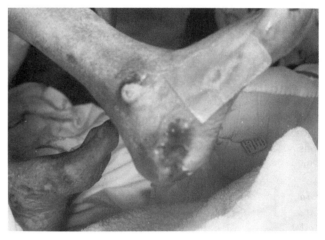

A

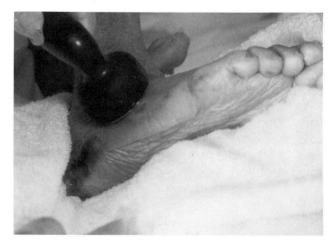

B

Figure 19–1 A and B, Application of US through a Hydroscan. Courtesy of Echo Ultrasound, Reedsville, Pennyslvania.

Underwater application is a useful method for transmission of US. A metal whirlpool tank is a poor choice to hold the water because the metal reflects sound energy and increases the intensity in the body area near the metal. A plastic or rubber basin or tub would be acceptable. Air bubbles need to be eliminated by running the water and letting it stand for a few minutes before using it for US transmission. Underwater application is a good choice if the region to be treated is irregular and the area to be treated can be conveniently placed in the container. This includes foot, ankle, hand, and elbow. Infection control requires proper disinfection of the water basin between uses. The applicator and the body part must be submerged throughout the treatment, and the applicator should not touch the skin. This would be advantageous if the area of treatment is painful. If possible, select a large container such as a baby's plastic bathtub where the target tissues can be placed a significant distance from the applicator. At that distance, the target tissues will be in the far field, where the spatial intensity is more uniform. It is recommended that the physical therapist wear waterproof gloves that trap US reflecting air, so as to minimize exposure to the sound energy. US at the kilohertz frequency is often delivered via a water bath so that the wound can be cleaned and debrided by it. Studies are in progress to demonstrate whether kilohertz US in a water bath is efficacious for wound debridement and healing.

Manipulation of the Applicator

Movement of the megahertz applicator throughout treatment is essential to avoid exposure of units of tissue to regions of high intensity; in the near field, where most treatments occur, the spatial peak (SP) intensity can be more than three times the SA. It is also essential to avoid excessive exposure to the peaks of pressure variation that occur in *standing wave fields* produced by the interaction of incident and reflected waves of ultrasound. Standing waves can damage tissue components, in particular endothelial cells, and exposure to them must therefore be avoided.

The applicator should be moved either in short linear strokes, a few centimeters long, ensuring that they overlap so that the entire region is treated, or in small circular movements, also overlapping, so that the movement is essentially spiral.

Set-Up for Treatment (Figure 19–2)

1. Explain the procedure to the patient and the caregiver.
2. Position the patient for comfort in a position that can be maintained for up to 15 minutes.
3. Remove clothing from the area to be treated.

Clinical Wisdom: *Use US for Blisters*

Treating blisters with US promotes absorption of the hemorrhagic material beneath the blister and healing of superficial and partial-thickness wounds. Absorption of hemorrhagic material may be due to enhanced macrophage activity via acoustic streaming and/or stable cavitation. Use the protocol for acute inflammation and apply as a periwound application or in a water bath. Continue after the blister roof is removed as long as hemorrhagic material is absorbed. Hemorrhagic material should shrink in size daily; when it is no longer shrinking, it has probably necrosed and will need to be debrided. *Color Plates 68 to 70* and Case Study 2 demonstrate a case in which US was the only treatment intervention, besides a transparent film dressing, until it was determined that focal area of necrosis needed debridement.

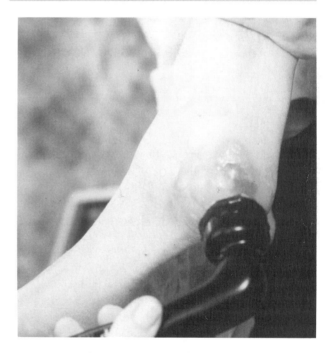

Figure 19–2 Periblister application of US gel.

4. Warm US gel by placing it in a warmer or between folds of a hot pack—always test a drop for temperature before applying to the patient.
5. Remove the wound dressing, unless it is a film or hydrogel sheet that is to be left in place. Check for bubbles under the dressing and bleed them from the edges if present.
6. Use either as a periwound treatment or direct application over a film or hydrogel sheet as described above.

7. Treat deep wounds by a periwound application around the margins of the wound.
8. Keep the sound head perpendicular to the surface in complete contact with the surface area throughout the treatment.

Clinical Wisdom:
Sonation of Undermined/Tunneled Areas

One-megahertz US is a very useful means to treat undermined/tunneled areas surrounding wounds. These areas can be "mapped" on the skin surface with a marker pen (see Chapter 4, Wound Measurements, about measuring undermining and tunneled areas) to guide the treatment. Imagine the wound with a grid over the area, or use a plastic screen with centimeter marking and divide the wound into quarters at the 12-, 3-, 6-, and 9-o'clock positions. Depending on the size of the applicator, sound at the rate of 1 min/cm². For example, a 5-cm² applicator would be used to stimulate a 25-cm² wound area for 5 minutes.

Aftercare

If the dressing is left intact, all that is required is to clean off excess US transmission gel/lotion. If a new dressing is to be applied, this should be done as soon as possible to avoid chilling of the wound tissues and slowing of epithelial migration and mitotic cell activity.

The US applicator must be handled carefully after use to avoid environmental contamination. After use, place the applicator in a rubber glove and transport it to a dirty sink area for cleansing with cold tap water and soap. Then place it on a cold disinfecting solution for the specified time, depending on the product used. This is usually from 5 to 20 minutes.

Adjunctive Treatments

It is an essential part of the clinical decision making to consider adjunctive treatments that may be given. Ultrasound may be the primary physical agent or it may be an adjunctive treatment along with another physical agent or electrotherapeutic modality. For example, for a deep wound, high-voltage pulsed current (HVPC) may be the treatment for the wound bed and US for the undermined periwound area. If this is done, do the HVPC treatment first and leave the packing in the wound bed to keep it warm and clean while the US treatment is given.

Ultrasound may be given as an adjunctive treatment to whirlpool when the whirlpool is used to soften necrotic tissue and the US is used to stimulate at the cellular level. Do the whirlpool first, then any debridement; flush out debris and any topical agents that could possibly be phonophoresed through the skin by the US. US should follow the whirlpool because cells are stimulated by US to release chemotactic agents; those chemicals should not be washed out of the wound.

Wound care products are part of the treatment regimen also, and should be considered in the treatment planning. Will the dressing be part of the US treatment as described above, or will the dressing be removed and replaced when the US treatment is given? Will the dressing be changed every other day? Can it be changed in conjunction with the US treatment to minimize disruption of the wound healing environment? Physical therapists need to check with nurses about the application of topical agents such as petrolatum or petrolatum-based products, which will interfere with the US transmission. This is another example of the importance of collaboration between nurses and physical therapists about treatment regimens to avoid conflicting treatment approaches and to improve utilization management of services for the patient.

SELF-CARE TEACHING GUIDELINES

Ultrasound should *not* be taught to a patient or a caregiver as a home treatment. Although it appears very innocuous, harm can be done by improperly trained and unsupervised individuals. To avoid harm, the many precautions listed earlier must be carefully considered. There are definite risks that are not readily apparent to the unskilled individual.

DOCUMENTATION

The functional outcome report (FOR)[37] is an acceptable method to meet Medicare and other third-party payer guidelines for documentation for the need for physical therapy intervention for wound healing. The cases presented here are examples of how to use the FOR methodology. More information on the method is available in Chapter 1. Documentation of US treatment outcomes is extremely valuable. The cases documented below are examples of the value of recording on film changes in wound healing that are produced by selected interventions. In both cases US was the only intervention given. For example, it would be difficult to do a controlled, double-blind study of patients with new hematoma formation as in Case Study 1. A single-subject design study would be one method of developing a body of knowledge about clinical outcomes. Case Study 2 was done as part of a student clinical affiliation projects to see how US affects hematoma formation under a blister. Photography was done every 2 days to track the change in the hematoma.

There are many ways that the thoughtful clinician can present information about treatment interventions and advance clinical practice as part of the documentation process.

Case Study 1: *Venous Ulcer Treated with US*

Patient: E.F. Age: 82 years

Functional Outcome Report: Initial Assessment

Reason for Referral

The patient was referred to physical therapy for evaluation of ulceration of her left leg. The patient had a long history of Alzheimer's disease and was noncompliant with all attempts to keep the wound dressed. Nurses in the nursing home where she lived were concerned about infection and healing of the ulcer and wanted a physical therapist's opinion.

Medical History

The patient had a cardiac pacemaker and venous insufficiency. As a consequence of her neurologic system changes associated with Alzheimer's disease, she was hyperactive and would not stay still more than a couple minutes at a time. Wound onset was 24 hours prior to referral.

Functional Diagnosis and Targeted Outcomes

Wound Examination. The wound is located above the left medial malleous. The surrounding skin is very friable, with extensive subcutaneous hemorrhaging and epidermal necrosis; petechiae surround the open area. There is mild edema, which is reactive to touching. The wound tissue is pink, with partial-thickness loss of the skin surface area (see *Color Plate 65*).
Functional diagnosis: impairment of the integumentary system; *targeted outcome:* wound closure; *due date:* 4 weeks.
Functional diagnosis: impairment of the venous system (venous insufficiency); *targeted outcome:* absorption of hematoma; *due date:* 2 weeks.
Functional diagnosis: acute inflammation phase; *targeted outcome:* rapid wound contraction; *due date:* 4 weeks.

Psychosocial Examination. The patient removed dressings and would not tolerate any topical medications, compression stockings, or staying off her feet. She walked all day long and was very accomplished at removing passive restraints in a flash. She was totally noncompliant during the last episode of wounding.

Functional diagnosis: impairment of mental functions. The functional loss causes undue susceptibility to venous ulceration of the legs and inability to heal without integumentary intervention. The patient has improvement potential and will heal after intervention, but she may continue to be at risk for venous ulceration.

Need for Skilled Services: The Therapy Problem

The patient has a history of recurrent ulceration above the left medial malleolus and impaired healing due to impairment of the venous system and impaired mental status. US is indicated during the first 72 hours after injury during acute inflammation. US would promote absorption of the hemorrhagic material and stimulate acceleration of the inflammatory phase, leading to rapid wound contraction.

Treatment Plan

Periwound ultrasound will be applied at 1 MHz, at 0.5 W/cm^2 (SA, TA), 20% pulsed for 5 minutes five times per week for 4 weeks. The nurses will attempt to do a wound dressing with a transparent film as tolerated.

Discharge Outcomes

Hemorrhagic material was significantly absorbed within 3 days. There was a change in wound shape and a reduction in size after 2 weeks. There was an 85% reduction in wound size at 4 weeks (see *Color Plates 65 to 67* for a pictorial review of the case).

Discussion

Behavioral information as well as medical history were important considerations in choosing the intervention. From all perspectives, US was the most practical choice for this patient. However, because of her noncompliance with any other treatment, it was also an opportunity to evaluate the effects of the US. The absorption of the hemorrhagic material was unquestionable. The patient required constant engagement and diversionary activities by a physical therapy aide to even tolerate the US by the physical therapist for 5 minutes. By the end of 4 weeks she refused to comply further. Since the wound was closing, physical therapy was discontinued.

Case Study 2: *Blood Blister on the Heel Treated with US*

Patient: M.M.   Age: 83

Functional Outcome Report: Initial Assessment

Reason for Referral

The patient was referred to the physical therapist because the nursing staff had identified a blood blister on a heel.

Medical History

The patient had had a below-the-knee amputation on the other leg due to peripheral vascular disease. The limb was at risk for amputation, and early intervention was requested for limb salvage. Patient was alert/confused and nonambulatory. She could reposition but not consistently. She had had a prior episode of a cerebrovascular accident. The following medical problems are associated with this request for service.

Functional Diagnosis and Targeted Outcomes

Integumentary Examination. The surrounding skin was erythematous, edematous, and tender.
Functional diagnosis: loss of function due to integumentary impairment; *targeted outcome:* accelerate the inflammatory response; *due date:* 2 weeks.

Wound Tissue Examination. The wound was covered with a bloody, fluid-filled blister. Bloody fluid suggests rupture of vessels beneath the blister.
Functional diagnosis: wound in acute inflammation phase; *targeted outcome:* debridement of blister, conservation of healthy tissue under the blister; *due date:* 2 weeks.
Associated impairment: possibility of necrotic tissue beneath blister; *targeted outcome:* clean wound bed; *due date:* 4 weeks.
Functional diagnosis: impairment of integument, depth to be determined; *targeted outcome:* exhibits granulation tissue; *due date:* 6 weeks.

Vascular Examination. Visual examination showed an inflammatory response to wounding. Palpation indicated weak but palpable pulses. Because of the prior vascular history the presence of peripheral vascular disease was assumed.
Functional diagnosis: vascular impairment; *targeted outcome:* enhanced perfusion; *due date:* 2 weeks.

Musculoskeletal Examination. The patient is nonambulatory, has limited mobility in bed, and needs verbal cues to reposition. Motor impairment from the stroke limits her mobility. Her Braden Risk Score is 15, indicating risk for pressure ulcers.
Functional diagnosis: undue susceptibility to pressure ulceration; *targeted outcome:* pressure elimination; *due date:* immediately.

Evaluation

The patient's loss of function in these systems is responsible for the undue susceptibility to skin breakdown on the legs and inability to heal without integumentary intervention. The patient has improvement potential, and the wound will heal with intervention to bring perfusion to tissues and relieve pressure.

Need for Skilled Services

The patient has a prior history of failed wound healing leading to amputation. Intervention that will enhance wound tissue perfusion to conserve tissues underneath the blister and stimulate healing will be required. Wound dressings will not address these issues. The blister needs to be debrided to assess tissue damage. Absorption of hemorrhagic materials will conserve healthy tissues and result in a healed wound. Pulsed nonthermal US is the choice for tissue perfusion in the presence of peripheral vascular disease and for stimulation of macrophage activity to absorb clotted blood in the tissues.

Treatment Plan

- Apply periwound nonthermal US to accelerate the inflammation phase and promote absorption of hemorrhagic material (0.5 W/cm^2 [SA, TA], 1 MHz, 20% pulsed for 5 minutes).
- Sharply debride the blister roof.
- Continue US until the extent of the wound depth is determined.

Outcomes

Periwound US and debridement were begun on August 26. On August 31 the blister was debrided, and a large hemorrhagic/necrotic area was seen under the tissues; inflammation in the surrounding tissues was subsiding. On September 2, there was a 50% reduction in the size of the hemorrhagic area and resolution of the inflammation in the surrounding tissues. Minimal reduction in the area of the hematoma in next 2 weeks indicated that the tissues had necrosed and debridement had begun. On October 8 the wound was progressing to the proliferation phase; there was a small area of necrosis (see *Color Plates 68 to 71*). The US seemed to have had maximum benefit and treatment was changed to HVPC.

continues

Case Study 2 continued

Discussion

Removal of the blister roof identified an area of focal necrosis or hematoma. The only other treatment intervention was transparent film dressing. The size of the hematoma was reduced 50% with seven US treatments. Inflammation was accelerated, and the wound progressed to the proliferation phase. At this point treatment was changed to HVPC. Closure was achieved on November 2.

REFERENCES

1. Dyson M. Role of ultrasound in wound healing. In: McCulloch JM, Kloth LC, Fudar JA, eds. *Wound Healing: Alternatives in Management.* 2nd ed. Philadelphia: F.A. Davis; 1995:318–346.

2. Ziskin MC, Michlovitz SL. Therapeutic ultrasound. In: Michlovitz SL, ed. *Thermal Agents in Rehabilitation.* Philadelphia: F.A. Davis; 1990.

3. Simpson SL, Hertzog MS, Barja RH. The plantaris tendon graft: an ultrasound study. *J Hand Surg.* 1991;16:708–711.

4. O'Reilly MAR, Massouh H. Pictorial review: the sonographic diagnosis of pathology in the Achilles tendon. *Clin Radiol.* 1993;48:202–206.

5. Karim A, et al. A novel method of assessing skin ultrasound scans. *Wounds.* 1994;6:9–15.

6. Lynch JA, O'Reilly MAR, Massouh H. A robust and accurate method for calculating the fractal signature of texture in macroradiographs of osteoarthritis knees. *Med Inf.* 1991;2:241–251.

7. Williams PL, et al. *Gray's Anatomy.* 38th ed. Edinburgh, Scotland: Churchill-Livingstone; 1995:417.

8. Gonzalez RC, Wintz P. Digital image processing. In: Gonzalez RC, Winter XX, eds. *Digital Image Fundamentals.* Reading, MA: Addison-Wesley; 1987:13–59.

9. Bamber JC, Tristam M. The physics of medical imaging. In: Webb S, ed. *Diagnostic Ultrasound.* Bristol, England: Adam Hilgerl; 1988:319–386.

10. Fornage BD, Deshayes JL. Ultrasound of normal skin. *J Clin Ultrasound.* 1986;14:619.

11. Whiston RJ, et al. Application of high frequency ultrasound to the objective assessment of healing wounds. In: *Proceedings of the 2nd Conference on Advances in Wound Management.* London: Macmillan Press; 1992:26–29.

12. Young SR, et al. Ultrasound imaging: a non-invasive method of wound assessment. In: *Proceedings of the 2nd Conference on Advances in Wound Management.* London: Macmillan Press; 1992:29–31.

13. Miller M, Dyson M. *Principles of Wound Care: A Professional Nurse Publication.* London: Macmillan Magazines Ltd; 1996:72–73.

14. Liong JL. *High Frequency Diagnostic Ultrasound as an Adjunct to Irritant Patch Assessment.* London: University of London UMDS; 1996. Thesis.

15. Van Holsbeek M, Introcaso JH. Sonography of muscle. *Musculoskeletal Ultrasound.* Chicago: Mosby–Yearbook; 1990:13.

16. Shafir R, Itzchak Y, Heyman Z, et al. Preoperative ultrasonic measurements of the thickness of cutaneous malignant melanoma. *J Ultrasound Med.* 1984;3:205.

17. Breslow A. Thickness, cross-sectional areas and depth of invasion in the prognosis of cutaneous melanoma. *Ann Surg.* 1970;172:902.

18. Sussman C. *Ultrasound for Wound Healing.* Monograph. Houston, TX: The Chattanooga Group; 1993.

19. Dyson M. Mechanisms involved in therapeutic ultrasound. *Physiother J Chartered Soc Physiother.* 1987;73(3):8.

20. Dyson M, Young SR. Acceleration of tissue repair by low intensity ultrasound applied during the inflammatory phase. Presented at the meeting of American Physical Therapy Association and Canadian Physical Therapy Association; 1988.

21. Hart J. The effect of therapeutic ultrasound on dermal repair with emphasis on fibroblasts activity. London, University of London; 1993. Thesis.

22. Gillet JH, Mitchell JLA. Acceleration of tissue repair of damaged skeletal muscle using ultrasound. *Orthop Prac.* 1989;2(4):36.

23. Harding K. Wound care: putting theory into clinical practice. In: Krasner D, ed. *Chronic Wound Care: A Clinical Source Book for Health Care Professionals.* Wayne, PA: Health Management Publications, Inc; 1990:19–30.

24. Hardy M. The biology of scar formation. *Phys Ther.* 1989;69:1014–1024.

25. Frieder S, et al. The therapeutic effects of ultrasound following partial rupture of Achilles tendons in male rats. *J Orthop Sports Phys Ther.* 1988;10:39–46.

26. Jackson BA, et al. Effect of ultrasound therapy on the repair of Achilles tendon injuries in rats. *Med Sci Sports Exerc.* 1991;23:171–176.

27. Consentino AB, et al. Ultrasound effects on electroneuromyographic measures in sensory fibers of the median nerve. *Phys Ther.* 1983;63:1788–1792.

28. Byl N, Hopf H. The use of oxygen in wound healing. In: McCulloch J, Kloth L, Fudar JA, eds. *Wound Healing: Alternatives in Management.* Philadelphia: F.A. Davis; 1996:365–404.

29. Knighton DR, Halliday B, Hunt TK. Oxygen as an antibiotic. *Arch Surg.* 1984;119:199–204.

30. McDiarmid T, Burns P. Clinical applications of therapeutic ultrasound. *Physiother J Chartered Soc Physiother.* 1987;73(4):14–21.

31. Parish L, Witkowsky J. Decubitus ulcers: how to intervene effectively. *Drug Ther.* 1983.

32. Dyson M, et al. Stimulation of healing of varicose ulcers by ultrasound. *Ultrasonics.* September 1976:232–236.

33. McDiarmid T, et al. Ultrasound and the treatment of pressure sores. *Physiotherapy.* 1985;71(2):66–70.

34. Byl N, et al. Incisional wound healing: a controlled study of low and high dose ultrasound. *Orthop Sports Phys Ther.* 1993;18:619–628.

35. Nussbaum EL, et al. Comparison of ultrasound/ultraviolet C and laser for treatment of pressure ulcers in patients with spinal cord injury. *Phys Ther.* 1994;74:812–825.

36. ter Riet G, Kessels AGH, Knipschild P. A randomized clinical trial of ultrasound in the treatment of pressure ulcers. *Phys Ther.* 1996;76:1301–1312.

37. Swanson G. Functional outcome report: the next generation in physical therapy reporting. In: Stuart D, Ablen S, eds. *Documenting Physical Therapy Outcomes.* St. Louis, MO: Mosby–Year Book; 1993:101–134.

CHAPTER 20

Whirlpool

Carrie Sussman

INTRODUCTION

Well-designed clinical trials with a whirlpool for the treatment of open wounds have not yet been reported. Absence of scientific validation should encourage thoughtful application. The basis for selecting whirlpool to treat wounds is the putative effects of controlling infection by softening and removal of debris and exudate, the enhancement of local tissue perfusion to transport oxygen and nutrients to the tissues, and the neuronal effects producing analgesia for comfort and increased mobility. The three putative effects will be discussed.

THEORY AND SCIENCE OF THE THERAPY

Infection Effects

Evidence to support use of whirlpool as a means of reducing infection is questionable. Two studies compared the effects of whirlpool treatment and whirlpool treatment followed by vigorous rinsing. Neiderhuber et al.[1] studied removal of bacterial load from the soles of the feet of 76 normal adults with intact skin. Factors considered in their investigation included temperature of the water, immersion time, agitation of the water versus soaking, spraying the part with clean water for 30 seconds, and agitation of the water during immersion followed by spraying of the part with clean water for 30 seconds.[1] Findings of the study were that temperature of the water was not a significant factor. There was a steady removal of bacterial load with longer duration treatment, 10 to 20 minutes being optimal. Agitation was best compared to either soaking or spraying in removal of skin surface bacteria, but the combination of immersion with agitation and spraying rinsed away 70% of the remaining contaminants

providing the best outcome. Bohannon[2] studied a single subject with a venous ulcer and compared bacterial load following whirlpool with low concentration of povidine-iodine without and with rinsing for 30 to 90 seconds at the maximum pressure tolerated by the subject. More than four times as many bacteria were removed when rinsing was added than without. Both studies appear to support use of whirlpool with rinse to reduce bacterial colonies present on skin and wound surface. There is considerable documentation in the literature that when the bacterial content of an ulcer exceeds 10^5 organisms per gram of tissue, healing is impaired.[3] However, neither study identifies the organisms isolated nor do they use the threshold standard of an infected wound as 10^5 organisms per gram of tissue measured by wound biopsy or culture.[4] Only one patient with a wound was evaluated. The strength of evidence is very weak that whirlpool controls infection.

There is other evidence that wounds treated in hydrotherapy are at risk for waterborne infection and other complications. Reports in the literature demonstrate *Pseudomonas aeruginosa*–associated skin disease after immersion in whirlpool.[5–7] Factors that influence host susceptibility include the anatomic and physiologic defenses of the skin, the skin surface microecology where the skin humidity is altered, and intrinsic factors including disease and age. The skin's relative dryness may be a defense mechanism to resist infection. The immersion in the whirlpool may negate the normal skin defenses. Chronic antibiotic therapy changes the normal flora of the skin and can lead to colonization and superinfection with organisms such as *Pseudomonas aeruginosa*.[5] Risk of infection for the patient who has a burn or wound has been documented. Shankowsky et al.[7] surveyed 202 burn units in the United States and Canada with 158 (75.7%) response and found that these facilities regularly use hydrotherapy as part of burn care. Whirlpool was implicated as a cause of nosocomial infection leading to sepsis with *Pseudomonas aeruginosa* (52.9%), *Staphylococcus aureus* (25.5%), and *Candida albicans* (5.2%).[7] Cardany et al.[8] found that hydrotherapy did not reduce bacterial load on burned or normal skin, but the water contained heavy contamination with viable organisms that have the potential for contaminating clean wounds and for patient cross contamination. A further documented complication is superhydration of the skin which allows penetration of bacteria.[5,7] Water content of the skin may increase to 55% to 70% following a 20-minute immersion.[5] Intrinsic factors such as immunosuppression and diseases such as diabetes are known to increase susceptibility to infection. Hospitalized individuals compared to healthy individuals have a decreased resistance to infection and have the highest risk of secondary health effects. Exposure to pathogens have been associated with many sources including whirlpool tanks. Infectious organisms, particularly *Pseudomonas aeruginosa,* have been identified in hydrotherapy equipment despite rigorous efforts to properly disinfect and monitor for cultures. For instance, Shankowsky et al.[7] reported a lethal outbreak of aminoglycoside-resistant *Pseudomonas aeruginosa* in a newly constructed burn center where stringent methods of disinfection were used and in spite of routine bacterial surveillance. Control of the outbreak was achieved when the hydrotherapy tanks were used for closed wounds during rehabilitation.[7]

Although the reports in the literature provide considerable evidence of risk of infection, hydrotherapy is used in 94.8% of the surveyed institutions. In spite of the reported high incidence of infection, hydrotherapy immersion continues to be used in 118 burn units. Only 27 respondents to the survey have discontinued immersion in favor of showers. Patients who are mechanically ventilated and or invasively monitored are regularly immersed at 47.6% of the responding burn units.[7]

Local treatment appears to reduce risk of lethal sepsis. Alternative measures of controlling wound infection with hydrotherapy using irrigation with sterile solution applied by a syringe or pulsatile lavage with suction are described in Chapters 7 and 17. Risk of infection due to immersion in hydrotherapy is becoming more widely recognized but has not yet significantly changed clinical practice.

Circulatory Effects

Cutaneous thermoreceptors are stimulated by heat and carry impulses to the spinal cord and to skin blood vessels, where a vasoactive mediator is released that stimulates vasodilatation. Heat also produces a mild inflammatory reaction through the release of histamine and prostaglandins. Bradykinin, which is a byproduct of an enzyme from sweat, is also released. Together, these chemical mediators enhance the permeability of the blood vessels. Vasodilatation allows increased blood flow, and this in turn increases capillary hydrostatic pressure. The result is fluid shifts from the vessels into the interstitial spaces, which produce a mild edema.[9] Vasodilatation is a benefit for a patient with reduced perfusion, but it can be disastrous for a patient with venous insufficiency, whose venous system has difficulty managing tissue fluids.[10] Fluid shifts also occur within the wound, with a loss of proteins, electrolytes, other nutrients, and growth factors found in wound fluid that pass out into the water. If the wound surface area is large, fluid shifts can lead to dehydration and depletion of nutrients needed for healing.[11] Use of saline instead of tap water will prevent loss of fluids. A saline whirlpool can be made by adding salt to the water. Immersion of one upper extremity can be a useful way of applying heat and producing generalized vasodilatation. This will cause increased perfusion to the lower extremities with minimal fluid shift and is an alternative approach that can be used to treat a wound in a patient with peripheral vascular disease. Increased perfusion is very important as a mechanism to help the body phagocytose and auto-debride necrotic tissue. Indirect application of heat would minimize the risk of infection.

Research Wisdom:
Whirlpool Implications for Venous Congestion

McCulloch and Boyd[10] reported that whirlpool treatment of a dependent leg resulted in increased hypotension and lower extremity vascular congestion, even in healthy individuals. The implications for the patient with a compromised venous system are very serious.

A benefit of increased blood flow is improved delivery of oxygen, nutrients, antibodies, leukocytes, and systemic antibiotics to the tissues and removal of metabolites. In patients with comorbidities such as diabetes, arterial occlusive disease, and limited mobility, there is a reduction of blood flow to the tissues. The impaired circulation compromises the effectiveness of antibiotics to control wound infection. Timing treatment to enhance perfusion and delivery of antibiotics to wound tissue is being tested with transcutaneous electrical stimulation.[12] Whirlpool-induced perfusion may be another way to enhance the delivery of antibiotic therapy. The physical therapy department and nurses who administer the antibiotics should consider collaborating in scheduling whirlpool treatment time to coincide with optimal delivery of antibiotics circulating in the blood stream to the tissues, because it could enhance the benefits of both treatments. A clinical trial would test this hypothesis.

Skin blood flow has an important function of maintaining constant core body temperature. This function is accomplished by the shunting of blood from the arterioles to the venules and venous plexuses located in the hands, feet, and face.

Neuronal Effects

Neuronal mechanisms that induce sedation, analgesia, and muscle relaxation and suppress the temperature regulatory system are affected by heat. For a patient experiencing severe pain, this may be calming and analgesic, but patients who are lethargic or semicomatose who have depressed central nervous system function would be neurosuppressed to a point where they could become totally unresponsive. These patients should not be put in the whirlpool. Analgesia from the warm water is often reported, but some wound patients, especially those with ischemic limbs or burns, find that the agitation stimulates pain receptors. Treatment at a very gentle agitation level directed away from the wound tissue can be used to soothe rather than stimulate the nerves. Patient tolerance should be evaluated and treatment modified as required. During the whirlpool treatment the patient should be encouraged to perform gentle exercise for muscle pump functions and strengthening. Joint range of motion extensibility is usually performed more easily and less painfully in the warm water. The gentle stretching forces around the wound may stimulate tissue regeneration. Of course, stretching and exercise of a newly sutured wound should be avoided until the sutures are removed.

THERMAL EFFECTS

Cellular

Another little-discussed benefit of heat is stimulation of cell mitosis and leukocytic activity. Research on pigs has shown experimentally that the speed of production of new epidermal cells is enhanced if the temperature is maintained at 37°C. Similar results have been reported following in vitro testing of human skin cultures. Leukocyte activity may fall to zero when wound temperature is cooled, such as during a dressing change. This will impair the phagocytic activity of the leukocytes.[13] It has been observed that it takes 40 minutes for a freshly cleaned wound to return to normal temperature, and 3 hours for mitotic cell division to resume.[14,15] Therefore, the effect of temperature on cellular mitotic activity is an important consideration when choosing a treatment temperature for the whirlpool and in prompt aftercare. Delayed phagocytosis and wound healing may be attributed to frequent changes in wound temperature. Careful choice

of water temperature and limited hydrotherapy treatment would cause less disruption in the tissue temperature.

Whirlpool Systemic Effects

- Increases heart and respiratory rates
- Induces sedation and analgesia
- Suppresses the temperature regulatory system
- Induces muscle relaxation

Water Temperature

Heat is transferred to the body from water by both conduction and convection. The body's response to heat is dependent on three factors: the area of a body surface immersed, the temperature of the water, and the duration of the application. Heat is dissipated through evaporation from the skin and exhalation from the lungs. Submerged skin does not transfer heat from the surface; therefore, heat dissipation is shifted to the exposed body areas that can sweat and to the lungs. The greater the body surface area immersed, the less transpiration can take place on the skin surface. Respiration and heart rates will increase to compensate. A tissue temperature rise of as much as 4°C at temperatures ranging from 37° to 42°C has been measured after immersion for 20 minutes in a whirlpool. In a study of effects of the whirlpool on circulation, pulse rates increased 1.3 to 1.5 times over the sitting or supine resting level, and the mean blood pressure increased 1.1 times over the supine resting values.[9] Autonomic neuropathy and pulmonary dysfunction, which are common comorbidities with wounds, interfere with evaporative cooling. Limit the body surface area, lower the water temperature, and reduce the treatment time in the whirlpool for patients with cardiopulmonary and neuropathic diseases so that they are less physiologically challenged. If this is not practical, choose another treatment modality.

The average skin temperature of the body is 34°C. The range of body indifference to temperature is 34° to 38°C. At 80° to 92°F (27° to 33.5°C) the temperature is tepid or nonthermal. The body may be chilled at this temperature range. Avoid hypothermia at this thermal range by treating only a limited body area. This is a good temperature choice for patients with venous disease. Neutral warmth is 92° to 96°F (33.5° to 35.5°C). Larger body areas can be treated at this temperature range. Warm the air to make the patient comfortable and avoid chilling. This should be the temperature range of choice when treating the patient with medical problems who would be stressed at a higher temperature. At both the tepid- and neutral-warmth temperatures, tissues will be soaked, softened, and cleansed and perfusion of the tissues will be increased.[9]

Clinical Wisdom: *Avoid Chilling*

When using lower temperatures, avoid chilling by maintaining warm room temperature and use only for single limbs, not the whole body. Reduce treatment duration from 20 minutes to 10 minutes.

Warm or thermal, 96° to 104°F (35.5° to 40°C) water temperature is associated with hyperthermia. Significant physiologic stress in the circulatory, nervous, and cardiopulmonary systems occurs under these conditions.[16] Water temperature choices are summarized as follows:

- Nonthermal/tepid: 80° to 92°F or 27° to 33.5°C
- Neutral: 92° to 96°F or 33.5° to 35.5°C
- Thermal: 96° to 104°F or 35.5° to 40°C
- Higher temperature levels are *not* recommended because of physiologic stress

Temperature Precautions

Water temperature modifies the effects on circulatory responses. There are some precautions that the physical therapist should use to modify the heating effects of treatment.

- Water temperature should not exceed local skin temperature (usually 34°C) in the presence of peripheral vascular disease.
- Water temperature should not exceed 38°C in the presence of cardiopulmonary disease. The heat stimulates peripheral vasodilatation with subsequent increased return of blood to the heart and increased cardiac output. The added load of blood volume can overtax a weak or decompensated heart muscle.[3]
- Water temperature of 32°C increases blood flow of 2.3 mL/dL of limb volume. Higher temperature increases blood flow volume.[9,16]
- Extremes of temperature should be avoided in patients with sensory loss, such as those with alcoholic- or diabetic-related neuropathy, who cannot feel the temperature and respond to the heat. Loss of thermal sensation can result in severe burns. Temperature sensation testing in a neuropathic patient is recommended before immersion in warm water. The procedure for testing is described in Chapter 3.

PHYSICAL AND MECHANICAL EFFECTS

The physical effects of immersion in water are soaking, saturating, loosening, and softening of tissues (Exhibit 20–1). Phagocytosis is aided by softening and loosening of necrotic tissue. In the process, exudate, sweat, and oils are removed. The wound will be deodorized, but prolonged soaking supersaturates the wound tissue and surrounding skin. This leads to maceration, which is the breaking down of the fibers of the skin. Soaking of the neuropathic foot that has already impaired sweat and oil production is not recommended. Dryness is a characteristic of autonomic neuropathy, and water will desiccate and macerate the tissue, leading to infection.[17] Agitation is used to cleanse and debride the wound tissue. The mechanical effects on circulation caused by agitation of the whirlpool are small.[18] It has been postulated that the mechanical stimulation of the cells stimulates granulation tissue formation. This remains anecdotal and requires further investigation.

In summary, the physical and mechanical effects of whirlpool are

Benefits

- Soaking and softening of eschar and other necrotic tissue
- Scrubbing and loosening of necrotic tissue and slough
- Debriding by mechanical action of turbulence
- Deodorizing the wound through cleansing
- Soaking to remove dried dressings

Exhibit 20–1 Whirlpool and the Inflammation Phase

Whirlpool affects the inflammation phase of healing by the following mechanisms:

- It increases vasodilatation of the superficial vessels.
- It increases blood flow, bringing oxygen and nutrients to the tissues and removing metabolites.
- It increases blood flow, bringing antibodies, leukocytes, and systemic antibiotics to the wound area.
- It shifts fluid into the interstitial spaces, contributing to edema.
- It softens and loosens necrotic tissue, aiding phagocytosis.
- It cleanses and removes wound exudate, controlling infection.
- It enhances mitotic cell division and leukocytic activity in a warm environment.

Clinical Wisdom: *Soaking Dressings*

- The whirlpool is often used to soak off dried dressings. However, if the purpose of using wet-to-dry dressings is mechanical debridement, do *not* soak off the dressing. Instead, pull off the dry dressing to remove necrotic tissues beneath before whirlpool treatment. This method of debridement is used to remove necrotic tissue but is not selective. Threads from the gauze that remain embedded in the tissue can then be soaked off in the whirlpool. Wet-to-dry dressings are best used on totally necrotic wounds, not on wounds with a combination of necrotic and granulating tissues.
- Wet-to-damp dressings may be appropriately soaked off in the whirlpool. Soak with the turbine turned off and remove all dressing material from the water. The dressing, if left in the tank, can become tangled in the agitator mechanism and cause mechanical problems or become a hidden source of infection.

Disadvantages

- Superhydrating and macerating skin[5]
- Changing of skin pH[5,6]
- Risk of infection[5–7]

CHOOSING AN INTERVENTION: CLINICAL REASONING

Applying Theory and Science to Clinical Decision Making

The previous sections reviewed the theory and science of intervention with whirlpool. The physical therapist would review the patient's medical history and do a systems review as guidelines for selection of an intervention with whirlpool. Whirlpool has the ability to affect body systems at the organ and tissue levels; however, there is little known about the effects at the cellular level except that warmth stimulates mitosis and leukocytosis.

Candidacy

Current health care practice standards rely on review of scientific literature. The Agency for Health Care Policy and Research (AHCPR) is the gold standard for this approach.

The value of a procedure is dependent on the quality of the scientific method used to establish efficacy. Recommendations in the AHCPR *Clinical Practice Guideline, No. 15, Treatment of Pressure Ulcers*[3] are graded high if the model is based on controlled clinical trials, while expert consensus is considered weak validity.

Two *AHCPR Pressure Ulcer Treatment Guidelines* recommendations affect use of hydrotherapy. First the guidelines state: "Heel ulcers with dry eschar need not be debrided if they do not have edema, erythema, fluctuance, or drainage. Assess these wounds daily for pressure ulcer complications."[3(p49)] It is the AHCPR panel's opinion that these findings indicate wound stability. The guidelines acknowledge that there is no research reported in the literature to support this recommendation. The recommendation does not take into consideration several issues. The expectation that eschar will be assessed daily is not realistic or practical in most care settings. The wound may appear stable, but the wound has an absence of inflammation phase. Inflammation phase may be suppressed for many reasons. Shouldn't the reason for suppressed inflammation be determined before deciding to debride the eschar or not? Functional mobility is a key indicator of risk for pressure ulcers. Eschar on a heel limits the functional activity of the patient, who is otherwise able, by limiting weightbearing on the eschar surface for transfers or ambulation. The patient with eschar on the heel cannot wear shoes and requires a special orthosis to remove pressure from the eschar. This precaution would be necessary until the wound healed. Leaving the eschar intact also means that the extent of the soft tissue injury cannot be determined. Wounds with eschar may have the potential for healing or deterioration. For example, documentation in the literature supports the potential for complete ulcer closure of heel wounds with eschar following debridement with hydrotherapy and collagenase.[19] When should the eschar be left intact? When the patient has inadequate circulation or is in a state of health that will fail to support healing, eschar should not be soaked or debrided. For example, wounds and adjacent tissues that look like *Color Plate 46* should not be debrided of eschar. If there is no report of vascular studies in the medical record, the physical therapist or nurse would consider performing noninvasive vascular testing or the patient should be referred to a vascular lab. Then candidacy for healing would be determined. For candidates, whirlpool is a quick and efficient way to soften eschar on the heels and enhance local tissue perfusion to facilitate debridement. In the case study used to illustrate clinical decision making for this chapter, circulatory status was evaluated in a patient with eschars on both heels and found to be adequate for healing. The patient was being positioned up in wheelchair and significant pressure was being supported on the heels during transfer, creating risk of trauma to tissues already compromised. Whirlpool was used to soften and debride the eschars. As it turned out, the outer eschar concealed two smaller eschars and these two needed to be softened and debrided revealing deep tissue damage. Once that was accomplished, the wounds were treated by other means to closure. Patient's functional outcome after heels were healed was the ability to do a standing pivot transfer with one person assist while weightbearing on both feet.

The second recommendation in the AHCPR guidelines regarding candidacy for treatment is the recommendation that whirlpool be discontinued "when ulcer is clean."[3(p52)] Clean is defined as being free of thick exudate, slough, or necrotic tissue. Clean ignores the potential for infection from waterborne organisms *before* the wound is clean. Wounds become clean of necrotic tissue and exudate over time; meanwhile, new tissues are laid down and exposed to infectious organisms. The AHCPR panel expressed concern for trauma to the granulating wound from high-pressure water jets. However, the issue of infection in the wound and cross-contamination of other wounds on the same patient and other patients is not addressed. Therefore, the use of whirlpool for the purpose of softening eschar for removal may be appropriate, but alternative methods of debridement should be considered until the wound is clean and also for patients with multiple wounds.

Patients with large amounts of necrotic tissue have a body system impairment of autolytic debridement and phagocytosis and need help from an intervention to hasten the process of removing the bioburden from the body. Whirlpool will hasten the softening of necrotic tissue and debridement. Wounds that contain debris, foreign bodies, and slough or that are highly exudative or malodorous and need intensive cleaning would benefit from whirlpool. Wounds of all tissue depths are treated in the whirlpool, but those that are deep, with undermining and tunneling would be at greater risk for transmitting infection into the body. All wounds and surrounding skin should be vigorously rinsed with clean warm tap water following removal from the whirlpool water to remove deposits of debris and bacteria.

Patients with impaired vascular perfusion of the lower extremities have risk for impairment of healing and undue susceptibility to pressure ulceration. These individuals may be candidates for whirlpool intervention as a prevention strategy because of induced vasodilatation by direct and reflexive stimulation as well as the enhanced perfusion by gravitational pull in the dependent position. A suggested method of preventive treatment strategy for individuals who have high risk of pressure ulcers or those with intact stage I pressure ulcers includes daily whirlpool at 38° to 40°C to stimulate peripheral circulation. The improved circulation

to the skin encourages skin growth and replacement which makes the skin more elastic and less susceptible to shearing and pressure.[19,20] Treatment of patients with circulatory impairment who have wounds with extensive necrotic tissue to soften for debridement may benefit from this treatment. Vetra and Whittaker[19] found that patients with limited circulation and extensive necrotic tissue who most likely would have had to have amputation of the affected limb received benefit from the enhanced perfusion associated with heating in the whirlpool combined with enzymatic debridement using collagenase.

Precautions

Historically wounds of nearly every type are referred for hydrotherapy. Appropriate use versus overuse of whirlpools is an issue. There has been a definite pendulum swing from treating every wound in the whirlpool to avoiding whirlpool entirely or limiting use to only necrotic wounds. Whirlpool benefits for treating some specific wound-related problems (eg, necrosis, thick exudate, circulation) have been described. The benefits and disadvantages must be carefully weighed. Whirlpool treatment can and should be modified to meet the intentions of the therapy. Patients with venous impairment already have more circulation to the area than the venous system can handle. Changing parameters are required if whirlpool is used. For example, if cleansing is the intention, tepid or neutral warmth (92° to 96°F or 33.5° to 35.5°C) will cleanse an ulcer in a patient with venous disease. Minimize the time in the dependent position (eg, treat for 5 minutes, not 20 minutes). Follow with compression therapy.[21] If the wounded limb is edematous or has friable skin around the wound and should not be immersed, perfusion can be enhanced by reflexive vasodilatation by immersion of the opposite lower extremity or an upper extremity.

Additional precautions should be considered to avoid potentially harmful effects when the following wound situations are present:

- **Clean granulating wounds:** Clean granulating wounds are easily traumatized by the force of mild agitation.
- **Epithelializing wounds:** Migrating epidermal cells may be damaged by even the least force.
- **New skin grafts:** Skin grafts will not tolerate high shearing forces and turbulence.
- **New tissue flaps:** New tissue flaps are very sensitive to shearing forces and vasoconstriction that may occur if the water or air temperature cause chilling.
- **Non-necrotic diabetic ulcers:** Callus often surrounds diabetic ulcers and will be softened and macerated. Macerated tissue will not tolerate pressure and the wound

will be enlarged. Moisture retention under the callus may become a source of infection.

Many whirlpool treatments are ordered twice daily. This requires twice-daily dressing changes and disrupts the wound environment. Dressings need to be selected that can safely and cost effectively be removed that frequently. Obviously, the physical therapist, nurse, and physician must collaborate on making a dressing selection that will provide the best wound environment and that is appropriate for twice-daily removal. A collaborative decision must be made as to who will replace the dressing. For example, if a saline-soaked gauze damp dressing is used and it is to be kept damp, there may be some shifts when the dressing is changed in the physical therapy department and another shift by nursing. Coordination is required to maintain the intended wound environment and the documentation requirements of both services.

Wound dressing technology can now provide the healing wound with a scientifically controlled environment of temperature and wound fluid to promote healing. Infrequent dressing changes are now considered the method of choice to promote healing. Limiting the number of whirlpool treatments and the frequency, duration, and extent is currently recommended by most experts.

Contraindications

Contraindications to use of whirlpool include the presence of any of the following:

- Moderate to severe extremity edema
- Lethargy
- Unresponsiveness
- Maceration
- Febrile conditions
- Compromised cardiovascular or pulmonary function
- Acute phlebitis
- Renal failure
- Dry gangrene (evaluate for ischemia)
- Incontinence of urine or feces (if whirlpool will be contaminated)

Patients who are noncandidates for whirlpool therapy are those who are febrile, who have cardiac or ventilatory pump failure or renal failure, who are lethargic, or who have venous system impairment. Patients with fetal posture contractures may not be able to be safely positioned in the whirlpool. Diabetics who have insensitivity of the feet may experience burns because of the inability to respond neurologically to thermal changes. Diabetics with callus formation on the plan-

tar surfaces of the feet should *not* be treated in the whirlpool because the integumentary system is impaired, calluses will be softened, and subsequent exposure to pressure from standing on the foot will result in skin breakdown. The break in the skin will become a portal for infection.

Patients with dry gangrene should not have the tissues softened because the dry gangrene is nature's method of walling off the tissues and encapsulating the area. Softening of the tissue will reduce the barrier and allow infectious organisms to enter the body. Autoamputation of necrotic digits usually occurs anyway (see Chapter 15).

Personnel Safety

Universal precautions should, of course, be followed by hydrotherapy personnel. The hydrotherapy personnel are exposed to airborne water vapor. Inhalation or contact dermatitis of water droplets containing bacteria and antiseptic or disinfection products presents health risks. Policies and procedures should be developed for each health care facility to minimize staff exposure.[22] Masks, gowns, and goggles are appropriate attire to use as barriers (see Chapter 17, Figure 17–2).

Clinical Wisdom: *Whirlpool Bathing*

One situation that needs clarification is the common referral of patients with wounds for whirlpool treatment and the expectation that this will serve as the patient's bath. The whirlpool is not a bathing pool or shampoo basin. The water in the tank is dirty with wound exudate and debris. Soap, shampoo, and disinfectants have ingredients that are harmful to wounds and may irritate delicate skin during soaking. For personal hygiene a shower is preferable because all substances are flushed away from the wound and the skin.

Delivery of Care

Thomson et al.'s survey[23] found that in most burn units (100 units polled) nurses perform hydrotherapy procedures although there is no consensus on who does it. Shankowsky et al.[7] found that in most of the responding 118 burn units using immersion hydrotherapy, both debridement and rehabilitation/physical therapy treatments were included in a single hydrotherapy session (71.7%) and that hydrotherapy continued throughout the patient's length of stay. According to Medicare guidelines, whirlpool is considered a skilled physical therapy procedure when the patient's condition is complicated by disease processes such as impaired circulation, areas of desensitization, open wounds (eg, stage III and IV pressure ulcers), or other complications that require the skills, knowledge, and judgment of a physical therapist. Diagnosis or prognosis are not the sole factors in deciding whether the service is skilled or not.[24] Recently some Medicare contractors have issued specific guidelines for physical therapy skilled services for wound care. The guidelines state that interventions that will increase function using treatment modalities specific to physical therapy require the skills of the physical therapist (eg, treatment of an open wound or burn over a joint while undergoing functional mobility training in the whirlpool). Wound care alone does not require the skills of the physical therapist.[25] There is no consensus on who should deliver the hydrotherapy procedure. Although hydrotherapy, defined as whirlpool, has long been considered a physical therapist procedure for patients with burns and wounds, it is unclear that there is reason to continue to classify hydrotherapy as requiring the skills of the physical therapist.

EQUIPMENT

Whirlpool Tanks

Whirlpool tanks are used for immersion of either the full body or extremity and are sized accordingly. Large hydrotherapy tanks are called Hubbard tanks and may be used for aquatic exercise as well as wound healing. They have either an attached turbine or a built-in turbine, or the turbine may be suspended from the side of a bathtub. The whirlpool is created by a mixture of water and air to create controlled turbulence. The more aeration the greater the turbulence. The mixture is adjustable but varies from one piece of equipment to another. Force and directions of the agitation are usually adjustable. The tank may be made of stainless steel, Plexiglas, or tile.

Tank Selection

Select a whirlpool tank sized for the wound or body area to be treated. If a patient has multiple wounds, the water should cover those that need soaking, cleansing, or debriding. The full body tank or tub will allow the patient to extend the legs fully and may be more comfortable. If the patient is contracted, select a tank in which the patient can be comfortably positioned. Hydraulic lift chairs and chaises or Hoyer lifts can be used to transfer a patient into the tank if the tank is too high or the patient is nonambulatory. If the patient is seated on a chair for a leg whirlpool treatment, be sure there is no pressure under the thigh.

PROCEDURE

Frequency and Duration

Frequency of hydrotherapy treatment has been traditionally tied to washing of burn wounds to remove topical creams used almost universally for patients in burn units. Protocols in burn facilities mandate washing the wound between each application of the topical agent. Soaking is also used to facilitate dressing changes. Topical agents commonly used to treat burns include silver sulfadiazene, sulfamylon suspension, and silver nitrate used for bactericidal effects. Survey results of burn units[7] show that hydrotherapy treatment is carried out at least daily (56.6%) and bidaily (33.8%). Although the same topical agents are used for other acute or chronic wounds, this is not universally the case. Therefore, the frequency of hydrotherapy treatment to cleanse the wound of topical agents should be modified to correspond to a different rationale of wound management. For instance, once daily 10- to 20-minute treatment for indicated wounds would be preferable in most cases to twice-daily 20-minute whirlpool treatments, which are still common. Once-daily or three-times-weekly whirlpool treatments minimize the frequency of dressing changes and exposure to infection, and maintain the wound temperature and the healing environment. Discontinue treatment when target outcomes are met, if the wound is not responding, or other treatment options would better meet the needs of the wound and the patient.

Water Temperature

Select water temperature based on the medical condition of the patient and the clinical objective of the treatment. All three temperature ranges will soak, soften, and loosen necrotic tissue and cleanse the wound. Keep in mind that the temperature of 37°C is considered optimal for epithelial cell migration, mitotic cell division, and leukocytic activity.[5] Use the temperature closest to the optimal that will be consistent with the medical status of the patient.

Monitoring Vital Signs

Patients who have a medical history of cardiopulmonary or cardiac disease, cerebrovascular accident, or hypertension should have vital signs monitored while in the whirlpool. Record the patient's respiration and pulse rate and take blood pressure. Observe for change in mental status and report of being lightheaded. The latter is common with immersion of large body areas. The feeling of being lightheaded should go away after the patient sits for 5 to 10 minutes outside the hydrotherapy area.

Infection Control

Use of Antiseptics

There remains controversy about the use of antiseptic agents in the whirlpool. Most burn facilities use a disinfecting solution for hydrotherapy.[7,23] Bacterial resistance to antiseptics is documented. In addition, antiseptics have limited effectiveness in reducing bacteria when high bacterial counts are measured and are inactivated by organic matter such as pus and wound exudate.[7,15] Research shows that the most commonly used antiseptic agents are harmful to the cells of tissue repair. AHCPR treatment guidelines for pressure ulcers say that antiseptic agents (eg, povidone-iodine, iodophor, sodium hypochlorite solution [Dakin's solution], hydrogen peroxide, and acetic acid) should not be used to clean ulcers because of their cytotoxicity to fibroblasts.[3,26] No controlled studies document that repeated application of antiseptics to chronic wounds significantly reduces the level of bacteria in wound tissues.[3,26] All commonly used antiseptic agents that are used in the whirlpool have cytotoxicity, even at very low dilutions.[27]

Chemicals in antiseptics are absorbed through the wound tissue, and some patients develop toxicity or allergic responses to the chemical agents. As described above under Personnel Safety, water vapor dispersed into the atmosphere during the agitation process contains droplets of the antiseptic and are inhaled by both patients and staff.

Although an antiseptic's use in the whirlpool is not encouraged, there are times when they should be used, such as for necrotic, heavily exudating wounds. Sodium hypochlorite solutions dissolve blood clots and may be useful in solubilizing the clotted material that constitutes a considerable portion of necrotic tissue. However, they may also delay clotting, and the wound exudate will become sanguineous. Be sure that the intention for using the antiseptic is clear, monitor carefully, and stop when the desired outcome is met (eg, the wound is exudate free or necrosis free). Use at low concentrations. Some commonly used antiseptics in the whirlpool are as follows:

- Povidone-iodine
- Sodium hypochlorite
- Hibiclens (chlorhexidine)
- Chlorazene (chloramine)

Appendix A describes each of these antiseptics, their action, indication, precautions, directions for use, and packaging.

Use of Tap Water

Questions arise about the safety of using plain tap water for wound cleansing. A comparison study on 705 wounds looked at infection rates following cleansing with tap water and saline. It was found that less infection occurred in wounds cleaned with tap water than with saline, and no bacteria were transferred to the wounds.[15] Monitoring of local water supply for organisms has been useful in controlling nosocomial infection.[7]

Vigorous Rinsing

When a body or extremity is removed from the whirlpool, a layer of residues remains on the surfaces exposed to the water, just like the bathtub ring residue after a tub bath. This residue has many contaminants associated with it. A proven, safe method to reduce bacterial count is to follow whirlpool treatment with vigorous rinsing of the patient's skin and wound tissue with clean, warm water to remove the residue. A shower may be the best method to cleanse a large body surface.

Aftercare

After the patient and wound are removed from the whirlpool and rinsed, the wound should be debrided of any softened and loosened necrotic tissue and then rinsed with warm tap water to remove loosened debris. After the final rinse, the wound should be protected from cooling, contaminants, and desiccation. The best approach would be for the wound to be dressed immediately in the hydrotherapy area. If the setting does not allow for a complete dressing application while the patient is in hydrotherapy, a protective moist dressing such as warm saline–soaked gauze should be placed in the wound and covered with a secondary dry dressing.

Infection Control for Whirlpool Equipment

The Centers for Disease Control and Prevention (CDC) and the American Physical Therapy Association (APTA) reviewed procedures for infection control in hydrotherapy and prepared a guide that is available through APTA.[28] The procedures described are adapted from the APTA guide. A copy of the guide would be valuable to all hydrotherapy departments.

Patients using whirlpools and other hydrotherapy tanks are often referred because of active infections. The infectious organisms and the organic debris are then deposited into the water. In the warm water, steady temperature and agitation make it easy for bacterial pathogens to become harbored in the hydrotherapy equipment water pipes, drains, and other steel components associated with the device. These regions are difficult to clean and to disinfect or sterilize. In addition, the *Pseudomonas* bacteria has the ability to assume a sessile form, secreting a thick protective glycocalyx that colonizes the components described.[7] This increases the likelihood that highly contaminated water will contact the sites of open wounds, Foley catheters, and other percutaneous devices. Besides the whirlpool tank and attached equipment, other equipment commonly used in the hydrotherapy department such as Hoyer lifts, wheelchairs, and other transfer equipment should be considered as potential sources for colonization.[28]

Procedure for Basic Cleaning of Hydrotherapy Equipment

1. Hydrotherapy equipment must be thoroughly cleansed to remove all foreign and organic materials from the object. Cleansing by vigorous manual scrubbing with detergents should precede disinfection procedures. The scrubbing should include the inside tank surfaces, the overflow pipes, the drains, the turbine shaft, and the thermometer shaft. The product chosen for cleaning should be an Environmental Protection Agency (EPA)–registered disinfectant.
2. Because the cleaning procedures often involve actions that may cause splattering, the cleaner should wear gloves and goggles while cleaning. Follow universal precautions.
3. Drain the hydrotherapy tank after each use.
4. Rinse all inside tank surfaces with clean water.

Procedure for Disinfection of Hydrotherapy Equipment

1. An intermediate level of disinfection is recommended for all hydrotherapy equipment after treatment of patients with open wounds. Be sure that the exposure time to the disinfectant at label-recommended dilutions is equal to or not less than 10 minutes. Check with the housekeeping department for different choices of disinfection products that are in this category.
2. After the cleansing and rinsing of the tank, the disinfection process can precede. Fill the tank with hot water and then add the disinfection product at the recommended dilutions. Expose all inside tank surfaces.
3. The agitator needs to be disinfected also and may be done separately by immersing it in a bucket with a solution of the disinfectant and running the agitator in the solution for 10 minutes.
4. Following disinfection, drain and rinse the tank.
5. *Dry* inside the tank with clean towels and keep the tank dry and covered until it is used again.
6. Wipe all related hydrotherapy equipment surfaces with germicide after *each use*.[28]

Disinfection Products. A great variety of disinfection products are on the market and each formulation must be EPA registered. These disinfectants are not interchangeable and should be reviewed for the varying performance characteristics of each.

Cleaning and Disinfection of Whirlpools with a Built-in Turbine Agitator. The procedure for cleaning and disinfection of whirlpools with built-in turbines/agitators differs slightly from the above procedures. The manufacturers of these whirlpools have specific instructions for spraying the internal turbine with a disinfecting solution. This disinfecting solution would need to remain in contact with the turbine for the time required based on the product used. In all other respects, the cleaning procedure would be the same as that for other whirlpool tanks.

Culturing the Whirlpool and Related Equipment

Culturing is a controversial topic in the hydrotherapy area. One rationale for culturing is to prevent infection. To contribute to the prevention of infection, the results must be interpretable. The best definition of interpretable is that certain results lead to specific actions.[28] One school of thought is that if the best methods of disinfection are already accepted procedures, routine culturing of whirlpool and associated equipment is not going to cause a change in procedure and therefore is superfluous. On the other hand, there are reports that careful monitoring of equipment and the water supply to identify potential sources of bacteria are useful in preventing outbreaks.[7]

EXPECTED OUTCOMES

Prognosis for wounds treated by whirlpool is a change in tissue function in 2 to 4 weeks. Expect a wound treated for exudate and odor to be odor and exudate free in 2 weeks. Wounds that are treated for debridement should be necrosis free in 2 to 4 weeks, depending on volume of necrotic tissue present. Wounds that have a wound healing phase diagnosis of chronic inflammation or absence of inflammation should progress toward a wound healing phase of *acute inflammation* phase in 2 weeks and to a wound healing phase of acute *proliferation* phase in 4 to 5 weeks. The signs and symptoms would include hyperemia, increased temperature of the skin, and mild edema followed by a decrease in temperature during the inflammatory phase and return to skin color like that of adjacent skin or comparable area on the opposite side of the body progressing to a granulating, contracting wound as seen in *Color Plates 8 and 9*. There are no reports in the literature about how long it takes for wounds treated with whirlpool to reach closure. Payer data say that wounds treated with whirlpool are usually treated for 3 months with presumed outcome of a clean wound.[29] Wounds treated with other physical therapy technologies have average lengths of treatment that range from 7.5 to 10.5 weeks with reported outcome of closure. To be competitive, treatment with whirlpool must have comparable outcomes. If the wound is not progressing on that trajectory, another intervention should be considered.

SELF-CARE TEACHING GUIDELINES

After completing the diagnostic process, the physical therapist may determine that hydrotherapy can be performed at home with a portable whirlpool unit attached to a bathtub. Grossly necrotic or purulent wounds are probably best not self-treated until the necrosis and purulence are reduced to a level where the patient and/or caregiver can manage them comfortably. Careful selection of the patient and caregiver must be made to have successful, noninjurious treatment results. The ability to understand and follow directions is critical.

- The patient and/or caregiver should be instructed in the correct water temperature, the duration of the immersion, how to rinse the wound after immersion, and the proper aftercare. A thermometer to take the water temperature should be used for safety to prevent burns. Some people believe that the water must be as hot as tolerable to be beneficial, and scald burns are common—especially in the elderly. Proper cleaning and disinfection procedures also must be taught for the tub and the portable agitator and thermometer.
- Patients with neuropathy should be instructed *never* to do home foot soaks or whirlpool because of the high risk of self-inflicted injury.
- Patients who are lethargic should have minimal soaking in tepid water, primarily for cleansing and softening of tissue, and this should be limited to single limb immersion. Instruct all patients and caregivers to monitor vital signs during the whirlpool treatment. Teach the side effects of the treatment and how to respond to symptoms such as lightheadedness, dizziness, or lethargy.
- Explain the desired effects of the treatment and any symptoms that are undesirable. If the patient is being seen through a home care agency, a demonstration and return demonstration in the home, including repetition of instructions, is essential to ensure the correct care delivery. If this is not possible, perhaps a mock set-up can be simulated in the hospital or clinic.
- Accountability is essential and encourages compliance. Set up a regular reporting schedule. A tracing of the wound by the therapist can be left with the patient and then laid over the wound for the patient or caregiver to compare changes in size and shape. It will also help reinforce compliance with the treatment regimen. The changes can be reported to the physical therapist by phone with periodic visits to monitor outcomes.

Case Study: *Patient with Eschars on Both Heels*

Functional Outcome Report

Patient Name: G.W.   **Start of Care Date:** 9/27

Medical History

84 yr old, alert confused black female. Nonambulatory resident of long-term care facility. Sits up in wheelchair and attends activity program. Medical diagnosis of Alzheimer's disease, prior history of cerebrovascular accident (CVA). No prior history of pressure ulceration.

Reason for Referral

1. Dry leathery eschars on both heels not responding to treatment with occlusive dressings. Indicates loss of healing capacity.
2. Need to determine severity of pressure ulcers on the heels.
3. Severely limited mobility and activity levels.

Systems Review and Exam

Circulatory System

Circulatory perfusion adequate for healing indicated by palpable pulses, warm feet, no significant leg edema and ankle-brachial index (ABI) of 0.8, but produces inadequate response to wounding due to motor and joint impairment of lower extremities (loss of muscle pump function for circulation).

Musculoskeletal System

Musculoskeletal impairments of the lower extremities due to weakness, joint pain, and stiffness with contractures

continues

Case Study continued

(10°) at the knees. Patient being positioned upright in wheelchair. Requires minimum assist to perform pivot transfer from bed to wheelchair. Weightbearing during transfer places stress on eschars. Unable to retain upright posture to ambulate and unable to reposition in wheelchair or bed for pressure relief. Braden risk assessment scores each for activity and for mobility 2/4.

Neuromuscular System

Loss of volitional movements due to impaired neuromotor system. Loss of cognitive awareness of position. Loss of protective sensation to reposition (sensory impairment).

Cardiopulmonary System

No clinical signs of cardiopulmonary impairment. Probable diminished oxygenation due to inactive mobility status.

Integumentary System

Adjacent and surrounding skin has normal skin color tones and turgor compared to adjacent areas. No pain responses in wounded tissues.
Wound Healing Tissue Assessment: Bilateral heels crusted with hard dry eschar; impairment of integumentary integrity. No thermal changes at the margins of the eschars compared to adjacent tissues. No edema or erythema (color changes) signifies impairment of inflammation response. Unable to see the tissue status under the eschar; unable to determine extent/severity of tissue loss.
Size: 25 cm² area of eschar on each heel.

Psychosocial

Patient unable to understand directions to reposition or exercise independently. Will follow guided movements. Needs caregiver intervention for repositioning, exercise, and transfers.

Functional Impairments and Functional Diagnosis

Loss of function in above systems causes the following:

1. Wound Severity Diagnosis unable to stage: impaired integumentary integrity associated with eschar on both heels. Removal of eschar needed to determine extent of wound depth.
2. Wound Healing Phase Diagnosis: absence of inflammation phase and absence of proliferation phase. Needs restart of the inflammatory phase of healing after conversion to a clean wound that will progress through phases of healing.
3. Associated impairment of mobility and activity secondary to neuromuscular disability (Alzheimer's disease and CVA).
4. Undue susceptibility to pressure ulceration on the feet due to motor and sensory impairment.
5. Low blood flow state but has adequate circulation to predict healing.

Short-Term Target Outcomes:	**Due Date**
Wounds: Softening of eschar	3 days
Debridement of eschar	7 days
Shows evidence of inflammation phase	14 days
Shows evidence of proliferation phase	28 days
Mobility: Nursing assistant will perform range of motion and guided exercise	3 days
Therapeutic positioning in bed and wheelchair will be performed by nursing assistants all shifts	7 days
Transfers with multipodus-type splint	5 days

Prognosis: A clean stable wound with potential for closure in 28 days. Undue susceptibility to pressure ulcers on the feet due to impaired mobility and cognition will continue after wounds are healed. Wound closure in 90 days both heels.

Plan of Care with Rationale for Skilled Services

1. Multiple debridement methods required to hasten progression to clean wound bed
   Procedures:
   - Score eschar—to allow penetration of moisture
   - Whirlpool to soak and soften tissue, enhance circulation daily
   - Sharp debridement—incremental as tissue softens and loosens PRN
   - Electrical stimulation—enhance microcirculation and stimulate cells leading to progression through phases of healing daily
   - Enzymatic debridement daily—to hasten solubilization of necrotic tissues
   - Autolysis with transparent film—to maintain moist wound environment to soften eschar
2. Therapeutic positioning to reduce risk of pressure and shearing to feet during transfers, in wheelchair, and in bed

continues

Case Study continued

3. Instruction of nurses' aides in range of motion and exercises to stimulate delivery of circulation to the tissues
4. Therapeutic exercise performed while in the whirlpool
5. Fitting of multipodus type splint

Target Outcomes Achieved at First Reassessment 10/1

Wound status:

1. Eschar softened, partially debrided by day 4
2. Removal of outer eschar revealed two focal areas of necrosis covered by eschar
3. Wound has evidence of inflammatory phase: edema, increased warmth in surrounding tissues

Mobility:

1. Patient lying on pressure relief support surface with pillows and multipodus splint to relieve pressure
2. Patient sitting up in wheelchair with feet supported with multipodus-type splint to relieve pressure during transfers
3. Range of motion and guided exercises by nurses' aide performed daily
4. Guided lower extremity exercise performed in the whirlpool

Reassessment 11/9

Wound status:

1. Eschar free, yellow slough
2. Wound depth greater than 0.2 cm
3. Two interconnecting wounds (medial and lateral sides of heel with viable tissue connecting)
4. Wound healing phase progressed to proliferation phase—presence of contraction and granulation tissue

Mobility:

1. Patient is participating in daily exercise and range of motion regimen
2. Therapeutic positioning is in place for all shifts

Functional Impairments

1. Integumentary impairment secondary to full-thickness pressure ulcer on the heels

Target outcome: clean proliferating and contracting wound—due date 21 days.

2. Absence of epithelialization phase and sustained contraction
Target outcome: Progress to epithelialization phase and sustained contraction—due date 21 days.

Revised Prognosis

Wound will heal to closure in 60 days.

Revised Treatment Plan and Target Outcomes

Need for Continuation of Skilled Services

Patient failed to respond to routine dressing and conservative management, is now responding to the treatment program. Treatment is done as a collaborative effort between the physical therapist and nurse. Change in treatment interventions required due to change in wound status. Patient has demonstrated potential for healing following interventions but will continue to be at risk for pressure ulceration.

Plan of Care (Intervention) with Rationale

- Discontinue whirlpool and sharp debridement tissue—neither needed to debride slough
- Continue electrical stimulation for microcirculation and stimulation of healing
- Discontinue enzymatic debridement—not needed to debride slough
- Change dressing to hydrogel and secondary dressing—to debride slough, for moist wound healing environment compatible with ES treatment regimen

Target Outcomes:

Clean wound bed	7 days
Proliferation phase: sustained contraction	14 days
Progress to epithelialization phase	21 days

Discharge Outcome

Wounds on both heels healed in 90 days from start of care.

Source: Functional Outcome Reporting System methodology used with permission of Swanson and Co., Long Beach, CA.

REFERENCES

1. Neiderhuber SS, et al. Reduction of skin bacterial load with use of the therapeutic whirlpool. *Phys Ther.* 1975;5(5):482–486.

2. Bohannon R. Whirlpool versus whirlpool and rinse for removal of bacteria from a venous stasis ulcer. *Phys Ther.* 1982;62: 304–308.

3. Bergstrom N, Bennett MA, Carlson C, et al. *Treatment of Pressure Ulcers.* Clinical Practice Guideline No. 15. AHCPR Publication No. 95-0652. Rockville, MD: Agency for Health Care Policy and Research, U.S. Public Health Service, U.S. Department of Health and Human Services; December 1994:45–65.

4. Swanson G. Hydrotherapy Use in Standard Physical Therapist Practice Project. Presented at class, University of Southern California, BKN 599. Los Angeles, CA, July 1997.

5. Solomon SL. Host factors in whirlpool-associated *Pseudomonas aeruginosa* skin disease. *Infect Control.* 1985;6:402–406.

6. Jacobson JA. Pool-associated *Pseudomonas aeruginosa* dermatitis and other bathing-associated infections. *Infect Control.* 1985;6: 398–401.

7. Shankowsky HA, et al. North American survey of hydrotherapy in modern burn care. *J Burn Care Rehabil.* 1994;15:143–146.

8. Cardany CR, et al. Influence of hydrotherapy and antiseptic agents on burn wound bacterial contamination. *J Burn Care Rehabil.* 1985;6:230–232.

9. Walsh M. Hydrotherapy: the use of water as a therapeutic agent. In: Michlovitz S, ed. *Thermal Agents in Rehabilitation.* Philadelphia: F.A. Davis; 1990:109–132.

10. McCulloch JM, Boyd VB. The effects of whirlpool and the dependent position on lower extremity volume. *J Orthop Sports Phys Ther.* 1992;16:169.

11. Guyton AC, ed. *Textbook of Medical Physiology.* 6th ed. Philadelphia: W.B. Saunders Company; 1981.

12. Alon G. Antibiotics enhancement by transcutaneous electrical stimulation. Presented at the symposium, Future Directions in Wound Healing; American Physical Therapy Association Scientific Meeting; June 1997.

13. Lock PM. The effect of temperature on mitosis at the edge of experimental wounds. In: Lundgren A, Soner AB, eds. *Symposia on Wound Healing: Plastic, Surgical and Dermatologic Aspects.* Sweden: Molndal; 1980:103–107.

14. Myers JA. Wound healing and the use of modern surgical dressing. *Pharm J.* 1982;229(6186):103–104.

15. Miller M, Dyson M. *Principles of Wound Care.* London: Macmillan Magazines Ltd; 1996:29–36.

16. Sussman C. The role of physical therapy in wound care. In: Krasner D, ed. *Chronic Wound Care: A Sourcebook for Health Care Professionals.* Wayne, PA: Health Management Publications; 1990: 327–366.

17. Levin ME. Pathogenesis and management of diabetic foot lesions. In: *The Diabetic Foot.* 5th ed. St. Louis, MO: Mosby–Year Book; 1993:46.

18. Cohen L, Martin GM, Wakin KG. Effects of the whirlpool bath with and without agitation on the circulation in the normal and diseased extremities. *Arch Phys Med.* 1949;30:212.

19. Vetra H, Whittaker D. Hydrotherapy and topical collagenase for decubitus ulcers. *Geriatrics.* 1975;30:53–58.

20. Novotne J. Efficient bathing systems benefit patients and care givers. *DON.* July 1987:28–30.

21. McCulloch J. Physical modalities in wound management. Preconference course. Presented at the Symposium on Advanced Wound Care; April 1985; San Diego, CA.

22. Baron R, Willeke K. Respirable droplets from whirlpools: measurement of size, distribution and estimation of disease potential. *Environ Res.* 1986;39:8–18.

23. Thomson PD, et al. A survey of burn hydrotherapy in the United States. *J Burn Care Rehabil.* 1990;11(2):151–155.

24. Health Care Financing Administration. Coverage of Services, 3132.4. Woodlawn, MD: December 1987.

25. Blue Cross of North Carolina. Medicare Bulletin Number 98-9. December 1996, Part A Office, Durham, NC 2:3.

26. Lineaweaver W, Howard R, Soucy D, et al. Topical antimicrobial toxicity. *Arch Surg.* 1985;120:267–270.

27. Kozol MD. Effects of sodium hypochlorite on cells of the wound module. *Arch Surg.* 1988;123:420–423.

28. American Physical Therapy Association. *Hydrotherapy/Therapeutic Pool Infection Control Guidelines.* Alexandria, VA: American Physical Therapy Association; 1995:8–11.

29. Swanson G. Use of cost data, provider experience, and clinical guidelines in the transition to managed care. *J Insurance Med.* 1991;23(1):70–74.

Guide to Topical Antiseptics, Antifungals, and Antibacterials

Source: Adapted with permission from *Topical Agents for Open Wounds: Antibacterials, Antiseptics, Antifungals,* G. Gilson, ed., reviewed by G. Rodeheaver, J.W. Cooper, D.R. Nelson, and M. Meehan, © 1991, Hill-Rom International.

INDEX TO TOPICAL ANTISEPTICS

Generic Name	Product Name(s)
Acetic acid irrigation	
Aluminum salts	Burow's solution, Domeboro®
Chlorhexidine gluconate	Hibiclens®, Exidine® skin
Hexachlorophene	pHisoHex®
Hypochlorites	Dakin's solution, chloramine-T
Oxidizing agents	Hydrogen peroxide, 1.5%, 3%
Povidone-iodine	Betadine™, Efodine®
Quaternary ammonium compound	Zephiran®

ACETIC ACID IRRIGATION

Description

A sterile solution of glacial acetic acid in water is used for irrigation. The pH range is between 2.9 and 3.3.

Action

The exact mechanism of action is unknown. Microorganisms will not proliferate at low pH, and all acids are bacteriostatic at low concentrations and bacteriocidal at higher concentrations.

Indication

Acetic acid is used to discourage bacterial infections in surgical wounds and to suppress growth by *Pseudomonas aeruginosa* in extensive burns; it is also a component in several dermatologic preparations.

Adverse Reactions

Acetic acid can cause irritation and inflammation. A solution of 0.25% acetic acid decreased bacterial survival by only 20% in cultured human fibroblasts.[1] The 0.25% acetic acid solution proved to be more damaging to fibroblasts than to bacteria whenever a difference in toxicity was observed.[1]

Dosage

Most physicians use acetic acid irrigant for wet-to-dry dressings. Acetic acid irrigant of a 0.25% solution is commonly used for bladder irrigation.

Packaging

Most institutional pharmacists prepare as a 1% surgical dressing.

Dermatologic lotion 0.1%
Irrigant 0.25%, 60 mL
Vosol 2% (Wallace Labs), 15 mL (multipack), 30 mL (multipack)

Other manufacturers of acetic acid: Kendall McGaw; Baxter Labs; Abbott Labs.

ALUMINUM SALTS (BUROW'S SOLUTION, DOMEBORO®)

Description

Aluminum salts have strong antibacterial effects. The general solutions containing aluminum salts are 1% aluminum chlorhydrate, 10% aluminum acetate, 30% aluminum chloride hexahydrate, and 5% aluminum diacetate.

Action

A mild astringent solution is made with Domeboro® tablets or powder.

Indications

Relief of inflammatory condition. One percent aluminum chlorhydrate, 10% aluminum acetate, and 30% aluminum chloride hexahydrate completely inhibit representative dermatophytes, yeasts, and gram-positive and gram-negative bacteria in vitro. Twenty percent aluminum chlorhydrate, 10% to 20% aluminum acetate, and 20% to 30% aluminum chlorhydrate salt are the most potent in vivo. The recommended concentrations (1:20 and 1:40) of 5% aluminum diacetate (Burow's solution) exert no in vivo bacteriostatic or bactericidal effects.

Precautions

Do not use plastic or other impervious material to prevent evaporation. For external use only. The enzyme activity of topical collagenase may be inhibited by aluminum acetate solution because of the metal ion and low pH. Cleanse the wound thoroughly with normal saline before applying enzymes.

Directions

Thirty milliliters of USP solution is diluted to 1 or 2 L with water, *or* Domeboro® tablets or powder may be dissolved in 0.5 to 1 L of water. Domeboro® tablets make a modified Burow's solution equivalent to 1:40.

Packaging

Pharmacy prepares Burow's solution.

Domeboro® 2.2-g packets of powder or tablets (Miles, Inc.)
Blue Boro® 2.2-g packets of powder or tablets (Herbert)
Burow's solution
  (J.J. Balan, Inc.), 480-mL solution
  (Paddock Labs), 480-mL solution, 3,840-mL solution
  (Wisconsin Pharm.), 480-mL solution, 3,840-mL solution

CHLORHEXIDINE GLUCONATE (HIBICLENS®, EXIDENE® SKIN)

Description

Chlorhexidine gluconate was introduced in the United States from Europe in 1977 as Hibiclens, which is 4% chlorhexidine gluconate with 4% isopropyl alcohol in a sudsing base. Hibitane is a chlorhexidine tinction for use as a skin preparation. It is an antiseptic and antimicrobial.

Action

Bactericidal on contact. Antiseptic activity and a persistent antimicrobial effect with rapid bactericidal activity against a wide range of microorganisms, including gram-positive bacteria and gram-negative bacteria as *Pseudomonas aeruginosa*.

Indications

Effective against a wide variety of gram-positive and gram-negative bacteria, molds, yeasts and viruses. Sporicidal only at elevated temperatures. Rapid acting—the reduction of bacterial flora on the skin occurs immediately. Repeated use produces further reductions. Safe to use on the skin. No significant problems with irritation, allergy, or photosensitivity. No evidence of toxicity if absorbed, and does not appear to be absorbed due to the protein-binding characteristic, which causes retention in the stratum corneum. It does not lose its effectiveness in the presence of whole blood.

Precautions

For external use only. Avoid contact with the meninges. Not recommended for full-thickness wounds.

Directions

Thoroughly rinse wound with sterile water. Apply sufficient Hibiclens and wash gently. Rinse thoroughly.

Packaging

Hibiclens skin cleanser (Stuart Pharm.) (4% chlorhexidine gluconate in a sudsing base), 120 mL
Hibistat germicidal hand rinse (Stuart Pharm.) (0.5% chlorhexidine in 70% isopropyl alcohol), 120 mL
Hibiclens antiseptic antimicrobial skin (Stuart Pharm.) (4% in sudsing base), 120 mL, 240 mL, ½ gal, 1 gal
Exidine skin (yttrium) (4% with 4% isopropyl alcohol)

HEXACHLOROPHENE (PHISOHEX®)

Description

Hexachlorophene is a chlorinated phenolic compound.

Action

Antibacterial cleanser. Its antibacterial action is unknown.

Indications

Active primarily against gram-positive bacteria, including staphylococci. Peak antibacterial effect of hexachlorophene is obtained only by repeated scrubs on successive days. It has very little effect on gram-negative bacteria or spores.

Precautions

Tends to leave a residual film on the skin that can persist for several days. Protective film can be easily disrupted by alcohol. It can be absorbed through the skin. Once in the blood stream, there is potential for toxicity to the central nervous system. Up to 3.1% of topically applied hexachlorophene could be absorbed through the skin.

Hexachlorophene contamination with gram-negative bacteria, *Klebsiella* species, *Pseudomonas aeruginosa*, *Escherichia coli*, and *Candida albicans* is possible.

Contraindicated for use on burned or denuded skin as an occlusive dressing, wet pack, or lotion, or on any mucous membrane. Do not use in deep wounds.

Directions

Clean area for 3 minutes with pHisoHex® and rinse thoroughly.

Packaging

PHisoHex® 3% (Winthrop-Breon), 5-oz bottle, 1 pt, 1 gal
Septi-Soft® 0.25% (Vestal), liquid, 240 mL
Septi-Sol® 0.25% (Vestal), solution, 240 mL

HYPOCHLORITES (DAKIN'S SOLUTION, CHLORAMINE-T)

Description

Sodium hypochlorite has germicidal, deodorizing, and bleaching properties. Henry D. Dakin, U.S. chemist, 1880–1952, developed this solution for cleansing wounds during World War I as a very dilute neutral solution (0.45% to 0.5%) of sodium hypochlorite and 0.04% boric acid.

Action

The exact mechanism of action by which free chlorine destroys microorganisms has not been established. The postulated mechanism is inhibition of some key enzymatic reactions within the cell, protein denaturation, and inactivation of nucleic acids.

Indications

For prophylaxis of epidermophytosis, diluted sodium hypochlorite solution is sometimes employed as a foot bath. It is employed in full strength, as a freshly prepared solution, in the management of suppurating wounds, often by continuous irrigation (Carrel technique). It is useful in the dissolving of necrotic tissue.

Precautions

Cellular damage occurs at concentrations of Dakin's solution formerly thought to be safe for use in open wounds (0.5%). Even at lower concentrations (0.25%), significant damage is seen in fibroblasts and endothelial cells.[2] Significant damage occurs at more dilute concentrations of 0.001% and 0.00001%.

In experiments done by Robert Kozol, cultured fibroblasts and endothelial cells exposed to Dakin's solution (2.5 × 10^{-2} or 2.5 × 10^{-3}) for 30 minutes showed a marked increase in cell injury characterized by convoluted nuclei, cytoplasmic vacuolation, dilated endoplasmic reticulum, and swollen mitochondria. They also found Dakin's solution to have an inhibitory effect on random and stimulated migration of neutrophils, a functional response rather than as a result of cellular damage.[2]

Chloramine-T, an aqueous hypochlorite antiseptic agent, retards the development of collagen in healing skin defects and prolongs the acute inflammatory response; therefore, healing is delayed. It is toxic to granulation tissue, leading to complete and irreversible capillary shutdown. Reepithelialization at wound edges is delayed in wounds treated with hypochlorite solutions.

Sodium hypochlorite solutions dissolve blood clots, delay clotting, and are irritating to the skin. It has been suggested that the use of hypochlorites can cause endotoxins to be released from gram-negative bacteria in chronic wounds such as pressure ulcers, which can initiate a clinical response varying from mild pyrexia to acute oliguric renal failure.

Directions

Most physicians order wounds packed with Dakin's solution and gauze three or four times daily.

Packaging

Most pharmacists prepare Dakin's solution as a 0.5% sodium hypochlorite solution. Even at this concentration, the solution is toxic to native cells. There is *no* safe concentration of Dakin's solution for use in open wounds.

Dakin's solution is prepared as a topical solution containing 0.15% to 0.5% of NaOCL. The full-strength solution contains 0.5% NaOCL. To prepare the 0.15% solution, it should be diluted 1:3.

Dakin's solution (Century Pharm.), 5% gallon solution
Chloramine-T (A.A. Spectrum), 250 g, 1,000 g, 2,500 g

OXIDIZING AGENTS

Hydrogen Peroxide Solution USP

Contact with tissues releases molecular oxygen, and there is a brief period of antimicrobial action. There is no penetration of tissues. It has been reported that the instillation of peroxide into wound cavities under pressure can result in oxygen passing into the blood stream, causing a life-threatening embolus.[3] Hydrogen peroxide has been documented to liberate oxygen that can spread along fascial planes, which causes swelling and crepitation and is frequently misdiagnosed as invasion by gas-forming bacteria.[3,4] It is toxic to exposed fibroblasts unless it is diluted more than 1:100.[4]

Packaging

A.A. Spectrum, 3% solution in water, 500 mL, 4,000 mL
J.J. Balan, 3% solution in water, 480 mL

Hydrous Benzoyl Peroxide USP

Can be bactericidal to microorganisms. When applied as a lotion, it is also keratolytic, antiseborrheic, and an irritant. May produce contact dermatitis. Its principal use is in the treatment of acne and seborrhea.

Potassium Permanganate USP

Consists of purple crystals that dissolve in water to give deep purple solutions. Tends to stain tissue and clothing brown. A 1:10,000 dilution applied in inert surfaces kills many microorganisms in 1 hour. Higher concentrations are irritating to the tissues. Its principal use is in treatment of weeping skin lesions with questionable justification.

Packaging

A.A. Spectrum, granules, 454 g
Humco Lab, Inc., granules, 120 g, 420 g, 454 g, 2,270 g

POVIDONE-IODINE

Description

Yellow-brown acidic water-soluble solution made of the polymer polyvinylpyrrolidone and iodine, creating a water-soluble agent that slowly releases free iodine.

Action

Potent antiseptic with a broad spectrum of antimicrobial activity, although its exact mechanism of action is unknown. Povidone-iodine is inactivated in the presence of blood and organic matter.

Indications

Povidone-iodine kills gram-positive and gram-negative bacteria, fungi, viruses, protozoa, and yeasts. Spore destruction is achieved only with moist contact for more than 15 minutes.[5] A 10% solution of povidone-iodine (1% of available iodine) kills 85% of cutaneous bacteria. Clinically indicated for prevention and treatment of surface infections, as well as to degerm the skin prior to invasive procedures.

Precautions

Stinging and burning of the tissue is a common side effect. One percent povidone-iodine is indiscriminate in toxic effects at full strength. A dilution of 1:1,000 is identified where no fibroblast toxicity occurs, while remaining bactericidal in in vitro studies.[1]

In vivo studies showed that povidone-iodine surgical scrub solution significantly potentiated ($P < 0.002$) the development of wound infection when compared with the incidence of infection in wounds treated with 0.9% saline solution.[6]

It is important to know that the Food and Drug Administration has not approved povidone-iodine antiseptic solution or povidone-iodine surgical scrub solution for use in wounds.[6]

For an antimicrobial agent to eliminate bacterial contamination, it must reach the bacteria in an active form. Because of the insolubility of iodine in water and its rapid complex formation with tissue and body fluids, its ability to reach and kill bacteria in a wound or tissue is highly suspect.[6]

Adverse Reactions

A continuous irrigation with Betadine™ in a 72-year-old woman, postsurgical debridement of a hip wound resulted in death 10 hours later. Her serum total iodine level at autopsy was 7,000 µg/dL, while the normal value is 5 to 8 µg/dL.[7]

Povidone-iodine has been reported to cause acidosis in burn patients. Lasting systemic side effects identified include cardiovascular toxicity, renal toxicity, hepatoxicity, and neuropathy.[8]

Povidone-iodine's toxicity directly interferes with wound healing at the cellular level and places the patient at a greater risk for wound infection.[9] Rodeheaver's studies showed that both aqueous iodine and povidone-iodine solutions significantly impair the wound's ability to fight infection.[6]

In separate studies it was found that povidone-iodine inhibits wound healing at the cellular level, and that the incidence and potential for infection are greater than if wounds are irrigated only with normal saline.[9]

Rodeheaver found that even though povidone-iodine solution significantly lowered contaminants in the wound, the wound was still heavily contaminated. He also found that povidone-iodine surgical scrub did not reduce the level of bacteria in the wound.[6]

Dosage

Topical: 0.5% to 10% to the skin
Solution: 0.5% to 1% to the skin

Packaging

Purdue Frederick, 10% solution, 8 oz
Generic, 10% solution, 8 oz, 480-mL, 3,840-mL

QUATERNARY AMMONIUM COMPOUND (ZEPHIRAN®)

Description

Benzalkonium chloride (BAC) is a quaternary ammonium compound commonly known as Zephiran. It is a cationic surfactant. The quaternaries are organically substituted ammonium compounds in which the nitrogen atom has a valence of 5.

Action

The bactericidal action has been attributed to the inactivation of energy-producing enzymes, denaturation of essential cell proteins, and disruption of the cell membrane.

Indication

Effective against some gram-positive and gram-negative bacteria, some fungi, and protozoa. Many bacteria grow in its presence. It is not effective against *Mycobacterium tuberculosis*, *Pseudomonas aeruginosa*, spores, and viruses.

Precautions

It is inactivated by anionic compounds such as soaps and detergents. Any residual detergent on the skin will neutralize the antiseptic effect. It is inactivated by blood and other organic matter. There are reports of contamination with *Pseudomonas cepacia*, *Enterobacter cloacae*, *E agglomerans*, and *Serratia marcescens*.

Directions

Rinse anionic detergents and soaps from the area first so that the antibacterial activity of BAC will not be reduced. Minor wounds and lacerations use 1:750 tincture or spray. Deep, infected wounds use 1:30,000 to 1:20,000 aqueous solution. Wet dressings use 1:5,000 or less solution.

Packaging

Germicin® (CMC), 50% solution, 1 pt, 1 gal
Benza (Century Pharm.), 1:750 solution, 60 mL, 120 mL
Zephiran® (Winthrop-Breon)
    Aqueous solution 1:750, 240 mL, 1 gal
    Disinfectant concentration 17%, 120 mL, 1 gal
    Tincture spray 1:750, 30 g/gal, 80 g/gal
    Tincture 1:750, 1 gal

INDEX TO TOPICAL ANTIFUNGALS

Generic Name	Product Name(s)
Amphotericin B	Fungizone®
Ciclopirox olamine	Loprox®
Clotrimazole	Lotrimin®, Mycelex®
Econazole nitrate 1%	Spectazole®
Haloprogin	Halotex®
Ketoconazole	Nizoral®
Miconazole nitrate	Monistat-Derm®
	Micatin®, Monistat®
Nystatin	Mycostatin®, Nilstat®
Tolnaftate	Tinactin®

AMPHOTERICIN B (FUNGIZONE®)

Description

Yellow-orange, odorless; may stain skin. A polyene antifungal for topical use, produced by a stain of *Streptomyces nodosus*.

Action

Amphotericin B binds sterols in the cell membrane with an alteration in permeability that results in leakage of intracellular materials.

Indications

Superficial *Candida albicans*, histoplasmosis, coccidiomycosis, and crytococcocis. It has no significant effect against gram-positive or gram-negative bacteria or viruses.

Precautions

Ineffective against dermatophytes. May stain skin. Rash may develop. Lotion may have a drying effect on some skin.

Vehicle

Cream: aqueous base containing titanium dioxide, thimerosal propylene glycol, cetyl alcohol, ceteareth-20, white petrolatum, methylparaben, propylparaben, sorbitol solution, glycerylmonostearate, polyethylene glycol monostearate, simethicone, and sorbic acid.

Lotion: aqueous base containing thimerosal, titanium dioxide, guargum, propylene glycol, cetyl alcohol, stearyl alcohol, sorbitan monopalmitate, polysorbate 20, glyceryl monostearate, polyethylene glycol monostearate, simethicone, sorbic acid, sodium citrate, methylparaben, and propylparaben.

Ointment: Plastibase® (plasticized hydrocarbon gel). A polyethylene and mineral oil gel base with titanium dioxide.

Dosage

Apply two to four times a day. Apply liberally to candidal lesions. Duration of therapy depends on individual response to treatment. May require 2 to 4 weeks of therapy.

Packaging

Fungizone® (Squibb Pharm.)
   3% cream and ointment, 20 g
   3% lotion, 30 mL

CICLOPIROX OLAMINE (LOPROX®)

Description

Effective broad-spectrum hydroxpyrimidinone antifungal agent that inhibits the growth of pathogenic dematophytes, yeasts, and *Malassezia furfur*.

Action

Inhibits the uptake of precursors of macromolecular synthesis. Acts by impairing transmembrane transport, thus preventing essential amino acids and electrolytes from entering the cell.

Indications

Tinea pedis, cruris, corporis due to *Trichophyton rubrum, T mentagrophytes, Epidermophyton floccosum*, and *Microsporum canis*. Cutaneous candidiasis (moniliasis) caused by *Candida albicans* and pityriasis (tinea) versicolor, due to *Microsporum canis*.

Adverse Reactions

Burning, stinging, pruritis, and erythema are reported side effects. Avoid eye contact.

Dosage

Gently massage into affected area and surrounding skin. Use twice-daily application (morning and evening). Treatment should last from 2 to 4 weeks. Avoid use of occlusive wrappings or dressings. There is only minimal absorption (1.3%) when applied topically to intact or broken skin.

Vehicle

Lotion: water-miscible lotion base consisting of purified water USP, cocamide DEA, octyldodecanol NF, mineral oil USP, stearyl alcohol NF, cetyl alcohol NF, polysorbate 60 NF, myristyl alcohol NF, sorbitan monostearate NF, lactic acid USP, and benzyl alcohol NF (1%) as preservative.

Cream: water-miscible vanishing cream base consisting of purified water USP, octyldodecanol NF, mineral oil USP, stearyl alcohol NF, cetyl alcohol NF, cocamide DEA, polysorbate 60 NF, myristyl alcohol NF, sorbitan monostearate NF, lactic acid USP, and benzyl alcohol NF (1%) as preservative.

Packaging

Loprox® (Hoechst-Rousell Pharm.)
   1% cream, 15 g, 30 g, 90 g
   1% lotion, 30 mL

CLOTRIMAZOLE (LOTRIMIN®, MYCELEX®)

Description

Synthetic imidazole agent that is an odorless, white crystalline and practically insoluble in water.

Action

Mechanism of action is unclear but probably involves damage to the cell wall, resulting in loss of intracellular electrolytes, similar to that of the polyene antibacterials.

Indications

Indicated for superficial fungal infections, *Candida albicans* infections, yeasts, and *Malassezia furfur*. Inhibits growth of most dermatophyte species as well as of some gram-positive bacteria. In high concentration clotrimazole is active against *Trichomonas* species. Also active against tinea pedis, cruris, corporis caused by *Trichophyton rubrum, T mentagrophytes, Epidermophyton floccosum*, and *Microsporum canis*.

Adverse Reactions

Occasional erythema at site of application has been reported along with urticaria, burning, edema, peeling, blistering, and stinging. Do not use in first trimester of pregnancy.

Note: Lotrisone is not the same as Lotrimin. Lotrisone contains a steroid.

Vehicle

Cream: vanishing cream base of sorbitan monostearate, polysorbate 60, cetyl ester wax, cetyl alcohol, 2-octyl-dodecanol, purified water, and, as preservative, benzyl alcohol (1%).

Lotion: emulsion composed of sorbitan monostearate, polysorbate 60, cetyl ester wax, cetyl alcohol, 2-octyl-dodecanol, purified water, benzyl alcohol (1%), and, as preservative, sodium phosphate dibasic sodium biphosphate to adjust pH.

Solution: nonaqueous vehicle of polyethylene glycol 400.

Dosage

Twice daily until eruption clears. Gently rub into the affected areas morning and evening. Clinical improvement should be evident in 1 week. Continue treatment for 4 weeks. Reevaluate after 4 weeks if no improvement. Use the solution four times daily.

Packaging

Lotrimin® (Shering Corp.)
   1% cream, 15-g tube, 30-g tube, 45-g tube, 90-g tube
   1% solution, 10 mL, 30 mL
Mycelex® (Milex, Inc.)
   1% cream, 15-g tube, 30-g tube, 90-g tube

ECONAZOLE NITRATE 1% (SPECTAZOLE®)

Description

Synthetic imidazole.

Action

Interferes with the biosynthesis of ergosterol (chemical needed by fungi to maintain cell wall integrity), resulting in the disorganization of the fungal plasma cell membrane.

Indications

For the topical treatment of tinea pedis, tinea cruris, tinea corporis (ringworm of the body), cutaneous candidiasis (caused by *Candida albicans*), and pityriasis (tinea) versicolor; effective against *Microsporum gypseum.* Effective against *Trichophyton rubrum, T mentagrophytes, T tonsurans, Microsporum canis, M audouinii,* and *Epidermophyton floccosum.*

Adverse Reactions

Three percent of patients complain of burning, stinging, pruritus, and erythema after 3 to 4 days of treatment. Avoid eye contact.

Vehicle

Cream: water-miscible base consisting of pegoxol F stearate, peglicol 5 oleate, mineral oil, benzoic acid, butylated hydroxyanisole, and purified water.

Dosage

Twice daily (morning and evening) for 2 or more weeks. There is only minimal absorption when applied topically to intact or broken skin. Occlusive dressings slightly increase the amount of absorption.

Packaging

Spectazole® (Ortho Pharm., Dermatological Division), 1% cream, 15 g, 30 g, 85 g

HALOPROGIN (HALOTEX®)

Description

Synthetic chlorinated ildopropynyl trichlorophenyl ether.

Action

The exact mechanism of action is unknown.

Indications

Topical treatment of dermatophyte infections and tinea vesicolor caused by *Malassezia furfur.* Active in vitro against staphylococci, streptococci, and *Candida albicans.* Indicated for tinea pedis, tinea cruris, tinea corporis, and tinea manuum caused by *Trichophyton Epidermophyton floccosum.*

Adverse Reactions

Local irritations, burning sensation, pruritus, erythema, scaling, folliculitis, vesicle formation are reported.

Vehicle

Cream: water-dispersible base composed of polyethylene glycol 400, polyethylene glycol 4,000, diethyl sebacate, and polyvinylpyrrolidone.
Solution: 75% alcohol and diethyl sebacate.

Dosage

Twice daily gently massage the 1% cream liberally onto the affected area for 2 to 3 weeks' duration. Interdigital lesions may require 4 weeks.

Packaging

Halotex® (Westwood Pharm., Inc.)
   1% cream, 15 g, 30 g
   1% solution, 10 mL

KETOCONAZOLE (NIZORAL®)

Description

Water-soluble imidazole derivative.

Action

Affects fungi by mechanisms involving increased membrane permeability, inhibition of uptake of precursors of RNA and DNA, and synthesis of oxidative and perioxidative enzymes.

Indications

Highly effective in chronic dermatophyte infections, including those resistant to *Candida* species, *Cryptococcus neoformans, Coccidioides immitis, Histoplasma capsulatum, Blastomyces dermatitidis*, and pathogenic dermatophytes. Effective for treatment of mucocutaneous candidiasis. Used in the treatment of tinea corporis, tinea cruris, and tinea versicolor.

Adverse Reactions

Stinging, irritation, and pruritus are reported.

Vehicle

Propylene glycol, stearyl and cetyl alcohols, sorbitan monostearate, polysorbate 60, isopropyl myristate, sodium sulfite anhydrous, polysorbate 80, and purified water.

Dosage

Apply 2% cream over affected area and the immediate surrounding area once daily for 2 weeks.

Packaging

Nizoral® (Janssen Pharm.), 2% cream, 15-g tube, 30-g tube, 60-g tube

MICONAZOLE NITRATE (MONISTAT-DERM®, MICATIN®, MONISTAT®)

Description

Synthetic imidazole antifungal.

Action

Destroys fungi presumably by inhibiting cell wall synthesis.

Indications

Effective against most dermatophyte species and against cutaneous candidiasis caused by *Candida albicans*. Effective against tinea pedis, cruris, and corporis caused by *Trichophyton rubrum, T mentagrophytes*, and *Epidermophyton floccosum*, the yeastlike fungus. Effective against *Malassezia furfur*, the organism responsible for tinea versicolor.

Adverse Reactions

May cause irritation, burning, erythema, maceration, and allergic contact dermatitis. Avoid eye contact.

Vehicle

Cream and lotion: water-miscible base consisting of pegoxol 7 stearate, peglicol 5 oleate, mineral oil, benzoic acid, and butylated hydroxyanisole, and purified water.

Dosage

Apply twice daily until eruption clears. Cream should be gently rubbed in thoroughly (to avoid maceration) on the affected areas and surrounding skin morning and evening. Clinical improvement should be evident (relief of pruritis) within 1 week. Continue treatment for 2 to 4 weeks.

Packaging

Monistat-Derm® (Ortho Derm. Div.), 2% cream, 15 g, 28 g, 85 g
Micatin® (Ortho), 2% cream, 15 g, 30 g
Monistat-7® (Ortho Pharm), lotion, cream, 45 g/tube with applicator

NYSTATIN (MYCOSTATIN®, NILSTAT®)

Description

Polyene antimicrobial derived from a species of the order Actinomycetales, *Streptomyces noursei.*

Action

Binds to sterols in fungal cell membranes, causing a change in the permeability of cell membranes and leakage of cell components.

Indications

Candidal infections of skin and mucous membranes.

Adverse Reactions

None known.

Vehicle

Nilstat®'s vehicle is composed of light mineral oil and Plastibase® 50W.

Dosage

Apply twice daily and gently massage into affected area.

Packaging

Ointment and cream, 100,000 U/g
    Mycostatin® (Squibb), 15 g
    Nilstat® (Lederle), 15 g
    Generic, 15 g
Nilstatin (Lederle), 0.1% triamcinolone acetonide cream and ointment
    Mycolog (Squibb), 15 g
    Generic, 15 g

TOLNAFTATE (TINACTIN®)

Description

Fungistatic and fungicidal agent.

Action

Mechanism of action is unknown.

Indications

Effective against *Trichophyton rubrum, T mentagrophytes, T tonsurans,* and various *Microsporum* and *Aspergillus* species. Effective against intradermal dermatophytic infections. Commonly used to treat tinea pedia (athlete's foot), tinea cruris (jock itch), tinea corporis (ringworm of the body), and tinea manuum when caused by the above fungal pathogens.

It is ineffective against *Candida albicans, Cryptococcus neoformans,* and *Aspergillus fumigatus,* and against bacteria, protozoa, and viruses.

Adverse Reactions

Essentially none, although local irritation and burning have been reported when applied to excoriated skin or lesions caused by multiple pathogens. Avoid eye contact.

Dosage

Dry the affected area first, then apply a small amount and gently massage into the area until the medication disappears. Apply twice daily for several weeks (may be required over 6 weeks with long-standing infections). Clinical improvement should be noted in 2 or 3 days. Only small amounts of the cream are necessary for therapy.

Packaging

Tinactin® (Sherring-Plough Healthcare Products)
    1% cream, 15-g tube
    1% powder, 45-g container
    1% powder, 120-g aerosol container
    1% solution, 10-mL container
Generic
    1% cream, 15-g tube
    1% powder, 45-g container

BACITRACIN (BACIGUENT®)

Description

Bacitracin is a polypeptide antibiotic produced from the Tracy I strain of *Bacillus subtilis* and licheniformin discovered in 1954. Bacitracin is stable in petrolatum and is available as an ointment or as a component of antibiotic mixtures.

Action

Bacitracin interferes with cell wall synthesis and has a wide antibacterial spectrum.

Indications

Topical bacitracin will eradicate susceptible bacteria in open infections such as infected dermatosis and cutaneous ulcers. Gram-positive cocci and bacilli, *Neisseria, Haemophilus influenzae*, and *Treponema pallidum* are sensitive to bacitracin 0.1/mL or less. *Actinomyces* and *Fusobacterium* are sensitive to 0.5 U/mL. Resistant strains are *Pseudomonas, Candida, Norcardia, Enterobacteriaceae, Cryptococcus* (formerly called *Torula*). Although bacitracin ointment has been applied to the nose of subjects colonized with methicillin-resistant *Staphylococcus aureus*,[10] two studies found it ineffective in eradicating nasal carriage.[11,12]

Precautions

Bacitracin patch tests may not show positive results for 96 hours after the usual 48 hours. Anaphylaxis (type I hypersensitivity) occurs almost exclusively in settings of topical application to sites of venous stasis dermatitis and ulcers, and presumably arises from systemic absorption of the drug. A patient sensitive to neomycin is probably sensitive to bacitracin. Local application of bacitracin has been associated with severe allergic disorders.[13]

Vehicle

Anhydrous ointment base, mineral oil, and white petrolatum.

Directions

Apply four to six times daily directly to the wound.

Packaging

Generic, 15-g tube (500 U/g), 30-g tube
Baciguent® (The Upjohn Co.), 15-g tube, 30-g tube, 120-g tube

GENTAMICIN SULFATE (GENTAMICIN, GARAMYCIN®)

Description

Gentamicin is a combination of three related aminoglycoside agents obtained from cultures of *Micromonospora purpurea*.

Action

Gentamicin is active against gram-negative organisms, including *Escherichia coli* and a high percentage of strains of species of *Pseudomonas* and other gram-negative bacteria. *Proteus* organisms show a variable degree of sensitivity. Some gram-positive organisms are affected, such as *Staphylococcus aureus* and group A ß-hemolytic streptococci. In general, higher concentrations are needed to inhibit streptococci than are needed to inhibit staphylococci and many gram-negative bacteria. The most important use of gentamicin is in the treatment of systemic gram-negative infections, particularly those due to *Pseudomonas* organisms.

Precautions

Gentamicin's antibiotic spectrum is similar to that of neomycin, and cross-resistance does occur. Widespread use is especially unwarranted because of the risk of increasing gentamicin-resistant organisms (since this drug may be very useful in eradicating *Pseudomonas*) and because equally effective drugs are available. Allergic reactions to gentamicin are unusual. As with any aminoglycoside, gentamicin should be avoided in patients with kidney disease or renal failure.

Vehicle

Cream: bland emulsion-type base consisting of stearic acid, propylene glycol stearate, isopropyl myristate, propylene glycol, polysorbate 40, sorbitol solution, and purified water.
Ointment: bland, unctuous petrolatum base.

Directions

Apply four to six times daily directly to the wound.

Packaging

Generic, 3.5-g cream or ointment, 15-g cream or ointment
Gentamicin (Schering, Fougera), 15-g tube
Garamycin® (Schering), 3.5-g tube, 15-g tube
Jenamicin® (Hauck), 2-mL vial

METRONIDAZOLE (METROGEL®)

Description

Contains metronidazole USP at a concentration of 7.5 mg/g. Classed as both antibacterial and antiprotozoal. The 0.75% topical gel, which is bactericidal, amebicidal, and trichomonacidal, is used for acne rosacea.

Action

The mechanisms by which Metrogel® acts to reduce inflammation are unknown, but may include an antibacterial and/or an antiprotozoal effect.

Indications

Topical application for the treatment of inflammatory papules, pustules, and erythema of rosacea. In the United Kingdom, it has been used on pressure ulcers, fungate tumors, and malodorous lesions with success.[14]

Precautions

Use with care in patients with evidence of, or history of, blood dyscrasia. Use care in administration to patients receiving anticoagulant treatment.

Vehicle

Gelled, purified water solution containing methylparaben and propylparaben, propylene glycol, carbomer 940, and edetate disodium.

Directions

Apply and rub in a thin film of Metrogel® twice daily (morning and evening) to the entire affected area after washing. Significant therapeutic results should be noticed within 3 weeks.

Packaging

Metrogel® (Curatek Pharm.), 30-g tube

MUPIROCIN (BACTROBAN®)

Description

Mupirocin 2% ointment is in a water-miscible, nonocclusive polyethylene glycol base. Mupirocin, or pseudomonic acid A, is produced by fermentation of the organism *Pseudomonas fluorescens.*

Action

Apparently exerts its antimicrobial activity by reversibly inhibiting isoleucyl–transfer RNA, thereby inhibiting bacterial protein and RNA synthesis.

Indications

For topical treatment of impetigo due to *Staphylococcus aureus*, ß-hemolytic streptococcus, and *Streptococcus pyogenes*. Highly active against all species of *Staphylococcus*, including methicillin-resistant *S aureus* (MRSA), *S aureus*, and most species of streptococci. It is ineffective against most gram-positive bacilli, anaerobes, and aerobic gram-negative bacilli, such as *Pseudomonas* species. In the treatment of MRSA and impetigo, mupirocin is usually used in combination with suitable systemic antibiotics.

Precautions

Caution should be used in pregnant and nursing women. Burning, itching, contact dermatitis has been reported. Prolonged use may result in overgrowth of nonsusceptible organisms, including fungi.

Vehicle

Bland, water-miscible ointment base consisting of polyethylene glycol 400 and polyethylene glycol 3,350.

Directions

Mupirocin 2% is usually applied topically two or three times per day for 5 to 14 days in adult and pediatric patients with primary or superficial skin infections.

Packaging

Bactroban® (Beecham Labs), 15-g tube

NEOMYCIN SULFATE (MYCIGUENT®, NEOSPORIN®)

Description

Neomycin is an active aminoglycoside against staphylococci, but less so against streptococci. Neomycin sulfate is obtained from species of the actinomyces *Streptomyces*.

Action

Neomycin acts by inhibiting protein synthesis, as do all aminoglycosides.

Indications

Neomycin is effective against most gram-negative organisms, except *Pseudomonas aeruginosa* and obligate anaerobic bacteria. Group A streptococci are relatively resistant.[15] Neomycin is active against staphylococci. Often neomycin is combined with bacitracin, which inhibits staphylococci and streptococci, as well as gram-negative bacilli.

Precautions

Neomycin is responsible for a greater incidence of allergic sensitivity and cross-sensitivity to other aminoglycosides than any other topical antibiotic, especially in wounds, because they have lost their epidermal barrier and cannot resist penetration.[16,17]

Directions

Apply four to six times daily to the wound.

Packaging

Generic, 15-g ointment, 30-g ointment
Neomycin (Burroughs-Wellcome)
Neomycin (various other manufacturers)

Neomycin-Containing Ointments and Creams

- Neodecadron® topical cream (Merck & Co., Inc.)
  Contents per Gram: 3.5 mg neomycin sulfate and 1 mg dexamethasone sodium phosphate

- Campho-Phenique™ triple antibiotic plus pain reliever (Winthrop)
  Contents per Gram: 400 U bacitracin, 5 mg neomycin sulfate, 5,000 U polymyxin B sulfate, and diperodon hydrochloride

- Myciguent® ointment or cream (Upjohn)
- Neosporin® ointment (Burroughs-Wellcome)
  Contents per Gram: 5,000 U polymyxin B sulfate, 400 U zinc bacitracin, and 3.5 mg neomycin sulfate (as base)
  Directions: Apply four to six times daily directly to the wound.
  Packaging:
    Generic, 15-g tube
    Neomycin (Burroughs-Wellcome), 15-g tube, 30-g tube

- Neo-Polycin ointment (Merrell Dow)
  Contents per Gram: 8,000 U polymyxin B sulfate, 400 U zinc bacitracin, 3 mg neomycin sulfate (base)
  Directions: Apply four to six times daily directly to the wound.
  Packaging:
    Generic, 15-g tube
    Neo-Polycin (Lakeside), 15-g tube

NITROFURAZONE (FURACIN®)

Description

Odorless, lemon-yellow, crystalline powder; pH between 5 and 7.5.

Action

The exact mechanism of action is unknown.

Indication

Effective against *Staphylococcus aureus*, streptococcus, *Escherichia coli, Clostridium perfringens, Enterobacter aerogenes*, and proteus. It has a broad spectrum of activity. Most bacteria of surface infections of the skin and mucosal surfaces are sensitive.

It has not been shown to be effective in the treatment of minor burns, wounds, or cutaneous ulcers that are infected. It has been successfully used in the treatment of second- and third-degree burns and in skin grafting where there are complications from bacterial infections that are refractory to the usual drugs of choice, but in which sensitivity to nitrofurazone is demonstrated by culture and sensitivity.

Nitrofurazone's antibacterial activity is inhibited in blood, serum, pus, and animobenzoic acid.[18] Phagocytosis is not inhibited, but animal studies have shown nitrofurazone to delay wound healing.[19]

Precautions

Burning, stinging, dryness, itching, local irritation, and erythema are reported side effects. Use with caution on patients with known or suspected renal impairment, since it contains polyethylene glycols, which may be absorbed and may produce adverse effects.

Vehicle

Water-miscible base consisting of glycerin, cetyl alcohol, mineral oil, an ethoxylated fatty alcohol, methylparaben, propylparaben, and purified water.

Directions

Nitrofurazone is a slow-acting drug, and at least 24 hours are required for it to take effect properly. Treatment should last at least 2 or 3 days. Only about 6% is absorbed.

The dosage interval and duration of treatment vary with the particular use and dosage form. Five days is the usual duration except in severe burns. The use in burn therapy is generally less than 1 week to avoid sensitization. Gently massage cream (1%) into affected and surrounding skin daily.

Packaging

Furacin® topical cream (Norwich Eaton Pharm. Inc.)
   0.2% cream, 28 g
   0.2% ointment, 28 g, 454 g
Generic, 0.2% ointment, 30 g

POLYMYXIN B (AEROSPORIN®)

Description

Polymyxin B is one of a group of cyclic polypeptides. The B represents *Bacillus polymyxa*, in which the polypeptides were derived from this organism found in the soil.

Action

Polymyxin B is a surface-active agent and is thought to alter the lipoprotein membrane of bacteria so that it no longer functions as an effective barrier, and thereby allows the cell contents to escape.

Indications

Polymyxin B is effective against *Pseudomonas* and other aerobic gram-negative bacilli, including *Pseudomonas aeruginosa*, but not against the *Proteus* and *Serratia* species. Polymyxin B has little to no effect on gram-negative bacteria. Polymyxin B is often used with neomycin and bacitracin. The triple combination is effective against a broad variety of gram-positive and gram-negative bacilli.

Precautions

Sensitization can occur after long-term usage.

Directions

Apply three to four times daily directly to the wound.

Packaging

Generic
Aerosporin® (Burroughs-Wellcome), 15 g

Polymyxin B–Containing Ointments

- Topisporin® (Pharmafair)—neomycin, polymycin B sulfate, bacitracin zinc
- Neosporin® (Burroughs-Wellcome)—polymyxin B sulfate, bacitracin zinc, neomycin sulfate
- Cortisporin (Burroughs-Wellcome), 5,000 U polymyxin B sulfate, 400 U bacitracin zinc, 3.5 mg neomycin sulfate, and 10 mg (1%) hydrocortisone
- Campho-Phenique™ triple antibiotic plus pain reliever (Winthrop)

Contents per Gram: 400 U bacitracin, 5 mg neomycin sulfate, 5,000 U polymyxin B sulfate, and diperodon hydrochloride

SILVER SULFADIAZINE (SILVADENE®, SSD®)

Description

White, odorless cream. Less than 1% of the silver content is absorbed, and up to 10% of the sulfadiazine may be absorbed.

Action

Acts only on the cell membrane and cell wall to produce its bactericidal effect. Silver, which is selectively toxic to bacteria, is slowly released. Both components in the complex are active.

Indications

Micronized silver sulfadiazine (1%) has a broad antibacterial spectrum, including many strains found in soft tissue infections: *Staphylococcus aureus, Escherichia coli, Pseudomonas aeruginosa, Proteus mirabilis,* and ß-hemolytic streptococci[20]; it is also effective against yeasts such as *Candida albicans.*

Although silver sulfadiazine is used commonly in chronic wound management, it has never been approved by the Food and Drug Administration (FDA) for such application.

Precautions

Patients with known sensitivity to sulfa drugs should not utilize silver sulfadiazine. Do a patch test prior to using. Silver may inactivate topical proteolytic enzymes. Silver sulfadiazine should not be used at term pregnancy. Avoid use of silver sulfadiazine in the presence of hepatic and renal impairment because of poor drug elimination.

Vehicle

The cream vehicle consists of white petrolatum, stearyl alcohol, isopropyl myristate, sorbitan monooleate, polyoxyl 40 stearate, propylene glycol, and water, with 0.3% methylparaben as preservative.

Directions

Apply with a sterile applicator once or twice daily in the amount of $\frac{1}{16}$-inch thickness to a clean, debrided wound. Because the vehicle is water soluble, it will be miscible in wound fluid; therefore, in most cases, less than 1 g is sufficient.

Packaging

Flint SSD® (Boots-Flint), 50-g jar, 400-g jar, 1,000-g jar
Silvadene® cream 1% (Marion), 20-g tube, 50-g jar, 85-g jar, 400-g jar, 1,000-g jar
Both are creams, 10-mg/g, in a water-miscible base.

ZINC BACITRACIN

Description

Zinc bacitracin (7% zinc) is prepared by the action of zinc salts on bacitracin broth. Zinc bacitracin is less water soluble than bacitracin and is more stable than bacitracin at room and elevated temperatures (shell life may be 5 years). Zinc bacitracin and bacitracin have different degrees of sensitizing potential.

Action

Zinc bacitracin is a cell wall synthesis inhibitor. Zinc increases the potency of bacitracin and also enhances its stability.

Precaution

May cause a generalized itching.

Vehicle

Special white petrolatum base.

Directions

Apply directly to the wound four or five times daily.

Packaging

Zinc bacitracin (Pharma-Tek, Inc.), 500 mU

Zinc Bacitracin–Containing Ointments

Costs and package size are very similar among manufacturers.

Cortisporin (Burroughs-Wellcome), 3.75 g
Neo-Polycin (Merrell Dow), 15 g
Neosporin® (Burroughs-Wellcome), 30 g
Polysporin (Burroughs-Wellcome), 15 g
Topisporin® (Pharmafair), 30g

REFERENCES

1. Lineaweaver W. Cellular and bacterial toxicities of topical antimicrobials. *Plastic Reconstr Surg.* 1985;75(3):394–396.

2. Kozol RA. Effects of sodium hypochlorite on cells of the wound module. *Arch Surg.* 1988;123(4):420–423.

3. Schneider D, Herbert L. Subcutaneous gas from hydrogen peroxide administration under pressure. *Am J Dis Children.* 1987;141:10–11.

4. Oberg MS, Lindsey D. Do not put hydrogen peroxide or povidone iodine into wounds! *AJDC.* 1987;141:27–28.

5. Strachan C. Antibiotic prophylaxis in "clean" surgical procedures. *World J Surg.* 1972;6:273–280.

6. Rodeheaver G, et al. Bactericidal activity and toxicity of iodine-containing solutions in wounds. *Arch Surg.* 1982;117:181–185.

7. D'Auria J, Lipson S, Garfield JM. Fatal iodine toxicity following surgical debridement of a hip wound: case report. *J Trauma.* 1990;30(3):353–355.

8. Aronoff TG, Friedman S, Doedens D, Lavelle K. Increased serum iodine concentration, serum iodine absorption through wounds treated topically with povidone-iodine. *Am J Med Sci.* 1980;279(3):173–176.

9. Thomas C. Nursing alert: wound healing halted with the use of povidone-iodine. *Ostomy/Wound Man.* Spring 1988:30–33.

10. O'Keefe JP, et al. Eradication of resistant *Staphylococcus aureus* on a surgical unit. *N Engl J Med.* 1985;312:858.

11. McAnally TP, et al. Antimicrobial agents. *Chemo.* 1984;25:422.

12. Yu VL, et al. *Staphylococcus aureus* nasal carriage and infection in patients on hemodialysis. *N Eng J Med.* 1986;315:91.

13. Vale MA, et al. Bacitracin-induced anaphylaxis. *Arch Derm.* 1978;114:800 (letter).

14. McMullen D. Topical metronidazole use in malodorous ulcerating skin lesions. IAET Conference Bulletin Abstract, 1990.

15. Reynolds JEF, ed. *Martindale the extra pharmacopoeia*, 29th ed. London, England: The Pharmaceutical Press; 1989.

16. Hirschman JV. Topical antibiotics in dermatology. *Arch Derm.* 1988;124:1691–1700.

17. Leyden JJ, Klingman AM. Rationale for topical antibiotics. *Curtis.* 1978;22:515–526.

18. Gennaro AR. *Remington's pharmaceutical sciences*, 18th ed. Mack Publishing Company; 1990.

19. Geronemus RG, Mertz PM, Eaglestein WH. Wound healing—the effects of topical antimicrobial agents. *Arch Derm.* 1979;115:1311–1314.

20. Kucan O, et al. Comparison of silver sulfadiazine, povidone-iodine and physiologic saline in the treatment of chronic pressure ulcers. *J Am Ger Soc.* 1981;29:232–235.

A Quick Reference Guide to Wound Care Product Categories

Diane Krasner

This listing of wound care products highlights the importance of generic product categories. Under each generic product category, up to four product examples are given (a mix of old and new products), to help familiarize the reader with each category. No endorsement of any product or manufacturer is intended. Within each category, products must be individually evaluated. All products within a category do not necessarily perform equally. Combination products may be listed in more than one category. Refer to manufacturers' instructions for specifics regarding product usage.

Absorptive Antimicrobial Dressings

Product	Manufacturer
Isosorb®	Healthpoint Medical
Iodoflex™	Healthpoint Medical

Alginate Dressings

Product	Manufacturer
Dermacea™ Alginate	Sherwood - Davis & Geck
Restore Calcicare	Hollister
Seasorb™	Coloplast Sween
5orbsan™	Dow Hickam Pharmaceuticals

Biosynthetic Dressings

Product	Manufacturer
BiobraneII®	Dow Hickam Pharmaceuticals
Silon®	BioMed Sciences

Cleansers

Product	Manufacturer
a. Saline	Multiple
b. Hydrogen Peroxide	Multiple
c. Skin Cleansers	
Peri-Wash®	Coloplast Sween
Royl-Derm™	Acme United
Skin Cleanser	Mentor Urology
Triple Care™	Smith & Nephew United
d. Wound Cleansers	
Constant-Clens™	Sherwood - Davis & Geck
Curasol™	Healthpoint Medical
Dermagran® Spray	Derma Sciences
RadiaCare™ Klenz	Carrington Laboratories

Collagen Dressings

Product	Manufacturer
ChroniCure™	Derma Sciences
Fibracol® (Collagen/Alginate)	Johnson & Johnson Medical
Medifil™	BioCore
SkinTemp™	BioCore

Note: All product names should be considered copyrighted or trademarked regardless of the absence of an ® or ™.
Source: © 1997, Diane Krasner.

Composite Dressings

Product	Manufacturer
Alldress®	SCA Mölnlycke
CombiDERM™ ACD™	ConvaTec
CovaDerm™/ CovaDerm™ Plus	DeRoyal Wound Care
Odor-Absorbent Dressing	Hollister

Contact Layers

Product	Manufacturer
Mepitel®	SCA Mölnlycke
Profore®	Smith & Nephew United
Tegapore	3M Health Care
Ventex™ Vented Dressing	Kendall Healthcare Products

Enzymes/ Debriding Agents

Product	Manufacturer
Accuzyme™	Healthpoint Medical
Elase® (Fibrinolysin/ desoxyribonuclease)	Fujisawa USA
Panifil® Ointment (Papain)	Rystan
Santyl® (Collagenase)	Knoll Laboratories

Foam Dressings

Product	Manufacturer
Allevyn®	Smith & Nephew United
Cutinova® cavity/ foam/thin	Beiersdorf-Jobst
Flexzan™	Dow Hickam Pharmaceuticals
Lyofoam®/Lyofoam® T	Acme United

Gauze Dressings
(also see Composite Dressings)

Product	Manufacturer
a. Woven	Multiple
b. Non-woven	
EXCILON®	Kendall Healthcare Products
NATURALON™	Kendall Healthcare Products
NU GAUZE General Use Sponges	Johnson & Johnson Medical
SOF-WICK™	Johnson & Johnson Medical
c. Packing/Packing Strips (Non-impregnated)	
Kerlix®/Kerlix® Lite	Kendall Healthcare Products
NU-BREDE™	Johnson & Johnson Medical
Packing Strips (Plain)	Multiple
TENDERSORB®	Kendall Healthcare Products
d. Conforming/Wrapping	
Conform®	Kendall Healthcare Products
Elastomull®	Beiersdorf-Jobst
Kerlix®/Kerlix® Lite	Kendall Healthcare Products
KLING™	Johnson & Johnson Medical
e. Debriding	
NU-BREDE™	Johnson & Johnson Medical
TENDERSORB®	Kendall Healthcare Products
f. Impregnated Gauze Dressings	
Dermagran™ Wet Dressing (Saline)	Derma Sciences
Gentell™ Hydrogel Dressing	MKM Healthcare
GRx Saline Wet Dressing	Geritrex Corporation
Vaseline® Petrolatum	Kendall Healthcare Products
g. Non-adherent Gauze	
Primapore®	Smith & Nephew United
Release®	Johnson & Johnson Medical
Telfa®	Kendall Healthcare Products
h. Specialty Absorptive Gauze	
EXU-DRY®	Exu-Dry Wound Care Products
SURGIPAD® Combine Dressings	Johnson & Johnson Medical
TENDERSORB® Wet-Pruf Abdominal Pad	Kendall Healthcare Products

Hydrocolloid Dressings

Product	Manufacturer
RepliCare™	Smith & Nephew United
Restore™/CX/Extra Thin	Hollister
SignaDress™	ConvaTec
Tegasorb™	3M Health Care

Hydrogel Dressings
(also see Impregnated Gauze Dressings)

Product	Manufacturer
Sheet	
CarraSorb™ M	Carrington Laboratories
Elasto-Gel™	Southwest Technologies
Gentell™	MKM Healthcare
Vigilon®	Bard Medical
Amorphous	
Carrington Gel Wound Dressing™	Carrington Laboratories
DuoDERM® Hydroactive Gel (Hydrogel/ Hydrocolloid)	ConvaTec
Hypergel®	SCA Mölnlycke
IntraSite® Gel	Smith & Nephew United

Leg Ulcer Wraps
Compression Bandages/Wraps

Product	Manufacturer
Coban®	3M Health Care
Dome Paste®	Miles
Elastoplast®	Beiersdorf-Jobst
Setopress®	Acme United

Multilayered Systems

Product	Manufacturer
Circulon™ System	ConvaTec
Profore®	Smith & Nephew United
Unna-Pak	Glenwood

Skin Sealants

Product	Manufacturer
Preppies™	Kendall Healthcare Products
Skin Prep™	Smith & Nephew United
Skin Shield®	Mentor Urology
3M No Sting Skin Protectant	3M Health Care

Transparent Film Dressings

Product	Manufacturer
BIOCLUSIVE™	Johnson & Johnson Medical
Flexfilm™	Dow Hickman Pharmaceuticals
OpSite®/Flexifix/ Flexigrid	Smith & Nephew United
Tegaderm™/HP	3M Health Care

Wound Fillers: Pastes, Powders, Beads, etc.

Product	Manufacturer
Bard® Absorption Dressing	Bard Medical
DuoDERM® Paste	ConvaTec
OsmoCyte™ Pillow Wound Dressing	ProCyte
Triad™	Coloplast Sween

Wound Pouches

Product	Manufacturer
Wound Drainage Collector	Hollister
Wound Manager™	ConvaTec
Adult and Pediatric Sized Ostomy Pouches	Multiple

Not Otherwise Classified (NOC)

Product Categories
Adhesives
Adhesive Removers
Adhesive Skin Closures
Adhesive Tapes
Antibiotics
Antimicrobials
Antiseptics
Bandages
Creams
Dressing Covers
Growth Factors
Healthcare Personnel Handrinses
Lubricating/Stimulating Sprays
Moisture Barrier Ointments/Creams/Skin Protectant Pastes
Moisturizers
Ointments
Perineal Cleansing Foams
Sterile Fields
Surgical Scrubs
Surgical Tapes

WOUND AND SKIN CARE PRODUCT MANUFACTURERS

3M Health Care
3M Center, Bldg. 275-4E-01
St. Paul, Minnesota 55144-1000
(612) 736-1723 or (800) 228-3957
Fax (612) 737-7678

Acme United Corporation
75 Kings Highway Cutoff
Fairfield, Connecticut 06430
800-TEL-ACME, (800) 835-2263
Fax (203) 576-0007

Bard Medical Div., C.R. Bard, Inc.
8195 Industrial Blvd.
Covington, Georgia 30209
(770) 784-6100 or (800) 526-4455
Fax (770) 784-6218

Beiersdorf-Jobst, Inc.
5825 Carnegie Blvd.
Charlotte, North Carolina 28209
(704) 554-9933 or (800) 876-3664
Fax (704) 551-8581

BioCore, Inc.
1605 SW 41st Street
Topeka, Kansas 66609
(913) 267-4800 or (800) 577-4801
Fax (913) 267-1900

Carrington Laboratories, Inc.
2001 Walnut Hill Lane
Irving, Texas 75038
(214) 518-1300 or (800) 358-5213
Fax (214) 518-1020

Colorplast Sween Corp.
1955 West Oak Circle
Marietta, Georgia 30062-2249
(770) 426-6362 or (800) 533-0464
Fax (770) 422-4324

ConvaTec
Customer Service, P.O. 5250
Princeton, New Jersey 08543-5250
(800) 325-8005
Fax (800) 523-2965

Derma Sciences, Inc.
121 West Grace Street
Old Forge, Pennsylvania 18518
(717) 457-1232 or (800) 825-4325
Fax (717) 457-1793

**DeRoyal Wound Care, A Div. of
DeRoyal Industries, Inc.**
200 DeBusk Lane
Powell, Tennessee 37849
(423) 938-7828 or (800) 251-9864
Fax (423) 938-6655

Dow Hickam Pharmaceuticals, Inc.
10410 Corporate Drive
Sugar Land, Texas 77487
(713) 240-1000 or (800) 231-3052
Fax (713) 240-0003

EXU-DRY Wound Care Products, Inc.
3830 Boston Road
Bronx, New York 10475
(718) 231-5200 or (800) 544-4325
Fax (718) 881-4917

Fujisawa USA, Inc.
Three Parkway North
Deerfield, Illinois 60015-2548
(847) 317-8800 or (800) 888-7704
Fax (847) 317-7296

Glenwood, Inc.
82 North Summit Street
Tenafly, New Jersey 07670
(201) 569-0050 or (800) 542-0772
Fax (201) 567-4443

Healthpoint Medical
2400 Handley-Ederville Road
Fort Worth, Texas 76118
(817) 595-0394 or (800) 441-8227
Fax (817) 595-0921

Hollister, Inc.
2000 Hollister Drive
Libertyville, Illinois 60048
(847) 680-1000 or (800) 323-4060
Fax (847) 918-3994

Johnson & Johnson Medical, Inc.
2500 Arbrook Blvd.
Arlington, Texas 76014
(817) 465-3141 or (800) 255-2500
Fax (817) 784-5459

Kendall Healthcare Products Co.
15 Hampshire Street
Mansfield, Massachusetts 02048
(508) 261-8000 or (800) 346-7197
Fax (508) 261-8271

Knoll Laboratories, A Div. of
Knoll Pharmaceutical Co.
3000 Continental Drive - North
Mount Olive, New Jersey 07828-1234
(201) 426-5655 or (800) 3-SANTYL
Fax (201) 426-5660

Mentor Urology
5427 Hollister Avenue
Santa Barbara, California 93111
(805) 681-6000 or (800) 328-3863
Fax (805) 681-6166

MKM Healthcare Corporation
1957 Pioneer Road, Bldg. H
Huntindon Valley, Pennsylvania 19006
(215) 957-1400 or (800) 462-3395
Fax (800) 888-1508

ProCyte Corporation
12040 115th Avenue, NE, Suite 210
Kirkland, Washington 98034
(206) 820-4548 or (800) 848-3668
Fax (206) 820-4111

Rystan Co., Inc.
47 Center Avenue
Little Falls, New Jersey 07424
(201) 256-3737
Fax (201) 256-4083

SCA Mölnlycke
500 Baldwin Tower
Eddystone, Pennsylvania 19022
(610) 499-3700 or (800) 992-9939
Fax (610) 499-3396

Sherwood - Davis & Geck
1915 Olive Street
St. Louis, Missouri 63103
(314) 241-5700 or (800) 325-7472
Fax (314) 241-3127

Smith & Nephew United, Inc.
11775 Starkey Road, P.O. Box 1970
Largo, Florida 34649-1970
(813) 392-1261 or (800) 876-1261
Fax (813) 399-3498

Southwest Technologies, Inc.
1746 Levee Road
North Kansas City, Missouri 64116
(816) 221-2442 or (800) 247-9951
Fax (816) 221-3995

Index

About the Editors

Carrie Sussman, PT, is President of Wound Care Management Services and Sussman Physical Therapy, Inc. and an alumni of the University of Southern California. Of her more than 30 years experience as a physical therapist, 20 years have been spent working to rehabilitate geriatric patients in long-term and subacute settings as both clinician and rehab director. More than 15 years ago, she developed a serious concern for the problems of trying to rehabilitate patients with chronic wounds. Her innovative and successful wound treatment program incorporating rehabilitation and use of PT technologies has been of interest to the medical, therapy, and payer community.

Carrie is a strong advocate of public policy issues and education that will help patients with chronic wounds to have the best functional outcomes. This has led her to involvement in groups and organizations that promote those interests. Since 1986, she has been an advisor to Blue Cross of California on matters relating to appropriate wound care guidelines and reimbursement issues. She currently serves as chairperson of the Committee for Practice of the Section on Clinical Electrophysiology Wound Management Special Interest Group and is a member of the Multidisciplinary Advisory Board of the University of Southern California (USC) Enterostomal Therapy Program. She also has the distinction of being the first physical therapist elected to the National Pressure Ulcer Advisory Panel (NPUAP) and is now co-chair of the NPUAP Public Policy Committee. She served as an expert panelist for APTA Integumentary Panel that has developed *A Guide for Physical Therapist Practice:* Vol. I, Part II, Preferred Practice Patterns for the Integument.

For nine years she has sponsored and chaired the Annual Physical Therapy Wound Care Management Services conference. The 9th Annual Conference was held September 28–30, 1997, in Torrance, CA. She is a national and international lecturer on topics relating to wound management issues, and has also published articles on this topic.

Barbara M. Bates-Jensen, RN, MN, CETN, is a graduate of UCLA with a master's degree in nursing with a focus on gerontology. As a clinical nurse specialist and an ET Nurse, she has acquired a wealth of information and experience with chronic wounds and pressure sores in particular which she shares enthusiastically as a frequent lecturer and author. As a part of her coursework at UCLA she completed a methodological study developing the Pressure Sore Status Tool. As a doctoral candidate at UCLA, she is pursuing the question of what clinical correlates are associated with pressure ulcer wound healing. She is currently Assistant Professor of Clinical Nursing at the University of Southern California and serves as coordinator of the baccalaureate junior level and the graduate ET Nursing Program. She and her partner, Patrick McNees, PhD, have completed a SBIR (Small Business Innovation Research Grant from the National Institute for Nursing Research) on automating the Pressure Sore Status Tool and continue their work on wound assessment with the computer program, the Wound and Skin Intelligence System. Her past experience includes an independent practice as a wound care consultant for acute care hospitals, home health care agencies, and long-term care facilities, and project coordinator for a National Institutes of Health research grant "Urinary Incontinence in Elderly Nursing Home Patients," with Joseph Ouslander, MD and John F. Schnelle, PhD.

Barbara is past President of the Pacific Coast Region of the Wound, Ostomy, Continence Nurses Society (WOCN) and served on the national board of directors for 4 years. She has served on the Editorial Board for *Ostomy/Wound Management Journal* and is past Wound Section Editor for the

Journal of Wound, Ostomy, Continence Nursing and is currently a reviewer. She is presently pursuing a doctoral degree in nursing at UCLA and has been elected to the National Pressure Ulcer Advisory Panel. She is the recipient of the 1997 Baranoski Founder's Award in recognition of creative practice strategies that have enhanced the care of wound care clients and the Bullough Award for faculty excellence.